Whytford's Works
– Jesus Psalter esp
beloved of Recusants

The Religious Orders in England

* * *

The Monastic Order in England

A History of its Development
from the times of St Dunstan to the
Fourth Lateran Council
943–1216

The Religious Orders in England I

The Old Orders 1216–1340
The Friars 1216–1340
The Monasteries and their World

The Religious Orders in England II

The End of the Middle Ages

PRIOR HOUGHTON

The Religious Orders in England

VOLUME III
The Tudor Age

BY
DOM DAVID KNOWLES

*Regius Professor Emeritus of Modern History
in the University of Cambridge*

Cambridge
AT THE UNIVERSITY PRESS
1971

PUBLISHED BY
THE SYNDICS OF THE CAMBRIDGE UNIVERSITY PRESS

Bentley House, 200 Euston Road, London, NW1 2DB
American Branch: 32 East 57th Street, New York, N.Y. 10022

© CAMBRIDGE UNIVERSITY PRESS 1959

ISBN: 0 521 05482 6

First edition 1959
Reprinted 1961
Reprinted with corrections 1971

First printed in Great Britain at the University Press, Cambridge
Reprinted in Great Britain by Lewis Reprints Limited, London and Tonbridge

CONTENTS

Frontispiece

An ideal portrait of Prior John Houghton. The original is in the Museo Provincial at Cadiz, No. 73, labelled "Beato Juan Houghton". It is the work of Francisco de Zurbarán (1598–1664), and was executed *circa* 1639 at a time when the master was painting the series of groups and portraits of Carthusian monks that made so strong an impression upon Théophile Gautier. Though face and figure are ideal, the iconography of mature appearance, halter and heart show that the memory of the London Charterhouse was still green in Spain after a century, possibly owing to the influence of the long-lived Duchess of Feria (see p. 227). *Foto Mas Barcelona*

Part One

The Tudor Scene

Part Two
The Gathering Storm

Part Three
Suppression and Dissolution

Part Four
Reaction and Survival

PREFACE

The final volume of this history covers almost exactly the reigns of the five sovereigns of the house of Tudor. It opens with the accession of Henry VII which a universal, if not a venerable, educational and literary convention has long accepted not only as the beginning of what is called a new period of English history, but as the moment of transit between the medieval centuries and the modern world. Absurd as this convention may be, it has profoundly affected English historiography, and its influence has been felt all the more because the eighty-seven years between the death of Henry V and the accession of Henry VIII have come to form a kind of interlunary period shunned by 'medievalists' and 'modernists' alike. In consequence, the dissolution of the monasteries has almost invariably been treated, both in outline histories and in monographs, by those primarily interested in the age of the Reformation, and their approach to it has been by way of a backward glance at the circumstances and tendencies that made, or seemed to make, the disappearance of the monasteries either inevitable or at least desirable. These writers have therefore done little to illustrate the manifold variety of character and conditions of life among the several religious orders in the forty-odd years that elapsed between Bosworth field and the fall of Wolsey. Froude and Dixon, Fisher and Gairdner, Gasquet and Baskerville, Constant and Hughes are all primarily occupied with and expert in the religious revolution of the 1530's. Their account of what went immediately before this in the monastic world resembles, all proportions guarded, the introductory chapter of a specialist monograph, which looks to the past for the traces and causes of what is to be the central theme of the work. Here, with the hope of somewhat redressing the balance, considerable space has been given to a review of particular achievements and activities of some of the orders and their representatives during the decades in question, when none could have foreseen the total destruction that was to come upon them so suddenly and so soon.

For a different set of reasons, many of the historians who have dealt with the suppression of the monasteries have ended the story with the last surrender of 1540, or at least with the gradual disappearance of the pensioned survivors. They have inherited, in part at least, from their predecessors in earlier centuries, a concept of the English Reformation as something that put an end, once and for all, to the monastic institutions of the medieval church. Yet the Marian revival was at least a tail-piece, a *coda*, to the medieval story, and it so happened that it provided a link, tenuous but real, with the reborn English monasteries of the Counter-Reformation, which have never since ceased to exist. Here, therefore, the narrative will be taken down to the days of James I, if only to show how

B

fittingly may be applied to another branch of the monastic body the words that have for long, and never more aptly than in recent years, been used as a device by the patriarchal abbey of Monte Cassino: *succisa virescit*.

In the account of monastic life before the final storm several additions have been made to the conventional picture. As in the two previous centuries, the breadth of the field and the dearth of contemporary biographies and chronicles have made it difficult to strike a mean between a summary account and a series of chapters on particular groups and topics, and it has seemed best to allow some characteristic figures of the time space in which to reveal themselves. The reader who wishes to know what manner of men the religious were immediately before their disappearance may see them here in light and shadow: he can travel up and down the country among the white canons with Bishop Redman; he can visit the moated manor houses of the Severn valley with Prior More, or listen to Robert Joseph with his humanist's gossip of Oxford and Evesham; he can see Huby at work at Fountains, Kidderminster at Winchcombe, and Islip at Westminster; he can note the gatherings in the White Horse tavern at Cambridge or watch the splendours of the liturgy at Durham; he must not omit from the reckoning the enlightened piety of Syon and the austere and silent adoration of the Charterhouse.

In more than one of these chapters sources of information have been used that hitherto have been neglected or unknown. Redman's Premonstratensian visitations and Prior More's *Journal* were printed for learned societies fifty years ago, but the former has been used only for controversial purposes while the latter, for all its rich variety of interest, seems to have escaped the notice of all historians of the period. Other sources are entirely new. The correspondence between the English Cistercians and the central authority at Cîteaux is still unprinted; it tells us much about the year-to-year administration of the order and reveals, in Marmaduke Huby of Fountains, a Tudor Cistercian of real distinction. The letters of the Evesham monk, Robert Joseph, are likewise unpublished; they lift for a moment the veil that covers the thoughts and interests of the 'university monk' in the age of Erasmian humanism. Both these collections of documents will shortly be published, the former by the Royal Historical Society, the latter by the Oxford Historical Society, and I owe a great debt of gratitude to the two scholars concerned, Dr C. H. Talbot and Dom Hugh Aveling, of Ampleforth Abbey, for the unselfish generosity with which they have allowed me to use their materials and to ply them with questions.

In the narrative of the Dissolution the unprinted reports of the commissioners of 1536 have been used more fully than by previous writers; they throw much light upon the social and economic conditions of the lesser monasteries. Similar help has also been obtained from a group of dissertations, still in typescript, that treat of the process of suppression in widely separated regions of England. Finally, in the account of the

Marian revival and the Westminster succession the reader will be introduced to a less familiar field, which has nevertheless been explored to
some purpose by modern Benedictine scholars. Here again my debt is
great to Dom Hugh Aveling, and to his older confrere Dom Justin (later
Abbot) McCann.

In addition to those already mentioned the following have given assistance in various ways: Mr Thurston Dart of Jesus College and those who
were his research students, with information about Tudor music; Mr
G. R. Elton, of Clare College, with much helpful criticism; Dom Andrew
Gray, of St Hugh's Charterhouse, Parkminster, with facts and documents
connected with the London Charterhouse; Professor H. Habakkuk, of
All Souls College, Oxford, concerning the sale of monastic lands; Mr
W. A. Pantin, of Oriel College, Oxford, who for more than twenty
years has continued to give encouragement and help of every kind;
Professor M. M. Postan, by reading and criticizing an economic chapter;
Dr J. J. Scarisbrick, with transcripts of Sussex visitations; Dom Aelred
Watkin, of Downside Abbey, with information and documents about
Glastonbury; and others whose names appear in the footnotes. Particular
acknowledgement is due to Mr G. J. Hodgett, of King's College, London,
to Mr J. Kennedy, and to Dr G. W. O. Woodward, of Nottingham
University, who have allowed me to use freely the information contained
in their unpublished dissertations. I must also thank all at the Cambridge
University Press and Bentley House who during twenty-two years have
displayed in their various ways so much skill and courtesy and goodwill
in my regard.

This volume completes a task that was undertaken almost exactly thirty
years ago. At a critical moment in the course of its accomplishment it
owed much (even if they did not know this at the time) to the advocacy
of four Cambridge friends: the late Zachary Brooke, Herbert Butterfield,
Philip Grierson and Munia Postan. *Hospes fui et collegistis me.*

CAMBRIDGE   DAVID KNOWLES
6 January 1959

A reprinting of this book has given me the opportunity to correct
small errors and make use of criticisms and information kindly given by
reviewers and readers. The principal revisions are on pp. 32, 166, 170,
175–6 and 345, for which I am indebted to Dr C. H. Talbot, Professor
G. Rupp, Dr G. R. Elton and Mr C. J. Hughes.

PETERHOUSE   M.D.K.
17 January 1961

LIST OF ABBREVIATIONS

*Full details of all works referred to in this volume are to be
found in the Bibliography*

AB	*Analecta Bollandiana*
AC	*Chapters of the Augustinian Canons* (Salter)
AJ	*Archaeological Journal*
BRS	*Bristol Record Society*
CAP	*Collectanea Anglo-Premonstratensia* (Gasquet)
Caniveʒ	*Statuta Capitulorum Generalium Ordinis Cisterciensis* (ed. Canivez)
CHS	Church Historical Society
CL	*Cistercian Letters* (ed. Talbot)
CPR	*Calendar of Patent Rolls*
CQR	*Church Quarterly Review*
CS	Camden Series
CYS	Canterbury & York Society
DAR	*Account Rolls of the Abbey of Durham* (Fowler)
DNB	*Dictionary of National Biography*
DR	*Downside Review*
DTC	*Dictionnaire de Théologie catholique*
DubR	*Dublin Review*
DV	*Visitations of the Diocese of Lincoln* (A. H. Thompson)
EcHR	*Economic History Review*
EES	*English Ecclesiastical Studies* (Graham)
EETS	Early English Text Society
EHR	*English Historical Review*
EM	*English Monks and the Suppression of the Monasteries* (Baskerville)
GASA	*Gesta Abbatum Sancti Albani*
HBS	Henry Bradshaw Society
Henry VIII	*Henry VIII and the English Monasteries* (Gasquet)
HMC	*Historical Manuscripts Commission*
JEH	*Journal of Ecclesiastical History*
LP	*Letters & Papers of the reign of Henry VIII*
LRS	Lincoln Record Society
MC	*Chapters of the Black Monks* (Pantin)
Memorials	*Memorials of Father Baker* (McCann)
MO	*The Monastic Order in England* (Knowles)
Monasticon	*Monasticon Anglicanum* (Dugdale)
MSAC	*Monasterii S. Albani·Chronica* (ed. Riley)
n.s.	new series
OED	*Oxford English Dictionary* (Murray)
OHS	Oxford Historical Society

OL	*Original Letters* (Ellis)
o.s.	old series (EETS); original series (CS)
PBA	*Proceedings of the British Academy*
PRO	Public Record Office
RO	*The Religious Orders in England* (Knowles)
RP	Record Publication
RS	Rolls Series (Chronicles & Memorials)
SC	Suppression Certificates
SL	*Letters relating to the suppression of the monasteries* (Wright)
SP	Suppression Papers
SPV	*State Papers (Venetian)*
SRH	*The Somerset Religious Houses* (Archbold)
SRS	Somerset Record Society
SS	Surtees Society
TBGAS	*Transactions of the Bristol and Gloucestershire Archaeological Society*
TRHS	*Transactions of the Royal Historical Society*
Valor or *VE*	*Valor Ecclesiasticus*
VCH	*Victoria County History*
WHS	Worcestershire Historical Society
YAJ	*Yorkshire Archaeological Journal*
YARS	Yorkshire Archaeological Society Record Series

Part One

THE TUDOR SCENE

CHAPTER I

THE REIGN OF HENRY VII

I. THE CHANGING SCENE

The advent of the first Tudor sovereign marked no epoch in the history of the religious orders in England. Neither the policy of the king nor the external events of his reign affected in any direct way the fortunes of the monasteries. Nevertheless, here, as in so many departments of the national life, the return of calm weather after a season of storms, and the steady hand of a single master at the ship's helm, allowed all the natural forces of the age full play, and tendencies hitherto latent or only seen by glimpses now became clear to every beholder.

Henry VII, as has often been remarked, was conservative and observant in religious matters. In this respect, indeed, he was a representative, almost a survival, of the last generation of simple medieval orthodoxy. Nothing in his outlook or behaviour differed in any significant respect from the ways of thinking and acting of Henry IV or still earlier monarchs. Neither humanism, nor Neoplatonism, nor neo-paganism, nor even the unethical political realism of Italy, had any direct influence on his attitude in religious matters. He was not personally interested in religion in its theological or devotional aspects, still less in its spiritual depth, but neither was he a critic or a libertine. His actions and policies, as we see them, were earthbound, and he did not understand the meaning of honour or integrity in affairs of state, but he was in his thought and behaviour in daily life a traditional and conventional Catholic, and he gave to religion, in his position at the summit of the social scale, the kind of service and respect, adequate but in no sense fervent or emotional, that was given on lower levels by the respectable country gentleman or city magnate.

The century between 1450 and 1550 was one of great and rapid change in England as in the whole of Europe. In the last twenty years of that period the changes in this country amounted to a revolution, and are familiar as such to every reader. It has not, however, been universally realized that the spectacular events of the reign of Henry VIII were rendered possible, though not inevitable, by the slow and almost imperceptible changes in outlook and opinion during the decades that preceded them. These changes may have been in some respects less arresting than contemporary developments in Italy, France and Germany, because the latter—the cultural and religious movements known as the Renaissance and early Reform—took place in the open and among the most influential and articulate classes of society, but they were none the less very important. If the movements on the Continent may be compared to a storm that agitates the waves, those in England were as the pull of the tide towards the shore. They were perhaps most significant in the social sphere and their results most obvious in a change of mutual relationships as between the religious, the upper classes of society, and the growing multitude of the well-to-do.

In the age of Chaucer and Langland the aristocracy and higher gentry, the upper ranks of the Church, the leading theologians of the universities, and the outstanding figures in the religious orders, were still the sections of the community from which the leaders and policies of every kind arose. Above them the king could impose his pattern upon events only to a limited extent and with great personal effort; below them there was little possibility of articulate opposition, save in the exceptional matter of Lollardy, and the ease and relative success with which even this was rendered innocuous may be taken as showing how strong and cohesive the ecclesiastical body still continued to be.

During the century that followed there was a great change. Though the older view that the nobility disappeared on the battlefields and scaffolds of the Wars of the Roses was an exaggeration of the truth, it is nevertheless certain that the great houses were sensibly fewer in number and far less secure in mind under Henry VII than they had been under Henry IV, whereas at the same time the classes of lesser landowners and rich merchants had greatly increased, while the king, in the person of the first Tudor, had risen well above the level of even the greatest of the nobles. As the master of all administration and initiative, indeed, he stood alone, or rather he stood supported by a powerful and talented group of lieutenants and executives of his own choosing, who were without any private strength save what was derived from the royal countenance. The fact that many of these officials were bishops did not diminish the king's prestige nor render any conflict of views possible, for they were government officials before all else.

During the same period of time, there had been a notable shift in the interests and occupations of the educated class. Until the reign of Henry V the schools of philosophy and theology at the universities were still filling something of the functions of intellectual leadership that they had taken from the monasteries some two centuries earlier. The majority of the professional minds of Europe had been trained first in the school of arts and then in the schools of divinity or canon law. At this very moment, however, the most brilliant men of Italy were being drawn away to humanism, to the classics, to philosophy, to mathematics, and to the beginnings of science. This movement had remarkably little echo in England until the middle years of the reign of Henry VII. Instead, while the universities gradually lost the initiative and the living power of the past, a steady and swelling tide was setting towards the Inns of Court. These young lawyers were not precisely of the same social class as had provided the poor clerks of Bradwardine's or Chaucer's day; they were the sons, often the younger sons, of the landowners, great and small, who were themselves a rapidly expanding class of men. But from the end of the Wars of the Roses till the end of the reign of Elizabeth, the Inns of Court harboured and trained the flower of the intelligence and energy and ambition of the country. Of the men who influenced policy and rose to high position and wealth by their wits and personality between 1490 and 1590 perhaps three out of every four were lawyers trained either in the civil or the common law, and of these two groups the common lawyers were by far the more numerous. The young Thomas More was brought back by his father from the useless humanism of Oxford to the study of law, and the foreigner Erasmus noted with surprise how young men of good family flocked to the Inns.[1] Aske and Cromwell, Audley, Rich, Layton, Legh, Christopher St German and Sir Thomas Eliot were all skilled in the law.

With the decline of philosophy and theology as formative intellectual disciplines, and with humanism still the pursuit of a very few, the level of culture of the civilized intelligent life fell to a uniform mediocrity. The reservoirs of the past, the monasteries and the universities, had lost their high quality, the aristocracy of the campaign and the council chamber had not only decreased in numbers but had lost the ideals of courtesy and chivalry, brittle and artificial as they had doubtless become. The poets and the patrons of Lydgate's day had alike disappeared. Between the age of Chaucer's Knight and that of Sir Philip Sidney there was no class of society which could claim to be an aristocracy either of mind or of manners. The two expanding groups of prosperous landowners and men of commerce were not intellectually as refined and as carefully trained as were their counterparts in Italy. The term 'gentleman' was indeed currently used, but the educated gentleman, one of a class, did not exist.[2] Almost all the energies and interests of Englishmen were directed towards purely material and personal ends: the acquisition of wealth and property, the founding of a family, the building of a house, the planning of a tomb and a chantry. Pecuniary values and economic gains were very nearly exclusive of all others. Perhaps in no other epoch of English history have purely material interests had such a monopoly in all the records of the age. Readers of the letter-books of the time—of the Pastons, the Plumptons, the Celys and the Stonors—are familiar with this: the cash value of a young man or a young woman is canvassed more eagerly than qualities of character or personal inclinations. Money and land are the only desirable

---

1 Erasmus, ed. P. S. Allen, *ep.* 999 (IV, 17): 'Quae professio [*sc.* Law] ut est a veris literis alienissima, ita apud Britannos cum primis habentur magni clarique qui in hoc genere sibi pararunt auctoritatem. Nec temere apud illos alia via ad rem et gloriam parandam magis idonea; siquidem pleramque nobilitatem illius insulae peperit hoc studiorum genus.' The letter is of 1519, but reflects the long experience of the writer.

2 The term 'gentleman' is notoriously slippery and impatient of definition save in its purely formal sense, but to how many of the leading men of the reigns of Henry VII and Henry VIII would we unhesitatingly attach it? To Reginald Pole, no doubt, and to Sir Thomas More, with a difference, but to whom else? To the fifteenth century the word had a strict connotation, e.g. to Godfrey Grene in 1464: 'There is a yong man, a mercer, in the Chepe ...a Norfolk man and of birth no gent. as I understand' (*The Plumpton Correspondence*, 11).

things.[1] For a brief space neither religious controversy, nor civil duties, nor the pursuit of adventure, nor the love of books or music, nor any theoretical or mental debate, had any appeal. The code of chivalry had gone; the code of loyalty and honour had yet to come. It is an earthy, selfish, grasping age.

When the interest lies neither in theology nor letters the only measure is the law, and there has never been an age in England when the letter of the law, as contrasted with the spirit of equity and justice, so dominated men's minds. If the letter of the law can be satisfied, justice counts for nothing; on the other hand, purely material rights must be safeguarded when on a higher reckoning a robbery or an injustice is carried through without scruple. Our own age, so susceptible to the claims of social justice and so abhorrent of personal suffering, has lost much of the sense of prescriptive and legal rights to property and privilege, but the early Tudor age can only be understood if these latter are reckoned with.

Deprived by Nominalism and theological formalism of the mental support of a reasoned philosophy and theology, and distrusting speculation of all kinds, the minds of the early Tudor age found security in two pillars of strength. The one was the common law of the land, tangible, acknowledged by all, and applied by experts taken from their midst. The other was the command of the sovereign, drawing its strength from his claim of obedience in conscience. In earlier times the royal authority, however violently or unreasonably it had on occasion been asserted, had in principle and often in fact been held in check by various limiting ideas at different times: by the counter-claims of the Church and canon law, upheld by popes and bishops; by the teaching of theologians and publicists on natural and divine law; by the integration of all law as a rational, ascertainable framework of the world and as a reflection of the divine order of the universe; and, finally, by the lack in the past of an organized, centralized machinery of government with adequate powers of execution and sanction, able to enforce the royal will and responsible to the king alone. At the end of the fifteenth century all these limiting factors had vanished or diminished; all that was now wanting was a king with sufficient intelligence, tact, and self-assurance to supply his subjects with the governance they desired and with the sense of security they needed. A firm government that did not outrage too violently the proprieties of common law and the material interests of the propertied classes could draw on a limitless fund of loyalty and submission.

1 Cf. the letter of the lovelorn Edward Plumpton from Furnivall's Inn in 1497. He has been brought 'into the sight of a gentlewoman, a wedow of the age of xl yeres and more... goodly and beautiful, womanly and wyse...she hath xx marc of good land within iij mile of London...she hath in coyne in old nobles c[li]...she is called worth m[li] beside hir land ...she and I are agreed in our mynd and all one'. Cf. also a letter of 1472: 'my Cosen Willyam hath ben with a full goodly Gentilwoman, and comynde with her after love's lore...suer yt is that of her ffader's enheritance she hath in possession C. markes of lande' (*The Stonor Letters and Papers*, I, 123–4).

These observations, like all such abstract generalizations about an age or a society, are no more than loose descriptions of the appearance of things. Instances, and important ones, of other and contradictory tendencies can readily be brought forward. Moreover, these sentiments and motives are at most only currents and ripples on the stream of human behaviour which in its essentials remains the same from age to age or, at most, only changes very gradually under the impact of some new external force. Beneath all the selfishness and materialism of the age, in which few historians have been able to find any admirable ethical characteristics, there can often be discovered the fairness, the kindliness and the love worthiness of undistinguished men and women.

Nevertheless, if we wish to understand, or at least to be aware of, the problems of Tudor history, we must be at pains to approach them with minds quick to perceive the movement of feeling. The age was, like our own, one of swift change in which the landmarks, social, intellectual and economic, which had been familiar for centuries, suddenly shifted or vanished. There is an analogy, even if only a partial and distant one, between the fortunes of the monks between 1450 and 1535 and the fortunes of the English landed aristocracy between 1900 and to-day. In both cases a class of great wealth and social influence lost much of its power and prestige not precisely through any degeneration on its own part, but by reason of revolutionary social and economic changes in the world around it, and through the consequent changes of sentiment in its regard. There are many still alive to-day who can well remember a time when the whole rhythm of society seemed to depend upon the movements and pursuits of a relatively small 'upper class', and when this or that great house dominated the life of half a county. Something of the same change took place with the religious orders in the sixty years with which we are now to be concerned. In the past historians have often assumed that while all else remained steady the monks fell rapidly into moral and pecuniary bankruptcy. It would be a truer view to see the world changing around them while they, for their part, were unable either to accompany that change or to adapt themselves to the demands and necessities of a different world. In that world both they and their neighbours round them were without any anchor save their ancestral and often now vestigial sense of spiritual realities, and a new sentiment of loyalty and obedience to the sovereign. They were to find every new influence a hostile one, in a grasping and acquisitive society which had as its characteristic quality a keen appreciation of the main chance.

II. THE BLACK MONKS

The abbey of St Albans, which almost alone of the greater abbeys provides for the historian an unbroken series of chronicles or records from the Conquest to the reign of Henry VII, bids fair, by the distinction of its sons, by its enduring love of letters, and by the indefinable quality which in an individual we call 'personality' or even 'greatness', to deserve the attention which it has always received. If, therefore, we begin our review of the last phase of English monastic life with a few pages on St Albans, it is partly because the records are still to hand, though progressively deteriorating as literary productions, and partly because the contrast between the abbey of William Wallingford and that of abbot Paul or Matthew Paris is itself a lesson in history.[1]

At St Albans, and there alone, we can follow the story of a monk who was in office before the Wars of the Roses began, and who lived to be abbot in the early years of Henry VII. This was William Wallingford, an enigmatic personage whose merits and demerits were canvassed in his lifetime in his own abbey, and have in recent years been debated, not without heat.[2] He and his brother Thomas come first into prominence during the abbacy of John Stoke, who was elected on Whethamstede's resignation. Stoke had been prior of the dependent house of Wallingford, and it is natural to suppose that the two brothers had been in some way his 'discovery' or his protégés. Certainly in his last years Thomas was sub-almoner and abbot's chaplain, while William, besides functioning as archdeacon, had also collected the offices of cellarer, bursar, forester and sub-cellarer; he was indeed known as the 'general official'. When Abbot Stoke died the community was divided in opinion. One party favoured the omnicompetent Wallingford, another the prior, William Albone, and for perhaps the last time the monks of St Albans enjoyed an electoral dialectic which was chronicled in language distantly recalling the golden age of Walsingham or Paris.[3] As the two rivals were well matched a compromise was effected by recalling the elderly Whethamstede from his retirement at his native manor. This course, hard to parallel in all the centuries of English monastic history, was surprisingly successful. Whethamstede, though no longer showing the elasticity or enterprise of his early days, was still a good diplomat and served the abbey well in the trying decade which witnessed the two battles of St Albans (22 May 1455 and 17 February 1461), in the second of which town and monastery were sacked and the abbot and community forced to scatter. Despite this misfortune and the uncertainties of the times, the abbot was able to continue his building and decoration. The records, indeed, give the impression that the economic position of the abbey was so strong that tolerably good management could always ensure a comfortable surplus, but the disaster of 1461 has been taken to mark the end of a chapter in the history of the house; after it we hear little of the visits of royalty, of great nobles and of

---

1 The best account of St Albans in the last century of its existence is still that of Miss M. Reddan in *VCH, Herts*, IV (1914), 403–8, together with the same writer's articles on Sopwell and Pré (*ibid.* 424–5, 431). Miss Reddan takes full account of the record and legal sources.
2 The contemporary accounts and criticisms of Wallingford are in *MSAC*, VI (i) (*Registrum Johannis Whethamstede*, I).
3 *Reg. J. Whethamstede*, I, 6–9.

embassies that for centuries had kept St Albans in the stream of the nation's life.

Whethamstede's first year in his second term of office had been marked by a domestic scandal of which the true story is probably lost beyond recovery. Two versions exist, and both are clearly biased, but in each the brothers Wallingford, and especially William, are accused of embezzlement and the misuse of funds on a large scale.[1] Whatever the exact truth, it seems impossible to acquit the general official of all fault. The elderly Whethamstede did not press the charges home, and William Wallingford, though deprived of most of his offices, retained the influential post of archdeacon.

When Whethamstede died in 1465 the ancients of the house must have exchanged memories of the world they had known more than forty years before, when the young abbot had stood for old customs against Henry V; they may also have exchanged more recent memories before electing William Albone, the prior, and his election seems to show that Wallingford had not yet fully recovered the confidence of his brethren. He was clearly indispensable, however, and held under Albone the offices of archdeacon and kitchener as well as that of prior, which at St Albans had so often been a step to the summit. When Albone died in 1476 Wallingford at last reached the top; he was the last abbot to take a notable place in the long list of those who for more than four centuries had rendered the abbey ever more magnificent and more beautiful. The chronicler gives a long catalogue of his works, which included the reredos, still to be seen, in the presbytery, and his own chantry and tomb. At the same time the decline in the prestige of the house and the growing power of smaller people are shown by the proceedings taken in chancery against him, and his difficulties with nunneries under his jurisdiction. All these and other troubles came to a head in 1490 in the affair with Archbishop Morton, and in the very serious charges made against the abbey at that time.

This affair of St Albans has been debated at great length by historians ever since Froude gave to it a controversial notoriety.[2] It must not be allowed to bulk too large in a general view of monastic life in the reign of Henry VII. Nevertheless, the last years of Wallingford's reign saw a decline setting in at St Albans from which the abbey never recovered, and the forty years that remained added nothing of note to the story of the house. Wallingford died in office in 1492 and was succeeded by his prior, Ramryge, who like his predecessor left a chantry in his church, but otherwise little of note either for good or for evil. On his death in 1521 Wolsey secured for himself the abbey *in commendam* and held it till his fall eight years later, leaving it impoverished, and the last years of St Albans were embittered by intrigues and rumours of the approaching end.

Yet the age was not the age of Wallingford alone. It was the age also

1 *Ibid.* 110 seqq., 116 seqq.
2 For a short account of the episode, *v. infra*, pp. 78–9.

of Richard Bere of Glastonbury, of Richard Kidderminster at Winchcombe, of John Islip at Westminster, and of Marmaduke Huby at
Fountains. In the pages that follow we shall see something of these men
and their world.

The machinery of government of the black monks continued in function[1] to the Dissolution. While there is no evidence to suggest that after the
elaborate re-edition of the statutes at the chapter of 1444 any further legislation of similar importance appeared, small additions and re-affirmations
continued to be made, the latest dating from 1516,[2] and in theory and on
paper at least, the discipline and observance suffered no great change
between the days of Thomas de la Mare and those of John Islip. Chapters
continued to meet regularly and to appoint visitors, who duly went their
rounds. From 1336, without a single exception, Northampton was the
venue of the triennial chapter till 1495; then, for no clear reason, the point
of assembly was shifted to Coventry, which had long been among the
four or five most populous towns of provincial England, and which had
held its prosperity during the fifteenth century. Coventry appreciated the
compliment, and was at pains to recognize the occasion with a civic
welcome, which took place on Wednesday, 4 July, when the fathers had
done their business at the cathedral priory. The reception is vividly described in the Leet Book.[3] After the final formalities the chaptermen

came forth at the south durre in the Mynstere & toke their wey thurgh the newe
bildyng downe the Bailly-lane. And the Maire & his Brethren in their scarlet
Clokes with all the Craftes in theire best araye stode under the Elme in Seynt
Mighelles Chirchyard. And all the pensels [pennons] of the Cite before them:
which pensels there went before the Crosse, & the Maire with his Brethren &
the Craftes stode styll till the presidentes cam whom the Maire toke be the
handes & welcomed them to town, & so folowed the procession...into the
Priory; & there was a solempne sermon seyde, where the Maire there satte
betwixt both presidentes, & after sermon doon they departed every man to his
loggyng & som with the Maire to dyner, as dyuers of them did before.

At Coventry the chapter stayed till 1519. In that year, possibly through
the influence of John Islip, then and thenceforth one of the presidents, a
move was made to Westminster, and there the meetings took place till
1532, when the last recorded chapter was held on 16 January.

III. THE FRANCISCAN OBSERVANTS

The Observant Friars were the only representatives in England of the
reform movements of the later Middle Ages which gave birth to a number
of new and zealous organizations among the monks and friars. Unlike
most of these, the Observants did not originate at a fixed moment as a

---

1 Cf. lists of chapters and references to Northampton (index, s.v.) in Pantin, MC passim,
vols. II, III.
2 MC, II, 224–6.   3 EETS, o.s., 138, p. 588, reprinted MC, III, 116–17.

branch of the Friars Minor. Rather, they counted among their spiritual ancestry all those, such as the *ʒelanti* and the Spirituals, who had in one way or another opposed the successive mitigations of the Rule of St Francis, especially on the point of the corporate ownership of property. The Observants, however, were not direct descendants of the Spirituals; they were the outcome of a swelling wave of fervour in the second half of the fourteenth century.[1]

As has been noted in passing in an earlier volume,[2] the bitter struggle between the Spirituals and the friars of the broader way had to outward appearance ended in a coalition, based on the victory of the Conventuals or followers of the mitigated Rule. The decisions of John XXII in his bulls *Ad conditorem canonum* (8 December 1322) and *Quorundam exigit* (7 October 1323) had seemed to put an end to idealism on both the practical and theoretical levels, by restoring to the Minors the ownership of property hitherto vested in the Holy See, and by denying that Christ and His Apostles had practised absolute material poverty. Nevertheless, a desire for the literal observance of the Rule had never become wholly extinct, and throughout the fourteenth century there were attempts by individuals or groups to return to the primitive observance, either while remaining within the order or by obtaining a papal privilege to withdraw from it. The numbers of friars acting in this way gradually multiplied, and the expedient was adopted of allowing certain houses to follow the stricter life, and in the latter half of the fourteenth century the number of such convents increased. Most of these remained within the order, but a few groups and individuals obtained papal privileges, enabling them to withdraw from it. As the movement spread in the early fifteenth century groups of houses in certain provinces were given papal permission to have provincial vicars and even (in 1414) a vicar-general of their own. It was in this epoch that the Observance gained lustre from three of its members who became luminaries of the order in the first half of the century, St Bernardine of Siena, St James della Marchia, and St John Capistran. The two first of these deprecated any cleavage among the Minors, and in 1430 Martin V endeavoured to restore unity by means of a general reform. The attempt issued only in a papal acknowledgement of the essential demands of the Conventuals, and there followed a strong movement towards secession on the part of the Observant Friars, led by John Capistran. This was only partially successful, and the Observants remained under the jurisdiction of the minister general of all the Minors, though with provincial ministers of their own; in addition, it was forbidden to monarchs or others to make any attempt to substitute Observants for Conventuals in existing houses.

1 There is no good account in English of the origins of the Observants. For what may be called their pre-history, *v.* D. L. Douie, *The Nature and Effects of the heresy of the Fraticelli.*

2 *RO*, 1, 245–7.

C

So matters stood when the first move was made to introduce the Observants into England.[1] The first request was made to no less a person than St John Capistran himself by Charles I, Margrave of Baden, acting for Henry VI. John replied (24 October 1454) that he could not come to England as he was about to go to Hungary, and the outbreak of the Wars of the Roses in the next year, followed shortly by the death of the saint, postponed the project indefinitely.

The next impulse would seem to have been due to the sister of Edward IV, Margaret of Burgundy, who was on a visit to England in the summer of 1480. Both her father-in-law, Philip, and she herself are known to have been both clients and patrons of the Observants, and in September 1481, acting with some English nobles, she obtained a bull from Sixtus IV authorizing the foundation of three Observant houses in this country. Nothing came of this immediately, but it is natural to see some connection between Margaret's action and the invitation issued by the king, probably in the autumn of 1480, to the vicar-general of the Ultramontane family of the Observants to make a foundation at Greenwich. He refused to act without papal licence, whereupon the king obtained a bull of 4 January 1481, licensing a foundation at Greenwich or anywhere else, and the house duly came into being on 2 July 1482. It was to be subject to a commissary of the vicar-general until the number of English convents should have grown. The first commissaries were foreigners and for some years, at least, a majority of the friars would seem to have been of foreign birth.

The new plantation did not increase rapidly. It had, however, the warm patronage of the new king, Henry VII, who on 11 December of the year of Bosworth gave his approval to what had been accomplished at Greenwich. Some thirteen years later an advance was made, but this took the form, not of a new venture, but of an endeavour to replace the Conventuals with Observants in five convents.[2] Such a measure, against which the Conventuals had of old endeavoured to protect themselves by a series of prohibitory bulls, was only rendered possible by a *non obstantibus* clause in the bull of 14 April 1498, issued by Alexander VI. This was given in response to a request from the king, who had stated that of the fifty-seven houses of Minors in England that of Greenwich was the only one where any observance worth the name remained, and that the total population of these fifty-seven houses did not surpass that of twenty-five in the past.[3] As the latter of these two sweeping statements is inaccurate, for the total number of Franciscans in 1490 was about two-thirds of the total of 1348, and had in fact risen slowly but steadily for many decades, so it is probable that the state of observance was considerably better than the petition to the pope had suggested. Indeed, the petition was itself incon-

[1] For this, *v*. A. G. Little, 'The Introduction of the Observant Friars into England', in *PBA*, x.

[2] This move is recounted in a second article by A. G. Little, 'The Introduction of the Observant Friars into England', in *PBA*, xxvii.

[3] Little, *PBA*, xxvii, 157.

sistent, for it had gone on to say that the convent of Greenwich was full to overflowing, and the king was consequently given permission to transfer the Conventuals from any particularly irregular houses to houses of better observance, and to fill the vacancies with Observants, unless indeed the original inhabitants were willing to adopt the observance of the newcomers.

Acting upon this bull, Henry effected the transference to the Observants of the friaries at Canterbury and Newcastle-on-Tyne, and on 19 May 1499 an English province was constituted independent of the Conventuals.[1] In the following year new foundations were made at Richmond (Surrey) and, some seven years later, at Newark. There the increase stopped, and for the remaining three decades of conventual life the Observants held these five houses, as against the fifty-five still occupied by the Conventuals. Introduced by the king into England, and settled as what in an earlier age would have been called a 'royal chapel' adjacent to the palaces of Greenwich and Sheen, the friars served as confessors, counsellors and preachers to the royal family, and as such were to bear the brunt of the royal displeasure when the private affairs of the king suddenly became part of a political and religious revolution.

IV. FIFTEENTH-CENTURY SUPPRESSIONS

If, as has been noted elsewhere, the numbers of the religious in England fluctuated considerably between 1300 and 1500, and showed a notable overall reduction between these two limiting dates, the numbers of religious houses remained remarkably stable. In a final analysis, this stability is eloquent witness to the even flow of English life between those dates, without revolution and without destructive warfare. There was, of course, the loss of the majority of the lesser alien priories in the decades immediately before and after 1400; in consequence, almost one hundred names disappeared from the monastic map. But these, with scarcely an exception, were small, dependent houses. Among the autonomous houses of all orders, and among the friaries, there were, with one partial reservation, practically no casualties at all between 1300 and 1500, despite the devastation of the pestilences. The rare exceptions to this statement (leaving aside for the moment the Austin canons) can be counted almost on the fingers of one hand, though the total number of houses was well over four hundred on any reckoning.

The small priory of Luffield (Northants), never really well off, was left desolate by the Black Death and never recovered. It was finally snuffed out in 1494. The abbey of Alcester, another cradle-sick child, was petering out in 1465, when it was annexed to Evesham and continued a tenuous existence till the end. The remaining casualties were either small dependencies such as Beaulieu (Bedfordshire), or victims of border warfare such as Cardiff. Even among the nunneries only two disappeared—

1 Little, *PBA*, x, 465.

Rowney (Herts) in 1457, and St Radegund's at Cambridge, the earliest
(1496) of the group of small houses of various kinds suppressed by Tudor
prelates in the interests of new educational establishments.[1]

The partial reservation made above concerns the Austin canons. Here,
within the century 1410–1510, some sixteen houses lost their autonomy,
and of these nine ceased to exist as religious houses.[2] In almost every case
the establishment was a small one, and since it was usual among the Austin
canons for the size of the original community to bear a direct ratio to the
income, a small decrease either of income or personnel could make regular
life impossible. Most of the casualties under review were caused either
by the family of three or four becoming extinct, or by a serious decrease
of the tenuous revenues, or by a combination of these two circumstances.
The Austin canons, alone of the religious orders, had autonomous houses
minute both in numbers and funds, and it was undoubtedly this that led
to a fair number of failures in the fifteenth century. At all periods the life
of the black canons had been the least austere and the least strictly organized
of any of the religious bodies, and in the fifteenth century their way of
life had to meet the competition of the numerous new collegiate foundations, which suited the taste of the age better. The sinking of these houses,
therefore, should not be set in a dramatic light. They had never been very
significant, and their disappearance was neither a catastrophe nor a portent.
Where practicable, these moribund priories were annexed to neighbouring
houses; in a few cases they were bestowed by king or patron on some
favourite educational establishment.

The reasons given for the disappearance of these houses may serve also
to explain the continued existence of many of their fellows. In a country
which for some four hundred years had not suffered a social or economic
revolution, a landed estate of moderate size, held by an undying community, had every chance of survival, and even of appreciation, and every
indication goes to show that until the very eve of the Dissolution the
prospect of a guaranteed livelihood, in combination with such attractions
as the religious life in itself might have, was enough to ensure a regular,
if modest, flow of recruits.

1 For these houses, v. D. Knowles and R. N. Hadcock, *Medieval Religious Houses.*
2 For these, v. J. C. Dickinson, 'Early Suppressions of English Houses of Austin
Canons'. The title and occasional expressions in Mr Dickinson's essay might give the careless reader the impression that the number of suppressions (as opposed to amalgamations)
was greater than was in fact the case.

CHAPTER II

SOME MONASTIC ACTIVITIES

I. MUSIC AND THE CHANT

In an earlier volume some account was given of the development of Gregorian chant and other music in the monasteries of England down to the beginning of the thirteenth century,[1] and the story was continued later with a few notes upon the thirteenth and fourteenth centuries.[2] Until very recently little was known of English music between 1350 and 1500, when the series of great composers began, whose Masses and motets opened what now for sixty years has been recognized as the golden age of English music. Within the last thirty years or so, however, musicologists in Europe and America have revealed with increasing clarity the eminence of the Englishman John Dunstable (d. 1453), and his importance in the history of continental as well as of English music. Between Dunstable and the sixteenth century something of a void seemed to exist, and it had been suggested that, as with poetry and literary prose an interlunary period had succeeded the age of Rolle, Hilton, Langland and Chaucer, so in music no master had immediately followed Dunstable. Now, however, a group of scholars can show this supposition to be false; throughout the fifteenth century music of a very high order of excellence was being produced, which set England in the van of a great movement and led without a break from Dunstable to the masterpieces of Taverner and Byrd, and through the age of the madrigalists to that of Henry Purcell.[3]

With this outpouring of musical genius we are not directly concerned, for it took place almost entirely outside the monasteries, and in the few cases where a monastery enters the story it is generally as the patron or employer of a composer who was not himself a monk. In the realm of music, as in that of literary and theological work, the monasteries had ceased during the thirteenth century to be the leaders of their world. The age of plainsong came gradually to an end, and the new forms of choral music, which had originated in the monasteries and had been developed by them, passed into the hands of musicians who were not monks and often not even clerics, whose works were performed by professional singers, the 'singing men' of cathedrals and colleges, and the children of song schools attached to great churches or forming part of a collegiate foundation. It was the age of chantries and colleges and, just as the stream of benefactions had been diverted from the religious houses to the college

---

1 *MO*, 545–60. 2 *RO*, I, 305–7; II, 296.
3 For what immediately follows, I must acknowledge the help given by Mr Thurston Dart, of Jesus College, Mr B. L. Trowell, of Gonville and Caius College, and Mr H. Baillie, of Corpus Christi College, who have been making pioneer study of fifteenth- and early sixteenth-century music.

and the memorial chantry, so the initiative in music passed from the monks to the master of the choristers in the great colleges and Lady Chapels up and down the land, and especially to the masters in such royal or splendid foundations as Eton, Windsor, the Chapel Royal, King's College, Cambridge, St Stephen's, Westminster, and Winchester College.[1]

While this change was taking place, the monasteries remained, as they had remained in other fields, strongly conservative. The Gregorian chant had always throughout Europe been the consecrated chant of the Gradual and Antiphonary, and it remained so to the end. How far it was blunted and degraded in England in the later middle ages has still to be discovered, but it is certain that the great mass of service books collected in the monasteries and largely destroyed at the Reformation contained Gregorian chant alone, and to the very end visitors recalled the religious on occasion to its execution.[2] The Gregorian chant, however, had never been exclusive. In the Anglo-Saxon and Anglo-Norman monasteries the presence of the children of the cloister had helped to encourage the early development of harmony and primitive counterpoint. When the children gradually disappeared with the cessation of infant oblation, it became customary at many houses to employ a few singing men to assist the monks with harmonized chant at Mass or Vespers, and while visitors continued to deplore artificial or falsetto singing on the part of the religious, they were ready to allow use to be made of lay singers to ease the task of the monks.[3]

Nevertheless, the monks and canons seem rarely if ever to have given a home in their choirs to the very latest developments of counterpoint in the fifteenth century. These were the province, as has been said, of the choirmasters of colleges, and seem not to have been connected with the liturgy but with the favourite extra-liturgical services of the age, the Lady Mass and the anthem of the Blessed Virgin sung before or after the evening *Salve Regina*. Here, however, there was a link between monastic and collegiate musical practice. The sung Lady Mass, first introduced at the great abbeys in the thirteenth century, gradually became universal. The performance of the chant for two Masses daily, in addition to the other offices, would have been an almost unbearable physical burden, and it was probably the need of assistance and the desire for elaboration in execution that gave birth to the monastic song-school, either as a separate establishment or as a part of the almonry school. By the end of the fourteenth century many of the largest abbeys had schools of this kind. The master, a layman, was engaged to teach the boys all forms of choral singing and to compose Masses and notes for them.[4]

1 For an interim report on this, *v. Musica Britannica*, x, 'The Eton Choirbook': 1, ed. F. Ll. Harrison, introduction, and the same author's article, 'The Eton Choirbook', in *Annales Musicologiques*, 1.

2 E.g. at Wenlock, injunction 25 in R. Graham, 'Roland Gosenell, Prior of Wenlock, 1521–6', in *E.E.S.* 142: 'gregoriana nota utatur'.

3 E.g. at St Mary's, York, visitation of *c.* 1393–4 (*MC*, III, 84).   4 *RO*, II, 296.

With the end of the fifteenth century another great change began. Elaborate choral compositions, hitherto generally restricted to the Lady Mass and motets or anthems, began to come in, not only for Masses of all kinds, but also for all the liturgical texts such as antiphons, responds and the various occasions of the liturgical year. By the early decades of the sixteenth century the offices at a great feast and for the Triduum of Holy Week had come to have a musical setting of great elaboration: indeed, it seems clear that a fair-sized collegiate or parish choir may well have performed a musical programme comparable to that of the very largest cathedral churches of modern times. It is strange that at the very moment when the liturgical traditions and monuments of the past were being swept remorselessly away, the musical setting of the liturgy in elaborate counterpoint was on the point of being brought to perfection by English masters in compositions that have never been surpassed.

As the variety and breadth of musical techniques developed, the choir-master at an abbey may well have introduced to the monastic choir some of the new forms of music that his colleagues were perfecting in colleges and royal chapels. Some idea of the musical repertory of a large monastic church may be gathered from the indentures made between the prior and convent of Durham and a succession of choirmasters. There are three such documents from the Tudor period alone, all couched in exactly the same terms. The last, dated 4 December 1513, sets out the duties of the post as follows:[1]

The said Thomas Haskewell [=Ashwell] shall give instruction, with assiduous care and as he best knows how, to such monks of the house as may be chosen, together with eight lay boys. He shall freely and to the best of his ability take pains to teach them both to play the organ and to acquire a knowledge of plain chant and harmonized chant by practising plain-song, prick-note, faburden, descant, swarenote and counterpoint.[2] He shall give them lessons carefully and

---

1 *Historia Dunelmensis Ecclesiae Scriptores Tres*, ed. J. Raine, no. cccxxiii, p. ccccxiii.
2 The text has: 'planesong, priknott, faburdon, dischant, swarenote et countre'. With the exception of plainsong, these terms are still of uncertain significance, owing partly to their various meanings in different times and places. Three categories of music seem to be included: plainsong, written polyphony and various kinds of improvised harmonization. Pricknote seems to have been written or 'pricked' polyphony, the notation being written in small dots or points. *Faburdon, descant* and *counter* are best taken as different forms of improvised polyphony. *Faburden* has many meanings and eludes definition, v. Scholes, *Oxford Companion to Music, s.v.* The *OED*, citing Stainer and Barrett, has 'a sort of harmony consisting of thirds and sixths added to a canto fermo', but perhaps Grove's definition is more in place: 'a type of descant [peculiarly English] in which the chief melody is transferred from the tenor [=our bass] to the highest voice [soprano]'. *Descant* is defined by Grove as: 'any polyphonic composition mensurable in every part, as distinct from the organum purum where the plainsong tenor is not measured'; but in common usage it is a form of extempore part-singing upon a plainsong melody. *Counterpoint* as an art-form has been defined as: 'the combination of simultaneous voice-parts, each independent but all conducing to a result of uniform coherent texture' (Scholes, *Oxford Companion to Music*, citing W. H. Hadow), but in the Durham indentures and elsewhere is probably merely another form of improvisation. *Swarenote* is the most difficult of all to define, since there is division of opinion as to whether it denotes a developed form of notation—the *ars nova*, the measured music of the fourteenth and later centuries, with 'squares' replacing 'points',—or whether it is merely

adequately four times a day on all ferial days, that is, twice in the morning and twice in the afternoon, and shall hear their renderings, keeping from them nothing of his knowledge in these matters. The said Thomas Haskewell shall also be bound to attend in person in the choir of the cathedral at all Masses, vespers and anthems of Our Lady at which prick-note, descant, faburden and harmonized music are performed, and he shall be present from start to finish of this chant. If needed, he shall play the organ in the choir, and sing the tenor part or any other part that suits his voice or that is appointed him by the precentor. Also he shall be present in person each day at the sung Mass of Our Lady in the Galilee and shall sing there either plainsong or polyphony.[1] . . . He shall also be responsible at the precentor's request for providing the chant, and every year he shall compose a new Mass of four or five parts, or some equivalent piece.

For all this he is to receive a salary of £10 a year and a livery, with a modest pension in old age, or if he is overtaken by infirmity.

From these indentures it is clear that polyphony and counterpoint, as well as other forms of harmonized chant, formed a normal augmentation of plain chant in the monastic choir, and that the young monks were instructed by a professional in all these forms of music. The chant was also accompanied with organ-music, and in this, too, the monks were taught to take part. As for the boys of the song-school, they certainly sang at the Lady Mass and evening *Salve*, and probably also on other festal occasions. At a large church, and with the kind of choirmaster Durham would attract, the repertory of music and the daily ration provided in choir may well have been generous and rich in quality. It is worth noting, however, that the formulae of the indentures were almost identical from 1440 to 1515,[2] whereas the developments in music during that time were very great. It would therefore be rash to suppose that the character and quantity of the music remained the same, while it would be equally rash to understand every term in the indenture with all its contemporary fullness; we cannot say, for example, on the strength of the indentures alone, that at Durham there were performed in the monastic choir Masses of the complexity and magnificence of Taverner's compositions. On the other hand, some of the very greatest names of the Tudor age occur as monastic choirmasters. Thus Robert Fayrfax was organist and director of music at St Albans from 1498 or 1502 for some twenty years, though he retained his connection with the chapel royal, and Thomas Tallis was organist and master of the choristers at Waltham for some years before the surrender of the house.[3] With such masters, and with a copious supply of good voices, some of the monastic churches must

another form of improvised singing in harmony. It may be added that the testimonial given in 1489 to a monk of Westminster about to migrate to Wenlock, that he could 'syng both playn song and prikked song', suggests that such an accomplishment was normal. Cf. E. H. Pearce, *The Monks of Westminster*, 163.

1 Cf. the account of this in *Rites of Durham, infra*, p. 136.
2 The earliest indenture of 1447 (*Scriptores Tres*, appendix cccxv) has all the above terms save 'swarenote', which appears first in the indentures of 1496 (no. ccc) and 1502 (no. cccx).
3 *V.* article in Grove's *Dictionary*, supplementing *DNB*.

in the early years of Henry VIII have enjoyed an abundance of splendid music in no way inferior to that of the great secular churches and chapels. The fifteenth century saw a swift and remarkable advance in the design and construction of the organ, which grew in a century and a half from the primitive instrument of the early Middle Ages into what is a recognizable forebear of the modern organ.[1] In its broadest lines the change was from an organ with a small and mainly diatonic range of notes, each controlling a large number of pipes and manipulated (if that is the word) by a blow of the fist, from which the only effect attainable was that of the 'full organ',[2] to a much more varied instrument controlled from a chromatic keyboard actuated by a touch of the finger and having stops to shut off individual ranks of pipes. This development, like the contemporary development of printing, was principally the work of German or Flemish mechanics, and the innovations reached England slowly; in many churches the primitive organ probably had a long survival. The 'great' organs in particular probably remained unchanged, and the improvements appeared only in small instruments. Generally speaking, by the last decades of the fifteenth century there were two kinds of organ in every large church: the 'great' organ, a melody instrument having as many as forty pipes to a note, and the 'little' organ, a harmony instrument with greater range and flexibility, varying in size according to its pitch. The former was used either for moments and occasions of emotion, when a loud or joyful noise was appropriate, or to support strong choral singing; the latter, the small organ, was used for the more delicate accompaniment of chant and polyphony, or for playing alternate verses of hymns, Magnificats and Masses, and for the first beginnings of instrumental music and improvisation. Most monastic churches would have had three organs: the great organ in the nave, transept or choir aisle; a small organ within the choir itself or on the choir screen; and another small organ in the Lady Chapel to accompany the choristers.[3] Thus at Waltham in Tallis's time there were a 'great larg payre' and 'a lesser payr' of organs in the choir, and 'a lytell payre of organes' in the Lady Chapel. The two small organs were probably of the kind that could on occasion be carried about the church; instruments of this kind were small enough to fit into a tribune or a gallery. Whethamstede's expensive organ at St Albans, probably still functioning in Tallis's day, was presumably an up-to-date piece of work for the mid-fifteenth century;[4] replacements were generally slow in coming. The great

---

1 *V.* article 'Organ' in Grove's *Dictionary,* and authorities there cited.

2 The Latin phrase 'organa pulsare' is still used in Roman rubrical directions. One is inclined to render 'thump the organ', but the term *pulsare* has a respectable musical ancestry with more gentle associations; it is used, e.g., of playing on the lyre by Virgil, *Aeneid,* VI, 647.

3 So Grove, *Dictionary, s.v.* Tallis, citing a Waltham inventory of 1540 in PRO, Exch. K.R. Church goods, 11/24. A 'pair of organs' simply = 'an organ'; cf. 'a pair of stairs' and Germ. 'ein Paar'.

4 Whethamstede's organ (Amundesham, *Annales,* I, 198, 259; *Registrum J. Whethamstede,* I, 455) cost £17. 6s. 8d. It was for the choir, and the additional expense of £43. 3s. 3d. for the organ and gospel stand suggests that it stood on a screen or gallery.

and small organs at Butley that were repaired in 1511 were old instruments, and the 'pair of organs' with two stops given by Henry Barrett to the Lady Chapel in the same year was clearly small and simple, whereas the 'organ of excellent voice and tone with five stops', given by the prior in 1534 was probably a more modern product.[1] Thus far only black monks and canons have been mentioned. Some of the other orders were stricter in their musical regulations. Thus organs and polyphony were forbidden to the Carthusians, and organs were officially forbidden at Syon, though the earliest surviving piece of English organ music appears to be associated with this house. The Cistercians for long did their best to prevent polyphony from coming in, but in the fifteenth century organs were normal. The Carmelites allowed faburden, but not motets.[2]

While none of the many great composers of the age is known to have been a religious, and Prior Dygon of St Augustine's[3] is almost the only monastic figure of any note, some of the greatest, as has been seen, were connected with religious houses. Fayrfax and Tallis were normal in their relationship, but John Taverner, in some ways the greatest of them all, though his life as an artist was short, has a less pleasant connection with the religious life. A Lincolnshire man, perhaps a native of Boston, he made his name at the neighbouring college of Tattershall, famed for its music, and was recommended to Wolsey by his diocesan, John Longland, when the cardinal needed a choirmaster for his Oxford college. There, in the choir that had been till recently that of the canons of St Frideswide's, his choristers gave expression to his rapid outpouring of majestic melody. His muse, however, failed to keep her hold on Taverner, and he began, like others at Cardinal College, to take up with the new learning. Wolsey tolerant as ever, and apparently appreciative of his genius, remarked to his accusers that he 'was but a musitian' and could do no harm.[4] The cardinal misjudged his man. Taverner, with the virus in his system, abandoned his harmonies for militant Protestantism and became a zealous agent of Cromwell in the suppression of the monasteries and the destruction of superstition. He composed no more, and died within a few years, to be buried beneath the great tower of Boston church, the 'beacon of the fens'.

The dissolution of the monasteries, followed after a brief interval by that of the colleges, must have given to musical composers and executants a shock almost as great as that received by architects and masons. It was not only that they lost the theatre and tools of their profession; they lost

---

1 *The Register or Chronicle of Butley Priory, Suffolk, 1510–35*, ed. A. G. Dickens, 28: 'unum par Organorum...cum ii obstructionibus'; 66: 'unum par Organorum bene intonatum et sonoratum cum quinque obstruccionibus'.

2 For these, v. Archdale A. King, *Liturgies of the Religious Orders*, 32f., 96f., 287.

3 For Dygon, v. *DNB* and Grove's *Dictionary*; and for a glimpse of him as prior, v. *infra*, p. 95.

4 The phrase is reported by Foxe, *Actes of the Martyrs* (ed. 1576, p. 1004), who notes that Wolsey 'excused him for his musicke'.

also the very matter of their art, the Latin liturgy and its robe of plainsong. Nevertheless, in spite of a barren decade which partly justifies Fuller's lamentation,[1] music rode the storm more successfully than architecture. Whereas Gothic designing came to a full stop, and reappeared only in the rarest examples, music, then in a new and virile phase of growth, unfolded its flowers as if there had been no storm, and even continued to use the old types and forms—the Mass, the Passion, the Motet—as the basis of its structure. What the Elizabethans made of some of the words to which Byrd set his music must remain something of a mystery. We wonder also whether the canons of Waltham, who heard the first performance of some of Tallis's Masses when their days in the cloister were already numbered, remained unmoved in Holy Week by his magnificent Lamentations and the call, nine times repeated, to Jerusalem to turn to her God, with its imploring address and the solemn cadences of the two bass voices.

II. BUILDING: THE LAST PHASE

Historians of the Tudor age have often declared that a period of activity in building, both ecclesiastical and domestic, opened with the return of peace in the reign of Henry VII. This statement, like so many others once made of the fifteenth century, has been challenged recently; we have been told that the Wars of the Roses were less catastrophic than earlier generations supposed, that many large areas were unaffected by them, and that English industry and commerce expanded steadily throughout the fifteenth century. There was, therefore, no *a priori* reason why building activity should slacken, and indeed careful examination of extant work has shown, and doubtless will hereafter show still more clearly, that parish churches all through the country were being rebuilt with larger naves or chancels, and with the towers and spires that are the glory of the regions that lie upon or near good freestone, such as Somerset, the Cotswolds and the upland country that runs north-east from Oxfordshire through Northamptonshire to Lincoln. It is easy, also, to cite some notable cases of large-scale building, such as that in the abbey church of Bury St Edmunds after the disastrous fire of 1465. Nevertheless, it is probably true that the half-century between 1440 and 1490 saw the inception of fewer large-scale undertakings than the periods immediately before and after, particularly at the highest architectural level, that of cathedrals, abbeys, and chapels royal. We remember the slow progress at Westminster at this time, and the virtual standstill at King's College Chapel, Cambridge. In contrast

---

1 The reader who has no music in his soul may care to have the sour comment of Erasmus (1516) on 1 Cor. xiv. 19: 'They have so much of it [*sc.* choral music] in England that the monks attend to nothing else. A set of creatures who ought to be lamenting their sins fancy they can please God by gurgling in their throats. Boys are kept in the English Benedictine monasteries solely and simply to sing hymns to the Virgin. If they want music, let them sing psalms like rational beings, and not too many of them.'

to this it is certain that the religious houses of England, during the last half-century of their existence, showed an undiminished activity in adding to their churches, in embellishing them, and above all in using all the new techniques and materials and designs of domestic architecture to adapt their buildings to the demands and tastes of a new age. No attempt will here be made to compile a catalogue of these works, or to distinguish individual or regional styles, but a brief glance at some of the noteworthy buildings of the Tudor age will show that the religious continued, up to the very end, to add to the great heritage of beauty that had been accumulating since the days of Lanfranc. Most of the examples will inevitably be taken from buildings that still exist, at least in ruin, but it must never be forgotten that some of the most magnificent have disappeared to the last stone, and have left scarcely a trace in the records of the time.

At Canterbury, where there had been something of a pause since Chillenden's day, the great central tower, known as the Angel Steeple from the gilt figure that once surmounted it, or Bell Harry from Eastry's great bell that hung within it, and which Erasmus was one of the first to note with admiration as he caught its gleam on approaching the city, was erected by Prior Goldstone II, c. 1495. At Gloucester, another far-seen church received its most familiar feature, the tower, c. 1460, and the noble Lady Chapel was completed c. 1500. Building at Gloucester was, indeed, almost continuous, and Leland could note that 'one Osberne, celerer of Gloucester, made of late a fayre new tower or gate-house at the south west part of the abbey cemiterye'.[1] At Winchcombe, not far away, 'Richard de Kidderminster, the last abbot saving one, did great cost of the church, and enclosed the abbey towards the towne with a maine stone-wall',[2] while a dozen miles away in the Vale of Avon 'Clement Lichfield, the last abbot of Evesham save one, did very much cost in building of the abbey and other places longing to it. He builded much about the quire in adorning it. He made a right sumptuous and high square tower of stone in the cemitory of Eovesham',[3] which still stands as evidence of the abbey's St Martin's summer of prosperity.

At Westminster the greater part of the nave received its roof and vault at the hands of Abbot Eastry (1471–98) and the final bay and west front, with the pavement beneath, were completed by Abbot Islip within a few months or weeks of his death. At Peterborough Abbot Kirton's 'New Building' with its fan vaulting recalling the nearby chapel of King's College was completed c. 1528. Away in the west at Sherborne the nave was reconstructed and the aisles and nave vaulted with the beautiful fan-tracery from 1475 to 1504, and the eastern extension of the chapel of St Mary-le-Bow achieved. At Bath almost the whole framework of the abbey as it stands to-day was the work of the last priors, continuing that of Bishop Oliver King and, as is well known, their work was unfinished

1 Leland, *Itinerary*, ed. L. Toulmin-Smith, ii, 62.
2 *Ibid.* 54.   3 *Ibid.* 52.

at the Dissolution.[1] At Glastonbury no enumeration can take the place of Leland's matter-of-fact but strangely impressive account of what must have been the most magnificent complex of purely monastic buildings in England, if not in Europe.

Richard Bere abbate [he writes] buildid the new lodging by the great chambre caullid the kinge's lodging in the galery. Bere buildid the new lodginges for secular prestes and clerkes of our Lady. Abbate Bere buildid Edgares chapel at the est end of the chirch, but Abbate Whiting performid sum part of it. Bere archid on bothe sides the est parte of the chirch that began to cast owt. Bere made the volte of the steple in the transepto, and under 2 arches like S. Andres crosse, els it had fallen. Bere made a riche altare of sylver and gilt: and set it afore the high altare. Bere cumming from his embassadre out of Italie made a chapelle of our Lady de Loretta, joining to the north side of the body of the chirch. He made the chapelle of the sepulchre in the southe end Navis ecclesie whereby he is buried sub plano marmore yn the south isle of the bodie of the chirch. He made an almose house in the north part of the abbay for vii or x poore wymen with a chapel.[2]

Some of those who worked as young men on the masonry of these edifices may well have earned good wages for pulling them down.

Other orders had been as active as the black monks. The Cistercian churches had in general been little altered since the great rebuilding epoch of 1180–1250, but in their last phase some of the abbots fell in with the fashion of their age and gave their church the tower which Cistercian statute had successfully forbidden in earlier centuries. A familiar example still standing is at Fountains, the work of that able man, Marmaduke Huby. Across the Pennines at Furness the western tower was still unfinished in 1536. The canons also indulged in western towers, as at Shap (c. 1500) and Bolton, where the tower was begun c. 1520 and never completed. Within the churches also beautiful things continued to accumulate: woodwork at Cleeve, chantries such as those of Tewkesbury, Peterborough and Bath; Wallingford's chantry and retable at St Albans, Islip's chantry at West-minster, Ramryge's chapel at St Albans, Lichfield's two chapels at Evesham.[3]

More numerous still and perhaps more characteristic of the age were the domestic buildings. Many have disappeared, many have been embedded in or absorbed by mansions, but a few remain. Two houses perhaps stand out in the memory above all others. The one is St Osyth's in Essex, where that great builder, Abbot Vyntoner, raised his majestic gateway and parish church and abbot's house in the rose-coloured East-Anglian brick and flint; the other at Forde on the confines of Dorset and Devon, where

1 *Ibid.* 1, 144: 'The residue of it [*sc.* Bath Abbey] was syns [Oliver King] made by the priors of Bath: and especially by Gibbes the last prior ther, that spent a great summe of mony on that fabrik.'

2 *Ibid.* 289–90.

3 For notes on these and other chantries, with illustrations of many, *v.* G. H. Cook, *Medieval Chantries and Chantry Chapels* (London, 1947).

Abbot Chard built his hall and door and cloisters *c.* 1528 and lived to surrender them a few years later. Forde, indeed, is a good example of the thoroughgoing domestic rehabilitation achieved by the Cistercians in the sixteenth century. It is a witness alike to their prosperity and to their acceptance of the new standards of living. Whalley in Lancashire provides another example of a Cistercian abbot's house with all modern conveniences, but perhaps the most notable extant example of reconstruction is at Cleeve in Somerset. Here the disappearance of the lay brethren, the increase in domestic amenities and the conventional position of the abbot were all frankly recognized in a scheme of architectural conversion. The long refectory, perpendicular to the south alley of the cloister, was dismantled and replaced by a smaller but more elegant hall parallel to the cloister walk and raised, like some of the black monk and college halls, on an undercroft; it was completed with staircase, screens and a large fireplace. At the same time the western or lay brothers' range was converted into an abbot's house, and a new inner gateway built. The black monks meanwhile were putting up domestic buildings fast. A notable example, still extant, is the mellow prior's house and infirmary at Much Wenlock; minor examples abound, such as the gatehouse block at Montacute and the abbot's house at Muchelney.

Where buildings have disappeared record often survives, sometimes in an unexpected place such as a commissioners' report of 1536. To those familiar with the sad tales of the visitation documents, with their leaking roofs, windswept dorters and dilapidated cloisters, and with the caustic comments of Layton or Legh on the dirt and squalor, the sober notes of these men may come as a surprise. The entries that follow are from the commissioners of Leicestershire, Norfolk, and Wiltshire:

> Owston. Moche of yt newe made with ffreston not fully fynesshed.
> Ulverscroft. Muche of yt withyn this iij yeres newe sett upp and buylt.
> Buckenham. The house newly built and in marvelous good reparacion.
> Maiden Bradley. Church and mansion with all the housing in good reparacion newly repayred and amendyd.
> Stanley. In very good state part newe builded.[1]

The same commissioners had their criticisms of some of the other houses, but these extracts show that the superiors, even of the smaller monasteries, had often both the money and the will to repair and remodel their home up to the very end of its existence.

III. MONASTIC PRINTING PRESSES

In the centuries when the monasteries were the main, if not the sole, reservoir of learning in western Europe, the monks were also the principal agents in the material production of books and writing of all kinds. By

---

1 For Owston, *v.* PRO, E 36/154/49; Ulverscroft, *ibid.* 51; Buckenham, PRO, S.C. 12/33/29, m. 2; Maiden Bradley, S.C. 12/33/27, m. 2; Stanley, *ibid.* m. 2ᵛ.

the time that printing had begun to replace writing by hand, the monks as a class had ceased to be leaders in the intellectual life of the age and to take any notable part in the physical production of books. It was, therefore, scarcely to be expected that the monasteries of England would play a leading part in the development of the new art of printing, all the less so in view of the banausic character of the craft in its earlier appearances. As it happened, only three English monasteries, so far as is known, were in any way connected with printing-presses: they were Abingdon, St Albans and Tavistock, and only in the last-named is there any evidence that the work was done by a monk. At St Albans, however, two presses were at work, separated in their activity by an interval of at least forty years. The subject is of considerable interest, and a few words will be said about all these ventures, but a true perspective will only be maintained if it is remembered that most of the early presses were very small affairs, resembling the amateur or 'toy' presses of to-day. They could be loaded upon a packhorse and moved from place to place like other heavy luggage. It was only by degrees that printing attained industrial status in the offices and workshops of Venice and Basel.[1]

The earliest by far of the monastic presses was that of the schoolmaster of St Albans, who worked between c. 1479 and 1486.[2] There is no certainty that he worked in the abbey precinct or that he was in any way patronized by the monks. He uses as his mark the saltire on a shield, which both town and abbey used as their arms. Nevertheless, the likelihood certainly is that he was patronized in some way by the abbey. His activities, as they are known to us, fall into two phases. In the first, 1479–81, he printed school books, including the *Nova Rhetorica*, compiled a year or two previously at Cambridge by the Italian Franciscan Lorenzo di Savona.[3] In the second, 1483–6, he launched out into more ambitious work, printing the *Chronicles of England* and the celebrated *Book of St Albans*, with its treatises on field sports and heraldry, which gave the printer occasion to use coloured inks.

It was forty years after this that the next in date of the monastic presses began work in west Devon. This was set up in Tavistock Abbey by the monk Thomas Richard, who had studied at Gloucester College from 1507 to 1515, when he proceeded B.D.[4] He was encouraged, but not neces-

1 Books, monographs and handlists dealing with early printing in England are legion. For the presses under review the best general account is perhaps still that of E. G. Duff, *English Provincial Printers to 1557*.

2 The most complete account of the first press at St Albans is in the article, 'Printing', by H. R. Plomer, in *VCH, Herts*, IV, 258–61 (1914). He disposed of the opinion, then recently propounded, that the press of 'Seynt Albon' was located in a house of that name at Westminster, and was set up by the schoolmaster there in collaboration with Caxton. The words *apud villam S. Albani*, which occur in the colophon of some of the books, should surely have prevented the opinion seeing the light of day. The books produced by the first press are described with some facsimiles by E. G. Duff in *Fifteenth Century English Books*.

3 For Savona, *v. infra*, p. 53.

4 The fullest account of the Tavistock Press is that of H. P. R. Finberg, *Tavistock Abbey*, Appendix D, 290–3.

sarily financed, by his friend Robert Langdon, a Cornish gentleman from St Martin's-by-Looe, who was also responsible for choosing the first book known to have been printed. This was the old medieval favourite, now with a millennium of popularity behind it, *The Consolation of Philosophy* of Boethius; it was presented in a translation, hitherto unprinted, done by John Watts, a canon of Oseney in 1410. This was not the first appearance of Boece in English print, as already *c.* 1478 Caxton had printed Chaucer's version. Richard's book bears the date 1525, with Robert Langdon's arms in the colophon. Three years later the printer became prior of Totnes, and it is quite uncertain whether his type had been used a second time. It remained at Tavistock, however, for in 1534 there appeared a small quarto containing *The Statutes of the Stannary*, being the customary laws of the tinners' trade as reissued in recent sessions of the Crockentor tinners' parliaments. After this the veil falls again, though there is evidence that the press passed out of the abbey with one of the monks at the Dissolution, and was still existing in his family thirty years later.

The third press was that set up at Abingdon, but here the printer was a professional, connected only accidentally with the abbey. The single book known to have been printed was a monastic Breviary of 1528, the work of John Scolar, who had published and possibly printed five books at Oxford in 1517–18.

Finally, and most productive of all, there is the second press of St Albans, set up *c.* 1526 and very active between 1534 and 1538.[1] The printer here also was a professional, John Herford, who worked under the patronage of Abbots Catton and Stevenage. The latter, who was interested in the press while still chamberer, had the family name of Boreman, and may well have been a brother of Nicholas Bourman, a London printer of the time. Herford began innocently enough with a Breviary of the use of St Albans (*c.* 1526) and a *Lyfe and passion of Seint Albon* by John Lydgate, done at the request of Cotton. He continued with a piece written by one of the monks, John Gwynneth, entitled *The confutacyon of the first part of Fryth's book* (1528). Finally, in 1539, when the great abbey was tottering, he produced a tract with the suggestive title *A very declaration of the bond and free wyll of man: the obedyence of the gospel and what the gospel meaneth*. Stevenage, challenged by Cromwell, disclaimed all knowledge of this;[2] he sent 'John Pryntare' up to London to answer to the Lord Privy Seal and the press was silent at St Albans, though Herford lived to resume business in the City.

Interesting as these early printing ventures are, they provide little evidence that the English monks realized, or wished to exploit, the potentialities of the new tool. In other lands, as for example at Ottobeuron

1 *V*. Plomer, *art. cit.* 261.
2 *LP*, XIV (ii), 315. Stevenage to Cromwell, 12 October 1538.

under Abbot Leonard *c.* 1508–11, printing was undertaken as the up-to-date equivalent of the earlier *scriptorium*, and the use of the press as a source of employment and as a contribution to the spread of learning was explicitly recognized.[1] In England there is no trace of this, and without pronouncing on a might-have-been of history, and imagining the monasteries of England spared to aid in the diffusion of humanism or post-Tridentine theology, we may say with assurance that in this field, at least, the Dissolution did not destroy anything of value.

1 Cf. Abbot Leonard Wildemann's preface to Alcuin's *De Sancta Trinitate*, printed at Ottobeuron in 1509.

CHAPTER III

THE CISTERCIANS

For students of the last fifty years of monastic life in England the deplorable lack of any intimate or personal records of the lives and fortunes of the white monks continues from earlier times. There is no domestic chronicler or annalist, and no Cistercian has left familiar letters or biographical material. Glimpses, however, can be obtained of the overhead organization of the order from the collection of letters received from English correspondents by the abbot of Cîteaux,[1] and from the scattered references to this country in the acts of general chapter,[2] while the domestic life of the abbeys is fitfully revealed by rare visitation documents, and evidence of prosperity and changing habits is afforded by records or remains of monastic building activity.

Throughout the period the Cistercians in England, Wales and Ireland were governed by the original constitutional machinery of the *Carta Caritatis*, modified in practice by the executive powers acquired by the abbot of Cîteaux more than a century earlier and by the practice, begun during the Great Schism and maintained by the virtual isolation of England from the Continent, of entrusting the oversight of the English, Welsh and (intermittently) Irish abbeys to two or more abbots-commissary, with full powers of visitation and reform.[3] By these means the primitive vertical descent of authority, which made each mother-house responsible for the discipline of daughter-foundations, was in large part abrogated, and a system of centralized national control was set up which had resemblances both to the regional 'circary' of the Premonstratensians and to the province of the mendicant friars. Besides their duties of visitation and supervision, the commissaries were responsible for collecting a tax or 'contribution', which was in essence a levy imposed on all Cistercian abbeys for the benefit of the central administration at Cîteaux, though it was sometimes diverted into, or replaced by, one to assist the building and furnishing of St Bernard's College at Oxford.

The appointment of the commissioners was normally in the hands of

1 These records, which passed, along with other documents from Cîteaux, into the archives of Dijon, were indicated by P. Gautier, 'De l'état des monastères cisterciens anglais à la fin du xv siècle', in *Mélanges d'histoire offertes à Charles Bémont*, 423–35; but this article did no more than give a brief introduction to half a dozen documents from the Archives de la Côte d'Or, without any suggestion of the richness and value of the collection. G. G. Coulton, likewise, used them occasionally but never systematically. They are now in process of being edited by Dr C. H. Talbot for the Royal Historical Society; Dr Talbot has kindly allowed me to use his transcripts, which I cite by the numbers he has given them. Their location is Dijon, Archives de la Côte d'Or, II, H. 19.

2 Edited by Dom J. M. Canivez as *Statuta Capitulorum Generalium Ordinis Cisterciensis*, vols. v and vi.

3 For this, *v. RO*, II, 127–9, 168–9.

the abbot of Cîteaux, who could specify the length of the term of office, but as the general chapter had sovereign powers his dispositions could be overruled or altered, while the death of an abbot of Cîteaux entailed a lapse of the commissioners' faculties. Though on the whole things ran smoothly, there are several instances of confusion.[1] At the opening of our period three commissioners were in function in each of the two ecclesiastical provinces; thus in 1486 England (save for the province of York), together with Wales and Ireland, was administered by the abbots of Stratford Langthorne, Combe and Cleeve; but in the early years of Henry VII it became the custom for three or two commissaries to be given authority over the whole country. Throughout the period, whoever else might be out or in, the abbots of Fountains, Stratford Langthorne and St Mary Graces (London) were almost continually in office. In earlier days Rievaulx had held the primacy in the north as the eldest-born daughter of Clairvaux; Fountains rose to the first place partly, no doubt, on account of its wealth but also by reason of the outstanding personalities of the two abbots, John Darnton and Marmaduke Huby, who ruled it for half a century. In the south Warden, eldest daughter of Rievaulx, gave place to Stratford and St Mary's largely because those two houses, of which the latter was a royal foundation, were so near the political and administrative centre of the kingdom that their abbots were inevitably in close touch with the court and the hosts of other Cistercians who might visit the capital.[2]

When the commissioners were three in number they did not always agree. In particular, the abbot of Stratford in the last decades of the century was a difficult man to work with, and disputes arose between him and the abbot of Fountains. The abbot of St Mary Graces seems always to have been the Lepidus of the triumvirate, and to have acted from time to time as peacemaker. For more than a quarter of a century the energy, ability and prestige of Jean de Cirey, abbot of Cîteaux (1476–1503) preserved continuity of policy, and it is perhaps significant that no English letters have been discovered for the dozen years following his death.[3] After that, some confusion crept in. Abbot Huby, joined for a time by the abbot of Rievaulx, held office almost continuously till *c.* 1520, but in the south there was less stability. An interesting letter of 1517 shows the

1 The English abbots write directly to the abbot of Cîteaux asking for powers as commissioners. Sometimes (e.g. in 1489 and 1495 (Canivez, v, 687, 692, nos. 43, 54; VI, 109, no. 32)) these are affirmed or confirmed by chapter, which at times also exercised its right of judging, correcting or suspending the commissioners (*ibid.* VI, 182, no. 43, 681–2, no. 42) but its approval does not seem to have been necessary to give the commissioners plenary authority.

2 As John Haryngton, the York lawyer and friend of the Cistercians, remarks (*CL*, 57), the abbot of Fountains, *nobilitate et opulencia*, and the abbot of Stratford, *favore regis ac dominorum spiritualium et temporalium*, will always be the most valuable agents *ex officio* for the Cistercians to use.

3 For Jean de Cirey as reformer, *v.* Imbart de la Tour, *Origines de la Réforme*, I, 504–5, and *DHG*, art. *Cîteaux*.

abbot of Fountains complaining of the multiplication of commissions.[1] There used, he says, to be only two commissioners, or at most four, two from each province. Recently five have been appointed and now three others have received commissions. The abbot of Cîteaux should take warning by what has happened to the English Premonstratensians. They were exasperated by the frequent bestowal and revocation of commissions, and succeeded in emancipating themselves from Prémontré and in passing directly under papal jurisdiction. We hear indeed about this time of the abbots of Vale Royal, Neath and Forde as commissioners in the south in addition to those of Stratford and St Mary Graces, and as only a very few appointments are registered in the acts of general chapter we must assume that there was a certain conflict of jurisdiction between the abbot of Cîteaux and the chapter.

Legally, the abbots were still bound to attend the annual general chapter at Cîteaux, at least at stated intervals, but wars and the Schism had long since broken the custom down, and the general leave of absence given to all English abbots in 1485 must have been a mere formality.[2] The abbot of Stratford was at Cîteaux some time before 1491,[3] and in 1497, after a recent visit, he writes that he hopes to come every two or three years.[4] Early in the sixteenth century lists of those present at Cîteaux are available. Out of the whole order only some forty or fifty abbots are present, and among them from time to time occur one or two English names; the last is that of the abbot of Forde in 1518.[5] Of traffic in the other direction there is little record. In 1490 Jean de Cirey proposed to visit England officially, but attempts to obtain a safe-conduct broke down.[6]

In 1502 there was talk of the abbot of Morimond coming, and in 1531 general chapter deputed the abbot of Chaloché to visit and reform, and sent a letter on his behalf to Henry VIII, but at that late date there could be little hope of the king's co-operation.[7]

The task of levying the contribution to the order was a standing charge upon the commissioners. This tax was intended to meet the overheads of administration, such as the expenses of general chapter and those of the abbot of Cîteaux and his staff throughout the year. The commissioners were allowed to deduct some, at least, of their own expenses on lawsuits and other extraordinary business; the residue, if the political situation permitted, was sent out to Cîteaux through the agency of a banker. The

---

1 CL, 123.

2 Canivez, v, 529, no. 91: 'Omnes de regno Angliae [excusati]'.

3 Letter of 19 August 1491 (CL, 69) '... quia advena capitulo jam antea generali adherens, nondum abbaciali nactus officio fidelitatem ultro [abbati Cistercii] promiserim'.

4 30 May 1497 (CL, 87): 'De biennio in biennium aut triennium...vestram visitare dominacionem, ubi teneor, diligentissime adnitar.'

5 Canivez, vi, 475 (Furness and Forde), 540 (Neath and Forde).

6 CL, 63.

7 Chapuys to the Emperor, 31 July 1531 (Spanish State Papers, IV, no. 775; Canivez, VI, 702, nos. 48–50).

yearly total at the end of the century would seem to have been fixed either at a notional figure of £76, or at the equally notional figure of £1 per abbey. We are never given the precise target by the commissioners, but it can scarcely be an accident that the sum of all the contributions in two successive years reached about £74 from a total of seventy-six houses (excluding nunneries),[1] and that twenty-seven houses contributed £26 in 1491 and 1492, while twenty-one abbeys sent £19. 16s. 8d. in 1493-5.[2] There was, however, no flat rate; and the quotas of the individual abbeys were fixed with a general, but not very clearly definable, reference to the wealth or numbers of the house. The curve rose steeply from the 3s. 4d. of a beggarly house such as Cwmhir, by intervals of 3s. 4d. or so, to the numerous class assessed at £1 and then up by stages to the £2 of rich abbeys such as Revesby.[3] These figures are of 1479; by 1491 the quotas of almost all houses had decreased by a percentage varying from 10 to 30 per cent. No details have come down from the northern province, but as we know that the total came to £27 from only thirteen houses, it is probable that Fountains and Rievaulx and Furness were assessed at £4 or £5.[4]

The benefits accruing to England from the central government at this time were not obvious to all, though they included the maintenance of a procurator in the Roman curia and the defence of exemption against the pressure of bishops supported by monarchs. The collectors of the tax were met by loud complaints, and by the evasive and delaying tactics that confronted all medieval tax-gatherers, but the commissioners were spurred on by the knowledge that they had to render an account to head-quarters, and that inefficiency might lead to a loss of their commission, which seems to have been an envied distinction. Occasionally, when times were unusually bad, they had to confess their failure;[5] in other years the money came in, but was almost wholly absorbed in litigation or in works on the fabric at Oxford; and when there was a contribution ready for despatch ordinances against the exportation of currency often prevented, or at least served as an excuse for not taking, any further action.[6] When things were bad, but not wholly desperate, they sent a moiety of the total sum, or one of the abbots concerned made up the deficit from his abbey's resources.[7] Failing even that, we find the abbot of Fountains sending out the constituents of a pewter table service for use at Cîteaux, or even lumps of tin from which to make platters and flagons.[8] In 1500 the commissioners send what they describe as a bouquet of preserved roses, lilies and violets as

---

1 The years are 1513-14 and 1514-15 (*CL*, 108, 109); an earlier list of 1478-9 gives a total of £48. 18s. 4d. for thirty-four houses, and the contributions vary within narrower limits; £2 is the highest and only one house.(Bindon) falls below £1 to 16s. 8d.

2 *CL*, 94.   3 *CL*, 94, 12.

4 *CL*, 114, 115.   5 E.g. in 1495 (*CL*, 87).

6 E.g. in 1488 (*CL*, 42).   7 So the abbot of Forde in 1517 (*CL*, 117).

8 The 'garnish' consisted of two large dishes, two fair dishes, twelve lesser dishes and twelve salters.

a token of their respect.[1] When the complete contribution was forth-coming the abbot of Cîteaux must have felt that the English connection was still a considerable asset, and if, as we are often bidden, we give to economic bonds and motives a strength above all others, it is a remarkable proof of the strength of the bonds of Cistercian charity that till within sight of the Dissolution the English abbeys were willing to send abroad an annual gift of £76, without hope of anything in return.

After the regular business of collecting and forwarding the annual col-lection and accounts the visitors had to wrestle with the perennial troubles of St Bernard's College. It is strange that the Cistercians, who were the first of the old orders to frequent both Paris and Oxford, should have been the last to get their college built, furnished and shipshape. As late as 1489 only one-third of it had been erected.[2] The period opens, however, not with building schemes, but with the vagaries of Richard Archbold, an Irish monk, who practised alchemy and wrote to the abbot of Woburn that he had at last been successful in turning the moon into the sun, that is to say, he had made gold out of a mixture of metals.[3] He gave figures to show that by ploughing back his gains into additional apparatus he could treble his output in a year. Meanwhile, with him, as with other men of genius, base coin is the chief need, and he appeals into the void for a loan of £5 to tide him over the winter; it will be refunded two or three times over next Easter or Whitsuntide. Archbold, like other inventors, was an expensive customer, and in 1479 had incurred debts for his degree feasts and other purchases almost equal (£50) to the whole contribution from the southern province. It is not surprising that his confrères heartily wished that he were out of the country and back in the land of his birth.[4] Even with Archbold out of the way the college continued to make heavy weather. In 1482 the provisor and students write to the abbot of Cîteaux that the place has become a reproach to the order.[5] Some years later, Marmaduke Huby took the matter in hand and in 1495 sought permission of the chapter to organize a collection of books, a dozen or so from each house, for the benefit of St Bernard's, and in the following year he tried to raise a subscription for the college.[6] More than twenty years later the building is still going forward; Huby has finished the hall and chapel, and the last quarter of the college is almost complete.[7]

1 *CL*, 105 (20 August 1500): 'Et quanquam viole hiis in partibus hoc praesertim anni tempore jam in[?de]crescunt, rosas tamen perpaucas artificiose non absque difficultate conservantes, quibusdam interjectis liliorum floribus, pro intersigno filialis dilectionis... transmittere decrevimus.' In the first edition (1959) of this book I was simple enough to take the floral terms literally, thereby missing Huby's witticisms. Dr C. H. Talbot has pointed out to me that *rosae* are rose nobles and *lilia* florins (? or *écus*).

2 *CL*, 53, Abbot Darnton of Fountains writes: 'collegium...adhuc...in terciam partem vix advectum'.   3 *CL*, 6: 'Ita quod luna sit in solem conversa.' The date is 1470.

4 *CL*, 16: 'Adeo se disposuit erga fratres, quod quasi omnes vellent quod esset extra patriam nostram, et quod remearet in terram nativitatis suae.'

5 *CL*, 31, of 11 May 1482.

6 *CL*, 30, in 1495. The request was granted by chapter (Canivez, VI, 108, no. 31).

7 Cf. letters of 1517 from Huby and Abbot William of Rievaulx (CL, 116, 120).

In the matter of discipline the powers of the commissioners were apparently plenary. They had the duty and right of visitation, with powers of deposition, and at elections they took the place originally reserved for the abbot of the mother-house.

Of the numberless visitations of the fifteenth century record of only one survives in the archives at Dijon. It contains the *comperta* and injunctions of a visitation of Warden in 1492 by the abbots of Stratford and St Mary Graces, acting as commissaries of the abbot of Cîteaux,[1] and it is worth remarking that both received a year later a laudatory testimonial from the York lawyer and friend of the white monks who has already received mention; he recommended the abbot of Cîteaux to retain them in office.[2] The *comperta* at Warden are somewhat disturbing. Besides accusations of bad attendance at choir, hasty recitation, failure to observe the rules of diet and of the closure of the dormitory at night, together with complaints of heavy rainfall (*plurimum pluit*) in the church, there is a consensus of testimony to more serious matters. Women of questionable character are allowed into the monastic buildings and even reside there.[3] Two of the brethren are accused of unchastity and one of these also of apostasy; the abbot himself is not above suspicion in this respect; he is also a bad administrator and has pawned many of the valuables of the church. It would seem that the aged prior was justified in leading off the depositions with the cautious remark that regular observance was worse than it used to be. The visitors issued a long list of injunctions setting forth regulations and penalties in full, but it is noteworthy that no individual penances were imposed. The visitation of Warden, indeed, is not reassuring. On occasion, however, the visitors acted with more decision. Abbot Huby in 1496 deposed an abbot of Strata Marcella,[4] and in 1497 moved with despatch and firmness when the faction-ridden community of Furness was split into two almost equal parts. He refused to recognize either of the ambitious rivals, and persuaded the community to elect a third, Alexander Banke, a young man of thirty years.[5] It was perhaps too much to hope that such a house could produce anything good, and in less than three years we find the general chapter rehabilitating Banke after his absolution from incontinence, irregularity, simony and other crimes,[6] and fourteen years later still the abbot of Stratford, who had failed to get to Furness in front of Huby in 1497, reached the abbey, which was in its normal state of faction, and after getting the better of Alexander's armed retainers, put in yet another abbot.[7] He proved, however, even less successful than Huby in effecting a permanent settlement; Alexander appealed to the king, and in the resulting confusion three years later the rival abbot of

---

1 *CL*, 76. Deposiciones Fratrum monasterii de Wardona.
2 *CL*, 82.
3 *CL*, 76. Dicit quod mulieres diffamate indies intrant et residenciam incongruam... faciunt at continuunt in monasterio.
4 *CL*, 91 (August 1496).   5 *CL*, 96–7.
6 Canivez, VI, 238, no. 25 (1500).   7 *CL*, 122 (29 April 1517).

Furness found himself in the Fleet.[1] Furness, indeed, was probably past praying for, and its sordid end twenty years later was of a piece with its recent history.

Furness, however, was in a class by itself. Elsewhere, the commissioners met with no prolonged opposition, though there are indications that old loyalties died hard. Thus the abbot of Whitland in 1496 tried to interfere with Huby's arrangements for Strata Marcella, his daughter-house; in the following year one of Huby's fellow-commissioners, the abbot of Stratford, claimed a right to order the affairs of Furness on the score of old Savigniac relationship, and, as we have seen, repeated the claim twenty years later.[2] In 1500 the commissioners report that some abbots, such as the abbot of Newminster, still claim their old rights, and that they are being warned away from Roche and Pipewell.[3]

How far the system of visitation worked in less desperate cases cannot, in default of evidence, be known. The accounts of only two visitations have survived, those of Warden (1492) given above, and Thame (1526), mentioned elsewhere;[4] here it is enough to remark that neither affair shows the visitors in a very favourable light. As for the state of discipline in general, we have part of a memorandum from the abbot of Combe written in 1521, in which he begs the abbot of Cîteaux to enforce in every way possible the enclosure of the cloister. The presence of women in the monastic buildings, he says, and even their residence with their families in the offices of the monastery, where they dispense hospitality to the monks, is ubiquitous and is a menace to the order besides being a public scandal.[5] The *detecta* at Warden in 1492 bear the abbot of Combe out, and it seems more than likely that it was this case that prompted the chapter of 1489 to remark that some British houses were in such a state that unless swift action were taken regular discipline would perish. A petition was in consequence made to the abbot of Cîteaux to visit the country in person.[6] He did his best to go, and Huby did his best to obtain a safe-conduct for him, but it was refused for what would now be called 'security reasons'.[7]

On another level, the efforts of some abbots to escape from the control of general chapter are frequently mentioned; they are willing, we are told, to fall in with the desire of the bishops to put an end to exemption and are even ready to call in the assistance of the king to make them free of control.

1 *CL*, 122 (29 April 1517). He writes, 'e carceribus by flet'.
2 *CL*, 96 (10 August 1497); cf. 122.   3 Canivez, VI, 235–6, no. 22; *CL*, 105.
4 For Warden, *v. supra*, p. 33; for Thame, *v. infra*, p. 70.
5 *CL*, 129. Failing this prohibition, he says: 'nunquam erit religionis honestas nec monasteriorum observantia in reputacione, quia multorum fuit et est ruina...quia non solum intrant...monasteria et loca tam regularia et alia sed eciam commorantur cum tota familia in diversis locis ordinis adeo prope claustra quod religiosi cum ipsis in suis mansionibus et ipsae cum religiosis confabulando, potando et omni hora diei...frequentando'.
6 Canivez, V, 687, no. 43.
7 Both the abbot of Stratford and Marmaduke Huby, acting for his abbot, seem to have made sincere efforts to obtain the safe-conduct (*CL*, 63).

This was in 1489 and 1490; similar attempts at defection *c.* 1517 are mentioned by Abbot Huby.[1]

In this miscellaneous and haphazard collection of documents from England one personality stands out from the list of names; it is that of Marmaduke Huby, abbot of Fountains from 1494 to 1526. He first appears in 1488 as collecting the subsidy for the abbot of Cîteaux on behalf of his own abbot, John Darnton, then a commissioner.[2] Darnton himself was a man of note, prudent, discreet and loyal, the most influential white monk of his day, zealous for the honour of his order and of high repute with all.[3] On his death in 1495 the provisor (or prior) of St Bernard's College quotes Propertius and Solon to illustrate his posthumous fame.[4] Huby, however, had a still higher reputation. His family, it seems likely, was established in York,[5] and he himself must have taken the habit at Fountains soon after 1460, for he tells us, in an autobiographical passage in one of his letters, that he was professed *c.* 1463, and that he began to take part in the administration of the order thirteen years before he became abbot, i.e. in 1482.[6] As abbot Darnton's bursar and confidant—'his Marmaduke'[7]—he accomplished reforms in Wales, and he succeeded as a matter of course to the abbacy in 1495. Thenceforward traces of his activity and tributes to his virtues abound. The provisor of Oxford asserts that no abbot of his time can bear comparison with him,[8] and twenty years later the abbot of Rievaulx is singing his praises.[9] During the greater part of his period of office he was commissioner and visitor, and his energy

---

1 *CL*, 58, 65. John Haryngton, the York lawyer, is insistent on the point. He testifies to the zeal and ability of Cardinal Morton. Huby in 1517 notes the presence of 'inventores novitatum et malorum, qui in Romana curia satagebant ordinem nostrum hic in Anglia per exempcionem Romano pontifici eidem immediate subicere et matrem nostram Cisterciensem ab omni jurisdictione ordinaria penitus excludere'. He blames Cardinal Bainbridge for encouraging this (*CL*, 123).

2 *CL*, 49; a letter of Abbot Darnton to the abbot of Cîteaux.

3 Haryngton writes of him as 'ordinis zelatorem et vestrae paternitati filium obsequentissimum ac generaliter virum laude et virtute in ordine dignum' (*CL*, 22 July 1493).

4 *CL*, 83, 12 August 1495. The quotation is from Propertius, III, i, 24: 'Maius ab exequiis nomen in ora venit.' Propertius was unknown to medieval England; the *editio princeps* appeared in 1471.

5 The Yorkshire antiquary J. S. Walbran, who edited the first volume of the *Memorials of Fountains Abbey* for the Surtees Society in 1863, gave what information he could discover about Huby on pp. 151 *seqq.* A William Huby of the city of York witnesses a Fountains indenture in Huby's day. Walbran gives the abbot's reputed arms (p. 153) and notes that a copy of the Coucher Book executed in 1509 is in B.M. Add. MS. 18, 276. The date of his profession is given approximately in an English letter to Lord Dacre written ?1523-4 (*Memorials of Fountains*, I, 239-42): 'I have beyn professyd in this Monastery of Fontaynes by the space of iiixx yeres.'

6 *CL*, 120, of 19 April 1517. He writes as bursar in 1489 (*CL*, 52).

7 The phrase is Haryngton's in 1493: 'Quid opus est verbis de eo [*sc.* Darnton] aut suo Marmaduco?' (*CL*, 82).

8 *CL*, 83: 'Neque esse neque temporibus nostris fuisse abbatem huic reverendo patri comparandum.'

9 *CL*, 119, of 17 April 1517: 'Cultor disciplinae, plantator religionis...et ruinarum domorum sedulus et novus reparator...certi enim sumus quod nullus in regno nostro Angliae tantam experienciam habet.'

and prestige made him the natural leader of his colleagues. He had differences with them and acted on occasion without their counsel, but the quarrels were always adjusted, and to the last his contemporaries clearly regarded him with admiration and respect. His official letters, though they reveal little of his personality, show a man of university training, not without some sparks of wit.[1] He stood high in favour with Henry VII[2] and twenty years later was on good terms with Wolsey, whom he advised the abbot of Cîteaux to sweeten with letters of confraternity illuminated with elegance.[3] He tells us that when he became abbot in 1495 there were only twenty-two monks at Fountains, whereas when he wrote (c. 1520) there were fifty-two professed, of whom forty-one were priests and the others in major orders. This is a remarkable achievement, even if in the same letter he tells of domestic caballing on the part of a monk who hoped to succeed Huby if he died or resigned—which he had not dreamt of doing[4] —and it throws welcome light on the only sphere of Huby's activities hitherto familiar to historians. He has long, indeed, been known as a great builder: every serious visitor to the ruins has been aware of his name as that of the builder of the great tower which, whatever may be thought of its architectural or religious propriety,[5] dominates every view of Fountains and even appears, when seen from a distance over the fields, as if rising out of the earth when all else is hidden in the narrow valley. The tower and the adjoining transept are marked with Huby's initials and arms, and are decorated with sentences chosen by him from the Cistercian liturgy.[6] In addition to the tower, he rebuilt part of the infirmary, providing additional private rooms for the sick; he almost doubled the accommodation in the abbot's lodging; he built, or at least largely rebuilt, the misericord and the gallery connecting the infirmary complex with the church;

1 Huby's trick of quoting Scripture, and especially the Old Testament, seems to reflect a training in the schools. His favourite witticism is the use of circumlocution for the English coin known as the angel (value 6s. 8d.); e.g. in 1517 he sends to Cîteaux 'sexaginta de angelicis spiritibus illius ordinis et ierarchie cujus sanctus Michael tenet primatum'. The 'angel' on the coin was St Michael. (CL, 120.)

2 The abbot of St Mary Graces remarks in 1497: 'habet cum omni gracia dominum regem faventissimum'. Cf. Huby's account of his interview in the same year with Henry, when the king regretted the absence of lay-brethren among the Cistercians, and offered to provide half a dozen. (CL, 97, 98.)

3 CL, 123. Huby cannot speak too highly of Wolsey: 'Virum sapientissimum... insignem justiciae cultorem, pauperum et oppressorum relevatorem precipuum...consulimus...ut littera suffragalis de confraternitate sapienter, pulchro dictamine ornata ac formosa manu scripta fiat.'

4 CL, 125: 'quod nondum facere cogitavimus'. Leland, Itinerary, I, 80–1, says Huby intended to found a 'cell' at Ripon, possibly to take some of the overflow or restless element from Fountains.

5 An early (1157) Cistercian statute forbade steeples and belfries (Canivez, I, 61, no. 16). Aesthetically, we may question the wisdom of placing a single lofty tower at the end of the north transept, or indeed of building a tower at all in a narrow valley. The original low tower over the crossing was in decay.

6 For an excellent description of the buildings at Fountains, with an elaborate plan, v. art. by Sir W. H. St J. Hope in YAJ, xv (1900), 269–402. Hope distinguishes all the remains of Huby's work.

and he added ovens and other fittings to the infirmary kitchen. His domestic buildings can usually be recognized by their characteristic white limestone. Marmaduke Huby stands out as by far the most distinguished Cistercian abbot of his age, and as the last of his race. We have no means of knowing whether he added to his gifts as an administrator the rarer gifts of a spiritual father, and we cannot guess how he would have confronted the crisis which he did not live to see, and in which his successors at Fountains made such a poor showing. No grave-slab of his has been found; his bones in all probability lie beneath the floor of the chapter house; his monument is the tower which still, in the 'surprise view' of the abbey, seems to stand as a living presence.

Among the other abbots who come fitfully into view in the Cistercian letters are those of Cleeve and Forde, both of whom, like Huby, can be found also to have left their mark upon stone. The earlier in date is Humphrey, abbot of Cleeve for some years before 1488 and later abbot of Beaulieu. He may well have been responsible for initiating the wholesale adaptation of his abbey to contemporary needs by constructing the large and beautiful refectory parallel to the cloister on the model of a black monk hall.[1] The other, the abbot of Forde, who first appears as commissioner in 1513 and is still holding the post in 1527, is Thomas Chard, who must rank among the greatest builders of his day, and whose hall and gateway and unfinished cloister, in which the rich panelling and fan vaulting of Tudor Gothic is set off with a frieze of Renaissance motifs, all built in the honey-coloured Ham stone, were scarcely handselled by his monks and guests before they were surrendered.[2] Chard appears in the letters as a somewhat ambitious administrator; he was concerned with the completion of the Oxford college, where he had probably himself resided, rather than with monastic reform, but it is interesting to note his attendance in person, with a single companion and ally on each occasion, at the general chapters of 1515 and 1518 at Cîteaux.[3]

When all the fresh evidence from the Cîteaux letters and the acts of chapter is added to the scattered testimony of buildings, the impression is received of a body better organized, better disciplined, and more firmly tied to the foreign centre of authority than has hitherto been realized. When all allowance has been made for the official and formalized character of the evidence, which may give an impression of order and regularity as deceptive in one direction as the mean and spiteful gossip of the visitation records is on the other, this impression, strengthened by the half-seen figures of the abbots of Fountains and Combe and Stratford, is not one of chaos or degradation. It does, however, reveal a flaw which,

---

1 For Cleeve, v. Proceedings of the Somersetshire Archaeological Society, XXXV (1889), 83–120; LXXVII (1931), 37–47; cf. also supra, p. 24.

2 For Chard's buildings, v. Royal Commission on Historical Monuments, West Dorset.

3 Canivez, VI, sub annis. His companions were the abbots of Furness and Neath. The abbot of Furness was presumably the unsatisfactory Alexander Banke; the abbot of Neath, of whom Huby disapproved, was an ally of Abbot Chard.

like the contemporary devolution of power practised by the papacy, might pass unnoticed in a static society, but which proved fatal in a time of change and crisis. The English Cistercians, like the English Premonstratensians, had no anchor in foul weather. Cîteaux, which in earlier centuries could give at least some advice and protection, let the cable slip when the storm broke; the commissioners of the moment thus lost their canonical stay, while lacking any constituent support from among their brethren; the white monks therefore were left in utter isolation to face the wolf who, as the medieval proverb had it, was not terrified by sheep, however numerous they might be.

CHAPTER IV

THE PREMONSTRATENSIANS

Though records of the white canons are scanty during the thirteenth and fourteenth centuries, we are fortunate in possessing, for the last quarter of the fifteenth, the copious register of visitations and other documents compiled by Richard Redman, abbot of Shap from 1458 to 1505 and bishop successively of St Asaph (1471–95), Exeter (1496–1501) and Ely (1501–5), who from 1459 to his death was commissary-general for the abbot of Prémontré in England and visitor of the English province, over whose triennial chapters he was *ex officio* president.[1]

Richard Redman[2] was a member of a Westmorland family which had already given more than one of its sons to public affairs. He was in all probability the great-grandson of Sir Richard Redman, Speaker of the House of Commons. The seat of the family was at Levens, near Kendal, where the Elizabethan mansion, with its formal gardens, still preserves the family name in one of its rooms, though the estate had already passed to others when the present house was built. Redman became a canon of St Mary Magdalen in the Valley of Shap, not many miles distant among the fells, and was while still young elected abbot. His great administrative talents were speedily recognized, and within a year he was acting for the abbot of Prémontré, who continued from time to time to give him commissions until he was permanently appointed commissary-general.

He had in the meantime acted for the king, and in 1471 was appointed to St Asaph, retaining nevertheless the comparatively wealthy abbey of Shap. Irregular as was this proceeding, it probably sprang from the desire of all concerned to retain Bishop Redman as visitor and president of the English 'circary' or province, and until his death the bishop maintained the keenest interest both in his abbey and in the order. He accomplished his duties as visitor with exemplary regularity, despite all other

---

1 The documents quoted are contained in Redman's Register (Bodl. MS. Ashmole 1519) and in the eighteenth-century antiquary Peck's transcript of a supposedly lost *Registrum Premonstratense* (B.M. Add. MSS. 4934–8), and were printed in a conflated form by Abbot Gasquet (later Cardinal) in CS, 3 ser., VI, X, XII (1904, 1906), with the title *Collectanea Anglo-Premonstratensia*. They will be cited as *CAP* with references to the volume of the edition and page of the volume. A criticism of the edition will be found in G. G. Coulton, *Ten Medieval Studies* (3 ed. 1930, 220–6), but his list of errors is by no means exhaustive and has been greatly extended by Mr H. M. Colvin.
Since this text and note were written Mr H. M. Colvin has signalized his discovery of the lost Register in Belvoir Castle Additional MS, 2 (*v. JEH*, VIII, i).

2 For Redman, *v.* article in *DNB*, and Colvin, *The White Canons*, 363–4. There is much confusion as to the date of Redman's permanent appointment as commissary-general; actually he obtained a commission for life in 1459; this was challenged, and he received one for twelve years in 1466. Gasquet (I, xix and elsewhere) gives 1478, which is clearly wrong, as can be shown from the documents he prints. The facts are set out by Colvin, *The White Canons*, 224–5, but the date of the final commission seems uncertain.

ties and offices, and visited every house with only two exceptions some six or eight times in his twenty-seven years of office.[1] As the Premonstratensian abbeys were scattered over England from Blanchland hidden in the moors west of Newcastle to St Radegund's near Dover, and from West Dereham near the Norfolk coast to Halesowen in Worcestershire and Torre in Devon his task was no light one. As a rule, the bishop visited all the houses in a single progress (there are seven complete tours in his register) and travelled with great despatch, but even so the circuit occupied him for more than three months of ceaseless movement. Moreover, the procedure of a visitation was both laborious and tedious; it brought no pecuniary gain and led to no advancement. Redman must therefore be given the credit of having acted from a genuine desire to serve his order and the cause of religion. His varied activities and relationships show him to have been a man of probity and ability; he had likewise a reputation for generosity, for which the means were supplied by the revenues of his offices as abbot and bishop; a careful perusal of his injunctions gives the impression of a man sincerely interested in the welfare of individual houses and religious, and with a real desire to promote good discipline; there is nothing perfunctory about his injunctions, and he was careful to compare one house with another, and each with its own previous state. At the same time he had neither the temperament nor the spiritual fire of a drastic reformer; the impression gained of him is of one ready to follow the promptings of good nature and to accept conventional standards whenever such a choice was consistent with a fair observance of canonical form.

Redman's register has a particular value not only because it includes all the houses of a homogeneous group, but also because it gives for all these houses the records of seven or eight consecutive visitations, together with lists of the communities concerned. It is therefore possible to get something like an adequate view of the state of the white canons shortly before the Dissolution. The register, moreover, has several characteristics due to the personal qualities of the compiler. The bishop was a canon himself; he knew, therefore, the spirit of his order; he was, besides, ready to praise as well as to blame; he.was willing, on occasion, to assess the relative excellence of a house among its fellows. Consequently, there is more to be gleaned from these injunctions than from the more formal, external acts of an Alnwick. On the other hand, we have only the final (and usually brief) report and injunctions of the visitor; the *detecta* and names of the deponents and indeed all the *procès-verbal* of a visitation are wanting. It may therefore well be that we are spared many trivialities and petulancies which would blur the larger issues.

Redman visited at intervals of four years (sometimes every three)

---

[1] Redman must have known the English countryside of the fifteenth century as well, if not better, than Leland fifty years later. Some idea of the distances he covered may be obtained from the interesting itineraries of Titchfield, printed by Professor Bruce Dickins in *Proc. Leeds Philosophical Soc.* iv, vi, 349–61.

twenty-nine abbeys: all the Premonstratensian houses, that is, in England and Wales save his own house, Shap, and the remote Welsh Talley in Carmarthenshire, which he visited occasionally by proxy, the abbot and a representative canon travelling to meet him at Halesowen. By and large his injunctions when read with care give an impression considerably more pleasing than might have been expected by those familiar with the episcopal visitations of Alnwick forty years earlier and those of the somewhat later bishops of Norwich. Taken as a whole the white canons were not a decadent body, and on many occasions, covering in a few cases the whole sequence at a particular abbey, Redman remarked that all was well temporally and spiritually. Not infrequently he bestows words of the warmest praise on the house and its abbot, and on the spirit of charity and obedience that prevailed. If it is thought that Redman was by nature indulgent, it may as fairly be urged that one who was himself a member of the order, who passed so repeatedly from house to house and who was besides the president of the provincial chapter, must have gained in time a pretty fair notion of the circumstances and reputation of each house, and was therefore less likely to be baffled or hoodwinked by collusive action, obstructive silence and hard swearing than if he had been a secular diocesan visiting perhaps for the first and last time. Indeed, the impression gained from the register is that Redman had a fairly accurate notion of what was going on, even if he did not always take the drastic steps in remedy of disorders which ardent zeal might seem to demand.

Of the twenty-nine houses visited some ten were entirely and continuously satisfactory. Of these Redman could write that their virtues and religious observance had been rewarded by an abundance of possessions;[1] that their abbot was a new founder of the house; that all neighbours conspire to praise the place and thus cause the visitor to exult in mind;[2] that there is perfect harmony between head and members[3] and that all serve God devoutly in regular observance by day and night;[4] that all is in flawless bloom;[5] that all thank God that they elected such an abbot as they have;[6] that not a shadow of blame, but widespread praise and fair fame is the abbey's portion;[7] that he has found nothing deserving of correction;[8] or even that all is so wisely ordered that Redman, were he not bound by obedience, would never come to visit the house while the present abbot held rule.[9]

---

1 *CAP*, II, 42 (Barlings, 1500).

2 *CAP*, III, 52 (Leiston, 1494): 'Nobis non modicam infert nostre mentis exultacionem.'

3 *CAP*, II, 85 (Beeleigh, 1488): 'Ibidem inter caput et membra caritas conexa est plena atque perfecta.'   4 *CAP*, II, 113 (Cockersand, 1481).

5 *CAP*, II, 161 (Croxton, 1494): 'Omnia circa religionis observancias divina officia et Ordinis instituta comperimus inviolabiliter reflorescere.'

6 *CAP*, II 146 (Coverham, 1500). The Abbot, John Askew, had received the warmest praise in 1491, 1494, and 1497.

7 *CAP*, II, 229 (Hagnaby, 1488): 'Nulla alicujus criminis comperimus umbracula', etc.

8 *CAP*, II, 57 (Beauchief, 1478); cf. III, 152–6 (Torre, 1494, 1497, 1500).

9 *CAP*, III, 223 (West Dereham, 1500). The Abbot, John Marten or Wisbeach, was highly complimented also in 1494, 1497 and 1503.

Of the remaining twenty-odd a dozen oscillated between a state of disorder that fell short of disaster and a degree of well-being that failed to reach absolute excellence. At these houses Redman had to deal with individual cases of incontinence and apostasy, with internal discord and with considerable relaxations. He was often able, on the other hand, to note that all was well or to confine himself to small points of discipline and ceremonial, and on the whole in this group a tolerable mediocrity was more frequently noted than a dangerous decline.

There remains a group of some seven abbeys[1] where conditions were unsatisfactory during the greater part of the twenty-five years covered by these records, or where at one time or another a serious scandal developed. Though it would be unfair to judge the whole order by these, and equally unfair to demand of a visitor that he should be able to give to a group of weak and unspiritual characters the inner vision and moral resolve which alone could effect true reform, it nevertheless remains true that Redman must be judged, if not by his success then at least by the serious efforts made to restore regularity to these houses.

It is not surprising to find that at several of them the abbot was guilty of immoral conduct, while in one or two cases the whole body was infected with corruption. The abbey of Langley may serve as an instance.[2] This house, a fairly large one in Norfolk, must count as one of the least satisfactory of all. When first visited by Redman in 1478 it was ruled by an aged and incapable abbot. The bishop gave two canons charge of the spirituals and temporals of the place, sent a canon convicted of incontinence to Titchfield, and imposed penances on two apostates. Four years later the abbey had a new head and a worse one. Abbot Mintling was justly accused of incontinence and dilapidation. Redman took the same course as before and appointed two administrators, the subprior and novice master. In 1488 the latter had become abbot and the bishop was able to express his satisfaction at the excellent state of the house. In 1491 conditions were less satisfactory, and in 1494 Abbot Alpe in his turn was accused of incontinence and dilapidation. On the former charge he was able to establish a technical innocence, though Redman's injunctions make it clear that he was seriously to blame;[3] on the latter he failed to justify himself, and a series of injunctions was directed towards limiting any further dissipation of property. Three years later Alpe had bettered the financial and economical position, but three years later again the whole house was an object of scandal to the neighbourhood; besides charges of

---

1 Viz. Eggleston (Yorks), Langley (Norfolk), Lavendon (Bucks), Newhouse (Lincs), St Radegund's (Kent), Sulby (Lincs), and Welbeck (Notts). The distribution of these houses forbids any judgment as to the relative decline of any particular district.

2 *CAP*, III, 15–30.

3 *CAP*, III, 25–6: 'Minime comperimus ex rei veritate prout publica circumvolat infamia ...attamen...mandamus quatenus dicte mulieris consortium...evitet, ulterius in monasterio suo nullo modo venire aut remanere permittat', etc.

incontinence against the abbot and others,[1] and cases of apostasy, there had been a conspiracy against the abbot. It is surprising to find Redman postponing action till the next visitation; he may perhaps have seen no way of getting the better of the moral chaos that prevailed. In any case, two years later Langley was in the depths of distress, and at last Abbot Alpe resigned, to be replaced by an outsider, Abbot Curlew of Lavendon, whose reputation had in the past been rudely blown upon, and who was once more accused and deposed at Langley in 1509.

Lavendon, indeed, an abbey in northern Buckinghamshire, had a history almost as unfortunate as Langley.[2] At Redman's first visitation in 1482 he had found a whole series of irregularities, among which was the conduct of the cellarer, this very William Curlew, who was charged with illicit relations with a named woman and with enriching his relations at the expense of the monastery's property. He succeeded in clearing himself technically of the first charge; Redman's injunctions show that he considered the second well founded. Six years later the whole fabric was in ruins, and in 1491, when Curlew had become abbot, two canons, one being the subprior, were convicted of incontinence. Three years later two were again convicted—one being again the subprior, whose punishment had been remitted previously, but who now had added to his misconduct an endeavour to poison his abbot. In 1500, however, the abbey was in better condition. The three offenders of the past had disappeared in manners unspecified, and Curlew had sunk the debts. It was shortly after this that he was elected to Langley.

A third example may be taken in Welbeck, the largest and proudest of the Premonstratensian foundations and the mother-house of a large family. Here we can trace the curve of prosperity through more than one sweep. At the earliest visitation all was in an excellent state under the aged Abbot Green.[3] Twelve years later, under Abbot Burton, a decline had set in; canons were sleeping outside the common dormitory, indulging in archery, and hunting in Sherwood. Four years later the collapse was complete; the house was ruined by the abbot's dilapidations; he himself was living incontinently and supporting his children on abbey revenues; he was besides gaming daily. There were two other cases of incontinence, together with apostasy and rebellion. Redman acted with firmness and deposed the abbot forthwith. Four years later things were mending, and in 1491, despite certain relaxations, the visitor was satisfied and could speak of the abbot as a second founder of the house. Henceforward, Welbeck was in good condition.

In addition to cases where the abbot was guilty of some canonical fault,

---

1 *CAP*, III, 29–30: 'Ne de cetero quoquomodo convencionem sive colloquium habeat cum illa muliere qua nuper permaximum contraxit scandalum, at non merito.' The last three words are contradicted by the context and are possibly a misreading or copyist's reduplication of the three that immediately follow, viz. *aut cum marito ejusdem.*

2 *CAP*, III, 35–42.

3 *CAP*, III, 177–96. The first visitation (1462) must have been one of Redman's earliest.

E

or where the house was in so decadent a state as to argue culpable negligence in its head,[1] Redman as visitor had to deal with a number of individuals guilty of apostasy[2] or charged with incontinence. Such cases amount to some forty in all,[3] excluding abbots. In a few instances the accused succeeded in establishing a technical innocence; the rest either failed to secure the requisite number of confrères to swear to their innocence, or spontaneously admitted their guilt. Careful readers of the register will no doubt differ in their judgments as to the adequacy of the punishment and the efficacy of the means employed in the enquiry and in the execution of the sentence. A wise authority would certainly draw a distinction between an isolated lapse of passion for which repentance was sincere, and a repeated fault or promiscuous relations with women. In the latter cases, protestations of repentance, however fervent, would carry little weight. The subsequent history of a number of these Premonstratensian cases shows that Redman erred, if at all, on the side of leniency. Whether this leniency amounted to complaisance, and whether the punishments (in particular that of exile) nominally inflicted were in fact enforced, can to some extent be ascertained by checking the culprit's movements from the lists of the houses. Whatever may be the judgment of a modern critic in a matter of discipline, which all must admit to present very great difficulties, it would at least seem clear that efforts to mend matters and the success attending these efforts were greater among the white canons than among any other body of monks and canons, the Carthusians alone

1 References may here be given, for the sake of completeness, to the remaining cases where superiors were gravely at fault.

At Beauchief in 1462, as the result of an appeal from the abbot of Welbeck, the mother house, Redman with the abbot of Welbeck and another held a formal trial of Abbot Downham, accused of dilapidation, rebellion, incontinence and other misdemeanours, and deposed and excommunicated him, along with his accomplices (II, 49–50). At Eggleston in 1502 two abbots deputizing for Redman at what appears to have been an extraordinary visitation found the abbey, both head and members, in a state of sickness. They commanded the abbot to reform himself under pain of deposition, but withheld sentence till the next visitation, of which no record survives (II, 221–2). At St Radegund's in 1497 abbot and community were at loggerheads with serious counter-accusations. Redman reserved judgment till the next provincial chapter. What happened there does not transpire, but in 1500 the abbot was accused of incontinence with loose women, and of frequenting taverns, where his ribald behaviour was a source of annoyance to the other *habitués* of the bar (*singulos audientes tedio maximo afficiens*). He was ordered to show discretion in his visits to layfolk and hostelries (*ne festivis diebus sive aliis, nisi tempore congruo, tabernas...frequentet* (III, 103–5)).

2 Apostasy, in the technical language of Redman's visitations, is absence without leave from the monastery precinct for some length of time, usually accompanied by temporary abandonment of the regular habit.

3 It is not clear how Gasquet obtained his figure of eighteen cases of incontinence (*CAP*, II, introd. xxii: 'Eighteen at most charged with any crime whatsoever against morality'). Apparently he is only reckoning culprits in the houses contained in his vol. II, though he gives the total of all canons in all houses when he endeavours to establish a percentage of crime, and by 'charged' he means 'convicted'. When he judges that those who succeeded in finding colleagues to swear to their 'innocence' were guilty of no crime whatsoever against morality, he would seem to neglect the evidence of the Register, as well as to be forgetful of Christ's words in Matt. v. 28. Moral innocence and forensic guilt are not correlatives.

excepted. But as the subject has been debated, not without warmth, by the apologists of the medieval religious and by their adversaries, it may be well to examine more closely the data afforded by the Redman documents.

First, as to the procedure followed. If accusations made to the visitor were serious enough to warrant further examination, he summoned the accused and charged him with the fault. He might either confess or deny; if he denied, he was given opportunity to purge himself canonically, i.e. to obtain testimony on oath as to his innocence from five of his confrères. If he was successful in this, the visitor had in practice no alternative but to declare him innocent, however great might be his private misgivings; if he failed, or if he had previously confessed, he became technically guilty, and the visitor pronounced formal sentence of punishment, reserving its execution, if he wished, to a future date or to the cognizance of the next provincial chapter. The customary punishment among the white canons was forty days of hard penance—fasting on bread and water—and banishment to another house of the order for a period of weeks or years, or in perpetuity. Where there were aggravating circumstances, the sentence might be made more severe by imprisonment for the term of the penance, or indefinitely. Corporal punishment is not specifically mentioned, perhaps because it was a sanction within the control of the immediate superior.

Such were the constitutional provisions, and they were severe enough. In practice, however, they were rarely applied in their full rigour. The culprit, when the terms of his punishment were promulgated, might promise amendment and appeal for mercy; he might also secure the intercession of his superior and some or all of his brethren. Moved by this, the visitor could suspend or even cancel his sentence. Here we are not concerned with the merits of exile as a punishment, with its probable effects on the culprit, and the mutual reactions between him and the family to which he came as a black sheep in a strange fold; we have merely to consider the manner in which this particular sanction was applied.

In default of a satisfactory index and cross-references it is not easy to trace a delinquent's career in Redman's Register; the following statistics may therefore not be exhaustive. In all, twenty-three cases have been noted where a sentence of exile was pronounced;[1] sixteen of these were passed on canons confessing to, or convicted of, incontinence, the remaining seven were guilty of serious rebellion or theft, or of repeated apostasy. In eight instances the sentences were remitted on the spot or its execution deferred indefinitely; of the remaining fifteen culprits three vanished altogether, presumably into apostasy, six de facto never left their

---

1 II, 19 (Alnwick); 36 (Barlings); 66 (Beauchief); 76, 78 (Bayham); 90–1, 92, 93 (Blanchland); 117, 121 (Cockersand); 130 (Coverham); 182 (Dale); 241 (Halesowen); III, 7 (Langdon); 16, 17, 24 (Langley); 39–41 (Lavendon); 68–9 (Newhouse); 112–15 (Sulby); 143 (Torre); 164 (Tupholme); 187, 189 (Welbeck); 203–7 (Wendling).

home, and six can be traced into exile. In other words, about one in four of those sentenced actually went into exile, while two-thirds of the total stayed at home either with or without authorization, though some of these soon disappeared, either by death or apostasy. Perhaps the most disquieting feature of the matter is the frequency with which those convicted of a serious fault, and condemned to an exile to which they did not proceed, are found continuing in, or promoted to, positions of responsibility or authority. Thus William Hynmers of Alnwick,[1] convicted in 1482 of dilapidation and embezzlement, and more than suspected of incontinence when warden of Brenshalgh, though condemned to deposition from office and permanent exile at Dale, is nevertheless found as rector of Brenshalgh in 1488 and 1491; Robert Wolfet of Beauchief,[2] convicted of rebellion, apostasy and incontinence in 1494, is *circator* or roundsman of the house (*quis custodiet?*) in 1497 and 1500; while William Bentham and James Skipton of Cockersand, condemned to exile for incontinence in 1488, are found in 1491 as subprior and cellarer respectively of their old home.[3] It is difficult to suppose that in all these cases, and in others which might be added to them, a thorough reformation of character had taken place, though in certain cases, such as that of the numerous delinquents at Newhouse in 1478, there is a fair presumption that four at least of the five implicated lived blamelessly in the sequel.[4] It must be remembered in justice, also, that in small rural communities the choice of suitable candidates for office was very limited.

In fine, three conclusions emerge from a consideration of all the cases; first, that punishment overtook a serious fault only in one out of every four instances; second, that a considerable number of those who remained unpunished continued in, or were subsequently appointed to, offices of responsibility; and thirdly, that of the six who went into exile five returned home, four of them to hold office, while the fifth remained in a position of trust in the house of his exile. In other words, that conviction for incontinence usually led to no serious consequences, even for officeholders, while exile, when submitted to, had no disastrous external aftereffects. Looked at more deeply, it may even be thought that only those whose repentance was sincere, and who therefore had a root of goodness in them, actually went into exile.

The above statistics include only those convicted at visitation and noted in the reports. The (unfortunately incomplete) records of provincial chapters somewhat unexpectedly yield notices of various canons transferred for unspecified reasons and whose names do not always figure in Redman's injunctions. Of these we are told simply that the chapter authorize the transference of such a canon of such a house to such another house for such a period of years, but as Redman presided at all the chapters concerned he presumably controlled the agenda, and it may be

1 II, 19, 21, 25.   2 II, 66 *seqq.*
3 II, 117, 120.   4 III, 68–9.

supposed that most of those concerned had already passed through his hands as visitor, though for some reason their names do not appear in his injunctions. We have therefore no means of knowing whether some secret or heinous fault, or merely some temperamental incompatibility, gave cause for the transference.

In all, some twenty changes are recorded, seven of which concern culprits known to us from Redman's Register; in these cases, which have already been analysed, the chapter either confirms the visitor's action or alters the destination.[1] Of the remaining thirteen canons affected eight can be traced from the community lists and are seen to have changed residence as commanded; of four all trace is lost, and it may be supposed that some or all apostatized. On the whole, therefore, the commands of chapter were in general more efficacious than those of the visitor.

By combining the evidence of visitations and chapters it is possible to follow the careers of several delinquent canons, and a few examples may be given here.

John Lincoln, who appears in all the lists of Barlings from 1475 to 1488, and who held several offices there, was perhaps convicted of incontinence at the visitation in the latter year; the record is fragmentary, breaking off at the beginning of one such conviction. He was presumably sent to Wendling by Redman, for the chapter of ?1488 gave a permanent transference thither. At Wendling he became subcellarer, but in 1494 was convicted by Redman of incontinence and theft, and banished to Langley for ten years. The sentence was confirmed by the chapter of 1495, but Lincoln never arrived at Langley and, as he disappears from all the lists, presumably apostatized.[2]

Robert Bredon of Sulby was convicted in visitation in 1491 of incontinence and apostasy, and received sentence for each crime, in addition to penance of forty days, being exiled to Alnwick for seven years and to Shap for three. As the sentences clearly could not run concurrently, it is not surprising to read that Bredon burst into tears and promised amendment. The pathos of the spectacle was increased by his abbot, who joined him on his knees and mingled his tears with those of his erring subprior.[3] The sentence was therefore duly suspended, and it is painful—though not perhaps surprising—to find that at the following visitation Bredon was found guilty not only of renewed apostasy and incontinence with the same partner in guilt, but of defaming his abbot to influential patrons and of appealing away from all domestic jurisdiction. For these crimes he was sentenced to an exile of ten years at St Agatha's, but at the provincial

---

1 I, 150 (1479); 153 (1485); 158–9 (?1487); 166 (1489); 171–2 (1492); 176–7 (1495).

2 I, 153, 177; II, 34–5; III, 204, 205. John Barlynges of the Wendling list of 1494 (III, 207) is clearly to be identified with Lincoln.

3 III, 112–13: 'Quibus [sc. Bredon and another] statim in lacrimis resolutis, misericordiam humiliter implorabant, melioris vitae reformacionem promittentibus. Et proprius illorum prelatus, coram nobis genibus flexis et similiter in lacrimis resolutus, pro eisdem veniam anxius postulabat.' Such scenes are not uncommon in the visitation records.

chapter of 1495 he was assigned to Dale during the good pleasure of Redman. To Dale he went, and apparently made good, as in 1497 he met Redman at West Dereham in Norfolk and obtained licence to accept a chantry or similar post.[1]

Finally, there is the curious case of Thomas Ludham of Langley. This brother, while still a deacon in that disorderly house, had in 1491 the misfortune to cut off the right hand of a Carmelite in the course of a prolonged brawl.[2] For this, in addition to forty days' penance, he was sentenced by Redman to exile and perpetual imprisonment at Sulby. He was already, it would seem, in durance at home. To Sulby he went; he was there in 1494,[3] and at Redman's good pleasure. Nevertheless, he speedily returned home and in 1497 could be seen as subprior at Langley.[4]

From a survey of all these figures and cases we gain the impression of a centralized disciplinary organization which is certainly functioning regularly, and cannot be described as wholly ineffective. Its efficiency is, however, incomplete; too often, we cannot help feeling, a well-merited punishment was remitted as soon as imposed; too often, for whatever reason, an unremitted sentence was disobeyed or given the go-by; and too often, whatever may have been the forcible reason urged in particular cases, past delinquents are found in office. The white canons were far from being wholly decayed. The fabric of their life and the machinery of their original constitution were still in existence, but if, even under the administration of the capable and influential Redman, a lack of vigour and true zeal for justice is to be deplored, it may be feared that a less gifted and more ephemeral superior would find it hard to maintain discipline at even a passable degree of tension.

A more favourable conclusion would seem to be valid in the sphere of economics. Three undoubted facts emerge from a study of Redman's visitations: first, that over the whole of the period covered the Premonstratensians as a body possessed abundant stores and credit;[5] secondly, that where debts or dilapidation were serious, an efficient abbot had little difficulty in restoring financial soundness; thirdly, that the aggregate liquid assets of the order were considerably greater at the end of Redman's life than they had been at the beginning of his career as visitor.

1 I, 176; II, 183; III, 112, 115, 116, 222 (the date of the grant is seen to be that of the Dale visitation). Robert Bredon must not be confused with Richard, a canon of Dale.

2 III, 24: 'Diu litigantibus et tandem manus violentas alter alteri nephande inferentes, manum ejusdem fratris Carmelite infortune[!] abscidit dexteram.'

3 His name appears last in the community list (III, 25) with the addition *in carcere*.

4 I, 177; III, 116, 28.

5 Redman's assertions to the abbot of Prémontré in 1486 and 1493 (I, 81–2, 91) that the English houses are *temporalibus pauperrima* occur in letters where there is question of financial subscription. They may be compared with his contemporary statements in visitation, e.g. 'Necessariis peroptime ac ditissime stauratum' (III, 148; Torre, 1492); 'cunctarum rerum opulencia habundantissime provisum' (III, 188; Welbeck, 1488); 'in granis et cunctis animalibus habundatissime stuffatum' (III, 64; Newbo, 1497). The white canons were not, of course, rich when compared with the largest houses of black monks and Cistercians.

Redman was visitor of the English houses in virtue of his office as commissary-general of the abbot of Prémontré;[1] the position carried with it the duty of convoking and presiding at the triennial provincial chapter. The acts of a number of these assemblies survive in his register, and here too a state of efficiency prevails which contrasts very favourably with the contemporary records of the black monks and Austin canons. The chapters were well attended; at some, indeed, all the abbots without exception were present,[2] and although the acts are concerned chiefly with liturgical and ceremonial matters it is clear that all outstanding disciplinary cases were considered and adjudged. Each set of acts ends with a list of canons transferred from one house to another; the majority of these had already been dealt with at least provisionally by Redman in visitation, but as has been noted the chapters (acting under his presidency) often changed the destination or prolonged the exile of the culprit.

The visitation records and Redman's *obiter dicta* give some interesting information regarding the daily life and fortunes of individual abbeys. The houses differed little in size; the very large and the diminutive communities of the black monks and black canons have no counterpart here. The largest during this period were St Agatha's (15–23 canons), Alnwick (21–26), Barlings (14–23) and Welbeck (18–24); the smallest Wendling (6–7) and Durford (8–11); the majority had an average of fifteen canons. There is no mention of *conversi* nor any trace in the lists; the column of names at Tupholme previously thought to be a list of *conversi* is an editorial blunder.[3] As regards prosperity, Redman wrote of Croxton in 1497 that it surpassed all the other houses in stores of grain and number of stock; the same encomium was passed on Barlings in 1500 and Newhouse in 1503.[4] Of Leiston he declared in 1488 that the liturgy was carried out there with greater solemnity and care than elsewhere, and in 1500 that all within and without was conducted in a manner more deserving of praise than at any other house.[5] The names of unworthy heads of houses have already appeared in these pages; among those who did good things, so far as records speak, the names of Abbot Wisbeach of West Dereham,[6] of

---

1 Cf. the terms of the commission in I, 74–6.   2 E.g. at Lincoln in 1476 (I, 140).

3 The list (III, 160) contains thirteen names, after the priests, which occur neither in the previous (1482) nor in the subsequent (1494) list. I originally (1959) suggested these were *conversi*; Mr Colvin points out that the names should appear in the 1491 Croxton list (II, 160, no. 345). In general, it is by no means clear that all the canons serving churches are included in these lists. The numbers in the text include 'novices', as the title often embraces all under the rank of priest. *V.* also Appendix II in Colvin, *The White Canons*.

4 II, 162–3; II, 42; III, 87.   5 III, 49, 50.

6 The encomium of Abbot Wisbeach of West Dereham (III, 223) may be quoted; it forms the whole of Redman's injunction for the visitation. 'Discretum pariter in spiritualibus et temporalibus non mediocriter comperimus prelatum, ad quem illud Salomonis reducere et assimilare merito possimus, Sapiens semper sapienter agit et gubernacula possidebit. Et tam intus quam foris cuncta sic disponit, quod nisi obediencia mihi preciperet ad dictum monasterium causa reformacionis illuc diebus quo vixerit minime descenderemus. Et ut quid de debitis aliquid loquamur, cum in omnibus tam animalium universis generibus quam granis suis omnibus superexcellit predecessoribus.'

Abbot Attercliff of Croxton (1491–1534) and of Abbot Dockett of Leiston (before 1488–1500) may be lifted for a moment out of time's oblivion.

The founder of the white canons had intended his sons to combine apostolic preaching with a quasi-monastic life based on that of the Cistercians. In England, even as late as Redman's day, something of this twofold vocation had been preserved. All the abbeys held churches, and at the end of the fifteenth century many, though not the majority, were served by vicars, perpetual or casual; the remainder were occupied by canons who, if their cure was a neighbouring one, were expected to return to the abbey at night and for meals. In some cases canons also served churches which they did not own, and as for all practical purposes they were off the strength of their abbey we find Redman on occasion ordering all home,[1] while, conversely, cases occurred where a temperamental canon was sent out to a church in the interest of domestic peace.[2]

For those of the community—never a large number—who had neither church nor office there remained manual work and claustral reading. How far serious horticultural or rural work entered into the normal life is not clear; there is, however, ample evidence that it was a practical reality, especially during the hay, grain and fruit harvest.[3] That Redman should have found it necessary to insist on obedience to all commands to field and garden work does indeed show that there was a tendency to shirk, but such injunctions would have been unthinkable among the black monks and canons, and casual references to employments other than these when the weather is bad, to garden as opposed to field work, and to the omission of the second daily sung Mass at harvest time and other heavy seasonal periods, shows that manual work was a reality for the white canons. Casual references, likewise, to reading in the cloister and to writing manuscripts to order show that these employments, too, still had their place.[4] The Premonstratensians had never been a student order, and most of the houses fell below the twenty-mark of the Benedictine Constitutions enjoining attendance at a university. Cases occur, however, of individual canons at study.[5]

References to less intellectual pursuits are more frequent. At lonely houses under the fells or in the heart of Sherwood the attractions of the chase had their appeal, and Redman found it necessary on several occasions

---

1 E.g. II, 97 (Blanchland).   2 III, 6 (Langdon).
3 E.g. III, 41 (Lavendon); 60 (Newbo): 'Omnibus horis diligenter insistant labori...et temporibus, quibus non permittit aeris temperies laborare, libris suis pro scientia adquirenda diligenter vacent.' *Ibid.* 85 (Newhouse, 1500): 'Fratribus omnibus et singulis precipimus quatenus tempore feni et messis ceterisque anni temporibus ad preceptum abbatis sine murmure debite laborent.' *Ibid.* 97–8 (St Radegund's, 1482): 'Precipimus toto conventui ut sicuti continetur in nostris statutis fratres a mane usque ad vesperam faciant opus in ortis sive ubicumque necesse fuerit.'
4 E.g. III, 113 (Sulby): 'Qui ibidem scriptores sunt precipimus ut quicquid de suo labore deinceps adquirerint prelato presentare non negligant.'
5 III, 178 (Welbeck)—a canon to be sent to the university; III, 224 (West Dereham)—a canon to be recalled from the university to teach at home.

to forbid the keeping of hounds, while at Sulby he noted with displeasure the fashion of keeping smaller dogs, rabbits and birds.[1] At Titchfield one of the canons was in the habit of leaving the house at night to poach fish from the abbey's stews.[2] Gambling was a more common fault; this usually took the form of throwing dice, but the newer game of card-playing finds mention,[3] and it is somewhat surprising that tennis is more than once forbidden in a context which implies that the gambling possibilities rather than the game itself constituted its appeal.[4]

Architecture and the arts of decoration had a particular interest for Bishop Redman. As bishop of St Asaph, he was responsible for erecting out of dilapidation the church which can be seen to-day, and he rested in death at Ely under what is perhaps the most sumptuous tomb in the cathedral. It is therefore natural to find him often issuing instructions (which were, perhaps, less honoured than any others) for the rebuilding of churches and conventual buildings.[5] As we have noted, the last decades of monastic life saw a considerable amount of new work undertaken. The Premonstratensian injunctions show this as occurring also in the last decades of the previous century; Redman had occasion in 1482 to remark on the beauty of the new buildings at Torre; at Newbo in 1491 he noted a beautiful new window at the end of the church; and at Beeleigh in 1500 he could write of the exceptionally beautiful work including a highly successful restoration of the windows.[6]

On the whole, it must be said that the white canons, though providing a number of distressing cases of decadence, do not give that extremely painful impression of stagnation and sordid vice that the reader of contemporary black monk and black canon visitations receives only too frequently from the records. The Premonstratensians, though not abounding in numbers and animated by no extraordinary fervour, were on the whole a well-disciplined body of which the members, with certain exceptions, lived a tolerably observant life.

1 II, 98 (Blanchland); III, 22 (Langley); III, 111 (Sulby): 'Ne aliquis fratrum aves, caniculos sive cuniculos habere seu alere presumat, quia magis curiositatem quam utilitatem pretendunt.' *Ibid.* 181 (Welbeck).

2 III, 128: 'Nocte exeundo pisces furtive lacubus infra monasterium situatis exstraxit.'

3 III, 100 (St Radegund's): 'Lusores deciarum vel ad cardes excommunicamus.'

4 III, 35 (Lavendon): 'Nullus...audeat...ad tenas aliquo modo ludere...seu ad aliquem alium ludum pro pecunia.' *Ibid.* 150 (Torre): Ludos insuper quoscunque pro turpi lucro inhibemus, presertim illum ludum vocatum vulgariter tenys.' Possibly 'tenys' is a game of cards or dice ('tens') and not (as Gasquet thought) tennis.

5 E.g. at Durford in 1494 he ordered the rebuilding of the ruined cloister (II, 198); nothing had been done by 1497 (*ibid.* 199) or 1500 (*ibid.* 200–1).

6 III, 147 (Torre): 'Plura et amena.' *Ibid.* 61 (Newbo); II, 88 (Beeleigh): 'Perpulcras ecclesie edificaciones fenestrarumque amenas reparaciones.' *Ibid.* III, 224 (West Dereham): 'Palam intuencium oculis apparent magna et laudabilia...edificia.'

CHAPTER V

THE FRIARS IN THE EARLY SIXTEENTH CENTURY

The seventy years that followed the death of the eminent Carmelite apologist, Thomas Netter of Walden (*ob.* 1430), make up the darkest period in the history of the English friars. Chronicles, biographies, literary work, and even theological treaties are lacking, and the fairly plentiful record material does little but tell us of the ordinations and academic successes of the friars, together with an enumeration of legacies appearing in the wills of townspeople all over England. By a significant coincidence, the two scholars who have devoted most labour to investigations in the sources of Franciscan and Dominican history use the same metaphor of sleep to describe the state of the two bodies of friars in the fifteenth century.[1]

Throughout the period, indeed, a small number of friars of both orders continued to be appointed to Welsh bishoprics, or to serve as suffragans to diocesans in England, but none of these made any great mark either before or after episcopal consecration. At Oxford the great controversy with the Lollards had died away, and no new crisis developed in which bishops might feel the need of a panel of expert theologians; although the Carmelite provincial, John Milverton,[2] took a hand in the early stages of the affair of Reginald Pecock, the final trial was a matter for politicians rather than for theologians. At the universities it was an age of routine, if not of decadence, in philosophy and theology, and with the foundation of numerous colleges the friars lost the pride of place that had once been theirs, and became only a group among the components of the academic body. Their interests and characteristics alike prevented them from being among the first humanists, and very soon they found themselves in opposition, passive if not active, to the school of Colet and Erasmus.

Numerically, however, they were still strong, and by the end of the fifteenth century they numbered some three thousand all told, a larger total than at any time since the Great Pestilence of 1348. Probably the percentage of the total number attending the schools at Oxford and Cambridge had diminished. It has been computed that at Cambridge, in the thirty-three years between 1455 and 1488, over a hundred friars were admitted to degrees;[3] at Oxford for a similar period a little later

1 Fr B. Jarrett, *The English Dominicans*, 151, wrote: 'Silent, dulled, asleep, they [*sc.* the Dominicans] took in the last century of their pre-Reformation existence hardly any place at all in the national life.' A. G. Little, in a letter to the present writer in 1941, remarked: 'After this [i.e. 1430] the province goes to sleep for fifty or sixty years.' The historian will not readily rest content with such judgments, but if we substitute some such phrase as 'remains undistinguished' for 'goes to sleep' the judgment is true enough.

2 For Milverton and William Goddard, the Franciscan minister provincial, in the *affaire* Pecock, *v.* V. H. H. Green, *Bishop Reginald Pecock* (index, *s.vv.*).

3 J. R. H. Moorman, *The Grey Friars in Cambridge*, 120.

(1505–38, with a few records wanting) there were about one hundred and forty.[1] In these numbers the Franciscans, as in the past, were the most numerous, at Oxford certainly, at Cambridge very probably. Save, however, for a few theological writings of a conventional character, scarcely anything is known of the activities of all these students. Almost the only humanist of early days is the Italian friar, Lorenzo di Savona of the province of Genoa who, while in residence at Cambridge, compiled in 1478 the *Nova rhetorica* that was printed almost immediately by both Caxton (*c.* 1479) and the printer of St Albans (1480).[2] Forty years younger than Fra Lorenzo, but possibly his confrère for a while at Cambridge, was Richard Brinkley, an early representative of the new learning in its scholarly and orthodox form. Brinkley knew both Greek and Hebrew, and as a borrower of books which he did not return he has interested modern bibliographers; it is thus that we know of a Greek New Testament lent him by his brethren at Oxford and of a Hebrew Psalter borrowed from St Albans which contains notes in his hand.[3]

Brinkley, however, who ultimately became provincial of the Minors (1518–26), is almost the last representative among the friars of learning pursued for its own sake or from personal enthusiasm rather than for purposes of controversy. His contemporary, Henry Standish,[4] was essentially a combatant and an inheritor of the tradition of the friars of Wyclif's day, at once opposed to doctrinal innovations and to clerical privilege. His rise, after taking his degree, was rapid. He became warden of the Grey Friars in London, and in 1505 minister provincial. Six years later he began his career as court preacher, and in 1515 found himself embroiled in the celebrated controversy with Abbot Kidderminster.[5] It is worth glancing for a moment at the oft-told story of what was the last public controversy in England on a great religious issue to be conducted according to the rules that had been honoured in Europe for more than four centuries.[6]

When parliament was ready to meet in 1515 it was realized that one of the laws about to expire unless renewed was an act of 1512 depriving clerics not in major orders of the benefit of clergy. The bishops and higher clergy, who had never felt easy about this act, moderate and reasonable as it may seem to the modern mind, were now in the throes of the *cause célèbre* of Richard Hunne, in which other clerical privileges were threatened, and the bishop of London, a few days before the question was to be reopened in parliament, put up the redoubtable Abbot Kidderminster to fulminate against the act at Paul's Cross. He presented the traditional case of the clergy with intransigence, and the lords, where the

---

1 A. G. Little, *The Grey Friars in Oxford* (OHS, xx, 1891), 54.
2 Moorman, *Grey Friars*, 207; Little, *Grey Friars*, 265–6.
3 For Brinkley, *v.* Moorman, *Grey Friars*, 155–6, and index, *s.v.*; Little, *Grey Friars*, 283.
4 *V. DNB*; Moorman, *Grey Friars*, 211; Little, *Grey Friars*, 271–4.
5 For Kidderminster, *v. infra*, p. 94.
6 The story is told at length in all histories of the period (e.g. Pickthorn, Fisher, Pollard, Hughes) and in biographies of Henry VIII and Wolsey.

spiritualty were in a majority, dropped the statute and a month later refused to pass a bill sent up from the commons renewing it. Meanwhile, the lower house had appealed to the king, and a committee of royal divines and canonists was set up to debate the issue at Blackfriars with counsel appointed by the clergy. It was at this meeting that Standish, warden of the Grey Friars, defended the Act of 1512 as making for the common weal and therefore not injuring the liberty of the Church; papal legislation in the past, recently (1514) reiterated by Leo X, had never, so he alleged, been received in England. In consequence, the commons demanded that the bishops should order Kidderminster to make a public recantation. So far from doing this, they reaffirmed their agreement with his position as correct and traditional. Meanwhile, during a parliamentary recess, Standish developed his position in a series of public lectures, whereupon the bishops summoned him before Convocation in November 1515, and demanded an answer to a series of crucial questions on the relations of Church and State. Standish, without answering, appealed to the king, and the whole question was twice debated in assemblies summoned by Henry in which counsel and commons and divines were represented at Blackfriars and Baynard's Castle. The whole affair, when it seemed about to develop into a dangerous crisis[1] in which the clergy would have been caught by a *praemunire*, was compromised. The clergy made what was in practice submission to the king; the offending statute was not re-enacted; Wolsey took steps to ensure that awkward incidents should not occur; and Standish, the 'minister and fomenter of all the trouble', was maintained in favour by the king and in 1518, against the will of Wolsey, promoted to the see of St Asaph's. Meanwhile, the fourteen years of Wolsey's 'personal rule' had begun, and the conflict was adjourned. It has an interest for the historian as being the last occasion when a monk and a friar stood forward as recognized spokesmen on a living issue of religious policy and theory, and it is noteworthy that each filled his historical rôle: the monk as the high churchman defending privilege, the friar as the advocate of the anti-clerical, anti-papal party.

For the rest, Standish was no reformer. He had come out against Erasmus in the storm that arose over the Greek New Testament of 1516, and had thus qualified himself for a place in the great humanist's gallery of obscurantists; his promotion as 'Saint Asse' in 1518 was a gift of the gods which Erasmus duly exploited.[2] Standish was likewise one of Wolsey's examiners of heretics, and as such one of those who tried 'little Bilney' in 1527. He was chief counsel for Queen Katharine, though not in fact very ardent in her support, and he joined with Stokesley and Longland in an endeavour to tone down the declaration of submission of the

---

1 *Lords Journals*, I, 57; *LP*, II, 1313–14.
2 Erasmus has many hard words for Standish, e.g. *ep.* 1126 (Allen, IV, 310): 'Habet [ed. Lee]...Standicium multis titulis insignem, primum Minoritam, deinde theologum, postremo episcopum.' *V. ep.* 608; Allen, III, 21; and the letter of More, *ep.* 481; II, 371–2.

clergy in 1532. On the other hand, he accepted the royal supremacy without demur. He was, in fact, a conservative of the type of Stokesley and Tunstall, and his death in 1535 relieved him of further choice between opposition to heresy and compromise with it.

Standish was the last distinguished friar of his generation. He had grown to maturity before the new theological learning had begun to trouble academic waters. The friars who were at their studies when he had become bishop were of another vintage. From 1520 onwards the opinions and writings of Luther were being diffused at Cambridge by a group of exceptionally gifted young men who were to be the leaders of opinion ten and fifteen years later and who were almost all, in one way or another, to suffer for their opinions.[1] Why Cambridge and not Oxford was the centre of the new theology is not at first sight clear. In part, it may have been that Lutheran teaching filtered into England through the ports of East Anglia and the fenland; in part because the dwellers in East Anglia, whence came a large proportion of the students at Cambridge, were more ready to absorb the new teaching than were the men of western England; in part, finally, much may have hung upon a few dominant personalities. In any case, the seeds of Lutheranism took root in Cambridge, and an informal society discussed its consequences; their meeting-place, the White Horse tavern, passed into legend as the cradle of one, at least, of the schools of English Reform; it was known to contemporaries as 'Germany', and the men who met there as 'Germans'.

To many of the young friars of the day the sudden impact of revolutionary doctrine which held forth a promise of spiritual refreshment to such men as Latimer and Bilney, and of freedom from numberless traditional inhibitions to those of the stamp of Coverdale or Bale, must have been both intoxicating and unsettling. Luther's three great pamphlets, attacking the papacy, undermining the whole system of the monastic and devoted life, and sweeping away its characteristic observances and prohibitions in the names of Christian liberty, of the word of Scripture, and of early Christian practice[2]—all this, before the forces of Catholicism had rallied, must have been a flood hard for individuals to stem, and it inevitably affected the friars more than the monks. The latter had lived almost all their lives in their age-old home, with the traditions of a family apart from the rest of the world, and few of them had any intellectual interests or love of religious dialectic. The friars, on the other hand, were in the world; their business was to preach and to argue; they had been, or were still being, brought up to a technique of speculation and dialectic that was outmoded, arid, and in many of its manifestations positively destructive of deep spirituality. To such men the new evangel from Germany and

1 The personalities and activities of this group have often been described; among the more recent and sympathetic pictures may be mentioned that by E. G. Rupp, *Studies in the making of the English Protestant tradition*, 15–46.

2 *De captivitate babylonica ecclesiae* (1520); *de libertate hominis christiani* (1520); *de votis monasticis* (1521).

Switzerland must have seemed at once as compelling and as dissolvent as Darwinism seemed to many a century ago or as Marxism appeared to many in the generation between the two European wars, while to simpler minds that lacked strong conviction or wise guidance it must have seemed at once as liberating and as dynamic as did the first call of John Wesley. The friars of early Tudor England were not, like their predecessors in the age of Aquinas, or their successors of to-day, the spearhead of orthodox theology, strong and confident in their possession of the truth and of means of defending it. They were rather a part of the world of their age, using outworn tools and lacking any sense of apostolic vocation or intellectual security.

Most of the leading spirits of the revolutionary group at Cambridge were from the colleges, and so secular clerics; such were Cranmer, Latimer and others. Of the friars who were of the party the ablest was the Austin friar Robert Barnes.[1]

Barnes was a Norfolk man from Lynn. He had taken the habit of the Austin friars as a boy, and was sent for part of his studies to Louvain, at that time entering upon the most distinguished period of its history and a noted centre of academic humanism. Barnes absorbed the Latin classics, and returned to lecture on them to a group of his confrères which included Miles Coverdale. He does not seem at this time to have had leanings towards the new opinions; he owed his new orientation, like Latimer, to Bilney but, unlike Latimer, he does not appear as the earnest prophet of reform; rather, he had many of the mental and social characteristics of the typical friar of the earlier satirists. As Gardiner, who knew him well over a long period of years, put it, he was 'a trim minion friar Augustine, one of a merry scoffing wit, friarlike, and as a good fellow in company was beloved of many'.[2] He attained notoriety, and began the series of his tribulations, with a sermon on Christmas Eve in 1525 in which he deprecated the worldly observance of festivals, criticized traditional religion on a number of counts, and passed on to expatiate upon the ostentatious splendours of Wolsey. His subsequent career falls outside the limits of this volume. After a long and not unfriendly examination, he recanted his expressed opinions under protest, but ultimately fled abroad, where he wrote as a convinced reformer and was ultimately used by Cromwell and the king to sound the German theologians in the matter of the divorce, and again in 1539 as an ambassador to Denmark and one of those charged with the negotiations for the marriage with Anne of Cleves. Finally, having returned to England, he insisted on parading his Lutheran opinions and was ultimately, in 1540, one of the group of six executed at Tyburn, three for Lutheran heresy and three for denying the king's supremacy in matters of religion.

1 For Barnes, *v. DNB*, and Rupp, *op. cit.* 31–46.
2 Gardiner gives a long and interesting account of his relations with Barnes in a letter to George Joye printed in J. A. Muller, *The Letters of Stephen Gardiner*, letter 81, pp. 164–78. The quotation in the text is on p. 165. Elsewhere (p. 334) he has a reference to Bale: 'ineptientis fraterculi latratus...frater Baal'.

Barnes had as his pupil in the classics at the Austin friary, and as his companion in the meetings at the White Horse, his confrère Miles Coverdale,[1] a man of greater mental gifts and of a less volatile temperament. He was a northerner, and the parts of Lutheran teaching that most attracted him were those that most resembled the tenets of Wyclif and the Lollards: zeal for the word of Scripture, hatred of images, and a disbelief in the value of a monastic or vowed religious life. He was in fact one of the earliest and most consistent 'puritans' of the first generation of reformers. He assisted Barnes in his trial for heresy before Wolsey and Tunstall in 1526, and then abandoned his habit and his vows and went abroad, where for twenty years he was active as a translator and controversialist. He returned in due course to be bishop of Exeter and a consistent upholder of what developed into puritanism.

Yet a third friar of great ability and unusual versatility of talent was at Cambridge with Barnes and Coverdale. This was the young Carmelite John Bale, destined to stormy career and many changes of fortune.[2] Bale, as he never ceased to proclaim, was a Suffolk man, and was born at Cove, near Dunwich, in 1495. He was entered by his parents at the Carmelite house at Norwich when he was twelve, and in due course was sent to Cambridge in 1514, where, unlike his contemporaries in the other three orders, he did not reside in the priory with his confrères, but became a member of the newly founded Jesus College. From Cambridge he passed to Louvain and Toulouse, where he is found in 1527; he returned to take his B.D. at Cambridge in 1529 and then passed immediately to be prior of the Carmelite houses of Malden, Doncaster (c. 1530) and Ipswich (1533). It was probably in Suffolk that he attracted the notice and patronage of Thomas, Lord Wentworth, one of the earliest men of position to take up with Lutheranism, and Wentworth was probably responsible for the final 'conversion' which led Bale to leave his order, marry and accept employment as a curate at Thorndon (Essex), though as early as 1531 at Doncaster he had taught one of his subjects that Christ was not really present in the Sacrament. As he tells us himself that he was a Carmelite for twenty-four years, his final break with the past must have taken place c. 1531. In that year he was in trouble with Stokesley, and in 1534 with Lee, the archbishop of York. Finally, he was accused of a string of quasi-heretical opinions (among which his extreme anti-papal bias was not reckoned) before Stokesley, but an old friendship with Cromwell, to whom John Leland also wrote as advocate, saved him, and during 1538–40 he appears to have been in charge of a group of strolling players under Cromwell's patronage, writing topical 'moralities' as anti-papal and anti-monastic

---

1 The literature on Coverdale is very extensive. For his life, v. *DNB*.
2 All previous accounts of Bale have been antiquated by two recent monographs by two scholars working independently though simultaneously; cf. *John Bale, dramatist and antiquary*, by Honor McCusker, and *John Bale, a study in the minor literature of the Reformation*, by Jesse W. Harris.

propaganda. From 1540 to 1548 he was in exile in Germany, whence he returned to receive the Irish bishopric of Ossory from the hands of Edward VI. With his further career we are not concerned.

Bale is not an amiable character. His controversial writings touch depths of scurrility and obscenity remarkable even for that age, and the epithet 'bilious' often attached to his name, though owing much of its vogue to its alliterative quality, is not altogether undeserved. Yet at the same time Bale has to his credit work of permanent historical value, and his very real industry and learning, coupled with his devotion to the memory of the past worthies of England, especially of his own order, have helped to temper the resentment which his bitter pen has provoked. Bale had a real sense of the value and interest of the past,[1] and a part of him, at least, had kinship with Leland and Abbot Foche of St Augustine's. As a young Carmelite and again presumably when prior in East Anglia, he had occupied himself in amassing facts about the history and ancient lights of his order.[2] He preserved with piety the collected notes of Leland, and himself published a bibliography of British writers which has ever since been a starting point for all who have attempted a similar task. Without Bale, Fuller, Pitts, Wood and Tanner would scarcely have known where to begin. He was, moreover, extremely learned in all matters concerning the English past, and even his excursions into ancient ecclesiastical history, though full of partisan acerbity and fantastic conclusions, are the work of a scholar who, in a more peaceful age, might have achieved something of solid utility. The notable example of Thomas Hearne and other antiquaries has shown that a certain type of scholarly industry and accuracy, together with a just appreciation of men long dead, is by no means inconsistent with a narrowness of mind and a bitter spirit of jealousy and intolerance towards the living. This is not to say that, on the balance, the good qualities of Bale's work outweigh the bad, still less, that his works of learning can in any way offset faults of character and lack of spiritual qualities. Yet devotion to any pursuit which is not purely selfish or mercenary has something in it that attracts sympathy, and Bale's application to his studies, even in advanced years, received quaint recognition from one of his own way of thinking:

> Good aged Bale, that with thy hoary heares,
>   Dost yet persiste to turne the paynefull Booke;
>   O happye man, that has obtayned such yeares,
>   And leavst not yet, on papers pale to looke.[3]

---

1 Cf. the passage in his *Summarium*, fo. 3, Q. 3, cited McCusker, *John Bale*, 123: 'Utque causam suscepti in hoc volumine laboris explicem, ad id me imprimis coegerunt historiarum dulcedo, literarum cupiditas, atque vehementer naturalis et officiosus erga patriam amor.'

2 He had, for example, compiled lists of the generals and English provincials, which drew from Fr B. Zimmermann, in *Monumenta Historica Carmelitana*, I, 264 n., the remark: 'qui nonobstante haeresi et apostasia de re historica Ordinis nostri optime meritus est'.

3 Barnabe Googe, *Eclogs, Epytaphes and Sonettes* (London, 1563), fo. E 6, cited by H. McCusker, *John Bale*, 128.

Besides these three notable figures, several other friars were on the edge of the great world, or were suspected of addiction to novelties, in the early decades of the century. Among the Franciscans of Oxford Nicholas de Burgo, a native of Florence and graduate of Paris, incorporated at Oxford in 1522/3, collaborated in 1530 with Stokesley and Foxe in writing a book on the king's marriage in favour of the divorce, and was probably used as negotiator with the university of Bologna in the same affair.[1] A colleague, Thomas Kirkham, opposed the divorce, but later became a Protestant. At Cambridge, Friar Stephen Baron, who became an Observant and provincial minister, was confessor to Henry VIII as a young man, and a noted preacher. He wrote a book of instruction for kings, *De officio et caritate Principum*, which he dedicated to Henry.[2] Gregory Bassett, on the other hand, who was at Cambridge from 1522 onwards, was suspected of heresy and imprisoned but later released. Whatever his views at that time, he ended as a conservative, and is noted in 1561 as a 'common mass-sayer'.[3] Another to incur suspicion was William Call, a Norfolk man and a Paston on his mother's side. In early life he was 'somewhat reclaimed to the Gospel's side' by Bilney, but as ten years later he was provincial the extent of his reclamation must remain uncertain.[4] More pronounced in his views was John Cardmaker, an Oxford graduate who spent some years at Cambridge. He was an active reformer, married, and ended in the fires of Smithfield in 1555.[5] A like fate probably overtook William Roy, an Observant of Greenwich, who spent some time at Cambridge and when there copied the Montfort Codex of the Greek New Testament at the instigation of Henry Standish, to help him in his controversy with Erasmus. Roy soon became unorthodox, and before 1524 fled to join Tyndale at Hamburg. He wrote a well-known satire on Wolsey, *Rede me and be nothe wrothe*, and a treatise against the seven sacraments, and was probably burnt as a heretic in Portugal in 1531.[6] Another friar who studied at both universities, Bartholomew Traheron, joined the reformers and went abroad, married, and returned to be keeper of the King's Library at Westminster, Member of Parliament and in time dean of Chichester.[7] Similar careers can be seen at other friaries. John Joseph of Canterbury became one of Cranmer's chaplains and a zealous reformer. George Browne, of the Oxford Austin friars, and later prior of the London house, was on terms of friendship with his London neighbour, Thomas Cromwell, and may have been the priest who assisted at the secret form of marriage between Henry and Anne Boleyn in 1533. He was appointed as one of the visitors of the friars in 1534, and was rewarded for his pains by a doctorate in divinity at Oxford and the archbishopric of Dublin.[8]

1 Little, *Grey Friars*, 280–2.
2 Moorman, *Grey Friars*, 151.
3 *Ibid.* 151–2.
4 *Ibid.* 160.
5 *Ibid.* 161, and *DNB*.
6 Moorman, *op. cit.* 205.
7 *Ibid.* 217.
8 *DNB*, and A. G. Little in *VCH, Oxon*, II (1907), 147.

F

From these brief notes it will be seen that for some fifteen years before the first clear indications of a general suppression of the religious orders, the friars had been exposed to currents of heterodox teaching, and had lost several of their number to the camp of the reformers. Doubtless the impact of the new theology was greatest at Cambridge, Oxford and perhaps London. The numbers known to have defected are few indeed from out of a body of nearly three thousand, and even if we allow for many nameless apostates the proportion is still small. Nevertheless, it is noteworthy that several of those who left their habit were men of unusual ability, and the effect upon others, not only of their defection, but of their opinions in the years before they went, and of the influences of all kinds that led to their going, must have been considerable. The friars, who in the days of Wyclif had showed themselves as a solid phalanx in the cause of orthodoxy, had been, to some extent at least, shaken and divided for some years before the end came. They were not, as a body, a bulwark of traditional Catholic teaching on the higher level in 1520–35 as they had been in 1370 and onwards.

Very little is known of the state of discipline among the friars in the decades immediately preceding the Dissolution. A rare, if not unique, piece of record evidence is found in a letter from the general of the Austin hermits, Gabriel of Venice, a convert Jew, to William Wetherall, the provincial of England, in the year 1527. This letter,[1] written by the superior who had had the task of containing the eruption of Luther and his first followers, gives a dismal picture of the friary at Canterbury. Sad stories had reached Rome: communal life and regular discipline is nonexistent; many of the friars eat and sleep in the city taverns and play at dice, cards and ball games in public; their morals are correspondingly lax. The provincial is ordered to restore order and to remove the ringleaders, Prior Roos and Friars John Parker and George Brum, from Canterbury. Should he fail in his duty, the general himself will consider sending visitors to the province. A note is appended to the letter giving permission to Friar John Toune to return to England. Toune was a Canterbury man, and it is natural to suppose that the general's impression of the friary was derived from him. If so, it is well to remember that two years previously Friar John, along with the then prior and others, had armed themselves with sticks and other weapons, and had prevented the coroner from arresting one who had taken refuge in the friary church.[2] As for George Brum, this can scarcely be other than Dr George Browne, who ten years

---

1 I owe this letter to the kindness of Fr B. Hackett, O.S.A., who procured a copy for me from the Archive of the Generalate of his Order in Rome, where the letter is in Regestrum Dd 15, fos. 126ᵛ–127ᵛ. It is dated from Padua, September 1527.

2 Canterbury City Archives MS. Bunce, fos. 99 ʳ⁻ᵛ. For this MS. see *HMC*, report 9, app. i, 176 a. I owe this reference, through Fr Hackett, to Fr Francis Roth, O.S.A. Fr Hackett points out that the charges against the London friar in *LP*, VII, 617, no. 1670, bear a striking resemblance to those in the above letter, and suggests that George Browne supplied Cromwell with a copy to use as common form.

later was to be appointed by the king general of all the friars in England. Too much weight must not be put upon this letter, a hearsay account of things depending upon the word of an undisciplined friar; it may, however, at least suggest that the restlessness of so many of the Austin hermits was a reflection of the prevailing lack of discipline and decorum in their houses. By contrast, the steadfastness of John Stone at Canterbury becomes still more remarkable.[1]

1 For Stone's refusal to admit the royal supremacy, *v. infra*, p. 364.

CHAPTER VI

SIXTEENTH-CENTURY VISITATIONS

I. THE LINCOLN VISITATIONS

Seventy years ago, the apologist of the Tudor monks appealed to the records as evidence of the regularity of monastic life immediately before the Dissolution.[1] At the time, few of the relevant documents were in print but nearly all have subsequently appeared. On the whole, they have proved less favourable in their verdict than Gasquet hoped, but they have also proved more difficult to interpret than he imagined. Some of their limitations as evidence have been noted elsewhere,[2] and these must always be borne in mind. Nevertheless, they remain important evidence. In the chapters that follow, we shall review the records of the bishops of Lincoln, next those of the bishops of Norwich, and finally the shorter and more varied records of other bishops and of some of the orders concerned.

The vast medieval diocese of Lincoln stretched from the Humber to the Thames, and from the slopes of the Cotswolds to the edge of the Fenland. Besides Lincolnshire, the second largest county of England, it included the shires of Leicester, Northampton, Rutland, Oxford, Buckingham, Bedford, and a large part of Hertford. Though somewhat smaller in area than the diocese of York, it was more unwieldy for an administrator, for much of the northern diocese was barren moor, and some outlying districts were in practice all but ignored by the ordinary, while for what remained York was far more conveniently situated as a strategic centre than was Lincoln, even if the archbishop of York never resided in the city itself. Moreover, the diocese of Lincoln was far more populous, and churches and religious houses were scattered over all the area save for a few inconsiderable tracts of forest. As regards religious houses, the diocese of Lincoln probably contained more than did York or any other diocese, but an unusually large proportion belonged to exempt orders. Cistercians and Premonstratensians had a fair number of abbeys within its ambit, and about three-quarters of the religious of the Gilbertine family, which had its origin and head house in Lincolnshire, dwelt in Lincoln territory. The houses of the black monks and black canons were numerous, but counted among their numbers relatively few abbeys or priories of the first rank: Peterborough, Ramsey and Croyland among the monks, Leicester, Oseney and Dunstable among the canons were the chief. Small and medium-sized houses, however, abounded and were evenly distributed, and we have records in the early sixteenth century of visitations of some forty-three establishments, a number sufficient to permit of a general judgment on the state of monastic life in the diocese. As

[1] Gasquet, *Henry VIII*, 10.   [2] *RO*, I, 83–4.

we also possess comparable records for the same territory a century earlier, we are in a position to see what, if any, changes occurred for better or for worse in the spirit of the religious and their discipline during the period.[1]

The bishops concerned in the sixteenth century are William Atwater (Nov. 1514–Feb. 1521) and John Longland (May 1521–47), and the visitations are of the periods 1517–20 and 1525–31. Atwater was a man of undistinguished family who had gradually climbed the ladder of preferment from a fellowship at Magdalen to the deanery of Salisbury and thence to Lincoln. Longland, of the same social class, was a more considerable figure.[2] Originally a Wykehamist, he also was a fellow of Magdalen and a doctor of divinity; he climbed the ladder steadily, followed Atwater to Salisbury and became confessor and almoner to Henry VIII before he was rewarded with Lincoln. He was, at least in his early years, regarded as a friend and ally by both the humanists and the conservative reformers. He corresponded with Erasmus and expressed high approval of his commentary on the New Testament. He was the friend of Richard Kidderminster, whose compendium of the Rule he circulated among the nuns of his diocese, and to whom he dedicated one of his printed sermons. More, always generous in his appreciations, referred to him as a second Colet on account of his homilectics and the purity of his life.[3] Later, as the king's confessor, he was caught up in (if he did not indeed originate) the great controversy of the divorce, in which he stood on the king's side; and he accepted the royal supremacy without much ado. In consequence of this, and of his readiness to implement the act of 1536 suppressing the lesser monasteries, he was one of the objects of attack for the Lincolnshire insurgents. Nevertheless, he remained till the end severely orthodox on all matters unconnected with the supremacy of the king; he consistently opposed Lutheranism, and approximated very nearly to Gardiner's outlook. He was therefore an alert and conscientious bishop at the time with which we are concerned, with no animus against the religious life as such, though he may have had a tinge of the Erasmian cynicism which had at one time affected even More. Neither Atwater nor Longland conducted all his visitations in person, and Longland in particular deputed much of the work to his vicar-general and chancellor, Dr John Rayne who, only a few years later, was to fall a victim to the fury of the mob at Horncastle.[4]

---

1 The sixteenth-century visitations have been published by A. Hamilton Thompson as *Visitations in the Diocese of Lincoln* (abbreviated title *Diocesan Visitations*) in LRS, 35, 37 (1944, 1947). The first volume of the series (LRS, 33, 1940) contains a long introduction, in the urbane and scholarly style characteristic of the author, which originally formed part of the Birkbeck Lectures delivered at Cambridge in 1935. For the earlier Lincoln visitations, *v.* RO, II, 208–12.

2 For Longland, *v. DNB*, and *DV*, I, xvii–xix, also the editor's note to Erasmus, *ep.* 1535 (Allen, VI, p. 1).

3 More's judgment, given in 1519–20 when Longland was dean of Salisbury, is in his letter to a monk (ed. Rogers, *ep.* 83, p. 192): 'Joannes Longland...alter, ut ejus laudes uno verbo complectar, Coletus, ceu concionantem audias, ceu vitae spectes puritatem.'

4 More precisely, on Ancaster Heath. *V.* LRS, 12, p. 20 n.

When a case of particular difficulty was imminent, however, Longland himself took command.

In order to clarify a mass of detail, it will be best to consider the monks and canons apart. Nine autonomous black monk houses were visited. Bardney, Croyland, Daventry, Eynsham, Humberstone, Peterborough, Ramsey, St Neots and Spalding. Bardney had long been a small and rustic house, without intellectual life or recognizable individuality. In 1519 Atwater found it in a slovenly condition, with hounds padding about the church and cloister and fouling the refectory and chapterhouse, while some of the brethren kept chickens and nesting-boxes in the cloister. Lay folk and women entered unopposed. No serious accusations were made, however, and when in 1530 Dr Rayne visited the place he had nothing to enjoin save the observance of silence. By that date, indeed, a fresh breeze from some quarter had blown into Bardney, for the younger half of the community had taken up with the new and not yet common fashion of taking as a 'religious' name that of a saint of ancient times, instead of adding to their Christian name their place of origin.[1]

Of Croyland there is only one record, that of 1519. Complaints were few and such as might be expected from a reasonably observant house; it is noted that the abbot had engrossed the offices of cellarer and receiver, but otherwise Croyland was going along tolerably well.[2] The same, so far as records go, may be said of Daventry, not always prosperous in the past, though there were two cases of apostasy and the monks, as was natural to men on the edge of the shires, were in the habit of taking a pack of harriers with them when out on their customary walk.[3] Eynsham, another rural house long fallen from fervour, was in 1517 in a state of torpor. Meat was eaten in the refectory; the porter's two daughters of doubtful reputation were about the place, and there was slackness in choir. An injunction insisted that monks should not learn grammar till they had the psalter by heart, and as no grammar master was available their intellectual attainments must have been limited. Three years later the house was unhappy, with an abbot who rendered no accounts and supported a sister and numerous other relatives on the house. When the visitation was ended, Atwater is recorded as having preached for two hours to the brethren, but the result of his zeal is not known.[4]

Humberstone, near Grimsby, a small and decayed Tironian house with only three monks, was by now little more than a farm. The abbot accused the brethren of absence from choir, of playing tennis in the village, and even of leaving the monastery altogether from time to time.[5] They in their

---

1 *DV*, II, 77–9.   2 *Ibid.* 108–11.   3 *Ibid.* 111–13.
4 *Ibid.* 138–44. 138: 'Ne aliquem ex monachis junioribus gramaticam cantum seu aliud quicquid addiscant quousque psalterium corditenus recordaverint et eciam impnos ac alia officia perfecte sciverint.' 144: 'Habita longa videlicet per spacium ij horarum et amplius saluberima exhortacione.'
5 *Ibid.* 167–70. 169: 'Ludunt ad tennisios in villa de Humberston.' Against this distressing behaviour severe injunctions were issued. But *v. supra*, p. 51 n. 4.

turn accused the abbot of withholding their stipends and of making them work in the hayfield for long hours; the share he took in their labours was one more item in the count against him. Peterborough was the largest, though not the richest, abbey in the diocese, with a community of fifty and a large income. Despite these advantages, and intellectual interests evidenced by a regular flow of students to Oxford, Peterborough throughout the fifteenth century had been a house liable to disorder in discipline and finance. It was not a happy house in 1518. The abbot, who had held office for more than twenty years, was Edmund Kirton. He had in hand six of the greater obediences, and the buildings depending upon the offices concerned were in disrepair. He rendered no accounts, and the monks complained that they were neglected both in refectory and infirmary, though they were able in part to find solace in the tavern kept by the house. Though unhappy, the community was nevertheless on the whole respectable, save for the sacrist, who was notoriously incontinent. Abbot Kirton, though he may have neglected his monks, did not wholly waste his considerable income. The beautiful fan-vaulted eastern chapel in the present cathedral was his work; he restored the abbot's lodging, now the bishop's house, and founded a grammar school in his native village.[1]

Ramsey, visited by Atwater four days before Peterborough, was the richest house in the diocese and one of the wealthiest in England. The abbot was John Warboys, elected in 1507 and in office till the Dissolution, which he survived for a number of years. In 1517 the condition of the house was considerably worse than that of Peterborough. The doors remained unlocked at night; the prior was a bad-tempered drunkard, easy with his friends and severe to brutality with others; despite many previous injunctions there was still no grammar-master for the young monks; both dorter and church let in the weather. Numbers had fallen from the statutory fifty to forty; only two or three attended High Mass and only eight or so the night choirs. The seniors, having sent the juniors to office, went off to dice for money, accompanying their gaming with hideous oaths; when they patronized the choir they talked to each other and left the reciting to the juniors. Much of this was doubtless the exaggerated outpouring of sore minds and soured tempers, but the impression given is of a sordid, though not of a morally decadent, house. Injunctions were given and censures duly imposed.[2] Thirteen years later Dr Rayne was at Ramsey. Numbers had increased slightly, and though Abbot Warboys was still in charge the general tone of the house had changed for the better. Abbot and prior led off with *Omnia bene* and the complaints centred round such

---

1 *DV*, III, 76–83. For earlier visitations, *v. RO*, II, 210. For the tavern, *v. DV*, III, 78: 'Infra monasterium est quedam taberna in qua fratres temporibus indecentibus aliquando nimis mane aliquando nimis sero bibunt.' Closing time was therefore fixed at 7 p.m. (winter) and 8 p.m. (summer). For the grammar school at Kirton-in-Holland, *v.* p. 79.

2 *Ibid.* 83–9. For the gambling, p. 88: 'Seniores...ludunt ad taceras et aleas et alios similes ludos temporibus nocturnis eciam pro pecuniis, et ibidem habent maxima juramenta per corpus dominicum et alia ejus membra.'

comparatively trivial matters as the kitchen drain and stray animals in the infirmary garden. There is no reason to suppose a conspiracy of silence, of which the Ramsey community of 1517 would have been quite incapable, and we may suppose that things had taken a turn for the better, as things will among men.[1]

Of St Neot's little is said. Between 1520 and 1530 the community increased, and at the latter visitation there was a chorus of *Omnia bene* which may or may not have been strictly justified. Spalding was in fair fettle.[2]

It would be tedious to review in detail the houses of Austin canons. They were very numerous, some thirty-three in all. Several were minute, with six canons or even less. Of most of these the records say little, whether for good or bad, but there are a few where it is possible to compare two visitations. Thus at Bicester in 1520 the frater was not kept, fleshmeat was always supplied and there was no public reading; likewise both novice-master and grammar-master were wanting. Ten years later some repairs were needed and numbers were still below the establishment, but otherwise all seemed well. In general the common faults were failure to keep the frater and lack of a grammar-master: the latter a very comprehensible failing in a small community with no regular intake of recruits.[3]

Some larger houses may be examined more closely. Dorchester near Oxford, the ancient seat of the bishopric, had been for more than a century one of the black spots of the religious world. There are only scanty remains of Atwater's visitation of 1517, but in 1529 and 1530 the place was apparently twice visited. In the earlier of these latter years the community of ten was in its chronic state of disorder; we may even suppose that the whole framework of the horarium had broken down, since Longland gave a long and detailed account of the daily routine, as well as injunctions bearing on particular abuses. In 1530 the prior and others were defamed, the doors stood open for all to enter, attendance at choir was scanty and had been neglected altogether, save for three appearances during the year, by one of the canons, who wandered out to fish or hunt, spending weeks at his brother's house, and had four or five times offered to fight the prior. Longland made a show of severity by suspending the abbot, prior and an incontinent canon, and by publishing a set of strict injunctions, but, as usually happened, the sentence on the abbot was immediately remitted, and there is little reason to suppose that the injunctions were observed. The virus was in the soil of Dorchester.[4]

1 *DV*, III, 89–94. 2 *Ibid.* 94–7 (St Neot's); 97–8 (Spalding).
3 *DV*, II, 79–82.

4 *Ibid.* 115–22. In addition, a long set of Longland's injunctions of 1529 was printed by Archdeacon G. G. Perry in a note, 'Episcopal visitations of the Augustinian Canons of Leicester and Dorchester', in *EHR*, IV, 304–13. These are discussed by A. H. Thompson in *DV*, II (App. II), 203–5, where he gives a probable scheme of the order of the documents. For the pugnacious sportsman, Dan Thomas Wytney, *v. DV*, II, 117: 'Quottidie vagatur ad venandum, piscandum...et est indoctus, verbosus, et nimium jurans ac ter aut quater paratus fuit ad pugnandum cum priore.'

At Dunstable, on the other hand, there was life in the body still. In 1518 the community numbered only seven and the prior rendered no accounts, but there were no other accusations and the bishop enjoined that the numbers should be increased. In 1530 this had been done; there were now sixteen canons, the prior was efficient and the place flourished.[1]

Leicester abbey was one of the largest and wealthiest houses of the order, with a community of twenty-five or so. The abbot, Richard Pexall, who was in office in 1518, continued till his enforced resignation in 1533; he was the abbot to whom Wolsey turned for his last haven, and who anointed and buried the cardinal. Pexall in 1518 had engrossed the revenues of cellarer, sub-cellarer, chamberlain and precentor but was otherwise efficient, save in his failure to control the servants, who did little work and kept a pack of hounds for their recreation. Emulating the servants, the boys of the almonry left their lessons to join the hunt. Clearly the example of Abbot Clown, that great hunter, had been of more avail than his precept.[2] Longland, at a visitation that has left no record, suspended the abbot from administration, but one of the two administrators was unworthy, and the abbot had forced his way back. When Longland came again shortly before 1528 the house had degenerated since 1518. The abbot rarely officiated in choir, and on the rare occasions when he appeared he brought with him his fool, who caused distraction and laughter among the canons by his sallies and snatches of song.[3] The unworthy administrator, Richard Lichfield the cellarer, was given to lavish entertainment of a mixed company in his checker. Shortly afterwards, in 1528, Rayne visited the abbey. He found that the canons went out early to hunt, often before daybreak, while hounds were ubiquitous in the monastery, leaving traces of their presence. Sick canons and boys were attended by women nurses, and the abbot had not improved his record of churchgoing, though the economic situation had improved. Rayne took the situation seriously and issued a set of injunctions; one of them, straying into several tongues either for the sake of clarity or through lack of a wide vocabulary, forbade the retention of 'ultra iii brase de lez grey-houndes et nulli alii canes nisi ii or iii cowple off spanyells pro le haris'.[4]

---

1 *Ibid.* 122–4. For the general contentment cf. the statement of the refectorer, 124: 'Dicit priorem esse nimium utilem monasterio et fratres caritatius (*sic*) se habere.'

2 *Ibid.* 183–6, and *v. RO*, II, 186.

3 The injunctions of Longland printed by G. G. Perry (*art. cit. EHR*, IV, 304–13) are connected in some way with this visitation, but, as in the similar case of Dorchester, it is not certain that Thompson has settled the order of affairs correctly. For the fool, who has some affinities with the Fool in *King Lear*, *v.* Perry, 306 (Longland is addressing Pexall): 'Quendam stultum ac scurram continue tecum ad confabulandum habuisti et habes, qui antecedit te quotidie quum ad ecclesiam transis [i.e. pass through the cloister] et in choro, cum tu ibidem existis [a rare occurrence to judge from the *detecta*], se stolide exercet, verbis, derisionibus, cantilenis at alias [*sic*], canonicis in choro occasionem risus et dissolucionis... prebens, etc.' He is forbidden to bring him to church.

4 *DV*, II, 186–95. The greyhounds are on p. 195. The complaint against the ubiquitous hounds (p. 189) is immediately followed by a request by the same canon for the liturgical observation of the feast of the Holy Name, for which *v.* also *DV*, II, 137.

Of Missenden, in south Buckinghamshire, records of three visitations remain, perhaps unfortunately for the reputation of the house. At the first in 1518 nothing very serious came to light; there were only five priests and the abbot was ordered to increase their number. In 1530 a new abbot had indeed multiplied his people, but had not thereby magnified joy. There were, besides himself, eight priests and five novices. The buildings were in disrepair, the discipline of the refectory was not observed, and the whole place was dominated by John Compton, the lay steward. Worse still, one of the canons was guilty of unnatural vice with the steward's son, one of the singing children. The culprit, who had had a previous conviction, was gated but apparently suffered no further punishment. Eight months later Longland himself appeared at Missenden on a special visitation arising out of new information. The abbot and a canon had been guilty of repeated misconduct with the wife of a villager, and the abbot's niece, whose mother was employed in the abbey brewery, had no good name.[1] When Longland delivered his injunctions, they were in the vernacular, in order that they might be understood. John Compton was to be dismissed, the guilty canon imprisoned, and a properly audited account to be presented by the abbot, who was to be overseen by two of the most discreet canons. A master was to look after the children, and a grammar-master to instruct the canons, who were to study this subject or practise writing, painting or carving daily.[2]

At St Frideswide's, Oxford, in 1517 all that is noted is one case of chronic insubordination and the lack of a grammar-master, but in 1520 there are other complaints. Six of the canons are out on Oxfordshire parishes, the prior has taken all offices into his hand and renders no accounts; he is accused of harshness and high-handed conduct. Four years later he handed the house over to Wolsey and became abbot of Oseney.[3]

Thornton, an important house near the Humber, well known to students of medieval architecture for its magnificent gatehouse and the remains of an octagonal chapterhouse, seems to have been in a flourishing condition with twenty-six canons under an abbot. Almost all agreed that all was well, and this prosperity may have been the reason why Thornton at the Dissolution was one of the few houses chosen for re-foundation as a college with school attached.[4]

Finally, at the small abbey of Wellow in 1519 Atwater showed himself unusually expansive. He exhorted the canons to cultivate cleanliness and good manners, and avoid every kind of rusticity, for which they had a bad name; every brother is to have a special altar, which he is to keep clean

1 *DV*, III, 16–27.

2 Longland's injunctions are not in *DV*, but were printed along with others by E. Peacock in *Archaeologia*, XLVII, 49–64.

3 *DV*, III, 47–50.

4 *Ibid.* 113–15. The notary, tiring of the repeated *omnia bene*, began to embellish the theme, e.g. 'Omnia bene asserit esse in consciencia sua', 'Dicit singula in cenobio salubriter se habere', etc.

and neatly apparelled, so that it may be said of each one: 'Lord, I have loved the beauty of thy house.' Every brother is to occupy himself with books and sound learning; everyone is to have a supply of paper and a pen. The bishop urges charity between the canons and their tenants and neighbours so that all contention, which is of the devil, may be avoided.[1] These injunctions are in their warmth of tone and spiritual appeal unlike any others in the collection, though this was by no means Atwater's first experience of visiting. Six years later the place was still prospering. Among the canons now was Robert Whitgift, uncle of the future archbishop of Canterbury; he succeeded to the abbacy in 1526 and remained in office to the end.

Looking back over the records of all these visitations, including many not specifically mentioned, certain faults are seen to be so common as to be endemic, over and beyond what may be called purely moral failings great and small. Superiors rarely gave the canonical annual audited account, and in the case of smaller houses rarely kept any accounts at all; regular instruction in the 'primitive sciences' (i.e. Latin grammar) was rarely available for the younger monks; the refectory was not regularly kept, in the sense that the religious habitually took their meals either in the misericord or with the abbot or in the frater with 'irregular' food; the religious, after a ceremonial retirement after compline, came down again and sat talking and drinking and (at the slacker houses) gaming; finally, the doors of the enclosure were left open, allowing even women ingress to the house to perform services such as nursing, washing and brewing for the religious.

None of these faults was new; instances of all occur in the very first visitations of which there is a complete record. It would be a mistake to treat them too dramatically, just as it would be a mistake to compile statistics; it is of the nature of this evidence that it gives no crisp data, and before judging severely we should make an effort to reconstruct the social conditions in the early Tudor countryside, when an abbey, deep in the fields or woods, with most of its inhabitants drawn from the surrounding hamlets, gradually let slip the formalities of canon law. There are, however, two respects in which old failings have become more insidious with the passage of years: they have become so common and so habitual that they are regarded as customs rather than as breaches of the law; and, when they result in moral faults, there is little or no attempt to punish them in any serious way.

Apart from the matter of faults and their punishment, two general conclusions on the state of the religious orders seem to emerge from the Lincoln records, and they are of the greater interest as running counter to generally received opinions. The one is that financial embarrassment or economic distress was not a common feature in religious houses of the age. Though there are several cases of inefficiency and waste and dilapidation, there is not a single instance in these Lincoln visitations of a house faced with ruin or decay on this score. The other concerns numbers. It has been noted summarily elsewhere[1] that no serious decline in the numbers of the religious is noticeable before the days of real uncertainty began from the early months of 1534. The Lincoln figures show that very little overall change had taken place between the days of Alnwick and those of Longland. If some communities had shrunk, others had swollen; indeed, if full statistics were available, we should probably find a slight aggregate rise. More significantly still, numbers often rose between the visits of Atwater and those of Longland. Thus Dunstable rose from seven in 1518 to sixteen in 1530; Chacombe from six (1520) to eight (1530), Missenden from five (1518) to fourteen (1530), St Neot's from ten (1520) to fourteen (1530), Wellow from eight (1519) to ten (1525), and there are no cases of spectacular decline. Moreover, at Dunstable and Missenden the earlier visitor had enjoined an increase, and it had been forthcoming. The inference is that recruits came, so to say, in response to advertisement; what the quality of such recruits was is another matter. Long before the date at which we have arrived, it would seem clear that in the majority of the houses almost all the recruits were local, and that they were adopting a way of life that promised a livelihood, rather than following a spiritual vocation.

In view of the paucity of information concerning the Cistercians, particular interest attaches to the notices we possess of two houses in the same district of England and during Longland's episcopate, even if the picture is an unattractive one. We must not forget that only exceptionable irregularity would set in motion the kind of unusual process that would leave record. The abbeys concerned are Thame, an Oxfordshire house near the Buckinghamshire border, and Bruerne, on the edge of the Cotswolds in the same county.

The bishops of Lincoln, owing to events in the twelfth century, ranked as founders and patrons of Thame, and in 1526 Longland learnt that the abbey was in a bad way. Canonically incapable of 'visiting' it, he appears to have adopted the course of going to the abbey and receiving depositions, which he forwarded to the abbot of Waverley, the mother-house, who proceeded to visit it himself. The articles[2] were chiefly concerned with the abbot: he was accused of expensive living, of dilapidation of the property of the house, and of allowing a favourite servant, one John Cowper, to obtain control of the establishment and to batten upon it. Furthermore, he was accused of dangerous intimacy with a boy, Cowper's son, and of excessive familiarity with other boys and youths boarding in

---

1 *RO*, II, 257 *seqq*.

2 The Thame dossier was printed by G. G. Perry in *EHR*, III, 704–22. He was stimulated to do this by the appeal, already noted, to the episcopal registers as testimonials to monastic virtue by Dom A. Gasquet in *Henry VIII* (p. 10). It is summarized by A. H. Thompson in *DV*, II, App. II. The Bruerne document has not been printed but is summarized by Thompson (*loc. cit.* 215–18) from a transcript from a Lincoln document made by the Rev. H. E. Salter and communicated by Geoffrey Baskerville.

the abbey. He allowed his monks to wander abroad, engaging in archery with the villagers and feasting in the local taverns. He kept useless servants, and did not forbid the entrance of women. A monk of the house, apparently a brother of Cowper, was accused of abetting him, of immoral relations with several women, and of promiscuous swearing. The abbot and his monks were totally ignorant of the Rule and monastic ceremonial.[1]

To these articles the abbot of Thame, who was clearly a man of considerable literary abilities, and enough of a humanist to make the conventional profession of lack of style,[2] returned long answers in a tone of suave insolence. So far from having an excessive attachment to John Cowper, he cherished towards him no more than the moderate love of one Christian for another.[3] As regards bad companionship, he would be delighted to avoid it for the future.[4] As for the relationship with Cowper *fils*, he admitted the impeachment but for the future would be most careful to avoid it.[5] The reports of his feasting were untrue; he and his guests (and would that visitors were not so rare) partook of the coarse food of the poor, so coarse that pilgrims, rich and poor alike, spurned it.[6] As for useless dependants, the householder who had none could call himself fortunate indeed, he himself would strain every nerve to get rid of the pest.[7] Little John Cowper, if he gives rise to gossip, shall go. Nothing, certainly, could be more detrimental to religious than female society; he will deprive himself and his brethren of it so far as he can honestly do so.[8] Slight as may be his literary talent, yet others will witness that he and his community are not so ignorant of the Rule as is alleged. Finally, he will observe all the injunctions most closely, and if he should relapse into the errors of olden days he will remember his plighted word and delay not a moment to retrace his ill-starred steps.[9]

Dom Chynnor, for his part, had never so much as dallied in imagination with the crimes imputed to him. As for swearing, he hardly ever used a bad word, but it might well be that one slipped out now and again accidentally, as one might say.[10]

1 Perry, *art. cit.* 706: 'Tu ignarus es, et fratres nescii ordinis religionis et sanctarum ceremoniarum ejusdem, nec ullus fratrum regulas [*sic*] Sancti Benedicti scit aut cognoscit.'

2 *Ibid.* 710: 'qualitercunque peritia Latinitatis rudes sumus'.

3 *Ibid.* 708: 'Nos...ut solemus erga proximos, eum ipsum mediocri quodam amoris et dilectionis vinculo prosecuto profitemur.'

4 *Ibid.*: 'Puerorum et juvenum consortia quam hilariter in posterum evitare conabimur.'

5 *Ibid.*: 'Obnoxios nos confitemur, unde et posthac solerti cura resecabimus.' Cf. 710, 'infantulum Cowper'.

6 *Ibid.* 709: 'Profitemur nos et convivas cum adfuerint (utinam adessent) vocari... magna penuria et grossis cibis epulari ita ut peregrini, superioresque et pares, id fastidiunt.'

7 *Ibid.* 710: 'Otiosos vero quis non alit? Atqui huic morbo summo conatu obviare studebimus.'

8 *Ibid.*: 'Mulierum autem frequentiam, quibus religioni nihil perniciosius, a fratibus omnibus et a nobis ipsis quantum decebit summopere destituemus.'

9 *Ibid.*: 'Si aliquando ex fluxu et fragili sensu aut tarda oblivione...delabimur, mox... pedem retrahere non elongabimus.'

10 *Ibid.* 711: 'Non sponte, immo incogitantia, inter loquendum nonnunquam decidunt verba non bene sonantia.'

The men who answered thus to a grave and just charge must have known what kind of person they had to deal with in the abbot of Waverley. Making no attempt to traverse their statements he composed a long résumé of the daily duties and behaviour of a good Cistercian, and exhorted the brethren to love their abbot and practise all the virtues inculcated by their Rule. Thus they will proceed not from bad to worse, but from holiness to perfection. St Stephen Harding, visiting Clairvaux, could scarcely have bettered his phrases. The document is a signal example of the false impression that may be conveyed by an unctuous amplification of platitudes.

The whole dossier was forwarded to Longland, who in a long and angry commentary demolished the abbot's defence and castigated the complaisance of the visitor. The abbot (writes Longland) is full of promises for the future, but what about the past? He asks, who is without idle mouths to feed? I reply, any prudent householder. He says he will forbid women so far as he can without discourtesy. When, pray, is it courteous for a cloistered Cistercian to entertain women of easy virtue? He says that pilgrims shun his coarse fare, but it is good enough to attract ladies of the neighbourhood. In short, the bishop concludes, you have allowed a bad abbot, a slack house, and a chaotic economy to escape without censure, and have merely treated the monks to a pious lecture on their time-table. If you fail to act, I as founder will find a way to put things right.[1]

Whether or not the abbot of Waverley acted we do not know, but within a year the abbot was replaced by Robert King, late abbot of Bruerne and soon to be the first bishop of Oxford. Thame's gain, if gain it was, was Bruerne's loss, for he was succeeded there by another rogue abbot, and the second piece of information mentioned above relates to the misdeeds of Abbot Chascombe. It is an account of a process in 1532, initiated by a royal writ, to enquire into the misdemeanours of the abbot, conducted by the abbots of Woburn and St Mary Graces, the 'general reformers' of the English houses appointed by the general chapter, and the abbot of Garendon, the official visitor of the house.[2] The abbot appeared, but only to deny the competence of the court as consisting simply of royal commissaries; he entered a tuitorial appeal to Rome, sheltering himself under the protection of Canterbury. It was an extraordinary step to take at so late a date. When he had retired the prior and nine monks accused him of simony (he had purchased his election from Wolsey), dilapidation and incontinence. The crimes were notorious and the charges amply substantiated. He failed to appear and was pronounced contumacious, but the end did not come for almost a year when, on 12 March 1533, he was found guilty by the same abbots as before, and deprived of office. No other monk was charged, either by the judges or by the abbot in self-defence, and it must therefore be assumed that flagrant misbehaviour, at least, was confined to the abbot.

1 Alexander (the Magnificent) of Lincoln had founded Thame in 1137–40.
2 Summarized by Thompson, v. p. 70, n. 2 *supra*.

II. THE NORWICH VISITATIONS

The second important collection of episcopal visitation records of the early Tudor period is that of the diocese of Norwich, and comprises Bishop Goldwell's visitation of 1492–3 and four visitations of Bishop Richard Nykke in 1514, 1520, 1526 and 1532.[1] Its value lies in the account it gives of a large group of houses visited at short intervals, thus presenting us with a comprehensive view of the religious life of East Anglia only a few years before the Dissolution. It differs in more than one respect from the contemporary collection of Redman: the houses of men are all Austin canons, save for half a dozen black monk communities and one of Trinitarians, and all, with few exceptions, small families of ten or less; in contrast to Redman's records the *detecta* and *comperta* are in many cases preserved and are sometimes lengthy, whereas the injunctions are very brief and never give an estimate of good and evil such as Redman habitually made; moreover Nykke, at least, was far less concerned than Redman with maintaining or restoring a fixed level of observance, and in many cases the examination was conducted by a suffragan or commissioners of the ordinary.

The general impression received differs little from that given by the collection of Alnwick eighty years earlier. Half a dozen of the houses, including the largest monastic establishment of the diocese, are extremely decadent, and there are a number of cases of incontinence. On the other hand, at one or two of the larger, and several of the smaller, houses of canons the visitands answered unanimously that all was well or made but trifling complaints. There is in general no reason to suspect collusion to hide gross faults, and at one or two of the priories (Pentney is perhaps an example though its later history is unsatisfactory) this silence may be taken as evidence of orderly content; in other cases, however, absence of desire to complain implies simply acquiescence in mediocrity. Many of the later visitations, indeed, give every sign of having been conducted with despatch as little more than a mere formality, two houses often being dealt with in a single day.[2]

The largest community was that of the cathedral priory of Norwich, which in 1492 still contained almost fifty monks. In the fourteenth century it had been distinguished by an enthusiasm for theological study and had produced more than one notable doctor; this enthusiasm had now vanished, and Goldwell's most peremptory injunction was one regarding the failure to send students to the university; two were to go without delay to Gloucester College.[3] No individual scandals were found, but the

1 These were edited by Dr Jessopp for the Camden Society in 1888. The notes and parts of the introduction are inaccurate, and the comments are thrown into a conversational form which fails to make contact with the real state of things as revealed by the documents themselves.

2 E.g. Buckenham and Wymondham, 23 July 1532 (pp. 307–8); Mettingham College and Bungay nunnery, 21 August 1532 (pp. 317–18).

3 *Norwich Visitations*, 7.

monastery, as was common with the larger black monk houses, was in
many ways slack in discipline. Women were living within the precincts,
the choir observance was faulty, and much time was wasted in useless
conversations. Twenty years later there had been something of a decline.
There was one clear case of incontinence and suspicions in other directions;
lay friends and relatives of the monks were being entertained in private
rooms; there was a curious accusation of monks dancing in the guest-
house, and the presence of sheep in the cloister garth seems to indicate
a slovenly administration.[1] Further visitations showed no great change.

St Benet's of Holme, by this time an undistinguished and lonely house
among the meres, was in all ways mediocre. Wymondham, till recently
a dependency of St Albans, was in a worse state. In 1492 it was noted that
the Office was ill celebrated, the monks kept neither cloister nor refectory,
but hunted and hawked; private ownership was common and the monks
traded with their allowances; the abbot had kept no accounts and held no
audit for years. There were no particular injunctions at this visitation, but
the abbot was banished to the manor of Downham with a substantial
dower, and the administration given to one of the monks.[2] Twenty years
later, the condition of Wymondham had still further deteriorated. The
abbot complained that the bolts of the cloister door had been broken by
monks whom he had not been able to identify, that the prior and others
had broken open a chest and extracted the muniments of the house, and
that he himself had been treated contumeliously by the prior's servants.
The prior for his part had complaints to make against the abbot, but was
clearly himself unbalanced if not insane, and a number of monks deposed
to his violent and irresponsible behaviour. It is not surprising that there
were accusations of incontinence and that the regular life was neglected.[3]
Six years later there was a new abbot of some learning from outside; the
former abbot and prior had disappeared, though the latter had been
replaced by a monk against whom serious accusations had previously been
brought. Various complaints of slackness and neglect were made, and the
injunctions did little to brace up the discipline. Finally, in 1526 a new
abbot from Norwich had apparently succeeded in re-establishing a better
order.

Perhaps of all the Norwich visitations those which have attracted most
attention are those of the Austin priory of Walsingham, where the shrine
of Our Lady was, during the half-century before the Reformation,
unquestionably both the most frequented and the richest in England, and
to which the visits of Erasmus, Henry VIII and Queen Katharine have
attracted the notice of historians. It is therefore somewhat surprising to

1 *Norwich Visitations*, 75: 'Dompnus Willemus Boxwell supprior dicit quod...in
hostiaria solent confratres saltare, favore hostilarii, tempore nocturno usque ad nonam.'
Ibid. 76: 'Dompnus Johannes Shilton...dicit quod...oves pascuntur in prato claustri in
nocumentum confratrum.' Six years later the same deponent was put to the pains of
stating that all was now well in the house save for these same sheep.
2 *Ibid.* 21–2.   3 *Ibid.* 96–100.

find the house in a far from satisfactory condition. In 1494 the complaints concerned comparatively minor matters—the partial behaviour of the prior, and his failure to present accounts. In 1514, however, a truly deplorable condition of things was revealed. The community was ridden by a couple of the prior's servants; the wife of one of these was the prior's mistress, who made free with the victuals of the house; in addition, the prior embezzled money and jewels from the shrine of Our Lady, and treated some of the priory lands as his own possession. Absence of respect and control reacted on the canons; a group were boon companions of the obnoxious servants John Smith and William Marshall, hunting and hawking by day and revelling by night, the rest were idle, unhappy and quarrelsome.[1] The bishop ordered the immediate removal of the two servants and set the prior of Westacre as coadjutor to the prior; the precise aim, as also the wisdom, of the latter step is not apparent, as only ten days previously the bishop, in a visitation at Westacre, had found the prior there negligent in giving accounts, heavily in debt, and the patron of a servant who was the exact counterpart, even down to his name and his wife's complaisance, of the more active of the precious pair at Walsingham.[2] The latter house, however, did not remain long in its wholly debased condition. Six years later a new prior was endeavouring to reform discipline, and meeting, as was to be expected, with insubordination and dissensions. Six years later again something of an equilibrium had been reached.

As has been said, many of the houses of canons of East Anglia, as also the convents of women, were extremely small in numbers and poor in resources. In the majority of these there were no serious scandals apparent, and still less evidence of fervour; the picture they present is not exhilarating, and the complaints show a state of slovenly and sometimes sordid disorder; they are not infrequently naïve in their want of any spiritual aims or ideals. At a few only is the impression given of a harmless and contented group of men or women living a regular and devout, if neither zealous nor austere, life.[3]

III. FROM ALL QUARTERS

Besides the three great collections from Lincoln, Norwich and the Premonstratensians, a considerable number of isolated records have been discovered and published by historians and antiquaries during the past

1 *Ibid.* 113–23.   2 *Ibid.* 101–5.

3 Cf. the records of the nunnery of Campsey, where the daughters of a number of notable families such as the Jerninghams, Willoughbys, Winters, Feltons and Bacons are found. At the two earliest visitations no complaints of any sort were put forward, and at the third the only nun to raise her voice was the precentrix, who deposed that in thirty-five years of religious life she had seen nothing worthy of correction save the dilapidated conditions of the antiphoners in choir. It is pathetic to note that six years later she and her sisters, under an ageing and parsimonious prioress, found it necessary to complain of the putrid meat served to the nuns and of negligence in the kitchen.

seventy years. They may be divided for our purpose into three groups
the visits of ordinaries and metropolitans between the accession of
Henry VII and the legateship of Wolsey; the visitations carried out by
the cardinal or his commissaries; and the normal visitations during the last
two decades or so before the royal visitation of 1536. There are also a few
visitations of the monastic authorities falling within these limits. The
diocesan visitations between 1535 and the disappearance of the greater
monasteries will best be considered on a later page when the last act of
monastic history is under review.

The first group is in almost every respect similar to previous records of
the fifteenth century. The new dynasty and the new learning had, however, begun to create an atmosphere of criticism and a sense that decay
and inefficiency must somehow be dealt with, and some of the bishops,
wholly unsympathetic to the monasticism of their day, were beginning to
judge their contemporaries with reference to a distant past and to the
letter of the Rule. Abroad, and especially in France, reform of the religious
orders was in the air. Influenced by French example, or perhaps merely
applying to the Church the policy of order and control that he was
following in secular government, Henry VII and his chancellor John
Morton, archbishop of Canterbury, decided in 1487 upon a fairly widespread visitation. The chief obstacle lay in the exempt orders—the
Cistercians, the Premonstratensians and the Cluniacs—and in a few
black monk houses, similarly exempt. Accordingly a bull was obtained
from Innocent VIII, *Quanta in Dei ecclesia* (13 August 1487) giving
him full powers to visit all save the Cistercians.[1] It is usual to regard
this as a measure of religious reform, but it may well have been at root
an administrative measure, characteristic of the age, directed towards
the centralization of power within a kingdom and proving also, from
the point of view of the papacy, to be a fatal measure of devolution of
authority.

So far as is known, Morton's only attempt to implement these powers
at the moment was in relation to the Cluniac priory of Northampton, and
to the abbey of St Albans. The priory of St Andrew at Northampton was a
fairly large house of some twenty-five monks. It must have had spacious
buildings, for as early as the thirteenth century it was occasionally the
rendezvous of the triennial chapter of the black monks of the Canterbury
province and, after the union of the northern and southern chapters in
1336, it was the invariable meeting-place until the end of the fifteenth
century. It was presumably chosen for its central situation, though
itself outside the jurisdiction of the chapter; the official chest of archives
was kept there, and the meetings were held in the Lady Chapel of the
priory church. The affairs of the priory had in 1487 for more than
fifteen years been appearing and reappearing in chancery; they are an
interesting example of the trouble that could be caused by a senseless and

1 The bull *Quanta*, as reissued in 1490, is in Wilkins, *Concilia*, III, 630.

gratuitous intrigue.[1] About 1470 the prior of La Charité-sur-Loire made a sudden attempt to regain the control of Bermondsey, Wenlock and Northampton that had been lost by his house almost a century earlier. He found an instrument in a restless and unscrupulous monk, a Welshman, William of Brecknock, a professed monk of St James's. Brecknock was duly appointed in 1473 vicar-general of the prior of La Charité in England, and he succeeded in getting his powers recognized in the royal chancery and at Bermondsey. When a vacancy occurred at Northampton he was collated by the prior of La Charité to the post of prior. The monks, how-ever, had elected Thomas Sudbury,[2] a monk of Bermondsey, who held his ground for almost eight years until Brecknock succeeded in getting the royal approval to his own appointment. He consoled his rival with the priorate of Wenlock (1482), but Sudbury after a while felt a desire to return to Northampton, and in 1485 secured letters patent from Henry VII empowering him to take possession. Six months later, however, Breck-knock obtained from the chancery confirmation of his own previous appointment, and endeavoured to implement this. Meanwhile, the feuds and expenses of the two rivals had reduced the priory to a state of chaos and bankruptcy, and early in 1487 Archbishop Morton decided to step in. His early attempts were unsuccessful, and even when his hands were strengthened by the papal bull it was not till 1491 that he secured the resignation of both pretenders and the election of a new prior.

The affair of St Albans, which came to a head in 1489, though earning less notoriety at the time, has in the recent past been treated by a series of writers from Froude to Coulton as a kind of test case for the condemna-tion of English medieval monasticism.[3] Abbot Wallingford's term of office, though marked by a series of successful manoeuvres that increased the influence and wealth of the abbey, and by numerous additions to its possessions and fabric,[4] had also its darker side. There were rumours of scandals and embezzlements in the community, and the abbot himself had several times been brought into chancery, not without cause, on charges of dishonesty and violent dealings, both with tenants of the abbey and with the nunneries under his control. It was presumably with a view of obtaining immunity for the future that Wallingford attempted in 1487 to secure complete autonomy for the courts Christian of the abbey and

---

1 The best account of this affair is by R. Graham, 'The English Province of the Order of Cluny in the Fifteenth Century', in *EES*, 82–7.

2 By a tiresome coincidence a Thomas Sudbury, monk of St Albans, figures in the docu-ments of the St Albans case; Coulton (*Five Centuries of Religion*, IV, 521 *et al.*) vexatiously conflates the two men.

3 For the modern controversy, *v.* Froude, *Short Studies on Great Subjects*, I, 401–42; J. Gairdner, *Lollardy and the Reformation*, I, 269–72; III, xxx–xxxiii; F.A. Gasquet, *Abbot Wallingford*; G. G. Coulton, *Five Centuries of Religion*, IV, 508–59. For a full discussion with a review of previous literature, *v.* M. D. Knowles, 'The Case of St Albans in 1490', in *JEH*, III, 144–58. On p. 155 therein (notes 1, 3, 4) for 160 read 151.

4 These are set out in the notice of his works in *Reg. J. Whethamstede*, I, App. (D). *V. supra*, p. 9.

episcopal orders for himself;[1] these requests, if granted, would have
rounded off the ancient immunities of St Albans by making the abbey and
its territory completely independent of any control short of the Roman
Curia: that is, of any control whatsoever. Wallingford's procurators were
in Rome in the spring of 1487; at the very same moment, Morton's were
there to demand extensive powers of visitation; while the abbot's men
returned empty-handed, the archbishop secured the issue of the bull
Quanta in Dei ecclesia. This, however, he did not at once use against
St Albans; possibly he was thwarted by appeals of which no record has
survived; but in 1489 the king appealed earnestly to the pope to strengthen
the hands of his archbishop. Wallingford may have got wind of this, for
he approached the Curia again, and was successful in obtaining a brief to
Morton bidding him protect the privileges of the abbey. It should be
mentioned that the pope of the day was Innocent VIII, under whose slack
hands the Roman Curia increased its reputation for venality and rapacity.
With two such rich prelates bidding for support the tactic of the officials
throughout was to issue favourable responses to both parties simultaneously. Thus exactly a month after the brief to Morton the pope
reissued in his favour the bull *Quanta,* and on its receipt the archbishop
conveyed to Wallingford a personal warning of his intention to set
St Albans to rights. Wallingford countered by appealing to the pope in
virtue of the special privilege enjoyed by his house which exempted it from
all visitation save by a legate *a latere* commissioned for that precise purpose. Without waiting for the issue of this appeal Morton on 5 July
despatched to the abbot the monition which has given occasion to so
much impassioned writing.

It is certainly an arresting document.[2] The abbot is accused of simony,
usury and dilapidation; of alienating the abbey's property; of failure to
maintain discipline and to punish monks guilty of sin with loose women
and with nuns; of making arbitrary and unworthy appointments in the
nunneries; of allowing monks to resort thither for immoral purposes; and
of allowing them to rob the shrine of St Albans in order to buy promotion.
We are left at first reading with the impression that the abbey had reached
the lowest depths of degradation.

That abbot and community were other than they had been under
Thomas de la Mare may be readily allowed. Wallingford seems to have
been an adroit, unscrupulous, ambitious opportunist,[3] able, clear-sighted
and free from gross vice; but his methods in defending and advancing his
own interest and those of his abbey had often been questionable, and it is
likely that he avoided trouble with his monks by making no attempt to
better their discipline. In a large abbey, under such an abbot, there were

---

1 *Reg. J. Whethamstede,* II, 287–9; cf. Knowles, *art. cit.* 153, n. 3.
2 Printed by Wilkins, *Concilia,* III, 630–2, and thence in *Monasticon,* II, 295–6.
3 The writer (?Whethamstede himself) of the Register four times uses the terms *politicus,*
politice, of Wallingford (*Reg. J. Whethamstede,* I, 5, 104).

probably serious delinquencies, but the community had not reached the degraded condition of a Dorchester or a Thame. A monition of the kind in question was a necessary step to be taken by a prelate who intended to visit under special powers an otherwise exempt community, and it was natrual that he should state the grounds of his action in the most emphatic terms. Morton's monition is not an isolated document; many of his charges are common form and were served upon other houses by other prelates; they are not the findings of an examination or the sworn depositions of witnesses, but reports that have been made to the archbishop by persons who have indeed a *prima facie* right to be believed, but who may well have had a grievance or a grudge against the abbot. While we are justified in thinking that such charges would not have been made by an archbishop against an abbot and community of unblemished virtue, it would be unsafe to conclude that all the charges were in every respect either *bona fide* or susceptible of legal proof.

Meanwhile, and with no reference to the monition, the proctors of both parties were exerting themselves in Rome, and were once more successful in obtaining apparently contradictory documents, the one (3 July) safe-guarding the abbey by giving it the right of appeal against any sentence passed against it, and of suspending the sentence *lite pendente*, the other (30 July) to the archbishop reaffirming the powers given by *Quanta in Dei ecclesia* in such a way as to cover most, if not all, eventualities, and with special reference to St Andrew's, Northampton.[1] Beyond this point we cannot go. There is nothing to show that Morton in fact attempted to visit St Albans, though he was at last successful in dealing with Northampton in the following year. On the other hand, the St Albans chronicler says that Wallingford was successful in maintaining his abbey's immunity in all respects.[2] The probability would seem to be that Morton realized that he would meet with resistance and would never find firm support at Rome, and that he therefore decided to hold his hand.

Besides his attempts to correct excesses in the exempt orders, Morton also visited parts of his province in virtue of his normal powers as metro-politan, and a short summary exists of his activities in the dioceses of Winchester, Salisbury and Exeter in 1492, and in the Midlands in 1498.[3] The details are very meagre; from three large houses of black monks and five priories of canons in the diocese of Winchester we learn little more than the numbers at each house; at St Swithun's and Hyde no serious

1 These and the other documents discovered by Gasquet are discussed in the article in *JEH* noted above. They are very diffuse and have not yet been printed, but the copies procured by the present writer from the Vatican Library were communicated to Dr I. Churchill, then librarian of Lambeth Palace Library, and presumably copies are there available to readers.

2 *Reg. J. Whethamstede*, I, App. (D), 478: 'Atque tandem...justissimam victoriam reportavit necnon nostra privilegia omnia illaesa et inviolata cum nostro magno honore... servavit.'

3 These have been described by Professor Claude Jenkins in his essay 'Cardinal Morton's Register' in *Tudor Studies presented to A. F. Pollard*.

faults came to light, but the administration was faulty; of the canons we learn next to nothing. Notes of the tour in Devon and Cornwall are still more jejune, and the frequency with which all witnesses stated all to be well, even at such houses as Launceston, of which little good was heard before and after, suggests that if the religious did not wish to expatiate, they were not encouraged by the archbishop to do so.[1]

A few years later, in 1500, Bath was visited by its bishop, Oliver King. He found no serious moral or disciplinary faults, but he entered energetically into the economics of the priory.[2] The cathedral church was in a ruinous condition owing, so he alleged, to the neglect of a series of priors, and the money that should have been spent on the fabric had gone in extravagant living. King therefore took drastic action. The income of the house was £480. From this the bishop assigned £54 to the prior and £80 to the convent; £40 were allotted to repairs and £10 to servants' wages. The rest, perhaps £250 when other necessary expenses had been deducted, was to go to the fabric fund. He added some observations upon this arrangement. His allowance to the convent, he said, gave more latitude than the literal observance of the Rule required. As the community numbered sixteen, his allowance of £5 per annum apiece was certainly adequate: he gave further evidence of his reforming temper by a rider that monks should be given food and clothes, but not a pension or money of their own. It was late in the day for a bishop to hold such language, and we may well wonder whether the injunction was observed. As for the fabric, it may be regarded as it stands to-day as Oliver King's monument, though the credit for the actual building is chiefly due to the last prior, in whose reign the work was seriously put in hand.

For Kent, some interesting information survives in Warham's register from his visitation of the diocese in 1511; some of the *detecta* and a number of injunctions are recorded.[3] Unfortunately, no details survive from Canterbury cathedral priory; it was still, as it had been for centuries previously, by far the largest community in England. Besides the prior and seventy-nine resident monks (including eight novices) there were six students at Canterbury College and two at Paris. At Dover, a dependency of Christ Church, the old troubles appear, though not in the aggravated form that might be expected from Layton's account twenty years later; the monks go about the town, the novices have no grammar-master, accounts have not been rendered. At Faversham the unusual step had been taken (we are not told when or by whom) of doing away with the monetary stipend or 'wages' in order to return to the communal issue of clothing. This had served as a deterrent to a number of prospective novices, though

1 Morton's Register, 51–5.
2 Bishop King's injunctions are in *Monasticon*, II, 270; also in J. Britton, *History and Antiquities of Bath Abbey Church*, Appendix, 200–1, and elsewhere. The bishop suggests that money belonging by right to the fabric has vanished *in voluptatibus*, i.e. dainty living.
3 *V*. 'Archbishop Warham's Visitation of Monasteries, 1511', by Mary Bateson, in *EHR*, VI, 18–35.

we are told that in fact the monetary value of the allowance of clothes and other necessaries exceeded that of the previous stipend; it was said that the monks were forced, through lack of a chamberlain, to make embarrassing application for clothing to the abbot himself.[1] Two houses of canons were visited: Leeds, a priory with twenty inmates, and Combwell, one with seven. At the former there is a rich crop of complaints against the prior. Besides the regular discipline in chapter, he used the lash on his subjects and even kicked the unwilling. At Combwell poverty was the rub; the canons went short in food, drink and clothing. Taken as a group, these Kentish visitations reveal a more respectable level of life than do many of those from Norfolk and Lincoln; their editor is, however, abundantly justified in seeing in the preoccupation with material and personal complaints a symptom of spiritual mediocrity.[2]

For the Austin canons elsewhere there are visitations at Merton in 1504 and 1509, and at Launceston and Barlinch in the latter year. Merton, one of the largest houses of the black canons, with a comfortable income of nearly £1000, was seemingly peaceful in 1504, but in 1509–10 all was going wrong. The prior, who was taking an interest in the rebuilding of St Mary's College, Oxford, and who in this very year (1509) had failed to give any account to general chapter of the moneys received for that purpose,[3] was clearly unsatisfactory. Bishop Foxe's injunctions[4] suggest that he had committed most of the faults possible to a superior: he was continually absent at Oxford; he was defamed with several women and noted for his disreputable male associates, young and old; he gave no accounts and could furnish no inventory; he was guilty of dilapidation; he refused to take counsel; he had allowed the number of canons to remain considerably below the statutory figure; and he was rarely present in choir. One might wonder how his continued presence as prior could further benefit the house, but apparently no attempt was made to shift him. Away in the west little had altered since the days of Bishop Grandisson. At Launceston the refectory was shunned and the infirmary had decayed; canons were out all day without permission. At Barlinch there were similar faults and the house lacked a grammar-master.[5]

The aims and endeavours of Wolsey, as legate *a latere*, to reform the religious orders are discussed on another page.[6] Here we are concerned

---

1 'Warham's Visitation', 28–30.

2 *Ibid.* 35. 'They lend no support to the theory that inmates of religious houses were steeped in inhuman wickedness. On the other hand, the decay of the monastic spirit is obvious throughout.'   3 *AC*, no. 56, p. 128.

4 These injunctions are printed as nos. cxlvii (*c.* 1504) and cxlix (1509 or 1510) in the appendix of documents in Major A. Heales, *The Records of Merton Priory*. It is noteworthy that in the year (1509) of the latter visitation the activities of the prior of Merton were on the tapis at the provincial chapter of the black canons at Leicester. No house was to pay to him its quota of the Oxford building fund until he had given a faithful account of past expenditure to the presidents (Salter, *AC*, 128). Nine years later he is seen handing in his books and reassuring the hysterical prior of Southwark as to the pure observance that prevailed in the order (*ibid.* 137–8).

5 *AC*, no. 94, pp. 183–4.   6 *V. infra*, pp. 158–60.

only with the visitations conducted under legatine powers. They are of a character that sets them apart from all others of the period. The earlier of the two surviving is from Wenlock, an important Cluniac priory, visited in September 1523.[1] There had been a disputed election in 1521, and a subsequent rebellion against the authoritarian conduct of the prior. The dispute over the election had gone to Wolsey; so now did an appeal against the prior, and Dr Allen, the cardinal's commissary-general, was sent down to visit. The *detecta* have not survived, but a long set of injunctions and a still more interesting series of counsels were taken down by the prior and preserved in his register. The injunctions, which are too long and minute to be summarized, have a twofold aim. The majority are directed against faults of the community or of individuals which had come to light; they are the familiar ones: drinking after compline, card-playing, rich clothes, open doors, absence of tuition for the young monks, maintenance of hounds in the monastery. In addition, however, Allen threw in a number of more constructive decrees: that custom should not be pleaded for a breach of the Rule;[2] that all, if not priests able to celebrate, should confess and communicate at frequent intervals; that all should sign permissions for financial transactions, those who might have opposed them noting the fact; that a system of fines should sanction silence in the refectory; that a dignified Gregorian chant should alone be employed in choir.[3] Not content with this, Allen handed out to Wenlock a list of 'counsels' which, if generally followed, would certainly have set the monks in a far stronger position in face both of their own consciences and of the outside world. The first among these is perhaps the most original; it is an exhortation to useful craft work in the monastery.[4] Among the rest we may note the substitution of two hours daily recreation in the monastery for absence at a grange for bleeding; reduction of the numbers of servants, especially those employed for display; the abolition of many ritual processions round the precinct in favour of a greater attention to the essentials of the liturgy.[5] It is not stated how much of this unusual document is due to Allen himself, but references to the recent legatine constitutions suggest that we have

---

1 They are printed in Latin (and also in translation) by Dr Rose Graham as an appendix to her article 'Roland Gosenell, Prior of Wenlock, 1521-6', in *EES*, 125-45; the injunctions are on pp. 139-44.

2 R. Graham, *op. cit.* 139: 'Ne sub nomine consuetudinis palleare sategant [*sic* both words] corruptelas pro ut de silentio, horis canonicis et jejunio.'

3 *Ibid.* 142: 'Gregoriana nota utantur, et quod distincte cantent longo sillabarum protractu.'

4 *Ibid.* 142, no. 1: 'Artes mechanice licite et honeste inter commonachos exerceantur, ne ociositas sit arma [*sic*] antiqui hostis captivandas [*sic*].' Dr Graham cites an interesting extract, from Preb. Clark-Maxwell, 'The Monks of Wenlock after the Suppression', where a contemporary death-notice is given of the priest William Corfill, sacrist of Wenlock in 1527 and subprior in 1540. He was a skilled bell-founder, 'a maker of organs, of a clock and chimes, and in kerving, in Masonrie, and weving of Silke and in peynting; and noe instrument of Musike beyng but that he could mende it'.

5 *Ibid.* 143, no. 8: 'Superflue circa monasterii ambitus deinceps non celebrentur processiones, et quod in servandis vere religionis ceremoniis sese magis dedant.' This was perhaps an attempt to get in ahead of the *novatores*.

here at least a selection of the decrees of reform proposed by Wolsey to the black monks in 1519, and found by them too severe.[1] In any case, one who proposed such a radical programme to Wenlock with hopes of a fair issue must have been of a sanguine, or of a very shallow, temperament.

Two years later, Allen, in virtue of the same powers, visited the cathedral monastery of Worcester, then under the rule of Prior More.[2] He delivered his injunctions, eighteen in number, a week after his arrival. No copy of them has been discovered, but seven months later, as a result of disputes and appeals, he promulgated amendments which annulled some of the previous decrees and glossed others. This document was confirmed by Wolsey a year later, and from the wording it is possible in some cases to catch the drift of the original injunctions, which can then be compared with those issued to Wenlock.[3] Nine are clearly identical, and a tenth corresponds to one of the Wenlock 'counsels'; probably some others which are abrogated without comment resembled items in the earlier set, thus making it still more probable that Allen had a scheme of general application based on Wolsey's constitutions. It is, however, clear that both he and the cardinal capitulated at Worcester to resistance, for besides the annulments, several of the glosses take all force out of the injunctions concerned. Thus the general prohibition against women entering the cloister and boys the dorter is interpreted in both cases to mean 'except with the prior's permission'.[4] These relaxations are all the more remarkable in view of the very severe indictment with which the original citation opens, and indeed the whole course of the affair suggests that the common form of such citations took a deliberately harsher line than actual fact warranted.[5]

The third group is of visitations of all kinds in the two decades immediately before the assertion of royal supremacy threw all into the melting-pot. The earliest is a tour of Somerset by Bishop Clerke's vicar-general in July and August 1526;[6] unfortunately, few details are forth-

---

1 *Ibid.* 143, no. 9. Food and clothing are to be given instead of money, as in the *novellae constitutiones legatine*. The reforming constitutions given by the cardinal to the Austin canons, however, do not show any marked similarities to the more original features of the Wenlock injunctions (Wilkins, *Concilia*, III, 683–8).

2 *V.* J. M. Wilson, 'The Visitation Injunctions of Cardinal Wolsey and Archbishop Cranmer'. Wolsey's injunctions, translated, are on pp. 359–64.

3 Canon Wilson (p. 360) writes that the original injunctions of 17 April 1525 were followed by 'a revised and corrected form...similarly lost', issued on 12 November 1525; lastly, on 3 November 1536, Wolsey 'issued the injunctions in the form' given in the paper. This is not correct. Allen did indeed revise and explain his original injunctions on 12 November 1525, but it was this revision, and not a second by Wolsey himself, that the cardinal finally ratified a year later (cf. pp. 363–4).

4 Injunction 3, on p. 361 of Wilson's paper; cf. the corresponding interpretation regarding women in the precinct (injunction no. 6, p. 362).

5 This is true also of Latimer's preamble; in both cases Canon Wilson rests too much argument upon the languages used (e.g. p. 357, 'a striking passage from the letter of Wolsey', and p. 358: 'Latimer is more outspoken...than either Wolsey or Cranmer').

6 Printed by Sir H. C. Maxwell-Lyte as 'Visitation of Religious Houses and Hospitals, 1526', in *SRS, Collectanea*, I.

coming. At Glastonbury the community of fifty, several of them bearing uncouth 'religious' names in the new fashion, met him with a chorus of *omnia bene* and were left with a few mild corrections. At Athelney all without exception pronounced all to be well; at Muchelney the only complaints were that few knew their way about the muniments and that the lay organist disturbed the brethren;[1] at Bruton, newly advanced to abbatial dignity, the canons were agreed that while repairs were needed in the guest-house and infirmary, all else was satisfactory save for the beer. At Keynsham, however, always a slovenly house, little had changed since the days of Bishop Bekynton; liturgical books were wanting, there was no instructor for the four young canons, the church and main conduit were badly in need of repair, and the visitor saw a pack of hounds making free with the stalls of the canons as with their kennel.[2] At Worspring the prior was at loggerheads with his six canons; he was a secretive, head-strong, tyrannical man, liable to outbursts of rage.[3]

In the following year a serious disturbance came to a head at Malmes-bury, and the president of the Benedictine chapter, the eminent John Islip, abbot of Westminster, delegated the visitation to the abbot of Gloucester.[4] The story is not unlike that of Whitby more than a century previously: a rough, self-willed abbot and a discontented community had destroyed the order and delicacy of the religious life, and a slovenly, sordid, and at times a positively vicious spirit had taken hold. The whole place was at sixes and sevens. The abbot accused ten of the monks of rebellion, and added apostasy, theft and fornication to the charge. The monks for their part accused the abbot of mismanagement and harshness; he beat them with a stick and listened to tales about them picked up in the town by a Mrs Alice Taylor, who was always in and out of his rooms, though no criminal charge was based on her visits. A group from the middle and lower parts of the community were, like Hawkesgarth and his friends at Whitby, definitely nefarious. Several had broken out of the house for longer or shorter periods without leave, and were charged with larceny and incontinence.[5] Finally, a company of eight, abetted by others and armed with bows, swords and clubs, had loosed a couple of friends from the monastic prison and laid siege to the abbot's lodging, putting him in fear of his life.[6] The prior, who was said to keep hounds, was fairly

1 Maxwell-Lyte, *Visitation*, p. 219: 'Organista monasterii perturbat conventum.' The ambiguous phrase leaves us uncertain whether the disturbing factor was the views of the organist or his voluntaries.

2 *Ibid.* 216: 'Prospiciens chorum una cum ecclesia esse nimis immundum atque canibus interdum plenum ac si spelunca esset eorundem.' No serious moral charges were made.

3 *Ibid.* 223–5.

4 The notes of this visitation are summarized in *LP*, IV (ii), 3678; they are printed in full by Pantin, *MC*, III, no. 284, pp. 124–36. Cf. also the account by Dom Aeldred Watkin in *VCH*, *Wilts.* III, 225.

5 *MC*, III, 126. For Thomas Hawkesgarth, *v. ibid.* 305, and *RO*, II, 206.

6 *MC*, III, 126: 'Arcubus, sagittis, gladiis fustibus et aliis armis invasivis januas abbatis ibidem obsiderunt...ac mortis periculum abbatis predicti crudeliter minantes.' No doubt both parties made the most of their stories.

impartial in his complaints, though inclining to the abbot's side. Nevertheless, he stated that the abbot held chapter in English, and shortened mattins when the clock went wrong. There was no reading in the refectory and guests slept in the dorter through lack of other accommodation.

Such was the state of the scandal when the visitor arrived. A careful examination showed that the right lay on the whole with the abbot, and six of the rebels were excommunicated: the precise effect of this does not appear. The abbot promised to refurnish the guesthouse and infirmary, to repair the clock, to restore the fare of yore and to be more kindly in correction. Nothing is known of the outcome of this.

Three years later, and a year after Wolsey's fall, Marton-in-the Forest (Galtres) a house of Austin canons in the North Riding, was visited by the dean and chapter of York.[1] On this occasion, indeed, nothing remarkable came to light but, on 9 May 1531, two canons presented Archbishop Edward Lee with a long list of articles against the prior; though clearly the issue of jaundiced minds, they cannot be wholly without a basis of fact. The prior, they say, originally intruded uncanonically, wastes his substance and affections on his relations, and provides the canons with 'sower drynke' and 'stynkyng bief with maggotts in it'; on occasion he threatens them with a drawn dagger. One of his relatives has the key of the dorter, and to prevent conviviality at nights follows the canons up the stairs after compline and then departs, jangling the keys and observing that 'he has loked the brethren in', to spend a pleasant hour in the local alehouse, while the imprisoned canons, even if one 'shuld dye for a drynke in the night', must perforce await the mattins bell with thirst unslaked.[2] If, however, the prior's side of the story is to be believed, these measures were not always successful in preventing nightly potations in the infirmary, or in hindering one George Sutton from wandering abroad by moonlight. Marton, in short, like many another Augustinian house, was in an advanced state of decay.

A year before the tour of the royal visitors began, Cranmer, in the second year of his episcopate, visited Worcester with metropolitan powers. The injunctions were not sent till the following February; they are a careful composition, following traditional lines in both matter and form, save for the first injunction of all.[3] The rest had all been heard before: the compilation of an inventory and accounts, the copying of all documents into the register before they are sealed, the engagement of a grammar-master, regulations for refectory and infirmary, mention of individuals by name. The only novel decree, which reflects the personal views of the new primate, is the establishment of a daily lecture of one

---

[1] The Marton documents were printed by Rev. J. S. Purvis among 'Notes from the Diocesan Register at York', in *YAJ*, vol. xxxv (1943), 393–403. The visitation was made by authority of the Dean and Chapter, *sede vacante*.

[2] This information is given by two canons in their accusation of the prior; they quote the janitor's words.

[3] They are printed in translation by Canon Wilson (*v. supra*, p. 83 n. 2), *op. cit.* 364–7.

hour on Holy Scripture, to be expounded literally. To ensure time for this, the office of Our Lady and the penitential psalms are to be discontinued as a choral function and recited in private.[1]

Finally, there are records from Yorkshire of a visitation undertaken by Archbishop Lee on the very eve of the royal enquiry, as a forlorn hope, it would seem, to forestall interference.[2] Details survive for three houses only: at St Mary's, York, a very wealthy house, the abbot was defamed of sinful relations with a married woman of Overton; he wore silk and velvet, and shoes with gilt buckles, and his horse had expensive trappings; he gave no accounts and kept an alehouse in the abbey precinct. The monks, also, wore luxurious clothes.[3] Lee's injunctions were delayed by various wrangles over jurisdiction, and were given only a few weeks before the general visitation began. In this Layton and Legh, though accusing some of the monks, made no charge against the abbot. The archbishop himself had done no more than reprimand. It has been suggested with some plausibility that as the archbishop had been obstructed for some time by the abbot's plea of exemption, he took his revenge by giving at least a show of credence to what was only insubstantial gossip, while on the other hand he did not use the inquisitorial methods of the royal commissioners to extract confessions from the rank and file. At the other houses that Lee (through his commissary) visited, such as Helagh Park and Warter, there were no open faults against morality, but the common life was largely at an end; the enclosure was not kept, and the canons were allowed no share in the administration. In addition, girdles and rings of precious metal were worn.[4]

1 Wilson, *art. cit.* 364.
2 *V.* 'Archbishop Lee's Visitations, 1534-5', in *YAJ*, vol. XVI. The article is unsigned; possibly Canon J. T. Fowler is the author.
3 *Ibid.* 446-7.
4 *Ibid.* 438-9 (Helagh Park); 445-6 (Warter).

CHAPTER VII

MONASTIC PERSONALITIES

I. WILLIAM SELLING

The life of William Selling,[1] monk and later prior of the cathedral monastery at Canterbury, was passed entirely within the bounds of the fifteenth century and, so far as the significant dates of his career go, it might have seemed more fitting to include his name along with that of Whethamstede, whose younger contemporary he was, than with those of the monks of the Reformation period. There is, however, a wider gulf between Whethamstede and Selling than between the latter and Kidderminster; Whethamstede passed through an awakening world with unseeing eyes while Selling, however limited his own creative powers may have been, at least recognized the new world and hoped to diffuse its spirit.

William Selling (?1430–94) took his monastic name from a village some four miles south-east of Faversham, and entered Christ Church as a boy. His family name was probably Tyll. He is found as prior taking an interest in the education of a boy, Richard Tyll, and Agnes Tyll, widow of William Tyll, was admitted to confraternity in the priory and granted, along with her husband, the privilege of sepulture in the cathedral near the body of St Thomas.[2] The young monk was sent to Oxford, where he was a member of Canterbury College from 1454 till 1464, attaining to the priesthood in 1456 and to the B.D. in 1458.[3] Letters written by him at this time are in a correct and concise Latin style that contrasts very favourably with that of Whethamstede; they show also a respect for the patronage of Prior Thomas Goldstone. At Oxford Selling attended the courses on Latin rhetoric of Stefano Surigone, and must have known Thomas Chaundler and perhaps Tiptoft, though it is not necessary to suppose that they alone were responsible for giving his studies a classical bent or suggesting a journey to Italy; in any case, he received in September 1464 leave to go abroad to study for three years in Italy at any university of his choice. He was accompanied by a confrère, William Hadleigh, later sub-

---

1 Contemporary records of incidents in Selling's life are not lacking, but the information they give is factual or insignificant, and lacks all intimacy. For such records v. *Literae Cantuarienses* and *Christ Church Letters* (both ed. J. B. Sheppard); W. G. Searle, *Chronicle of J. Stone*; W. A. Pantin, *Canterbury College, Oxford*, vol. III; J. Gairdner, *Letters and Papers ...of Richard III and Henry VII*. Among modern works the article in *DNB* is remarkably inaccurate; there is useful information, needing control, in Gasquet, *The Eve of the Reformation*, 30 *seqq.*, and excellent sketches in W. F. Schirmer, *Der englische Frühumanismus*, 154–62, 181, and R. Weiss, *Humanism in England*, 153–9, and 'Humanism in Oxford'.

2 Pantin, *Canterbury College*, III, 122–3; *Lit. Cant.* III, 315. The date of the admission to confraternity is 7 February 1491. Cf. also Gasquet, *op. cit.* 22 n. 1.

3 *V.* details supplied by Pantin in Schirmer, *op. cit.* 181.

prior at Christ Church (1471–99).[1] The two monks visited Padua, and stayed for some time with a widow lady, Johannita Bely, whose good offices were subsequently recognized by the grant of a letter of confraternity;[2] they also stayed at Bologna, where both were admitted to the doctorate in theology, a rare privilege for any save friars; they were indeed two of the only four monks on the Bologna lists between the creation of the faculty in 1364 and 1500.[3] Selling can have been in England only a short time when he undertook a second journey from October 1469 till some date in 1471; his companion on this occasion was Reginald Goldstone, who became on his return warden of Canterbury College but was recalled to Christ Church later to be Selling's right-hand man.[4] This journey had as its ostensible purpose a visit to Rome to secure from Paul II plenary indulgences for the customary jubilee in honour of St Thomas, held every fifty years and due in 1470, the tricentenary of the martyrdom. The petition was backed by letters from the king and queen; it was duly granted, and a Roman citizen, Pietro Mellini, received from the grateful convent the same recognition as Signora Bely for similar offices of hospitality.[5] It was probably on this journey, returning from Rome, that Selling stayed at Florence, made the acquaintance of the eighteen-year-old Angelo Poliziano, already celebrated as the translator of Homer, and was initiated into Greek studies by Demetrias Chalcondylas.[6] On his return, Selling held for a short time the post of chancellor, which had acquired some of the duties originally discharged by the precentor, but within little more than a year he was elected prior, a position which he held till his death on the feast of St Thomas, 29 December 1494. He had, however, a third opportunity of visiting Italy, for early in 1487 he was the fifth of ten ambassadors sent to offer the homage of Henry VII to Pope Innocent VIII. The arrival of the embassy on 8 May, and its audience of the pope on 14 May are duly recorded by Burchard, the papal master

---

1 Pantin, *op. cit.* 107–8; *Lit. Cant.* III, 239.

2 Printed by Sheppard, *Christ Church Letters*, nos. xxxviii–xxxix. As the lady's husband was a Venetian, it has sometimes been stated that Selling stayed in that city. Actually she lived at Padua and was English by birth. Cf. Paduan archive cited by Weiss, *Humanism in England*, 154 n. 3.

3 S. Mazetti, *Memorie storiche sopra l'università di Bologna*, 309. For *éloge* of Hadley, *v. Chronicle of J. Stone*, fo. 92 a.

4 The date of their departure *c.* 19 October 1469 appears in a letter of one Robert Hill, who obtained a safe-conduct for them (*Christ Church Letters*, no. xxiii); their expenses 'pro indulgencia adquirenda contra annum jubileum' are in Pantin, *Canterbury College*, III, 108–9. For Goldstone, *v.* long *éloge* in *Chronicle of J. Stone*, fo. 58 b. He is referred to by J. B. Sheppard (*Christ Church Letters*, p. xxii) as 'the Prime Minister' of Selling, and Schirmer, *op. cit.* 156, echoes the phrase—'eine Art Premierminister des Abtes'. The word in the text is perhaps more suitable.

5 *Lit. Cant.* III, 244–8, where the petition is printed, and *Christ Church Letters*, xxxix–xli. Mellini was a canonist who had acted for English monasteries.

6 Leland, *De Scriptoribus Britanniae*, 482, confuses the journeys of 1464 and 1469; he is followed by Gasquet. For correction, *v.* Schirmer, *op. cit.* 156. Selling may, however, have learnt Greek either at Oxford or on his first journey; cf. Weiss, *Humanism in England*, 159 n. 6.

of ceremonies. Selling, he tells us, rode in a black habit and black hood, with a black hat, but Thomas Milling, whilom abbot of Westminster and now bishop of Hereford, was less correctly dressed.[1] The prior was the orator of the party, and acquitted himself well; the draft of his oration, in Selling's hand, is still extant, as is also the petition which he presented to the pope, and which has the autograph *fiat* of the pope against each clause.[2]

On this journey Selling took with him Thomas Linacre, a native of Canterbury and the son of a Kentish landowner, who may have been his pupil for a time at Canterbury and who had recently, in 1484, become Fellow of All Souls. Linacre was introduced to Poliziano and Chalcondylas at Florence, and remained there to join their pupils, the sons of Lorenzo de' Medici, not returning till 1499.[3] As for Selling, his success on this diplomatic mission was recognized by his frequent employment on subsequent embassies, including one in 1490 to Tours, where he met Robert Gaguin, the great French humanist who was acting for Charles VIII. In addition to his diplomatic activities, Selling appears as an active prior, as a preacher against heresy,[4] as the personal friend and mentor of several of his monks, the patron of Canterbury College and the authority responsible for the erection and possibly some of the details of the design of the great central tower of Canterbury, Bell Harry, of which he expected to see the completion but which was in fact finished a few months after his death.[5]

William Selling has received honourable mention in every recent account of English humanism. As a scholar or writer his contribution to the English renaissance was not large. Besides his Roman oration and some notes, the only surviving composition of his is a translation from the Greek of a sermon of St John Chrysostom dated 1488, which is of interest as being perhaps the first translation made by an Englishman from that language in the fifteenth century.[6] These works, indeed, together with his letters, are by themselves evidence that he approached the humanists of Italy with a receptive mind, to absorb a culture higher than that of his own country. Selling's significance, however, depends not so much upon his own writings as upon his activities as a collector of books and a transmitter of learning. For Selling's manuscript collection there are several witnesses, including Leland, who tells of a *De Republica* of Cicero and other books that perished, and of some that survived. Among these may well be the Homer and the Euripides now at Corpus Christi College, Cambridge, and

1 *J. Burchardi Rerum urbanicarum commentarii*, ed. L. Thouasne, 257–9.
2 B.M. MS. Cott., Cleop. E. III, fos. 123–32; Canterbury Cathedral Chartae Antiquae C. 187. For Selling's Italian hand, *v.* W. A. Pantin, 'English Monastic Letter Books', 209.
3 For Linacre, *v.* Schirmer, *op. cit.* 162–3, and *DNB*.
4 *Chronicle of J. Stone*, 108–9.
5 *Christ Church Letters*, no. lviii, Selling to Archbishop Morton, *c.* 1494.
6 B.M. Harleian 6237 and Additional 15,673. For William of Worcester on Selling's interest in Greek philology, Gasquet, *Eve of Reformation*, 25 n., cites B.M. MS. Cott. Julius, F. VII, fos. 118.

a Latin Chrysostom at Trinity College.[1] The prior improved the library over the prior's chapel, and provided a room in the eastern range of the cloister with glass windows for students.[2] Seemingly, however, his books never reached the conventual library, but remained in the prior's lodging, where they were for the most part destroyed by the fire that broke out during Layton's visitation in 1535.[3] It has generally been assumed that Selling bought the books for his convent rather than for himself, but the practice of earlier days, and the fact that the books never reached the library, does not encourage this opinion. Similarly, the frequent references in modern works to the cloister school at Canterbury in which Selling is said to have taught rest upon no contemporary evidence or similar practice. Selling resided very little at Christ Church before he was prior, and even if there is some evidence that he lectured on Greek grammar[4] this would have been to a small group of monks, not to a 'school' in the renaissance or modern meaning of the word. If Linacre was in any sense of the word his pupil, it must have been when he was a boy in the prior's household; Linacre learnt most of what he knew at Oxford and at Florence.

No tradition of Greek learning or of any unusual devotion to humanistic studies seems to have survived at Canterbury. The monks of Canterbury College in the first decades of the sixteenth century resembled in all respects their brethren at Gloucester or Durham Colleges, and there is no suggestion in the correspondence of Erasmus that Christ Church or its monks were in the van of the new learning. In short, Selling was a notable example of the first generation of English humanism in the age of the philologists and collectors which preceded that of the great scholars of the religious and critical 'enlightenment', when humanism became a philosophy of life in the hands of such men as Erasmus and Jacques Lefèvre, but he made no great or original contribution to literary or monastic history. He had the fortune to be the patron of Linacre, and to introduce Greek to Canterbury, but he holds no important place in the development of the Renaissance.

1 For this, v. M. R. James, *The Ancient Libraries of Canterbury and Dover*, l–lii. The Homer and Euripides are now MSS. 81 and 403 in the library of Corpus Christi College, Cambridge; the Chrysostom is MS. 100 at Trinity College.

2 A Canterbury obituary, printed by H. Wharton, *Anglia Sacra*, I, 145–6, gives many details of Selling's successful administration, e.g. 'Aedificavit turrim quandam camerae Prioris vocatae La Gloriet contiguam...Librarium etiam supra Capellam Prioris situatam perpulchra coelatura adornavit; quam etiam nonnullis libris instaurari fecit, ad usum maxime literarum studio deditorum, quos miro studio et benevolentia nutrivit et fovit. Australem vero partem Claustri ad usum studiosorum confratrum vitreari fecit.' There follows an account of Selling's work on the manors which recalls Henry of Eastry rather than William More.

3 Leland, *De Scriptoribus*, 483; *LP*, IX, 669.

4 The authority for this is William of Worcester, who gives notes on Greek orthography and accents as taught by Selling; cf. B.M. MS. Cott. Julius, F. VII, fo. 118[r].

II. RICHARD KIDDERMINSTER

During the greater part of the period covered by this volume the most distinguished English monk was undoubtedly Richard Kidderminster (c. 1462–c. 1532), monk of Winchcombe and abbot of that house for almost forty years (1488–1527).[1]

Winchcombe, which had been of considerable importance after its first foundation in 798, and again on its revival under King Edgar, had been affected less than many of its sister-houses by the Norman plantation and had remained thereafter a house of the second or third rank, distinguished neither by any eminence on the part of its abbots nor by the literary and artistic work of its monks, nor by any great architectural magnificence, though it had maintained a sound financial position, and in the early sixteenth century ranked among the well-to-do houses such as Malmesbury and the New Minster at Winchester. It had, indeed, in the person of its prior, Aldwin, rekindled the fires of monastic life in the shrines of the north, but this had been a personal enterprise rather than a corporate achievement; it was in fact an attempt on the part of three individuals to escape from the conventional mediocrity of the south. Kidderminster, therefore, owed his prestige almost entirely to his personal qualities, though he himself pays tribute to his predecessor, Abbot Twyning (1477–88) who, himself an Oxford man, sent the young Kidderminster to Gloucester College at the age of twenty-two.[2] There he studied letters: that is, no doubt, the new humanism, which included a study of literature and prose and verse composition, and practice in letter-writing, on a scale hitherto unattempted in the claustral and other elementary schools. After less than four years, Abbot Twyning died, and the small community, probably of less than twenty monks, elected the promising young Oxford student. Unlike many abbots in similar case in the past, he was determined not to let his studies suffer. He taught himself theology in his own cloister, and when he had attracted a group of promising young recruits, he decided to implement fully the traditional machinery of monastic studies, which had rarely been put fully into motion save at the largest monasteries such as Durham and Canterbury.

1 For the main outlines of Kidderminster's life and activities, v. DNB, s.v. Kedermyster. There are notices of him also in a long note by P. S. Allen in Erasmi Epistolae, IV, ep. 1061; D. Royce, Landbok de Winchelcumba, II, xxxiii–xxxv; and R. Graham, VCH, Glos, II, 71. Some of our information comes from a history of Winchcombe compiled by Kidderminster himself in 1523. The MS. of this appears to have perished in the Great Fire of London, but extracts made by Brian Twyne and R. Dodsworth survive, and of these parts were printed in Monasticon, II, 301; they were also used by Anthony Wood. Kidderminster's public activities find mention in all the sources for the history of the early decades of the sixteenth century. For his achievements at Winchcombe, v. W. A. Pantin, 'Abbot Kidderminster and Monastic Studies', in DR, XLVII.

2 This autobiographical passage is cited from Bodl. Twyne MSS. XXIV, 551 seqq. by Pantin, art. cit. 199–200.

The Winchcombe community had increased to twenty-eight, and a regular system of studies was imposed, two bachelors of divinity lecturing daily on the Old and New Testaments, while the abbot himself lectured twice weekly on the Sentences. Kidderminster, writing many years later, in 1523, but giving no date for the circumstances he describes, dwells with some complacency on his achievements:

It was [he writes] a fine sight to see how the brethren devoted themselves to sacred learning, how they made use of Latin even in their familiar conversations, and how the cloister at Winchcombe at that time had all the appearance of a young university, though on a minute scale. Added to this, regular observance was so ardently observed among us, and brotherly charity was so honoured, that you would have said that there could not possibly be another such family, so united, so harmonious and yet so small, in the whole of England. The good God alone knows what a joy it was then for me to be immersed in sacred studies with my brethren in the cloister. There day and night I passed the time at my books in a little study I had constructed; would that I had allowed it to stand till the present day! My industry was such that practically all the learning I have in Scripture and divinity was gained there in the cloister. I have written all this that those who come after may learn that theology may be as fruitfully studied in the cloister as at the university.

And Kidderminster goes on to instance the achievement of Bede the Venerable, and to wish that monks would follow his example and join monastic observance to their studies, rather than repeat that nothing can be done outside a university.[1]

This passage, which owes its preservation to the attraction it had for two seventeenth-century antiquaries, has often been quoted without reference to its historical background. Meritorious as was the achievement of Kidderminster and charming as is his picture of the cloister at the foot of the Cotswolds, the programme was not original[2] and the results were not in fact remarkable, though only two years before he wrote a grace was passed at Oxford allowing the monks of Winchcombe who had learnt logic and philosophy in their monastery to dispute immediately after the masters and bachelors at Oxford.[3]

Kidderminster never lost his enthusiasm for studies or his zeal for regular observance. He compiled some sort of translation of the Rule and drew up an important Register of his house which contained its history from the earliest times along with lives of the abbots and other treatises. He also used the opportunities given him as visitor of other

1 The passage is quoted by Wood in *Historia et Antiquitates Universitatis Oxoniensis* (ed. J. Gutch, 1647), I, 298; cf. also Wood's *Athenae Oxonienses*, I, 61–3.

2 Pantin, *art. cit.*, shows that Kidderminster's programme was little more than an up-to-date version of the claustral school in *scientiae primitivae* and the theological lectures prescribed by Clement V and the Council of Vienne (decree *Ne in agro*) and in the Benedictine Constitutions of 1336. For such a school elsewhere, *v. Rites of Durham*, 96–7.

3 Cf. Wood, *Historia...Oxoniensis, s.a.* 1521.

houses to explore their records. He himself has left an interesting record of one of his finds:

Coming in due course [it was in 1513] to the abbey of St Mary's at York, and spending a long time there discussing points of observance with the monks, I learnt from what they said that their house owed its beginning, and the manner of its monastic discipline, to Evesham, while the monastery of St Cuthbert at Durham was similarly beholden to Winchcombe.

This, he says, was news to him; he pondered over it, and when he passed on to Whitby, and made enquiries there also, he was shown an ancient volume giving an account of it all. Overjoyed even to the shedding of tears at his discovery, he came in due course to Durham, where he kept his counsel till he had finished his visitation. He then related his discoveries to the monks, and told them that they owed their monastic life to little Winchcombe.

This [he continues] was not received with great enthusiasm by the ancients of Durham, who politely but tersely conveyed the impression that they had never heard anything of the kind in their lives. When I perceived this I begged them to be so good as to produce an account of their foundation. The prior, an excellent man, at once ordered the document to be produced, and on the very first page I found what I had dearly wished to know [the foundation, that is, of Durham priory by Aldwin]. Let all the brethren of Winchcombe, present and future [he concludes], reflect what a glory and a joy it is to them (and will be, as I hope, while the world endures) to think that such a famous monastery as Durham, and one which in regular observance surpasses all others in the realm, should have taken its origin from such a poor little house as ours.[1]

Despite the modest size of his abbey, Richard Kidderminster soon rose to eminence among his brethren in the habit. As early as 1492 he was general collector of the contributions to a benevolence levied upon all members of the general chapter for the war in France;[2] in 1513, as has been seen, he was appointed visitor of a number of houses including all those of the northern province,[3] and in 1519.–20, at the time of Cardinal Wolsey's attempted reform, he was third president of the chapter.[4] Meanwhile, he had achieved celebrity in a wider field. In 1512 he was chosen, along with Silvester de Giglis of Worcester, John Fisher of Rochester and Sir Thomas Docwra, Prior of St John, to represent the country at the council of the Lateran.[5] It was probably not his first journey to Rome, for we hear of his having preached on several occasions before the pope, and of having done some historical research at St John Lateran.[6] Three years

---

1 Bodl. MS. Twyne, xxiv, p. 544. I must thank Mr Pantin for providing me with a transcript of this.
2 *MC*, iii, 192.
3 The certificate for this visit to Durham is extant and has been printed in *MC*, iii, 234.
4 *MC*, iii, 119.
5 *LP*, ed. Brodie, i, 1048, 1067, 1170 (1). The two last references suggest that Kidderminster did not reach Italy with the others.
6 This is in an unpublished part of the Twyne MS.

after the council he attained national fame with his sermon at Paul's Cross upholding to the full the clerical privileges which had been attacked by the Franciscan, Dr Standish, in the heat of the controversy over the death of Richard Hunne.[1] Besides his work on the history of his own monastery and his compendium of the Rule, he wrote against Luther defending the doctrine of indulgences. His work on the Rule has not been preserved, but it impressed Bishop Longland of Lincoln so much that he proposed to send copies to all the religious houses of his large diocese.[2] Another humanist among his friends was Edward Lee, the antagonist of Erasmus and later archbishop of York, who bears testimony to Kidderminster's good nature.[3] This last quality, or something akin to it, is seen in the few letters of his that have been preserved, such as that congratulating Wolsey on his elevation to York in 1514, when he descants upon the Chancellor's early promotion and congratulates Oxford on her distinguished son, or his later letter to the cardinal, accompanying four pies each containing two Severn lampreys,[4] or his two letters, dating from the last years of his life, conveying his best wishes and compliments to Cromwell.[5] All this, comprehensible as it may be, seems to indicate that his resounding defence of clerical privilege at Paul's Cross was rather a professional's defence of his order than a confession of religious principle. Certainly one of the last extant references to him is in a letter of the king to his representatives at Rome, urging that his marriage suit should be referred back to England, and suggesting that the judges should be Archbishop Warham and Kidderminster, 'a man of remarkable learning and experience'.[6]

Some years before this, Kidderminster, as a man of sixty-five, had resigned his abbacy, though he is still occasionally alluded to as 'the abbot of Winchcombe'. He retained his old prestige, however, as the king's letter and those of Robert Joseph of Evesham show; perhaps also he retained a measure of responsibility for his house, which might account for the necessity of keeping in good odour with Cromwell. The date of Kidderminster's death is not known. It appears as 1531 in works of reference, but in fact the last known letter is that to Cromwell of 13 January 1532, when he was in good health and making his plans for the coming summer.

Kidderminster, though a somewhat shadowy personality, is one of the most attractive figures among the black monks of the generation before the deluge. One of the group whom the new learning affected in different ways, he is an antiquarian rather than a humanist, but his enlightened and orderly rule at Winchcombe shows that he had the interests of religion, albeit perhaps a conventional religion, at heart, while his history of his house and his interest in original documents show him to be of the age of

---

1 *LP.* II, 1313. For Standish, *v. supra*, pp. 53–4.
2 Cf. Allen, *Erasmi Epistolae*, IV, 163.
3 Cf. *Erasmi Epistolae* IV, 62–3; *ep.* 1061 (from Edward Lee): 'Winchelcumbensis nemini male vult.'
4 *LP*, I, 3925; III, 668.   5 *Ibid.* V, 510.   6 *Ibid.* VI, 327.

Leland and Bale rather than of Whethamstede. The results of his reorganiza-
tion of studies at Winchcombe were not spectacular; we know of no
literary work due to his teaching, and the Winchcombe monks who appear
in the correspondence of Robert Joseph of Evesham, or in the Cromwell
papers, are not distinguishable from those of other neighbouring houses.
There is no reason to suppose that Kidderminster, had he been ten years
younger, would have joined Richard Reynolds and the Carthusians, or
even that he would have made bones about surrendering his abbey, but
we feel that for him, at least, such a surrender would have caused more
than a private anguish. Certainly, if what we have of his writings reflect
his inmost feelings, he would have felt what many of our own age feel,
that an institution of venerable antiquity was receiving a hasty judgment,
and that something of value was being lost to England beyond recovery.

Among the many secondary results of the humanist and critical activity
of the Renaissance was a new interest in antiquities of every kind, and the
birth of antiquarian pursuits and studies. An early harbinger had been
William of Worcester, that diligent pacer of churches, but the class may
be said to have achieved full citizenship only with the work of John
Leland. Shortly before the Dissolution there are signs that the monks and
religious, who in other lands were so soon to excel as antiquaries, were
beginning to take up with the new interest. Richard Kidderminster, as
we have seen, eagerly searched for records of the past both at Winchcombe
and when acting as visitor at Whitby and Durham, and Bale began his
excavations among the Carmelite archives from his early days in the habit.

We have a glimpse of another abbot-antiquary in the writings of John
Twyne (?1501–81), in early life schoolmaster at Canterbury and always
a conservative, himself an antiquary and the father and grandfather of
scholars. Among his friends at Canterbury in early manhood were the
abbot and prior of St Augustine's. The former, John Essex or Foche
(abbot, 1522–38), was interested both in the Latin classics and in ancient
British history; the latter, John Dygon, who was, as has been seen, a
musician of note, was also a classicist. Twyne gives us a sketch of the
abbot, summering in his manor at Sturry in the Stour valley east of
Canterbury and visited by his prior and the young lawyer Henry Wotton,
soon to be Cranmer's first dean. It is a pleasant conversation piece of four
accomplished men, two elderly and two young, and Twyne pauses to
reflect upon the sad turn the abbot's fortunes were to take when he, once
a Lord of Parliament, was left to decay in grief and squalor. The picture
is overdrawn, for Abbot Essex, after surrendering his abbey, spent the
rest of his life at his manor of Sturry with a comfortable income suited to
the life of a country gentleman.[1]

---

1 *Joannis Twini Bolingdunensis Angli, de rebus Albionicis, Britannicis atque Anglicis
Commentariorum libri duo*, 4–40. Twyne laments that his friend after the Dissolution 'in
luctu et squalore senex contabuit' (p. 6). As the abbot had the manor house at Sturry,
together with a pension of £61 (say, at least £3000 at present (1957) value) his surroundings
need have reflected no more than a moderate degree of squalor.

III. JOHN ISLIP

John Islip was born at the village of that name in Oxfordshire on 10 June 1464.[1] The manor was part of the ancestral inheritance of Westminster, the gift of Edward the Confessor, whose birthplace it was; the splendour of medieval Westminster came and went with a child of that quiet village.[2] John entered Westminster on the feast of St Benedict, 21 March 1480, and was ordained six years later; in 1487 he became chaplain to Abbot Estney, holding the post till 1492. In an earlier age public opinion in many monasteries had insisted on a rota of the abbot's chaplains, fearing favouritism and the presence among the monks of the cloister of a devoted 'abbot's man', but such checks had long ceased. The post was one, like that of a bishop's secretary in modern times, which put a young man's foot on the first rung of the ladder of promotion, and Islip soon became subalmoner (at an unspecified date), treasurer and warden of the churches[3] (1492–9), warden of Queen Eleanor's manors (1492–9), abbot's receiver (1496–7) and cellarer (1496–9). His mind had no speculative or literary bent, and he was never sent to Oxford or Cambridge,[4] but it is an interesting sign of the times that he was admitted to Gray's Inn in 1492. At the end of the fifteenth century the common law was a fashionable education for the land-owning classes and ambitious young men; the realistic and acquisitive Englishmen of the day thought it more profitable than a university education; and monks were beginning to follow the fashion, as they had followed the friars to the universities in a previous age; the common law was more useful than the canon law to an administrator.

Abbot Estney died in 1498; Abbot Fascet who succeeded him immediately appointed Islip as his prior; two years later, after more than a year's illness, Fascet died, and on 27 October 1500 the prior was elected abbot by acclamation.[5] His ability in subordinate office had no doubt become apparent, and he had in addition taken a principal part in what might well have become an epoch-making move in Westminster history, and one which in any case gave to the fabric its final and in many ways its most beautiful appendage. Some years before 1498 the popular devotion to Henry VI had become so widespread and so intense that Henry VII determined to petition Rome for a canonization and a shrine at Windsor.[6]

---

1 For his career, v. E. H. Pearce, *The Monks of Westminster*, 167–8; H. F. Westlake, *Westminster Abbey*, I, 157–80 et al.; and J. A. Robinson, 'The Benedictine Abbey of Westminster', in *CQR*, LXIV. His family name may have been Giles; the arms of that family appear beneath his portrait in his Obituary Roll, and St Giles is pictured assisting at his deathbed.

2 The place has a passing familiarity to many as the first (or last) port of call on the leisurely journey that helps to emphasize the distance and the sense of adventure for the traveller who passes from one of the ancient universities to the other.

3 *Sc.* of Ashwell, Staines and Oakham.

4 The connection of Westminster with Cambridge began in 1499.

5 The account of his election and installation in R. Widmore, *History of Westminster Abbey*, 234–44, is drawn from documents in the muniments of the Abbey.

6 Westlake, *op. cit.* II, 358–65.

The claims of Windsor to the relics were immediately contested by the existing rivals Chertsey (the original tomb) and Westminster, and after a trial before the Lord Chancellor and the Privy Council judgment was given in favour of Westminster on 5 March 1498. The successful claimant now became the party most interested in the proposed canonization of the king; Henry VII was to expedite this and obtain (for a consideration) licence to translate the body, while Westminster went ahead with the preparation of a shrine, the new Lady Chapel, in which both the king and his mother, the Lady Margaret, took considerable interest. As is well known, neither canonization nor translation took place. The canonization was delayed, either because Henry VII recoiled from the necessary expense or because it was agreed to wait till the building was ready to receive the shrine. In the event, Henry died before the chapel was completed; his son showed no interest in the project of canonization, while the late king's directions for his own monument and Masses were on the most lavish scale. In the sequel, the chapel became his in popular esteem, and his son was spared the awkward situation that might have arisen had he found it necessary to discourage superstitious practices by confiscating the treasures accumulating at the shrine of a recently canonized predecessor.

Meanwhile, the care of the building operations had from the beginning rested with Islip, at first as prior acting for Abbot Fascet (1498–1500) and then as abbot. The two abbots before him had engrossed the important spending and administrative offices of sacrist and warden of the new work, and Islip kept the two posts in hand for the thirty-two years of his rule,[1] thus becoming responsible both for the completion of the vaulting and paving of the nave and for the construction and furnishing of the new Lady Chapel.[2] In addition, he added the Jericho Parlour to the domestic buildings[3] and constructed the Jesus Chapel as his own place of burial.[4] For all this he deserves an honourable position in the last generation of great monastic builders.

Islip was on easy relations of friendship with Henry VII,[5] and the young king Henry VIII made an even more extensive use of his services, though he never became a political figure. He joined the Privy Council in 1513, was a trier of petitions in Parliament from 1510 onwards and from 1512 was on the Commission of Peace for Middlesex. In 1513 he was noted in the Navy List as part owner of the *Kateryn Fortileza*, and he was associated in various ways with both More and Wolsey. During the second and

---

1 Pearce, *loc. cit.*   2 Westlake, I, 193–5.

3 *Ibid.* 181 and plate 23.

4 The identity of the Jesus Chapel with Islip's chantry was finally established by J. A. Robinson, *art. cit.*, and is accepted by Westlake, I, 181. It is the chapel between those of St John the Evangelist and St John the Baptist, i.e. between the south-east corner of the east aisle of the north transept and the westernmost chapel of the *chevet*. For illustrations, *v.* drawing in the Obituary Roll (*v. infra*, p. 98) and Westlake, I, pl. 22.

5 There is record of the king's dining with the abbot and of the latter presenting him on another occasion with two marrowbone puddings. For what follows, *v.* Westlake, I, 164 *seqq.* and refs.

third decades of the century his name occurs frequently in the records of
public events and services though rather at the circumference than at the
centre. A few of his activities may be instanced: thus in 1525 he was at
Glastonbury arranging for the election of a successor to Abbot Bere, and
it was probably he who suggested the name of Whiting to Wolsey. From
1526 onwards he was connected with several trials for heresy, some of
which took place in the chapterhouse of Westminster where, in particular,
Thomas Bilney was tried in 1527. In 1529 he took a minor part in the
divorce proceedings, and duly signed the petition to the pope in July
1530. A year later he was proposed, as a 'good old father', as an alternative
to Kidderminster if an assessor to Warham were needed for a trial in
England.[1] A little earlier, in 1529, there had been a move to include him,
among others, in the Praemunire indictment drawn up against Wolsey;
proceedings had been stayed, to the king's material advantage. In the last
year of his life Westminster joined the growing number of monasteries
paying a large annual fee to Thomas Cromwell. In monastic affairs,
Islip gave practical support to both Gloucester College at Oxford and
Buckingham College at Cambridge. He took his share in the work of
the monastic general-chapter, by which he was often appointed visitor of
the London and midland district, and of which he appears as president
in the only two chapters (in 1520 and 1527) of the period between
1500 and 1536 for which the name of a president is recorded. It was in
1527 that he took cognizance of the deplorable condition of Malmesbury
abbey.[2]

Islip died at his manor of La Neyte by the riverside at Chelsea on Sunday
12 May 1532. His funeral was conducted on a scale of the greatest
magnificence; the hearse, escorted by monks, retainers and heralds, was
followed by multitudes of the city folk, the procession filling the whole
road between Chelsea and Westminster. After Dirge and Mass in the
presbytery of the Abbey, the coffin was removed to the place prepared for
it where the principal mourners were entertained to a refreshment of
sweet bread, spices and 'marmylate', of which they partook 'over the
Chappell of the defuncte' what time 'they of the Churche did burye the
defuncte in the said Chappelle'.[3] His obituary roll, the last and perhaps
the most sumptuous example of its race, was decorated by an artist of
remarkable talent—the name of Holbein has been suggested—but was
never fully completed.[4] It contains several large drawings, one of the
deathbed of the abbot, where he is assisted by saints and angels as well as
by his monks, another of the great hearse approaching the high altar, and
yet another of Islip's chapel, showing its two stages and thus illustrating
the account of the funeral refection. Of even greater interest, perhaps, is

1 *LP*, v, 327.   2 *MC*, III, 124–36. *V. supra*, p. 84.
3 The document is cited in Widmore, *History of Westminster Abbey*, 206–10.
4 It has been excellently edited by W. H. St J. Hope, 'The Obituary Roll of John Islip,
Abbot of Westminster, 1502–32, with Notes on other English Obituary Rolls'.

the large drawing of the abbot in his habit surrounded by flowers[1] symbolizing the cardinal and theological virtues and the gifts of the Holy Ghost; with his right hand he holds the stem of the lily of piety, while with the left he breaks or 'slips' that of the rose of love. All these sketches, in addition to their beauty of line and composition, show an individuality of feature and a realism of detail which never becomes grotesque.

Little is known of the personal character and private life of Islip, save that they were externally blameless. As with other notable men of Church and State at that time, as with Wolsey himself, the unparalleled outward magnificence of ceremonial and building and hospitality contrasts strangely with the absence of any direct indication of the inner wealth of a creative intellect or a loveworthy personality. Islip's motto: 'Seek peace and ensue it', if understood in a material sense, might well in early Tudor times have taken a man fast and far from his sea-mark and polar star. If his funeral was the most splendid that had been accorded to any abbot of Westminster, he died at the very moment when such monastic pageantry was about to fade into thin air. The funeral of 'the last great abbot of Westminster—perhaps the greatest of his line'[2] has been called, with singular aptness, 'the funeral of the Middle Ages'.[3] On the day before it took place, Convocation made submission to the king with acknowledgement of his headship of the Church; on the very day of the funeral Sir Thomas More returned the Great Seal to the king.

---

1 The flowers are as follows: (faith) pink; (hope) pansy; (charity) rose; (prudence) marigold; (justice) borage; (temperance) daisy; (constancy) gillyflower; (fear of the Lord) columbine; (piety) lily; (counsel) violet; (fortitude) honeysuckle; (knowledge) flower-de-luce; (understanding) lily of the valley; (wisdom) cornflower.

2 J. A. Robinson, *art. cit.* 77. It is not easy to agree with this judgment.

3 A. P. (Dean) Stanley, *Memorials of Westminster Abbey*, 335.

CHAPTER VIII

HUMANISM AT EVESHAM

By a fortunate accident of survival there has come down to us from the abbey of Evesham, only fifteen miles distant from Worcester in the Vale of Avon east of the far-seen Bredon Hill, a book which opens a window upon the monastic world of the day giving a view very different from that of visitation records. This is a collection of letters written at Evesham by a monk of the house, one Robert Joseph Beecham[1] or Willis.

These letters, about one hundred and sixty in number, were all the work of a single hand during two, or at most three, years. Only thirty or so in the whole collection bear a date, but there are indications that the chronological order is on the whole preserved, though with a few patent disarrangements.[2] In the whole series only three or four external events are mentioned,[3] but by a fortunate chance they combine with the sole precise date in the whole collection[4] to assign a long run of letters to the autumn of 1530, and the whole series to a date between Christmas 1528 or 1529 and Christmas, 1531. No less than sixty correspondents are addressed, but at least seventy letters, or almost half the total number, are directed to eight of the writer's friends, while forty correspondents are the recipients of but a single letter apiece.

1 The letters are in Peniarth MS. 119, fos. 604–735 in the National Library of Wales, Aberystwyth. They were transcribed by Dom Hugh Aveling of Ampleforth Abbey to be used in an edition by Mr W. A. Pantin in a forthcoming volume of the Oxford Historical Society. I am greatly indebted to Dom Hugh and Mr Pantin for permission to use this typescript, and to the former also for allowing me to draw upon the results of his researches. For Robert Joseph's possible surname of Beechem or Beecham, v. infra, p. 104. It may be noted that the Beauchamp family lived near Alcester, where their name is perpetuated in a farmhouse Beauchamp Court. Dom Aveling, however, suggests another surname, viz. Willis, and identifies Robert Joseph with Dns Robert Willis, who became vicar of All Saints, Evesham, in March 1546 and of Cropthorne on 11 January 1559; he made his will 28 June 1569 (proved 16 July). Robert Joseph was prior studentium at Gloucester College on 17 December 1537 (Oxf. Univ. Records Reg. B (rev.), fo. 194ᵛ).

2 E.g. the sequence lxv–lix was written from Ombersley during August and September, whereas lxiii to the vicar of Ombersley, recalling the visit, is dated 20 November, and the letter between (i.e. lxiv) is that which is precisely dated 30 September 1530. Similarly lxxiii is of 6 December, whereas lxxiv is of 21 September. But such demonstrable misplacements are rare and in general the order seems to be chronological.

3 lxx: 'Ingens pervolitat rumor de Tracei contestamento variis haeresium virulentiis differto.' Sir William Tracy died in 1530; he was a Gloucestershire man, buried at Todding-ton (dioc. Worcester), and the matter would be of interest at Evesham. lxxi (30 November): 'Plusculum novorum internos recens dispervit fama de Cardinali illo Eboracensi episcopo.' Wolsey was arrested for treason at Cawood, near York, on 4 November 1530. lxxviii (undated): 'Quid de Cardinali Eboracensi Archiepiscopo apud vos popularis circumsemi-navit rumor libenter audirem ex te.'

4 lxiv: 'Die veneris festo divi Hieronimi.' September 30 fell on Friday in 1530. As regards the total period covered by the letters, iii was written shortly after Christmas; lxxx–lxxxiv date from early in January a year later; cxxx–cxxxii date from the following Christmas season. But it is possible that three (not two) years are covered, v. infra.

The writer was a young monk of Evesham, who had studied in arts for some years at Oxford, and had returned, apparently without finishing his course, to fill the office of abbot's chaplain at Evesham, from which post he was removed in 1530 to receive the charge of educating the novices in letters.[1] Most of his correspondents were monks of other black monk houses, such as Abingdon, Bury St Edmunds, Eynsham, Glastonbury, Gloucester, Pershore, Ramsey, Tavistock, Winchcombe and Worcester, but Cistercians of Combermere and Hailes, and an Austin canon of Studley, are addressed, together with several secular priests, a number of Masters and Doctors, and one or two of the writer's relatives. Almost all can be recognized on the internal evidence of the letters as being, or as having been, students at Oxford, and those most frequently addressed are clearly old companions of the writer.[2] A few can be identified as persons with a small niche in the annals of the times,[3] or at least as appearing in contemporary lists of their communities, and two in particular bear names familiar to all students of the period: the aged abbot of Winchcombe, Richard Kidderminster,[4] and a young monk, the most admired of all the writer's friends, who was destined in the troubled years to come to be Dean of St Paul's and abbot of Queen Mary's refounded Westminster.

The reader's first impression, as he makes his way through the collection, is one of resentment with a letter-writer in such a crucial time who could spill so much ink and tell us next to nothing of his world. The only references to public events occur in two or three letters close together in date, and mention the controversy over the will of Sir William Tracy or allude to the rumours of Wolsey's final disgrace.[5] Nor is Robert Joseph more communicative either as to domestic happenings at Evesham, or to his own personal doings and opinions. No one familiar only with ancient or modern collections of letters would believe that a writer could use so many words to convey so little information or thought, but this will scarcely seem surprising to a medievalist, and the monk of Evesham though a humanist in language, has much of the medieval man about him. If, however, we cease to look for what we shall not find, these letters are by no means without interest or value; they are far from being (save for a few examples) mere literary exercises. Robert Joseph is not precisely the kind of young monk we should expect to find at Evesham. To begin with, he writes in an excellent, idiomatic, conversational Latin which derives its vocabulary from Plautus and Terence rather than from Cicero. His style, in fact, immediately proclaims him for what he is, a fervent

1 lix. For his previous post, v. xxv: 'sacellanus magistro meo sum ad manum'.

2 In addition to explicit references the easy equality with which he addresses monks from other monasteries presupposes previous companionship, and in fact a dozen or more can be identified as Oxford graduates of this generation.

3 E.g. Richard Smith (lxxii, cvi, etc.) is almost certainly the volatile controversialist who crossed the fence more than once, dying at last in exile at Douai; cf. *DNB*. Wye (xxxiii) is probably William Way, later Fellow of Corpus Christi College, Oxford (*DNB*).

4 Only one letter (clxv) is addressed to him.

5 *V. supra*, p. 100 n. 3.

disciple of Erasmus. References to the great humanist are frequent, and the terms used are those of warm admiration; the works of Erasmus are quoted and some of his turns of phrase are recognizable.[1] Robert Joseph had indeed taken from him his ideal of a life spent in the service of letters. Further than this, however, he does not go. He has nothing of the 'modernism' of Erasmus, nothing of his violence towards theologians and obscurantists, nothing of his hostility towards the friars or of his criticism of the 'ceremonies' of the religious life. He is not in sympathy with the religious innovators and iconoclasts, and, although he is aware that an addiction to undiluted theology is apt to have a bad effect upon one's Latinity, his final advice is for a mixture of the two. He writes to his friend Ethelstan of Glastonbury:

He who avoids extremes does best. While those deserve censure who pass their whole life without ever doing more than weaving incredibly subtle syllogisms, yet I would not fully acquit those who, as the phrase goes, snap their fingers at scholastic arguments and say that nothing that smacks of Scotus is worthy of attention. Slip between each extreme; you will pass safest by the middle road.[2] For my part, I would handle Scotus and his followers in such a way as to take my opinions from them while borrowing a pure style from writings of a finer temper. If you do this, you will satisfy the Scotists with your skill in reasoning and please men of taste with your Attic charm of style.[3]

His own virtuosity is considerable. He writes easily, and is never at a loss for a word, and when the reader is driven to a dictionary it is his own ignorance of Roman comedy and lexicography, not the writer's barbarism, that stands revealed.[4] Robert Joseph knows familiarly not only Plautus, Terence, Virgil, Horace and Ovid, but Juvenal, Epictetus, Theophrastus, Cato, the younger Pliny and among later writers Jerome and Lactantius; and he asks for Quintilian on rhetoric to be sent to him. Of his contemporaries, besides Erasmus, he knows Budé, Judocus Clicthove, Lily, Pace and above all the Carmelite poet Giovanni Battista Mantuano, whose *Eclogues* and *Carmina* he quotes very frequently. It was on these last, and the *Eunuchus* of Terence, that he proposed to nourish his novices.[5] He is also a clever versifier: his common practice was to turn an English distich or proverb into an elegiac couplet in a dozen different ways, but he is equally at home not only with hexameters, but with sapphics and asclepiads.[6] His Greek was apparently in a rudimentary stage, but he writes to Oxford for a Greek lexicon and other books for learners, together with the *Chiliades* of Erasmus.[7] The accomplishment and training

---

1 Cf. vii, xv, xxiv, liii, lvi, lxxii, xcvi, cxxxi, cxli; especially xxiv: 'Ego omnibus Erasmum lacerantibus obici cupiam illa Lilii [William Lily, high-master of St Paul's, *ob.* 1522] "Doctus ab ignavo coetu laceratur Erasmus, Attamen huic saeclo lumen Erasmus erit".' Also xcvi: 'Erasmus nostre decus etatis.'

2 Ovid, *Metam.* II, 137.   3 xxi.

4 E.g. words such as *bolus, blatero, congerro, Grecanicus, strena.*

5 lxxxii. For Mantuanus (Giovanni Battista Spagnuoli, 1448–1516), *v.* article in *Enciclopedia Italiana.*

6 Cf. lxiv, c.   7 lxxii.

par excellence of the humanist was, he held, the frequent writing of letters, and he denounces his correspondents who write in English, and abbots who discourage their monks from correspondence:

I cannot sufficiently express my astonishment at certain prelates who cling so scrupulously to the letter of the Rule of St Benedict, that they warn their subjects against the exercise of letter-writing as they might keep them from a brothel. Is not this the shortest of all ways of forbidding the whole study of literature to their monks?[1]

As not a single letter of his correspondents survives we cannot be sure that all of them were as fluent and correct as Robert Joseph, but the mere fact that he could address lengthy letters in idiomatic classical Latin to some sixty correspondents, some of them country priests and the majority young monks, is an impressive witness to the high level attained by the literary education of the period at Oxford.

Of the personal history of the monk of Evesham we have all too little information. When the correspondence opens he has recently returned from Oxford[2] and is abbot's chaplain, but after a time, when a new prior was to be appointed in place of one carried off by the pestilence, his candid criticisms of the individual who was in the event successful earned the disapproval of Abbot Lichfield, and he was sent back into the cloister to instruct the novices.[3] He was naturally sympathetic when a friend had a similar misfortune,[4] for the traditional attitude of Jocelin of Brakelond to the 'poor monks of the cloister' as opposed to the obedientiaries had persisted through the centuries, but his downfall seems to have been only one move in a general post at Evesham in which Clotsall the kitchener became chamberlain, Acton the chamberlain became guestmaster, Broadway the precentor fell to being kitchener, while Studley rose to the precentorship.[5] To Robert Joseph, however, it was an imprisonment, and he quotes feelingly from the Scriptures of a similar experience of his namesake the patriarch, with the appeal to a successful friend to 'remember Joseph'.[6] A year or so later he has hopes of returning to Oxford and is found enlisting the support of the aged abbot of Winchcombe, the influential Kidderminster; whether he was successful or not does not appear, though the abrupt end to the collection of letters is followed by two short copies of verses composed at Oxford.

His residence at Evesham was interrupted at least once during these years by the approach of the pestilence; the young monks were dispersed over the countryside and Robert Joseph took refuge at Ombersley, a

1 xxviii. The reference is to ch. 54 of the Rule of St Benedict.
2 Cf. v and cxxix, which would seem to give 1528 as the year of departure.
3 lix.   4 xciv.
5 l. These names, and others such as Fladbureus, Uptonus, etc., are 'sweet symphonies' to those familiar with the district.
6 liv. The friend, 'inclitus ille praesul Politensis', is John Stonywell, last abbot of Pershore (1527–39), late suffragan bishop in York with the title *in commendam* of Pulati in Epirus. *V. infra*, p. 340.

village north of Worcester on the road to Kidderminster, where the church and manor had long been the property of Evesham abbey. Here, in the depths of the country, only a few miles from Prior More and his aubades at Grimley, the Evesham humanist found a kindred spirit in Robert Dorning the vicar, to whom he writes in after days with nostalgic memories.[1] The fever, to which he had for the moment given the go-by, caught him six months later in February at Evesham itself. Abbot Lichfield, with whom he was never on cordial terms, showed a very practical solicitude for him in this crisis,[2] but he was hard hit by the sickness and complained (without apparent justification) that his pen had lost its fineness and his hand its strength; he could scarcely endure the effort of writing. Worse still, the illness had been costly and had eaten up his savings.[3] A few other personal glimpses are given; he begs the good offices of the prior of Alcester for his father, of the surname of Beecham, whose illness has been augmented by a bereavement;[4] he commits a brother to Smith at Oxford as a sizar, and a young cousin or nephew to Taylor as an inmate of his hall.[5] He sometimes tells us where he is writing: often it is in the dormitory between lauds and prime when he is sleepy; occasionally it is in the cloister, the school or the library.[6] The conclusions of his letters are almost all different: 'thine beyond all flattery', 'thine while life lasts', 'thine while boars haunt hills and fishes streams', 'thine while there's skin on my bones', 'thine till death's dart'.[7] His signature likewise varies: he is 'the cloisterer of Evesham', 'the cowl-wearer', 'a little Benedict', 'a cloister-walker'.[8] While his affection for the generality of his correspondents seems only conventional, for one at least his admiration was undoubtedly sincere; it is an early and notable testimony to the character and personality of one who, a quarter of a century later, was to set his faith before ambition when the way stood open to Canterbury. The name of John Feckenham occurs in the very first letter: Joseph's

---

1 lxiii. These visitations seem to have been the plague, not the sweating sickness; cf. C. Creighton, *A History of Epidemics in Britain*, I, 292 seqq.

2 xci: 'Magistrum nostrum [he is writing to Feckenham] ut erga me sit animus nescio, satis tamen munifice febricitantem tractavit. Non semel enim me sua dignatus est pecunia beare.' This is a characteristically sixteenth-century interpretation of the Rule, ch. 36: 'Cura maxima sit abbati ne aliquam neglegentiam patiantur [infirmi].'

3 xci: 'Febris universam devoravit pecuniam.'

4 lxxxv. He writes to the prior of Penwortham (a Lancashire cell of Evesham) who is apparently in charge of Alcester, once an abbey, but now a mere cell of Evesham.

5 xvi, cv.

6 E.g. xlix: 'E somni officina sive malis e dormitoriolo nostro post peractas matutinas.' xxxviii: 'Raptim a prandio e pedagogio nostro.' xlvi: 'Ex cistula ['box', here = carrell] nostra claustrica.' clxiv: 'Ex bibliotheca.'

7 i: 'Tuus citra omnen fucum et Gnatonismum.' Gnatho is a parasite in the *Eunuchus* of Terence. xvii: 'Tuus dum superstes fuerit.' xxviii: 'Tuus dum juga montis aper', etc. [cf. Virgil, *Eclog.* v, 76]. cxviii: 'Tuus dum cutis carnem texerit.' cxx: 'Tuus ad mortis spicula.' One is reminded of the conclusions of Lord Fisher's letters to Winston Churchill at the Admiralty: 'Yours till hell freezes', 'Yours till charcoal sprouts', etc.

8 l: 'Eveshamius claustricola.' cxxiv: 'Cuculliger.' cxxviii: 'Benedictiaster.' clv: 'Claustrambulus'.

feelings towards him are such that he would love even his dog for its master's sake; he is the light of Evesham, honey-sweet to Joseph and more than half his soul.[1] He is his dearest brother; he would rather be at Oxford with him than hold the richest benefice elsewhere,[2] and one of the few letters where the note of piety is sounded is that in September 1530, when he writes of Feckenham's coming ordination to the priesthood.[3] No correspondent receives more letters than he; yet despite this admiration the letters to Feckenham are on the whole disappointing; they are usually short, and tell us nothing of the addressee. Equally favoured as a correspondent is John Neot of Glastonbury, but here there is more of equality; indeed, Robert Joseph is almost his mentor. Neot had other interests besides books. He would spend a whole afternoon on the bowling-green or with rod and line by Isis and Cherwell, or simply calling on friends for a drink, and his Joseph half humours his fancy. He writes to him on a spring morning when April was tossing bounty to the cherries in the Vale of Evesham:

See, the air is mild, and the breeze light from the west; the thickets ring with bird-song, and are merry with the sight and scent of blossom. Up, then! Drop Scotus, take up your bowls and be off to the green; you will bring back a bushel of health as well as a sixpence or two. If you don't feel like bowls, go fishing.[4]

The Evesham monk rarely touches on religious topics. His relations with his abbot, to whom he always alludes by a current convention as his 'Master', were distant, and he more than once expresses a wish that his behaviour might accord with his name.[5] When he is condoling with a Gloucester monk who has lost office he joins to the Psalmist's reassurance that he has never seen the just man abandoned the Virgilian anticipation of pleasant memories of past hard times.[6] Perhaps the deepest note he strikes is a reverence for the priestly office, never held so low as in his own day.[7] He writes to his friend the vicar of Ombersley of the high position that a cure of souls gives;[8] more unexpectedly, but certainly sincerely, he writes to a Cistercian friend of a boy who had chosen the life of a secular priest rather than that of a monk: 'I am sure his character will be an

---

1 i: 'Vel catulum non possim non diligere quem diligit ille.' clviii: 'Illum domus nostre lucernulam, Josephi mel merum et animae plusquam dimidium Fecknamum.'

2 cix: 'Mallem tecum Oxonicolam esse quam vel pinguissimum munus possidere.'

3 lxxiv. This letter would seem to be of 21 September 1530, and would thus show Feckenham's date of birth to have been c. 1505–8, or some seven to ten years earlier than the approximate date usually given.

4 cx. Spheristerium, though often a tennis-court, here seems to have its more common meaning of bowling-green. Bowls were a monastic sport, and the phrases spherarum jaculatio and globulis mittendis suggest bowls rather than tennis. John Neot took his B.D. in 1535, and was still at Glastonbury in 1538–9 (cf. A. Watkin, 'Glastonbury, 1538–9', 450). Cf. also infra, p. 347.

5 lix: 'Plane videatur sui proprii nominis [sc. Clemens] oblitus.'

6 xciv; cf. Virgil, Aeneid, VI, 203, 207.

7 lxxiv (to Feckenham on his ordination): 'Magna dignitas sacerdotium, verum nunquam ita ut nostris temporibus pedibus conculcatum proque vili habitum.'

8 lxxvi.

example to the country folk, and to my mind there is no life more truly calm than that of a secular priest provided that he is chaste, devout and well-educated.'[1]

Towards the end of the series there is a glimpse of an interesting correspondent, one William Dalam, a canon of Studley priory, some fifteen miles north of Evesham between the forests of Feckenham and Arden. Dalam was an outspoken man; he had visited Evesham and had later criticized the lavish table of the monks.[2] Joseph objects that he was given a hospitable reception, and now finds fault with his hosts; surely the most meritorious form of self-control is that exercised in the midst of plenty. Dalam was not to be repressed, and proceeded to complain of the intolerable garrulity of Robert Joseph and his friend, the schoolmaster of Evesham. Letters upon letters, he says: one is knocked down and buried under them.[3] If all Joseph's letters have survived from the period, Dalam's complaints seem excessive; as for Evesham, it was in fact passing through a phase of real prosperity, which was doubtless reflected in its living, but it is interesting to find an Austin canon of a minor house, only a few years before the end, commenting adversely upon black monk extravagance.

Occasionally Robert Joseph gives us glimpses of contemporary life, not devoid of a trace of humour. The letters, we gather, were carried by a variety of agents: there was Galatea, a maiden of sixty, a beauty white as the mythical raven;[4] there was a fishmonger, whose beat took him to Evesham and Combermere in Cheshire;[5] there was a drunken rascal who put Joseph's letter deep in his wallet, where the sun could not burn it by day, nor the moon by night,[6] until it was found on his return to Evesham and his senses many days later.

Taken altogether, our debt to Robert Joseph is less for what he tells us directly than for what impressions his letters as a whole convey. He and his friends have no fear for the morrow; they have not a glimmer of foreboding that within four or five years they will be taking the Oath of Supremacy, and four years after that surrendering their abbeys.[7] They feel no urgency to be defending the faith or reforming themselves. The picture is of a life still following the immemorial pattern of the past. Yet in one way the pattern has altered. The monks have caught the new humanism; they write of books and events in the new idiom which is half-way between

1 clxi: 'Nec video qui tranquilliorem degent vitam his sacrificis qui appellantur saeculares, modo caste, sancte et humaniter mores componant.'
2 cl: 'Exuberantia ciborum et potorum.' Dalam is an unfamiliar name, but the bearer appears (with the same spelling) as subprior on the list of those who took the Oath of Supremacy (*Deputy Keeper's Reports*, VII (1846), 301).
3 cl–clii.
4 xxvii: 'Galathea quaepiam, puella annorum fere sexaginta, pulchra valde, nec corvi albedini cedens.' For the raven's original whiteness, v. Ovid, *Metam.* II, 541 *seqq.*
5 lix: 'Volitans piscivendulus.'
6 lxx: 'Ita marsupio immersas epistolas. . .ùt nec per diem sol ustulavit eas neque luna per noctem.' Cf. Ps. cxx. 6 (Vulgate).
7 The lists of signatories from Evesham to the oath and the deed of surrender appear not to have survived, but many of the correspondents from other houses can be traced.

that of Matthew Paris and our own. They are not the bucolic, earthbound creatures that visitation records suggest; Robert Joseph's correspondents at Hailes and Winchcombe are not merely the sour, disgruntled, tale-bearing monks of Cromwell's letters, nor would Robert Joseph have become a comfortable squire like Prior More. They are rather of the family of Longland and Tunstall. Yet we must not exaggerate their learning. They have the foundation of classical letters, but they are not scholars or learned in the sense that Erasmus and Budé and Melanchthon are learned. What they and their likes would have become had they been granted peace in their time can only be guessed, but we know what became of Feckenham, and another of Joseph's correspondents, Richard Smith, became successively Regius Professor of Divinity at Oxford and Chancellor of Douai University.

All that we can say with certainty is that these letters show that a culture, a mental agility, a love of letters existed in some, at least, of the houses of all the orders on the eve of the great upheaval. It is not unpleasing to think that at Winchcombe and Evesham, whence, almost five hundred years earlier, monks had gone to revive the ancient glories of the north, there was, even at the end, a stirring of life, and that Abbot Kidderminster may have had a decisive influence upon the formation of Feckenham, the last black monk of the old order to win a place in the history of his country and in the esteem of his countrymen.

Note The Evesham letters have now been published as *The Letter Book of Robert Joseph*, edited by H. Aveling and W. A. Pantin (Oxford Historical Society, new ser.vol. xix,1967 for 1964). The numbering in the notes has not been adapted to the printed text, which follows the same order but after a time runs first one and then two digits ahead of the typescript from which my numbers were taken, e.g. letter lxx = 71 and letter clxi = 163.

CHAPTER IX

WILLIAM MORE, PRIOR OF WORCESTER,
1518–36

Several times in the course of this history of the monastic order in England an individual has been taken as the representative of his age. In earlier centuries reasons for the choice of this man rather than another were found in some quality of eminence that he possessed, whether holiness of life, intellectual or practical ability, or a combination of these qualities. Lanfranc, Ailred of Rievaulx, Hugh of Witham, Henry of Eastry, Uthred of Boldon and Thomas de la Mare were all men who, in one way or another, stood out among their contemporaries. For the last phase of the monastic life before the Dissolution an individual presents himself who, though holding for long the headship of an important house, cannot properly be described as eminent or distinguished either in mind or in character or in achievement. His inclusion in a gallery of portraits is due primarily to the aptness with which his career at all points illustrates the trend of the age; it is due also to the copious material from which the course of that career can be traced.[1]

William Peers, who on entering religion took the surname of More from the hamlet near Tenbury that had been his home,[2] was born in 1471

1 The principal source is the *Journal of Prior William More*, edited for the Worcestershire Historical Society in 1914 by Miss E. S. Fegan. The editor, with a diffidence which we may regret, disclaimed any qualifications for introducing or annotating the text, and the editorial matter is in fact very scanty. This is unfortunate, as the Journal is a mine of information on economic, social and linguistic matters, which might well have afforded scope for wide and valuable comment. The indices also are very inadequate, partly because a somewhat unusual general rule was adopted of noting only the first occurrence of persons and subjects. Fortunately, the editor was not always consistent in her application of this, but it remains true that the reader or student can never be certain from the index that he is relieved of the task of searching the whole volume for a word or name which he failed to make a note of; he will also find that a number of other idiosyncrasies render the indices less useful than they appear. The reader would also have been greatly helped if the current year and quarter had been indicated on each page.

The only writer to make copious extracts from the Journal while it was still unprinted was the gifted Worcester antiquary John Noake, who in his still valuable *Monastery and Cathedral of Worcester* devoted a long chapter to More, giving an admirable selection of short passages illustrating the prior's activities. Miss Fegan's remark (p. vii) that he 'overlooked very little' is, however, somewhat too emphatic, for the economic and monastic historian will find many details which did not, and could not have been expected to, interest Noake almost a century ago; in addition, some misstatements and omissions show that his knowledge of the Journal was not perfect.

In addition to the Journal a very large number of account rolls of the priory survive from the early sixteenth century. A number of these have been printed in *The Almoner's Book of the Priory of Worcester*, ed. by J. H. Bloom, and in *Accounts of the Priory of Worcester, 1531–2*, ed. by J. M. Wilson, together with *A catalogue of the Rolls of the Obedientiaries*, ed. J. H. Bloom and S. G. Hamilton.

2 More nowhere indicates his native place, but le More was a manor of the priory in the parish of Lindridge near Tenbury. It is now a farmhouse in a countryside of small villages

or 1472 and was shaven and clothed with the monastic habit in St Mary's cathedral priory in 1488. He became kitchener in 1501 and later subprior under John Wednesbury.[1] When the latter died in 1518 he was elected prior with the approval of Richard Foxe, bishop of Winchester and at that time still a person of influence.[2] Thenceforward for some seventeen years he kept, or rather caused to be written up for him, a day-book in which were entered in detail his receipts and expenses throughout the year. It is thus possible to follow his movements and activities week by week, to note his tastes and interests, and so to form an impression of his personality and worth.[3]

His Journal is unique of its kind, as being the only record known to survive of the daily expenditure of the head of a house in the sixteenth century, but its uniqueness is purely accidental and due to its chance survival; its form has in it nothing remarkable. Every obedientiary, every bailiff of a manor, and thus every head of a house, kept a journal of expenses and receipts to serve as a basis for the figures presented to chapter at the annual audit. It is, however, fortunate that the one surviving example of such a journal kept by the head of a house should cover a long period which happens also to include the supreme crisis of the monastic life in England, and that its author should be one whose career, especially in its later stages, can be followed in other sources.

Nevertheless, too much must not be demanded from the Journal. An account book, even if detailed and absolutely complete, is like a visitation record; it contains only facts of a certain kind and reveals only certain aspects of life; it is very far from presenting a complete and accurately focused picture. The prior does not note events of national interest save by accident; there is no intimate self-revelation or criticism of others. The coronation of Anne Boleyn and the birth of the Princess Elizabeth are noted because on each occasion a gratuity was given to the royal messenger

(VCH, Worcs, III, 442–3). The prior stayed there more than once, and I received the impression that it was his name-place—an impression shared, as I afterwards found, by Noake, op. cit. 134. More was there for over six weeks in the summer of 1521, and it is perhaps significant that his departure coincided with the death and funeral of his mother (Journal, 137–40). Mrs Peers had been living near her son at Grimley, but she may have returned to le More for care in her last illness.

1 Journal, introd. i and p. 3; Accounts of the Priory of Worcester, xvi.
2 LP, IX, 656.
3 The Journal runs from October 1518, shortly after the prior's entry into office, to within a week of midsummer, 1535. About six weeks are missing in spring, 1535, and leaves have been cut out at the end which may have contained a month or two more. According to the editor, the Journal is in three hands, one of which may (possibly, but in her opinion not probably) be that of More himself. The Journal contains many notes of payments to scriveners for various purposes and at least one (p. 80) 'to Richard skryvenar for writing my Jornall', but this and several other occasions where the first person is used (e.g. 'I gyff') need mean no more than that the scribe is copying More's notes. Miss Fegan also prints (pp. 416–25) valuable extracts from a companion volume (probably the 'new Jornall' to which the prior refers more than once) which contains inventories of Crowle, Grimley and Battenhall in 1532, together with accounts of work done and payments made on these and other objects; this was certainly written by 'John skryvenar' (p. 404).

who brought the news;[1] the fall of Wolsey, the submission of the clergy, the imprisonment of Sir Thomas More and the taking of the oath of Succession receive no mention.

Prior More's Journal is only one of a very rich collection of compotus rolls of all the obedientiaries of the cathedral priory. For some years, indeed, the set is absolutely complete, and we can study the full presentation of the accounts of the house as they passed through the annual audit. One such set, containing the prior's rolls, has been printed. It covers the financial year running from Michaelmas 1521 to Michaelmas 1522. With this, and the receipts and expenses for the year given in the Journal, it might be thought that we should possess a clear picture of the prior's financial position. A few moments' inspection, however, will show that this is not the case, and it is well to draw attention to this at the outset, lest a reader of these pages, or of the Journal itself, may think the picture he obtains is more complete and accurate than in fact it is. Indeed, these accounts, in common with almost all accounts, modern as well as medieval, present an appearance of completeness and simplicity that is illusory. When they are examined more closely, discrepancies (or what seem to be such) appear at every point. The chief cause of the great difference between the Journal and the rolls is, however, easily discoverable. While the expenses in the Journal are real outgoings, the sums debited against income in the rolls are a piece of book-keeping. At cathedral priories the income of the superior had never been charged, as at most abbeys, to sources entirely separate from the revenues of the convent, and though in practice certain of the Worcester revenues were by custom earmarked for the prior, strictly speaking all were the property of the prior and convent together. The prior, therefore, in financial theory, was not supported by the revenues of the property which was by custom assigned to his support, but by a number of annual grants made for specific purposes. It is these grants which, at the annual account, are debited against the sources of income. Of these grants, some are real: thus there is a grant for household expenses and another for what might now be called petty cash which seem to correspond fairly closely with the actual expenses for those purposes recorded in the Journal, but other grants, such as those for clothing for the prior and his servants, are clearly notional and are not reflected in the Journal. Whether money was actually paid, and then used at the prior's discretion for any purpose he might wish, or whether clothes were issued without money changing hands, is not clear from the rolls. Furthermore, a careful study of the Journal reveals that important expenses find no place there. Thus the travelling and lodging costs for the prior's regular and lengthy visits to London do not figure in the Journal, though purchases and gratuities in London do so appear, and a number of important normal

1 A 'letter concernyng the coronacon' is noted in the first week of May 1533 (p. 367). About 14 September of the same year a note occurs (p. 373) of the birth of a 'princes... whose name is Elizabeth'.

expenses appear so rarely that it is likely, if not certain, that they must often have been met without leaving record. These observations, though seemingly technical, are in fact necessary to a complete understanding of the Journal, for they all tend to show that the prior did in fact receive and dispose of considerable sums for which no record exists, while remaining within the framework of an annual system of accounts in which the balance was struck, not between income received and cash spent, but between sources of revenue and a number of grants and allowances. On this reckoning, it would seem that Prior More as a rule broke even, and indeed a complete view of the Journal suggests that he was a tolerably good man of business and that there were no large losses to the house through incompetence or prodigality. The real criticism that a reformer, whether economist or monk, might make would rather take the form of questioning the need, in the circumstances of the age, for the head of a monastery to live in such a way that an income equivalent to a quarter of the revenue of the house was needed to maintain him, together with a large following of servants, and to equip with all domestic furnishings and amenities three or four large manor houses.

For the Journal makes it abundantly clear that during the years of his priorate William More spent comparatively little time at the cathedral priory. Though the need to supervise great estates and to live off their produce had long ago vanished with the change from an economy of exploitation to one of rents, the external pattern of the prior's life is almost identical with that of the peregrinating abbots and priors of an earlier age, with that of Abbot Wenlock of Westminster or Prior Darlington of Durham. Though More had commodious lodgings in the priory, with all facilities for hospitality, he spent the greater part of the year on his manors, no longer devising and executing an agricultural policy, but living the life of a country squire in relatively long spells of residence at three or four manor houses, which priors of the past had selected as places to be kept when other manors had been leased with hall and demesne. Thus in the accounting year 1527–8[1] More spent only nine weeks at the priory, which he visited for some of the greater liturgical seasons of the year, such as Christmas, Quinquagesima, Easter, the Rogations and Whitsuntide; of the forty-three weeks that remained nineteen were spent at Battenhall, a manor only a mile from the cathedral, nine at Crowle, four miles to the north-east of the city, and fifteen at Grimley, four miles to the north in the valley of the Severn.[2] This was one of the few years in which fell no visit to London, which often took up from four to six weeks. The pattern of

1 *Journal*, 254–79. Henceforward all figures, unless otherwise noted, refer to pages in this book.

2 For descriptions of Battenhall, Crowley and Grimley a hundred years ago, *v*. Noake, *op. cit.* 155–6, 62–3. The manor house at Crowle was still standing when Noake was first making his observations. More also stayed once for some weeks at Corting (189–90, the year being 1524) and he spent odd nights at one or two other manors.

the year 1532–3[1] was much the same: eleven weeks at Worcester, fourteen at Grimley, twelve at Battenhall, ten at Crowle, two in London, and the remaining three broken with journeys to town or between one manor and another.

As the estates at Worcester, which had always been a cathedral priory, were not divided between prior and convent, the manors not specifically appropriated to one of the obedientiaries were administered by the cellarer. In the early sixteenth century there were some twenty-seven under his control, and of these some fifteen had come to be regarded as furnishing the income of the prior;[2] the major part of their rents therefore passed directly into his hands. With the exploitation of such parts of these manors as remained unleased he would seem to have had no concern; that was the cellarer's business. The tools and gear and labour for which More pays are those devoted directly to constructions and repairs at the manor houses, and to the maintenance of sluices, floodgates, moats, fishponds, parks and warrens. As only rents and dues are recorded among the receipts, with no mention whatever of sales of stock or grain or dairy produce, and as on the other hand his accounts include each week 'expenses on howsolde' without particulars, it is not possible to say how far his manors supplied grain, vegetables, milk and cheese, and whether the cost, whatever it may have been, was debited to the cellarer or never appeared at all upon the books. All that can be said is that the prior's visible expenses on provisions are for wine and 'spices' only, with an occasional 'byff' when a great company assembles.

Prior More, in his early years in office, spent considerable sums upon setting his houses, especially those at Crowle and Grimley, in good order. He tackled Crowle, which he found 'in decay', in his very first year, and in that and the year following he spent upwards of £34 on carpentry work alone; this, in that country of half-timber houses, would account for by far the larger part of the cost of a new fabric. In the next few years most of his attention was given to Grimley, where the fabric was fairly sound, and where he was consequently able to attend to furnishings, decorations and fitting up the chapel, of which the altar was consecrated shortly after Easter in 1523 by the bishop of Ascalon.[3] By this time More had returned to finish Crowle, and in the years 1524 and 1525 the house and chapel were glazed from top to bottom, large quantities of glass being brought down from London and fitted by 'Edmund glasyer of Alceter'.[4] A further large

1 357–75.

2 The manors can be traced in More's receipts (15 ff.). For the distribution of the receipts of the manor of Bradwas between the prior and others, v. *Accounts*, 42–5.

3 The bishop, Ralph Heylesdon, was acting for the absentee Geronimo Ghinucci. He had 6s. 8d. 'for his labour' (171).

4 139. More's glaziers came from Alcester (139, 196), Abbot's Bromley (266, 312) and perhaps Coleshill (cf. cornesshe colsull, 196, 219, 222); for further lavish details, v. 422–3. Habington, *Survey of Worcestershire* (ed. WHS, 1895), I, 540, writes of Grimley with 'its fayre demesnes...inryched with the ryver of Severn'. Habington is also the authority behind Noake (*op. cit.* 135) when he describes Grimley windows as filled with the arms of its

undertaking was the hanging of all the living rooms with painted cloth or serge. This was bought in bulk undecorated and then painted *in situ*. Entries such as the following are frequent: 'Item to thomas Kynge peynter for peynting the borders in the grene chambur conteynyng xxxiii yeards price the yeard peynting 2d'.[1] From Crowle the work passed to Battenhall, which was glazed on the grand scale in the last weeks of 1524 by 'cornesshe colsull'.[2] Finally, when the rooms had windows and hangings, furnishings and upholstery came pouring in, with beds, tables, bedspreads, cushions, sheets and table napery.[3] When the prior had finished, Crowle and Grimley and Battenhall, as their inventories show, were comfortable and well appointed houses by any standards which exclude the amenities of modern plumbing and what are called the public utility services.

Prior More, as we have seen, lived on a substantial and secure income paid at regular intervals either by the tenant in person, or through bailiffs and rent-reeves, or by one of his own monastic officials. He carried with him a retinue of some size: four gentlemen, ten yeomen and ten grooms, in addition to a chaplain and monk-steward,[4] and he maintained in addition the numerous indoor and outdoor servants that encumbered every large house of the age. He had no agrarian problems to exercise him; his unavoidable expenses consisted primarily in finding wages and maintenance for his household, and his only cares were for the three or four available sources of what may be called the 'heavy' provisions—the deer park, the fish stew, the rabbit warren and the dovecot. For each of these we have details over a long course of years. Not only are we given the numbers of deer, rabbits and pigeons delivered yearly from the manors, but we can watch the expenses of fencing, ditching, hunting and snaring. Of the fish-stews in particular a very full account is given. The ponds and moats of Crowle and Grimley and Battenhall were clearly a personal interest, almost a hobby, of the prior. What with nets and weirs and floodgates, with clearances of sedge and slime, with renewals and selections of fish, they took up a considerable amount of his time and money. Each spring, at the end of March or in early April, when Lent was nearly past,

---

builder Prior Wednesbury. These were 'gules, on a fesse sable, between three strawberry branches slipped, with berries proper, as many birds close, or'. This device might certainly seem to have a canting reference to Wednesbury's name, and were probably newly granted. More likewise purchased a coat for himself in 1520 (119): 'payd to ij herrawds of Armes of the kyngs for Armes...£4.' Grimley was duly adorned (266): 'Item for xii skochions of my Armes to a glasear of abbots bromley, 8 s. 4 d.' So apparently was Crowle, *v*. Noake, 206.

1 216; cf. 84.   2 219, 222.

3 Cf. inventories, 416. More seems to have had a liking for comfortable bedding. In the first fortnight of his rule he bought: 'iij fetherbedd with iij bowsters v peyer of blanckettes viii Coverletts ij Grete Coveryngs viii peyer of Shetes iij mattres iiij pyllowes of Down... vi quysshoons' (73).

4 The numbers in the text are as given by Musard, not a very reliable witness, in January 1536 (*LP*, x, 216). It is not easy to ascertain from the *Journal* (e.g. 72) what were the numbers in 1519. The chaplain receives only incidental mention in the *Journal* (e.g. 99). 'Dan Roger bewdeley my steward' occurs in 1529 (301, 309).

the ponds were drained and the fish counted before restocking took place, usually with fish bought elsewhere.[1] The moat at Crowle, in particular, with a surface width of forty feet narrowing to thirty at the bottom 'from under the bruge to the formust tornell ayenst the pyggion hows' was one of the achievements of his period of office.[2] Worcestershire is to this day a country of moated farms and manors, where the shallow pools, overhung by branches of pear or cherry, are stirred only by the moorhen or the birds of the farmyard. In the century following More's death the placid girdle of water was often to save from surprise and capture both recusant and royalist; in his more peaceful day it was regarded only as the home of tench and bream and eels. When Grimley mere was drained in 1527 there were found to have survived Lent seventeen great tench, fifty-eight store tench, seven chub, a multitude of roach, two great eels, and many small eels and pike.[3] In the Low Week of 1532 forty-three tench, two carp, four perch and three hundred roach were put into Hallow pond; forty tench and a great number of roach and perch into the nether pond there; thirty-eight bream and twenty tench into the moat at Crowle; eighteen small pike into Ashenshall and Whitnell pools.[4] Each expanse of water carried also its swans, and every May the prior noted their increase: 'Md. that the Eyght day of may the Eyre of Swannes withyn the mott at batnall did ley ix eggs & v of them wer Addle and iiii of the eggs wer Signetts this yere. Item the Swannes in the poole at Grymley did ley vii eggs iiij beyng addyll iij of them wer signets.'[5]

There is no indication that the prior himself hunted or entertained his friends with the sport. He kept a huntsman, however, who was the regular recipient of a small present on Christmas Day, and for whom on one occasion he purchased 'a grete horne' for 3s. 4d.[6] It was no doubt for the chase that three of the servants were provided with 'bowes & Arrowes to shote with' at a cost of 3s. 8d.[7] Besides clearing the parks, hounds on occasion crossed the Croome country as far afield as 'Bredon

---

1 127, 149, 169 show the quantities of 'store fish' put in from year to year. V. also 269 where a purchase of store fish is recorded from 'sir Richard stone of ryppull [Ripple (Glos.) on the Severn below Tewkesbury]'.

2 272. A note in a Worcester MS. Library of Dean and Chapter, Axii, cited by Miss Fegan in Journal, 426, gives the measurements of Crowle moat as 111 yards (east side), 62 yards (west), 51 yards (north) and 74 yards (south). Noake, who saw the house before its destruction c. 1863 writes (op. cit. 155–6): 'This most interesting building...consisted of a half-timber structure of considerable size, enclosing with its two wings a large court-yard. It included a chapel, galleries opening from rooms above...a fine dining hall... kitchen with enormous fire-place and encaustic tiles in great abundance. The moat round the house was complete.' The moat, according to VCH, Worcs, III, 329, can still be traced.

3 243. The word used for chub is 'botlyng'.

4 347.   5 404.

6 For the first occurrence of this Christmas gift, v. 97; for the horn, 270. Both Noake and Fegan read 'hunt' for 'hunter' (i.e. huntsman) in these and other places, but as the latter often reads 'hunt' where the functionary is clearly indicated (e.g. 13, 283), both writers probably overlooked some small mark of abbreviation. Though not a hunting man, the prior may have hawked: cf. reference to 'my goshawke' (138).

7 210. They were apparently made of wych-elm; cf. 'v wicheon bowes' (372).

hulls',[1] but this was a non-recurrent expense, as was also, somewhat unexpectedly, a sum given to Mrs James Badger 'for my kennells howndes'.[2] For other forms of hunting desultory payments occur: in 1529 Mr William Skull is rewarded for 'hunting the otters'; three years later Mr Badger is employed.[3] Foxes and cats were snared promiscuously by Harry Mownforde in 1519, and a casual reference to a 'foxe-net' in 1523 shows that this must have been a constant need.[4] 'John the taker of moldewarts at Grymley' does not appear before or after 1528, but he was an expert, for in that year a second payment is recorded to 'John the moldyer taker for takyng molls at batnall parke'.[5] Similarly, nothing is heard of measures against another pest till William Broke in 1532 opens a campaign against 'rokes, crowes and cheowes', for which he is paid twopence a dozen over a series of weeks.[6]

More, indeed, when out on his manors of Crowle and Grimley, sinks deep into the landscape, and the whole cycle of village life passes before us:

> When Tom came home from labour,
> And Cisse to milking rose.

It is in 1527 that the first payment (1s. 4d.) occurs 'to the maydens at grymley for syngyng on maye day'; this became an annual expense: thus in 1528, 'on may day to maydens at grymley, 16d', and in 1531, 'rewards to them that singeth on maye mornyng men and women at grymley, 3s.'[7] The prior in these years was at Grimley in person, but he did not escape subscriptions to vocalists elsewhere; thus in 1528 we find a shilling given 'to syngers on may day at Worcester', and eightpence 'to the maydens box at Crowle'.[8] Crowle, indeed, a village not primarily associated with music in the mind of a Worcestershire man of to-day, had a turn for song in early Tudor years. In 1532 a reward of 16d. goes 'to the yong men of crowle for syngyng on maii day in the morenyng', while in the same week we read: 'to the maydens of crowle for syngyng on holyrowde day [3 May] in the morenyng towards our lady light, 20d., and to other syngers 12d.'[9] In 1533 the maidens have replaced the young men on May Day, and in 1534 the usual 16d. goes 'to vi mayds at crowle that did syng in the morenyng on seynt philip & Jacob day (1 May)'.[10] At Worcester, however, male voices predominate; thus in 1533 a shilling goes at Battenhall 'to John Acton, William parker & John tylar for syngyng on

---

1 283.   2 395.   3 296, 353.

4 80: 'Rewarded to harry mownford as concernyng the foxes...for takyng of foxes & catts.' Cf. 377.

5 289, 293. The editor indexes 'moldewart' under 'molewort', giving the meaning as 'arabis or wall cress', but hazarding the remark that 'here it seems to have some connection with moles'. At my childhood's home on the Worcestershire-Warwickshire border moles were always known as 'moldiwarps' to the gardener. Cf. *OED*, *s.v.* 'mouldwarp' and its innumerable variants.

6 368–70.   7 247, 327.

8 270. 'Box' here and often in the Journal is clearly a collecting-box; the term is the equivalent of our 'collection' or 'subscription'; cf. 'Christmas box'.

9 348.   10 386.

maii morenyng' and in the same week 16d. 'to iiii of worceter singyng men for the same syngyng'.[1] Another occasion celebrated with early morning song was the dedication of the priory church, which fell often in Whit week. Thus in 1528 there were 'iiii syngers on our dedicacion day in the morenyng', and in 1531 something of a festival with 16d. 'to the singers of the town on our dedicacion day in the morenyng', a shilling 'to mynstrells on our dedicacion day', and 20d. 'to dauncers of the parasshe'.[2]

April, May and June, with their early sunshine and long evenings, were the season for every kind of entertainment. There were the 'iiii syngyng men craftsmen of Worceter upon seynt georges day in the morenyng at crowle'; the 'dauncers of seynt sewthans' in Ascension week, and a whole series of parish 'shows'—'Seynt Sewthans', 'the box of seynt Andres sheowe on the dedicacion day', 'the box at the showe of sent peturs' and a number of shillings 'to other boxes'.[3] Many of the entertainments were organized for the benefit of the church; thus the parishioners of Grimley on one occasion prepared for Whitsuntide with a 'churche Ale and a pley', towards which More subscribed the large sum of 7s. 6d.[4] Another year saw the same amount given 'to the church Ale at kyngs Norton', while in 1530, when More was at his native village, 4s. 6d. went to 'costs & expenses at pensax church Ale' and 2s. 4d. 'to pleyers at the more on the Assencion day to the uce of a churche'.[5] Bottom and his fellows were active about midsummer in every village; in 1519 the last week in June saw 'rewards to Robin Whod and hys men for getheryng to tewksbury bruge'; ten years later it was 'certen yong men of seynt Elyns that pleyd Robyn Whod' in May; in 1530, in the week after Trinity Sunday, 'the Dauncers of claynes' received 10d. and a shilling went to 'the box of Robyn hood'; in 1531 6s. 8d. went as late as 26 July 'to the tenants of clyve, pleying with Robyn Whot, mayde marion & other', and in May 1535, entertainment is provided by 'Robyn Whod and little John of Ombresley'.[6]

The climax of the village season came early in July. In 1533 More notes the gift of a noble 'in rewards to alhalland church at the pley holden at hynwycke hall seynt Thomas yeve beyng sonday and on seynt Thomas day beyng monday, which pley was kept to the profett of alhaland churche'.[7] The characteristic event of St Thomas's Day (6 July) was not, however, a play; in 1524 a shilling goes to wine 'at the bonfire at crowle on seynt thomas yeven'. In later years more details are given; thus in 1529 the prior records that he 'spende at the boonfyre at the crosse in crowle on seynt Thomas nyght amonge the hole neypurs of the seid towne iii pens in kakes, a potell and a quarte of red wyne and a potell of sacke'. A similar celebration took place at Grimley; thus in 1529 a

1 367.   2 272, 329.   3 385, 329, 387, 327.
4 308.   5 371, 308.
6 87, 293, 309, 332, 405. V. E. K. Chambers, The Medieval Stage, I, 174 seqq.; II, 337-9.
7 370.

shilling goes 'for a potell of secke & a potell of redwyne for the bonfyre'. No details, however, are given of the refreshments provided by the much larger sums distributed 'to the wyffes of more and Newenham, of burraston and of Pensax, to make mery amongs them'.[1]

The winter solstice, and the ten days between Christmas and the Epiphany, were another season of amusement. More's first Christmas as prior is marked by a series of entries: 'rewarded to a harper of the Dowke of bokyngham, 12 d.; rewarded to syngers of carralls at cristmas day at nyght, 16 d.; rewarded for carralls, 4 d., 4 d., 2 d., 1 d., 2 d., 2 d.; rewarded to iiii pleyers a pon the Epiphani Day belonging to sir Edward beltenop, 3 s. 4 d.; in rewards to pleyers children, 12 d.'[2] The pattern of the festivities included one or more dinners to the corporation of Worcester. Thus during Christmas in 1520–1 we find: 'for wyne to dyner on cristmas Day 1 quarte of mawmesey, 3 d. To brawne for the balyffs at nyght in the grete hall; ii dosen of wafurnes. A potell of osey & a potell of rumney, 12 d.' The dinner was accompanied by 'carrolds' and rewards were given 'to William the Lewter for his syngyng & pleying in the cristamas wycke'. Another dinner followed a week later: 'rewarded to iiii pleyers of glowceter a pon sonday when the balyffs and the xxiiii dyned with me in the grete hall, 3 s. 4 d.'[3] On New Year's Day 1525 a touch of colour is given: 'At Worceter the balis & all skarlet gownes dyned with me.'[4] In More's last year, the Christmas of 1534–5, further invitations were issued: 'the bayliffs & ther wyffs & other of the citie with ther wyffs xviii dyned with me sonday seynt Johns day. £3. 3 s. 11 d., ultra byff 12 s.' The entry does not state what entertainment was provided, but we note: 'to mynstrells Innocents day [28 December] and a popet pleyer 2 s. 0 d., to singers of carrowls, 8 d., to iiii pleyers on Innocents day 2 s. 8 d.'[5] On occasion the city fathers had to be satisfied with less severe amusements; 'rewards to ii childurn that tumbled before me & the balyffs & others, 12 d.'[6]

In addition to his subscriptions to the amateur theatricals of Crowle and Grimley, More found himself also patron of the professionals, strolling players and instrumentalists and conjurors of the king or queen, or of a magnate of Church or State. It might be 'the mynstrells of my lord of Shrewsbury', the 'kyngs Jugeler and his blynd harper William More', who was to be in trouble ten years later, or maybe 'the kings pleyers John slye and his company' or 'William slye and his company beyng the queen's pleyers'.[7] 'The kyngs Jogellar, Thomas brandon' was a frequent visitor both at Worcester and Grimley; his 'chylde' earns 8 d. 'for tumblyng';[8] among other visitors were 'my lord cardinal's mynstrels', 'a mynstrel of sir George throckmorton', and 'the dewke of

1 193, 310, 296, 158.   2 76–7.   3 123.
4 223.   5 399.   6 145.
7 88, 102, 252, 405. Miss Fegan suggests, probably with reason, that 'sly' is an occupational surname like 'scrivener', 'dawber', and the rest.   8 255.

Suffolke's trumpeturs'; in lieu of a circus the prior could command 'the
kyngs bereward at batnall havyng ii beres there'.¹ When alone he had
his fool, Roger Knight, whom he had seemingly inherited from his
predecessor and for whom, alone of all his following, he makes individual
purchases of clothes, including motley, and for whose laundry also he
regularly pays. These expenses cease in 1524, when Roger may have died,
and there is no indication that a successor was found.² Of the prior's own
recreations there is only one hint, the purchase in the summer of 1520 of
'ix bulls [bowls] to bull with all, 8 d'. We may note with interest a later
entry: 'Item for a bagge pype, 2 s. 8 d.'³

More, like Abbot Wenlock and many another prelate, came from a family
of middling circumstances in the countryside, and, again like Wenlock
and many another son who had risen to a position of influence and wealth
in the church, he maintained an affectionate and generous contact with
his relatives. In his first years of office his parents came to live at Grimley
and received many marks of attention; thus in 1519 we find 'to my mother
3 s. 4 d. ayenst Easter', and the same sum 'rewarded to my father &
mother a yenst cristmas'. Indeed, a gift 'before I went to London',
suggests that his parents were in some way dependent upon him, as does
another entry 'payd to sir William chylde for 40 bus. of whete for my
father's rent, 70 s.'⁴ This note is followed almost immediately by a whole
series of purchases of material and payment for labour 'at my father's
house at grymley'.⁵ Clearly this was a new and substantial building, with
a thatched roof, but Richard Peers did not live to see the house-warming.
He must in any case have been well stricken in years and he died suddenly
towards the end of February 1520. When he was buried on the 20th at
Grimley the little place could seldom have seen a costlier funeral: what
with candles and Masses and breakfast for the monks at Worcester and
sundry other provisions the obsequies brought a bill of more than £9.⁶
This however, was exceeded when Mrs Peers died. The funeral was
celebrated at Grimley manor by the black and grey friars of Worcester, in
addition to a dirge at the cathedral, and Anne Peers was laid to rest in the
chancel of the parish church at a cost of £10. 10 s.⁷

His father and mother were by no means the only beneficiaries of the
prior's easy circumstances. His brother Robert was apparently a wine and
general merchant of Bristol, and received the custom, by no means
negligible, of More's household; he was the recipient on one occasion of
'a gowne cloth' costing 20 s., but it can scarcely have been he who benefited
from the gift of 'a tonne of wynne to my brother costing £5', though his

1 296, 269, 373, 288.

2 For motley and the laundress, 'mawte catur' [= Maud Caterer], v. 83, 121; for 'a pety
coote & a peyer of socks to Roger knyght', v. 118. Roger clearly intrigued Miss Fegan,
who indexed all his appearances. He vanishes like Lear's Fool after a broken entry recording
the issue of 'a New sewte' in Lent 1523/4 (187).

3 155, 354.   4 83, 97, 101, 121.   5 121 ff.
6 127.   7 140.

wife is doubtless indicated by the 'rewards to my syster law of Bristowe when she was here'.[1] Other members of the family occur, and receive gifts: 'my sister Ales and her children', 'my sister of cropthorne', 'myne awnte of Astley', 'Thomas martley my unkell', 'Agnes [or Anne] my cosen', 'Annes purser of London summe tymes peers'. On occasion the reference is more general, as 'gyff to certen of my kynsfolke of oxford-shire' when on the way to London, or simply 'rewards to dyvers of my por kynsfolke'. Most of these relations disappear as the years pass, but cousin Anne continues to the end to live in one of the houses controlled by the cellarer, and to do household needlework for More, who pays her rent.[2]

His largesse extended far beyond the family circle, especially on the occasion of a wedding. Often the bride can be identified as the daughter of a servant. Thus in a single week of 1522 occur 'rewards to master croft's dowgter lawe at her wedyng, 6s. 8d.', and 'rewards to thomas astones dowghthers wedyng, 20d.' If 'Thomas bolt that maryd my cosyn' was duly requited with 20s., a reward of no less than £3 went to 'Jone tomes, thomas the pantlers dowghter, who was maryde to William Tommes draper on seynt Cecilie day the virgyn'.[3] Occasionally servants were sent to represent their master, as 'to six of my servants ryding to Alice foster wedyng, 6s. 8d.', and 'to Anne pritchett wedyng to Hervington and for costs of my servants ther, 15s.' The most vivid picture of all is on one of the last pages of the Journal: 'Md. that Jone, John herford Dowgter of the more [perhaps an old family friend] was maryde to Robert Wod-ward of ynckebarowe on seynt Emerencian day the xxiii day of Januarii to whom I gaff 40s. Item for ther drynckyng at Richard hygons in the hye strete as they cam rydyng throwgh Worceter from the more to ynckebarowe in wyne and cakes, 5s.'[4]

The Journal has more than once taken us into the world of Mistress Ford and sweet Anne Page; as we read on we might think ourselves to be in Justice Shallow's orchard or by the table dormant in the hall of Chaucer's Franklin. Provisions must necessarily bulk large in any account book, but the impression is given by many documents of early Tudor England that they served almost as a medium of exchange or a form of accumulated wealth. Prior More records his New Year gifts for 1519: they come from a miscellaneous group of friends, clients and henchmen, ranging from the landlords of the Plough and the Cardinal's Hat to 'John yks wyff': between them they contributed twenty capons, four dozen larks, two peacocks, two peahens, two geese, eight partridges, a shoulder of brawn, one lamb, one pig, six snipe and teal, one lamprey, a dish of trout and grayling, another of roach, and two cheeses, one of them being 'grete'. This score, however, was passed easily the following year,

1 110, 88. There was also an Edmund Peers at Bristol who may have been another brother; cf. 78, 270.

2 94, 164, 356, 258, 272, 119, 242, 270.   3 146, 311, 397.   4 304, 250, 400.

when the total of capons was twenty-three, with five peacocks, thirteen dozen larks, six woodcock, eight partridges, one 'feysand', four 'Stikkes of birds', three geese (one of them 'green'), one duck, one cygnet, a hundred warden pears, twenty 'oregges' and two 'boxes of bisketts'.[1] On the other hand, the presents appear to become more varied as the years pass. In 1519, the only friend who made no contribution to the larder was the abbot of Winchcombe's cousin, a mercer, who sent 'a fyne hand napkyn'. In 1532, besides game and delicacies including 'a peece of marmylade' and three 'pownd gardeners', we notice 'a corporas case', 'a fygur of our lord', 'a peyer of gloves', 'A tothe pycke garnesshed with selver & gylt', 'a pyllows bere', 'a peyer of knyffes' and 'a case to putt pennes & ynke in'.[2]

Intermingled with the material or social expenses are a fair number with a religious purpose. The friars of Worcester, black and grey, often received gifts at Christmas, sometimes of a shilling, at other times of a dish of lampreys,[3] and there are several entries such as the following, which must represent responses to a mendicant's request: 'to the prior of the fryurs of wyche [i.e. Droitwich] when he went to his generall chapter, 8 d.'[4] All indications, indeed, show that the friars were still poor and dependent upon charitable gifts. Besides personal gifts, a number of benefactions to churches occur: 'peyd for ii pax to gyff to grymley church and hallow, 12 d.'; 'selver crewetts at grymley church, 22 s.'; 'new schowryng and reparyng of the Alablaster tabull to the hye Awter of Grymley church, 4 s. 6 d.'; 'new rowde lofte at hymulton churche, 11 s. 3 d.'; 'I bowght & gyff to hallow churche a chales all gylt weying xx unces, £5.'[5] Not all these gifts went to churches belonging to Worcester priory. There are, for example, subscriptions 'to seynt martins newe tower, 6 s. 8 d.', 'to the Sextone of moche malverne to the byldyng of the parisshe churche there, 3 s. 4 d.', 'to the priur of little malverne towards the losses of his chalesses stolen, a noble'.[6] Gifts on the occasion of a priest's first Mass are frequent,[7] and the prior several times gave attention to the needs of an ancress, as 'payde in brycke lyme and sond to the reparacon of the Anckras hows by the charnel hows ex devocione, 10 s. 0 d.'[8] Other instances of devotion occur; thus in 1527 he was admitted to the Third Order of St Francis: 'to the grey fryurs for my brotherhood, to ther relevyng, 12 d.'[9] and once he

---

1 77, 98.

2 361–2. The word 'marmalade' was first used of a conserve of quinces, and then for plum jam (*OED*); it had a consistency like that of our 'candied' fruit. A 'poundgardner', sometimes written by More as 'li. gardener', was a pomegranate; 'corporas' = corporal; 'pyllows bere' = pillow-case.

3 121 (Christmas, 1531): 'For iij pyes of lampurnes bake & gyff amongs all the grey fryurs, 12 d.' 340.

4 88, 214, 275.   5 80, 83, 149, 243, 179.   6 168, 377.

7 E.g. 114: 'The offryng to master porters son furst masse, 10 s. 0 d.' Cf. also 247, 284, 330.

8 136. This was presumably the ancress whom the Bishop of Dover found so difficult to eject (*LP*, XII, ii, 49); cf. 322.   9 281.

notes a short pilgrimage: 'for expenses rydyng to hayles from cropthorn in pilgrimage, 2 s. 4 d.'[1] On the other hand, the seven shillings given 'to Symonds of byrmychame to be brother of the yelde there' was probably not *ex devocione*.[2] Cases of distress are met with help: 'rewarded to Nicholas the clerke of the church when he was Robbed, 12 d.'; 'In rewards to a por man of overbury beyng brent 12 d.'; and once a payment of 20 d. is recorded 'for ii shurts to William begger a por yong man'. It may have been the spirit of the season that led the prior one Christmas week to risk a shilling in reward 'to certen persons be syde the rodes for redempcion of a gentilman in turkey'.[3]

If Prior More's life was in great part that of a country squire, the payments that reveal his personal tastes best are those traditional to monastic superiors of the Middle Ages. In his early years he was at pains to equip himself and his chapels with service books. There are several payments to Richard scryvener for writing breviaries and the like, and 'to sir Thomas Edwards [doubtless a priest] for lymnyng gyldyng and drawyng of certen of my masse bookes'. It is noteworthy that monks are not employed on this highly skilled work, whereas one of his early entries is of a shilling to dan Thomas Blockley 'for makyng and floresshyng of the begynnyng of the register'.[4]

The yearly visit to London was used for negotiating large purchases, as well as for ordinary shopping. In 1520 the prior bought a ring, two chalices and four pieces of plate for £20, and cloth of gold and orphreys to the value of £87 for a set of vestments comprising 'ii coops, a vestment [i.e., a chasuble], ii tynnacles, iii albes, ii stoles, iii fannells [i.e. maniples] ...price of the hoole charge £90. 18 s. 14 d.'[5] In 1521 his stay in town saw purchases of furniture for the monastic choir: 'ii grete dextes [i.e. desks] with ii egulls...on to be in the qyur, the other to the hye Awter to rede the gospell upon with iiii candilsycks', together with 'ii grete candilsyckes for Johannis Awter for tapers', the whole costing £18.[6] In 1522 came the most costly purchase of his life, a precious mitre bought of John Cranks, goldsmith, for £49. 15 s., and a pastoral staff for £28. 15 s.[7] Whether or no More heard any criticism of these large expenses at the time cannot be known, but it is worth noting that they were to be brought against him more than ten years later, and that in the remaining thirteen

---

1 314.
2 156. Pre-Reformation Birmingham was a place of some note; the prior was probably invited to join as a county magnate; his gild may have been that of the Holy Cross, for which v. *VCH, Warwicks*, II, 347–8.
3 247, 376, 97.
4 120, 74, 79–80, 82, 116. Elsewhere (87) Sir Thomas Edwards appears as repairer of the prior's clock for 16s.
5 103–4; cf. 419. The orphrey (fr. *orfèvrerie*) is the strip of precious material covering the seams of the vestments. The 'vestment' is clearly the priest's chasuble; the 'tynnacle' [tunicle] is the vestment of the deacon and subdeacon; 'fennel' [v. *OED, s.* 'fanon'] is the modern maniple. Egulls = eagles (for lecterns).
6 153; cf. 419.
7 163, 419; cf. *A catalogue of the Rolls of the Obedientiaries*. Appendix III, 47–8.

years of his rule he made only one purchase at all comparable to them. This was in 1525, when the acquisition of a 'grete byryles stone with the garnesshyng of hym at london' cost £10 with a considerable further sum for carriage when, three years later, the stone came down to Worcester and was placed in position before St John's altar.[1] It was intended to be the prior's tombstone; like many other costly monuments erected during the lifetime of eminent men it never covered the body of its purchaser.

Among the London purchases books often figured. Some were certainly bought for the convent library, others for himself. So far as can be ascertained, almost all the books purchased for cash were printed books, and many were patristic, scholastic and canonistic works that had long been classics—Seneca, Cyprian, Jerome, Gregory, Ambrose, Richard of St Victor, Aquinas, Hostiensis, Innocent IV, Zabarella. These were presumably bought as useful modern editions of books that had long been in manuscript at Worcester. A few are more personal: the prior twice bought copies of Bishop Langland's translation of the Rule of St Benedict, and copies of the English chronicles and the Life of Christ by Ludolph of Saxony may have been for private reading. On the whole, however, the number of books clearly bought to satisfy More's personal needs was small.[2] Most notable of all in some respects is a group of five collections of early and recent statutes of England, going down to 1534. The prior, as will be seen, was for many years on the commission of peace, but the purchase may also remind us that all men in public place had to keep abreast of the prolific legislation of the Reformation Parliament.

The Journal says little of the prior's relations with his convent, and only once records the appointment of an official.[3] We learn casually that he himself exercised the functions of kitchener in the year 1530–1, and in the latter year there was an extensive 'renewyng of disshes in the covent kychion'.[4] As has been noted, More spent little time at Worcester, and then only at festival seasons, when guests must have taken up most of his leisure. He appears to have given a number of customary entertainments to the community—at Christmas, at 'quytide' (Quinquagesima Sunday), and most elaborately after the Maundy on Holy Thursday, when a greater

---

1 211, 217, 273. The whole cost £13. 6s. 1d. Byryle = ? beryl (cf. *OED* s.v.).

2 E.g. 111 (1520): 'bokes to the library'; and *LP*, x, 1272, where More asks that he may have the books in his chamber at Worcester. Miss Fegan, in an interesting appendix, pp. 409–15, lists all his purchases of books and identifies the editions of many of them, indicating those which still survive in the Worcester Chapter Library. Still greater precision might now be attained by using A. W. Pollard's catalogues and N. Ker, *Medieval Libraries*.

3 The appointment is that of the scrutators in 1520 (127). Other scattered references are to gifts, especially to student monks. There are two payments for writing, on p. 74 to Dan Thomas Blockley for the register and pp. 347, 350 to Dan William Wolverley 'for prycking of iij Exultavit of v parts, 2s.' This presumably refers to the setting of the alternate (chorus) verses of the *Magnificat* (*Et exultavit*, etc.) to 'prick-song'.

4 For the prior as *coquinarius*, *v.* 330, 336. We may draw what inferences we will from the allusion on p. 258 (just before Advent, 1527) to the purchase of 'a peyer of slippers for mattens, 10d.'

expense on wine is recorded than on any other day. He also paid regularly 10s. a quarter for the ten o'clock Mass, and 2s. 4d. yearly at Michaelmas for geese for the convent's breakfast.[1] He had with him a chaplain and a monk-steward, to whom he paid 6s. 8d. a quarter, but of other monks we hear little. Battenhall was not, like Bearpark at Durham, a place of holiday for the brethren; the rewards 'to the iiij Novices at batnall the iii day after their profession' were probably made on the occasion of a formal visit.[2] On the other hand, Battenhall was sufficiently near Worcester for monks to visit the prior without appearing in the accounts, and an entry occasionally occurs, when the prior is elsewhere, of sums paid to visiting brethren. The only group of these to figure at all frequently are the students at Oxford. Worcester had from the first sent a regular stream to the college—then Gloucester College—which now perpetuates the connection by its name, and it may have become customary that the prior should bear the expenses connected with the inception of masters and bachelors. Entries of such payments are not rare, as 'rewarded to dan John Lewarne to be bachelor of divinite in oxford, 40s.', and 'rewarded to dan Roger neckham to be Doctor of Divinite, 40s. 2d.' The prior's legal advisers were similarly assisted; thus in 1524 a gift is recorded 'to mr Richard foxfords to his commencement to be doctor, 53s. 4d.'[3] The students at Oxford frequently received small gifts, usually when the prior was passing through the university town on the way to London. The first of these payments is in 1519: 'rewarded to scholars of oxforde, viz. of caunterbury and mawmesbury, 2s. 8d.', and once a large payment occurs which More takes care shall not serve as a precedent: 'to dan bartholemes stoke student at oxford ex benevolo animo meo hoc anno £7'.[4]

Two Worcester monks receive exceptional mention. The one is dan Robert Alchurche the sexton. An early entry shows him to have been trusted by More, and another, unique of its kind, notes his death 'in the Sextry a bowte vii of the clocke at nyght' on 10 December 1531. Thenceforward at intervals the prior pays a considerable sum for Masses for his soul.[5] The other name has still more significance in the light of after events. In the autumn of 1527 and thenceforward for a considerable time, and again for a period in 1531, a series of payments is made to dan John Musard for working in the library on binding and repairing books.[6] This

---

1 E.g. 208 (1525): 'a galand & half of claret, 18d.; a galand & half of Red wine, 18d. A galand of secke 12d. A potell of mawmesey 8d.' For the celebration of the Maundy three centuries earlier, v. Lanfranc's Monastic Constitutions, 31–5. For the Mass, v. (e.g.) 189; for the geese (seven for 2s. 4d.), 254.

2 366. On the third day the newly professed, who had worn their hoods over their heads since pronouncing their vows, presented themselves for a ceremonial unpinning. It is typical of the age that they should have received a cash 'reward' of 4d. apiece.

3 79, 232, 215.

4 86, 335. 'Mawmesbury' in the first passage is presumably the part of Gloucester College belonging to Malmesbury Abbey; cf. RO, I, 27. A gift to students from Glastonbury is recorded on p. 135.

5 127, 360, 389.   6 256–62, 322, 324.

is almost the only payment of its kind to a monk in the diary, and it is natural to suppose that Musard may have been in some way an object of the prior's encouragement or care—a conjecture which receives some support from the note at New Year, 1531, of a gift 'of musard a potell glasse of aquavite'.[1] If this were so, the care was ill requited, for at midsummer, 1531, there is the entry: 'the takyng of musard. Item rewarded to Roger bury, Lewes the bedull, John tyler and Richard the cellarer's horsekeeper for the fatching and conveying dan John Musard home from overbury after he robbed his master of certen plate & other things, 6 s.'[2]

Although Prior More made no great figure in the social or political life of the country, he could not, as head of a great house and a landowner of importance, escape certain public duties. For some years he can be seen entertaining the justices at times of sessions; in 1526 he is himself of the quorum, and his first appearance on the bench is recorded by the payment of 3 s. 4 d. to the constable of the castle 'for the leying the quysshon for me at the sessheons'.[3] Henceforward he is always at Worcester when the justices are sitting. He was also of necessity a professional dispenser of hospitality. As a rule, his guests do not appear by name in his Journal, but at Crowle and elsewhere we catch glimpses of the gentlemen of Worcestershire and Warwickshire, the Winters of Huddington and the Throckmortons of Coughton, whose descendants in the third and fourth generations were to earn a tragic notoriety. Occasionally the name of a great lady appears. At Worcester, in the last week of August 1523, we note: 'Item for swete wyne spended upon my lady sannys, 12 d., 10 d.' The entry is followed by another: 'my lady sonnes [? a misreading of 'sannys']. Item rewards, 6 s. 8 d.' Lady Sandys was a Worcestershire woman, a Bray by birth; she had married a young courtier who was to remain one of the king's favourites and to give her a beautiful home, 'The Vyne', in Berkshire. In 1530 we find her sending More a rosary: 'a peyer of grete Amber bedes of v settes', and, as we shall see, her friendship with the prior was to have issue in later years.[4]

An exception to the casual entries of hospitality occurs in 1526. Early in that year the Countess of Salisbury, Margaret Pole, arrived with her charge, the nine-year-old Princess Mary, then still heiress presumptive of England. Her arrival was preceded by some hasty decorating, and attempts to make her apartment weather-proof,[5] and expenses rose considerably during her stay. The princess was in the priory for five weeks, and then

1 321.   2 330–1.
3 238. He also appears as sitting on commissions of customs (247) and corn (255).
4 177, 311. Lord Sandys built 'the Vyne' near Basingstoke, from which he took his title 'Baron Sandys of the Vyne'; v. also DNB.
5 222: 'To John Taylor, 7 s., moris taylor and Annes purser 20 d. for sowyng of the hangyngs in the corte chamber.' 'To colsull the glasyer for glasyng of a hole in the entrie next the chappell.' 'Item to hym for glasyng of the wyndow at the steyer heed at the stone chambur durr, &c.' Cf. also 224.

moved to Battenhall for a month, returning to Worcester half-way through Holy Week, and departing again after Low Sunday, her retinue being the better by £7. 13s. 4d. from gratuities received from the priory.[1] Mary's offerings at the prior's Mass on St Wulstan's Day (19 January), Candlemas, Easter Sunday and the Assumption are recorded. The princess returned at the beginning of August and Thomas Brandon, 'the king's Joguler' was on hand;[2] when she left the prior escorted her to Cropthorne and Evesham. Shortly before this visit there is a note of three payments for wine 'for my lady salesbury sons', one of them being 'my lord mowtigeowe'.[3] The imagination rests for a moment on the guest-hall at Worcester that year. England in 1526 must still have seemed a settled country with the future predictable, when Anne Boleyn and Thomas Cromwell were still in private place, and the sword that was to divide kinsmen so sharply lay still sheathed. Yet the four visitors who sat there with the prior were all to know sorrow, and were all in their fashion to suffer, or to cause suffering, for their faith. The Countess and her elder son were to perish at the hands of the executioner, while the younger son was to die in exile haunted by the disaster that he had helped to cause. They must often have spoken of the absent brother, Reginald, also in part to be the cause of their fate, who was himself to die, a prince of the Church, on the same day as the little girl, his cousin, each of them alone in the new, harsh world which they had hoped to sweeten, but had only the more embittered.

During all these years we can see Prior More from another angle among his fellow prelates. Abbot Kidderminster of Winchcombe and the abbots of Gloucester and Reading were occasional visitors;[4] he was summoned to Westminster to hear Wolsey's scheme of reform in 1520,[5] and found the cardinal expensive on more than one occasion, as: 'Md. of £20 delyvered to the A. of Winchecombe for my lord cardinall as all other abbotts did [Low Week, 1520]'; 'Md that I have bowght to lend to my lord cardinall towarde his Jorney to calys for to treate of pease...vi horsses, the price of them £12. 4s.', with more than £3 in addition for harness and carriage to London in July 1521.[6] He had commitments also in the diocese. The see of Worcester was held for many years by a succession of Italians and, when it became vacant in 1522 on the resignation of Giulio de' Medici, More honoured a venerable tradition by straightway sending out his subprior and a notary as visitors of the diocese *sede vacante*. For this year, too, the prior as official acted as receiver and disburser of all moneys coming officially to the see, or expended by it on routine acts and salaries.[7] Three years later his peace was disturbed by a visitation conducted by Dr John Allen, who shared with Cromwell among

1 227, 233, 235.
3 233. Mowtigeowe=Montague.
5 96.
7 3–11.

2 37–9, 235.
4 93, 114, 404.
6 106, 136.

Wolsey's servants a notoriety for violent and rapacious conduct.[1] His injunctions, however, though interesting in themselves as showing Wolsey's conception of reform, were not drastic and were probably not observed. Other clouds, however, were soon on the horizon. The years after 1529 were full of vital changes, with rumours of more impending, and even if we had no further knowledge we might guess that it was not a time when a great monastery could prosper in peace of spirit while its head spent his days among the rewards and fairies of Grimley. In fact, the cathedral priory was not at peace, and the interplay within its walls of selfishness and frailty with the designs of the powerful minister who for some years before the end had been receiving a large annual fee from the prior, might be taken as an exemplary instance of the combination of agencies that brought about the downfall of the monasteries. Sources of friction and weakness, which had existed for decades or centuries without fatal consequences, were now to bring the fabric down.

We shall glance on a later page at the last days of Worcester. The prior himself, so far as can be gathered from the copious available evidence, was not directly responsible. His life, though it may have had little of the monastic in it, was morally blameless. His expenses, if occasionally large, and if sometimes they exceeded his income, were not ruinous or prodigal, and the general impression to be gained from his Journal is that of a good administrator, open-handed but alert. In all respects he was the child of his age. When the moment came, he and his community duly subscribed to the Oath of Succession and to the series of declarations repudiating the pope. He followed, in fact, both for good and for evil, the way of the world.

1 The visitation took place on 8 April 1525. The injunctions are printed by Canon J. M. Wilson in 'The Visitations and Injunctions of Cardinal Wolsey and Archbishop Cranmer'. The first of Wolsey's injunctions (p. 360) is that the subprior and cellarer are deprived of office. These were presumably Neckham and Fordham, perhaps already suspended by More. Cranmer's visitation took place 17–19 August 1534 (*v. Journal*, 391), not 14 August as stated by Wilson, *op. cit.* 357. The injunctions are printed by Canon Wilson, pp. 364–7. Latimer's visitation is in W. H. Frere, *Visitation Articles and Injunctions of the Period of the Reformation*, II, 12–14.

CHAPTER X

BUTLEY AND DURHAM

I. THE BUTLEY CHRONICLE

A monastic chronicle of the decades immediately preceding the Dissolution is so rare as to be almost unique; the register of Butley Priory, therefore, though in itself jejune, and rendered still more so by curtailment in transmission, deserves for this reason alone a brief mention.

Butley, a house of Austin canons founded in 1171 by Ranulf Glanvil, had enjoyed throughout its history an uneventful and tolerably prosperous existence.[1] It lay at the head of a creek in East Suffolk between Aldeburgh and Felixstowe, where the salt marshes gave way to heath and rough pasture, and these in turn to the great oaks and solitary rides of Staverton forest. The tidal waters in the medieval centuries washed the timbers of a wharf within little more than a hundred yards of the monastery, and stone for the fabric of the church had been floated thither from the valley of the Yonne in France. The fabric was large, and the endowment substantial from both manors and churches in the neighbourhood. The armorial frieze of the gatehouse, one of the most remarkable works of its kind to survive, is an impressive instance both of the ability of a remote house to commission craftsmen of the first rank and of the ramifications of its patronage among the regional nobility and gentry. Appropriately enough, the relations of the house with these people is one of the chief interests of the chronicle.

The short register or chronicle,[2] in form a mixture of both types of book, runs from 1510 to 1535 and was probably the work of the subprior, William Woodbridge. The author has no pretensions to historical skill, and he lacks altogether the humanistic facility of composing in classical Latin which was not uncommon at the time; his entries are of interest partly for a few vivid glimpses of daily life, partly for the number of names and dates they add to East Anglian *fasti*, and partly for the impression they give of a languid religious life being overtaken unawares by great events.

The last forty years of Butley's life are tolerably well documented. Besides the chronicle, there is record of four visitations between 1505 and 1535 by the long-lived Bishop Nykke of Norwich or his commissioners,[3]

---

1 For Butley, v. art., 'Butley Priory', by J. N. L. Myres, in *AJ*, xc, and 'Butley Priory' by the same writer in *Oxford Essays in Medieval History presented to H. E. Salter*. For the gatehouse, v. articles, 'The later history of the priory and the gatehouse', by W. J. Caroë, in *AJ*, xc, 229–81, and an heraldic description by J. G. Mann in *Country Life*, 25 March 1933.

2 This has been edited with a long and informative introduction as *The Register or Chronicle of Butley Priory, Suffolk, 1510–1535*, by Professor A. G. Dickens.

3 *Norwich Visitations*, ed. A. Jessopp, 131, 177, 216, 285.

and notices and correspondence concerning two elections and the process
of dissolution. The economic scene is illustrated both by the *Valor* and
by a catalogue of the household at the moment of liquidation.[1] From all
this a fairly coherent picture is obtained of a community, peaceful and
observant when compared with many of the decayed or sordid houses of
canons in Norfolk and Suffolk, but mediocre in talent and spirituality, and
showing no disposition or capacity to oppose the forces that were gradually
to overwhelm it.

The priory had a gross income of about £400, and a community of
some twelve canons and a prior; it was therefore comfortably off, and as
it also enjoyed efficient administration during the period covered by the
chronicle it was never in any serious straits. Building and furnishing
continued; a prior's house had recently been built, a new infirmary was
ordered at a visitation and apparently constructed; the roof of the great
chamber of the prior collapsed entirely in February 1531, and was repaired
by Pentecost, and in the same year most of the kitchen roof was destroyed
by fire and repaired in three weeks; this kitchen had itself been built only
a dozen years previously.[2] In the church the rood fell and was repaired,
organs great and small were repaired in 1511, when an organ with two stops
was presented to the Lady Chapel, and in 1534 the prior installed at his
own expense a new organ with five stops.[3]

To the reader of the present day perhaps the most interesting entries
are those recounting the visits of patrons and the great. The first of these
to be recorded was that in 1516 of the twenty-year-old Mary Tudor who,
after a brief year as Queen of France, had given herself *en secondes noces*,
in spite of her royal brother's disapproval, to Charles Brandon, Duke of
Suffolk. She was received with the usual ceremonial accorded to exalted
personages, and the chronicler records the copes and procession, with
lights, incense, holy water, silk cushions and the rest.[4] Then, after an
interval, we hear of the visit of Thomas, third Duke of Norfolk, in 1526.
He arrived on Sunday, 16 September, in time for supper, with William,
Lord Willoughby (who was to die a month later), and forty others, and
after dinner on the following day spent the afternoon and evening till ten
o'clock hunting the fox in Scuttegrove Wood with his friends and their
sons. On Tuesday he took a survey of other woods, and the prior, who
was soon to purchase land from him, rode with him. The Duke was at
Butley again in July 1529, with the young Earl of Surrey and twenty-three
servants.[5] The following year the Duchess of Suffolk was at Butley once
more. She and her husband arrived in the evening of 12 July and stayed,
save for short visits to friends, until 22 August.[6] That month provided
seasonable weather, and the queen (as the chronicler calls her) took her

---

1 Printed by Dickens, 71–3. It may be noted that Prior Thomas Sudbury of Butley
(1529–38) became bishop of Ipswich in 1536.

2 *Ibid.* 59, 35.   3 *Ibid.* 47, 28, 66.   4 *Ibid.* 33.
5 *Ibid.* 50.   6 *Ibid.* 51–2.

supper on several evenings in the various gardens that clustered to the east of the claustral buildings; probably the officials concerned bore part, at least, of the charges and sat at the ducal table. On the last recorded occasion, 21 August, when the party met in the sacrist's garden north of the church, a heavy storm broke up the *al fresco* meal; the tables were carried into the church which, it is to be hoped, resisted the weather more efficiently than complaints at a previous year's visitation had suggested.[1] The queen, we are told, gave half-a-crown at two solemn Masses, and five shillings when she departed to sample Benedictine hospitality at Eye. Next year the ducal pair returned on 11 September, and two days later hunted the fox in Staverton park, where they had dinner and games under the oaks. A week later they repeated the performance in Scuttegrove wood, with a successful supper, and the queen remained till 16 November.[2] During this stay she made offerings which reached the convenient accounting total of 16s. 8d.; this even sum can hardly have been by chance, as the odd eightpence was contributed as a parting gift. The death of the duchess is duly recorded in 1535, when it was apparently hoped that the obsequies would be at Butley. In the event, Bury St Edmunds had that distinction, and the prior of Butley had to be content with singing the epistle at the solemn requiem.[3]

Too much should not be made of these social events, spread over a long space of time. It may even be that it was their rarity that earned them a record, and in any case such functions, nowadays as ever, are the food of mediocre chroniclers. In one respect, times had changed but little since the first fathers of Cîteaux stood firm against the feudal lord of the land holding his court in the monastery. More significant, perhaps, is the characteristic Tudor exploitation of a religious house without any evidence of gratitude or patronage of its best interests.

II. THE RITES OF DURHAM

The Journal of Prior More of Worcester allowed us to see, as in a frame, the very texture of the fabric in which was woven the pattern of daily life at a great monastery on the eve of suppression. With all its limitations and omissions, it is something we can handle and hold to the light, as one feels the roughness and knots of a web and notes the varied and irregular flaws

---

1 *Ibid.* 52: 'Et 21 die Augusti in Orto fratris Nicholai ex parte boriali Ecclesiae hujus, scilicet ante Cenae finem coacta fuit Ecclesiam intrare et cenam ibidem finivit pluvia pre nimia.' Cf. *Norwich Visitations* (26 June 1526), 217: 'ecclesia conventualis est ruinosa in tectura videlicet plumbo et pluit in diversis locis in ecclesia'.

2 *Ibid.* 54: 'Regina et Dux...vulpes apud parcum de Staverton venati sunt et ibidem Prandium suum sub Quercubus sumpsere cum Joco et Ludo satis Jucundis...et die veneris ...equitabant ad boscum vocatum Stuttegrove Wood vulpes venantes et ibidem prandium suum cordis jocunditate et alacritate sumebant.' The editor, perhaps inadvertently, gives the impression (p. 23) that Lady Mounteagle stayed behind at Butley for her confinement; it is clear (p. 55) that she remained at Glemham.

3 *Ibid.* 60 and n. 8.

of colour. A very different picture is given by another document, more than half a century later in date, that has had the fortune to survive. This is the so-called *Rites of Durham*,[1] a detailed but in many ways incomplete and disorderly account of the ritual and other furnishings of the cathedral church, and of certain ceremonies connected with them, together with a summary description of the monastic buildings and an account of the duties of some of the monastic officials shortly before the suppression of the house.

The compilation is anonymous, but the year of composition is given as 1593, and nothing in the book is inconsistent with such a date. The familiarity shown throughout not only with the customs of the monastery and with the names of the monastic and other officials, but with details of the furniture and daily practices which had long since been removed or changed, offers a strong indication that the writer is drawing upon his own recollections. Fifty-eight years had passed since Cromwell's visitors had made their first appearance at Durham, bringing with them the beginning of sorrows for those who wished no novelty, but an old man of seventy-five or upwards might have retained a very vivid memory of half-a-dozen or more impressionable years on one side or other of his twentieth birth-day. Internal evidence would suggest (though no stronger word can be used) that the writer was not a monk himself, though intimately connected with the life of the house and having had access to some of its records.[2] He has been identified with one George Bates, the clerk of the feretory of St Cuthbert and keeper of the priory register shortly before and after the Dissolution, but the evidence for this is not compelling.[3] Whoever he may

1 The *Rites of Durham* is a treatise without title or author's name, contained in a number of manuscripts both at Durham itself and in private hands. The relationship of these to each other has not been fully worked out, but the oldest is certainly a manuscript roll of c. 1595 apparently written by two or more otherwise unknown scribes, and beginning at chapter xv, almost one-quarter of the way through the work. Another manuscript, containing the whole treatise, was written c. 1620 and came shortly after that date into the hands of the excellent Cosin, not yet bishop of Durham, who emended it in places and added notes in sympathy with the author. The date of composition appears to be fixed by a statement that 'the collection of this memorial of Antiquitie was in the year of our Lord god A thousand five hundreth Nuntie & thre', which statement follows closely upon a reference to an event which took place 'of laite in the yeare...1589'. The author nowhere gives any indication of his identity or alludes to any personal experience; a note in one of the manuscripts (*Rites*, ed. Fowler, xiv) said to be in the hand of the Cambridge antiquary, the northerner Thomas Baker (*ob.* 1740), identifies him with 'George Bates the last Register of the house', adding that there are indications of this in the book itself. George Bates and his duties certainly figure more than once (e.g. 78, 94), but the present writer does not feel that the attribution is at all certain. The *Rites*, which had been printed in part in 1672, was one of the first documents to be published by the Surtees Society, as edited by James Raine the elder in 1844. This volume had fallen out of the market before the end of the century and was still in demand; it was therefore re-edited in 1903 by Canon Fowler, who used additional manuscripts and added copious and very valuable notes. He did not, however, attack the question of authorship. References in what follows are given to this second edition.

2 Allusions to the monks and their ceremonies and their edifying life seem to indicate a spectator rather than an actor; post-Dissolution events, on the other hand, seem to be described by an eye-witness who was not a member of the new capitular foundation.

3 *Rites*, 29, and *supra*, n. 1, for the date of compilation.

have been, he was a man of the old way of thinking in religion, as were so many in Durham and about the neighbourhood. Though his aim is antiquarian, not controversial, and though he avoids harsh personal or doctrinal references, his sympathies are warmly with the past, and he uses the old, traditional phrases, as when he speaks of 'the Blessed sacrament' or 'our blessed Ladie', or refers to the 'godlie Religiousnes of monasticall life' of the past. Moreover, his language, when writing of the monks and their ceremonies, is always sympathetic and uncritical, and we shall surely be right in thinking of him as a Catholic at heart and probably also in action, still moving about the cathedral and its precinct, but never reconciled to the destruction of so much beauty and dignified ceremonial that had been part of his daily experience in the morning of life.

Many of the details from his pages have been cited elsewhere in these volumes, but it may be worth while to give a glimpse of the whole picture. It is precisely that which a loyal and simple-minded dependant might be expected to paint, without any theological or spiritual depth, but with a tenacious memory in which past sunshine lingers. Several of his vignettes are familiar from frequent quotation by apologists of recent years:

Over against the said Treasure house door, there was a fair great stall of wainscott where the Novices did sitt and learn, and also the master of the Novices had a pretty stall or seat of wainscott adjoyning on the south side of the Treasure house door over against the stall where the Novices did sitt and look on their bookes, and there did sitt and teach the said Novices both forenoon and afternoon, and also there were no strangers nor other persons suffered to molest or trouble any of the said Novices or Monkes in their Carrells, they being studying on their bookes within the Cloyster, for there was a Porter appointed to keep the Cloyster door for the same use and purpose....[1]

Also the mounckes was accustomed every daie aftere thei dyned to goe thorowgh the cloister ... to the centorie [cemetery] garth wher all the mounckes was buried, and ther did stand all bair heade a Certain longe Space, praieng amongst the Toumbes and throwghes [grave-slabs] for there brethren soules being buryed there, and when they hadd done there prayers then they did Returne to the cloyster, and there did studie there bookes untill iii of the clocke that they went to Evensong.[2]

The said mounckes weare the onelie writers of all the actes and deades of the bushoppes and priors of the abbey[3] church of Durham, and of all the Cronacles and stories: and also did write and sett furth all thinges that was wourthie to be noted, what actes and what miracles was done in every yere and in what moneth. Which there doinges were most manifestly and vndoubtedlie to be[4] most Just and trewe and was alwaies most vertuouslie occupied, never Idle, but either writing of good and goddly wourkes or studying the holie scriptures to the setting furthe of the honour and glorie of god, and for the edifieinge of the

---

1 *Ibid.* 84–5. In all the passages which follow the spelling, with its many inconsistencies, follows Fowler's text. 2 *Ibid.* 87.

3 Durham, though never an independent house under an abbot, is frequently given the title of abbey in medieval documents, and this has survived in local use till recent times.

4 So Fowler's text, but some omission would seem to have taken place.

people, as well in example of good life and conversac'on, as by preaching the worde of god. Thus yow may se and perceave howe the mounckes and Religious men wer occupied in most godly writing and other exercissis in auncient tyme.[1]

Within the fermery in onnder neth the master of the fermeryes chamber was a stronge presonne...the which was ordeyned for all such as weere greate offenders as yf any of the Mounckes had bene taiken with any felony or in any adultrie he should haue syttin ther in presonne for the space of one hole yere in chynes without any company, except the master of the fermery who did let downe there meate thorowgh a trap Dour in a corde, being a great distance from them....[2]

There was a famous house of hospitallitie called the geste haule with in the abbey garth of Durham on the weste syde towardes the water...ther interteynment not being inferior to any place in Ingland, both for the goodness of ther diete, the sweete and daintie furneture of there Lodginges, and generally all thinges necessarie for traveillers....This haule is a goodly brave place much like unto the body of a church with verey fair pillers supporting yt on ether syde and in the mydest of the haule a most large Raunge for the fyer.[3]

On the right hand as yow goe out of the cloysters in to the fermery was the commone house and a Maister thereof, the house being to this end, to haue a fyre keapt in yt all wynter for the Mounckes to cume and warme them at, being allowed no fyre but that onely. Except the Maisters and officers of the house who had there severall fyres. There was belonging to the common house a garding and a bowlinge allie on the Backe side of the said house towardes the water for the Nouyces Sume tymes to recreat them selves when they had remedy[4] of there maister he standing by to se ther good order. Also within this howse dyd the maister therof keepe his o Sapientia ones in the yeare, viz.: Betweixt Martinmes and christinmes (a sollemne banquett that the prior and couent dyd use at that tyme of the yere onely) wher ther Banquett was of figes and reysinges aile and caikes and thereof no superflwitie or excesse but a scholasticall and moderat congratulac'on amonges them selves.[5]

These idyllic glimpses of monastic life were undoubtedly intended to present an aspect of the past that controversialists and pamphleteers of the preceding fifty years had neglected, and they cannot be taken as a complete picture. The old conservative, however, is not primarily an apologist, but a ritualist and an antiquary, and some of his pages give a more vivid impression of the interior of a great monastic church than can be found elsewhere.

His [i.e. St Cuthbert's] sacred shrine was exalted with most curious workmanshipp of fine and costly green marble all limned and guilted with gold hauinge

1 *Rites*, 88.
2 *Ibid*. 89. The language is vague and does not imply a recent or habitual use of the prison. Visitation records of the early sixteenth century suggest that such drastic penalties had become very rare if not almost unknown by that time, but it is conceivable that the prison was used for cases of violent lunacy.   3 *Ibid*. 89–90.
4 Remedy, in the sense of 'recreation', 'holiday', is still current at Winchester College.
5 *Ibid*. 88–9. This passage seems to reflect a somewhat blurred memory. The monks as well as the novices doubtless used the bowling green, and the feast mentioned was only one of several.

foure seates or places conuenient under the shrine for the pilgrims or lame men sittinge on theire knees to leane and rest on, in time of theire deuout offeringes and feruent prayers to God and holy St Cuthbert, for his miraculous releife and succour which beinge neuer wantinge made the shrine to bee so richly inuested, that it was estimated to bee one of the most sumptuous monuments in all England, so great were the offerings and Jewells that were bestowed uppon it, and no lesse the miracles that were done by it, euen in theise latter dayes....In the time of deuine seruice they were accustomed to drawe upp the couer of St Cuthbert's shrine beinge of Wainescott wherevnto was fastned vnto every corner of the said Cover to a loope of Iron a stronge Cord which Cord was all fest together over the Midst over the Cover. And a strong rope was fest vnto the loopes or bindinge of the said Cordes which runn upp and downe in a pully under the Vault which was aboue over St Cuthbert's feretorie for the drawinge upp of the Cover of the said shrine, and the said rope was fastned to a loope of Iron in the North piller of the ferretory: haueing six silver bells fastned to the said rope, soe as when the cover of the same was drawinge upp the belles did make such a good sound that itt did stirr all the peoples harts that was within the Church to repaire unto itt and to make ther praiers to God and holy St Cuthbert, and that the behoulders might see the glorous ornam'ts therof:... which cover was all gilded over and of eyther side was painted fower lively Images curious to the beholders and on the East End was painted the picture of our Saviour sittinge on a Rainebowe to geive Judgment very lively to the behoulders and on the West end of itt was the picture of our Lady and our Saviour on her knee And on the topp of the Cover from end to end was most fyne brattishing [i.e. cornice] of carved worke cutt owte with Dragons and other beasts moste artificially wrought and the inside was Vernished with a fyne sanguine colour that itt might be more perspicuous to the beholders.[1]

The shrine lay immediately behind the high altar, and in front of it those in the monastic choir would have seen the pyx containing the Sacred Host which, as generally in England, was not reserved in an aumbry but suspended over the *mensa*:

Within the said quire ouer the high Altar did hang a rich and most sumptuous Canapie for the Blessed sacrament to hang within it which had 2 irons fastened in the french peere [i.e. *franche pierre*, freestone] uery finely gilt which held the canapie ouer the midst of the said high Altar...wheron did stand a pellican all of siluer uppon the height of the said Canopie uerye finely gilded giuinge hir bloud to hir younge ones, in token that Christ did giue his bloud for the sinns of the world, and it was goodly to behould for the blessed sacrament to hange in, and a marueilous faire pix that the holy blessed sacrament did hange in which was of most pure fine gold most curiously wrought of gold smith worke, and the white cloth that hung ouer the pix was of uerye fine lawne all embroydered and wrought aboue with gold and red silke, And 4 great and round knopes of gold maruelous and cunningly wrought with great tassells of gold and redd silke hanginge at them, and at the 4 corners of the white lawne cloth. And the crooke that hung within the cloth that the pix did hang on was of gold and the cords that did draw it upp and downe was made of fine white strong silke.[2]

1 *Ibid.* 3–5. 2 *Ibid.* 8.

Yet both shrine and pyx would have been hidden from Maundy Thursday till a week after Ascension Day by the vast erection known as The Paschal:

Also there was a goodly monument pertaininge to the Church called the pascall . . . that did stand uppon a foure square thick planke of wood . . . before the high altar . . . and at euerye corner of the planke was an iron ringe wherunto the feete of the pascall were adioyned, representinge the pictures of the foure flyinge dragons, as also the pictures of the 4 Euangelists aboue the tops of the dragons underneath the nethermost bosse, all supportinge the whole pascall and in the 4 quarters haue beene foure Christall stones, and in the 4 small dragons 4 heads 4 christall stones as by the holes doe appeare[1] and on euerye side of the 4 dragons there is curious antick work as beasts and men uppon horsbacks with bucklers bowes and shafts, and knotts with broad leaues spred upon the knotts uery finely wrought all beinge of most fine and curious candlestick mettall glistring as the Gold it self having six. . . . Flowers . . . comminge from it three of euerye side wheron did stand in euerye of the said flowers . . . a taper of wax and on the height of the said candlestick or pascall . . . was a faire large flower beinge the principall flower which was the 7 candlestick; the pascall in latitude did containe almost the bredth of the quire, in longitude that did extend to the height of the uault, wherein did stand a long peece of wood reachinge within a mans length to the uppermost uault roofe of the church, wheron stood a great long square taper of wax called the pascall; a fine conueyance through the said roofe of the church to light the taper withall; in conclusion the pascall was estimated to bee one of the rarest monuments in all England.[2]

Involved as this description may be, the impression given is one of very great magnificence. Scarcely less impressive is the account of the ceremony on Easter morning, a relic from the distant past of Dunstan's England and the monasteries of the Dark Ages that has never found a place in the Roman rite:

There was in the abbye church of duresme uerye solemne seruice uppon easter day betweene 3 and 4 of the clocke in the morninge in honour of the resurrection where 2 of the oldest monkes of the quire came to the sepulchre, beinge sett upp upon good friday after the passion all couered with redd uelvett and embrodered with gold, and then did sence it either monke with a paire of siluer sencors sittinge on theire knees before the sepulchre, then they both risinge came to the sepulchre, out of the which with great reverence they tooke a maruelous beautifull Image of our saviour representinge the resurrection with a crosse in his hand in the breast wherof was enclosed in bright Christall the holy sacrament of the altar, throughe the which christall the blessed host was conspicuous to the behoulders, then after the eleuation of the said picture carryed by the said 2 monkes uppon a faire ueluett cushion all embroidered singinge the anthem of christus resurgens they brought to the high altar settinge that on the midst therof . . . the which anthem beinge ended the 2 monkes tooke up the

---

1 The wording suggests that the despoiled base of the candlestick was still preserved in the church when this passage was written. The whole description recalls metalwork of the early twelfth century such as that of the much smaller Gloucester candlestick in the Victoria and Albert Museum.   2 *Rites*, 10–11.

cushines and the picture from the altar supportinge it betwixt them, proceeding in procession from the high altar to the south quire dore where there was 4 antient gentlemen belonginge to the prior appointed to attend theire comminge holdinge upp a most rich cannopye of purple ueluett tasled round about with redd silke, and gold fringe, and at euerye corner did stand one of theise ancient gentlemen to beare it ouer the said Image, with the holy sacrament carried by two monkes round about the church, the whole quire waitinge uppon it with goodly torches and great store of other lights, all singinge reioyceinge and praisinge god most deuoutly till they came to the high altar againe, wheron they did place the said Image there to remaine untill the assencion day.[1]

The writer then passes in review many of the altars and decorations of the church, dwelling especially on the Jesus altar before the great rood at the entry of the choir:

Also there was in the hight of the said wall from piller to piller the whole storie and passion of our Lord wrowghte in stone most curiously and most fynely gilte, and also aboue the said storie and passion was all the whole storie and pictures of the xii apostles verie artificiallye sett furth and verie fynelie gilte contening from the one piller to thother, a border very artificially wrowght in stone with marvelous fyne coulers verye curiouslye and excellent fynly gilt with branches and flowres, the more that a man did looke on it the more was his affection to behold yt. . . and also aboue the hight of all upon the waule did stande the most goodly and famous Roode that was in all this land, with the picture of Marie on thone syde, and the picture of John on thother, with two splendent and glisteringe archangels one on thone syde of Mary, and the other of the other syde of Johne, so what for the fairness of the wall the staitlynes of the pictures and the lyuelyhoode of the paynting it was thowght to be one of the goodliest monuments in that church.[2]

When he comes to describe the Galilee the writer is at pains to make it clear that there were sermons in the cathedral of a Sunday long before Dean Whittingham came back from Geneva:

Euery sonnday in the yere there was a sermon preched [by one of the monks] in the gallely at after none from one of the clocke till iii and at xii of the clock the great Bell of the gelleley was toulled euery sonndaie iii quarters of an howre and roung the forth quarter till one of the clock, that all the people of the towne myght haue warnyng to come and here the worde of god preached. . . ii men of the kitching was charged with the Ringing of on Bell, and the iiii men of the church that dyd lye allwayes in the church was charged with the Ringing of the third Bell, and vi othere was alwaies charged with the Rynging of the great Bell, viz., ii of the back howse, ii of the Brew house and ii of the killne. And in the latter dayes of kyng Henrie the eighte the house was supprest, and after that tyme the said Bells was neuer Rounge.[3]

The bells thus hanging idle were, we are told, noticed by the Calvinistic dean, who determined to break them up and sell them as scrap metal. The suffragan bishop of Berwick, Thomas Sparke, however, sometime monastic

1 *Ibid.* 12–13.   2 *Ibid.* 33.   3 *Ibid.* 39.

chamberlain of the priory, was too quick for him, and had three of the bells removed to form a chime in the belfry of the central tower. The writer goes on to describe the Lady Mass in the Galilee:

With in the said gallelei in the Cantarie being all of most excellent blewe marble stood our Ladies alter, a verie sumptuous Monument fynly adorned with curious wainscott woorke both aboue the head, at the back, and at either end of the said alter, the wainscott being devised and furnished with most heavenly pictures so lyuely in cullers and gilting as that they did gretly adorne the said alter where our Ladies masse was song daly by the master of the song scole, with certaine decons and quiristers, the master playing upon a paire of faire orgaines the tyme of our Ladies messe.[1]

These extracts will have made it clear that the sympathies of the writer lay with the old world. He had lived to see all these things go—the shrine of St Cuthbert dismantled by the commissioners of Henry VIII under the expert eyes of 'skilfull lapidaries';[2] he had seen the plate taken away for melting, and the vestments to furnish brocades and velvets for the mercers; he had seen the retables defaced and the altars despoiled. He had seen Dean Whittingham tearing up the tombs of the priors, breaking up the brasses and carved chalices and carrying away 'the Residewe' to 'make a washinge howse of many of them for women Landerers to washe in', and had watched him uprooting from the pavement of the cathedral 'two Holy Water stones of fyne marble very artificially made and graven' in order that they might be 'caryed into his kitching and put vnto profayne uses: and ther stoode during his liffe in which stones thei dyd stepe ther beefe and salt fysh'.[3] He traces for us the further progress of these stoups; the larger one passed from the kitchen of the deanery to the buttery and finally, in part, to 'Lambes shop the black smyth vpon fframygaite brige end'. As for the lesser one, it had been found so useful by Mrs Whittingham (née Calvin) that on moving out of the deanery after her bereavement she 'browght yt into her howse in the bayly and sett it there in her kitchinge'.[4]

For all his love of the old ways (perhaps, indeed, because of his love of them) the writer gives evidence enough that life in the cathedral monastery was dignified rather than austere. The monks of Durham, as we can learn also from their copious account rolls, were living on 'wages' in a monastery that had been made tolerably comfortable by Tudor standards. The anchorite in the cathedral[5] and the prisoner in the dungeon were alike legendary figures. Yet, whatever their life may have held of ease and mediocrity, the beauty of the setting remained, and the display on high days and holy seasons of the treasures of artists and craftsmen that the centuries had accumulated. The lights still 'did burne continually both day and night' in the great cressets before the high altar, 'In token that

1 *Rites*, 43–4.　　2 *Ibid.* 102.　　3 *Ibid.* 60–1.　　4 *Ibid.* 61.
5 *Ibid.* 17: 'The Amanchoridge...being in antient time inhabited with an Anchorite.'

the house was alwayes watchinge to god',[1] and the sound of bells at mid-night 'in the lanthorne called the new worke',[2] clear in the magical silence of midsummer or borne fitfully across the Wear in winter storms, gave assurance to the townspeople and the countryside 'in the deep night that all was well'. In the great church itself the shrines of St Cuthbert and of Bede the Venerable took the mind back to the earliest days of the faith in Northumbria, while the silver pyx with its lights bore witness to a presence more sacred than that of the Temple. Throughout the days and years sunlight and taperlight had rested upon the blue and gold and crimson and cream and silver of the vestments and vessels. The old con-servative did not live to see the final desecration, when thousands of Scottish prisoners, famished, sick and dying, tore down the screens and tabernacle work for firewood, and filled the cathedral with flame and smoke,[3] but he had seen the shrine and the pyx disappear. The glory had departed from Durham, for the ark of God had been taken away.

1 *Ibid.* 14.   2 *Ibid.* 22.
3 *Ibid.* (a later insertion).

Part Two

The Gathering Storm

CHAPTER XI

ERASMUS

Although the story of the suppression of the monasteries in England has been told repeatedly and by writers of very different views and aims, what may be called the pre-history of the destruction of the religious life and the denial of its ideals has never been studied in any detail. English historians, whatever period of history may be their theme, have always shown themselves reluctant to look beyond the Channel for the well-springs of currents of English thought and action, and not only the suppression of the monasteries, but the whole great political, social and religious revolution of which it was a part has very generally been treated as if it were a relatively sudden and entirely insular affair. Many of the most familiar accounts of the Reformation in England take their start well on in the reign of Henry VIII, and make little allowance of influences from abroad before the emergence of Luther.

With the Reformation and its distant origins we are not directly concerned, but even such a small part of the revolution as the suppression of the monasteries has a wide background. It may indeed be true that the last decisive impulse was due to purely material considerations as they appeared to an all-powerful minister, but the ease with which the work was done, the propaganda by which it was accompanied, the general acquiescence with which it was received, and it may be added, the facility with which the consent of the king was obtained, can only be explained by the presence of ideas unsympathetic to the traditional framework of religious society in the minds of the generality of the small class of Englishmen who inspired or criticized high policy. It has, indeed, often been said by critics abroad that Englishmen are prone to attribute all their actions of public policy to a zeal for righteousness; certainly, the destruction of the monasteries has often been attributed to the inevitable, if long delayed, eruptions of moral indignation at the sight of luxury and vice. Yet even if the existence of such corruption be granted, history can show few if any examples of a great revolution (which is by definition a sudden phenomenon) accomplished solely by moral indignation. Revolutions are rather the final transference into the clumsy and intractable medium of action of ideas that have been germinating long enough to affect the mental climate of an epoch.

The mental climate that could approve, or at least tolerate, the disappearance of the monastic ideal, seen in all the varieties of the religious life, had been constituted in part by the fusion of two great streams of thought. There was what may be called, for want of a better term, the radical, puritanical current, impossible to define and manifesting itself chiefly by its antagonism to ecclesiastical institutions of every kind—to the sacraments, to the hierarchical, mediating priesthood, and to classes and degrees among those calling themselves Christians. The ancestry of such an outlook was long, reaching back at least as far as the twelfth century to the Waldenses, the Poor Catholics and the Humiliati of Lombardy, Provence and the Rhineland; it had been given full citizenship in England by Wyclif and the Lollards, and it has endured as a powerful and even as a characteristic force for four centuries wherever the so-called Anglo-Saxon culture has penetrated. In its extreme form, as enunciated by Wyclif and preserved by his followers, it reprobated any set of man-made rules and practices as unwarranted complications of the simplicity of the gospel, and regarded monks and friars as deviating from the pure ideal of the Christian and hence as intrinsically harmful. How strong this current was in the first decades of sixteenth-century England is extremely difficult to say, since those who held such views were invariably heretics on other counts, and remained on the whole mute and elusive until the invading flood of Lutheranism gave them courage and a voice.

The second great current, hitherto unduly neglected, yet undoubtedly very pervasive and powerful in the higher and educated levels of society, whence came the wielders of power and the diffusers of propaganda, was the new enlightenment, of which Colet and More were early English representatives, but of which Erasmus was above all others the prophet. This was a more complex stream, of which the waters can be made susceptible of infinite analysis, but no account of early Tudor England can afford to leave it out of the reckoning.

Its head may be found in the religious movement originating in what is now the heart of Holland towards the end of the fourteenth century, with its centre at Deventer around Gerard Groot and the Brethren of the Common Life, expanding into the Augustinian congregation of Windesheim and the schools of the Low Countries, and expressing itself in a phase of religious sentiment which came to be known as the *devotio moderna*.[1] This, while fully Catholic and orthodox, was, if the minds of those who adopted it could be analysed by some psychological spectroscope, at one extreme of the range of colours in which the Spanish-Italian minds of the Counter-Reformation occupied the place furthest removed in the opposite direction. It was an orthodoxy which accepted but set little store by the hierarchical framework of the Church, with its technical discipline of theology and complicated machinery of canon law, with the world-wide resources of the papacy and the policies of the centralized orders; which preferred in their stead the family, the group of associates, or the independent houses of Austin canons, as the foci of religious action, and turned from elaborate liturgical services and fixed ceremonial practices and scholastic meditations to the simple, direct imitation of Christ which, as

1 There is no satisfactory and complete account in English of the *devotio moderna*, but the subject is touched upon by E. F. Jacob in *Essays in the Conciliar Epoch*, 121–53.

often among peoples of Germanic origin, could on occasion lose its dogmatic firmness and become an emotional pietism, but which in its most characteristic form could rise, in the school of Thomas à Kempis, to a classical expression of Christian and Catholic life, accepted as such even by a St Teresa and a St Ignatius. Although Gerard Groot had known Ruysbroeck and spent some years in a Charterhouse, the Brethren of the Common Life and the canons of Windesheim drew apart from the mystical traditions of Eckhart, Tauler and the Dominicans and Carthusians of the Rhineland, and the mystical element still present in the *Imitatio Christi* is not typical of the latter half of the fifteenth century.

As this century wore on, the *devotio moderna* extended its influence and in part changed its character. One of the forms it took, significant in view of later developments, was a piety based on a reading of the synoptic gospels and St Paul rather than on the theological doctrines expressed by the definitions of the Church; this tended to emphasize the practices of primitive Christianity as revealed in the career and writings of the Apostle, and tended to seek in the gospels the simple, human, historic incidents rather than the declaration of theological truths or the recognition of types and symbols and prophecies that had formed such a large part of medieval exegesis. It was probably from this wind of sentiment, rather than from direct Wycliffian teaching, that Colet first drew his taste for the simple exposition of Scripture, and of St Paul in particular, as also his distaste for pomps and ceremonies of all kinds.

This piety of Deventer, streaming southwards towards the end of the fifteenth century, encountered another current flowing northwards from Italy, that of the critical, historical and philological approach to the New Testament elaborated by Lorenzo Valla[1] and his imitators. The Brethren of the Common Life had always been great educators, and their pupils were therefore well able to receive the scholarship, technically more advanced than theirs, of the Italian and later of the French humanists, now beginning to be diffused by the new invention of printing. When to the purely linguistic and critical analysis of Valla were added the achievements of the humanistic editors and commentators on the early Fathers and historians, it might well seem, in the first flush of enthusiastic discovery, that a scholar now had all the equipment needed for the reconstruction of the framework and attitude of mind of the early Christian Church. This intoxicating New Learning, clothed in the nervous and flexible language of the great humanists, claiming to show for the first time the early age of Christianity in something approaching to a clear historical light, and contrasting so strongly with the outward show of the Church under the Borgia papacy and of the schools dominated by a nominalist theology, produced an intellectual shock comparable to that which the writings of Darwin were to produce upon the sheltered minds of a later generation in England. The

1 Valla's *Annotationes* on the gospels were not printed until 1505, but Erasmus had seen them when a student.

New Learning, indeed, gave to the Wycliffian and Hussite doctrine of the all-sufficiency of Scripture the intellectual instrument that had hitherto been lacking. Individual, 'private', judgment as to the meaning of the Scriptures and the teaching of the early Church seemed no longer, as with the first Lollards, a mere whim or a personal preference. In men of scholarship it could appear to be the inevitable result of the critical examination of literary texts and historical facts.

Among all those influenced by these currents of thought and religious sentiment in north-western Europe one man, in the early years of the sixteenth century, emerged and shone out as at once the standard-bearer and the prophet of his kind. We are not concerned here with Erasmus[1] as the focus of a critical phase of European religious history, still less with his relationship to the leaders of the conservative and revolutionary forces in the great controversy that began at Wittenberg. Erasmus, however, like Voltaire in a later age, was a revolution in himself, and his influence upon all educated men, whether of letters or action, was so individual and so pervasive, that his responsibility in forming a climate of opinion cannot be neglected, least of all by Englishmen since his influence in English circles of thought has been somewhat obscured. While his direct contacts, as a young and still impressionable man, with Colet and More have often been described,[2] the influence upon a younger generation of 'Erasmism' as it appears in his writings and those of his imitators, has rarely been noticed by historians of the English Reformation.

Erasmus, in this respect resembling an Abélard or a Newman, is one of those men of genius whose complex minds present so many facets that any summary judgment stands self-condemned, and any precise label can at once be criticized. With Erasmus, also, as with Newman again or with Cicero, the marvellous style acts as a charm; while he is speaking to us, all criticism is stilled; he has won us, and we cannot believe that the mind of the master is less sincere than his voice, or that his arguments are less adequate than his language. He is so sane, so persuasive, so humane, that

---

1 The literature on Erasmus is enormous, and the varieties of judgment upon him as numerous as the books. Some measure of his influence on his age may be obtained at a glance by referring to the pages occupied by the editions and translations of his works in the catalogue of a great library such as that of the British Museum or Cambridge University. Within the last fifty years the materials for the understanding of his life and mind have been rendered notably more accessible by the monumental edition of his letters by P. S. and H. M. Allen, *Opus Epistolarum D. Erasmi Roterodamensis* (Oxford, 12 vols.; completed by index volume, 1906–58). Reference will henceforth be made to this edition by volume and page. This has given opportunity to M. A. Renaudet to analyse the development of Erasmus's thought, with a justice and penetration never before achieved, in a series of articles and books of which *Études Erasmiennes* (1521–9), published in 1939, is the most valuable for our purpose. At the same time, the researches of M. M. Bataillon, culminating in his great work, *Erasme en Espagne* (Paris, 1937), have served to establish the existence, in the second decade of the sixteenth century, of an 'Erasmian' movement throughout Europe.

2 In particular by F. Seebohm, *The Oxford Reformers* (Oxford, 1887), which, appearing when J. R. Green was at work on his *Short History*, passed substantially into the consciousness of generations at school and university.

it is only with an effort that we can bring ourselves to examine his words for their implications, their ambiguities, and their failure in direct assertion.

Erasmus was accused during his lifetime of heresy, laxism, Lutheranism and double-dealing; his followers were being persecuted and punished in Spain at the very moment when, towards the end of his life, Pope Paul III desired to admit him into the Sacred College; though a succession of popes for thirty years had accepted his dedications, praised his work and requested his aid against the enemies of the Roman Church, his books, long after his death, were put upon the Roman Index. It was left to the eighteenth century to hail him as the first great rationalist of the modern world.

To-day all would agree that he desired to be, and considered himself to be, an orthodox Catholic throughout his life and to the end;[1] he was in fact so considered by his contemporaries, including all the popes who reigned during his long literary career, and a short time before his death he received, not for the first time, an official hint that a cardinal's hat could be his for the asking.[2] Most historians would also be in agreement that, whatever may be said of the wisdom or theological acumen or moral courage of his decisions as to how to act and write and speak in the face of Luther's assaults, he showed a remarkable consistency throughout his literary life in proposing a certain ideal of the Christian life, and a no less consistent attitude towards all forms of extreme opinion. As to the precise doctrinal formulation of this ideal, however, and still more as to its essential orthodoxy, there has always been a variety of opinion, and writers, both within and without the Catholic Church, have been found to admire it and to reprobate it, to maintain its orthodoxy, and to regard it as subversive of the traditional faith.

Perhaps it would be fairly near the truth to say that while it would not be easy to isolate from his writings any theological proposition that was contrary to any pre-Tridentine formula of doctrine, his whole expression of the Christian revelation, and his attitude to revealed truth, differs very significantly from that of one who follows by instinct or desire the 'mind of the Church'.[3] Thus, while never denying what had been defined, or

1 So much is certain, but the extent of his daily conformity to normal Catholic practice is, like so much about him, obscure. Thus, for example, he undoubtedly approached the Sacrament of Penance at times, but whether he frequented it is another matter; he never abandoned belief in the Real Presence and undoubtedly attended Mass, but whether he habitually offered the Holy Sacrifice as a priest, or communicated, seems unascertainable. He died with words of Christian faith and trust on his lips; Luther's bitter fling that he died *sine cruce, sine luce, sine Deo*, is thus far unjustified; but it does not seem to be either recorded or denied that he asked for, and received, the Last Sacraments. Similarly, the severe judgment of Godet in the *DTC* that Erasmus was a priest 'sans vocation et sans piété, non sans foi', might seem scarcely justified in face of the years spent by Erasmus in editing and commenting upon the New Testament.

2 Cf. *ep.* 3048 (XI, 217) and briefs to Erasmus of Paul III, *ibid.* 3021, 3034 (XI, 137, 188).

3 Perhaps the most sensitive analysis of Erasmus's outlook is that of M. Renaudet, *Études Erasmiennes*, ch. iv, 'Le Modernisme erasmien', esp. pp. 122–30. M. Renaudet writes without a trace of *odium theologicum*, but with a just appreciation of traditional Catholic doctrine, which is, indeed, a necessary condition of any criticism of Erasmus, and without which many otherwise gifted writers have repeated meaningless platitudes.

flouting what had been ordained, by the supreme authority of the Church, he remained as it were agnostic to the thesis that a religious truth could be contained within a theological formula, or a virtuous life regulated by a disciplinary code. He inherited, directly from his Dutch masters, and indirectly from the victorious Nominalism of the previous century, a distrust of metaphysics and of theological speculation and formulation,[1] but for the mysticism and 'fideism' in which many other religious minds took refuge he substituted a positive, practical religious ideal based on the teaching of the gospel as interpreted by personal, critical study of the text,[2] and for the traditional scheme of the soul's holiness deriving from the supernatural virtues and gifts of the Holy Spirit he substituted a picture of the good life in which the moral wisdom of the past, as seen in the ethical writings of Greece and Rome, was joined to the teaching of the early Christian Fathers. The 'philosophy of Christ', which he preaches in the *Enchiridion* and in the *Commentaries* and in many another work, is one in which a wide culture and a humanistic moral outlook form the basis of a life modelled on the gospel teaching presented in a purely human fashion. It is a persuasive, seductive ideal, and Erasmus never denies the need of divine illumination and help for the man who is to live a Christian life, nor does he omit to tell of the price that has been paid by the Son of God on behalf of mankind. Nevertheless, it is impossible to feel satisfied that the theology and ascetical teaching of Erasmus adequately recognize the wholly supernatural plane on which the life of Christ moved,[3] and to which the life of the Christian is potentially elevated by baptism, and joined in fullness by the Holy Eucharist—a life which implies depths of love and wisdom and of redemptive suffering of which the unaided human mind could not dream and to which the unaided human will could not attempt to attain. Similarly, Erasmus never denied the affirmations of the Virgin Birth and the divine motherhood of Mary as defined in his day, but the mother of Christ is for him the young mother of Bethlehem; that in her divine motherhood are contained her Immaculate Conception, her universal advocacy for all, and her supreme excellence among God's creatures, the readers of Erasmus, and Erasmus himself, were far from realizing. His religious ideal, though presented with all the seductive charm of reasonable argument and salted wit and grace of language, is a kind of 'low-tension' Christianity, a de-spiritualized religion, that has

1 Renaudet, *op. cit.* 124, writes of 'son pyrrhonisme un peu sommaire, son goût personnel et profond pour une certaine humilité de pensée en face du mystère du monde', and continues (125): 'Il estime l'esprit humain à jamais incapable de saisir les réalités suprêmes.'

2 *Ibid.* 130, where Renaudet writes of his 'méfiance irréductible à l'égard de toute spéculation; il est une sorte de positivisme théologique, fondé sur la sainte Écriture, et qui demande à la seule Écriture le sens du mystère divin caché dans le monde.'

3 Renaudet, 170–1, remarks justly: 'Pourtant l'esprit de cette critique, si prudent, si respectueuse de tout ce qui représente un effort de la pensée, n'est déjà plus catholique …il affirme trop haut que dans la vie religieuse, l'esprit seul compte, et que le reste est indifférent…on pourra l'accuser d'offrir de Jésus une image trop humaine….Sa conception de la grace est d'un moraliste.'

been well called by a sensitive modern critic the 'modernism' of Erasmus, and it was this that spread far and wide in all the cultivated circles of north-western Europe in the two decades that immediately preceded the papal condemnation of Luther.[1]

The extent of the influence of Erasmus in creating a critical, untraditional climate of mind can scarcely be exaggerated. Perhaps Voltaire is the only writer and thinker in the modern world whose influence on his generation during his lifetime has been so widespread. For our purpose, however, the direct criticisms of Erasmus are more significant than his presentation of the Christian life, or his tireless advocacy of humane learning, or his influence in the field of critical scholarship. There was in him, for all his dislike of violence, a very strong dissolvent force.[2] Indeed, it was the vigorous and determined criticism of what he deemed serious abuses in the Church that earned for him the remorseless enmity of numberless individuals in the groups that were his targets; it was in reaction to his attacks that they formulated their accusations of doctrinal unsoundness. It may perhaps be added, that it is the manner of these attacks, rather than their aim and object, that arouses a feeling of uneasiness in the mind of a reader of to-day. The tireless iteration of the same charges over a space of thirty years and more recalls the not dissimilar methods of Gerald of Wales and John Wyclif; this, and the use of the weapons of satire and irony and fiction, seem to place the great debate upon the dialectical, if not even upon the rhetorical and the recreational level, rather than upon the purely spiritual or even the purely moral one, where the high serious-ness can be maintained that alone carries conviction and troubles con-sciences and so justifies its severity.

Here, we are directly concerned solely with Erasmus's criticisms of the religious life and of those who followed it. Two introductory observations must be made. The first is, that Erasmus had himself in youth entered the

1 Renaudet, 122, thus defines this 'modernism': 'Refus d'admettre que l'intelligence du dogme chrétien ait. . .atteint une formule complète et définitive. Affirmation du bienfait que chaque progrès réalisé dans tout domaine de savoir apporte à la pensée chrétienne. . . .Refus d'admettre que les règles de la vie chrétienne se trouvent à jamais codifiées dans la discipline d'une Eglise; affirmation de l'aide qu'apporte, à la pratique de l'Évangile, chaque progrès réalisé dans l'art de vivre.' True as this is, it could perhaps, like all 'modernism', be put still more succinctly; in the last resort, Erasmus as a theological writer does not fully admit the traditional implication of the doctrine of the Incarnation—the assumption of human nature, Christ's and the Christian's, into the divine life: Christ's by the hypostatic union, the Christian's by the sonship of adoption.

2 The very real difference between the Erasmian and the Lutheran, and still more the Calvinistic, conception of reform and the well-known riposte to Luther's epigram on the origin of the Reformation, must not lead us to suppose, as some writers have suggested, that Erasmus's reformed Church would have been wholly Catholic in character, as would, let us say, Thomas More's. It would be truer, though again an over-simplification, to say that the Erasmian conception of reform mingled with that of Luther in some, at least, of the programmes of the sixteenth century. Even Cranmer, though not by temper an Erasmian, owed something to the great humanist, and Erasmian ideas can be found at various moments in the Anglican and other communions—which is perhaps no more than to say that Erasmus, like Ockham or Descartes, was the first to give firm expression to a way of thought which had perennial appeal.

religious life and assumed its obligations; he had subsequently abandoned his vocation as irksome and uncongenial many years before he obtained the papal dispensation which on the forensic level 'regularized' his position. Whatever the circumstances may have been (and so far as any external judgment can be made at such a distance of time it would seem clear that his entry into religion was neither wholly spontaneous nor wholly spiritual in motive, and that the surroundings in which he found himself were narrow and harsh) there can be little doubt that he retained throughout his life, at least on the subconscious level of his mind, not only a sense that an injustice had been done to him, but also the need to prove to himself that he had lost no opportunity for spiritual progress by abandoning the life of his profession.[1] The second observation is less important, but may serve to prevent misunderstanding. When Erasmus is speaking of the religious life, and even of the monastic life, he has in mind almost invariably the religious who were most in evidence in the urban centres in which almost his whole life was passed, and who were his enemies for the greater part of it. The friars, and especially the Dominican and Franciscan friars, were, as a class, devoted to the formal theology of the schools and were the enemies of the *bonae litterae*, the literary culture and attainments, of the humanists; they were therefore on a double count the opponents of Erasmus, and as the controlling force in academic decisions, and as holding a monopoly of popular preaching, they were in a position to condemn his writings and to stir up indignation against his every action. This type of friar was most numerous in the university towns of the Low Countries, Germany and France; in England though, as we have seen, it was not unknown, the friars were in general less distinguished and therefore less in evidence.

The gravamina of the charges which Erasmus repeated so often in his published writings and his private letters and also, one may suppose, in his private conversations were: that the religious were as a class Pharisees and hypocrites; and that they found in regulations and ceremonies (by which Erasmus understood formal, external practices and prayers of all kinds) the essence, the sign, and the test of sanctity, thus exalting empty observance before mercy and love. This criticism was in fact an application of the leading thesis of Erasmus's *philosophia Christi*: that there was only one way of Christian life, that of following the teaching of the gospel, and only one promise to make to God, that of the baptismal vows. All beyond this might be tolerated in those who found it useful, but was inessential and in general undesirable. This typically 'Erasmic' position which, while not explicitly destroying the traditional Catholic ascetical tradition, nevertheless gave it the go-by as something inessential, may be regarded as a complete reversal on the part of the new learning of the attempt of the Gregorian reformers, St Bernard and even St Francis, to 'monachize' the

---

1 For Erasmus's own account of this, *v*. his autobiographical letter to Gerard Geldenhauer dating from 1523 to 1526 in *ep*. 1436 (v, 427); cf. *ep*. 447 (II, 291).

whole Church. The careful reader of Bernard's Sermons on the Canticle or the genuine writings and sayings of St Francis—and, it may be added, the reader of Walter Hilton's *Scale of Perfection* or à Kempis's *Imitation of Christ*—will be able to judge for himself what justification there was for the charges made by the opponents of Erasmus that he debased and de-spiritualized the following of Christ, by depriving it alike of the arduous degrees of ascent to a perfection beyond that of a human standard, and of the union of the mind and will with God, of the lover with the Beloved, following the Incarnate Word to Calvary, which Christian tradition had always preached as the crown of a Christian's endeavour.

A few extracts from the writings of Erasmus may serve to give precision to these general statements; they will show also that Erasmus, alike in his critical and his creative thought, was consistent, not to say stationary, throughout his literary life. Thus in the *Enchiridion* of 1504 he wrote:

> Indeed, if truth be told, do we not see members of the most austere monastic orders maintaining that the essence of perfection lies in ceremonies or in a fixed quantity of psalmody or in manual labour? And if you come to close quarters with these men and question them on spiritual matters you will scarcely find one who does not walk according to the flesh.... The monastic life should not be equated with the virtuous life: it is just one type of life that may be either advantageous or not according to the individual's dispositions of mind and body. I would no more persuade you to it than I would dissuade you from it.[1]

The same contention, phrased a little more harshly, appears in a letter written to his sometime fellow-religious Servatius Rogerius, once the object of his ardent affection and now, as prior of Steyn, endeavouring to recall Erasmus to his old home: 'I will make bold to say', Erasmus writes,

> that Christian piety has taken no little harm from the so-called religious orders, though their first origins may have been due to genuine devotion.... What can be more loathsome or more impious than these orders when they become relaxed? And if you look at those whose reputation is fair or even excellent I doubt whether you will find anything but cold Jewish ceremonies without a trace of a likeness of Christ.[2] It is in these that they pride themselves, by these that they judge and condemn others....

'There are here', continues Erasmus, writing somewhat more warmly of his Cambridge colleagues than in other letters, 'colleges in which the spirit of religion and the simplicity of life is such that you would think nothing of any religious order in comparison with them, if you could see them'. But perhaps the fullest and most explicit statement is made in the long letter to Paul Volz, himself abbot of the Benedictine house of

---

1 *Enchiridion*, ed. Cantab. (1685), 169–70, 291: 'Monachatus non est pietas, sed vitae genus pro suo cuique corporis ingeniique habitu, vel utile, vel inutile.'

2 *Ep.* 296 (1, 567–8), of 8 July 1514: 'Praeter figuras quasdam et Judaicas caeremonias, haud scio quam Christi reperias imaginem.'

Hügshofen, which Erasmus set as a preface to the new edition of the
Enchiridion published by Froben in 1518:

I do not blame Franciscans or Benedictines for cherishing their Rules, but
I blame those of them who think their Rule more efficacious than the Gospel....
I have no quarrel with them because some live on fish, others on vegetables and
herbs, and others again on eggs, but I do most earnestly warn of their mistake
those who, like the Jews of old, base on such practices a conviction of their own
virtue, and prefer themselves to others on account of trifles of this kind devised
by mortals of no importance,[1] while at the same time they fail to see anything
wrong in attacking the good name of others with calumnies....And I wish
most earnestly that canon law forbade anyone to be caught in snares of this kind
[*sc.* the vows of religion] under the age of thirty, before he has self-knowledge
and before he knows wherein the heart of true religion consists....My own
earnest wish would be (and I am sure all truly devout men would wish the same)
that the religious life of the gospels might be so deeply rooted in the hearts of
men that they would be content with this, and would not seek the Rule of
Benedict or Francis...for I feel that the three vows devised by man could add
very little to one who in purity and sincerity had observed that first and only
vow which we take in baptism, not to man but to Christ.[2]

In these and many similar passages Erasmus launched upon his world
an attitude towards the traditional monastic life, and indeed towards the
traditional practice of the 'counsels' of the gospel, that was to have a great
future. Though in the last analysis—in what it implied rather than in what
it expressed—it differed little from that of Wyclif and Hus, it was far
more persuasive (or, as Erasmus's opponents would say, insidious) by
reason of the justice of many of the observations, and the moderation and
humanity and ambiguity of the language. Like so much else in the
Erasmian programme, it gently deflated the Christian ideal, replacing it
with what seemed to be the spirit of the gospel, but was in fact its wraith.

Nowhere is his method more characteristic than in his well-known
biographical sketch of Jean Vitrier, the Franciscan of St Omer whom he
puts alongside of Colet as his *beau idéal* of a Christian priest. The picture
he draws is indeed an attractive one and, though we know little of Vitrier
save what Erasmus tells us,[3] there is no need to suppose it to be anything
but true in its main lines. We are given clearly to understand, however,
that Vitrier's virtues owed nothing to his religious profession, to which,
indeed, his attitude was so Erasmian that we are left wondering how far
the disciple is speaking of his master, or how far that subtle artist is reading
his own experience and opinions in his friend's mind:

Although [Erasmus writes] he was indeed by no means an enthusiastic supporter of that way of life into which he had slipped, or had been drawn, in

---

1 *Ep.* 296 (III, 373): 'Ex huiusmodi nugis ab homuncionibus [*sc.* SS. Benedicto et
Francisco] repertis.'

2 *Ibid.* III, 373–5. Volz, a few years later (1526), joined the Reformers.

3 Vitrier, the propagator of a 'paulinisme singulièrement libre' (Renaudet), was censured
as a 'Hussite' by the Sorbonne in 1498.

youthful ignorance.[1] He would often say to me that it was the life of idiots rather than of religious men to sleep and wake and sleep again, to speak and keep silence, all at the sound of a bell...and to do everything by human regulations rather than by Christ's law.[2] Nothing, he said, was more inequitable than the equality observed among those who were unequally gifted, especially when, as often in monasteries, heaven-sent genius meant for better things is buried under ceremonies or human regulations or jealous confinement. Yet he neither suggested a change of life to anyone else nor attempted anything of the sort himself.

Compared with these radical opinions, the criticisms of individuals and the *ad hominem* arguments, which Erasmus scatters throughout those of his writings which, with the *Encomium Moriae*, the *Adagia* and the *Colloquies*, became a part of the mental furniture of all the cultivated minds of Europe, seem unimportant, but they penetrated deep into the consciousness and memories of his age. The rich abbot of sporting tastes and bucolic mind, who can see nothing but waste of time in learning, even if it is scriptural or patristic;[3] the friars and nuns who boggled at a rubric or a minute regulation while engaged in the pursuit of luxury or lust;[4] the overfed, lazy monk, the proud, worldly, licentious friar—all these and many more recur in narratives of exquisite urbanity, salted with every art of satire and irony. Numberless other men of the period, from orthodox and high-minded thinkers like More to pamphleteers or popular preachers, were willing to jeer or laugh or storm at the worldly or vicious monk and friar. Erasmus did more: he aimed at showing, often with sincere respect and courtesy towards individuals, that the vowed life of the gospel counsels was at best an unnecessary formalism and more often a pharisaical hypocrisy. It was an accretion of the ages, not to be rudely destroyed, but to be allowed to disappear if its hour had passed. It was a more civilized treatment of the topic than Wyclif's, a more Fabian approach, but the end would have been no less inevitable.

Erasmus first visited England in the summer of 1499, when he was probably approaching his thirty-third birthday and was already well known in the world of letters. He was still remarkably receptive, and his

---

1 *Ep.* 1211 (IV, 508) of 13 June 1521 to Jodocus Jonas: '...illud vitae institutum, in quod per inscitiam aetatis fuerat vel delapsus vel pertractus'.

2 *Ibid.*: 'Denique nihil non facere ad praescriptum humanum potius quam ad Christi regulam.' Erasmus had a genius for ambiguity, but the ordinary reader might be excused for thinking the whole passage to be a complete denial of the traditional Christian teaching that the doctrine and command of duly constituted authority in the Church is to be accepted as that of Christ himself. Contrast with the text of Erasmus that of St Benedict, *Regula*, c. 5: 'Quia obedientia quae maioribus praebetur Deo exhibetur.'

3 Cf. *Colloquium abbatis et eruditae.* The remark is made there 'olim rara avis erat abbas indoctus, nunc nihil vulgatius' (*Colloquia*, I, 273). The abbot in the dialogue believes in keeping his monks ignorant to ensure their submission.

4 Cf. the dialogue on fish-eating (*ibid.* II, 34 *seqq.*). Much of this is a favourite topic of Erasmus and the stories have many of the marks of a *ben trovato*. More takes up the motif, though not the story, in his letter to a Monk (*Correspondence*, ed. Rogers, pp. 196-7).

enthusiastic letters to and about his newly-made English friends might well be those of a man ten years younger. His English visit had been arranged by his whilom pupil and life-long friend, William Blount, Lord Mountjoy, and after staying with him at various houses (from one of which at Eltham he paid a call upon the youthful royal family in company with More) he proceeded to Oxford in the early autumn. As he was technically still an Augustinian canon, it was natural that he should stay at St Mary's College, of which Richard Charnock was then prior. Charnock, whose tenure of office at Oxford (c. 1492–c. 1501) fell between periods of rule at Dunstable and London, was a man of some culture and urbanity, whose admiration for the celebrated young humanist was warmly reciprocated by Erasmus.[1] He was the friend of Colet, and is linked with him more than once by his guest, who would be willing to live in their company even in the depths of Scythia.[2] He is compounded of humane learning, kindliness and integrity, the light and ornament of his order, a prior of all the Graces.[3] He advanced money to Erasmus, and the latter notes his presence at a dinner given by Colet, perhaps at Magdalen, which was followed by a disputation of which we are given details; he was partly responsible for persuading Erasmus to undertake the task of collecting proverbs for the first edition of the *Adagia*; he was a nonpareil, the ornament and glory of English religious.[4]

Erasmus paid a second visit to England from the autumn of 1505 to midsummer 1506, and now Richard Whytford of Syon is among his friends. His third stay was in 1508, and it was then, when an inmate of More's household, that he threw off his brief masterpiece, the *Encomium Moriae*. His fourth and longest stay was at Cambridge, from August 1511 to July 1514, when he worked at Queens' upon the Greek New Testament. It was then (1512) that he visited Walsingham, thus acquiring material for one of his most celebrated colloquies a dozen years later.[5] It was perhaps then also, when staying with William Gonnell in the summer months at Landbeach, that he visited the nearby Denney, where some years later two sisters of his friend Thomas Grey were Poor Clares.[6] In 1514 he left Cambridge for Louvain, and save for a short visit in 1519 never returned to England, though he corresponded with his friends and patrons till the

---

1 *Ep.* 108 (I, 249): 'Humanissimus praesul Richardus Charnocus.' For him, *v.* Allen's notes *ad loc.*

2 *Ep.* 115 (I, 267) of November 1499 to W. Blount: 'Cum his duobus amicis [*sc.* Colet and Charnock] ego vel in extrema Scythia vivere non recusem.'

3 *Ep.* 116 (I, 268): 'Richardus prior, ille Charitum antistes...homo non minus mirabili mixtura ex omnium literarum generibus omnibus quam ex summa humanitate summaque item integritate conflatus.'

4 *Ep.* 126 (I, 290), being the preface to the *Adagia* addressed to W. Blount: 'Deum immortalem, qua humanitate qua integritate viri [*sc.* Blount and Charnock], ut quam tu nobilitatis, tam ille Britannicae religionis unicum ornamentum ac decus mihi videatur.'

5 *Ep.* 262 (I, 513) of 9 May 1512 to A. Ammonius: 'Ego, mi Andrea, pro felici rerum ecclesiasticarum successu votum suscepi. Jam scio religionem probas. Visam virginem Vualsingamicam atque illic Graecum carmen votivum suspendam.'

6 *Ep.* 1927 (VII, 283) of 1527–8.

end of his life, and always looked back with affectionate regrets, as to a lost paradise, to the glimpses he had had, under Thomas More's roof in Bucklebury, of that happy childhood he had never himself known.[1] In no country, perhaps, did Erasmus make fewer enemies and more distinguished friends than in England, but with all his freedom from ties of family or loyalty he was never physically or psychologically at home outside the comfortable, well-furnished houses of the cultured cities near the Rhine.

If the writings of Erasmus were widely read in Spain, whither he had never gone and where there were few who knew him personally, it may be taken for granted that they were familiar in England wherever the new learning had penetrated.[2] We are not left without numerous indications: among those known to have been friends or correspondents of Erasmus are all the distinguished men of the generation immediately before the Reformation and many of the younger men who helped to bring it about—Henry himself and Queen Katharine, Wolsey, Foxe, Warham, Longland, Tunstall, Stokesley, Fisher, Colet, Grocyn, Linacre, More, Gardiner, Whytford, Lupset, Pace, Mountjoy, Grey; it is a remarkable litany, and it could be extended indefinitely. In England, also, he had his opponents: John Batmanson the Carthusian, Edward Lee, Richard Kidderminster, and the unknown monk of More's long letter,[3] but they were neither many nor inveterate. There can, indeed, be no question that the works of Erasmus were as familiar to all who could enjoy Latin, 'to ilka man o' decent feeling', as, let us say, the essays of Macaulay were to educated men of the 1840's. Indeed, the public of Erasmus was wider still. From 1525 onwards a broadening stream of translations began to flow from the English presses. Characteristically enough, these were for several years chiefly the educational and devotional works; it was only in 1533 with the *Enchiridion* (reprinted 1534, 1540, 1541, and twice in 1544) that the chief manifestos of the Erasmian programme began to be read far and wide.[4] In other words, prior to the decision to move against the monasteries the influence of Erasmian criticism and 'modernism' could have been felt only among the intellectual leaders of the country.

1 *Ep.* 2212 (VIII, 274) of 6 September 1529 to Margaret Roper, on receipt of Holbein's drawing of the More family. 'Frequenter illud apud me soleo optare, ut semel etiam ante fatalem vitae diem intueri contingat charissimam mihi sodalitatem; cui meae, qualis qualis est, vel fortunae vel gloriae bonam partem debeo, nec ullis mortalium debeo libentius.' This letter, written in Erasmus's sixty-third year, is one of the most sincere and moving of the whole collection. *Si sic omnia dixisset.* It is one of the characteristics of that enigmatic personality that he can thus, in the turn of a sentence, dissolve all hostile feelings.

2 The remarkable vogue, and subsequent extirpation, of Erasmism in Spain has been the subject of study for M. M. Bataillon (*v. supra*, p. 144 n. 1).

3 For Edward Lee, *v.* the letters of 1520–2 *passim*; for Batmanson, *v.* Allen, *epp.* 1099, 1113, and *infra*, p. 154; for Kidderminster, Allen, *epp.* 1061, 1126 (IV, 309–10), and *supra*, p. 94; for the monk, *infra*, p. 469.

4 For the works of Erasmus printed or translated in England before 1540, *v.* A. W. Pollard, *Short-Title Catalogue.* They were seventeen in all.

Nowhere is the influence of Erasmus more striking than in the writings of Sir Thomas More. More's mind and character were essentially simple, inasmuch as he always approached intellectual questions with a realist, common-sense outlook and judged his own actions and those of others by straightforward, homely moral standards. Yet he had a mind of great brilliance which was at the same time extremely receptive, and he was both a cautious man and a humble one. Throughout his public life until the last crisis he was showing different facets of his personality to different groups: to his humanist friends he was the admired wit and the inquisitive, critical author of *Utopia*; to Wolsey and the king he was the capable and loyal subordinate; to his family he was the affectionate and generous father. Only Margaret, and perhaps even she not fully, knew the real More and his lonely sanctity that gradually for many years, and then rapidly in time of trial, ripened into fullness.

More in early years accepted and admired the intellectual pre-eminence of Erasmus, and for a time at least he made his friend's opinions his own. Though as a young man he had lived in the Charterhouse, he had chosen another way of life, and though he retained his admiration for the monastic ideal he had no illusions as to the shortcomings of the normal monk and friar of his own day. It is, however, surprising, and it is the measure of the strength of Erasmus's influence, to find that in *c*. 1520 he still makes his friend's arguments his own. The document in which this appears most clearly is a long letter to a monk who has attacked Erasmus's edition of the Greek Testament.[1] More's anonymous correspondent may well have been the Carthusian John Batmanson, but More builds no argument on his precise status or personality. He does accuse him roundly, however, of ignorance and pride for venturing to correct Erasmus in a matter of scholarship, and also for supposing that holiness consists in outward rites and garments, and in the mechanical observance of rules, ceremonies and exercises. The letter as a whole is not among More's most attractive compositions: it is long, and repetitions abound. Its chief interest lies in showing how Erasmus could dominate a mind as profoundly conservative as More's. How far it may be thought to show that what Erasmus took to be the monastic mentality really existed in England must be a matter of conjecture.

A dozen years after More's letter another admirer of Erasmus, a younger man, set down his thoughts on monastic life with particular reference to England. Thomas Starkey[2] had for long moved in conservative circles. Born *c*. 1495–9, he had been a Fellow of Magdalen, Oxford, and had subsequently taken orders. Like More, he stayed for a time in the Charterhouse; then he became chaplain to the Countess of Salisbury, and was ultimately caught up by Cromwell into the group of humanists who wrote

1 For More's letter, *v*. Appendix I, *infra*.
2 For Starkey, *v*. DNB. *A Dialogue between Reginal Pole and Thomas Lupset* was edited by K. M. Burton in 1948.

pamphlets for the government; he was at this time a royal chaplain. He died in 1538; had he lived longer he would have shown more clearly where his real sympathies lay.

Like his fellows in Cromwell's circle Starkey had savoured Renaissance Italy and had been among the intimates of Reginald Pole. How far the opinions he attributed to Pole are in character and how far imaginary or personal to Starkey himself is irrelevant to our present purpose; we can take them as being current coin among the advanced young humanists of the day. Lupset opens the topic of monasticism by praising it as the haven of a few wealthy men who fear the world's temptations; he himself anticipates Milton in preferring a bold conflict with evil to a fugitive and cloistered virtue. After several pages Pole raises the burning Erasmian questions:

Pole. And how think you by the law which admitteth to religion of all sorts, youth of all ages almost, insomuch that you shall see some freres whom you would judge to be born in the habit, they are so little and young admitted thereto?

Lupset. Surely of this, after my mind, springeth the destruction of all good and perfit religion....

Pole. And what think you by the law which bindeth priests to chastity?

Lupset. ...I will say as Pope Pius did, that great reason in the beginning of the Church brought that law into the order of the Church, but now greater reason should take the same away again.[1]

Pole then continues with a condemnation of the 'great sort of idle abbey-lubbers which are apt to do nothing but to eat and drink', and Lupset returns to his original thesis, that monasteries, few in number, should exist for the benefit of men tired of the business and vanity of the world, where they might 'wholly give their minds to prayer, study and high contemplation'.[2] Pole then sketches a programme by which a few houses should be kept for such people, none of them young, and that these or other monasteries should be appointed as schools for children of the nobility; Westminster and St Albans are noted as particularly suitable for this purpose. As for abbots and priors, they should be elected for three-year periods as are 'the order of the monks of Italy', and they should live among their brethren so as 'not to triumph in their chambers as they do, which causeth all the envy in the cloisters'. Finally, he would admit 'none under thirty year of age'.[3] We need scarcely be told that this was all 'written in our days of the most famous divine, Erasmus, whose counsel I [Starkey] would in our studies we might follow'.[4] Little did Starkey know that his old patron Pole would, within a few years, be presenting to the pope himself criticisms of the religious more searching, and proposals more drastic, than any put forward in this dialogue for their reform.

1 Starkey, *Dialogue*, 121, 125.   2 *Ibid.* 140–5, 169.
3 *Ibid.* 180–1.   4 *Ibid.* 187.

M

Among the intellectual leaders of the country may fairly be counted the king. Recent historians, considering principally the omnicompetent activity of Cromwell, and the evidence both of Henry's distaste for paper work and his love of hunting, have perhaps allowed themselves to forget what a versatile and, within its limits of depth, what an admirable instrument the mind of the king was. As late as 1529, thirty years, that is, after his first visit to England, Erasmus is still speaking of Henry in terms of admiration only surpassed in warmth by his eulogies of More.[1] Erasmus, no doubt, had his fair share of a client's tact and of sixteenth-century king-worship, but his phrases are precise and impressive. With all the wealth of documents that make up the story of the fateful 1530's, we are all but entirely in the dark as to what the king himself was reading and thinking, and what influences, other than those of passion and immediate policy, were working upon him to effect the great change in his religious outlook. But he, whose mind was so active, and so receptive of anything that chimed in with his personal designs and desires, cannot but have read the *Adagia*, the *Encomium Moriae*, the *Enchiridion* and the *Colloquia* of Erasmus. That they had a decisive influence upon the direction of his plans need not for a moment be supposed. But that they supplied in part the categories of thought and expression that suited his interests well is more than possible. Henry, so apt at justifying all his actions to himself and to others, must have had some specious reasons with which to cover the crucial step that lay between the desire to mend, and the decision to end, monastic life in England. It may well have been that here again the egg laid by Erasmus proved, when hatched, to be a bird of another feather than that intended by the great humanist.

---

1 *Ep.* 2143 (Allen, VIII, 129) of 1 April 1529 to John Cochlaeus: 'ingenium erat [*sc.* in the youthful Henry] vividum, erectum et, ad quodcumque se vertisset, supra modum habile.... Dices illum ad omnia natum.' The whole letter deserves study; and cf. *epp.* 855, 1342 (Allen, III, 356; V, 223).

CHAPTER XII

REFORM AND SUPPRESSION UNDER WOLSEY

The suppression of the alien priories, which had been preceded by demands on the part of a small but fanatical minority for confiscations of a more comprehensive character, did not in the event point the way towards a more general dissolution. Such an end would not have appeared desirable, even if practically attainable, to Henry V or his son. It did, however, set a precedent of another kind by making lands and endowments available for royal and other colleges. Henceforward, prelates or kings who contemplated founding academic colleges or collegiate churches looked about for decayed monasteries within their jurisdiction whose revenues and lands might be transferred to what appeared to be more useful purposes, and it is not surprising, in view of the multitude of religious houses and the vicissitudes of the times, that they seldom looked in vain. The second half of the fifteenth century did not lack munificent bishops interested in foundations at Oxford and Cambridge: thus Waynflete of Winchester acquired for Magdalen College the decayed or derelict priory of Selborne in Hampshire and the whilom alien house of Sele in Sussex;[1] at the end of the century Alcock of Ely suppressed the vanishing nunnery of St Radegund's at Cambridge, and converted it into Jesus College, while Smith of Lincoln transferred Cold Norton to his college of Brasenose at Oxford.[2] At almost the same time Henry VII obtained bulls suppressing Mottisfont for the benefit of Windsor, and by uniting the priory of Luffield, a royal foundation, with Westminster rendered most of its revenues available for the same purpose.[3] The procedure in all these cases was ostensibly canonical: after an enquiry in which the forms, at least, of impartial justice were observed, permission was obtained from Rome for suppression and transference, and though it is possible to see, in the causes and circumstances alleged, exaggerated or unfair charges not unlike those made later by Cromwell's visitors, no serious objection could be taken to the procedure. Later still, in 1524, Fisher of Rochester did not hesitate to obtain the decaying nunneries of Bromhall (Berkshire) and Higham or Lillechurch (Kent) for St John's College, Cambridge.[4] Used thus with modera-

1 For Selborne, v. VCH, Hants, II, 179; for Sele, VCH, Sussex, II, 62. Sele was later taken over by the Carmelites from Shoreham.

2 CPR, Henry VII, 1494–1509, p. 72.

3 For Luffield, v. VCH, Northants, II, 97. The king was patron of the house, which was dilapidated and contained only three monks. Compensation was given to Westminster, whither the monks were transferred. For Mottisfont, v. VCH, Hants, II, 174. Here, however, the bull of suppression was not acted upon, and the house remained till the Dissolution.

4 For Bromhale, v. VCH, Berks, II, 81; for Lillechurch, VCH, Kent, II, 145–6, and Monasticon, IV, 379. At the latter house there were only three nuns, of questionable reputation, and the former, also reduced to three inmates, was in a state of decay. G. Baskerville, EM, 102–3, is misleading in his treatment of these wholly justified suppressions. Cf. his

tion and discretion the practice of transferring to quasi-religious purposes revenues which had ceased, and could not easily again be adapted, to further the cause of regular monastic life might have proved a valuable means of shifting property from effete to vigorous institutions. It received, however, a somewhat new and sinister significance at the hands of Wolsey.

The great cardinal, too often in the past regarded by historians wise after the event as a royal minister *sui generis* who opened the door inevitably to Caesaropapism, was in fact one of a group of eminent prelates in the Europe of that epoch who gained for a time an all but supreme control of the churches of their respective countries. The growth of national sentiment, the development of power and efficiency by the central government in Spain, France and England, and the simultaneous absorption of the papacy in the cares and struggles for its temporal dominions in Italy, led to a devolution by successive popes of all save the supreme jurisdiction in church matters to a single powerful ecclesiastic in the country concerned. Paradoxical as it may seem, history can show examples of secular monarchs, also, who have thus stretched their prerogative to the limit in order to devolve powers which they were too weak to exercise themselves. In the case of the eminent Observant friar, Francis Jiménes de Cisneros (1436–1517), in Spain, these powers were used for a strengthening of discipline and doctrine that was in time of the utmost value to the papal and Catholic cause; in France Georges d'Amboise (1460–1510), and in south Germany Cardinal Matthew Lang used their high position less purely, but with no immediate ill consequence for Rome. It was only in England that the characters of Wolsey, his king, and Wolsey's successor as chief minister combined to direct the use of similar powers to dissimilar purposes and with an issue very different.

Wolsey had none of the spiritual qualities of a reformer, but when he became what his ablest biographer does not hesitate to call Prime Minister,[1] his energy and efficiency alike prompted him to reduce to better order the religious houses which must long since have appeared a fit subject for reform to his realist gaze. Here again he cannot have been ignorant of the labours of Jiménes in Spain, or of the movements, in part spontaneous and in part controlled, towards reform in the monasteries of France.[2] Any reform worth the name, however, manifestly needed to be directed by an authority regionally and personally universal, and for this a jurisdiction in all dioceses and over all the religious, including the exempt orders, was essential. Such jurisdiction, under the pope, belonged only to a *legatus a latere* with a permanent tenure of office; it is not surprising, therefore, to find the reform of the monasteries, exempt and non-exempt, specified in

comment that 'the bishop's behaviour was no worse, but was certainly no better, than that of the King's visitors in a few years' time'. By a curious chance Fisher's bulls follow (24 September 1524) hard upon Wolsey's second bout of suppression (4 May 1524).

[1] This is the title of ch. iv of A. F. Pollard's *Wolsey*.
[2] For France, *v.* Imbart de la Tour, *Les Origines de la Réforme en France*, vol. i.

the bull of 27 August 1518, directed to the two cardinals only three months after Wolsey's appointment to a joint legacy with Campeggio. Ten months later a similar bull gave the same powers to Wolsey alone, and henceforth he enjoyed full legatine authority, though this did not of itself, without a special commission, give powers of visiting and reforming the exempt orders. These he obtained, finally and fully, by a bull of 24 August 1524.[1]

The first notable sign of his reforming activity is a long set of constitutions for the non-exempt Austin canons, given in March 1519, and intended to continue in force till the provincial chapter at Trinity, 1521. They were largely a reproduction of the Benedictine Constitutions of 1336, with a few additions.[2] No meeting between Wolsey and the canons is recorded, but in the autumn of 1521 the abbots and priors of the black monks were summoned to York Place on 12 November to discuss reform, and a provincial chapter was summoned to meet at Westminster at the end of the following February.[3] No official account has survived of this November meeting but, according to Polydore Vergil, Wolsey rated the monks for their irregular lives and avarice, and by way of impressing the hesitant, proceeded straightway to visit the abbey of Westminster with a considerable parade of severity, which was only relaxed when sufficient cash was forthcoming.[4] This account, though not wholly trustworthy, may well rest on a basis of fact; the cardinal's vexatious visitations provided an article for the charges brought against him after his fall.[5]

Before the Lent chapter took place, Wolsey sent round the monasteries a book of statutes which he proposed to enforce. It has been lost, but the regulations probably resembled the injunctions already given to the black canons. Whatever their nature, they were too much for the monks, and a letter exists in which they beg the cardinal to reconsider his proposals. The monks are so numerous, they say, that any attempt to effect a sudden return to the rigours of regular observance may produce widespread apostasy or rebellion, while recruits will be discouraged. Few nowadays wish for austerity, and if all the monasteries had to follow the rule of the Carthusians, the Bridgettines or the Observants they would soon be depopulated.[6] The letter is interesting, both in its frank *non pos-*

---

1 *LP*, II, 4399 (27 August 1518); III, 475, 510, 557, 600, 647, 693; IV, 610, 697, 759. Cf. Rymer, *Foedera*, XIV, 15–18, 23.

2 They are in Wilkins, *Concilia*, III, 683–8.

3 The dates and documents of this episode are in Pantin, *MC*, III, 117–24.

4 *Anglica Historia*, xxvii (ed. D. Hay, CS, 3 s., lxxiv), 258: 'Ut fidem verbis majorem habeant [monachi] ex improviso coenobium Westmonasterium adiit...intemperanterque omnia agit, miscet, turbat ut terreat caeteros, ut imperium ostentet, ut se terribiliorem praebeat.'

5 The twenty-fifth article dealt with this; others with the pillaging of monasteries (Pollard, *Wolsey*, 259).

6 *MC*, III, no. 283, pp. 123–4: 'In hac nostra tempestate [say the monks] mundo jam in suum finem declinante perpauci sint atque rarissimi qui vitae austeritatem et observanciam regularem cupiant.' It is interesting to note that the same three religious bodies are linked together for praise by Pole in his *Pro ecclesiae unitate defensione* (ed. 1536), 103.

sumus and in its tribute, so soon to be endorsed in letters of blood, to the three families of religious that stood apart from the rest.

There is no evidence that Wolsey attempted to enforce his statutes. He lacked entirely the ardour of a reformer, and he was too absorbed in personal and diplomatic interests to give even a statesman's attention to the matter. In no point is the contrast more strongly marked between him and Cardinal Richelieu a century later. He did, however, continue to make sporadic efforts by means of visitations conducted by commissaries, as at Wenlock in 1523 and Worcester in 1525. The surviving injunctions from Worcester are not remarkable for either severity or originality, but the lengthy injunctions and counsels given at Wenlock by the much-abused Dr Allen are unique for their date.[1] In them, somewhat unexpectedly, the recent legatine statutes, which are the basis for some of the injunctions, are referred to as a desirable norm rather than a strict law of obligation.

Meanwhile, Wolsey had been active in obtaining and exercising powers of visitation over the friars. The main bodies of the 'ordres foure' gave little trouble, but the new offshoot from the Minors, the Franciscan Observants, used more obstructive tactics. Noted as a body alike for their zeal and for their turbulence, and extremely influential at Rome, they did all they could to resist. On 7 July 1521, both the pope and Cardinal Quinones, the eminent general of the order, wrote to Wolsey begging him not to visit, and three weeks later Clerk, Wolsey's agent in Rome, wrote again, asserting that the pope had begged Wolsey 'for Goddes saake to use mercy with thois friars, sayeing that the be as desperatt bestes past shame, that can leese nothyng by clamours'.[2] The Observants certainly proved themselves noisy enough, but the high esteem in which they were held, and to which both Clement VII and Quinones testified, make it reasonable to suppose that Clerk translated the pope's words somewhat freely to please Wolsey, unless, indeed, they are thought to voice the impatience of a weak man bullied by the English diplomat and caught, here as elsewhere, between the upper and nether millstone. In any case, Wolsey waited more than two years before visiting the Observants; the friars proved true to their reputation, and the arrival of his commissaries was the signal for the exit of nineteen intransigents; the visitation was adjourned, and the popular preacher, Friar John Forest, was put up to anathematize the truants, some of whom returned and were clapped into the prison of the porter's lodge at York House.[3]

---

1 For these, *v. supra*, pp. 82–3. The Worcester articles are in 'The Visitations and Injunctions of Cardinal Wolsey', ed. J. M. Wilson; those of Wenlock are in *English Ecclesiastical Studies*, by R. Graham, 139–44. The *novellae constitutiones legatinae* are referred to among the *consilia et exhortaciones* on a point that had been law from the time of monastic origins, viz. the prohibition of a money salary to monks.

2 *LP*, IV (i), 477–8 (7 July, letters of Pope and Cardinal); 1521 (28 July, Clerk to Wolsey).

3 The episode is noted by Hall, *Chronicle*, ed. C. Whibley, II, 26 (February 1524), and *Grey Friars Chronicle* (in *Monumenta Franciscana*, RS, 4), II, 190 (16 January 1524). The Observants later became known in government circles by the cant name of Friars Obstinates.

That Wolsey's projects of reform had no foundation of spirituality is shown clearly by his more personal contact with the religious. His well organized staff of commissaries took cognizance of all the external relations of the monasteries. Abbots and priors were deprived or impelled to resign, often unjustly, and whenever vacancies occurred the cardinal's habitual practice was to induce the community to entrust the election to himself.[1] In almost every case, to judge from surviving records, the favoured candidate was expected to make a handsome contribution towards Wolsey's colleges or other interests, and from 1522 the cardinal permitted himself to hold *in commendam* the abbacy of St Albans, one of the two or three richest in England.[2] It was an abuse hitherto almost unknown in this country. Demands for contributions towards his expenses were frequently received by the wealthier houses, and the need for his favour forced compliance. It should be said, however, that his appointments often strengthened the regular life of an abbey, and it seems clear that he, and not Henry, was on the side of the angels in the case of the Wilton election.[3]

Wolsey's personal interests, which influenced so many of his dealings with the religious, were the chief motive also of his entry upon a course of suppression hitherto without parallel. Between 1524 and his fall in 1529 a stream of bulls and royal writs authorized the disappearance of some twenty-nine houses of monks and canons and nuns.[4] The series began when St Frideswide's in Oxford was suppressed in order to make way for Wolsey's college, and later in the same year this permission was confirmed and authorization given for the annexation to the college of other small monasteries to the same aggregate value of three thousand ducats.[5] The suppressions actually carried out were in value many times greater than the sum allowed. One of the charges against the fallen cardinal was of having suppressed monasteries uncanonically,[6] and as no further bull is discoverable before 1528 it must be presumed that Wolsey acted as if the papal grant had given him *carte blanche*. In all, between April 1524 and December 1525, some twenty monasteries were suppressed in addition to St Frideswide's, and their revenues transferred to Wolsey's college at Oxford. The houses thus eliminated, modestly described by the cardinal as 'certain exile and small monasteries', were certainly not among the

---

1 This was another of the charges against Wolsey; cf. Pollard, *Wolsey*, 259, and *ibid.* 200–4, for many instances of high-handed behaviour and bribery.

2 Rymer, *Foedera*, XIII, 775 (8 November).

3 A number of writers, including Pollard, *Wolsey*, 202–4, have been misled in this somewhat complicated business by the king's letters, which are a good example of Henry's skill in throwing a screen over his own very questionable conduct by an assumption of righteous indignation expressed in pious reproof. For the actual sequence of events, *v.* article by the present writer, '"The Matter of Wilton" in 1528'.

4 Incomplete lists are given in Gairdner, *The English Church, 1509–58*, 419, and there are others in *LP*, but discrepancies between papal bulls and royal letters patent, together with obvious clerical errors and misspellings, make it difficult to attain complete accuracy. For a list with dates, *v.* Appendix II, *infra*. For the acts of dissolution, *v. LP*, IV (i), 1137.

5 Rymer, *Foedera*, XIV, 23.

6 Lord Herbert, *Henry VIII*, 412; abridged in *LP*, IV, iii, 6075.

greatest in the land, but in the aggregate they yielded a sizable net income of about £1800, which was approximately the income of Abingdon, one of the wealthier (though by no means the wealthiest) of the contemporary abbeys. More than half this sum came from four houses; the average income of the remainder was a little less than £50. The total number of monks, canons and nuns concerned was probably less than eighty, that is, a little more than the contemporary community of Christ Church, Canterbury, so that the whole transaction was equivalent to the suppression of a single great abbey. As only four of the houses concerned had a community of eight or more, and several had three or less, Wolsey's further statement that 'neither God was served, nor religion kept' in them may probably be accepted as reliable. Recent writers by drawing attention to the four or five larger houses among the twenty, have questioned the customary assumption that all these monasteries were ciphers in the religious world.[1] It is true that five had an income well over £100, but St Frideswide's, which alone had a fair-sized community, stood apart from the rest as forming the material nucleus of the new college; the four others, Bayham, Daventry, Lesnes and Tonbridge, had communities of ten or less and might reasonably be considered as decayed, though it is not possible to discover why Wolsey's eye fell upon these individuals among all the houses of England. It is perhaps noteworthy that the only public protests recorded were concerned with two of this group. The fate of Daventry is hard to account for; it had an income greater even than St Frideswide's and in a recent visitation it had seemed to be tolerably observant. Possibly the disproportion between income and inhabitants attracted Wolsey's attention to a friendless house.

The strong personal bias behind these suppressions, together with the cardinal's arbitrary and sometimes uncanonical actions and the violent and rapacious behaviour of his agents evoked numerous protests.[2] At Tonbridge the townsmen petitioned for a continuance of the priory, which they preferred to the promise of a school with scholarships at Cardinal College,[3] and at Bayham in Sussex gentlemen of the neighbourhood assembled in disguise and reinstated the canons for a time,[4] while complaints against Dr Allen, Wolsey's chief agent, and against Cromwell, reached the king from all sides, and were passed back to Wolsey by More.[5]

---

1 G. Baskerville, *EM*, 104–5.

2 Cf. the entry in the *Chronicle* of the biased Hall (II, 31–2, March 1524): 'Wherefore sodainly he entered...into the saied houses, put out the Religious and tooke all their goodes, moveables and scarcely gave to the poore wretches any thyng, except it were to the heddes of the house.'

3 For Tonbridge, *v. LP*, IV (i), 1470–1 (2 and 3 July 1525), where Warham is found disclaiming any share in the protest. Cf. *LP*, IV, 4920.

4 *LP*, IV (i), 1397; Ellis, *OL*, III (ii), cxlv.

5 E.g., *LP*, IV (ii), 3360 (19 August 1527), where Knight writes to Wolsey: 'I have heard the King and noblemen speak things incredible of the acts of Dr Aleyn and Cromwell', and Ellis, *OL*, II (ii), xcix (=*State Papers*, I, 154). For Henry's criticisms, *v.* his letter in *LP*, IV (ii), 4507 (14 July 1528).

Undeterred, the cardinal continued on his course, and after an interval of three years November 1528 saw the issue of two bulls, the one authorizing the suppression of monasteries with less than six inmates to the value of eight thousand ducats, the other allowing for the union of monasteries and nunneries with less than twelve religious with larger houses. A second bull of the same tenor reached Wolsey at the end of August 1529.[1] The first of the earlier bulls seems to have been directed towards the financing of the cardinal's college at Ipswich; the others were perhaps part of a wider policy. Acting on these Wolsey proceeded against seven small houses. Three were dependencies and were merged in the houses to which they belonged; the others were liquidated save for one, which for some reason escaped the cardinal's hands only to fall into those of the local landowner a few months later. In all these the total amount of income actually confiscated was probably less than £200 and the number of religious concerned only twenty-five. We must therefore suppose either that the wide powers given by the bulls of 1528 were never used, or that they were intended by Wolsey to afford tardy confirmation of what he had already achieved uncanonically. It is noteworthy that according to the terms of one of these later bulls the suppressions were to be made in favour of Windsor and King's College.[2] Whether or not his was a move on the part of the king to follow Wolsey's suit in the interest of royal foundations, it was not in fact effective.

Throughout the business of suppression Wolsey employed a group of able, overbearing and unscrupulous agents who applied in varying degrees the violent and dishonest methods later used on a larger scale under the direction of the cardinal's trusted officer, Thomas Cromwell. The religious were either turned out without ceremony or were persuaded to endorse a form of surrender admitting their faults; the necessary inquests were then held, and it was found that the religious had voluntarily forsaken their house which duly escheated to the king, who could be claimed as founder of a large number of monasteries on very dubious grounds.[3] The inmates were given their choice between transference to another house or return to secular life (presumably with a legatine dispensation) assisted by a small sum of money. The buildings were then rifled, dismantled or converted just as were those of their fellows ten years later.

Wolsey had thus, at the time of his fall, carried his dealings with the monasteries to the precise point that had been reached in his broader

---

1 Rymer, *Foedera*, XIV, 270–2, 272–3, 345.
2 *Ibid.* 270–2. At that date the Cambridge college must be meant.
3 When property escheated or fell in any way to the Crown the verdict of a local jury as to the facts—technically known as an 'office'—was legally requisite (*Statutes of the Realm*, II, 252, 306, i.e. 8 Hen. VI, c. 16 and 18 Hen. VI, c. 6) as a solemn act of record. One of the charges against Wolsey was that he obtained these by collusive methods; cf. Hall *Chronicle*, II, 32: 'Then he caused thexceter [the escheator] to sit and to find the houses voyde, as relynquished, and founde the kyng founder, where other men were founders', etc.

ecclesiastical policy. While remaining technically and indeed sincerely within the limits of orthodoxy and a rather loose canonical practice, he had collected into his hands all the strands of power and had perfected a technique of destruction which might well have perished with its creator, but which was in fact inherited by an agent bound by no ties of education or of caste or of ambition to the law and tradition of a centralized church.

Towards the end of his career of spoliation the cardinal, as general overseer of the Church in England, was maturing a scheme of a totally different character. This was a project to create an unspecified number of new bishoprics out of the confiscated revenues of an equal number of abbeys. The church was to be used as a cathedral, and the monks were to be retained either as a monastic chapter or as a body of secular canons. Monastic chapters were, of course, as old as the English monastic order, and more than one abbey had in the past been converted into a cathedral. A wholesale reshuffle of the kind proposed was, however, something novel, and still more strange was the acquiescence by Rome itself in the proposal that monks should change their profession for the less exacting status of secular canons. In the first bull Clement VII, voicing the feeling of his cardinals, refused permission to act and did no more than authorize Wolsey and Campeggio to make investigations and submit proposals; in the second, six months later, he gave permission for the transformation and allowed the legates, *pro hac vice tantum*, to appoint the reigning abbots or others as bishops.[1] It was, however, too late. Campeggio was leaving England and for Wolsey, also, the sands were running out. The scheme was shelved, to be revived and partially implemented eight years later.

---

1 A bull of 12 November 1528 authorized Wolsey and Campeggio to make enquiries as to the procedure followed in the past when new monastic chapters were created by suppressing abbeys (Rymer, *Foedera*, xiv, 273–5); that of 29 May 1529 (*ibid.* 291–4 and *LP*, iv (iii), 5607–8), repeating the order for careful enquiry, gave the definite permission to erect new sees with the arrangements noted in the text (i.e. the monks could become secular canons *salvis tribus votis substantialibus*).

CHAPTER XIII

EUROPEAN PRECEDENTS

English historians in the past, and indeed all writers who have touched upon the subject, have tended to treat the suppression of the English and Welsh monasteries as a purely domestic affair, conducted in an insulated area, and brought about solely by causes to be found in the remote or immediate past history of the country. This may be, on a wide view, a true judgment. It is, however, possible that recent writings and events in other countries of Europe had their effect upon English opinion and royal policy: books, travellers and diplomatic agents kept government in touch with the foreign scene. In any case, the suppression of the religious life in England loses all historical context unless it is seen as an act in a great drama that was being played all over Europe.

We have seen in the preceding chapter how pervasive were the raillery and criticism of Erasmus, at first in humanistic circles only, but later among all those of the New Learning, until finally the Erasmian strictures on the religious life became part of the stock-in-trade of all those hostile to the old religion. This attitude of sarcastic or caustic mockery had already become a characteristic of the mental climate in educated Europe when it was adopted and intensified by Luther, who made of the pleas and suggestions of the humanist an immediate and burning practical issue.

Luther, himself an Augustinian friar, remained for some years after his first public outburst without renouncing his own profession or attacking the theological principles upon which it rested. In 1521, however, when in the Wartburg, he composed and sent to Wittenberg a number of theses directed against monasticism.[1] His attack was based on two of his main assumptions: that salvation was to be found in faith alone, and not in works; and that liberty was the birthright and hall-mark of a Christian. The monastic ideal, in his view, rested upon an unwarranted distinction between the counsels and commandments of Christ; the religious relied on his Rule and works of piety or penance, and he neglected the service of his fellow-men in a selfish quest of personal perfection and salvation. Luther was still prepared to allow those who did not trust in works to continue in their monastic life, and he himself did not as yet propose to dispense himself from the vow which to him was always the religious vow *par excellence*, that of chastity, but perpetual vows were in his view unlawful, as alienating the Christian's inalienable birthright of spiritual liberty.

Luther always moved rapidly, without ever feeling the need for consistency, and within a few months he had developed his opinions very considerably. In the autumn of 1521 he wrote his treatise *De votis*

1 For these, *v.* J. Mackinnon, *Luther and the Reformation* (London, 1929), III, 22–34.

monasticis,[1] which in after days he considered the most powerful and irrefutable of all his writings. It had indeed an immediate, an immense, and a lasting influence, and though there was little in it that had not been said before by Wycliffites, Hussites and others, the various arguments were powerfully massed and pungently expressed, and very little has been added in the centuries that have since elapsed to the case against monasticism and the scriptural anthology in support of it which Luther now brought forward.[2] The monk relies on practices and Rules, thus becoming a Jew, if not a Manichee; he thus goes clean against the apostle's law of liberty. Moreover, his vaunted poverty is actually a sham and his profession of chastity quite unavailing to preserve the virtue. The true Christian life consists of active works of mercy, not in wearing a cowl, shaving the head, scourging oneself, fasting and repeating sets of prayers. Luther is now ready to absolve monks as well as secular priests from their vows: the vow of chastity, in fact, is invalid from the start, as being in most cases a promise of the impossible and in all cases derogating from Christian liberty.

This pronouncement of Luther suited well with current sentiment. At a special chapter of the Augustinian Friars, summoned at Wittenberg in the same year, the assembled fathers, guided solely, as they declared, by Scripture and not by human traditions, and convinced that all that is not of faith is sin, proclaimed that all those under vows were completely free to choose their future state. At the convent of Wittenberg itself all the members save the prior took advantage of the freedom thus asserted.

Luther's pronouncements on the religious life and monastic ideal were not long in finding a sympathetic reception in the northern kingdoms.[3] In Denmark King Christian II was already interested in the teaching of the Reformers, and his policy was continued by his successor Frederick I (1523–33). During the reign of this monarch occurred the crucial action which, followed by the Ecclesiastical Appointments Act of 1534, severed the administrative and disciplinary links between the Danish Church and Rome without as yet making any formal repudiation of papal authority as such or any change of doctrine. The occasion was the Diet or meeting of the Rigsraad at Odensee in 1526, where papal confirmation and papal receipt of fees for newly elected bishops were abolished. 'Freedom of conscience' was proclaimed in 1527, while in the matter of the vow of chastity and the equivalent undertaking by all in major orders, the Diet

---

1 *Werke,* ed. Weimar, VIII, 573–669.

2 E. de Moreau, however, remarks (*Histoire de l'Eglise,* ed. Fliche et Martin, XVI, 92 (1950)): 'Malgré les jugements contraires, cet ouvrage nous paraît, en beaucoup d'endroits, d'une insigne faiblesse.'

3 There is no completely satisfactory and detailed account of the origin of the Reform in Scandinavia by a German, French or English scholar. In what follows, the account in vol. II of the *Cambridge Modern History,* E. H. Dunkley, *The Reformation in Denmark,* J. Wordsworth, *The National Church of Sweden,* J. G. H. Hoffmann, *La Réforme en Suède,* and H. F. Holmquist, *Die schwedische Reformation,* have been used.

allowed all spiritual persons, including religious, to choose between marriage and celibacy.[1]

The mendicant orders were prominent in Denmark, and more in view than the relatively few abbeys; the Carmelites in particular counted many men of ability and influence, who were in the event to join the Reform and occupy official positions in the Church. They were on the whole unpopular on account of their considerable wealth. In Scania, the southern part of modern Sweden which was then directly governed by the king of Denmark, monastic houses were of greater significance, and their lands were coveted by the nobles. The Diet of Odensee and the king's action effected the confiscation of some fifteen Franciscan houses between 1528 and 1532, but the other religious continued for a time, and it was only under the next king, Christian III (1536–59), that further steps were taken. In 1537 a Church Ordinance forbade the mendicants to preach, beg or hear confessions. Other religious were allowed to leave their houses at will, and the property so abandoned was taken over by the Crown.[2] In the sequel the orders of friars rapidly disintegrated, but the Cistercian houses continued to exist for some decades, not becoming extinct till c. 1580.

In the kingdom of Sweden the pattern of change was different. Religious houses were not numerous in comparison with those of England or France, but the number of religious probably bore an equal proportion to the total population, and their proportionate wealth was even greater. Friaries existed only in Stockholm and a few other towns, but there were a number of large Cistercian and Premonstratensian abbeys, two important Bridgettine houses, and a recently founded Charterhouse, that of Mariefred, which had received royal endowment. Taken as a whole the monks and canons, like the small group of bishops, were very wealthy landowners, and Gustavus Vasa is recorded as saying in 1527 that the lands of the Crown and nobility together did not equal a third part of the possessions of the Church. The religious had, besides, with the bishops, great social and jurisdictional power as 'feudal' magnates.[3] On the other hand, there was less animus against the religious and less desire for religious change in Sweden than in Denmark, and had the political situation been stable it is possible that Sweden, like Ireland, would have taken no initiative in the direction of the Reform.

It so happened, however, that Sweden was at a crisis of her national history. The union of Kalmar of 1397, by which the three Scandinavian kingdoms had been united under one elective Crown, had been in abeyance at the middle of the fifteenth century and again from 1471 onwards, and

1 For what follows, v. B. J. Kidd, *Documents of the Continental Reformation* (Oxford, 1911), 233–4.

2 Kidd, *op. cit.* 327.

3 Feudalism of the Carolingian or Norman types had never been established in Sweden, but by the fifteenth century the great landowners had come to occupy much the same social position as their English contemporaries.

the country was governed by members of an elected royal family, calling themselves sometimes king and sometimes regent. All administrative power in the country, save in the city of Stockholm, was in fact in the hands of the nobles and the relatively small group of landholding bishops.

A change came with the accession of the energetic Christian II to the throne of Denmark in 1513. He resolved to make the union of the three kingdoms a reality. Sweden was divided between two parties, that of Sten Sture the younger, the representative of the national royal family, and that of Gustaf Trolle, archbishop of Upsala, who was recognized as administrator by a group favouring close union with Denmark. In the confused disturbances that followed, Sten Sture, who had had the better of the struggle, deposed and imprisoned the archbishop, who appealed to Denmark for help and succeeded in obtaining papal confirmation of the excommunication of his rival, Sten Sture, by the archbishop of Trondhjem who claimed metropolitan powers. Christian II thereupon, being violent and ambitious, set out to gain control of Sweden, identifying himself with the cause of Gustaf Trolle and papal jurisdiction. He defeated and mortally wounded Sten Sture and was crowned king of Sweden at Stockholm on 4 November 1520. A few days later he took treacherous and terrible vengeance on the opponents of Archbishop Trolle in the series of summary executions known to history as the Stockholm bloodbath. Though in fact wholly personal and political, the massacre was conducted on the pretext that those who had deposed Trolle were guilty of rebellion against the pope and had ignored the papal excommunication. Thus, at this fateful moment of Swedish history, the papacy was identified in the minds of all both with a great crime and with the cause of Denmark, the enemy of national aspirations. The cause of traditional religion was further weakened, as it was later weakened in England, by the vacancy of several sees owing to the Stockholm murders.

It was at this juncture that a national leader of genius appeared in the person of Gustaf Eriksson, better known as Gustavus Vasa. Gustavus was one more of that group of young and gifted rulers whom destiny had called to decide what was to be the path to be chosen by a Europe at the crossways. Born in 1496 and thus five years younger than Henry VIII, he had served as a young soldier under Sten Sture, and after his death had endured a period of wandering and adventure in his native province of Dalecarlia, thus becoming a figure of legend in Swedish history comparable to Alfred the Great or the Young Pretender. Finally, collecting a band of his dalesmen he began a campaign of guerrilla warfare which ended in 1523 with the capture of Stockholm and Kalmar and the election of the young leader as king.

The new ruler had at first no intention of changing the religion of the country though, as a young, clearsighted and efficient autocrat, he was prepared for drastic reforms. A friendly papal legate of native birth, John Magnusson, was in the country, and he was soon elected archbishop of Upsala in place of the exiled Trolle, though his position was not regularized at Rome till he himself was an exile in turn. Meanwhile, the out-standing man in the Swedish Church was the orthodox and patriotic Brask of Linköping. Gustavus demanded heavy loans from the clergy, and confiscated the recent royal benefaction of Gripsholm, which had been given to the Charterhouse of Mariefred, but took no further revolutionary step for the moment. Lutheranism, however, had begun to enter the country, with the great reformer Olaus Petri (Olaf Petersen), as its spokes-man, and made rapid progress among the educated. Gustavus began to favour the new opinions and to countenance clerical marriages, that of Petersen among others; at the same time he harassed the monasteries by quartering troops upon them, by getting control of their affairs, and by finding legal pretexts for reclaiming lands given them by his ancestors. Finally, in 1527, a Diet was summoned to Västerås in June 1527 to discuss points of theology, including the papal claims. The constitution of this gathering was novel, and the four remaining bishops, whose order had always previously sat next to the king, were degraded to lower seats; by way of riposte they drew up a protest against Lutheranism and asserted the authority of the pope. The Diet was then asked by the king to provide a larger revenue, which was undoubtedly needed, and church property was indicated as a source. Brask, speaking for the bishops, maintained a firm refusal to spoliation and was supported by others in the Diet. Gustavus then passionately declared that he would lay down the crown unless he was given what he asked, and left the assembly, which after three days of deliberation recalled him and promised obedience to all he might demand. A few days later, at the dictation of the king, the celebrated decrees known as the Recess of Västerås were promulgated.[1]

Among these decrees were some touching the religious orders. All ecclesiastical property deemed by the king superfluous to the needs of the religious was to be handed over to him. All land of the kind that was exempt from taxes (the equivalent of that in England given in frankalmoin), bestowed since 1454, was to be returned to the families of the donors. All taxable land whatsoever was to be returned, with no retrospective time-limit. A few days later further ordinances were passed: no prelates were to be appointed without royal confirmation, and various items of the Lutheran programme were introduced, including the surveillance of monks by the civil authority. The aged Brask, despairing of the republic, joined the exiled Archbishop Magnusson at Danzig; new bishops were consecrated by command of the king; the monasteries lost most of their property and many ceased to exist. There was, however, no direct persecu-tion or imposition of oaths as in England, nor was there a wholesale suppression. Instead, the monasteries gradually and one by one became extinct. The Bridgettine nunneries, which more than any other houses were regarded as a national institution, were pensioned by the king and were the last to disappear, half a century after the crowning of Gustavus Vasa.

1 Kidd, *op. cit.* 234–6.

The attack on the monastic and mendicant orders, which in Scandinavia was primarily inspired by economic motives and conducted by the king for his own benefit or that of the nobility, was launched almost simultaneously in Switzerland by democratic or oligarchic public authority desiring to implement the programme of a religious reform. Thus, in the last month of 1524, the Council of Zürich dissolved the religious houses in their territory, devoting their revenues to education or the relief of the poor. The procedure anticipated in many respects that later adopted by the king of England, as when in 1523 nuns were given permission to marry. A year later, in December 1524, we find the abbess of our Lady's Minster offering to surrender her convent under her seal and hand, on the understanding that she might remain there, well-found, for life.[1] At the same time the friars were offered the choice of leaving the order to learn a trade, those who had brought possessions with them to the convent being allowed to remove them, and those in need being given public assistance till they were self-supporting. Those who wished to remain were, for the time being, gathered into the Carmelite friary, where they were provided for. Naturally, all soon disappeared into the citizen body or went into exile. A little later in 1530, the Council of Zürich, supporting Vadianus and the local town council, took the opportunity during a vacancy to seize and secularize the ancient abbey of St Gall.[2] Basel accepted the Reform fully and with all its corollaries in 1529; Geneva did not expel its religious, and then only with some regret, till 1530.[3]

While the suppression of the religious life in Switzerland was more drastic, and the course of events there probably more widely known in England than the gradual and less catastrophic events in Scandinavia, the Swiss proceedings, which were unmistakably the translation into action of the doctrines of Luther and Zwingli, could in England be openly approved only by those of Lutheran sympathies. The Danish and Swedish events, on the other hand, could provide valuable practical lessons to a monarch more concerned with financial gain than with doctrinal reform. Whether Henry VIII was in any way stimulated or guided by the actions of the king of Denmark and Gustavus Vasa cannot be decided, but it is at least certain that an influence from the north upon England is chronologically admissible. The events in Sweden and Denmark bear a remarkable resemblance to those in England eight or ten years later, if allowance is made for the disturbing influence of Henry's divorce suit, for the greater efficiency of a long-established central government controlled by Thomas Cromwell, and for the far greater numbers, both of religious and of educated men, in England. No doubt some of the similarity is due to the racial and therefore the psychological kinship between Englishmen and Scandinavians. The relative lack of contacts between the countries in modern times, and close relations with France, Germany and the English-speaking lands overseas, has obscured for most Englishmen their close

1 Kidd, *op. cit.* 441, 443.   2 *Ibid.* 468.   3 *Ibid.* 501, 516–17.

kinship with Denmark and Sweden. Nevertheless, it is a noteworthy fact that the Scandinavian way of life and the reaction to new political and social demands are closer to our own than are those of any other European nation. For this reason it would not be strange to find that the Scandinavian behaviour at a time of national revival and religious change resembled that of England. It is, however, difficult to prove that news of Swedish or Danish happenings penetrated to England. There is no trace in the papers of the time of a diplomatic representative of England at Stockholm. Nevertheless, the agents of Wolsey and Cromwell were in Hamburg and other German ports, and it is difficult to suppose that they or their royal master remained wholly ignorant of what was happening in the northern kingdoms. Any such knowledge would have served to give them confidence and perhaps even to suggest lines of policy when an attack on the monasteries was first envisaged. Certainly, there was by 1533–4 no lack of recent and attractive precedent, no lack of trenchant arguments, for a monarch who wished to better himself at the expense of the Church and to acquire the property of the religious without incurring the odium of sacrilege.

The precedents hitherto considered had been set by reformers or despoilers who had no scruples in breaking with the past and in destroying venerable institutions. This section may perhaps be ended appropriately with mention of a group of reformers who, though entirely orthodox of belief and without a thought of violent or lucrative action, produced a document that even now startles us with its drastic recommendations. The historian when he contemplates it must feel anew the difficulty of recapturing the thoughts of a past age. At the very moment when the lesser monasteries of England were disappearing, when such of the Carthusians as had not been done to death were being driven into schism or heresy, and when the Pilgrims of Grace were hazarding their lives in protest against the suppression, a group of earnest ecclesiastics in Rome were presenting the Farnese Pope Paul III with a report that pilloried the decadence of many of the religious orders in Italy and suggested the wholesale abolition of numerous branches of the great orders. The report,[1] as a spring of action, was strangled at birth by the protests of interested

---

1 The report, the *Consilium de emendanda ecclesia*, presented (9 March 1537) by the papal commission of reform, which included among its members Cardinals Contarini, Caraffa, Sadoleto and Pole (it is printed by Kidd, *Documents of the Continental Reformation*, 307–18), recommended that all the 'conventual orders' be allowed to die out and be forbidden to receive novices ('conventuales ordines abolendos esse putamus omnes'). This recommendation is referred to in somewhat ambiguous terms by Pastor, *History of the Popes*, Eng. trans. XI, 165 *seqq*. It would seem to refer to the 'conventual' branches of the orders of friars. The report was strictly confidential and its publication was never intended, but it speedily became common property. Several of the members—Caraffa, for example, and Pole himself—were by temperament vehement and drastic, particularly in these, their early years, and it is probable that they intended their suggestions to have a strong galvanic action rather than to serve as a considered programme. Later, when Caraffa became Paul IV, he placed the report on the Index (1555). Cf. H. Jedin, *The Council of Trent*, Eng. trans. 423–33.

N

parties, by political manœuvre, and by the inertia of the pope; its unauthorized publication raised a gale of satire and criticism in central
Europe and its effect for speeding the cause of reform was virtually nil.
Appearing as it did in 1537 it could have had no effect on opinion in
England in 1535, and there is no evidence that it made any impact at all
in this country. It is nevertheless well to bear it in mind, for it shows how
deeply the need for reform had been felt by the most serious and forward-
looking minds even in Rome itself; it shows also, more clearly than any
other episode, the 'double time', as of different ages or worlds, that
existed simultaneously in the Europe of these decades. The one, urgent
and swift-moving, was the time of Luther and Cromwell; the other, slow,
almost stationary, was that of the pre-Tridentine Roman Curia and of the
romance lands in general, who pursued their own policies unaware of the
chasm in the religious world that was opening at their feet.

CHAPTER XIV

ACCEPTANCE OF THE ROYAL SUPREMACY

With the disgrace and death of Wolsey there began, for the Church in England, a period of stress and revolution without parallel in the past. Though the waters of domestic discontent and imported revolution had, throughout the cardinal's long lease of power, been mounting against the dykes, and far-sighted observers had long been anticipating a catastrophe, no one dared to prophesy what form it would take. No mortal prevision, indeed, could possibly have embraced those two imponderable forces, the will of the king and the genius of his new minister, which gave to events in the decade 1530–40 the particular impulse which determined their direction.

Throughout the changes of those years, in which there occurred a breathless sequence of events so pregnant with consequence, we are here concerned solely with the attitude and behaviour of the religious. To what extent was their conduct in the supreme crisis from the autumn of 1535 to the end of 1539 predetermined, or at least predisposed, by their action in earlier years? To answer this question it is necessary to begin our review some months before the death of the cardinal.

The precise degree of causal relationship between the king's 'great matter' of the divorce and the subsequent ecclesiastical revolution has always been a controversial topic, but it can at least be said that some relationship of cause and effect existed. Almost equally impatient of solution is the allied problem as to the connection in the minds and conduct of individuals between disapproval of the king's matrimonial designs and disapproval of his rejection of papal supremacy, for it was not until the second half of 1533 that the two issues were in fact fused by the papal condemnation of the Boleyn marriage. Two observations, however, seem to be justified: the one is, that generally speaking those who are known to have acted or pronounced in a public way in favour of Queen Katharine are found also to have made at least the beginning of a protest against the royal supremacy, and *vice versa*; the other is, that the royal supremacy was used as a principal means of clinching and compelling adhesion to the validity and consequences of the Boleyn marriage. It may be added that Henry never forgot or forgave those who had pertinaciously defended the validity of his marriage with Katharine.[1] It would, however, be a mistake to assume, with some historians, that an intelligent individual's decision

---

[1] No one knew this better than Sir Thomas More. Although he died, as he said on the scaffold, 'in and for the faith of the Holy Catholic Church', he could also say, immediately before the verdict was pronounced against him at his trial: 'It is not for this Supremacy so much that ye seek my blood, as for that I would not condescend to the marriage' (Harpsfield, *The Life and Death of Sir Thomas More*, 196).

on the divorce suit was based merely on a technical, or alternatively on an emotional, judgment, as it would also be untrue to say that the severe treatment meted out to opponents of the supremacy was little more than delayed punishment for opposition to the divorce. The fact that the solemn recognition of the royal supremacy, accompanied by a repudiation of all papal jurisdiction, was a denial of accepted Catholic teaching, whereas assertion of the validity of the Aragon marriage was a personal, private expression of opinion on what was ostensibly an open legal issue, does not in truth differentiate the issues as completely as might be thought. In the last resort, when emotions had passed and canonists had said their say, even before the final papal decision, judgment on the divorce question was a moral one, resting upon assessments of the honesty and veracity of the queen, of the sincerity and reliability of Henry, and upon the whole deep Christian issue of the lawfulness of a man's ruining the life of his putative wife and daughter for motives which might well appear base or at best mere worldly expediency. To pass such a judgment, and to abide by it, needed both clear insight and high moral qualities; the same qualities were needed still more urgently in one who proposed to take his stand against the royal supremacy. Similarly, when More, with his clear mind and careful judgment, said at the end of his trial that this was the final outcome of a pursuit which began when he opposed the king over the divorce, he was speaking of what he knew of the king's character, not of the intrinsic connection between issues. The test of the Oath of Succession or of the denial of papal supremacy was not a device to ruin the opponents of the Boleyn marriage only, but a means of eliminating opposition of any kind. Thus in spite of the clear distinction between the two questions, each was in a sense a religious issue, decided in large part by an awareness of spiritual motives, and though it was some years before the causal connection between the two decisions became clear, to take the king's part in the divorce suit was in fact to set one's foot upon a slope where it became ever more difficult to call a halt or to retrace one's steps.

In the summer of 1530, when Wolsey was already in disgrace and the divorce suit appeared to have reached a complete deadlock, the king decided to promote a letter to the pope in support of his case, signed by a number of spiritual and temporal lords, but not in any sense appearing as a memorandum of parliament. Some of the signatures were obtained at a meeting summoned by the king, others by commissioners sent into the country for that purpose. The text of the letter, after rehearsing the unity between head and members of the nation in England, and the difficulties and future disasters likely to occur in a kingdom without an heir male, went on to beg the pope to grant the king's request. The most significant part, however, is the hardly disguised threat of direct action if the request is not granted. 'If the pope is unwilling', the writers say, '. . . we are left to look after ourselves, and to find a remedy for ourselves elsewhere. . . if Your Holiness does not grant our request. . . our state will certainly be an unhappy one...but not altogether without remedy... some remedies are indeed extreme ones, but a sick man seeks relief in any way he can find.'[1] The pope, in his carefully worded reply, made it clear that he had taken the point.[2]

This letter received relatively few signatures. Wolsey, newly arrived in the diocese which he had not visited previously in his sixteen years' tenure of the see, would doubtless have signed any letter the king put before him; Warham may have been asked in the royal presence. Besides these two, only four bishops signed, of whom Longland of Lincoln is the single notable name. This, however, gives considerable significance to the signatures of the abbots, twenty-two in all, and all drawn from the group of parliamentary prelates. Though the letter contained no denial or limitation of papal jurisdiction, it nevertheless held a language which was, as the technical phrase of later days had it, 'offensive to pious ears'. Moreover, the signatories, whether they realized it or not, had taken a step, which it would not have been easy to retrace, along the road of submission to the king. In view of later events, it is worth noting that the abbots of Glastonbury and Reading were signatories.[3]

In the years that followed, the monks and canons were implicated, however unwillingly or mechanically, in all the stages of the ecclesiastical revolution, for their prelates, the *personae* of their houses, were all members of Convocation, and twenty-six black monk abbots, one cathedral prior (of Coventry) and two abbots of the Austin canons were members of the House of Lords. As regards the latter, we have direct information of the share taken by individuals, for the extant journals of the House of Lords begin in 1533; as regards the former, we have no exact figures of attendance, but all abbots and priors of independent houses were summoned to attend the Upper House of Convocation in either the northern or the southern province. Nunneries were not represented, and the Carthusian priors were by custom not cited; the mendicants also were out of the reckoning. With these exceptions, the religious superiors were all members of one at least of the two legislatures of medieval England. As such, those who attended took part, no doubt as a rule formally and almost automatically, in the series of momentous acts and decisions that marked the five years following Wolsey's death. On 7 February 1531 they were of the Convocation that acknowledged the king as Supreme Head, 'so far as the law of Christ allowed', and on 15 May 1532, by the agreement known as the Submission of the Clergy, they abandoned their right of independence in legislating for the Church. In the session of parliament beginning on 4 February 1533 the Act for Restraint of Appeals was passed, issuing in a statute which has been

1 N. Pocock, *Records of the Reformation; the divorce, 1527–33*, I, 429–32.
2 *Ibid.* 434–7.
3 The others were Westminster (Islip), Gloucester, Abingdon, York, Peterborough, Ramsey, Croyland, Thorney, Selby, Bardney, Holme, Hyde, Evesham (Lichfield), Malmesbury, Winchcombe (Kidderminster), Tewkesbury, Waltham and Cirencester.

characterized as 'the most important in [English] constitutional history of the sixteenth century, if not of any century'.[1] Shortly after, Convocation was asked to pronounce (5 April) on the question of law and fact in the matter of the Aragon marriage. Could the pope dispense from the impediment of affinity with a brother's widow, when the marriage had been consummated, and had the evidence of the suit established that the marriage of Katharine and Arthur had in fact been consummated? To both these questions the desired negative and affirmative answers were returned by overwhelming majorities. Of those present only sixteen gave an affirmative answer to the first question—among them the abbots of Winchcombe and Reading, and the priors of Ely, Walsingham and St Gregory's, Canterbury—and only six a negative one to the second query.[2]

In the following month (11 May 1533) the bishops and abbots were required to follow Cranmer's example, given a few months back, by repudiating the oath of obedience to the pope which they had taken on their appointment or election, and on 1 June they were present in large numbers at the coronation of Queen Anne at Westminster, which the monks of the house attended in copes. In the following year, in the session of parliament beginning 15 January 1534, the House of Lords received, and read three times (14–17 March), the Dispensations Act, which the writer of the Lords' Journal entitled 'the bill concerning the usurped authority of the Roman Pontiff'. At these readings twelve abbots were present, including those of Reading and Colchester.[3] Nine days later, a second version of the submission of the clergy went through, followed shortly by the Heresy Bill, which decreed, *inter alia*, that speaking against the papal claims was not heresy; then, in the presence of the king, members were solemnly reminded of the oath 'to observe all the effects and contents of the act' foreshadowed in the recently passed (first) Act of Succession as applicable to all the king's subjects.[4] The sanction of Praemunire had already been attached to the submission of the clergy and the Statute of Appeals, and the control of the exempt monasteries had been vested in the king.

Hitherto the abbots in parliament and the prelates summoned to Convocation had been the only ones to bear whatever personal responsibility attached to those who allowed the king and his minister to have their way. Now for the first time each individual religious was compelled to take personal action. The procedure in this difficult business of swearing-in the whole population above the age of childhood seems to have been that the Ordinary (or some other exalted commissioner) took the oaths of abbots, priors and curates, and that these produced lists of their subjects who were

---

1 Pickthorn, *Henry VIII*, 201. The lesser clergy and laity were justified in holding that the 'spirituality' had sold the pass. One John Heseham was apprehended by Sir Piers Dutton in 1536 for remarking 'that if the spirituall men had holden togeder the Kyng cold not have by [*sic*] Hed of the Churche' (*LP*, XI, 486).

2 Pocock, *op. cit.* II, 457–8.   3 *Journals of the House of Lords*, I, 75.   4 *Ibid.* I, 80–1.

sworn by lesser commissioners.[1] As is familiar to all, the Oath of Succession ostensibly did no more than secure allegiance to the offspring of Henry and Anne as lawful heirs to the Crown; it did, however, also imply a great deal that was not specifically asserted: the unlawfulness of papal dispensation, the validity of the Boleyn marriage and, indeed, a wholesale renunciation in practice of papal authority. To the reader of to-day its implications, enforced and interpreted by the cumulative effect of the past year's legislation, proclamations, and acts of power, are clear beyond a doubt. Ostensibly, however, and even plausibly to contemporaries, it was concerned solely with domestic issues, in particular the (to the lay mind) inextricably tangled question of the divorce, and the purely practical matter of the succession. Only those who had clear convictions on the validity of the Aragon marriage, and who realized that the papal jurisdiction had long ago been flouted and abandoned, could be expected to make a stand. Outside the religious orders only Fisher, More, Dr Nicholas Wilson and one or two others refused to take the oath. The Carthusians, as will be seen,[2] submitted after a time of hesitation and heart-searching, 'in so far as the law of God permitted', the Bridgettines also swore the oath.

The Oath of Succession, however, was not enough for Cromwell and the king. Even before it was imposed the bishops had been specifically sworn to the royal supremacy, which was to be proclaimed resoundingly on 9 June 1534. By that time the process of imposing the new doctrine on the clergy was in full swing. A beginning was made with the friars, who received special and very drastic treatment. There were several reasons for this. In the first place, preaching was their *raison d'être*, and they had long combined the functions, divided in the world of to-day, of popular preacher, political agitator, and broadcaster. Secondly, they were, as the monks and canons were not, members of a fully organized international order pivoted, however loosely, upon the papacy. Thirdly, the Observants in or near the capital, who stood high in popular esteem, had throughout the vicissitudes of the divorce suit kept up a vigorous protest in favour of Queen Katharine. Clearly, smooth progress with the new settlement of church affairs would be more likely if they could effectually be brought to heel.

A visitation was therefore decided upon, and for this purpose Cromwell appointed two agents upon whom he could rely, Friar John Hilsey, prior provincial of the Dominicans, and Friar George Browne, provincial of the Austin friars,[3] with powers to visit all the orders of friars and to secure

---

1 Cf. the letter of the bishop of Winchester to Cromwell on 5 May 1534, in Pocock, II, 536 (= *Letters of Stephen Gardiner*, ed. Muller, 56).

2 *Infra*, pp. 229–30.

3 The commission to Browne and Hilsey, dated 13 April, is in *LP*, VII, 587 (18). Bale, in his 'Catalogus Priorum Generalium', printed by Zimmerman, *Monumenta Historica Carmelitana*, I, 245–65, has paragraphs on Browne and the last Carmelite 'general' John Byrde.

their adhesion to a sufficiently comprehensive set of articles.[1] According to these, not only did they take the Oath of Succession (article 2), but they explicitly admitted the validity of the Boleyn marriage, accepted the king as supreme head of the Church, and denied that the bishop of Rome had any more authority than that of every diocesan bishop. In addition, they were to agree never to refer to the bishop of Rome as pope, and in their sermons they were to declare his power to be a usurpation. Two special directions were reserved for the Observants: they were to insert the king's name in the place of the pope's in their formula of profession, and to accept Friar Browne as their provincial. At all friaries a list of valuable and precious objects was to be drawn up.

The visitation of the four original orders appears to have gone off smoothly and without protest.[2] The Observants, as was to have been expected, were less compliant. In consequence, as will be related elsewhere, the two London houses were emptied of their communities, and the rest of the order were either imprisoned or driven into exile or quartered in confinement upon their Conventual brethren.[3]

Concurrently with the visitation of the friars, commissioners toured the country in the second half of 1534 demanding adherence on oath from members of chapters, monastic communities, colleges and hospitals to a series of assertions and undertakings, of which the first was the acceptance in perpetuity of the king as Supreme Head of the Church, and the second a declaration that the bishop of Rome, who had usurped the title of pope, had no more scriptural warranty for exercising any jurisdiction over England than had any other foreign bishop. These were followed by prohibitions against calling the bishop of Rome by the papal title and observing any of his laws that had not been ratified in England, and by commands to preach in favour of the royal supremacy and against the pope. Something over one hundred certificates of this oath-taking by religious houses are preserved, and there can be little doubt that the absence of the remainder is purely accidental.[4] Among the surviving lists there are no Cluniac, Cistercian, Premonstratensian or Gilbertine houses, but we know from other occasional evidence that some of these took the oath, and there is no reason to think that any were omitted. Nor is there any reason to suppose that any individuals refused to take the oath or to make the undertakings so far as words went. In this matter Baskerville's comment, that if any had refused to swear 'they and we would have heard about it', is

---

1 An inadequate précis of these is in *LP*, VII, 590. They are printed in full by H. de Vocht, *Acta Thomae Mori*, Appendix II, 208–9.

2 In a letter from Exeter of 21 June, Hilsey says that he has 'not found any religious persons who have utterly refused the oath of obedience' (*LP*, VII, 869). Constant, *Reformation* (Eng. trans.), 131, has 'many' for 'any', which presumably misled Hughes, *Reformation*, I, 276, into writing 'few'. The assent of all the London houses of friars is in Rymer, *Foedera*, XIV, 487–9 (17–20 April).   3 *V. infra*, pp. 210–11.

4 The list of houses with the name of the superior and one or two others is in Rymer, *Foedera*, XIV, 485–527. A complete and accurate list is in *Deputy Keeper's Reports*, VII (1846), App. 2, pp. 279–306.

probably valid.[1] It is true that the assistant keeper at the Record Office, who transcribed the lists for governmental publication more than a century ago, noted that many of the signatures were not autographs, as the lists were all written in a single hand, but this cannot be pressed to imply that the community were unaware of what was going forward.[2] The operative act was the 'corporal oath', taken upon the Scriptures in the presence of the commissioner by the whole community, and no doubt the list was prepared beforehand to expedite matters. We know of at least one individual who successfully evaded 'corporal' action, and of another who gave his assent by an ambiguous declaration which left his conscience free.[3] Others may have done the same, and some may even have made themselves scarce during the visit of the commissioners, while many doubtless swore with a mental reservation, or with no intention of binding themselves: Ἡγλῶσσ' ὀμώμοχ', ἡ δὲ φρὴν ἀνώμοτος.[4] In the external forum, however, all were regarded as having sworn, and the abbots and priors could certainly not evade responsibility for their action, either as individuals or as heads of families. No doubt many acted against the grain, and as a concession to present evils, and hoped for the day when England would once more acknowledge the pope. It is not for the historian to say how many or how few were thus disposed. It is, however, within his province to record the facts. In the words of More's trenchant apologue, they were first deflowered that they might afterwards be devoured.[5] It was not a question of conciliarist or Gallican opinion. By this action of compliance, which was not taken blindly or on a sudden impulse of fear, the monks did in fact admit a lay ruler to supreme power in spiritual matters and thus cut themselves off from the Roman Catholic Church of which the pope was head, and when we have no evidence of any expression of remorse or any word of recantation we have no grounds for supposing that they returned into her fold.

1 *EM*, 117.

2 *Deputy Keeper's Reports*, VII, 279: 'The signatures in my opinion are not all autographs, but frequently in the same handwriting, and my impression is, that the writer of the deed often added many names.'

3 The evasive monk was of Woburn (*LP*, x, 1239); the astute (or simple) one was the young sacristan of Beauvale who, 'when the king's Commissioners asked for the supremacy and how he took the king, answered plainly: "I take him as God and the Holy Church take him: and I am sure he taketh himself none otherwise."' With this simple answer (so we are told) they were contented (Hendriks, *The London Charterhouse*, 304–5). *V*. Appendix v, *infra*.

4 'My tongue swore, but my heart is unsworn.' The notorious declaration of Hippolytus by which Euripides incurred such odium (*Hippolytus*, 612) was unconsciously echoed by Friar Forest, who 'took the oath with the outward man, but his inward man never consented thereto' (*v. infra*, p. 370).

5 *The correspondence of Sir Thomas More*, ed. Rogers, p. 521. The various shifts of the perplexed minds of the day were catalogued once and for all by More in the Tower in August 1534, when he said to his daughter: 'Some may doe [i.e. take the Oath of Succession] for favour, and some may doe for feare... and some might hap to frame himself a conscience and thinke that while he did it for feare God wolde forgive it. And some may peradventure thinke that they will repent, and be shryven thereof... and some may peradventure be of that minde, that if they say one thing and thinke the while the contrary, God more regardeth their harte than their tonge.' Cf. also *ibid*. 527.

Throughout the summer and autumn the monasteries up and down the land were being sworn to the supremacy and repudiation of the pope. On 17 August the commissioners visited Worcester, and Prior More and his monks duly took the corporal oath. They did not know that two days previously, on the Feast of the Assumption of the Blessed Virgin, another company of men were taking an oath of a different kind. On that day a group of unknown students, of varying ages and nationalities, Peter Faber, Francis Xavier, Laynez, Salmeron, Bobadilla, Le Jay and Rodriguez, with their leader, Ignatius of Loyola, took their first vows in a chapel on Montmartre in Paris, thus laying the foundation-stone of the Company of Jesus.

While the commissioners were still on tour Cromwell and the king drove the last rivet into the fetter of royal supremacy. What had been proclaimed in June was given statutory record early in November by the Act of Supremacy, and a prospective and retrospective sanction was given for any oaths that might be imposed in its support.[1] This was followed by the Treasons Act,[2] which imposed the penalty for treason on all who maliciously spoke, wrote or acted in such a way as to 'deprive' the king of any dignity, title, or name of his royal estate. The first day of February was appointed for the act to come into force, and a few days before that date the title of Head of the English Church was solemnly added to Henry's style. It was by this combination of statutes that Fisher, More and the Carthusians were finally brought within the net. The penalty for refusing the Act of Succession had been no more than imprisonment and loss of goods, and the swearing-in of prelates and communities to the maintenance of the Supremacy had presumably been accomplished by the order of Head of the Church and his vicar-general; there had been no statutory penalty attached to a refusal to swear, and for reasons of policy Cromwell had been unwilling to bring the Carthusians and Bridgettines sharply up to the brink; the Observants were a more pressing problem, and could be dealt with by an act of power, but the others, as enclosed religious, were at once less of a nuisance and more difficult to eliminate; with them the process, as we shall see, was slow.

The adhesions to the Supremacy, which had been collected during the autumn of 1534, were still incomplete when the first move was made to appoint visitors for the monasteries; and these appointments were followed almost at once by those of the commissioners for the tenth, the compilers of the *Valor Ecclesiasticus*. When at last the visitors began their work in the late summer of 1535, the first of the injunctions that they carried with them ordered the abbot and community 'faithfully, truly and heartily to

---

1 Act of Supremacy, 26 Henry VIII, c. 1:2; Act of Succession, *ibid.* c. 2. Chapuys heard of the passing of the Supremacy Act on the morning of 17 November (*LP*, VII, 1437; cf. 1377, 1482). For the decree of 15 January 1535, announcing that the title of Supreme Head of the Church would be assumed by the king on 1 February, *v.* Rymer, *Foedera*, XIV, 549.

2 Treasons Act, 26 Henry VIII, c. 13.

keep and observe, and cause, teach and procure to be kept' the observance of the Acts of Succession and Supremacy; the second enjoined that all should 'observe and fulfill by all the means that they best may, the statutes of this realm, made or to be made for the suppression and taking away of the usurped and pretended jurisdiction of the bishop of Rome within this realm'. It was thus a harassed and submissive body, habituated to royal visitations of every sort, who had nothing to fear or to hope from papal action, that faced the interrogatories and injunctions of Leigh and Layton.

The successive stages of acquiescence on the part of the religious, and the several degrees of oath-taking have been set out in some detail because it is very easy for a reader to lose his bearings in the rapid and confused succession of events and legislation. Even careful historians continue to make misleading statements. Many confuse the statutory oath to the Act of Succession of 1534 with the non-statutory oath renouncing the papal jurisdiction in the same year, or with the process consequent upon the denial of the king's title of Supreme Head after 1 February 1535. Others make the mistake of denying that any oath to the supremacy was ever exacted. In consequence, many of the apologists of the monks have shown themselves ignorant or forgetful of the fact that by the end of 1535 all the monks, with the rarest individual exceptions, such as the remnant of the London Carthusians (and apparently also the Bridgettines), had repeatedly and solemnly rejected the pope and explicitly accepted royal supremacy, while some of the critics of the monks reduce unduly the admittedly small number of those who refused one or other of the oaths.[1]

1 Baskerville, whose scholarly accuracy has often been assumed without question, is often in fact inaccurate, and sometimes tendentiously so. Thus, e.g. on pp. 116–18 of *EM*, he confuses the oath of succession with the oath abjuring the pope, and reduces and confuses the number of those among the Carthusians, Bridgettines and Observants who refused to take the anti-papal oath. To those just named must be added the rare but notable individuals, such as the monk of Jervaulx, Friars Browne, Cooke and Stone, and the secular priests and laymen, who during the next eight or ten years refused the oath of supremacy and died for it.

CHAPTER XV

ELIZABETH BARTON

The first series of happenings that embroiled a number of monks and religious with the government was connected with the career of Elizabeth Barton, the Maid of Kent. It was the lot of this unfortunate woman to be the object of the most diverse judgments when alive, and historians have not succeeded in reaching an agreement which was never achieved by contemporaries.[1] The problem is indeed perplexed beyond hope of certain solution, for not only have we to deal with evidence provided by interested, dishonest and terrified parties, but we are also called upon to make, at least by implication, a spiritual judgment of a kind peculiarly difficult in any age or variety of circumstances. Was Elizabeth Barton, in her days of freedom, a hypocrite, or a hysteric, or a sincere recipient of some kind of supernatural influence, or a mixture of two or more of these characters? Did she in fact, freely and frankly, confess to imposture, or were the words imputed to her falsely or wrested from her by trickery, threats and mal-treatment, and twisted into a meaning which she did not intend them to bear? Or was it rather that her faith failed under physical or psychological duress and, once lost, was never recovered? Though the issue may seem trivial, or at least outside the scope of an historian, he cannot avoid making a judgment, at least by implication, for the matter affected the fate and reputation of the Nun's clientèle of monks and friars, of whom the most notable were two monks of Christ Church, Bocking and Dering, and two Franciscan Observants, Risby and Rich, who were closely associated with her career, and shared her fate.

Elizabeth Barton was a servant maid of one Thomas Cobb, steward of the archiepiscopal estates that lay around the Kentish village of Aldington, which lies on the lower slope of the downs that face westward over Romney Marsh. At Easter, 1525, she became to all appearance seriously ill, and remained so for several months; the illness was accompanied by trances, in which she foretold coming events and asserted that the Blessed Virgin had appeared to her and foretold her cure at the neighbouring

---

[1] The episode of the Nun of Kent occupies considerable space in relevant volumes of *LP* and figures at length in contemporary chronicles and propaganda, especially Hall's *Chronicle*, II, 244–5, 247–59, and Richard Morison, *Apomaxis calumniarum*, pp. 73–5. All modern historians have devoted space to her; in the nineteenth century Lingard showed himself unfavourable, as did also Froude, while Gasquet attempted a rehabilitation; the most balanced judgment was perhaps that of Bridgett in his *Life* of Fisher. The article on Elizabeth Barton in the *DNB*, by the editor Sir Sidney Lee, is violently biased and full of historical errors, as is also that on Bocking. References to her also abound in the works and letters of More, Fisher, Cromwell, Cranmer and Tyndale. In more recent times A. D. Cheney, 'The Holy Maid of Kent', in *TRHS*, n.s., XVIII, gives a useful account of her early days, and the Rev. L. E. Whatmore published the text of Capon's sermon at Paul's Cross in *EHR*, LVIII.

chapel of Court-at-Street. The cure duly took place amid a great throng of people on the Feast of the Assumption (15 August), and the chapel became a place of pilgrimage, with a fame that endured even after its originator had suffered a disgraceful death. Meanwhile, Richard Masters, the rector of Aldington, had informed Archbishop Warham, who took the traditional step of setting up a commission of enquiry, appointing as its head Dr Edward Bocking, cellarer of the cathedral monastery of Christ Church. The commission reported favourably, and at the archbishop's orders the Maid entered the Benedictine convent of St Sepulchre near Canterbury, where Warham appointed Bocking to be her confessor and director. This was in the autumn of 1525, when Elizabeth was sixteen years of age.

She remained at Canterbury for almost eight years, but as the rule of enclosure was not strictly applied at that time she was able to travel to London and elsewhere on visits of devotion, or in her role of spiritual counsellor and comforter of those in distress. Her illnesses and trances continued to occur, especially at the Feast of the Conception of the Blessed Virgin (8 December),[1] and she believed herself charged with messages of hope and warning to great and small alike. At the same time her life was blameless and edifying, and she won and retained the confidence and love of many who found in her advice and encouragement a strengthening and inspiring force.

When in 1527 the matter of the king's marriage began to be bruited, the Nun of Kent, as she was now called, was steadfast in her opposition, which was, so she said, repeatedly encouraged and given precision by what she saw or heard in her trances. It must be remembered that in the early stages of the affair the king consulted widely all and sundry, and professed to have an open mind on the question, while the trials and negotiations of the long-drawn suit gave the utmost publicity to every aspect of the question which, as has happened so often with the matrimonial difficulties of those in high place, was a burning topic of general interest for six weary years. The Nun's pronouncements, therefore, whatever may be thought of her sincerity or spiritual wisdom, were not in the beginning as rash or dangerous as they came to appear, or as they have seemed to unsympathetic historians. Her reputation was clearly great. Warham himself, in 1528, obtained for her an interview with Wolsey[2] whom, so it seems, she rebuked sharply both for his general neglect of his responsibilities and in particular for his share in the divorce proceedings. She also obtained access to Silvester Darius, Auditor of the Rota, and Giovanni Antonio Pulleo, and sent by them messages to Clement VII, threatening him with disaster if he encouraged the king.[3] She pressed Queen

---

1 So the prior of Christ Church in Wright, *SL*, VII, 21–2.

2 *LP*, IV, ii, 4806 (1 October 1528). Warham refers to Elizabeth as 'a well-disposed and virtuous woman, as he hears from her sisters'. He seems to have been consistently favourable to her, introducing her to Fisher as well as Wolsey, and he clearly believed in her sincerity and apparently also in her spiritual pretensions.

3 So Capon in *EHR*, LVIII, 467–8, and the preamble to the attainder (Hall, II, 257).

Katharine for an interview, but the queen steadfastly and, as it proved, wisely, refused to allow her to enter her presence.[1] Henry himself sent for her and granted her an audience in which she spoke plainly against his project and of the catastrophe that would overtake him if he persevered with it. The king, uncertain as yet of his success and perhaps still affected by scruples of conscience or superstition, took her visit ostensibly in good part, but did not forget it. Whether her exhortations, as was later asserted, had any real effect upon the conduct of Wolsey and Warham cannot be known with any certainty, but in the years when all the spiritual élite of London and its environs—More, Fisher, the Friars Observant, the Bridgettines and the Carthusians—were known to be hostile to the divorce the influence of a reputed saint and visionary cannot have been negligible.

During all this time Dr Edward Bocking was her adviser and impresario,[2] and, like William Flete almost two centuries before, the centre of a group that recalls the *famiglia* that gathered round their 'mother', St Catherine of Siena. Besides Bocking and Dering, there was another monk of Christ Church and Dan John Hawley of St Augustine's, along with several of Bocking's 'novices'. Then there were Dr Risby, a Wykehamist of both foundations and now warden of the Grey Friars at Canterbury, and Dr Rich, warden of Richmond; Henry Gold, one of Warham's chaplains, and his brother; Robert Colens, a Canterbury anchorite, Christopher Warener, anchorite at the Black Friars in the same city,[3] Thomas Lawrence, registrar to the archdeacon of Canterbury, Edward Thwaites, a Kentish gentleman, and, on the fringe of the circle, Dan Henry Man, a Carthusian of Sheen, and several other monks from there and from the London Charterhouse. Elizabeth Barton was a familiar and honoured visitor at Syon, and on at least one occasion gave extremely salutary and effective counsel to a woman of London who claimed to be a visionary.[4] During this long period of eight years nothing in her conduct invited criticism; the innuendoes in subsequent government documents are common form and are patently unjustified. Though young in years the Nun established an immediate ascendancy over men of mature age. Thus Henry Gold, Warham's chaplain, wrote to Dering that he was now about to visit her monthly: 'I promise you, I think every day a year till the month days, and that day of her presence (alack for pity) is no day, ne worthy to be called an hour',[5] and Henry Man the Carthusian, to whom she was 'my good mother Elizabeth, in whom is my trust', could write: 'Let us magnify the name of the Lord, who has raised up this holy virgin,

---

1 *LP*, VI, 1419. This probably explains Chapuys's neutral attitude towards the Nun, whom he might have been expected on general grounds to favour.

2 The term is used by H. A. L. Fisher, who gives what is on the whole the best short narrative of the episode (*Political History of England, 1485–1547*, 331 ff.).

3 *LP*, VI, 1336. He writes of 'her perfect life and virtue'.

4 More, *Letter* 197, p. 484.

5 *LP*, V (1531–2), 1698.

a mother indeed to me, and a daughter to thee, for our salvation—she has raised a fire in some hearts that you would think like unto the operation of the Holy Spirit in the primitive church.'[1] She was, in addition, well known to three eminent men, two of whom, at least, in honesty, experience of the world, prudence, mental acumen and a sense of spiritual values were unsurpassed by any of their contemporaries. In a judgment of character the concurrent testimony of Warham, Fisher and More, and their esteem for Elizabeth Barton over a series of years, must carry considerable weight, and it goes far towards eliminating the possibility of complete and long-standing fraudulence.

The quality of her experiences, however, is another matter. Mystical theology, and in particular the discernment of spirits and the criteria of authentic spirituality, were unfamiliar topics in early Tudor schools of divinity, and neither Warham nor Fisher would have claimed expertise in the field. Dr Bocking was a trained divine, but there is no indication that he had had any experience in guiding contemplatives. The directors of the Nun, therefore, lacked any assistance comparable to the classic treatises which the great Spanish mystics and theologians were to produce in such luxuriance before the century was out, and sixteenth-century England had made few demands upon directors of souls. Several of the experiences related by or claimed for Elizabeth Barton were such as would immediately have put a cautious mind on the alert, and they did in fact thus affect Sir Thomas More. At the same time, symptoms of trance and physical illness, which to-day would unhesitatingly be classed as hysterical or psychopathic, have frequently appeared in the early stages of the lives of those who have later been distinguished by virile sanctity,[2] and the same may be said even of the more disquieting experiences of the Nun of Kent. Moreover, the best known of the medieval ecstatics had been distinguished by the abnormality of their lives. If those who knew her best were correct in their judgment of her essential goodness and sincerity, Elizabeth Barton, who unquestionably exhibited symptoms of hysteria in her youth, may perhaps be regarded as an instance of a type described with such precision by St John of the Cross fifty years later. More than once he gives instructions how to deal with one fundamentally sincere and receptive of spiritual influence and called to the contemplative life, but still clouded by psychological weaknesses and unable to distinguish between true spiritual knowledge and the workings of imagination or hysteria. To such the same wise advice was given again and again by the Carmelite doctor: to disregard entirely all apparently distinct visions and revelations and emotions as if they had never been, and to give all one's care to loving and serving the invisible God, known by faith

---

1 *LP*, VI (1533), 835, 1149 (2).
2 Cf. the illnesses recorded in the autobiographies of St Teresa of Avila, a younger contemporary of the Nun (*Life*, ed. Peers, ch. v), and St Thérèse of Lisieux in the 1880's (*Histoire d'une Ame*, ch. III).

alone.[1] Dr Bocking lived in a world where this sane doctrine was not familiar, and indeed in a very few years men more learned and experienced than himself were to be at odds over similar phenomena in one greater and more fortunate than Elizabeth Barton.[2] Bocking is indeed the most elusive figure in this story. None of his relevant correspondence has been preserved, none of his contemporaries has any personal allusion to him; we hear nothing of his part or conduct in the final *débâcle*. From his antecedents and attainments, as prior of Canterbury College, we should expect to find him a conventional, dry, practical, unspiritual and unenthusiastic man. Whatever he was, he undoubtedly acted unwisely in making much of the Maid's prophecies and still more in publishing them and abetting others in doing so. He can scarcely be acquitted of fostering any proclivity there may have been to fantasy on the part of his protégée, and it is very probable that the encouragement of Bocking and others, who were admittedly hostile to the royal divorce, had its effect, if only a subconscious one, upon the subject-matter of the Nun's auditions. It is, however, most unlikely that he practised elaborate deceit or trickery; his fault was that of entering waters too deep for him, and of exploiting the outward and visible and fallacious accidents where he should have sought first the kingdom of God.

Even so, the good character of Elizabeth Barton and her powerful well-wishers might have protected her, as they had protected previous holy women of the Middle Ages who had spoken of the testimonies of God before kings and popes, and had not been put to the blush. For some eight years her case had been treated on traditional lines: enquiries by the ordinary; assignment to a convent; appointment of a qualified confessor; and she had enjoyed the respect accorded to one who had survived formal examination and might well be a privileged witness to the unseen. The wisest man in England, the ex-Chancellor himself, old enough to be her father, had addressed her as his 'good Lady, and right dearly beloved sister in Our Lord', and had subscribed himself her 'hearty loving Brother and Beadsman'.[3] But in 1533 circumstances had changed. The great divide had been crossed and the control of things had shifted. Warham was dead, Henry was married to Anne, and Cromwell and Cranmer were in charge of Church and State, the one bent on eliminating all opposition to what was now *fait accompli*, the other deeply and personally committed to the change and devoid of all respect for mystics, whether genuine or

---

1 Cf. *The Ascent of Mount Carmel*, book II *passim*, esp. c. 18, which, had Dr Bocking been able to read and follow it, would have saved both himself and his penitent from much sorrow. The saint showed himself well able to detect false mysticism (*Works*, ed. Peers, III, 299–300, 366).

2 St Teresa, *Life*, ch. xviii (ed. Peers, 185): 'They used to tell [my confessor Fr Baltasar Alvarez] that he must be on his guard against me, lest the devil should deceive him into believing anything I might say to him, and they gave him similar examples of what had happened with other people.' Cf. p. 189: one of her confessors told her 'it was clear I was being deceived by the devil'.

3 More, *Letter* 192, pp. 465–6.

counterfeit. Events suddenly began to move swiftly. On 15 July the Carthusian Henry Man, writing to Bocking, had rejoiced that there were left a remnant who had not bowed the knee to Baal.[1] On 19 July or thereabouts Cranmer, acting on orders from Cromwell who had himself been commanded by the king, sent to the prioress of St Sepulchre's with orders to bring Elizabeth Barton to the archbishop at Otford in Kent.[2]

It is natural to ask why a move was made at this precise moment, after so long a delay. In default of explicit evidence it would seem likely that the king was moved by news or forecasts of his impending excommunication, which took place on 4 July in Rome. In the sequel, the chief aim of the king and his minister was to deprive both excommunication and prophetess of their credit by representing the former as effected by the latter, and the latter as deluded or criminal. Whatever the reason for the move, Cranmer, as on other occasions, acted with deceptive gentleness, and was for sending the Nun to Court-of-Street in the hopes that new and more dangerous revelations might be forthcoming.[3] Cromwell, however, had followed up his first letter with a questionnaire to be used by the archbishop, and this had the desired effect of eliciting answers bearing on the king's marriage. At the end of September the minister was ready and Sir Christopher Hales, the Attorney-General, was at Canterbury rounding up the selected victims. 'As I can catch them, one after other', he wrote, 'I will send them to you.' 'The two religious men', he added, with reference to Bocking and Dering, 'are of as good reputation as any in their degree.'[4] After a first examination, it seems, the Nun was sent back to Canterbury, and enquiries were made of all those to whom she was known to have spoken. Early in November she was arrested again and taken to the Tower, for Chapuys had heard of her imprisonment by 12 November.[5] From this moment onwards we are in the realm of uncertainty and conjecture, with fragments of information that are at best unreliable and for the most part either biased or patently tendentious. It is clear that the Nun was examined several times by the Council and in the Star Chamber, and on or before 20 November a great gathering was got together of which the Council formed the nucleus, but which included also the principal judges, a number of bishops and many nobles from every part of England.[6] Once assembled, they debated for three whole days together what Chapuys

---

1 *LP*, VI, 835. The reference is no doubt to those who still disapproved of the king's second marriage.   2 *LP*, VI, 869.

3 *LP*, VI, 967. Richard Gwent, Dean of the Arches, writes to Cromwell on 11 August: 'My Lord doth yet but dally with her, as he did believe her every word: and as soon as he hath all he can get of her she shall be sent to you.'

4 *LP*, VI, 1148 (24 September).

5 *Spanish State Papers, 1531–3*, no. 1149 (*LP*, VI, 1419). Chapuys speaks of Elizabeth Barton as 'a nun who had always lived till this time as a good, simple and saintly woman'.

6 The fullest account is that of Chapuys, *Spanish State Papers*, no. 1153 (*LP*, VI, 1445). It is confirmed by Capon, ed. Whatmore, *art. cit.* 473, and in part by Cromwell himself (Wright, *SL*, no. xi, p. 31), who speaks of 'as greate assembly and counsel of the lordes of this realme as hath beene seene many yeares heretofore out of a parliament'.

calls 'the crimes, or rather the foolish superstitions, of the Nun and her adherents', no doubt in the wider context of the threat from Rome. The principal charge against Elizabeth Barton was of having spoken and influenced opinion against the king's divorce and second marriage, and she was accused of having influenced Warham, Wolsey and even Clement VII in this sense. At the end of it all Chancellor Audley warned the assembly not to take any notice of papal sentences induced by the 'damnable and diabolic instrumentality' of the nun, or of her prophecies that the king would shortly have to face rebellion and dethronement, with an ultimate prospect of damnation. At this, so Chapuys relates, the gathering, which so far had listened in silence, broke out with the cry: 'To the stake with her!' The king, indeed, proposed that the Nun and her associates should be condemned as traitors and heretics, but verbal treason was not yet criminal by statute, and the men of law were not prepared to condemn for misprision of treason those who had merely heard what the Nun herself had told the king face to face.

The Nun had been present throughout the Chancellor's speech, listening with perfect equanimity, and avowing that all that had been said of her activities was true.[1] The phrase is ambiguous, but it would seem certain from other sources that at some time during her examination Elizabeth Barton had 'confessed' that her alleged revelations were imaginary. What lay behind this confession cannot be known. She had been in the Tower, and repeatedly examined, not only by the Council, but apparently also by Cranmer and Latimer, who makes an unexpected appearance for a moment.[2] There is no evidence that torture was used, but the possibility cannot be ruled out;[3] she was certainly exposed to searching and pitiless interrogation, mingled with cajolery and threats, from a group of extremely able and unscrupulous lawyers. The letters of Cromwell to Fisher and More, and the reports of the trials of the two latter, give us some idea of the mental and moral pressure that was brought to bear upon those whom the government wished to trick or to break. Joan of Arc a century before, and Edmund Campion fifty years later, lost their balance for a moment when hard pressed by great intelligence devoid of truth and mercy. Whatever the circumstances, Elizabeth Barton would seem (more

---

1 *Spanish State Papers*, no. 1149: 'All this time the Nun was present in the room without exhibiting the least fear or astonishment...but, on the contrary, openly confessing and avowing that all that had been said of her was perfectly true.' Even if accurate, this account is ambiguous, as we do not know what had been said previously. Whatmore, *art. cit.* 473, n. 1, takes it as an 'open and intrepid admission of opposing the divorce', which might seem at first glance plausible. It would, however, appear to be undeniable that the Nun made some sort of damaging confession at least four or five days before 23 November, and this brings us very near the date of the council. Moreover, Capon on 16 November refers to a confession (*LP*, VI, 1433; cf. *EHR*, LVIII, 473), while on 23 November he asserts this to have been made before the great assembly.

2 Hall, *Chronicle*, II, 244, notes the share of 'one called Hugh Latimer'.

3 Constant, *Reformation in England* (Eng. trans. I, 210 n.), asserts that torture was used, citing Morison, *Apomaxis calumniarum*, 75, but there is no such statement in Morison.

than that cannot be said) to have declared that her revelations were imaginary,[1] and had been suggested and encouraged by Bocking and others. This, however, was not the end. Almost immediately after her 'confession' she chanced to meet Thomas Gold, one of her associates, in the Tower, and told him that her confession was due to a divine inspiration that had come to her to deny her revelations, since God's good time for their fulfilment had not yet come. Gold, who was not a prisoner, passed this on to his brother, and it reached Bocking and Risby at Canterbury.[2] However garbled and untrustworthy the incident may be, it seems to indicate that Elizabeth Barton's 'confession' was a failure of constancy, rather than an admission of fraud, and that she endeavoured to prevent its consequences. In the sequel, she seems to have gone back upon her disavowal, and to have reiterated her confession.

Whatever the truth of the matter, she had broken up her company and destroyed her credit once and for all. The government decided to bring contempt and ridicule upon the whole affair by a public denunciation at Paul's Cross, Canterbury, and elsewhere. John Capon (*alias* Salcot), abbot of Hyde, a protégé of Anne Boleyn who was expecting a bishopric, allowed himself to be put up to preach and to vilify the Nun. His sermon, which has been preserved,[3] is confused, inaccurate and scurrilous, but it seems certain that Elizabeth Barton and her leading associates, who were present, signed some sort of confession.[4] No further steps were taken for some time against the Nun, though she and her friends remained in prison.

1 Capon says this (*EHR*, LVIII, 469, 473) and, though his word is intrinsically worthless, he was speaking in the presence of the Nun herself, who had previously shown herself ready enough in self-defence. We may of course suppose that she had been rendered harmless by physical or psychological torture, but there is no direct evidence of this.

2 Capon's account (*EHR*, *loc. cit.* 473–4) of this recantation is the most interesting addition to our knowledge furnished by his sermon when printed *in extenso*. He twice emphasizes that it had been made very recently, 'within these four days past' (p. 473), 'within these four days' (p. 474). It is not easy to agree with the editor, Father Whatmore, when he maintains that the Nun made no confession of guilt of any kind. Capon's account receives some corroboration from the anonymous informer who gives in his letter to Cromwell (Wright, *Letters*, VI, 18) among other 'revelations' of the Nun: 'How the angell of God hath comaundyd hur to say that all ar but yllusions, for the tyme is not cum that God wille put forth the wurk.' All this evidence, however, comes from tainted sources; it is possible that the Nun revoked her confession without any appeal to supernatural warnings.

3 Summarized in *LP*, VII, 72 (3), and printed by Whatmore, who shows that the sermon with the necessary alterations was repeated a week or two later at Canterbury by Dr Nicholas Heath. This makes it very probable that the sermon as delivered by Capon at Paul's Cross was prefabricated in Cromwell's office.

4 *Art. cit.* 473: 'And these persons here present...have confessed themselves to be greatly to blame that they have given so light credence unto her upon her own saying, without due examination and proof had thereupon, and have confessed that they surely believe her said revelations to have been falsely forged, contrived, feigned and counterfeited.' From this it is clear that they confessed to having been deluded by the Nun, and deplore their credulity. They make no confession of having used her as a tool. The preamble to the attainder, however, assumes that they took an active and deliberate part in the deceit, and this insinuation was made still more precisely by Hall, *Chronicle*, II, 245: 'These... confessed their feigned hipocrisy, and dissimuled sanctitee [this slip surely indicates that Hall is extending the Nun's confession to all]...and signed [a bill] declaryng their subtile, craftie and supersticious doynges.'

The king and Cromwell were far more interested in implicating the more distinguished opponents of the divorce. Queen Katharine, by steadily refusing to see or to correspond with the Nun, had kept herself out of range, but More and Fisher seemed vulnerable. As the lawyers still boggled at admitting a case for misprision, it was decided to proceed by the novel method of attainder, thus obviating the necessity for trial. In the bill as originally presented, the names of both More and Fisher were included. More's defence was so strong that the king grudgingly agreed to omit him; Fisher was more deeply implicated and more forthright in defence; his name remained. The bill as finally passed, not without difficulty, went over the whole affair in a long, rambling and untruthful preamble, drawing freely upon the story as given in the official version of the previous November.[1] On 21 April 1534, Elizabeth Barton, the Benedictines Bocking and Dering, the Observant Risby and the priest Henry Gold, were executed as traitors at Tyburn. A confession, purporting to be the Nun's last words at the gallows, is printed by the chronicler Hall.[2]

As has been said, the two monks Bocking and Dering remain dim figures, but on no sober interpretation of the story does the crude villainy attributed to Bocking in the sermon and preamble of the attainder, and repeated by many historians, appear probable or indeed morally possible. All the evidence goes to show that he believed in the basic sincerity of Elizabeth Barton until the *débâcle* of November 1533. In other words, she was not his tool or 'medium' in any criminal sense. On the other hand, he can scarcely be acquitted of gross indiscretion as a spiritual director, which in the circumstances was also gross imprudence. Even on the most favourable interpretation of her character, the Maid had more than a touch of hysteria and fantasy, which were as apparent to clear minds of the sixteenth century as they are now. It should have been his task to restrain and conceal all such questionable manifestations, to screen her from all publicity, and to advise her to make nothing of her visions and auditions. It should have been clear to him that she was nearer of kin to Margery Kempe than to Joan of Arc or Catherine of Siena. Instead, attracted by the superficially marvellous, and searching for parallels in the ecstatics of the past, he acted as a showman rather than as a director. The others, with a natural but regrettable excitement at contact with a reputed mystic who shared their opinions on current events, were unable to maintain a prudent reserve. They cast their pearl, if pearl it was, before insensitive eyes, and the consequence was inevitable.

As for Elizabeth Barton herself, her career must always remain enigmatic through lack of reliable evidence at the crucial point. As has already

---

1 As statutory authority was not yet available to support a charge of verbal treason, care was taken to insert in the bill such phrases as might imply actions, e.g. 'the sayd Hugh Rych actually travayled, etc.' The preamble opens with a resounding declaration of the sanctity of the king's second marriage, and is throughout full of untruthful and tendentious statements.

2 Printed by Hall, *Chronicle*, II, 259, and reprinted Cheney, *art. cit.* 119–20.

been suggested, the most probable interpretation would seem to be that she was basically sincere, a mystic *manquée* who never learned, either owing to her own lack of fidelity or to unwise direction, how she might reach the depth of spiritual vision that sustained the Carthusians, More and Fisher in their hour of testing. When left alone to face the confusion of falsehood and cruelty she showed herself lacking in the simple heroism and humility which had ultimately saved Joan of Arc. She has been called the first of the conservative martyrs,[1] and in so far as she died because with her, as with almost all those who died martyrs' deaths under Henry VIII, the head and front of her offending was an adverse judgment on the king's divorce, she may be counted to have died to uphold Christian morality, but in fact her equivocal conduct deprives her of a right to the title. Yet her death, and still more that of her supporters among the monks and friars, was a not unimportant moment in the chain of events. It was one more warning that neither the religious habit, nor a reputation for sanctity, nor a skill in divinity, counted for anything with those now in power; one more instance of the failure of traditional piety to justify itself to the world; one more warning to those who fain would have called a halt to the march of events but who loved too well their life and the England that they knew. Cranmer informed his friends with great satisfaction and some inaccuracy of the discomfiture of the queen's enemies. The community of Christ Church felt called upon to dissociate themselves, in abject and fulsome terms, from their unfortunate colleagues, and the archbishop followed up their appeal to the king with a supporting letter.[2] 'I suppose', he adds persuasively, 'they will desire me to offer unto your grace for a plesure ii or iii c lib.' The monks of St Augustine's, for their part, indulged for the last time that spirit of emulation which for nearly a thousand years had distinguished the relations of the two Canterbury churches to each other.[3] Of Elizabeth Barton herself, the only personal memorial is the list of her scanty belongings—'an old matteres,vii corsse schettes....A lyttell old dyaper towell....An old mantell and a kyrtell'—which escheated to the Crown as a traitor's goods, but were in part bought back by her prioress and her sisters.[4]

---

1 H. A. L. Fisher, *Political History of England, 1485–1547*, 334.
2 The letters of Prior Goldwell and his monks are in Wright, *SL*, VII, VIII. Cranmer's letter to the king in favour of 'my priory' is *ibid*. LXXXI (13 December 1533) on p. 271 of the Parker Society's edition.
3 *Chronicle of a Monk of St Augustine's, Canterbury* (CS, o.s. 77, pp. 280–1).
4 Wright, *SL*, x.

Part Three

SUPPRESSION AND DISSOLUTION

CHAPTER XVI

BEFORE THE DISSOLUTION

I. THE OUTLOOK OF THE AGE

Before embarking upon a narrative of the events leading to the dissolution of the monasteries, it may be permissible to note some characteristics of Tudor society which in the past have often been overlooked by those unacquainted with the age.

One such characteristic is that the modern tradition of public service, and even the outlook of a mechanical impersonal bureaucracy, had not yet come into existence. The agents of government great and small, from an Audley or a Cromwell downwards, were the servants of their immediate superior who might be the king himself or a minister directly appointed by him. They had their living and their career to make, and this could only be done by executing his commands and meeting his wishes; to suppose that they had any of the modern civil servant's or police officer's sense of duty to the public is to transfer the outlook of the present day to an age which had another way of regarding life. The same consideration applies, *mutatis mutandis*, to the holders of all other positions or offices that are to-day considered of trust or 'public', such as those of members of parliament, lawyers or even the judiciary. Among men of these classes there was a complete absence of the ethical conventions or the professional etiquette of their modern counterparts, save perhaps among men of the law when the issue was between private parties. All were the servants, mediate or immediate, of the king.

This was of itself no new circumstance; it had been thus during the latter medieval centuries; what had changed was the position of the king. In the past the king in his public capacity had been, so to say, in solidarity with his servants and his subjects, the linchpin of a system of which he himself was an integral part. Now the king was, or could be, the authority using all his servants and services to implement a policy or design in which they as a body had no interest or share, and towards which they might feel dislike or disapproval. It was a peculiarity of the early sixteenth century in England, as distinct both from the fifteenth and from the seventeenth, that there was no class or group or profession or party sufficiently strong or resolute or self-confident to hamper the sovereign in the exercise of his initiative and executive powers. The Church and the baronage had had their day: the landed gentry and aristocracy and parliament were not as yet conscious of political power.

The Tudor sovereignty, especially in the later years of Henry VIII, has sometimes been described as the rule of a tyrant, and the decade of Cromwell's ascendency, in particular the years following the Treasons Act of 1534, has often been called a 'reign of terror'. The phrase, or its equivalent, first used by historians committed to no party allegiance, was taken up by Catholic apologists, and has recently been as energetically repudiated. It is perhaps a misleading phrase in this context. First applied to an episode in the French Revolution, it can properly be used only of a situation in which a whole class, whether social, political, racial or religious, is doomed to extinction irrespective of any personal act of resistance or submission on the part of its members. The French aristocracy at a particular stage of the Revolution, the propertied class politically opposed to the Russian revolution, the Jews in Hitler's Germany are examples of such a class. Henry VIII and Cromwell were often ruthless towards individuals, but they never wished or attempted to eliminate a class or party as such. The imposition, with extreme sanctions, of an oath such as that to the succession of Anne's children, or against the pope's jurisdiction, was a tyrannical act, and the imposition of the death penalty for verbal treason was so likewise, but in neither case was a particular class marked down for destruction which could not be avoided by any act of submission on the part of the destined victims. Save perhaps in the case of the Pole family, where purely personal and dynastic motives were allowed play, Henry VIII and Cromwell destroyed only those who opposed, or refused to accept, their measures and policies.

Nevertheless, our reaction must not go too far. The repeated operation of the policy of exacting oaths from some or all of his subjects, taken together with the legal doctrine of verbal treason and misprision of treason and the official encouragement of delation, did in fact put great numbers of the king's lieges in a predicament and a state of potential danger such as has rarely, if ever, existed in this country either before or since. In all the specifically religious persecutions of the sixteenth century the accused could at least escape the supreme penalty by renouncing his beliefs. Verbal treason, on the other hand, once committed, could not be undone or atoned for by any subsequent recantation or protestation of loyalty or change of heart. An idle or ill-tempered sally or complaint, a justified criticism of government policy, spoken among acquaintances round a fire or on the road to market, could be hoarded in an informer's memory and produced by a spiteful enemy or an officious time-server a year or two afterwards with fatal consequences to the speaker. That Cromwell and his agents, for reasons which are hidden from us, let many cases drop even where the evidence was clear, should certainly be borne in mind by historians, but their behaviour, while it spared many, brought others, equally guilty or innocent, to the block and gallows.

A second characteristic of the age, less important but still of significance for the historian, is the language of piety used by all men of every class and under all circumstances. This habit, indeed, of commending one's employers or correspondents to the care of the Holy Spirit, and of attributing the success of one's policies to the direct favour of God, is so common and is found in men so unashamedly mundane that it would be a mistake to regard it as a cloak or as a piece of hypocrisy; it was simply a conventional survival. Religious hypocrisy, indeed, appearing in a habit of attributing godly motives to worldly policies and profitable enterprises, has often, and perhaps with reason, been alleged as a peculiarly English characteristic, and the public men of the Tudor age, from the king downwards, were not exempt from the fault, but since a use of the language of devout faith when writing of human relationships and business affairs has dropped out of fashion in the present century we are apt to take professions of religious feeling as evidence of a sincere (even if of a misguided) religious outlook. To make this assumption of the public men of the reign of Henry VIII is most unwise.

The early Tudor age was not one in which artistic or wide intellectual interests were common, as they were in contemporary Italy. We must not take More as the typical Englishman, nor must we apply to any realm save that of linguistic achievement the extravagant praises of the young Erasmus. Henry himself, Fisher, Gardiner, Cranmer, Longland and the rest were all well-educated men of considerable intellectual power: the king, indeed, in his early manhood, had seemed an admirable Crichton. Yet none of these men is sensitive, cultivated and percipient in such a way as are, let us say, Sir Philip Sidney, John Donne, Charles I, Falkland or Clarendon. Even such men as More and Erasmus, though eminently learned and richly gifted, are not citizens of the wide world as are Leonardo or Shakespeare. Foreigners noted the wealth, the domestic prodigality, the public display of England, but the English scene was very different from that of the contemporary Venice or Florence, with their elegance and grace and subtlety of thought and emotion. Nor was there any sense of adventure or romance, or of a great ideal, in the English air. The aim of all was material prosperity, cash, land, high place, physical ease; devotion to an idea or to a cause or to learning and art were rare if not unknown. Selfishness, ambition, faithlessness, venality and hypocrisy are human failings in every age and country. They were certainly not lacking in the Italy of Leo X, where Michelangelo could wish for the oblivion of marble and sleep, 'while scathe and shame endured'. Rarely, however, have they been found all together and so universally as in the reign of Henry VIII. Other vices and failings are not typical: lawlessness, irresponsibility, profligacy, spendthrift dissipation, bitter cruelty—these have been seen more clearly in other ages and in other countries: but it is difficult to think of an age in which unselfishness, devotion to an ideal, faithfulness to a master or a friend were rarer in public life, or one in which lust for material gain was greater.

One idea and ideal remained, and was used to give a veneer to every design. This was respect for the office and person of the king, which made submission and obedience to him the first and ultimate principle of political and national life. This is not the place to attempt a discussion of the historical and psychological origins of this devotion; they exist and can be defined; we can say what we mean by 'the *mystique* of the Tudor kingship'. Every age, our own included, has such overpowering sentiments that seem obsessions to those who come after: 'reason', 'equality', 'rights of man', 'progress', 'self-determination'. Here it is enough to realize the paramount and ubiquitous influence of the Tudor devotion. It is found in the most courageous and clearsighted—in a More or an Aske—as well as in the thoughtless, the simple and the servile. Of all the leading men of the age Fisher, perhaps, shows least infection; More, who had it deeply, was nevertheless clearsighted enough to recognize both it and its dangers long before the latter were apparent to all. In a very real sense it was not Henry, but his subjects, who made of him supreme head of the Church on earth; long before 1535 they had, without knowing it, made of the king the sole object of their devotion and obedience, and they had no reply when Henry took them at their word. The lion, as More had feared, had come to know his strength at last.

For us, in what follows, it is enough to remember that these two most characteristic features of contemporary public life—the materialistic, cautious, realist outlook and the complete submission to the king—were present in varying degrees in all Englishmen of whatever rank or order. Monks, friars, priests and bishops show them as clearly as do courtiers, members of parliament or agents of Cromwell. It is only by remembering that the religious were Englishmen of their day that we shall begin to understand the sequel. The assumption, tacitly made by many of the apologists of the monks in the past, that the religious, men and women alike, were a class apart, with another outlook and other ideals, is without foundation in fact. It would be true of the Jesuits and seminary priests fifty years later, and true of the clergy and religious in France at the opening of the present century, but it is not true of the early Tudor religious. Monks and clergy alike were children of their age and country; it was this that made the Dissolution, and indeed many of the religious changes of the reign, not only possible but relatively easy of accomplishment.

II. THE PLAN OF CAMPAIGN

No evidence has hitherto come to light as to the precise moment when the design for suppressing the religious houses in general was conceived in the form that was to be translated into action, or as to the immediate author of the scheme. There is no reason to suppose that Henry, at the time of the cardinal's fall, had any clear intention of following the examples of Germany and Scandinavia. Cromwell, on the other hand, with his experience of the profits that had accrued from winding up decayed and disorderly houses, and with his keen interest in European conditions, may well, even before 1530, have fixed upon some project of partial dissolution as the most promising expedient for raising revenue. Even here there can be no certainty; when Cromwell made his will in 1529, he left a small legacy to the four London houses of friars.[1]

The government's need for funds increased very rapidly after the cardinal's death: shrinking revenues, the king's extravagance in building and in buying estates, troubles in Scotland and Ireland and, a little later, defence preparations against continental enemies of the divorce, all combined to make action of some kind inevitable. More than one observer noted about this time that Henry's early liberality had given way to avarice;[2] his father had been accused of this characteristic, and its gradual appearance in the son was partly due to real need, partly, perhaps, to heredity, and partly also to the general hardening of his character. There is good evidence that Cromwell, perhaps on more than one occasion, promised to make his master extremely wealthy;[3] when he did so, he must have had in mind some scheme for liquidating a part of the Church's wealth. In the event, several sources were tapped before the monasteries were laid under contribution, and the various moves no doubt often supplied a topic for discussion at the interviews between minister and king; but of these no word has survived.

Yet if the moment of final decision is unknown we can watch the gradual movement towards action of some sort. As early as April 1529, Cardinal Campeggio is found writing in some anxiety to Sanga, a papal secretary in Rome, about the free circulation of Lutheran books at the English court.[4] According to the cardinal, these books contained promises of full acceptance of orthodox doctrines if the king would reduce the clergy to the conditions they enjoyed in the primitive Church by taking away all their temporal possessions. When he remonstrated with the king and cited conciliar statements as to the right of the Church to own property, Henry replied that it was churchmen after all who held those views. What books were in question is not known, but it was possibly in this year that Simon Fish's short tract, *A Supplication for the Beggars*, was scattered abroad at the royal procession on Candlemas Day, and subsequently broadcast over London.[5] Fish did little more than warm up some fragments of Wyclif's programme, with a characteristic recklessness of statistics, but he undoubtedly went straight to the point. Bishops, abbots and their like, he told the king, 'have gotten ynto theyre hondes more then the therd part of all youre Realme. The goodliest lordshippes, manors, londes and territories are theyrs'. In addition, let him consider, 'the

---

1 *Life and Letters of Thomas Cromwell*, by R. B. Merriman, I, 62. Too much should not be made of this modest bequest.

2 R. Pole, *Apologia*, 92, stresses the king's avarice, as does the French ambassador, du Bellay, in *LP*, IV, 4649 (20 August 1528). The abbot of Colchester's remark nine years later (c. 4 November 1537) 'that the King and his Council were driven into such inordinate covetousness that if all the water in the Thames were flowing gold and silver, it were not able to slake their covetousness' (*LP*, XIV, ii, 458), doubtless reflected current gossip.

3 Pole, *op. cit.* 121 *seqq.*

4 *LP*, IV, iii, 5416 (3 April 1529).

5 Fish's work was ed. by F. J. Furnivall in EETS.

infinite nombre of begging freres; what get they yn a yere?'[1] Allowing fourpence a year as alms from each person in the realm, and a population of some two-and-a-half millions, the friars will net £43,333. 'And what', he adds, 'do al these gredy sort of sturdy, idell, holy theves?...Truely nothing', save seducing wives to the number of a hundred thousand.[2] Besides these private disasters, the clergy are a constitutional menace:

Are they not stronger in your owne parliament house then your selfe? What a nombre of Bisshopes, abbotes and priours are lordes of your parliament. Are not all the lerned men in your realme in fee with theim, to speake yn your parliament house for theim?[3]

In view of what was so shortly to happen in the parliament house, Fish's outlook cannot be considered realistic, but his remedy was practical enough:

Set these sturdy lobies a brode in the world, to get them wives of theire owne, to get theire living with their laboure in the swete of theire faces,[4]

as no doubt Fish and the other pamphleteers did. It has been suggested that Fish's was the book brought to the king by the merchants George Elyot and George Robinson, and read to him at his request in his closet, after which, we are told:

the kyng mad a long pause, and then sayde: if a man should pull downe an old stone wall and begyn at the lower part, the upper part thereof might chaunce to fall upon his head: and then he tooke the booke, and put it into his deske.[5]

Was Henry still pondering over the talk with Campeggio, and Fish's advice, when he sent to Convocation at Oxford for a copy of the articles for which Wyclif was condemned?[6] In any case nothing more is heard of this topic in official circles for some three years, when an event of some significance occurred.

The community of Austin canons in the priory of Christchurch, London, long in debt owing to inefficient administration, suddenly in 1532 threw themselves upon the king's charity by surrendering the house to him as founder.[7] Their motives are not clear; other houses had been in worse case, and it would seem both that Cromwell had been at work and that

---

1 Fish, *Supplication*, 2.   2 *Ibid.* 46.
3 *Ibid.* 8.   4 *Ibid.* 14.
5 Foxe, *Acts and Monuments*, cited by Furnivall, *op. cit.* introd. viii–ix. M. Creighton in *DNB* article on Fish accepts this, and adds: 'just before the reassembly of Parliament in November [1529] London was flooded with copies of it [*sc.* Fish's *Supplication*] in a way which suggests the connivance of someone in authority'.
6 *LP*, IV, iii, 6546 (2 August 1530).
7 For this episode, *v.* E. Jeffries Davis, 'The Beginning of the Dissolution: Christchurch, Aldgate, 1532', in *TRHS*, 4th ser., viii. The writer, while rightly emphasizing its interest, possibly exaggerates its significance, relying on Fuller, *Church History*, book VI, iii (ed. J. Brewer, vol. III, 358–62), who represents this suppression as a *ballon d'essai* on Henry's part. Similar methods were, however, employed still earlier elsewhere by Cromwell when need arose as, e.g., at Calwich (Staffs), 1530–2; cf. F. A. Hibbert, *The Dissolution of the Monasteries*, 36–7. Calwich was suppressed without a papal bull, by 'finding an Office'.

some of the canons genuinely expected relief from the king. Actually, they were dispersed to other houses, and the foundation was suppressed; much of the property went to Audley, the new Chancellor. No papal permission was obtained or solicited. This was the first example of complete secularization, and thus provided the spectacle of all the elements of the finished technique of suppression appearing together at the same moment. The case is also of interest for another reason. When property escheated or fell to the king, it was necessary for a jury on the spot to hold inquest and give their verdict—in technical phrase to 'hold an inquest of office' or 'find an office'—that the property was without an owner and so rightly reverted to the Crown. Wolsey had obtained a number of such verdicts by questionable means, when no surrender had taken place, and his conduct had provoked one of the articles brought against him. In the present instance, offices had been found for property outside London, but it may have been felt that a city jury might give trouble before it decided that the members of a corporation, of which the head was *ex officio* a City alderman, could legally and unreservedly make away with all their rights in perpetuity; they might also have questioned whether the king was in fact founder of the house. In any case, Cromwell consulted Audley, who advised a retrospective act of parliament to record and validate the transaction. His advice was taken, and proved a valuable precedent for future action.[1] At the same time, the long interval between this surrender and any further move against the monasteries must tell against the opinion that has been expressed that the king and Cromwell were flying a kite, and that when no disaffection ensued they felt free to proceed to a more wholesale spoliation.[2]

Henry's mind, however, continued to brood over the matter, and in course of time the voice of conscience began to make itself heard. In March 1533 he broached the subject with Chapuys, who found him 'determined to reunite to the Crown the goods which churchmen held of it, which his predecessors could not alienate to his prejudice, and that he was bound to do this by the oath he had taken at his coronation'.[3] A year later rumours of confiscation were again in the wind. Both Chapuys and John Husee, Lord Lisle's agent, expected it in the parliament that met in January of that year, and Nicholas Olah, in a very ill-informed letter,

---

1 All difficulty of this kind was circumvented in the end by the Act of May 1539, securing to the king unreservedly all surrendered property. A still more awkward legal situation had been avoided in anticipation by Cromwell when he proposed as an Act for the parliament of 1533: 'Any...Abbot, etc., convicted of high treason, to forfeit lands held in right of their corporations'. Thus in the last days of medieval monasticism the king regained in a magnified and sinister form the complete financial control which the abbeys of the twelfth century had eluded by separating the establishment and the liabilities of the abbot from that of the community.

2 *V. supra*, p. 200 n. 7. Fuller, *op. cit.* 360, says that the king intended 'to make a discovery in people's affections...and if he had found the people much startled thereat, he could... retrench his resolutions'. There is no evidence to support this opinion.

3 *LP*, VI, 235 (15 March).

could write from Brussels to Erasmus that he has heard that Henry has distributed the monasteries to his nobility to use as they liked.[1] In fact, the parliament that spring had other fish to fry, but in September the scheme was at last beginning to crystallize. Cromwell, to whom is attributed language curiously like that of Olah's letter, told Chapuys that he understood that in the forthcoming parliament the king would distribute among the gentlemen of the kingdom the greater part of the ecclesiastical revenues to gain their goodwill.[2] This may have been a preview of a document, calendared in November 1534, which contains a plan of expropriation, on the Swedish model, in the interests of the Crown. According to this, all episcopal revenues are to be reduced to a flat rate of 1000 marks, save for Canterbury and York (2000 marks and £1000 respectively), and the king is to have half the revenues of all cathedral and collegiate churches. All monasteries with less than thirteen monks are to be closed down out of hand, the revenues going to the king. In the remainder, a maintenance fund is to be set up by which priests will receive some £7 and other religious £5 a year apiece, while the abbot is to have as much as all the rest together; the residue is to go to the king. Nuns are to have £3. 6s. 8d. a year each.[3] Once again, nothing was done for the moment, but the schedule perhaps indicates Cromwell's original intention. Whatever may be thought of it, it was at least a reasoned, ordered scheme; events were to modify it into something much more haphazard.

In any case Cromwell was boasting to Chapuys in December that he would make his master more wealthy than all the other princes of Christendom, and thenceforward events moved swiftly.[4] Commissions to Cromwell, as vicar-general, to visit religious houses, and to his subordinates Tregonwell and Bedyll were probably drafted in December 1534, and those to the abbots of Stanley and Forde to visit named Cistercian houses followed early in January, but the commissioners were almost immediately side-tracked to give the road to more urgent traffic.[5] On 30 January another set of commissioners were appointed, those for the inquests for the tenth which issued in the *Valor Ecclesiasticus*, and which gave the government information without which they could scarcely have carried through their programme of suppression so rapidly. The reports of the commissioners came to hand in the summer, and in August, as we shall see, the royal visitation began which led speedily and directly to suppression.

1 *LP*, VII, 24, 114 (28 January); in Erasmus's letters *ep.* 2915 (Allen, x, 368, 12 March 1534): '[Rex dicitur] monasteria distribuisse suis baronibus, quibus demolitis uterentur suo arbitrio.'

2 *LP*, VII, 1141 (10 September).   3 *Ibid.* VII, 1355.

4 *Ibid.* 1554 (Merriman, *Life of Cromwell*, I, 17): '[Cromwell] deust promettre de le faire le plus riche que oncques fut en Angleterre.'

5 *LP*, VIII, 73–5. It was presumably for an earlier project of this visitation that Layton composed his articles of enquiry to which he refers in his letter of 4 June 1535 (*ibid.* 822).

Much has been written of the supposed motives behind the momentous decision which, far more than any of those concerned in it could have foretold, was to be of revolutionary significance not only in the religious, but also in the social and economic life of the nation. Did Henry and Cromwell, or the latter alone, see from the first, whatever the date of that 'first', a massive if not total secularization as the end to which all lesser moves were directed and by which they were determined? Or did they, or at least did the king, sincerely aim originally at mending, and only when that seemed hopeless decide on ending the monasteries? The latter opinion, though persistently and unrepentantly maintained by one more widely acquainted with English monastic history than any other of his day, can scarcely be considered tenable.[1] Long before the visitors went forth in August 1535, with their questions and injunctions, the most fervent houses of religious had already been either disbanded or severely mauled, and even though this was nominally a political action, it is scarcely conceivable that a sincere and wise reformer would have gratuitously destroyed what all recognized as the mainstay of English monastic life. Moreover, and more significantly still, it is certain that no opportunity was given to the visitors to complete their work, or to the monks to show their readiness to obey the injunctions, before the irrevocable step was taken by the Act of Suppression of 1536. Finally, an argument might be drawn from Ireland, where the project of suppression was regarded from the first in a purely financial light.[2] Yet, as we shall see, the king, at least, acted in 1536 and later as if there was a future for some, if not many, of the monasteries, though these were not necessarily to show signs of drastic reform. The available evidence, in other words, though in some ways so plentiful and explicit, fails us in our enquiry both for the exact moment, and for the exact form, in which decisions were taken. We can, however, say with some confidence that financial, and not religious, motives were uppermost in the minds of both king and minister; less confidently, but still with fair certainty, that both proceeded resolutely but as it were experimentally, as was natural to men who were both opportunists, though in different ways: Cromwell with the ruthless determination to seize what chances fortune might present of increasing his master's revenues; Henry, primarily eager for pecuniary gain, but uncertain of the risks and still retaining (what Cromwell had never had) something at least of the conservative's recognition of the religious way of life.

But whatever may have been Henry's mind in the last months of 1534, his attitude in after years is certain. If he did not plan and will the whole pattern of events, he approved it and made it his own when it was accomplished. There are two illuminating *aides-mémoire* written by the king

[1] For Coulton's views at the end of his life, *v. Five Centuries of Religion*, IV, especially ch. lviii.

[2] Cf. the memorandum (*LP*, XI, 1416) of 1536 listing the monasteries in the Pale of Ireland, and stating that if suppressed suddenly the king will get £3000 (Irish money), whereas if warning is given he will lose £1000 of this.

respectively five and eight years later than 1535 to his envoy in Scotland, which have not received the attention they deserve.[1] In them Henry lays bare, with considerable frankness, what he wished to be understood as his past designs. The first document is a series of instructions to Ralph Sadler, once factotum to Cromwell, who in 1540 was sent to Scotland with good advice for James V, towards whom the king of England habitually adopted the attitude of tolerant patronage suitable to their relationship. Henry had heard that his nephew had recently had recourse to the sordid expedient of driving off the sheep of his poorer subjects in order to augment his revenue. Such petty traffic was unworthy of a king; James would be better advised to follow his uncle's example and realize the monastic wealth of his kingdom, thus putting to far better use what was at present spent on 'untruth and beastly living'. As one recounting with satisfaction a successful *coup* for the benefit of a junior, he mentions that he himself had taken 'good and politic means to increase his revenue' by gathering into his hands such houses 'as might best be spared'. Should James be attracted by the proposal,

we shall not only give unto him our best advice and counsel, but also therein to aid and help him, to bring his good determination to a perfect end and conclusion. But, if he will ever do any thing this way, he must keep it very close and secret; for, if any of his clergy shall smell it, they will not fail, either by suggesting him to the wars, or by procuring some other prince or potentate to make war upon him, or by provoking of inward rebellion and treason, or by some false and untrue mean or other, to keep him in business and extreme need, or else utterly to destroy him. And therefore he must in this case... keep it close to his own heart, making very few, and these tried and trusty, of his counsel to be foreseen therewith, lest if they should savour it, he live not (as the King's Majesty trusteth he shall) till he have an hoary head.

In the sequel, James died before he could profit from the avuncular counsel, but in 1543 the Regent, Arran, appeared to be a fit recipient of advice, and Henry forwarded a full programme to Sadler.

As concerning the second point [he wrote], for the extirpation of the state of monks and friars, the enterprise whereof requireth politic handling, it shall be first necessary that the governor send substantial and faithful commissioners, as it were to put a good order in the same, and to provide that they may live the more honestly without wasting of such things as they have in their possession. ...Which commissioners must have secret commission most secretly and groundly to examine all the religious of their conversation and behaviour in their livings, whereby if it be well handled, he shall get knowledge of all their abominations; and that once gotten, he with the chief of the noble men, agreeing with them for the distribution of some of the lands of the abbeys to be divided to himself and among them, which shall be to their great profit and honour,

---

1 The letters are calendared unobtrusively in *LP*, xv, 136 and xviii, i, 364, but have escaped comment, since they appear long after the Suppression. The earlier is in Nat. Lib. Scot. Advocates, MSS. 33. 3. 10, the later in B.M. Addit. 32650, fo. 123. They are cited in the text from M. St C. Byrne, *The Letters of King Henry the Eighth*, 288–9, 315–16.

and also admitting the bishops into the plan, with the promise of 'some augmentation' of their 'small portions', he shall take care 'to allot a good portion of those lands of the abbeys to the augmentation of the state of the king'. If he acts thus, and makes

a reasonable provision for the entertainment of the religious men now being in them, and for term of their lives, the proceeding to the execution in the suppression of the same will be the more easy and facile among such as will understand the truth.

Whether or no this advice follows exactly the course of Henry's own decisions a few years earlier, or whether, like lesser men, the king is simplifying the story of a lucky deal which had given unexpected results, it is at least permissible to conclude that neither the desire nor the hope of reforming the religious of England had any part in determining the actions of Henry and Cromwell in the years preceding the Act of Suppression of 1536.

It will probably never be possible for the historian to show by documentary evidence the precise degree of responsibility of Thomas Cromwell for initiating, planning and expediting the downfall of the monasteries. Henry, the effective as well as the titular head of the state, must have known and acquiesced in the scheme as it unfolded, even if we suppose that in his notes to Scotland he was claiming as his own a successful plan of Cromwell's when his minister was no longer able to vindicate it for himself. Yet it is possible that the Dissolution would have taken place less violently and less rapidly had another than Cromwell been in power. One of the most perplexing traits in Henry's complex character is the readiness with which he allowed those whom he trusted for the moment—his grandmother and his wife early in the reign, and Wolsey and Cromwell in later years—not only to execute but also to originate and plan high policy. Self-willed, obstinate and able as he was, resourceful as he always showed himself in self-defence, he nevertheless, whether from indolence or lack of invention or a still more carefully concealed sense of insecurity, allowed his two greatest ministers to commit him long and deeply to courses of action which in different ways brought odium and imminent disaster upon him. It was as if, once convinced of the absolute fidelity and ability of a servant, he allowed him to set the course and hold the wheel through dangerous waters until, without a warning, the captain came on deck to throw the helmsman into the surf. Certainly, no one who studies the policy and administrative acts of the two decades from 1520 to 1540 can fail to note the very great change, not only in external aims, but in mental climate, between the essentially traditional, orthodox, unbloody rule of the cardinal, and the revolutionary, secular and ruthlessly bloodstained decade of his successor. In the manner of the destruction of the monasteries everything bears the mark of Cromwell rather than of the king; to Cromwell supreme power was delegated, he could use it as he would.

CHAPTER XVII

THE END OF THE OBSERVANTS

The fate of the Observants was closely linked with that of Elizabeth Barton. Early in the reign of Henry VIII, as has been recorded above, a prelate of the black monks had complained of the strictness of the reforming regulations of Wolsey. It was not given to all, he said, to emulate the austerity of the Carthusians, of the Bridgettines, or of the Franciscan Observants.[1] The collocation of these three bodies is significant: it was precisely they who, in different ways and tempers, opposed the designs of the king and were in consequence silenced or dispersed by authority before the general assault was delivered upon all the religious orders. Of the three, the Observants were the first to challenge Henry, and they were to prove at once more vocal, more violent and more unanimous in their opposition than any other order.

The Observants were the only representatives in England of the reforming movements of the later Middle Ages which had given birth to a number of new and zealous organizations among the monks and friars. In origin one of the successive waves of fervour which in every century had endeavoured to spiritualize and rejuvenate the institute of St Francis, the Observants had, as we have already seen, counted in their number three of the great Franciscan luminaries of the fifteenth century, St Bernardine of Siena, St James della Marchia, and St John Capistran. The English province, which had increased to seven houses with a population of some two hundred religious, was closely connected with the order abroad and was visited regularly by foreign superiors; the early history of the order had given them living connection with Rome. A certain number of French and Flemish friars were members of the province, but the composition of the whole body was predominantly English.[2] They had a tradition of strict observance, uncompromising if uncultured theological orthodoxy, and a forthright bluntness of speech that was in striking contrast to the conventional outlook of the majority of the other friars of England and to the tendency towards the new heretical theology shown by individuals. They were, in a word, most 'Catholic' in temper, resembling very nearly the Spanish and other Latin friars of the time; no doubt it was this kinship of feeling that attracted Queen Katharine and her household so strongly to them; Observants were always her confessors, both at Court and in her last phase of retirement; when at Green-

---

1 *MC*, III, no. 283, p. 124 (*v. supra*, p. 159).
2 Some writers have asserted the contrary, but the names of the friars who took a leading part in the struggle are all English, as are all save two or three of the list of 143 in *LP*, VII (1534), 1607. Peto (Peyto, Petow) appears to have been English; he was related to Sir George Throckmorton.

wich she attended their Office, and in her will she left directions for her burial in one of their churches.[1]

Of their seven convents the two near London were the most notable. That at Richmond was in close touch with the Carthusians of Sheen and the Bridgettines of Isleworth. That at Greenwich, another royal foundation, lay by the palace and supplied preachers and confessors to the court; thus during the divorce negotiations Father John Forest was confessor and director to the queen, while Father William Peto, the Provincial, was confessor to the Princess Mary. Henry himself, in the early years of his reign, had favoured the Observants, and forwarded a petition on their behalf to Leo X.[2]

The Roman sympathies of the order, their personal relations with the queen and her daughter as well as with More, Fisher and Reynolds, and, it may be added, the outspoken bluntness of approach to questions which the more sophisticated or the more cautious treated with reserve, all combined to make of the Observants ardent opponents of the royal divorce. Their opposition to the king's will, manifested already in the connection of Fathers Rich and Risby with Elizabeth Barton, came to a head on Easter Sunday, 31 March 1532, at the moment of crisis when the clergy were about to submit; Peto, the provincial, openly indicted the king's passion and his evil counsellors in a sermon at Greenwich at which members of the court were present. Henry, as was his way in this, the irresolute phase of his reign which was rapidly drawing to a close, summoned the critic to an interview in which Peto once more spoke his mind. At the same time he obtained permission to go abroad, ostensibly to attend the chapter at Toulouse, actually, it would seem, to arrange for the publication in the Low Countries of a treatise against the divorce which rumour said had been written by the bishop of Rochester. In his absence the king put up Dr Curwen, one of his chaplains, to preach at Greenwich in a sense contrary to Peto. Curwen permitted himself to wish that his adversary were there to answer him, whereupon, like the ghost in the play, Father Elstow the warden appeared in the rood-loft and offered to respond for his minister. Further exchanges took place between the two before the sermon ended, greatly to the king's annoyance, and when Peto returned, after no long absence, he was commanded to deprive Elstow of office. On his refusal, both were imprisoned; it was on this occasion that Peto is reported to have met a threat of drowning with the reply that the way to heaven was as short by water as by land.[3] A fortnight later Henry was writing to Rome for a commission to try the two, while Chapuys and the Papal Nuncio were putting in a counter

---

1 Cf. Katharine's will in *LP*, x (1536), 40; for the visits of Observants to her in retirement, *v. LP*, vi, 889; Rich, Peto, Curzon, Robinson and Forest are among the names given in various documents.

2 *LP*, i (1513), 4871; Ellis, *O.L.* ser. iii, i, 66.

3 Chapuys describes the incident in *LP*, v (1532), 941. The chroniclers also mention it with some inaccuracies, e.g. Stow, *Annals*, 559 (ed. 1615).

plea.[1] In the event, Peto and Elstow were released, and immediately crossed the Channel for Antwerp, where they continued their activities of all kinds against the divorce and were in frequent communication with the convent of Greenwich.[2] Elstow was succeeded as warden by another of the same opinions and an even more intransigent temper, Father John Forest, Queen Katharine's confessor.

The majority of the Observants throughout the country undoubtedly were of their provincial's way of thinking; besides Elstow, Forest, Rich and Risby two others, Fathers Robinson and Curzon, were steadfast in opposition and were elected 'discreets' of Richmond and Southampton.[3] Superiors were in consequence bidden to enforce conformity, or at least silence, where necessary; as their public utterances show, they did not mince matters, and it is unlikely that difficult subjects were handled with any squeamishness. There were certainly cases of imprisonment and apostasy, and shortly before Peto's clash with the king one Raynscroft died in durance at Greenwich, his end perhaps hastened by his confinement. Nevertheless, the province held together in a truly remarkable way, and though Cromwell's papers contain a memorandum showing a list of leading friars reputed to be for or against Peto, no real rift took place before the final dispersal.[4]

There were, however, at Greenwich, the centre of things, two malcontents whom Cromwell encouraged as agents and informers.[5] In the sequel both left the order, but in the years 1532–3 each was responsible for a considerable amount of mischief-making. The first of these was a priest, John Lawrence, whose extant correspondence with Cromwell and the king opens at the crisis of the opposition to the divorce in the spring of 1532. Lawrence, who complained of ill-treatment in his convent for his defence of the king, and who was ready to preach in favour of the divorce, delated his superiors and brethren to Henry and Cromwell without scruple, and also passed on to them the decisions of the provincial chapter. Forest and one Robinson were his especial enemies; the former eventually forbade him to write to Cromwell or the king. Before the end of the year he is found applying to Cromwell for a dispensation.

Lawrence's letters become infrequent at the end of 1532, but the tale is immediately taken up by Richard Lyst, who introduces himself as a supporter of Lawrence against Forest. Lyst had been a servant of Wolsey and later a grocer and apothecary in Cheapside. He had also some connection with Anne Boleyn, to whom he wrote asking for money and

---

1 Chapuys in *LP*, v, 989. In spite of this friction the king is found authorizing alms of £6. 13s. 4d. to the Observants in chapter at Richmond in the autumn of 1532 (*LP*, v, 1346). Cf. also *LP*, VI, 1057.

2 *LP*, VI (1533), 726, 899–902, 917, 934.   3 *LP*, v, 1259.

4 *LP*, v, 1312. This list must date from before May 1532, as Elstow figures as warden of Greenwich. Forest, rather strangely, appears among those *contra Petow*.

5 For letters of Lawrence and Lyst, *v*. index of *LP*, v–VI. Some are printed by Ellis, *OL*. ser. III, ii, ccix–ccxiv.

promising Masses. He had become a lay brother, since he was ineligible for orders owing to an existing contract of marriage; he was now free, the lady having died. Restless, neurotic and unhappy, he was prepared to accuse his superior, Forest, of having murdered Raynscroft in prison. He delated Forest's interviews with the king to Cromwell and demanded to see Henry before the warden's next visit; 'if the King had followed my advice', he remarked, 'things would have been better ordered,'[1] adding later that 'it would be a meritorious deed if you had Forest removed to Newcastle or Newark'.[2] In default of external assistance Lyst acted himself, and when the newly appointed French Commissary visited Greenwich he was presented with a 'long pistyll' of Forest's misdeeds. The warden was, in the event, removed to the North, probably owing to the commissary's desire to placate the king, but Lyst, who had repeatedly urged both this and the transference of the whole convent across the Thames, did not stay to enjoy freedom from Forest's supervision; within ten days of sending the news to Cromwell he left the order and was to be found, six months later, studying at Cambridge for the secular priesthood.[3] As for Lawrence, after an absence of some months he proposed to return to the cloister, but fearing ill-treatment, asked Cromwell for the position of superior at Canterbury or Richmond, not, he was anxious to assure him, for reasons of private ambition, but in order to advance the king's honour.[4]

Forest may well have been relieved to depart from Greenwich, but the Observants as a body maintained their ground with remarkable unanimity and determination, and neither the exile of Peto and Elstow, and the disgrace of Forest in 1532, nor the arrest and execution of Rich and Risby in 1534, had any marked effect in shaking them. They were, in common with the other orders of friars, singled out for early attention by Cromwell, owing to their influence as special and itinerant preachers. Instructions were given that all must be examined separately, take an oath of allegiance to Henry, Anne and their issue, acknowledge the king's supremacy and deny that of the pope, and make a number of further undertakings.[5] Though all others yielded, the Observants held firm. At Eastertide Pecock, the warden of Southampton, was 'wanted' by Cromwell for a sermon upholding papal supremacy delivered at Winchester on Passion Sunday; he was duly sent up by the mayor of Southampton, but apparently gave a satisfactory explanation.[6] In May, Legh and Bedyll failed, as it would seem, to extract the oath from Richmond and a fortiori from Greenwich.[7]

---

1 LP, VI (1533), 116 (4 February): 'I can take my natiral rest scarce two nights in the week, and I fear sickness.' Ibid. VI, 512 (20 May): 'I am fearfully troubled various ways in the night, and can get no rest.'

2 LP, VI, 334 (12 April, Holy Saturday).

3 LP, VI, 1264 (12 October). He hoped to serve God thus 'with more quietness' than was possible among the friars.   4 LP, VII (1534), 139.

5 LP, VII, 587, xviii (commission of visitation to George Browne and John Hilsey); ibid. VII, 590 (instructions to visitors).   6 LP, VII, 448–50, 472–3.

7 LP, VII, 622. The wardens of Richmond and Canterbury had been executed only a few weeks previously (20 April).

A month later the pair tried their fortune again, and after parleying persuaded the community of Richmond to commit the decision to their four 'discreets'; the outcome is not clear. The commissioners then proceeded to Greenwich, but here the convent was unanimous in its refusal either to agree to the articles proposed or to commit the decision to delegates. They were above all firm in refusing to abandon papal supremacy, alleging a passage from their Rule which assumed it. To this argument Legh and Bedyll made three mutually incompatible answers, but had finally to complain to Cromwell that 'all this reason could not sink into their obstinate heads'.[1]

At precisely the same time Hilsey, Cromwell's commissioner to the friars in general, was chasing a couple of Newark Observants from Bristol through Devon and Cornwall and back again to Cardiff, whither they had shipped themselves in secular attire. There, they were arrested by the authorities and taken up to Westminster, but their captor still felt danger in keeping the slippery pair 'so near the sanctuary'. They were accused of upholding the pope and condemning the king's new marriage. In particular, it was alleged that when asked, as assistants at Princess Elizabeth's baptism, whether the infant had been christened in cold water or hot, they had replied 'in hot, but it was not hot enough'. Despite their bravado, they broke under durance and denied that they had spoken against the king.[2]

The different activities of these and other Observants, who were liable at any moment to voice from pulpit or parish-cross sentiments which many of their auditors had long been cherishing in their bosoms, must have caused intense annoyance to Henry and Cromwell. They hesitated no longer to take drastic action, and on 17 June two cartloads of friars were driven to the Tower.[3] By 11 August 1534, Chapuys could write to his master that of the seven houses of Observants five had already been emptied for refusing to acknowledge the royal supremacy, and that the remaining two were expecting orders to go.[4] A little more than a fortnight later a clean sweep had been made, and the same observer noted that the friars were in chains in various convents of other orders and were being hardly treated.[5] An interesting letter fell into Cromwell's hands from a London friar imprisoned with a companion for refusing the oath; they wished to know whether their brethren who were still in London had sworn.[6] From a slightly later period a list survives giving the names of one hundred and forty friars: of these forty-odd are in confinement in monasteries or with ecclesiastical or lay magnates; thirty have fled to Scotland or abroad; thirty-six are 'exempt', and thirty-one have died.[7] The manner of the deaths of the last group is not specified, but the number

1 *LP*, VII, 841 (15 June).
3 *LP*, VII, 856 (19 June).
5 *LP*, VII, 1095 (19 August).
7 *LP*, VII, 1607.

2 *LP*, VII, 939 (3 July); 1020, 1652.
4 *LP*, VII, 1057 (11 August).
6 *LP*, VII, 1307 (written at Stamford, 25 October).

is too large to represent the normal toll of nature, and the tradition that these died in prison from hardship and torture is very probable. Thomas Bourchier, who was a member of the Greenwich friary restored by Queen Mary, relates the incidents of a number of martyrdoms about this time, among which are those of Anthony Brockby, a scholar of distinction in past years at Magdalen College, Oxford, who was severely tortured before his death by strangulation in prison; others were Thomas Cortt, who had preached against the king, and Thomas Belchian, who had written against the divorce.[1] The number of these victims will never be known, nor even their names. They died untried and uncondemned. Their end was without honour: but they should be counted among those who witnessed even unto death the faith they had received.

The king refounded Greenwich, presumably with Friars Minor, and the community existed for a few years until it passed away with the rest of the province.[2]

---

[1] Accounts of these are in Bourchier, *Historia Ecclesiastica de Martyrio Fratrum* (ed. 1582), 11–17. His pages, though inaccurate in details, are probably reliable for the main facts. Cf. A. G. Little in *VCH, Kent*, II, 197; he inclines to identify Brockby with Browne (*v. infra*, p. 371).

[2] *LP*, XII, i, 795 (44); *ibid.* XIII, ii, 34.

CHAPTER XVIII

SYON

The second of the religious bodies regarded by the black monks of Wolsey's day as examples of rigid observance was that of the Bridgettines, represented in England by a single house, Syon abbey on Thames-side, between the villages of Isleworth and Brentford. The community, as has been noted in an earlier volume, had been in existence for little more than a century when Cardinal Wolsey died.[1] It was extremely wealthy, with a net income, far exceeding that of any other nunnery, of £1735, which gave it the tenth place in order of revenue among all the religious houses of the kingdom. The large numbers had been maintained, and the vocation continued to attract recruits from the first families of the land. The house was distinguished not only by its good observance, but by its informed devotional life, based largely upon the spiritual writers of the late medieval period, including the English mystical writers of the fourteenth century; it possessed a magnificent library, particularly rich in modern religious works,[2] and the brethren were in close contact with the Carthusians across the river at Sheen, and with those of the House of the Salutation in London. The community was by statute made up of sixty nuns (including a small number of lay sisters) and twenty-five religious brethren (of whom seventeen were in holy orders), and in the early sixteenth century it fell little short of this total. In the lists which survive from 1518 and 1539[3] many well-known family names appear among the nuns. The prioress in both years was Margaret Windsor, sister to Lord Windsor, and the names of Scrope, Strickland, Nevill, Brereton, Conyers, Fitzherbert, Bourchier, Newdigate, Tresham, Montague, Fettiplace, Knottesford, Monington and Vaux are at once a clear indication of the circles from which the house drew its recruits and a strangely complete epitome of recusant lists of a succeeding age.

The religious men who acted as chaplains and directors to the nuns were of a type very different from the covey of nondescript clerics who

---

1 For the foundation of Syon, v. RO, II, 176–81. For further incidents in the early history of the house, the most useful work (pending the appearance of the article in the relevant volume of VCH, Middlesex) is still G. J. Aungier, History of Syon Monastery, etc. This work, which is largely concerned with the topography of Isleworth, contains only a brief and incomplete account of Syon; it is, however, carefully compiled and there are useful appendices of records and documents which are not to be found in full elsewhere. There is no adequate recent monograph on medieval Syon. Mr F. R. Johnston (for whose thesis on the cult of St Bridget, v. RO, II, 387) has for some years been engaged on research for a work of this kind, and has kindly allowed me to see an annotated list of the brethren that he has compiled.

2 For this, v. RO, II, 347–8. It should perhaps be repeated that this great collection of books was for the use of the brethren. The nuns no doubt had a smaller and more conventional selection of books.　　　　3 Aungier, History of Syon, 81, 89.

celebrated the liturgy and dispensed the sacraments at many of the larger nunneries. They were recruited principally from the small class of academic clergy, or from beneficed priests who wished for a stricter life, and not from local sources. Fellows of colleges had from the beginning left Oxford and Cambridge for Syon, and in the second and third decades of the sixteenth century the brethren reckoned among their number several of intellectual distinction who had entered the order with a university degree and often after several years in the priesthood. In this the Bridgettines resembled the Carthusians, but there was a difference between them. Whereas the Carthusians were by profession solitaries, and only by exception scholars or divines, the Bridgettines had, at least in England, a constant tradition of learning. They formed, indeed, a group without parallel in Tudor England; men who combined personal austerity of life with theological or devotional competence, and who by their books, by their direction of a fervent and aristocratic nunnery, and by their influence as counsellors and confessors of leading laymen, were a power to be reckoned with in a religious world which contained all too few centres of enlightened piety.

In the early sixteenth century, when Cambridge had in many ways taken the leadership from Oxford in things of the spirit, it was from Cambridge that the Bridgettines came. During the last thirty years of Syon's life, at least six Fellows of Cambridge colleges joined the community, and during the century of Syon's existence at least six Fellows of Pembroke College, Cambridge. These men brought with them their books, which they left to the house at their death. Among them were John Fewterer,[1] sometime (1506) Fellow of Pembroke and later confessorgeneral; John Copynger,[2] Fellow in 1511 of Christ's College; William Bond or Bunde,[3] Fellow in 1506 of Pembroke, who died in 1530; and Richard Lache,[4] Fellow in 1523 of St John's College, Cambridge. Fewterer, though an ambiguous figure in his last years, had a high reputation in the early years of trouble; he had been the trusted confidant of Fisher, More and Houghton. Two, however, stood out from the rest, Richard Whytford and Richard Reynolds.

Whytford,[5] who came from a landed family of Flintshire, had been a Fellow of Queens' College, Cambridge, in 1495 and chaplain, first to William Blount, Lord Mountjoy, and next to Bishop Foxe of Winchester.

1 For Fewterer, v. Venn, *Alumni Cantabrigienses*, I, ii, 135, and M. Bateson, *Catalogue of the Library of Syon Monastery, Isleworth*, xvi, xxiv.
2 For Copynger, v. Venn, I, i, 396; Bateson, 115, xxiv.
3 Venn, I, i, 177; Bateson, xxiii.
4 Venn, I, iii, 33. He died rector of Fakenham, Norfolk.
5 Whytford has received a passing mention in numberless works, but still awaits adequate treatment. Meanwhile, reference may be made to *DNB*, Venn, I, iv, 393, and the editions of his printed works; also to *Harpsfield's Life of More* (ed. Hitchcock and Chambers), notes 16, 19/21 (p. 310); H. S. Bennett, *English Books and Readers, 1475 to 1557*, esp. 163–4; and E. M. Nugent, *The thought and culture of the English Renaissance*, 376–83. [See now note at end of chapter, p.221.]

In the last years of the reign of Henry VII he was the close friend of both Erasmus and More,[1] and he is said, in a well-known anecdote, to have warned the latter not to trust his episcopal patron.[2] He joined the community of Syon c. 1507, when he was already some forty years old, and thenceforward devoted himself to literary work for the benefit of his fellow-countrymen. He was a prolific writer, with fifteen or so works, either original or translations from Latin, to his credit. They include versions of the Rule of St Augustine, of the Sarum martyrology,[3] of St Bernard's *De praecepto et dispensatione* (*The Pype or Tonne of the lyfe of perfection*), as also two treatises for lay people or 'householders', the one a short 'introduction to the devout life'[4] and the other an instruction for preparation for Holy Communion. The majority were printed by Robert Redman or Wynkyn de Worde. Whytford, who habitually refers to himself as 'the wretch of Syon' or 'the old wretched brother of Syon', gradually developed a melodious and finely cadenced English style, which is seen at its best in the only translation of his still current, that of the *Imitation of Christ*.[5] He was also most probably the author, or at least the effective editor and reviser, of the most popular devotional manual of the English Catholics throughout the Penal Times, the so-called *Jesu's Psalter*.[6] In the anecdotes that occur occasionally in his works,[7] and in the prefaces which he writes for his translations, glimpses of Whytford's personality may be caught. They show a man with many of the qualities of Colet and More, though without the urgency of the one or the genius of the other: conservative, distrustful of 'heresy', retiring to the point of diffidence, orthodox to the full and yet with a kind of spiritual timidity and tenuity that contrasts so strongly with his Italian contemporaries St Gaetano and St Antonio Maria Zaccaria, who are on fire with an overflowing, self-effacing charity. Whytford, like his greater countrymen Fisher and More, might ennoble his age, but had no call to reform it.

His most distinguished colleague at Syon, though no more of a reformer than Whytford, had more of steel in his character. Richard Reynolds,[8] another Cambridge graduate and a Fellow of Corpus Christi

---

1 Cf. the letter of Erasmus (*ep*. 191, Allen, 1, 422) to Whytford in praise of More written 1 May 1506, with Allen's notes.   2 R. W. Chambers, *Thomas More*, 97–8.

3 Ed. Procter and Dewick, *The Martiloȝe in Englysshe* (HBS).

4 For this, *v*. Helen C. White, *The Tudor Books of Private Devotion*, 157–61.

5 His translation of the three first books of *The Imitation* (the fourth is by the Lady Margaret) was republished in 1872 by Dom Wilfrid Raynal and again, with useful if uncritical notes on Whytford, by Dom Roger Hudlestone in 1908. I have not been able to see the Yale doctoral dissertations on Whytford by E. J. Klein (1937) and on Syon by Mrs E. P. Sheridan (1950). Fr. Klein has also republished *The Imitation* (1941).

6 No recent critical discussion of the authorship exists. The fullest is still the scholarly booklet of S. H. Sole, *The Jesus Psalter*. The attribution appears to go back to Anthony Wood.

7 Sole, *op. cit*., cites three such, one of which shows that Whytford had visited Holywell (Flints).

8 For Reynolds, *v*. Venn, I, iii, 445, and *The Angel of Syon*, by Dom A. Hamilton. For Pole's testimony, *v. Pro ecclesiasticae unionis defensio*, F. ciii. The tract by Corvinus (*v. infra*, p. 217 n. 4) has: 'vir angelico vultu omnibus gratiosus', and he continues to say that he had

College in 1510, was as a theologian perhaps second only to Fisher in England. Like Whytford the friend of Erasmus and More, and well known to Reginald Pole during his residence at Sheen, Reynolds impressed all who knew him well alike by the depth of his learning and the unsullied purity of his life, which was reflected in a countenance to which more than one of his contemporaries applied the epithet angelical. The records are strangely silent upon the origin and early life of Richard Reynolds. He was probably of a Devonshire family distinguished by the learning of several of its members, and he may have been brother of Thomas Reynolds, dean of Exeter.[1] After graduating in arts at Christ's he became Fellow of Corpus Christi and took the doctorate in divinity, but about 1515 joined the community of Syon. Adept in Latin, Greek and Hebrew, he was probably, as Pole said, the keenest intelligence among the religious of his day, combining the best qualities of the old learning and the new. He left to Syon no less than ninety-four books, a number greater than that bequeathed by any other donor. Although he does not figure as a letter-writer or correspondent in the collections of the time, his personality and the manner of his death marked him out among his fellows, and as 'the father of Syon' he took his place, along with Fisher and More, in the memories of religious conservatives, and more than two years after his execution we find Sir George Throckmorton, lately converted to the king's party by a perusal of the New Testament and the royal *Institute of a Christian Man*, telling Henry how Reynolds, many years since, had advised him to stick 'to the death' to his opinion of the validity of the Aragon marriage, and not to hold his peace in parliament in 1532, when the anti-papal measures were being debated, even though he might think that his words would be of no avail.[2]

The flourishing condition of Syon, its excellent observance, its aristocratic connections and the intellectual distinction and virtue of Reynolds and Whytford and others made of it something unique in Tudor England, an orthodox Port Royal, a key position in the religious life of the country. When the divorce was mooted, Syon was all but solid in opposition. Reynolds was in the counsels of More and Fisher, so far as they admitted anyone to their confidence, and various depositions in the next few years show that, besides the religious, a group of dependants and neighbours were among the king's severest critics.

The various negotiations and stratagems employed to persuade the two families of Syon to take the oaths to the Act of Succession and the Royal

known Reynolds when in England in the suite of Cardinal Campeggio. For other tributes, *v. LP*, VIII, 666 (Chapuys to Charles V); *ibid*. 786 (Dr Ortiz to the Empress): 'a very learned man'; *ibid*. 616 (Cranmer to Cromwell): 'a learned man', and *ibid*. 801 (Starkey to Pole, a letter written at the king's command to explain the execution): 'Reynolds, whom I have often heard praised by you...a man of such virtue and learning.'

1 This conjecture (based on some evidence) was first made by Dom A. Hamilton, *The Angel of Syon.*
2 *LP*, XII (ii), 952.

Supremacy can be seen only by glimpses, and it is difficult to reconstruct the whole story from the scattered letters that have survived. These are, however, numerous enough to show that Syon, though ultimately yielding at least a tacit consent, struggled long in the clutch of circumstance, that both the king and Cromwell set great store by its submission, and that to achieve their end they were willing to go through a long and tortuous process of persuasion, oppression and intimidation.

As early as the beginning of January 1534, Stokesley, bishop of London and ordinary of the community, was enlisted by Cromwell in an endeavour to get some sort of signed approval of the king's second marriage out of Syon. The ubiquitous Bedyll and one Mores or Morris, a lay steward of the house, were also in the business which broke down, at least in its earliest form, through the unwillingness of Stokesley to subscribe to an inaccurate statement drawn up by Bedyll, and an equal unwillingness on the part of the nuns to sign an alternative draft.[1] Early in May Rowland Lee and Bedyll, who had failed in their first attempt to persuade the London Carthusians to take the oath of Succession, but who had been more effective at Sheen, were preparing to try their fortune at Syon.[2] There is no record of the issue, but though there is no certificate of any oaths received, and though it is difficult to suppose that Reynolds took the oath, it is equally difficult to suppose that Syon was allowed to remain unsworn.

For almost a year (May 1534–April 1535) nothing is heard of Syon, save that in the early autumn of the former year the nuns received a visit from Queen Anne, then lying at Richmond. The only record of this is in a late and partisan account, composed with the purpose of vindicating a place in the movement of Reform for Queen Elizabeth's mother, but the fact of the visit may be accepted, the more so as the obvious reluctance of the ladies of Syon to admit the royal visitor, whom most of them would have regarded as an unprincipled adventuress, is made clear enough. It is not, however, necessary to believe that they were as speedily converted to the light of the gospel by her dark eyes and 'sweet words' as the narrator suggests, or that they immediately substituted the English Primers which she distributed in choir for the Latin psalter and antiphonary.[3]

It is most unfortunate that no information exists of the events leading up to, and immediately following, the arrest of Reynolds in the spring of 1535, for his name is absent from all the letters written from Syon. He was presumably chosen for severe treatment like the Carthusians owing to his resolute refusal to admit the royal supremacy, and an endeavour was made to break up the nest of discontent on the fringe of

---

1 *LP*, VII, 15, 22.   2 *Ibid.* 622.

3 This incident is described by William Latimer the younger (chaplain to Queen Elizabeth) in a sketch of Anne Boleyn's career preserved in Bodleian MS. Don. c. 42. Written forty years after the event it is tendentious but is presumed to contain a kernel of fact. It is cited by C. Butterworth, *The English Primers* (1529–45), 54–5.

Isleworth.[1] Feron, a young man of the neighbourhood, and John Hale, an aged priest of the place, were arrested and examined, while Henry himself had interviewed Morris, the steward, whom he apparently distrusted or suspected of some sort of collusion with Stephen Gardiner, then under a cloud. When Morris failed to give satisfaction, he was handed over to Cromwell to be 'groped'.[2] Of the circumstances leading up to the arrest of Reynolds nothing is known, but we know from his own words that he was lodged in the Tower on 20 April, the day on which the three Carthusian priors were finally examined.[3]

When interrogated, Reynolds spoke with exceptional self-possession and force.[4] He would seem to have been less affected than most of his contemporaries by the paralysis that invaded all who opposed the king; he was doubtless well aware of his superiority to his judges in theological learning and sincerity; his words were therefore fearless and trenchant. He meant no malice to the king, he said, but would spend his blood in the pope's cause; whoever might oppose him in the England of that day, he had with him a thousand thousand of the past.[5] Later, when on trial before Audley and others, he was asked why he remained obstinate against so many peers and prelates. He replied that if it were a question of reasons, his were stronger than theirs; if of numbers, all Christendom was on his side, and the larger part of England itself, though many through fear or through ambition professed the contrary. At this point Cromwell asked with some interest for the names of those who were with him. 'All good men of the kingdom', replied Reynolds, and he continued to assert that the king was in error and that certain bishops had misled him. This was not the kind of information the judges wished for, and he was ordered to be silent. He answered with dignity: 'If you do not wish me to speak further, proceed with the judgment according to your law.' When condemned to death he asked for three days in which to prepare for his end. He had lived in the Tower away from regular observance, he said, but he

1 John Hale, vicar of Isleworth, an elderly man executed with Reynolds, was condemned on a different charge, that of seditious conversation and criticism of the king's second marriage. Robert Feron, a young clerk of Teddington, and Scudamore of Syon were also in the party, and there was a good deal of counter-accusation among them when examined; Hale was executed, Feron pardoned (*LP*, VIII, 802 (5), 565, 567).

2 *LP*, VIII, 592 (Henry to Cromwell, 7 May, with Morris's answers). He was as compliant as could be desired, and opined that 'the Holy Ghost is as present at such an act [i.e. the passing of the Act of Supremacy] as ever He was at any General Council'. He apparently endeavoured, not unsuccessfully, to run with the community of Syon and hunt with Bedyll; the latter commends him warmly more than once (*v. LP*, VIII, 1125).

3 According to the Italian account (*LP*, VIII, 661) Reynolds on 29 April said he had been in the Tower for eight days. The tract in *Historia martyrum* (*v. infra*, n. 4) gives 15 April as the date of his first examination.

4 The fullest account of Reynolds's examination is in a Vatican MS. given in *LP*, VIII, 661; details are added in the letter (*ibid.* 1096) of (probably) Philippe Dumont. The tract, *de D. Reginaldi Theologi martyrio*, which along with others precedes M. Chauncy's *Passio Major*, is not by him but is based upon the two accounts just mentioned.

5 *LP*, VIII, 566: 'He also says that he doth this as thousand thousand that be dead.' These, doubtless *ipsissima verba* of Reynolds, occur in an official memorandum.

wished to make himself ready for death as a religious should. He had his wish, and went forth joyfully with the Carthusians on 4 May.

At Tyburn he was the last to be executed. According to a reliable narrative, he encouraged the Carthusians during the butchery. He was noted as a preacher, and when his turn came he spoke to the people at length with calmness and eloquence. It was probably his sermon that provoked the wrath of Henry and led him to give less publicity to future executions. Then he died, like the Carthusians, with heroic fortitude. In equanimity, in strength of character, and in constancy he takes rank with More and Fisher among the noblest of the age. He was the first to die of that trinity of lucid intelligence and holy life who were found intolerable by their king and removed from among men within two summer months, because they were contrary to his doings.

When next the community of Syon is seen again, almost two months have gone by since the death of Reynolds, and Bedyll and Stokesley are trying to ascertain the state of feeling among the religious. They have 'found the lady abbas and susters as conformable in every thing as myght be devysed', and the confessor-general and 'ffather Cursone, which be the saddest men ther and best learned', showing themselves 'like honest men'. Two of the brethren, however, were stubborn, and might need, in Bedyll's phrase, to be 'weeded out'. These were presumably Whytford and Lache.[1] A month later he reported that the abbess and nuns were satisfied with the king's title of Supreme Head and that the confessor-general, Fewterer, had preached and had 'done his duty' (i.e. had 'set forth' the title), but that Whytford had preached without reference to the king's headship, and that when one Ricot had prayed for the king as Supreme Head nine of the brethren, including Copynger, had walked out of the church. In Bedyll's view Whytford and Lache (Leeke, Legge) were 'heads of their faction', and should be 'attached'. There was a possibility, Bedyll added, that some of the brethren might attempt to run away to avoid the strain of the situation. In his opinion, 'if they did so, so men shuld never here tidings of theim, nouther know where they became, it were no greate lost'.[2] In the sequel, Whytford would seem to have been left at liberty, but there is some evidence that Lache was in the Tower for a time.[3]

Despite Bedyll's optimistic opinion of the 'honesty' of all concerned at Syon, matters had progressed little in December, when Cromwell himself went down but met with small success. It would seem that since Reynolds's execution no actual violence had been used to bend or break

---

1 *LP*, VIII, 1125 (Bedyll to Cromwell, 28 July), also in Wright, *SL*, xvi.

2 *LP*, VII, 1090 (Bedyll to Cromwell, 28 August). This is printed by Aungier, *History of Syon Monastery*, 435–8, with inaccurate date. In *LP* this letter is erroneously printed (following the date given by Aungier) under the year 1534. The mistake is noted in *LP*, IX, 200. Bedyll, in the later letter, clearly refers to his visit with Stokesley described in the letter of 28 July.

3 *LP*, VII, 756 (misplaced in 1534; W. H. (? W. K[ingston]) to Fewterer): 'Mr Legge your chaplain was sent to the Tower, by commandment of Mr Secretary Cromwell.'

those who still refused to swear to the king's new title. Layton tried his hand in mid-December, using the methods he had found profitable else-where, and swept together a number of charges against one Bishop, who had long been a source of tribulation to Fewterer and Copynger by his irregular ways. He now added to the prevailing state of tension by declaring the king's title in a sermon to a church full of people, whereupon one of the lay brothers 'openly called him a false knave'. Layton then went on to supply some details of an alleged intrigue of Bishop with one of the nuns which involved breaking the convent grates with the assistance of a clumsy accomplice; he adds, *more suo*, with a glance at his unctuous colleague, that had Mr Bedyll been in the plot he would have brought the matter to a successful issue with far less ado—'such capacity hath God sent him'.[1] The worthy Bedyll, for his part, less than a week later gave a further account of Syon. The brethren, he said, were still obstinate, and as Cromwell's presence had proved unavailing other help had been enlisted—on Tuesday Dr Butts the king's physician together with 'the quenys amner' to 'convert' Whytford and Little, and on Wednesday a batch of no less than four doctors of divinity sent down by the king him-self. Syon was indeed taken even more seriously than the Charterhouse. When all else had failed with Whytford Bedyll himself 'handled him in the garden both with fair words and foul', accusing him of soliciting the nuns in confession, and thereby furnishing an occasion for the abolition of auricular confession throughout England. Whytford, however, was not to be terrified. 'He hath a brazen forehead, which shameth at nothing', the shocked archdeacon concluded, and he had to be content with for-bidding Whytford and Little to hear the nuns' confessions. Bedyll then summoned Lord Windsor to do his best with his sister, the prioress, and finally Stokesley and Fewterer attended in the nuns' chapterhouse and 'took it upon their consciences and the peril of their souls that the ladies ought to consent to the king's title', and repeating Warham's expedient of 1532 they 'willed all such as consented to the king's title to sit still', while dissidents retired. None was found to depart, though 'one Agnes Smyth, a sturdy dame and a wylful' later in the day 'laboured diverse of her susters that we should not have their convent seal'.[2] In the same letter Bedyll stated that Copynger and Lache had been sent to stay with Stokesley. When there, Copynger had an interview with Cromwell, and Stokesley wrote that he had been 'continually labouring' with him and was hopeful as to the result, especially if Bishop, whose 'irreligiosity' troubled him, could be removed.[3] His hopes were justified; Copynger and

1 *LP*, IX, 954; Wright, *SL*, xvii; Aungier, 85–6 (Layton to Cromwell, 12 December).
2 *LP*, IX, 986; Wright, *SL*, xviii; Aungier, 87–8 (Bedyll to Cromwell, 17 December). The Queen's almoner was John Skip, later (1539) bishop of Hereford. A letter from Rygote (Ricot) to the king asking for a dispensation is in *LP*, VII, 1092; this probably belongs to 1535 or 1536. Rigot is not among those pensioned in 1539.
3 *LP*, VIII, 77 (21 January 1536 = 1535 o.s.). This letter is wrongly put under 1535; it is clearly a sequel to that of Bedyll on 17 December 1535.

Q

Lache capitulated and shortly afterwards wrote at length to the brethren of the London Charterhouse urging them to submit and pressing them with reasons. To this letter the confessor-general Fewterer added a postscript of approval.[1]

Thenceforward little is heard of Syon in Cromwell's correspondence, though in September 1536 Copynger is found writing to the vicar-general thanking him for the books he has sent, one of which is being read to the brethren at dinner.[2] Any literature recommended by Cromwell may be assumed to have had a tendentious character; perhaps the *Defensor Pacis*, which had failed to impress the Carthusians, was now sent down to Isleworth. A few days after this letter had been written the confessor-general, Fewterer, left; Copynger was appointed in his room, and showed himself adequately subservient. For a year or more the brethren had been banned from preaching; when the new confessor-general applied for permission, shortly after a visit from Cromwell in June 1537, he reminded the vicar-general that the disciples of Christ had received grace by the coming of the Holy Ghost and then did preach; the implication that Cromwell's visit might be followed by a similar outpouring of grace shows sufficiently how far Copynger had moved since the days of Reynolds.[3]

Nevertheless, authority still remained curiously indulgent to Syon, possibly because any harsh treatment of such a numerous and high-born community would have produced repercussions throughout court and government circles that might have been hard to control. In the event, Syon fell by means of a legal quibble. In June 1537, the steward, John Morris, was knocked up one morning by the constables of Brentford, who had arrested Sir William Knotton, a professed priest of Syon, in the purlieus of the village. Sir William, who had found the religious duties irksome, had 'departed thence over the walls' and explained to the watch that he was going to see Cromwell to ask for a release.[4] Nothing more is heard of this for almost a year; then, on 29 May 1538, Stokesley was served with a writ charging him with violating 16 Richard II, c. 5 (Praemunire) and 28 Henry VIII, c. 10, the Act extinguishing the authority of the bishop of Rome.[5] He had, it seems, taken the profession of William Knotton in February 1537, and in so doing had acknowledged a papal bull and the papal name (specifically Martin V). So, of course, had every prelate present at a profession since 1 April 1420. Stokesley, after a moment of alarm, in which he wrote to Cromwell excusing himself—'you know what pains I took to persuade them of Syon to renounce the bishop of Rome'[6]—took the point and sued out a pardon, but the legal position had now been established. Nothing was done for eighteen months; then, probably in the early autumn of 1539, a series of jottings appears among Cromwell's

1 *LP*, VIII, 78, also wrongly calendared under January 1535. It is printed in full by Aungier, 430–4.
2 *LP*, XI, 487.
4 *Ibid.* 67 (10 June).
6 *Ibid.* 1096.
3 *LP*, XII, ii, 33 (5 June 1537).
5 *LP*, XIII, i, 1095.

'remembrances': 'Touching the monastery of Syon, the king may dissolve that by *praemunire* and [=an, if] he will.' 'The monastery of Syon to come by *praemunire*.' 'The suppression of Syon.'[1] And so, in the final sweep of the great monasteries that had refused to extinguish themselves by voluntary surrender, Syon fell under the hammer shortly before 25 November, the date on which the pensions were assigned.[2] There is no record as to whether all the nuns and brethren formally took an oath to maintain 'the king's new title'. It is difficult to suppose that they escaped doing so; it is equally hard to assert that Whytford and one or two others, after their long resistance, capitulated at last. Whytford certainly received a pension, but his retirement into the household of Charles, Lord Mountjoy, the son of his old patron, where he continued to put out a series of writings wholly Catholic and conservative in character until his death, shows at least that he remained at heart a brother of Syon. As will be seen later, the sisters of Syon, in this unique among the nunneries of England, retained and made effective their desire to continue their life under their Rule. Not all the nuns, however, were thus faithful. The abbess, Agnes Jordayn, accepted and enjoyed the lavish annuity of £200, and her executors were well able to afford the handsome sepulchral brass which still commemorates her in the church of Denham. Dame Margaret Dely, the treasurer, with a mere £13 (or twice the allowance of the rank and file of the community), spent what remained of her life within sight of her old home, and her more modest brass can be seen in the church at Isleworth.

1 *LP*, xiv, ii, 424, 425.   2 *Ibid.* 581.

Note Since this chapter was written Whytford's authorship of the translation of the *Imitation* has been convincingly disproved by Professor Glanmor Williams. His article 'Two neglected London-Welsh clerics: Richard Whitford and Richard Gwent', in *The Transactions of the Honourable Society of Cymmrodorion*, 1961 Part 1, pp. 25–32, is authoritative.

CHAPTER XIX

THE LONDON CHARTERHOUSE
AND ITS SISTER HOUSES

The House of the Salutation of the Mother of God at Smithfield does not appear to have been distinguished from its sisters during the fifteenth century by any superior degree of fervour. Like them, however, it had preserved intact the essentials of the Carthusian way of life, and thus provides a striking example of the reward that comes to a body of men, perhaps of no remarkable virtue, who are faithful to the prescriptions of their Rule: the coals remain alight and, though dull, may be kindled to flame by a breath of the Spirit. The London Charterhouse was to give to English monastic history one of its brightest pages, and it is possible for us to see that the heroism of so many of its sons in the hour of flood and whirlwind was no sudden impulse or unpredictable accident, but the native resistance of a fabric not built upon the sand. We are fortunate in being able to assemble, from various sources, materials which, if far from complete, are yet sufficient to enable us to reconstruct in its main lines the story of the last years.[1]

Among these sources one is, for better or worse, pre-eminent. The brief history of the last years of the London house, composed by one who had been a member of the family, stands alone among the documents of the time as supplying a picture drawn by a contemporary of the intimate life of a religious community immediately before the Dissolution.[2] The

1 By far the fullest account of the last years of the English Carthusians is in Miss E. M. Thompson's *The Carthusian Order in England*, 371–485, where many of the documents, printed and unprinted, are quoted in full. A less critical narrative, which is, however, based on the sources and contains additional details, is in *The London Charterhouse*, by Dom Lawrence Hendriks. For an account of the buildings and the plan as revealed by the excavations of 1948–9, v. *Charterhouse*, by D. Knowles and W. F. Grimes. A suggestive picture of Carthusian life and relationships is given by Archbishop Mathew and Fr Gervase Mathew, O.P., in *The Contemplative Life and the Reformation*.

2 Dom Maurice Chauncy's *Historia aliquot martyrum* was first printed at Mainz in 1550 and has often been republished, though the latest reprint is the *édition de luxe* of Montreuil-sur-Mer of 1888; this is the edition to which references are given in these notes. It remains a rare text, and a critical edition of all the versions would be welcome. The work has a complicated history, which is not yet completely clear. Chauncy wrote his original account for the Carthusians of Val de Grace in February 1546 (not 1539, as was generally supposed till recently); this version, long thought to be lost, has recently been rediscovered by Mr H. G. Richardson, who has identified it with an anonymous account in Guildhall (London), MS. 1231. Mr Richardson is engaged on editing this text, of which Fr Andrew Gray, of St Hugh's Charterhouse, Parkminster, has kindly supplied me with a transcript. It frequently differs verbally from the printed text, but references to the latter have been retained as more convenient. Almost simultaneously Chauncy wrote a similar account for the prior of the Grande Chartreuse, in order to justify the request he and his companions were making for reception at the Charterhouse of Bruges. This latter text was the version published in 1550, with its Latinity somewhat polished by the editor, Dom Vitus à Dulkem, and reprinted by Dom V. M. Doreau in 1888. Some fifteen years later, in 1564, when anxious

method and outlook of Dom Maurice Chauncy, together with the temperament and character which they reflect, fall far short of the simplicity and clarity that comes from perfect mental self-control. He is seriously deficient in critical powers and is frequently inaccurate in small matters of fact; he had a love of the marvellous, not to say of the fabulous, which exceeds all reason and conveys to the reader the probably unjustifiable impression that the whole community was equally superstitious;[1] he is prolix, even in his shortest narrative, and overlays a little information with a mass of scriptural allusion. Nevertheless, there can be no question of his sincerity and general trustworthiness, and he was an eyewitness of the events he describes. To his narrative can be added a number of casual letters and documents dating from the early sixteenth century, and part at least of the *dossier* assembled for the processes conducted against the monks.

Although the history of the London Charterhouse in the fifteenth century may not have been remarkable, the situation of the place, so different from that of the earliest and latest foundations of the province, must always have ensured a certain celebrity for its withdrawn and austere vocation. It would seem in consequence to have attracted throughout the period a steady flow of recruits with a genuine desire for a life of monastic perfection; it also attracted—as the Carthusian order has always attracted from the days of St Hugh to our own—a number of aspirants of enthusiastic or neurotic temperaments some of whom succeeded, then as now, in winning through at least the early stages of the difficult probation, to prove a source of infinite vexation to all in authority by their mental and moral vagaries, and by their graceless, spiteful or ill-grounded accusations against those who had endeavoured to wean them, and to protect others, from their habits of selfishness and irresponsibility.

Among the genuine vocations of the later fifteenth century was one which perhaps did more than any other to determine the subsequent fortunes of the house; it was that of William Tynbygh or Tenbi, Irish

to solicit papal support for the English Carthusian exiles, Chauncy wrote a shorter version in which some details are added, together with historical sections of a tendentious nature, while much valuable matter was omitted. Finally, in 1570, he composed yet another narrative, a somewhat expanded version of the 1564 account. The narration addressed to the prior of Val de Grace, an abridgement apparently derived from this, and the recension of 1564 (the so-called *Passio Minor*) have been printed by Van Ortroy in *Analecta Bollandiana*, VI, 36–51, XIV, 268–83, and XXII, 54–75. The recension of 1570, of which the manuscript is in private hands, was printed as *The Passion and Martyrdom of the Holy English Carthusian Fathers* by the Church Historical Society in 1935. For editions and manuscripts, *v.* E. M. Thompson, *The English Carthusians*, 343–52, and *The Passion*, etc., 30–3 (by Miss E. M. Thompson), and the introduction to the *Passio Minor* by Fr van Ortroy in *AB*, xxv.

The author, Maurice Chauncy, came of a landed family in Hertfordshire; he was born in 1509 and took the monastic habit *c.* 1531–2. He left England to resume his religious life in 1546, was prior of the restored Sheen 1555–9 and subsequently of the exiled Sheen Anglorum in the Low Countries. He died on a journey at Paris in 1581.

1 Hence, e.g., the allusion by H. A. L. Fisher in *History of England*, 343, to 'this somewhat morbid and superstitious community'. For Chauncy's inaccuracies see the notes to the 1888 edition and Miss Thompson, *passim*.

or Anglo-Irish by race, and of good family,[1] who joined the community
c. 1470 and became prior in 1500, holding office for thirty years. Whatever
be the facts lying behind the extraordinary story of Chauncy, who
received it as a family myth when it was already sixty years old,[2] Tynbygh
had no doubt experienced a radical conversion as a young man, and his
subsequent life was ascetic to a degree; it was no doubt he who set up in
the house such a high standard of fidelity to the statutes of the order. It
was shortly before Tynbygh's rule began that the young Thomas More
lived in the precincts for four years; it was Tynbygh who received John
Houghton into the community, and it was in his last years that there set
in a remarkable flow of ardent and distinguished recruits who were to
form the core of the resistance to the king in 1534.

Lying as it did at the edge of the city, with its orchards and gardens
running up among the town houses of the great, the Charterhouse could
scarcely fail to be a centre of religious influence. The solemn devotion of
the liturgy, the contrast between the silence and austerity there and the
noisy, restless, ambitious and sordid whirl of the city streets, the presence
within its walls of a number of men of gentle birth and high abilities,
attracted to its gatehouse many of the *âmes d'élite* of the time, and facilities
seem to have been given for those in need of spiritual direction to visit
and confess themselves to the priests,[3] and even to make a prolonged stay
in the guest quarters.

Tynbygh was succeeded by Dom John Batmanson,[4] who was a man of
sufficient learning to be chosen by Edward Lee, the friend of More and
future archbishop of York, to criticize the edition of the New Testament
by Erasmus. That hypersensitive scholar's reaction to Batmanson's attack
need not be taken as a pondered judgment, but the Carthusian, who continued his work with an attack on Luther and who wrote treatises in the
medieval manner on passages of Scripture, was clearly not one of the new
learning and was probably no match for its masters. In any case, his rule
was short.

In his successor, John Houghton, the strict monastic life brought to
blossom for the last time on English soil a character of the rarest strength
and beauty—a last flowering, a winter rose, of English medieval monachism. When all allowance is made for the youthful hero-worship and later
hagiological aim of Maurice Chauncy, the picture that emerges is of a man
capable not only of inspiring devoted attachment, but of forming in others
a calm judgment and a heroic constancy equal to his own. He found him-

1 In the story of his conversion there is an allusion to a chapel in his father's house
(*Historia*, 74).

2 *Historia*, 74. Taken prisoner on a pilgrimage to the Holy Land, he was miraculously
transported to his father's house in Ireland. The history of Tynbygh does not appear in the
Passio Minor.

3 Chauncy describes the cloister as being empty during the day 'nisi aliqui saeculares
colloquii gratia fortuitu supervenissent' (*Historia*, 66).

4 There are articles in *DNB* of varying merit on Tynbygh, Batmanson, Boorde and
Chauncy. For the confusion of two John Batmansons, *v.* Appendix I.

self head of a family in which youth was predominant; more than half the community were under the age of thirty-five when he began his short rule;[1] no doubt they were impressionable enough. But it was not the most impressionable who followed him to the end of his journey; Chauncy and others like him were left orphans, remembering with sorrow the golden days of spring; the seventeen who did not fail had learnt from him to depend on no human guide, to fear neither sharp pain nor material want, and to be true, through all extremes of suffering and desolation, to the purpose of their profession.

Houghton had joined the Charterhouse early in the reign of Henry VIII. Sprung of gentle family in Essex, he had taken a degree in laws at Cambridge from Christ's College, but instead of embarking on a career, he had studied in retirement for the priesthood and lived for some years as a secular priest before taking the monastic habit in 1515. Seven years later he became sacrist and after five more years, to his great distress, he was appointed to the distracting office of procurator. From this he was taken, in 1530–1, to be prior of Beauvale in Nottinghamshire, but after a bare six months he was recalled by the unanimous vote of the community, in 1531, to become prior of the London house.

As prior he was able to develop his character to the full. Much of Chauncy's long account of his virtues is wordy and conventional, but a few individual traits can be clearly seen.[2] The prior, we are told, was reserved and somewhat stern with aspirants for the first few years of their training; with the elder fathers, jealous, as always in a strict community, of custom and precedent, he was tactful and easy of approach. Mindful of his position in public, he required an exact performance of the ceremonial of courtesy and respect; when he entered another's cell he put his dignity aside and spoke as an equal, not as a superior. His life was abstemious beyond the demands of the Rule, and he had an exceptionally deep love of the Office, in which he noticed the least haste or failure, and would even leave the choir as a sign of disapproval. An extant letter of his is witness that he followed the contemporary stream of his order's devotion, and esteemed highly Denis the Carthusian;[3] his confessor, however, was William Exmew, who is known to have prized highly the *Cloud of Unknowing* and its companion treatises, and the younger man may have taken his bent from his superior. Houghton was regarded as a saint by those who knew him in the years when a martyr's death for one in the London Charterhouse would have seemed an impossibility. Whatever his methods, he achieved a result rare in any religious order and most rare,

---

1 *Historia*, 58: 'Circiter enim viginti erant in illo Conventu qui annos triginta octo non attigerant.' There were thirty monks and eighteen converses (*ibid.* 65).

2 See Chauncy's fourth chapter *De sancto et discreto regimine Prioris*.

3 The letter is printed by Hendriks, *The London Charterhouse*, 366–8. In it Houghton writes: 'Is [*sc.* Dionysius] adeo corda nostra suis sacratissimis scriptis et documentis sibi allexit, ut eo carere sine gravi molestia minime possimus. Nobis etenim sapiunt opera ejus ...prae ceteris paene omnibus sacris scriptoribus.'

perhaps, in one long established and rooted in tradition: he joined his community to himself in a new and joyful realization of the splendour of their vocation and in an ever-fresh, never-failing hope of a still nearer approach to God. Before the sudden gathering of the clouds, when the world outside seemed full of costly splendour and empty show, and of the 'packs and sets of great ones', the House of the Salutation was a green valley where those of goodwill could find pasture and clear water. In Chauncy's pages, written when the old age had gone downstream in the cataclysm, there is a poignant, if inarticulate, cry to Time to cease his passage: *Verweile doch, du bist so schön.*

The monks whom Houghton guided were as a body worthy of their prior. He himself looked upon them as angels of God,[1] and visitors who sought of them counsel and help involuntarily echoed the words of the patriarch: 'Verily God is in this place.' It was commonly said that if a man wished to hear the divine service carried out with due reverence he should visit the London Charterhouse.[2] The rules of fasting and silence were kept in their strictness, and such alleviation as the fire in the cell were often forgone save in extreme cold. The night choirs in winter, when the lessons were long, began shortly after ten and lasted till three in the morning. Fear of distraction was so real among the brethren that the intention had been formed of asking the king to take over ownership of the property of the house, allowing the monks only a pension from it.[3]

The life of the Charterhouse, contrasting as it did so strongly with the turmoil of the city and the display of the court and of the cardinal of York, and with the worldliness of so much in the church life of the country, could not but prove a powerful magnet to what generous aspirations still existed. Chauncy tells us that many of the monks were of wealthy or distinguished family, and that many even of the lay brethren had given up property or the expectation of affluence in order to enter the house. Though his canons of distinction may have been those of a bourgeois rather than of an aristocrat, his statement can in several cases, besides that of Chauncy himself, be corroborated from his own pages or other sources.

After Houghton, the figure most clearly seen is that of William Exmew. Like his prior, he was of good family and a Cambridge man of exceptional ability; at the Lady Margaret's recent foundation of Christ's College he had become familiar with Greek as well as Latin. In 1534 he was still but twenty-eight, though distinguished by both ability and holiness; he had been first vicar (or second in command) and then procurator of the house, while Houghton's choice of him as confessor is a sufficient proof of his maturity and spiritual insight. The impressionable Chauncy, to whom Exmew in his radiant young manhood appeared the *beau idéal* of a monk, has recorded several personal details of him, and in particular of his self-reproach as he, the procurator, left the night-choirs early, likening himself

1 *Historia*, 76: 'Prior crebrius dicere solebat sese Angelos sub sua obedientia habere.'
2 *Ibid.* 69.
                                              3 *Ibid.* 70.

to Judas who was unworthy to hear the last words of his Master.[1] More valuable still, perhaps, is the evidence of a manuscript that Exmew knew well, and nourished his spirit on, *The Cloud of Unknowing*, which he caused Chauncy to copy.[2]

Yet a third, like Exmew still young, has left a mark on the records of the time.[3] Sebastian Newdigate, bearer of a name which since his day has more than once left a notable impress on English life, sprang of a family settled at Harefield in Middlesex and later also at Arbury in Warwickshire.[4] Through his mother, Dame Amphylis Nevill, he was related to the county families of Lincolnshire; an elder sister Jane, who married Sir Robert Dormer, was ancestress of a family ever to be distinguished among the English Catholics; another sister, mother of the recusant Lady Stonor, stood at the head of a long line faithful to the old allegiance; two brothers were knights of Malta and two other sisters became nuns in the observant convents of Syon and Dartford.[5] The young Sebastian, tall, handsome, gallant and with great charm of manner, had gone to court as a page, where he attracted the notice of the king and became a gentleman of the Privy Chamber. When the royal divorce was first mooted his sister, Lady Dormer, summoned him to visit her and warned him of the danger of the king's example. The young courtier at first defended his master, but finally promised that if his sister's judgment proved correct, he would remember her advice. 'Remember it and act upon it', she retorted. 'I shall', he said. 'I fear for you', she replied. He paused, leaning his head upon his hand, and then asked what she would think if she heard that he had become a Carthusian monk. 'A monk', rejoined his affectionate sister, 'I fear, rather, I shall see thee hanged.' A few months later, Newdigate was in the Charterhouse, though Lady Dormer would not be

---

1 *Ibid.* 77–8. Chauncy describes Exmew (p. 77) as 'primo Vicarius, postea Procurator' and later (p. 107) as 'remotus a Vicariatu Procurator factus' while, on the same page, Middlemore in 1535 is 'tunc Vicarius antea Procurator'. Unless Exmew changed offices twice this would seem to imply that these two monks changed places shortly before the death of Houghton.

2 So Sir H. Chauncy in his *Historical Antiquities of Hertfordshire* (1700), 58.

3 Most of our knowledge is derived from H. Clifford, *Life of Jane Dormer, Duchess of Feria*, ed. J. Stevenson, S.J. Although this account did not leave its author's hands finally till 1643, it was composed *c.* 1616 and is a valuable source of information. The writer was for some years, *c.* 1600–9, a kind of major-domo in the Spanish household of the widowed duchess. This lady, born in 1538, was granddaughter of Jane Newdigate, later Lady Dormer, Sebastian's elder sister, and had been brought up by her grandmother who survived till 1571, her eightieth year. She must often have told the child of her martyred brother only a few years after his death, and on all important family traditions Clifford's record may be accepted, even though on other matters he often repeats uncritically a later Catholic *on dit.*

4 Sir J. Newdigate (1719–1806) perpetuated his memory by his University prizes, and the holder of the baronetcy during the childhood of Mary Ann Evans figures in George Eliot's first novel under the name of Cheveril. A mid-Victorian Newdigate was distinguished by his antipathy towards Catholicism.

5 Clifford (*op. cit.* 39) says that the sister at Syon became abbess; a Maria Newdigate duly appears in a list of nuns at Syon in 1518 (Aungier, *History of Syon*, 82) but not in any subsequent list, nor in the list of abbesses (*ibid.* 108).

persuaded of the authenticity of his conversion till she had called upon Tynbygh herself.[1]

Chauncy tells us, and those with any experience of observant religious communities will readily believe his words, that the converses fell not a whit short of the choir monks in holiness. He says—and this again is a familiar experience—that many were men of prayer and often surprised the more learned by the spiritual wisdom with which they spoke of what they had heard read in church or refectory. In the event, a number of them proved able to hold their own even more successfully than the choir monks in confessing their faith and in the endurance of prolonged suffering.

It was not, however, to be expected that all the inmates of the House of the Salutation would find or follow perfectly their calling, and such a life, lived so purely, imposed a severe strain on those less pure and inevitably provoked psychological or moral reactions among those not of the finest temper. Even some who desired to imitate their leaders followed false, or flickering, lights. It is noteworthy—and again true to the experience of the ages—that those who, like Dom John Darley or Chauncy himself, delighted in the marvellous and the visionary, should have failed when confronted with unlovely reality. Others, in whom neurotic or psychotic tendencies existed, alternated between imaginary terrors and real irregularities in an endeavour to escape from solitude and from themselves. Finally, there were not wanting some who by their irresponsible vagaries or by sheer treachery helped to ruin the house that had sheltered them. Of these the least malicious was perhaps the ingenious, restless Andrew Boorde, who had made profession at a very early age. Temperamentally unsuited to a life of silence and monotony, and perhaps also unfaithful to his vocation as he knew it, he ultimately obtained a dispensation of some kind through the agency of Prior Batmanson, though he lived on at the Charterhouse until he was freed by Cromwell, to set out on his travels for the purpose of studying medicine, which occupied him for the rest of his life. Less amiable than Boorde were such men as Dom George Norton, who became desperate in solitude; Dom Nicholas Rawlings, who entered the Charterhouse after a fault in clerical life, made his profession after a few months when his life was despaired of in illness, and subsequently recovered to lodge a series of unfounded charges against his superior; Darley, the seer of visions, who heard at least one true word from beyond the grave, and who ended as a chaplain at Salisbury; and the discontented and backbiting Dom Thomas Salter.[2] To these may be added

---

1 Clifford, *Jane Dormer*, 19–23; cf. also 37: 'This gentleman, as he hath been described to me, was somewhat tall of stature, his body well proportioned and comely...he had a great courage.' Chauncy, *Historia*, 108, vouches for his education at court: 'fuerat nutritus in domo domini Regis'.

2 For all this, *v.* Chauncy's eighth chapter *De fratribus reprobis*, and the accounts and letters in Thompson, *English Carthusians*. The ghost of old Dom Raby appeared to Darley, and spoke of the martyrdom of Fisher and Houghton. When Darley asked him 'ffather, what elles?' he replied 'the angelles of pease ded lament and murne withowt mesur'; and so vanished away (Wright, *SL*, XII).

the anonymous renegade who provided Cromwell with a series of charges against the statutes of the order, intended to show that their austerity and withdrawal from the world was unnatural and anti-Christian.[1]

Such acts of treachery, however, and all thought of revolution, lay in the womb of time when Houghton began his rule, and the young community of the House of the Salutation asked only to be allowed to go its way forgotten of the world. They were, however, too near the centre of things to escape all contacts with the life of men unblest. Many were aware that Newdigate, and perhaps others also, had sought there a refuge from the iniquity of the times; thither turned the thoughts of Sir John Gage, vice-chamberlain of the court, when he felt that he could no longer serve the king,[2] and thither, we may suppose, came many for counsel and strength when the divorce and its sequels began to cause much searching of hearts, though the London monks were never in any way compromised with the Nun of Kent. The Charterhouse, therefore, though its members evaded rather than courted public notice, was in spite of itself an influence to be reckoned with, for even its enemies acknowledged the holiness of life of the inmates.[3] It was an influence that worked invisibly when the course of public affairs was normal, but which could not be ignored when the government was making excursions into the spiritual realm, and claiming control of consciences or of beliefs.

The Carthusians, in common with all other subjects of the king, were required in the spring of 1534 to swear to the first Act of Succession, and by so doing to acquiesce in the annulling of Henry's first marriage and in the legitimization of Anne Boleyn's offspring. Their sympathies had unquestionably lain with Queen Katharine, and they were personally persuaded of the validity of her marriage; when the commissioners first arrived on 4 May to tender the oath Houghton replied in the name of all that what the king might do was no business of Carthusians; they asked only to be left in their peace. When urged to assemble the community to swear he replied that he could not see how such a long-standing marriage could be declared invalid. He was therefore conveyed to the Tower along with the procurator Humphrey Middlemore. There they were visited by Edward Lee, archbishop of York, and others, and persuaded that the faith was not at stake; it is possible that they never saw the preamble to the Act, with its implicit repudiation of papal authority, which formed the obstacle in the way of More and Fisher; in any case they agreed to take the oath,

---

1 This, and the letters of these unsatisfactory inmates of the Charterhouse, supply ample evidence of the rigour of the life and the high level of discipline. See in particular the complaints referred to in the text (*LP*, VII, 1047, and Thompson, *English Carthusians*, 390–2) and Andrew Boorde's inability to abide the 'rugorosyte' of the observance (*LP*, IX, 12).

2 *LP*, VII (1534), 14.

3 E.g. Bedyll to Cromwell, 28 August 1534: 'If it were not for the opinion whiche men had and some yet have, in thair apparent holinesse, which is, and was, for the moost part covert hypocrysy, it made no greate mater what became of thaim so thair soules were saved' (*LP*, VII, 1090).

so far as it might be lawful, and were sent home. They had, however, gone too fast for the community, most of whom were still for refusing to swear. When the commissioners returned to administer the oath, they apparently obtained no adhesions; at a second visit, Houghton and half a dozen swore, and it was only at a third visit, at the prior's instant wish and surrounded by men-at-arms, that all took the oath. So far as can be seen, their opposition rested on a strong disapproval of the king's action rather than on a clear sight of the ultimate principles involved; when they swore, therefore, it was without doing utter violence to their consciences in a matter of faith.[1]

Houghton's expressed forebodings that they would not long be left in peace were speedily realized. In the same session of parliament the Treason Act was passed, which extended the definition of that crime to include treason by word, and specifically such speech as might 'maliciously' deprive the king of any of his 'dignities or titles'. Under this act, which came into force on 1 February 1535, a charge of high treason could be brought against anyone who denied, or who even refused to acknowledge, that the king was Supreme Head on earth of the Church in England. No oath was attached to the act, but in the spring of 1535 commissioners were appointed to require acknowledgement of the king's headship of the Church, and this was usually obtained by administering an oath upon the gospels in general terms of acceptance of the king's headship. All religious houses were visited for this purpose in due course.

When it was clear that they would not be ignored the Carthusians realized that the day of trial had come. Houghton's chief anxiety was for the many young members of his community whose vocations he had doubtless fostered and whose professions he had received. He feared for their perseverance if the house were suppressed, and he even considered the possibility of outward compliance, with words of reservation, in order to save his monastery if he alone could swear for all.[2] Meanwhile, he set aside three days of preparation for the trial: on the first, all made a general confession; on the second all, led by Houghton himself, asked pardon of each of his brethren in turn for all offences; on the third, the prior sang a Mass of the Holy Spirit for guidance. When he did so, and the moment came for the elevation of the consecrated Host, all felt in their hearts, and

---

1 There is no doubt that the Carthusians took the Oath of Succession. Certificates of Bishop Rowland Lee are extant stating that he has received oaths and fealties at the Charterhouse on 29 May from Houghton and five others, and on 6 June from the bulk of the community (*LP*, VII, 728). The suggestion of Dom Hendriks (*The London Charterhouse*, 125) that a special form of oath was allowed has nothing to commend it.

2 Such at least is the probable meaning of the ambiguous sentence in *Historia*, 93: 'Si solummodo pro meo consensu negotium fuerit, exponam me misericordiae Dei, et ero anathema pro his fratribus meis minimis, ac consentiam regiae voluntati, si licite fieri possit, ut praeservem istos a tot et tantis periculis futuris.' We cannot be sure that Chauncy preserved the exact words of Houghton; in any case, he omitted them from the corresponding passage of the *Passio Minor* of 1564, probably because he considered his readers would be scandalized.

to some it seemed that they heard, either as a gust of wind or as an echo of harmony, a breath of the Spirit Whose counsel they had implored. The celebrant was for some minutes unable to continue the Mass, and at the subsequent chapter he spoke of his experience thankfully indeed, but with an exhortation that all should abide in God's grace with prayer, humble and fearful. His own constant prayer was that of Christ for His disciples: 'Holy Father, keep them whom thou hast given me in thy name.'

While Houghton thus awaited the summons he was visited by his fellow priors of Beauvale and Axholme. The former, Robert Laurence, was in origin a monk of London; the latter, Augustine Webster, had professed at Sheen. They decided to forestall the commissioners by seeking an interview with Cromwell in which to ask for exemption from the obligation of the oath. This was refused, and after a series of three interrogations conducted by the vicar-general they were lodged for their pains in the Tower, where Fisher and More already lay on the matter of the Oath of Succession, and were examined by some of the Council. Houghton took careful notes of their various examinations, and these, after being read by Fisher, were conveyed to the Charterhouse, where Chauncy saw them.[1] Unfortunately, these papers have not survived, but Chauncy's account may be presumed to be essentially trustworthy. According to him, when they expressed willingness to consent 'so far as the law of God might allow', Cromwell roughly brushed aside all qualifications; when they asserted that the Church had always held otherwise, and that St Augustine had set the authority of the Church above that of Scripture, the vicar-general replied that he cared naught for the Church and that Augustine might hold as he pleased. All he wished to know was whether they would swear a direct oath or no. They then refused absolutely. It seems clear that in taking this decision they were influenced solely by their conviction that a matter of divine faith was at stake. The Carthusian Order, as such, was in no direct dependence upon the papacy, as were the orders of friars, nor did the pope figure in their statutes. Nor had Houghton and his companions any concern with the unity of Christian nations, whatever may have been the case with More. All that Chauncy says, and all that can be extracted from the fragments of Houghton's notes and record sources, goes to show that the Carthusian priors and their followers, many of them men of education and wide reading, stood purely and simply by the traditional faith of the Church in the divine commission to Peter. They were thus in the most literal sense martyrs of the faith.[2]

They were in due course tried in Westminster Hall on 28–29 April, and

1 *Historia*, 106: 'Omnia interrogata et responsa sua in hoc negotio scripsit propria manu in pugillari; quem misit ad Patrem Guillelmum Exmew...qui mihi misero dedit.' Exmew, before his own arrest, compiled an account of Houghton's trial and death to be sent to the Grande Chartreuse. Chauncy, in his turn, gave the notes to a Spaniard to take to Rome, and it is possible that the account printed in *LP*, VIII, 661 from an Italian source is taken from them.

2 See Appendix III, *infra*, p. 471.

an unwilling jury was browbeaten by Cromwell into pronouncing the verdict of guilty.[1] After their condemnation Cranmer made one of his characteristically cautious attempts to save their lives at the expense of their convictions, but his offer to argue with them was not acceptable to Cromwell. As they left the Tower for Tyburn on a May morning (Tuesday, 4 May) they did not know that they were watched by one who had long known them and wished them well. With his customary humility More, who was standing with his daughter by a window, attributed their early release from this world's prison to the long years of penance they had spent while he had lived at ease, and he called the attention of his Margaret to their joyful alacrity, as of men going to their marriage. By the royal command they were executed in their monastic habits, with the hair shirts of their Rule beneath. Each at the foot of the gallows was offered pardon if he would submit, and on their refusal the barbarous sentence was carried out with every circumstance of cruelty. Houghton, the first to die, embraced his executioner and addressed the vast crowd, taking them to witness against the day of judgment that he died rather than deny the teaching of God's Church. He bore the agony of the butchery, aggravated by the tough hair shirt, with what seemed a more than human patience; conscious to the end, he died invoking the Lord he had loved and followed to the Cross. He was forty-eight years of age.[2]

When the prior had been taken to the Tower the government of the House of the Salutation fell to the vicar, Humphrey Middlemore, who acted in all things with the counsel of the procurator, William Exmew, and of Sebastian Newdigate. On the very day of the execution Cromwell sent his 'owne Thomas Bedyll' to the Charterhouse, furnished with copious anti-papal literature. The three seniors, at his request, spent the rest of the day perusing the books, but found nothing in them to alter their convictions. Bedyll, meanwhile, had been taken sick, but he summoned the Carthusians to his bedside and warned them of the dangers of hypocrisy and vainglory, not to speak of the direct action of the lying spirit who had deceived the prophets of Achab.[3] Still unconvinced, the three monks were removed to the Marshalsea, where they remained for a fortnight chained by the neck and legs to posts without the possibility of moving or the relief of a minute's freedom. Here, according to a tradition which may be reliable, Newdigate, the ex-courtier, received a visit from his old master,

---

1 There seems no reason to doubt that threats were used, though Froude endeavoured to disprove it. Chauncy asserts (*Historia*, 101) that this was so, as does an anonymous contemporary (BM. Arundel MS. 153, fo. 308, cited Thompson, *English Carthusians*, 397), and in a letter written to Lord Lisle two days before the trial (27 April) John Husse relates that Cromwell has had much trouble with the judges and sergeants about the case (*LP*, VIII, 606).

2 *LP*, XIV, 200. Pole, *Apologia ad Carolum Quintum*, 98–9. The details of the execution probably reached Chauncy from Antonius Rexius, O.P., a friend of Houghton, who was present.

3 MS. Cleopatra, E. VI, fo. 259 (Thompson, *English Carthusians*, 404–5).

who made a last attempt to win his submission by alternate blandish-
ments and threats.[1] But neither fair words nor the frown of the
instant tyrant could shake the Carthusian, and in due course this
second trio were examined by the Council and (11 June) tried at Westminster. Gallant, high-spirited young men as they were, unbroken by
their long ordeal of pain, they adhered steadfastly to their refusal and
put forth their reasons with energy and ability.[2] A week later (19 June),
like the three priors, they went to their death as to a feast, with eagerness
and joy.[3]

The plight of the London Charterhouse, thus deprived by public
execution of its spiritual and administrative superiors, may readily be
imagined. Those that were left were called upon to follow a most exacting
Rule without the confidence that comes from submission to those with
canonical and personal claims to obedience, and they were exposed to all
the assaults upon the citadel of the soul that are delivered by the waves of
doubt and despondency that swell and eddy in times of stress within the
walls of an enclosed community. Above their gateway the severed arm of
their late prior provided a text for visitors. They were, in addition, subjected to every form of vexation and petty persecution. Two servants of
Cromwell, John Whalley and Jasper Fyloll, were put in, the one to undertake the duties of procurator, the other to use all his endeavours to convert
the monks. The former underfed the community by progressive stages,
while he himself and his cronies lived in plenty and wasted the revenues;[4]
the latter, in addition to his own arguments, let loose upon the brethren
a series of visitors and *conférenciers* of the new way of thinking. When one
of these had been received with ridicule, Whalley forwarded to the vicar-
general a proposed course of treatment which, were the issue not so fateful,
would appear ludicrous in its ponderous futility. A series of discourses by
'honest learned men' was to be followed by public sermons against the
pope, ending in a crescendo of exhortations by the bishops of York,
Winchester, Durham, Lincoln, Bath and London. If these charmers
failed, the monks were to be called before the priors of all the Charterhouses of England and the temporal and spiritual peers of the realm. 'No

---

1 Clifford, *Jane Dormer*, 27–32. This tradition, reaching Clifford from Lady Dormer
(Jane Newdigate) through a single intermediary, her granddaughter Jane Dormer, may be
accepted in its main lines. Clifford asserts that Henry interviewed Newdigate both in prison
and in the Tower, and recounts long speeches which are certainly not the *ipsissima verba*
of the parties.

2 *Historia*, 108: 'Audacter allegantes de Scripturis Sanctis ante tribunal Judicum.'

3 *Ibid.*: 'Iveruntque ad mortem quasi ad epulas...alacritate corporis et hilaritate
vultus.'

4 The monks also received the attentions of Bedyll and others. The statement in the text
is from Chauncy, *Historia*, 109; Miss Thompson prints the relevant letters from the pair.
According to Fyloll the expenses of the Charterhouse in food alone exceeded the clear regular
annual revenue, which according to the *VE* was £642. This is scarcely credible, even taking
into consideration the recent steep rise in prices, the high cost of fish at all times, and the
falling-off of gifts to the monks. Either the converses purposely confused Fyloll or he gave
false figures.

question of it', the writer adds, 'they be exceedingly superstitious, ceremonious and pharisaicall, and wonderly addicted to their old Mumpsimus.'[1]

In the sequel they were deprived of their books, even of the statutes of their institute, the house was put under a brutal and inquisitorial 'order', and their privacy was invaded by hostile or curious visitors who badgered and even struck the monks.[2] Members of the Council and others harangued and argued in the chapterhouse so as to disorganize the horarium, and the few brethren who were discontented or malevolent were encouraged to communicate their grievances and suspicions to Cromwell, and to receive from him dispensations from any points of discipline they might find hard. Their friends failed them, and the Bridgettines of Syon, who had formerly encouraged their resistance, now wrote urging that submission was reasonable and meritorious.[3] If anything were yet lacking to the bitterness of the cup which they were daily required to drink, in surroundings where every corner spoke of the past and all that they held precious was blown upon and ridiculed, they were permitted to find it in a message addressed to them by the head of their order, the prior of the Grande Chartreuse. Their late confrater, Andrew Boorde, in the course of his long continental tour of medical academies, visited the Chartreuse to make enquiries about the dispensation he had received, and apparently felt called upon to suggest to the authorities there that the London house was making unnecessary trouble to the government and king, and would be the better for a rebuke. Dom Jean Gaillard accordingly, in August 1535, asked Boorde to convey his wishes to London; he also wrote to the bishop of Lichfield, Rowland Lee, in the same sense. The erring brethren, he said, were not to fail in obedience to the Defender of the Faith, lest they might be deprived of his kindly interest in these troublous times. They were also to pay more attention than they had hitherto done to the punctual observance and transmission of obits. As a further measure to assuage any soreness of feeling that might exist, and to ensure harmonious co-operation from all parties in the future, the prior of the Grande Chartreuse admitted Cromwell and the bishop to full confraternity of the order, and instructed his sons to do nothing without their counsel.[4]

---

1 Whalley to Cromwell, printed by Thompson, *English Carthusians*, 415–16. *Mumpsimus* and its variant *Sumpsimus* were cant terms current among those of the new way of thinking in religion, denoting a superstitious ceremony (cf. 'hocus-pocus'). Both were used by Henry VIII in his well-known last charge to the Parliament of 1545.

2 *Historia*, 109: 'Qui illuderent et colaphis caederent nos.'

3 *The English Carthusians*, 434–5. The letter, from B.M. MS. Cott. Cleopatra, E VI, fo. 172–4, is printed in full by Aungier, *History of Syon*, 430–3.

4 Boorde's letter (*LP*, IX, 11) is in *English Carthusians*, 413–14. The letter of the prior to Rowland Lee is in *LP*, IX, 8. It is badly mutilated but some phrases are clear, e.g. 'continua oratione...ad Deum pro ipso serenissimo rege, Fidei Christianae Defensore... filii nostri errantes inter haec tempora nubila, clementissima...facie privemur', etc. Boorde's letter should be pondered by those who sympathize with the indulgent treatment accorded him by some historians, e.g. in the *DNB*.

The oppression of the Charterhouse lasted for two years. There is evidence that the king would have made short work of the opposition had it not been that Cromwell, presumably for reasons of policy, was unwilling to outrage public sentiment with the spectacle of the sudden and complete destruction of a community so highly esteemed, and therefore delayed long to accomplish the royal wishes.[1] After all other devices had failed, the tactic of division was attempted. On 4 May 1536, four of those accounted most stubborn were sent to other houses; Chauncy and one Fox to Beauvale; John Rochester and James Walworth to Hull.[2] A little later eight more were sent for a time to the Bridgettines at Syon, where they were like to find learned men who, having argued themselves into support of the king's position, would be doubly anxious to persuade others. The Bridgettines did their best, but their success was not great.[3]

Hitherto, the unanimity of the brethren, or at least of the respectable majority, had helped to protect them, as Tynbygh had long ago foretold. At last, however, the king became more instant, and a little later, in May 1537, a division was at last effected in the sorely tried family. The Council threatened to suppress the house out of hand, and a number of the monks, exhausted by the persecution and hoping to save their monastery, agreed to renounce the authority of the pope and to accept that of the king as supreme head; this they swore to so far as words went though, if we may believe Chauncy who was ultimately one of their number, their hearts and consciences always gave the lie to their lips.[4] It was not, however, thus with all. Ten remained, 'unmoved, unshaken, unseduced, unterrified', who would not swear; three were priests, one a deacon, and six were converses. They were immediately lodged in a filthy ward of Newgate; it was the Friday before Whitsunday, 18 May.

The first martyrs had been executed as a public spectacle. The publicity had not told against them, and the second group had been despatched without advertisement. The third and most numerous band was denied even the dignity of a formal trial and execution. They had asked to live as hidden servants of Christ; they died, silent witnesses to His words, hidden from the eyes of all. Chained without possibility of movement in a foul atmosphere, and systematically starved, they were thus left, as Bedyll put it, to 'be dispeched by thand of God'.[5] Abandoned by all, and dying slowly of hunger and fever, they received a moiety of succour and a more precious instance of love from a devoted woman. Margaret Gigs, the adopted daughter of Sir Thomas More, had learnt from him to practise

1 *LP*, xii, 501 (27 September 1536).

2 Chauncy does not give the names in his first account; they can be discovered from the account of 1570 (ed. Church Historical Society, 108, 112; B.M. Cott. MS. Cleopatra, E. iv, fo. 298), and from the letter (from the same MS. fo. 247) printed in Aungier, *Syon*, 438–9.

3 *Historia*, 113–14; Cott. MS. Cleopatra, E. vi, 172–4; E. iv, 247.

4 *Historia*, 115–16; 'Taedio affecti commiserunt se in periculo misericordiae divinae licet non absque gravi conscientiarum suarum laesione...et certissime scio quod revera ita acta sint, sed non in hoc justificati sumus.'

5 Bedyll's letter is printed in *English Carthusians*, 480–1.

R

charity and knew well of her father's admiration for the Carthusians. She now bribed her way to their prison and, acting the part of a milkmaid, carried in a bucket on her head food, which she placed with her own hands between their lips. Besides food, she brought also clean linen which she put on them, and cleansed them as they stood unable to move hand or foot. The effects of her ministration betrayed her; the authorities, finding the prisoners still alive, reprimanded the gaoler and Mistress Clement (as she now was) was denied entrance. Undeterred, she obtained access to the roof and endeavoured, by removing some tiles, to let food down in a basket.[1] She failed in her design, and the Carthusians died one by one through the summer months; the last to die in chains was Thomas Johnson on 20 September, but a converse, William Horne, was for some reason removed to a more tolerable durance and lived on in prison till he was drawn to Tyburn to suffer as his prior had done on 4 August 1540. 'And so this child, tried longer and more severely than any other, followed his father, and died for the love of Jesus, and for the faith of His bride the Catholic Church',[2] thus completing the tale of eighteen martyrs, for two of those exiled from London had been hanged at York in 1537.

Rarely indeed in the annals of the Church have any confessors of the faith endured trials longer, more varied or more bitter than these unknown monks. They had left the world, as they hoped, for good; but the children of the world, to gain their private ends, had violated their solitude to demand of them an approval and a submission which they could not give. They had long made of their austere and exacting Rule a means to the loving and joyful service of God; pain and desolation, therefore, when they came, held no terrors for them. When bishops and theologians paltered or denied, they were not ashamed to confess the Son of Man. They died faithful witnesses to the Catholic teaching that Christ had built His Church upon a rock.

Those who had taken the oath to save their house were quickly to find, as More had put it a few years before, that, once deflowered, they would soon be devoured. Within three weeks after the last arrests the surrender

---

1 The authority for this is the *Life of Mother Margaret Clement* preserved in two MSS. of the English Austin Canonesses now at Haywards Heath and Newton Abbot. The relevant passage, together with much information about the Clements, is given by C. S. Durrant in *A Link between the Flemish Mystics and the English Martyrs*, 183. The author of this *Life*, Sister Shirley of the convent of English nuns at Bruges, did not complete her work till 1611, but, as with Clifford's information about Sebastian Newdigate, what she says has excellent credentials and may be in gross accepted. She was for years the intimate assistant of Mother M. Clement, who was herself a daughter of Margaret Clement (*née* Gigs). As the mother (like Jane Newdigate, Lady Dormer) lived to an advanced age, dying in exile at Bruges in 1570, substantial error, in view of the good faith of the parties, is not possible. The incident in the text may therefore be accepted as historical. It receives confirmation from another incident recorded by Sister Shirley. When Margaret Clement (the elder) lay dying, but in complete possession of her faculties, she repeatedly told those with her that she could not stay long, for the fathers of the Charterhouse stood around her bed, calling her to come away with them.

2 *Historia*, 117: 'Sicque patrem secuta est sua proles, inter omnes diutissime et durissime vexatus, et necatus pro amore Jesu et pro fide sponsae suae Ecclesiae Catholicae, potius quam falsum dicere aut jurare voluisset.'

of the monastery had been demanded and obtained. It was still more than a year before the remnant of the community was expelled; in the interval Chauncy and a companion, who had been removed to Beauvale and Syon to shake their constancy, were induced to take the oath, still hoping to save their house.[1] The hope was empty: the House of the Salutation was suppressed on 15 November 1538; the church and buildings, desecrated and forlorn, were used as a store for the king's pavilions and arms; the altars were found convenient as gaming-tables by the workmen.[2]

The conduct of the other Carthusian priories was less heroic than might perhaps have been expected from a body living such a strict life.[3] None of them had had a Houghton to train them to war. As will be noted on another page, those that were legally liable to suppression under the Act of 1536 as lesser houses had in fact been spared, so that seven remained in 1538–9, when the drive to liquidate what remained of monastic capital began. Sheen, the richest of all and of considerable repute, the near neighbour of the Bridgettines of Syon, and distinguished by the residence of Dean Colet and Reginald Pole, put up little opposition. As will be remembered, Henry Man, Henry Ball the vicar, John Mitchell the procurator, and William Howe the sacrist had been among the most enthusiastic and perhaps unthinking of the supporters of the Maid of Kent. When the *débâcle* took place in the autumn of 1535 they disowned her memory with equal alacrity. Cromwell realized that they would give no further trouble and saw to it that two of them were appointed to higher office. Man was sent first to Witham, and when after a few months he was recalled to be prior of Sheen, Mitchell took his place in the west; the two were appointed visitors of the province by the vicar-general. When therefore Rowland Lee and Bedyll came on 7 May 1534, to sound the community on their attitude to the Act of Succession, Man did his best to forward their mission, and the commissioners had nothing but praise for their compliance. Next year, however, when the issue of principle was plain and their London confrères had given them a lead, the community of Sheen was not so unanimous. While Man, the prior, was compliant to the point of obsequiousness, the vicar, Henry Ball, and several others were unwilling to admit the supremacy. They begged for permission to remain silent, or for time to change their minds, and whatever the upshot of their letters to Cromwell and others, there were in the sequel no martyrs from Sheen. As previously in the affair of Elizabeth Barton, we catch glimpses of an ineffectual piety which wished, but dared not, to make a stand, and which was thwarted by the treachery of a discontented element which was so common and so lamentable a feature of Tudor monastic life.

Witham, the cradle of the province, showed no trace of the spirit of

---

1 *Historia*, 119. 'Spei quidem frustratae innixi vanisque persuasionibus et promissionibus illecti, abstracti et seducti.'

2 *Ibid.*: 'Super altaria sancta saltantes choreis luserunt et aleis.'

3 For what follows, details and references will be found in the accounts by Dom Hendriks and Miss Thompson (*English Carthusians* and *Somerset Carthusians*).

St Hugh and his redoubtable converse, who had spoken his mind to Henry II. The monks satisfied Layton in 1535 and surrendered easily enough in 1539. At Hinton, Prior Horde, a monk of London who had a high reputation in the order, was in earlier days unfavourable to the divorce, and on the subject of the royal supremacy and surrender of his house was divided in mind and will to the last, but his brother Alan, a bencher of the Inner Temple, represented to him the dangers of resistance, and he gave way.[1] In his resistance to surrender he was upheld by a majority of his community including one Nicholas Balland, who openly denied the king's supremacy, asserting that of the pope. His friends endeavoured with success to rescue him from the consequences of such opinions by representing him as suffering from bouts of lunacy, and in the event he signed the surrender with the rest. There was, however, method in his madness, for sixteen years later he was one of Chauncy's companions in the revived Charterhouse, and he lived for more than twenty years in religion, dying at Louvain in 1578.

Of the rest Axholme, having lost its martyred prior, a monk of Sheen, made an inglorious end in an atmosphere of intrigue. At Beauvale, when the commissioners arrived on 16 April 1535 and examined the community on the question of the royal supremacy, Trafford the procurator affirmed his belief in papal supremacy, and declared his willingness to abide by this to death. He was in consequence sent up to London to see Cromwell, and arrived there a few days after the execution of his prior, Robert Laurence. There, for whatever reason, his conviction disappeared; he was sent to Sheen, and a year later he was put in charge of the remaining monks at Smithfield as Cromwell's puppet prior to surrender the house. Bedyll, who found Exmew and Newdigate vain and hypocritical, thought him 'a man of suche charite as I have not seen the like'.[2] Cromwell, however, had a long memory, and when it came to allotting pensions Trafford received an annuity of £20 as compared with that of £133 given to the prior of Sheen.

Coventry, which had been respited in 1536, gave little trouble at the end, but Hull and Mount Grace were at first disposed to resist; they were won over by the arguments of the archbishop of York. The two London monks however, who had been exiled to Hull, stood firm, and one of them, John Rochester, wrote to the Duke of Norfolk a letter, which deserves more respect than it has received from historians, in which he begged for the opportunity to meet the king face to face and demonstrate to him that the royal supremacy over the Church was 'directly against the lawes of God, the fayth cathole, and helth of his hyghnes bodie and Sowle'. Norfolk forwarded the letter to Cromwell, with the remark 'I beleve he is one of the most arrant traytours of all others that I have heard of', and suggested that he should be sent up to London to be 'justified there'. The

---

1 For Horde, v. also Ellis. *OL*, II, 2, cxxx, and *LP*, XIV, i, 145, 269.
2 Letter in *English Carthusians*, 481.

execution of Rochester and his companion, Walworth, took place in the sequel at York, on 11 May, and the Duke reported the event to the king, with the comment that 'two more wilful religious men, in manner unlearned, I think, never suffered'.[1] The indictment contained no charge but that of denying the royal supremacy.[2]

Mount Grace, the northernmost house, was second only to London in repute. We saw elsewhere that towards the end of the fifteenth century Richard Methley set down his spiritual experiences in a group of writings which still exist.[3] A younger contemporary of Methley, John Norton,[4] who entered religion in 1482–3 and became in turn procurator and sixth prior of the house, wrote a series of short tracts on the monastic virtues, on the imitation of Christ and His Passion, and on the Blessed Sacrament, in which he set down the thoughts that had come to him in prayer as the words of the Lord speaking in his heart. His reflections are diffuse and doctrinally commonplace, and there is nothing to indicate specifically mystical experience; he has none of the fire of Rolle or the direct vision of Dame Juliana, but there is no extravagance or ineptitude in what he writes. His pages are indeed a distant reflection of the style that found its highest expression in Denis the Carthusian. He is one more witness to the sincerity and high ideals of his order, of which, like Methley, he is extremely proud, and the admiration felt for his compositions by the distinguished chancellor of York, a Cambridge man of note, William Melton, is still further evidence of the place held by the Carthusians in contemporary opinion.[5]

Mount Grace continued to flourish, with a tradition of fervour and a steady intake of notable recruits, till the end.[6] When the crisis came there was a painful struggle. Two monks refused to take the oath of Succession in the summer of 1534, but apparently without fatal consequences. When it came to accepting the Supremacy in 1535 there was more hesitation. The prior, John Wilson, was at first set upon refusing, but he took counsel of the two northern bishops, Tunstal of Durham and Edward Lee of York. Both were men of real learning and conservative temper, but both had, with differing degrees of hesitation, capitulated to the king when it was

---

1 *LP*, xii (i), 777–8, 1172 (3). The date is as in Chauncy, *Historia*, 118.
2 The indictment is in part printed by Thompson, *English Carthusians*, 466 n.
3 *RO*, ii, 224–6.
4 Norton occurs as prior 1527–8, 1531–2 in *VCH Yorks*, iii, 193. His treatises, *Musica Monachorum*, *Thesaurus Cordium vere Amancium* and *Devota Lamentacio*, are preserved in Lincoln Cathedral MS. A 6. 8. I owe a knowledge of them to Dom Philip Jebb, who kindly lent me a copy of his transcript.
5 Melton (d. 1528) was master of Michaelhouse at Cambridge, and himself the author of a sermon printed by Wynkyn de Worde; cf. art. in *DNB* by Mary Bateson.
6 The flourishing state of Mount Grace can be seen in a letter (? c. 1530) of Prior Wilson in which he writes of building works that are going forward, of a recent recruit, Sir William Maleverey, commissary and official of Bishop Fisher, and of a waiting list of five (including the Benedictine subprior of Burton) for the unfinished cell. The letter from B.M. Add. MS. 48965 was printed along with others by T. C. Skeat in 'Letters from the Reign of Henry VIII.'

no longer possible to temporize. They were therefore deeply pledged to uphold the royal supremacy and anxious on every count to convert others. With a combination of patristic quotation and appeals to their own example they worked successfully upon Prior Wilson's scruples. Two of the monks, however, tried to evade the issue by a flight to Scotland; they were brought back and lodged in the convent prison. Eventually all accepted the Supremacy, kept themselves carefully out of trouble during the risings of 1536–7, and in due course surrendered the house on 18 December 1539. It may, however, be remarked that Prior Wilson, another monk, and two converses of Mount Grace were among those who joined Chauncy at the Marian revival of Sheen in 1555, and that no other Charterhouse provided him with so many recruits.

CHAPTER XX

THE ECONOMY OF THE MONASTERIES
IN 1535

No account of the monastic world immediately before the Dissolution would be complete without some assessment of the economic background that lay behind the proposals and events of the time. It has often been asserted in the past that financial distress, or inefficient administration, would alone have made some great readjustment necessary. It has been no less often held that the wealth of the monasteries, and their wasteful and luxurious habits, invited and justified confiscation. Many of these opinions were no more than hypotheses, or rested on a few contemporary statements or charges, but until comparatively recently no attempt was made to find a more reliable basis for judgment. Yet, by a piece of singular good fortune comparable to that enjoyed by students of the Norman Conquest, the monastic historian has at his disposal a comprehensive survey of the financial and economic state of the religious houses of England taken on the very eve of the Dissolution. This is contained in the returns of the royal commissioners who in 1535 were given the task of cataloguing the revenues of the Church; the final outcome of their labours is the collection and digest of returns known as the *Valor Ecclesiasticus*.[1]

The occasion of the great survey was as follows. It had been the custom since 1306 that the first year's income, known as the first fruits, of episcopal sees, should go to the papal treasury. This had often given rise to complaints and, in the sporadic outbreak of anti-papal feeling in the years immediately following the disappearance of Wolsey, dislike of this tax had found expression in the Convocation of 1532, which petitioned the king for the parliamentary repeal of annates, as the levy on first fruits was called. This manifestation of an anti-papal mood in a very practical context exactly suited the circumstances of the moment in the king's 'great matter', and Henry and Cromwell proceeded to exploit the situation with remarkable adroitness. A bill was passed through Parliament restraining the payment of annates, but allowing the king to compound with the pope for their transformation into a charge of not more than 5 per cent on the net income of a see; assent to the bill was suspended at the king's pleasure, thus providing Henry with a bargaining counter in his negotiations with the pope. When the final break with Rome occurred in 1534 the bill

1 The *Valor Ecclesiasticus* was printed by the Record Commission in six folio volumes, 1810–34, edited by J. Caley and J. Hunter, the latter of whom contributed a valuable introduction. The only critical and tolerably comprehensive study of the data provided by the *Valor* is that of Professor A. Savine, being the first part of vol. 1 of the *Oxford Studies in Social and Legal History*, edited by Sir P. Vinogradoff (1909). Savine's work will be discussed on a later page.

became law, but within a few months another bill went through parliament securing the first fruits of all spiritual benefices and offices to the Crown, and furthermore imposing a new annual tax of 10 per cent on the net incomes of all spiritual benefices, to take effect from 1 January 1535.[1] Annates thus reappeared in an amplified form, with the addition of a heavy annual tax on the net income of the Church.

Before a levy of the latter tax could become practicable a survey of all ecclesiastical incomes was essential. Accordingly the chancellor, Sir Thomas Audley, was empowered to send inquisitors into every diocese to ascertain the value of all ecclesiastical benefices. For this purpose commissions were set up on 30 January 1535 for each shire, before which all clergy and officials were bound to appear with full information, to be given on oath; the returns were to be completed by the first Sunday after Trinity (30 May) in the same year. Detailed instructions were provided as to the taking of evidence and the inspection of registers and account books. Here we are concerned only with the religious houses; the commissioners were instructed to compile a list of all such, specifying their manors, farms, rents and other temporal revenues, together with the names of all rectories, vicarages, tithes, oblations and other spiritual revenues owned by the religious. The final issue of all this was to be a statement of the exact annual amount coming in from every separate source of revenue, the total of which was to represent the gross annual income of the house. From this the commissioners were to deduct, as tax-free, any pensions, rents and alms for the payment of which the house lay under testamentary or other legal obligations, together with all fees due annually to the lay administrators, such as receivers, bailiffs, auditors and stewards, as also (in the case of spiritual revenue) fees due for synodals and proxies. Together, these two kinds of allowance amounted to some 5 per cent + 3 per cent of the total income. After the local returns had been assembled, a book for every diocese was to be compiled and returned to London, as has been said, by the first Sunday after Trinity.

The chancellor chose as his commissioners and sub-commissioners men of the classes that had for long been used as agents of the government: bishops, mayors, sheriffs, justices of the peace, official auditors and local gentry. A feature of the lists was the predominance of the lay element; the only clerical member of each commission was the bishop, and, although he was usually chairman and conducted negotiations with the government, the total absence of representation on the commissions of the great class which alone was the victim of the new taxation is noteworthy, and significant of the 'new look' which had come in with Cromwell. It is eloquent proof alike of the technical excellence of the administrative organization, of the high level of efficiency among the local 'unprofessional' agents, and of the drive imparted to the whole corps by the vicar-general, that such a widespread and detailed enquiry should have been scheduled for completion

1 *Statutes of the Realm* (26 Henry VIII, c. 3), III, 493–9.

within five months, two of which were bad for travelling, and should in fact have been achieved within a little more than nine. Naturally, in such a vast undertaking, executed so speedily, omissions and inconsistencies were to be expected; the *Valor*, like Domesday, often needs and sometimes baffles exegesis; but on the whole, with the latter document as with the former, admiration rather than criticism is the reader's first reaction.

The commissioners, as laymen and agents of the government, are not to be suspected of laxity or favouritism towards the religious; they were unpaid, and their hopes of future reward or recognition could best be served by a zeal displayed in the exact and inflexible performance of their instructions.[1]   On the other hand, they were not as a class prejudiced against the religious, to whom many of them were linked by relationships of tenancy or official service, while in many cases, as descendants of founders, patrons or benefactors, they were on easy terms with the monasteries, in whose churches their ancestors were buried and in whose cloisters, in not a few cases, their sons and daughters had taken the habit or received their education. As for the monks, they, like the rest of the great body of churchmen, probably took the enquiry as but one more of the many impositions they had endured at the hands of Wolsey and his successor for a quarter of a century. Some, indeed, may have felt that the red light was now showing so plainly that it was scarcely realistic to haggle about taxation when their very existence was threatened.

The final lists, duly digested, were in the hands of the exchequer officials early in 1536. The greater part of them still exists, and is preserved at the Public Record Office in twenty-two volumes and three portfolios. Eighteen of the volumes contain the commissioners' returns for England and Wales, another contains Irish information, and the remaining three form the official digest of the returns; the portfolios contain part of the survey as it came in from the various shires. The commissioners' returns are in fact not complete: six counties (Berkshire, Cambridgeshire, Essex, Hertfordshire, Northumberland and Rutland) and parts of two others (Middlesex and Yorkshire) are missing, but the monastic statistics of these can be supplied from the exchequer digest. Of the eighteen volumes mentioned above two are known officially as the *Liber Regis*; they contain copies of the commissioners' returns, written carefully on vellum with painted miniatures, and tradition has it that they were made in duplicate for the king by a monk of Westminster, where the abbot, William Benson, was a king's man.[2]

---

1 Savine, 5–13, where the correspondence that passed between the commissioners and the government, as summarized in *LP*, is discussed. There are several instances of that effusive zeal combined with self-commendation that is a familiar characteristic of Cromwell's correspondents.

2 Some of the entries were apparently made by the monks on behalf of the commission, as, for example, at Eynsham, where the facts and figures are in a clear and handsome script. The figures and tables of the *Valor* can be controlled in certain cases by surveys and extents made by individual houses earlier in the century (e.g. those of Whalley and Glastonbury;

The *Valor* has a number of limitations as an instrument of research. Besides the omissions and mistakes inevitable in a hasty compilation of such magnitude, three large monasteries (the Cistercian Kingswood and Kirkstall and the Augustinian Bristol) and two small (Holy Trinity and St Andrew's, both at York) are missing.[1] Furthermore, the only total of income available for all the thirty-nine counties of England is that of the net or taxable revenue, that is, the total income less the allowable expenses. The gross income can be ascertained in twenty-three of the counties, but only in the case of twelve is it possible to recover the gross and net income from both temporal and spiritual sources.[2] To provide an estimate of the totals that are wanting it is necessary to supply average figures constructed to show the same proportional relationships as are shown by the totals that exist.

There remains the further question as to the general accuracy of the sums and valuations given by the commissioners. It would obviously be unreasonable to expect that numerous groups of men, bound to each other by no ties of association, training or professional code, and working under pressure of time, would produce exactly the same details and totals as another set of men on another occasion. Moreover, fidelity to fact was undoubtedly lessened by the tension inevitably present in every age and in every class of society between the fiscal agents of government and the taxpayers who are undergoing assessment. Nevertheless, there seems to be no reason to suppose that the commissioners would do more than give the benefit of the doubt to the treasury whenever possible, and that this would be offset by the conservative estimates handed in by the religious. That this was the current opinion at the time can be seen from the action of the officials at the centre who, in going through the lists, docked the monks of many of the allowances that had been claimed.

In point of fact, if we doubt the veracity of the *Valor* there are documents to hand for controlling its figures. In a few instances, two independent returns are given in the *Valor* itself, either because the exchequer itself required or received them, or because dependencies of a house situated in a different county were surveyed by two commissions.[3]

cf. Savine, 47, 57), and those made after the *Valor* by the agents of the government, such as the Northern Surveys of 1536–9, the Exchequer or 'Paper' Surveys of about the same time, the Suppression or Receivers' Accounts of 1536–40, and the detailed Pollard-Moyle survey of Glastonbury. For this last, *v. Monasticon*, 1, 10–21; for the others also, Savine, 42–70.

1 Savine, 32; but he does not notice the omission of Kirkstall, which does not appear either in his text, lists or index. Its net income was £336. Kingswood was in fact twice valued in documents not printed in the *VE*; *v.* art. 'Kingswood Abbey' by E. S. Lindley. Its net income was £239 or £244.

2 *V.* tables in Savine, 98–9.

3 The double returns for Oxfordshire, Bruerne and Burton-on-Trent are discussed by Savine, 34–41. He did not suspect fraud in the case of Burton but Hibbert, *Dissolution of the Monasteries*, 72–91, seems to have established this. The only other instance noted of serious fraud was at St Mary's, Winchester, where the figure in the *Valor* was admitted to the commissioners of 1536 as having been too little by no less a sum than £150. As this piece of deceit had the unforeseen effect of putting the nunnery into the class of smaller houses liable to be suppressed in 1536 it was from the governmental point of view a happy fault, and went unpunished.

Furthermore, a year after the completion of the *Valor* all religious houses with an income not exceeding £200 were liable to be suppressed, and special commissions were sent to make another survey, this time including a detailed survey of the demesne.[1] Of a similar character, but still more elaborate, is the survey taken immediately after the dissolution of Glastonbury by Pollard and Moyle, two of Cromwell's agents.[2] Then, a little later, come the Exchequer Surveys of the demesne (the so-called Paper Surveys), and the receivers' accounts of moneys paid into the Augmentations Office after the suppression of the monasteries. Finally, in a few cases terriers or surveys made by individual houses shortly before the Dissolution still exist.[3] From all these sources it is possible to estimate the general worth of the figures of the *Valor*. On the whole, these additional materials confirm the substantial accuracy of the great survey. There are, however, two exceptions of some importance, the one regional, the other common to all the commissioners' work. There seems little doubt that the income of the northern houses—those in the ecclesiastical province of York, together with some in other parts of the country, notably Staffordshire—is on the average rated so much lower in the *Valor* than in other documents that a serious undervaluation is to be suspected. In the north this might be attributed to the difficulties inherent in the task of a small commission working in a wide and wild region, or to a certain partiality towards the monks on the part of the gentry and others who only eighteen months later were to be the leaders in the Pilgrimage of Grace.[4] No circumstantial or regional explanation, however, will account for the consistent undervaluation of monastic demesne held in hand, and of monastic woodland in general. Here, the figures of the *Valor* were largely conjectural, as the property had never been fully exploited for cash, and the owners, when valuing for tax, would inevitably suggest a conservative figure. For the woods, indeed, the *Valor* commissioners appear to have worked on different principles in different districts, and not infrequently omitted many, or all, of the woods, or concealed them in other sources of income. The later surveyors, on the other hand, appear occasionally to have estimated what we should now call their capital value, viz. the value of the whole wood if sold at maturity, whereas their value as income could have been, and often was, estimated roughly by discovering the average area yearly ripe for felling; sometimes, however, they adopted a third method, that of giving an estimate of the value of the timber if felled immediately for sale. On the whole, therefore, taken by and large, the *Valor* underestimates the monastic income (or rather the potential income of the monastic estates) by a percentage which is certainly as large as fifteen for the whole country, and which for some districts may be as large as twenty, or even forty. In many ways such an undervaluation was inevitable in a decade when all prices were rapidly rising, and when rents had not caught up

1 Savine, 42–7, and *infra*, ch. xxiv.   2 Savine, 49–59.
3 *Ibid.* 42–49, 57.   4 *Ibid.* 46–9.

with the increase. A valuation subsequently made, with a view to the realization of the property by keen exploitation or by sale on the open market, would naturally advance both prices and rents, especially when the demesne, hitherto estimated at its yield in produce, was now being set out to lease or rent for the first time.

Thus far we have been considering the data provided by the *Valor* and the accuracy of the figures given by the commissioners within their terms of reference as understood by them. But it must be remembered that several types of asset escaped their attention altogether, as not falling within their definition of revenue. These were, speaking generally, what would now be called fixed assets and current assets. The former, comprising the buildings, furnishings and equipment of the monastery were inevitably (and rightly) left out of the reckoning, though they were in the sequel to be realized so soon. The treasure of the house was also left out. Most of this might indeed be considered as part of the furniture of the place, and in part as sacred and inalienable, but a part, especially at the larger houses, was the nearest to liquid or free capital of anything the monks possessed, for there is no doubt that not only gifts but also surplus income was in the fifteenth century 'banked' by conversion into plate or jewellery. It was, nevertheless, dead as regards productive power. In addition, however, there were several classes of current asset. The commissioners, unlike the accounts for a wardship, took no notice of standing crops and only occasional notice of livestock, and made little or no mention of the stores of all kinds, such as grain and hay, which must at all houses have represented what was in fact a return in kind for cash expended. Nor is there any mention of surplus cash in hand, which in some monasteries stood at a considerable figure, even when a balance had been struck between credits and outstanding debts. It is true that in the practice of the age all this was sterile, that is, it produced no visible income, but some of it, at least, could at need be used in lieu of income till it was exhausted, and therefore in a modern balance-sheet would be expressed in terms of accruing interest. In other words, even excluding all fixed assets, the actual liquid wealth of the monasteries, all question of undervaluation apart, was considerably greater than the figures of gross or net income would suggest and these amounts would, if expressed, emphasize still more the great inequalities of wealth among the houses.

The *Valor Ecclesiasticus* was analysed, now almost fifty years ago, with patient and scholarly thoroughness by a Russian scholar, A. Savine.[1]

---

[1] Savine's work is careful and impartial, and a great deal of information can be extracted from it by a patient reader, but the treatment is not always lucid, and some names and figures, which might well have been printed in appendices, cumber the pages and interrupt the flow of the argument. Naturally, it is vain to seek in Savine's pages for a treatment of points of financial and economic history which have only become fashionable or controversial since he wrote. Moreover, he had little familiarity with the sources of monastic history in the later Middle Ages, and he occasionally uses the silences or omissions of the *Valor* to establish general conclusions which can be invalidated by positive evidence from another source. Nevertheless, his work remains very valuable after fifty years, though it can

Within his self-imposed limits of enquiry, Savine's work was accurate and definitive, and it would be a waste of time for another to work through the *Valor* again in search of answers to the same questions. Savine, however, though remarkably alert on all economic and agrarian problems, was more interested in figures and statistics than in trends and developments, and there are many questions now commonly asked by economic historians which he never put to himself. Moreover, though he made good use of other quasi-contemporary surveys, he did not take a view of his subject from the different angle which even fifty years ago was provided by printed monastic accounts such as those of Durham and its dependent priories. These would have shown him (what has been shown still more amply since his day) that the monastic income was underestimated by the commissioners of 1535 even more than he supposed, that errors in valuation and computation are so frequent in the *Valor* as probably to affect even the statistical percentages obtained from large groups of entries, that in particular the amount of industrial activity, especially in coal-winning, was a notable feature in the economy of monasteries in County Durham and Northumberland and elsewhere, and that the area of waste and spoiled land, especially in the north, was greater and more significant than he realized.[1] Nevertheless, his general statistics and conclusions are in the main valid, and as the figures in the *Valor*, which are themselves not fully complete, can be replaced by more accurate ones only for scattered groups of houses, it will be best to use the figures of the commissioners of the tenth throughout, unless otherwise noted, though the reader must bear in mind that the aggregate incomes given, whether gross or net, are probably less by some 20 per cent than the actual income of the house in cash or cash value during the last decade of its history. Thus Glastonbury, with an income in the *Valor* of £3311 net, may easily have handled a sum much nearer £4000.

The total income of the religious houses as extracted from the *Valor* is of little significance when the total national income is unknown. For England alone, it has been calculated that the total gross income of monks, canons, nuns and knights hospitallers amounted to some £165,500.[2] Three-

and should be supplemented for the regions concerned by the studies of W. J. Archbold, *The Somerset Religious Houses*; J. W. Clay, *Yorkshire Monastic Suppression Papers* (YAS, Rec. Ser., XLVIII); D. Hay, 'The Dissolution of the Monasteries in the Diocese of Durham'; and F. A. Hibbert, *Dissolution of the Monasteries of Staffordshire*. I have also used an unpublished Ph.D. thesis of Trinity College, Dublin, by Mr G. W. O. Woodward, *The Benedictines and Cistercians in Yorkshire in the Sixteenth Century* (1955).

1 This emerges clearly from D. Hay's article, as also from several of the Durham account rolls of the preceding century.

2 This is Savine's figure (p. 100), with the addition of £1500 to cover the four houses omitted by him and another £1500 or so for the hospitallers. It must be remembered that he includes neither Wales nor the friars. Allowing for the wide margin of undervaluation, the real value for the same houses was perhaps £200,000. For a present-day (1957) equivalent we should have to think in terms of £20 m. or so, but that sum would of course be a far smaller part of the national income to-day than was the aggregate total of the religious in 1535. Savine's figure is for 553 houses, and his list is in many ways an arbitrary selection. The

quarters of this were made up of temporal income, the spiritual income accounting for the remainder. About one-sixth of the gross income was recognized as tax-free; this was undoubtedly a smaller proportion than justice and an equitable interpretation of the statute would have demanded. It seems useless to enquire what total acreage of land lay behind this income. The surveys rarely give acreage at all fully, and attempts to translate incomes from rents into acres are fruitless. Moreover, any reckoning based on income would fail to take account of unexploited land or moorland grazing.

Of greater interest for the monastic historian is an analysis of the houses according to wealth. Here it has been reckoned that if all are classed in five divisions, made up of the very small (under £20 per annum), small (£20 to £100), medium (£100 to £300), large (£300 to £1000) and very large (over £1000), the first class contains about 9 per cent, the second and third each 35 per cent (the second being slightly the smaller of the two), the fourth 16 per cent and the fifth 4 per cent. If, on the other hand, the aggregate wealth of the various classes be considered, the last class, that of the very rich monasteries, some twenty-three out of 550 in number, accounts for more than a quarter of the total sum.[1]

From the details supplied by the *Valor* and other surveys, it is possible to gain a very fair idea of the sources and kinds of monastic income, and a careful analysis shows, what is apparent from all earlier indications, not only that the monks stood in the position of *rentiers* for most of their income, but that the practice of farming all kinds of revenue was universal; this is true of the spiritual revenue as well as of the temporal.

The spiritual income formed about a quarter of the gross total income of all the houses, and perhaps one-fifth of the taxable amount; it should, however, be added that the proportion was much greater than this in the counties of Durham and Northumberland, owing to the harrying that much of the land had suffered in the past fifty years.[2] The bulk of this income was obtained from the churches, many of which the monks had held from the earliest times. Its sources were tithes, glebe, pensions from churches and offerings. Of these tithe in one shape or another yielded the most, some five-sixths of the whole. These revenues might be gathered in detail by bailiffs or receivers, or by local agents who collected the other rents or farmed the manor, but very often they were leased out to a farmer by virtue of episcopal or papal permission; whole rectories had been so

estimated number of religious houses in c. 1530, excluding 187 friaries and all hospitals, is in the region of 650 (cf. Knowles and Hadcock, *Medieval Religious Houses*, 364). The difference is largely accounted for by the merging of dependencies with the owning house in the *Valor*; the discrepancy scarcely affects the validity of Savine's general conclusions.

1 Savine, 114–15. For a comparison of the relative wealth of the largest houses in the Domesday survey, *v.* Appendix IV, *infra*.

2 This is another point demonstrated by Hay. He does not add, however, that even the spiritual income of the lands beyond Tyne had fallen greatly from its fourteenth-century peak for similar reasons (*v.* RO, II, 317).

leased, as we have seen, long before the sixteenth century, and in such cases all connection was severed between the monks and their parishioners. Of the remainder, offerings accounted for an insignificant fraction; in earlier centuries the body of a saint, real or reputed, or a celebrated relic had often been a principal source of wealth; by the sixteenth century this had ceased; two of the most famous shrines of an earlier age, those of St Thomas of Canterbury and of the Holy Blood at Hailes, now received only £36 and £10 respectively. Walsingham alone, with an income in offerings of £250, recalled the generosity and faith of the past.[1]

Of the temporal income perhaps one-eighth came from urban properties and from quaestual and industrial sources of all kinds. Monasteries in the city of London or on its outskirts naturally owned much house property and urban land, but only in a few cases, such as the London Charterhouse, the Cistercian St Mary Graces and the Austin St Mary of Southwark, did such revenues amount to more than a half of the temporal total.[2] Industrial and commercial concerns occupied a still less important place. They had indeed recently been banned to the monasteries by statute, and even the growing of grain for market had been banned to the larger houses,[3] but there is no evidence that this had led to the extinction or transference of business on any appreciable scale, though it may well have led to judicious suppressions in the statements provided for the commissioners. If we except mills, which had from the beginning yielded income to the religious of a kind more feudal than industrial, the small tanneries, fulling mills and mines of salt held by the monks were insignificant. Only the Tyneside coal of Durham and its satellites, and the Cornish tin of Tavistock were of any consequence, and unfortunately the former of these is far from fully accounted for in the *Valor*, and the latter not at all. Durham and Finchale, in particular, had been exploiting coalpits for more than two centuries, and in the fifteenth century had often leased them for appreciable sums, but so far as can be ascertained from the accounts, they had the pits in hand at the time of the Dissolution, and used the produce lavishly for their own needs. Other houses, also, with properties in coal-bearing districts, such as Furness, Newminster and Flaxley in the Forest of Dean, used coal for fuel and thus made use of a source of invisible income that

1 Savine, 103. In the year of the translation of the relics of St Thomas in 1220 the oblations at the shrine amounted to c. £1142 of the then currency (J. B. Sheppard, *Literae Cantuarienses*, II, xlvia, d; R. A. L. Smith, *Canterbury Cathedral Priory*, 12) the offerings at Durham had shown a corresponding fall. *V.* also J. C. Dickinson, *Walsingham*, 60, citing *VE*, III, 386.

2 Savine, 118–19.

3 *Statutes of the Realm*, III, 292–6 (21 Henry VIII, c. 13). Breweries and tanneries were specifically forbidden. Agriculture and stock-raising beyond the needs of domestic consumption and hospitality were forbidden to the greater houses with over 800 marks (£533) of revenue; the smaller houses were allowed to cultivate any demesne which they had exploited during the previous century. Traffic also was forbidden (par. 5): 'Spiritual persons shall not buy any merchandise for resale.'

never appeared in the *Valor*.[1] As for the markets, which had once formed an item of importance, they had now ceased to be a significant source of profit, and the fisheries had lost their value in the face of competition from the increasing quantity of deep-sea fish now being supplied throughout the country, though here again it is certain that the religious had useful sources of invisible income not registered in the *Valor*. Another dwindling revenue was that from the courts of manor and hundred controlled by the monks, for even if the admission fines of leases, which were paid to the manor court, are reckoned in, the curial revenues did not greatly exceed, on the average for the whole country, some five per cent of the total income.[2]

There remains the temporal income drawn directly from the land, whether from demesne or whole manors put out to farm, from tenements, from rents for smaller holdings, from woods, and from produce of the land supplied by such of the demesne as was still exploited by the religious. This, which accounted for some two-thirds of the total income of the religious houses, was the foundation of the whole fabric. Of the six divisions just mentioned, by far the most important were the leases of manors and the rents from small holdings.[3] By the sixteenth century the estimated receipts from demesne in hand and from the woods that had not been leased amounted to something less than one-tenth of the total rural receipts, though this fraction could be slightly lessened or considerably increased, as has been suggested above, by consistently treating the woods either as interest-paying capital or (as contemporaries seem to have regarded them) as liquid assets comparable to a store of grain or hay. In any case, the figures given are alone enough to indicate that the days of high farming were over for the monasteries, and the figures of the *Valor* accord so well with those in compotus rolls and surveys of a slightly earlier date that it is unlikely that the disappearance of farming for the market was due in any notable degree to the statute of 1529. Of the two main classes of holding, manors, that is, and separate tenancies, the former accounted for the larger part of the income; thus the important abbey of Battle kept only one of its twenty-three manors in hand, and the wealthy nunnery of Shaftesbury drew almost all its landed income from leased manors.[4] Within the manors the distinction between demesne and

---

1 Savine, 122 *seqq.* There is no adequate study of monastic coal-mining; the only survey is the paper by Dr J. B. Simpson, 'Coal-mining by the monks', in *Transactions of the Institute of Mining Engineers*, 39. Dr Simpson shows that not only in Tyneside, but at Beauchief and the houses mentioned in the text, the monks made use of local supplies of coal. He states (without references) that Tynemouth in 1538 leased a pit for £50 p.a. In 1532 the Bursar at Durham spent £7 in wages to winners of coal (*lucracio carbonum*) in addition to £3. 4s. for picks, baskets (? shovels, *scopae*), rope and *pro exasperacione* (i.e. sharpening) *le pykkys*. Cf. *Durham Household Book*, 184–5.

2 Savine, 138. The figures of curial revenue are particularly difficult to interpret, and the amount in the *Valor* seems to have been a notional, estimated one, not an actual receipt; in some cases admission fines were included, elsewhere not.   3 *Ibid.* 141 *seqq.*

4 *Ibid.* 153, 155. At St Augustine's, Bristol, out of fifteen manors *c.* 1500, five were farmed out entirely, five had their demesnes farmed, and five were managed for the abbey by a bailiff (BRS, IX, 40).

tenancies still existed, and within the demesne itself there were often tenurial holdings, but on monastic estates as elsewhere the intermingling of strips had in great part disappeared with the cessation of week- and boon-works on the one hand, and with enclosures and concentration of strips on the other; the demesne had often simply become a large farm, with house and offices. The minor tenancies were of all kinds; freehold, copyhold, leasehold and tenancies at will. Where the whole manor was farmed the tenants had no direct connection with the monastery; where the demesne alone was leased or where the monks kept it in hand the rents were collected and repairs effected by the monastic officials or their representatives.

The need for the direct exploitation of the land by the monks for their own household consumption had always been and still was lessened by the existence of payments in kind. These were still surprisingly common in 1535, and it is almost certain that they were in fact more numerous than the pages of the *Valor* suggest. Not only was tithe often paid in grain, but renders in kind were not uncommon in lieu of rent for tenancies and demesne that was leased out. They were of all kinds: corn, hay, poultry, eggs, cheese, pigs and cattle; and they varied very greatly in relation to money rents as between house and house. Thus at Furness in Lancashire one-seventh of the total income was in kind, and at St Augustine's, Canterbury, almost one-fifth of the very large income (£309 out of £1684), whereas at the neighbouring priory of Christ Church there is record in the *Valor* of only £7 in kind out of an income even larger.[1] Such payments in kind as remained were chiefly from demesne, and are no doubt a survival of the old food-farms of the manors; the only house where payments in kind by customary tenants in lieu of rent were large was Worcester, and it is interesting to note the persistence there of the system that had been in vogue five centuries before in the days of Wulfstan.[2]

The monasteries still owned considerable flocks of sheep, herds of cattle, and studs of horses, and here till the end, after satisfying their own needs, they looked to the market for income, but the *Valor*, unlike *Domesday*, is very inconsistent in its mention of beasts. While the returns from Dorset contain accounts of numerous flocks, those of Somerset and Suffolk, even more celebrated as grazing counties, make no mention of sheep; the profits there are no doubt merged in the general sum put to the credit of a manor, though we may suspect that here, even more than in other matters, the calculation of average sales would err considerably in a conservative direction. The whole question of livestock on the eve of the Dissolution is, however, surrounded with difficulties. In addition to

---

1 This, however, is almost certainly a case where the silence, or method of composition, of the *Valor* is deceptive. As recently as 1504–5 the garnerer's accounts of Christ Church show 686 bushels of corn received as food farm (R. A. L. Smith, *Canterbury Cathedral Priory*, 201).

2 Savine, 163; cf. *MO*, 442.

our ignorance of the effect of the act of 1529,[1] it is certain that even before 1535 some houses were selling off their stock for cash, and the number of head owned by Fountains, once so rich in herds, when the final survey was taken, is almost negligible. On the other hand, even small nunneries appear in their surveys as owners of sizeable flocks which must have produced far more mutton and wool than the religious would need for themselves.[2]

It has often been stated in the past, and repeated at second-hand till the present, that the religious were as a class insolvent, and that their economy was on the point of collapse, even when they had no external enemy. So far as can be seen, this opinion was based partly on a few scattered accusations of Tudor writers and visitors, and partly on the assumption that all aspects of the monastic life were in a process of steady deterioration during the fifteenth and early sixteenth centuries, and that if occasional financial failures took place in 1400, an almost general bankruptcy would ensure a century later. Such a result, in an age when the wealth of the country was still almost entirely in the hands of landholders, and when the religious were great landlords with all the advantages of undying possession, could only result from universal mismanagement resulting from either simplicity or incompetence or corruption, and, of these, the last alternative was usually chosen, however unconsciously, by historians. It will be well, therefore, to consider first whether the religious were as a body insolvent, and then to review the manner in which they spent their vast aggregate wealth.

The *Valor*, being of its very nature an assessment of income for taxation, gives no information as to the balance between income and expenditure, but we have the account rolls of representative houses in the early decades of the sixteenth century and, as giving still more precise information, we have exact statements of the amount of debt with which numerous monasteries were burdened at the time of the Dissolution. Some of these are supplied by incidental letters of the religious themselves, or of the governmental agents, but the majority come from the findings of the commissioners sent round to survey the lesser houses prior to suppression, or appointed to wind up the affairs of a larger house that had surrendered to the king. The account rolls, which survive chiefly from the large and well-ordered houses,[3] make it clear that at these the chief officials (and by the sixteenth century the administration was generally centralized for all practical purposes in the hands of a single superior or obedientiary) had

---

1 The statute of 1529 does not seem to have covered sheep farming.

2 Savine, 178, concludes: 'In spite of the fact that pasture was twice as valuable as arable land, that monasteries were in a large way of business, and that they had particular reasons to reduce the amount of their arable [*sc.* both the statutory prohibition and the need to reduce overheads], yet up to the last the monks tilled almost as much land as they kept for grazing purposes.'

3 Three notable examples are Durham (numerous vols. in SS), Worcester (vols. in WHS) and St Augustine's, Bristol (BRS, ix).

no difficulty in keeping expenditure within the limit set by income, and of having a surplus from year to year, or when required.

The commissioners of 1536, charged with reporting on the finances of the smaller houses recently declared to be liable to suppression, were specifically instructed to discover the sums owed by, and owing to, the house, and from their returns exact figures are available for more than fifty monasteries of men and women scattered over all England south of the Trent and west of the Pennines.[1] To these may be added some other isolated entries from Yorkshire and elsewhere. Many of these are cited by Savine, and a review of the whole number does nothing to weaken his general conclusion that the monastic property 'was not encumbered by enormous debts'.[2] Among these houses every degree of financial liability is found, from a positive credit balance to a burden of debt exceeding the annual income of the house, but heavy debts of the latter class are exceptional. The case of Athelney, often quoted, where the abbot pleaded debts of £860 against a net income of perhaps £240, would appear to be unique, and the list of his debts, with which he furnished Cromwell, has several curious features.[3] For the smaller houses a rough calculation from the figures of thirty taken from among the monks, canons and nuns of Norfolk, Hampshire, Leicestershire and Warwickshire suggests that the aggregate debts amount to something less than 40 per cent of the aggregate annual net revenue. For the larger houses that were not affected by the act of 1536 we have to depend on other and more scattered evidence provided by the suppression commissioners and incidental sources of information; the general picture is similar, but the overall indebtedness would seem to reach a considerably smaller percentage of the much greater incomes, and some of the greatest houses, of which Worcester and Durham may be taken as examples, seem to have been virtually clear of debt.

1 Abstracts of these are in *LP*, x, 916–17; *ibid.* 1191 (i)–(v); and *LP*, xi, Appendix 2, p. 2. These cover Leics, Warwicks, Rutland, Sussex and a few houses in Hunts and Lancs. Others, covering Norfolk, Hants, Wilts and a few houses in Glos, were noted and in part printed by F. A. Gasquet in 'Overlooked testimonies to the character of the English monasteries on the eve of their suppression', in *DubR*, cxiv (April 1894), 245–77. These last, strangely enough, have continued to be overlooked by historians, including their editor, who never inserted their evidence in his other work, and Savine. For this and subsequent chapters transcripts of all these documents were obtained, and the facts and figures are based on the texts.

2 Savine, 216–17. He concludes: 'It is evident that they [*sc.* the monastic debts] did not seriously affect the financial results of the Dissolution.' With this Hibbert (*Dissolution of the Monasteries*, 187) agrees: 'Their normal debts represent only the casual credit of ordinary life.... In the ordinary course of events [they] would have been discharged in due course.'

3 The abbot's letter and list are in Archbold, 29–33. The largest items are £66 due to the king, £90 to Glastonbury and £80 to the abbot of Dunkeswell, a Cistercian house in Devon. These total £236. Creditors, seemingly 'private', account for another £260. Abbot Robert was clearly the classical type of debt-addict; he lived in the rosy unreality of Mr Micawber, and could hope that Cromwell would 'prouyde som remedye', specifically if he 'cowlde have a frynd that wold lene me iiij or v hundret poundes wtout ony prophete or lucoure' he would easily be able 'to paye the reste out of hande'. Oddly enough, the neighbouring Muchelney, like Athelney a house closely linked with Glastonbury, had the unusually heavy debt of £400. *V.* letters in Archbold, *S.R.H.* 29 *seqq.*, 68 *seqq.*

Furthermore, it is by no means clear that the load of debt was in fact as solid and formidable as it appears at first sight. In many cases the government commissioners, and occasionally the superiors or officials of the houses concerned, set out their debts in detail. The general pattern of their statements is the same, from whatever part of the country they hail,[1] and it warns us that, before any pronouncement on the quality of a debt, the total sum must be broken down and examined. Every kind of liability and creditor is included: arrears of tax to the king, or of synodal and other dues to the bishop, pensions to vicars, even clothes-money to the monks.[2] Among individual creditors tradesmen, merchants and lawyers appear indeed, but they rarely account for a large part of the debt. This is in almost every case, whatever the size of the house, owing to private individuals, both ecclesiastics and laymen, who have lent to the house. A careful examination of a number of these lists, with all their local and social implications, would form a valuable contribution to Tudor economic history. The impression given is that a number of these loans were either goodwill contributions to a building fund or even virtually savings deposits, and in any case regarded by their owners as long-term transactions. In other words, much of the debt could be kept floating indefinitely by small annual payments which would prevent arrears from accumulating and would satisfy private individuals of substance almost as would the payment of interest or a dividend to-day.

Moreover, it would be a mistake to look at the debts *in vacuo*, so to say, without at the same time considering assets which would appear on the other side of a modern balance-sheet. Thus, quite apart from the capital value of buildings, lead, treasure, woods, etc., which the commissioners reckon separately, many of the houses had very large stores of grain and fodder wholly in excess of what was needed by the community before the next harvest, as also much livestock with young beasts suitable for sale or slaughter. Thus the Cistercian Netley, with a debt of only £144, had stores and stock to the value of £114; the nearby Quarr, with £45 of debt, had stores of £241; while Stanley (Wilts) could place stores of £189 against a debt of £272.[3] In these cases and many others, the bulk of these stocks might be counted a liquid asset with as much reason as are the unsold flour of a miller or the stores of a grain merchant at the present day.

Finally, it must be remembered that no mention is made in any of these assessments of what would now be found as cash in hand on current

---

1 The Benedictine abbot of Athelney's debts may be compared with those of the Cistercian abbot of Dieulacres (Hibbert, *Dissolution*, app. v, 243–4), of the Augustinian abbot of Lilleshall (M. E. Walcot, 'Inventories and Valuations of Religious Houses at the time of the Dissolution', in *Archaeologia*, XLIII), and of the prior of St Thomas at Stafford (*ibid.*), whose debts were almost all to regional gentry. In the last case Hibbert (*op. cit.* 187) does well to point out that the prior was doubtless largely behindhand owing to the necessity of paying a fine of £153 for licence to exist.

2 Walcot, *art. cit.*   3 PRO, S.C. 12/33, 27, m. 1; *ibid.* m. 2.

account at the bank. We know from other sources that many houses had a considerable overall profit on the year's working,[1] and that almost all had a common treasure chest or reserve fund, though there is very little information as to how far surpluses on the year's working remained as book-entries or some elementary form of credit or tally, and how far they stood for coin in the common chest, but that there was somewhere a pool of money, and that every obedientiary must have had a considerable store of ready cash is unquestionable, and at a house such as Durham, where surpluses sometimes ran to £1000 or more, the amount must at times have been considerable.[2] All this, again, would count against the debts in a modern balance-sheet. In short, from whatever angle we look at the matter, the financial state of the monasteries taken as a class appears far less unsound than might be suggested by the rehearsal of a list of debts. It would be misleading to confuse the centuries, and to think of the age of Henry VIII in terms of the age of Henry II. Then, when the quantity of cash in circulation was relatively small, and reserves were held by very few, the great abbey of Bury could be for a time completely in the clutches of a few Jewish moneylenders. In Wolsey's day the wealth of the country, and the number of men with money, had greatly increased, and at least some ease of credit and space for manœuvre existed. The resources of the monasteries, save for a few very small or very badly mismanaged houses, were well able to carry the normal expenditure and overhead costs, and they would in due time doubtless have adjusted rents to meet the price rise that may have been temporarily shaking their balance. Indeed, the whole question of monastic solvency requires more careful treatment than it has received. Too often it has been regarded superficially and censoriously, in much the same temper as prosperous Victorians regarded the bankruptcy of a tradesman, and the fact that the house concerned did in fact survive without either catastrophe or wholesale repudiation of debt has not been taken into account. Only a very careful examination, for which documentary evidence is often lacking, would distinguish between debts of culpability and prodigality, debts of misfortune and miscalculation in a period of economic change, and debts which, both financially and ethically, differed little in character from periodical overdrafts or mortgages raised on the credit of the house.

No one can study, however superficially, the figures of monastic finance in the later Middle Ages without asking himself how these great incomes were absorbed and whether the waste was great. In other words, did not the income of the larger houses far exceed any reasonable needs of a body professing a life of self-discipline, if not of self-denial, of simplicity, if not

---

1 Durham in 1536–7 had a profit of about £9 and a 'superplus' of £844 ('Rotuli Bursarii, 1536–7' in *DAR*, III, 690–707).

2 The bursar of Durham had a store of coin of high denominations; cf. *Durham Household Book*, 92, where 40 shillings are paid to the subprior *in auro in scaccario bursarii*; the archdeacon of the East Riding paid *in auro*; the master of the infirmary paid *in auro, viz.*, George Nobyls.

of austerity, in common life together? Where, for instance, did the £4000 odd of Glastonbury's income go after fifty monks had been fed?

To these questions, if they are understood in a purely spiritual sense, a direct answer can certainly be given. Not only at the epoch of the Dissolution, but for an undefined and very long period previously, the monks and canons of England, with a few notable exceptions, had been living on a scale of personal comfort and corporate magnificence, and with a variety of receipts and expenses of all kinds, which were neither necessary for, nor consistent with, the fashion of life indicated by their rule and early institutions. It would, however, unduly simplify monastic history to be content with this answer, which is, indeed, not one with which the historian as such is concerned. His task, rather, is to discover whether the income of the religious houses was, from a purely financial and economic aspect, excessively great: whether, to speak in modern phrase, the yearly balance-sheet showed, or could be made to show, a profit which was, economically speaking, too great; whether such profits were justified by the use to which they were put, or whether, on the other hand, waste and superfluous expenditure drained away at the source what should have been a fair profit. These are questions which, if they are to be satisfactorily answered, require the data of a whole series of studies covering particular houses and orders and periods of time; nevertheless, from c. 1400 onwards, the general stability and similarity of practice and economic conditions among all classes of religious throughout the country allows of a generalization which is perhaps reliable in its essentials.

First, then, if we regard the monastic finances from an accountant's point of view, without, that is, considering the intrinsic value or relevance of the objects upon which the expenses are incurred, we shall not find that the profits under normal good management were excessive. If we consider a large house of over £500 net income, the pattern of expenditure will be of the following kind.[1] Royal and papal subsidies, including taxes, aids, benevolences, subsidies and dues of all kinds; payments and presents of every description to officials and magnates, together with the routine spiritual fees to bishop or chapter, regularly absorbed a portion of the revenues which might be as great as one-sixth over a period of years. The expenses of maintenance, administration and restocking the property and manors normally consumed at least one-fifth of the income, and another large fraction went as an allowance, or to meet the expenses, of the abbot or prior and his household. An abbot would receive anything from one-fifth to one-quarter; a prior considerably less, perhaps only one-tenth. Finally, one-third or more went to the clothing and feeding of the monks, the household and the guests. The balance, which in a good year at a well-ordered house might vary from one-tenth to one-fifth of the whole, was

1 What follows is largely a conflation of the data obtainable from the very full sixteenth-century accounts of Durham, Worcester and St Augustine's, Bristol; cf. also the précis of Huntingdon in Gasquet, *Henry VIII*, 1st ed., II, 507.

available for building or for extraordinary repairs or for sinking a debt, or it might be simply carried forward as surplus. In practice, however, a whole series of charges, individually extraordinary but statistically normal, such as lawsuits, loss or damage from wars, tempests, unseasonable weather or animal diseases, cut down the profits, while the costs of maintenance and repair mounted with every decade that passed and with every new addition to the buildings. Thus what might have been a profit amounting to 30 per cent or more of the income was often all but absorbed in the recurring expenses of taxation, litigation and repairs.[1]

Regarded more particularly from an economist's point of view, the monastic system had throughout the later Middle Ages three very weak spots: the separate establishment of the superior; the decentralization of finances; and the wasteful and superfluous elements in the household.

The first, in which must be included also the allowances, generous in amount though of sporadic occurrence, to ex-superiors, had existed for four centuries. The circumstances which had partially caused or partially justified the system had largely ceased to operate with the decline of feudalism and of the position of the monastic superiors in public life, but the ideas which it reflected had taken such root that nothing short of a social revolution could have removed them. The radical vice of the system was that it earmarked a large fraction of the income of the house to the support of a second household that was economically superfluous, and put a large sum every year at the free disposal of one of its members. The detailed accounts of the spending of Prior More of Worcester from 1518 to 1535 show what a great deal of economically useless spending was possible to a superior of a medium-sized house while remaining well within his allowance. More's elaborate reconditioning and furnishing of several of his manor-houses, to say nothing of his large and purely ornamental staff and his purchases of vestments and jewellery, were all economically superfluous. The almost contemporary career of Richard Bere at Glastonbury is an instance of similar, or even greater, expenditure on like objects.

The decentralization of administration was likewise of very old standing, and equally indefensible on the economic level. Some of the efforts to diminish its evil effects have already been noted;[2] on the whole it may be said that, while they had effected considerable improvements in administration and accountancy, there still remained unnecessary expenses of duplicated staffs and overhead charges, together with multiplied chances of

---

1 The Bristol accounts give precise figures for the accounting years 1491–2 and 1511–12, which the editors tabulate as in a modern balance-sheet. In the earlier year the expenses were £704, with a credit balance of £14; in the latter £528 with a credit of £90. The difference in expenses was due almost entirely to items in 1491–2 of £112 and £40 in taxes and litigation, compared with £24 and £1 in 1511–12. In each year the abbot's portion of the income was upwards of £160 (i.e. one-quarter of the earlier total and one-third of the later); provisions, clothing and wages were constants at £28–32, £12 and £26 respectively (BRS, IX, 60–3).   2 RO, II, 312.

inefficiency. At many houses, however, the early Tudor practice of superiors in taking into their hands one or more of the most important spending offices had removed some of the worst dangers of the system.[1]

The third weakness, that of the over-great and wasteful household, was not peculiar to the religious, but made itself felt in all great establishments, from the court downwards. It was in a sense inevitable in a society where the material needs of life were met very largely from stocks produced automatically from the resources of the consumers themselves, and not bought on the market strictly according to need; where the custom of life-long attachment in return for service had not yet fully given place to a wage economy, and where hospitality was comprehensive and lavish in scale, and irregular and sudden in its demands upon resources; where charity was occasional and equally lavish; and where, finally, provision had always to be made for several households under one roof. Under such conditions, the supply of staple commodities in normal seasons must often have exceeded the average demand, with the inevitable consequence of waste in the preparation and consumption, as also in the disposal, of such surplus stock as must almost always have accrued. Even in modern society, where commercial organizations exist in all centres of population to dispose of surplus and spoiled products at a lower level of subsistence, the waste of bread, vegetables, milk and all perishables at a large school or catering establishment is very great, and possibly even greater *per caput* in private households. At a medieval monastery it must have been much greater, for the fixed measures and double portions, and the traditional gift of all broken meats to the poor, encouraged and almost sanctified lavish provision, and the example of promiscuous hospitality and charity must have encouraged dependants of every degree to pass on superfluous food and stores to their families and friends outside the gate. Finally, the price of both food and clothes rose relatively far more steeply once the roughest and commonest fabrics and commodities were left behind than it does in the modern world. A roll of fine cloth or a box of spices, for example, stood relatively far higher in comparison with a carcass of mutton or pork than it does to-day. It was here that the religious spent a great part of their income, for there is general agreement that the black monks and canons, at least, used good quality cloth both for their own habits and for their gifts of gowns and liveries, as there is also general agreement that, even apart from a fair measure of sheer waste, the monks of the larger abbeys enjoyed, if not a more abundant, at least a more expensive and *recherché* fare than all save the most prosperous classes in the land.

When we consider the monastic economy from a social and a human, rather than from a purely economic point of view, we can make a series of observations. First, the sums of money, both absolute and relative to the total income, spent on food and drink appear excessive, and this con-

1 *RO*, II, 328–9.

clusion is borne out by all detailed examinations of the quantity, quality and variety of the materials consumed. Secondly, while the revenue was—at least as a long-term income for all except the very largest and the very smallest houses—fixed, the expenditure was very elastic, and this not only in the sense that many expenses, such as lawsuits and taxes, repairs and replacements, were either very irregular or could be deferred for an indefinite time, but also that at any given moment, provided that no scheme of retrenchment was already in operation, lasting economies could be effected out of hand by drastic sumptuary measures and reductions of staff, without in any real sense affecting the well-being of the religious. Only thus can we explain the remarkable resiliency shown by monasteries of all orders and sizes when controlled by a superior who earnestly desired to sink debt or find cash for building schemes. No doubt, especially for the latter purpose, an abbot would often mortgage the future by converting customary rents to leases with high admission fines, but opportunities for this expedient were limited, and a long series of remarkable and swift recoveries, from the days of Samson to those of Bere, shows that there was almost always a wide margin between necessary and normal expenditure. The economic crisis of 1929–35 and the two World Wars have amply demonstrated that private families and institutions of all kinds can retrench very drastically without serious loss to health and happiness for themselves, though it is also true that the cultural and economic well-being of the whole population could not easily be maintained if private expenses never rose above the level of those abnormal years. When all is said and done, perhaps two impressions remain most clearly in the minds of those who have pondered over a long series of monastic account rolls. The one is that, even in the wealthiest houses, there was very little wasteful and uneconomic spending, save for the important items of the abbot's income and foodstuffs, though it is also probable that the wealthier houses had none of the spurs to economy such as are automatic in a modern business concern that judges success by large profits rather than by the achievement of an easy balance. The other is that, even granted all this, yet there is something fundamentally amiss, socially as well as spiritually, when a community of fifty or less men or women, vowed to the monastic life, administers vast estates and draws large revenues which are not used for any spiritual purpose, just as they have not been earned by any work of mental, material or spiritual charity.

CHAPTER XXI

SERVANTS, ALMSGIVING AND CORRODIANS

No feature of the monastic economy in Tudor days has been more severely criticized than the alleged superfluity of servants and dependants. The numbers are certainly formidable when seen in the aggregate at a large house, and when compared with the numbers of the religious. Thus at Rievaulx there were, at the Dissolution, one hundred and two 'servants' to twenty-two monks; at Gloucester the ratio was eighty-six to twenty-six; at Byland eighty to twenty-five; and at Butley seventy-one to thirteen.[1] Moreover, quite apart from precise figures, there are the recurrent complaints of visiting bishops over two or more centuries, while the satirists and reformers dilate upon the hordes of lazy dependants who do nothing but eat and sleep; the term 'abbey lubber' was indeed coined to describe such men and their likes.

There is, therefore, every excuse for the general reader to suppose that the monastic servants were a principal cause of any insolvency that might exist, and there has been a marked tendency on the part of both critics and apologists of the monks to stress, if not to exaggerate, the figures for their different purposes. The strictures of Coulton and others are familiar to all; on the other hand Gasquet, writing seventy years ago and concerned to emphasize the disturbance to society caused by the disappearance of the monasteries, did not hesitate to say, after fixing the number of dispossessed religious at eight thousand, that 'probably more than ten times that number of people were their dependents or otherwise obtained a living in their service'.[2] If these words have any definite meaning, and are not intended to include the families of employees or the large outer circle of shop-keepers and middlemen occupied chiefly with monastic traffic, they imply that the religious of England maintained either by wages or alms the stupendous total of over eighty thousand servants and dependants. It is not surprising, therefore, to find a moderate writer such as Trevelyan alluding to the 'large companies of monastic servants'.[3]

That a superfluity of hands existed at many monasteries need not be denied. Few large establishments in any age, least of all those charged with catering for a fluctuating or seasonal household, are entirely successful in eliminating waste or securing the maximum output of work. Large households and troops of servants and hangers-on of every description were characteristic of the Tudor age, and did not disappear with the abbeys. Travellers and satirists continued to gird at the system throughout the

---

1 The figures for Rievaulx and Byland are taken from Woodward, 72, citing PRO, S.C. 6 Henry VIII, 7452; those for Gloucester, from Savine, 225; for Butley, from the *Chronicle*, ed. A. G. Dickens, App. 1.

2 *Henry VIII*, 359–60. 3 *History of England*, 284.

Elizabethan age. A large monastery in or near a town, or lying on a main road, would have been of all households the most difficult to rationalize under medieval conditions. Nor need we doubt that at the larger houses of black monks and canons the separate household of the prelate, with the files of liveried servants kept chiefly for display, were an obvious, not to say scandalous, target for the critics. But before accepting the vast numbers alleged, and the assertion of their redundancy, it is well to control such statements by means of some reliable figures of the numbers employed and of the precise categories of employment or dependency into which they fell.

Fortunately, such figures are available in some abundance. The commissioners sent round in the spring and summer of 1536, to survey anew the resources of the smaller houses that had become forfeit by the act of that year, were required to give the numbers of those dependent in any way upon each house, and in most cases they understood these instructions as requiring them to state precisely the categories of employment and dependency into which they fell. Though they differ both in the details they give and the nomenclature they adopt, these lists do in fact give a fairly accurate picture of the staff on the pay-roll and the persons on the alms-list of each house.

Some of these lists may have perished; others may still await discovery; but already full returns of this kind are available for the counties of Leicestershire, Warwickshire, Norfolk, Sussex, Hampshire, Wiltshire and Gloucestershire, together with partial returns from Yorkshire, Lancashire and Essex.[1] They cover some fifty-four houses of men of all orders (excluding friars) and some twenty-six houses of women, and the numbers of religious concerned are in the region of 424 men and 274 women.[2] All the houses are 'lesser' houses with an income below £200 per annum, save for two Yorkshire abbeys, Rievaulx and Byland, and St Mary's nunnery at Winchester, which fell into an inappropriate category owing to a fraudulent return of its income made at the assessment for the tenth, but there is no reason to suppose that the picture at a small or mediocre house differed greatly from that at one of the larger houses save in scale and in the existence in the latter group of the class of personal attendants upon the superior that has been referred to already.

The houses of men in these lists had depending upon them some 1360 souls; the nuns provided a livelihood for 516. The respective ratios of religious to dependents are therefore in the neighbourhood of 1 : 3·2 (men)

1 The printed (and in some cases abbreviated or summary) versions of these have been listed *supra*, p. 253 n. 1. In what follows I have used transcripts of the original documents. The references are: *Leics, Warwicks, Rutland*: PRO, E. 36/154/48 to 63; BM. Cott. Cleo. E. IV, fos. 336-40ᵛ (=old pagination 280-4ᵛ) covering Huntingdon A. canons, Sawtrey Cist. and Stonely A. canons. *Lancs*: B.M. Cott. Cleo. E. IV, fo. 343 (=288). *Hants, Wilts and Glos*: PRO, S.C. 12/33/27 (M 1-3). *Norfolk*: PRO, S.C. 12/33/29 (M 1-8). *Sussex*: PRO, S.C. 5/3/128.

2 For the calculation in this paragraph houses for which no return of servants is available have been ignored.

and 1 : 1·9 (women). This, however, means little, for among the dependants the commissioners reckoned not only all the agricultural and pastoral labourers and servants, but all those kept at alms or on a pension, and also (in the case of the nuns) the chaplains and clerics. All these, in the abbreviated lists such as those surviving for the half-dozen Lancashire houses, are included under the heading of servants. To be of significance for our purpose the figures must be broken down, and here the commissioners in most cases give us fairly adequate assistance. To begin with, those who are in any way a charge on the establishment as beneficiaries by alms or covenant must be eliminated: corrodians, children, pensioned servants and simple almspeople. This class, in all the lists where details are available, gives a total of 170 at the houses of men, and forty-four at those of women. Next, the labourers or 'hinds' as they are universally styled, must be dismissed. They form by far the largest class: 919 at the forty-four houses of men where they are distinguished, and 413 at the twenty-six houses of women. Along with the hinds the dairywomen, some seventy in all, must go. These last, as is to be expected, come chiefly from the houses of men. In the case of the nunneries, they are concealed in the general class of 'women servants'.

When all these categories have been subtracted we arrive at last at the domestic staff, those who in one way or another kept the establishment running for the benefit of the professional inmates, whether as chaplains (for the nuns), or as salaried servants of the superior grades who as 'gentlemen' or 'yeomen' waited upon the community and its head in a semi-ceremonial capacity, or in the lower ranks of church-cleaners, grooms, cooks, bakers, brewers, barbers, porters and infirmary servants. This miscellaneous group, which included a few very responsible officials such as surveyors and under-stewards, totals some 330 for the forty-four houses of men and 144 for the twenty-six nunneries concerned.[1] As there were roughly 200 male religious and 274 nuns in the houses concerned the final ratio of employers to domestics is a little over 1 : 1·1 for men and (if priests are not counted) a little over 1 : 0·4 for women. This may probably serve as an overall average for small and medium-sized houses throughout the country, but whereas for the nuns the average figure for all districts is also, within very narrow limits of difference, the average figure for every component group, the figures for the houses of men vary greatly from district to district. Thus in the Midlands and Sussex the ratio is almost exactly 1 : 1 between religious and servants, in Wiltshire and Hampshire it is as low as 1 : 0·7 and in Norfolk as high as 1 : 2·5. This last figure is perhaps partly to be explained by the very small numbers of religious at many East Anglian houses; these, when the needs of hospitality and of fair-sized churches and buildings had to be met, could not easily be accompanied by a correspondingly reduced staff. It is perhaps

---

1 These are the houses for which detailed information of the categories of servants is available.

worth noting that at the medium-sized Butley, which is in East Anglia and where we happen to have full details of the establishment from the domestic chronicler, the staff comes fairly near the Norfolk ratio of 1:2. On the whole, however, the average figure of 1:1 is probably valid for the whole country. We must not, however, forget that this census was taken at a moment when the number of religious had fallen considerably owing to the discharge of the youngest age-group by the commissioners of 1535 and the paralysis of recruitment for some years. This decrease was probably one of 10 per cent at least and if allowance is made for it, would bring the number of male religious at the very least to a parity with the number of servants.

True, these figures are almost all taken from the lesser monasteries, and it was at the larger houses that redundancy was most noticeable, or at least most noticed, but there is no reason to suppose that the ratio was very different even in the great abbeys. The bursar of Durham, who handled all but £200 or so of the annual income (£1600) of the priory in 1531–2, had less than sixty servants on his pay-roll, and while some of these were employed outside the house, at Bearpark and elsewhere, very few were personal or merely domestic servants.[1] The great majority were engaged in operating or servicing the offices of the priory, such as the bakery, brewery, storehouses, furnaces and the rest. Save only when he lay in the infirmary, a monk of the cloister, even in the sixteenth century, would seem to have received no routine personal service or attendance from a dependant so long as he remained within the monastery. There is no evidence, for example, that the service received in many modern religious houses either from paid servants or from lay brothers, such as the sweeping of cloisters, making of beds, cleaning of footwear, fuelling of fires, and the rest, were ever received by the medieval monks unless they were superiors or major officials, who disposed of all-purpose attendants.[2] Indeed, the one and only considerable group of largely otiose and merely ornamental attendants was that which formed the corps waiting upon the abbot or prior. Even here, some of these no doubt assisted in dealing with guests who would otherwise have needed attention from other members of the staff; but the large and separate household, and the state kept by at least some of the greater abbots and cathedral priors, undoubtedly led to an unnecessary multiplication of functionaries, and there is very little to be said for the ten yeomen and twenty-odd servants who were regularly employed by Prior More of Worcester as staff for his manors and as companions on his journeys.

The foregoing pages have not been written to suggest that there was no waste or redundancy in the monastic staff, such as there tends to be in the

---

1 *Durham Household Book*, 92–9.
2 In the Durham list is a *claustrarius*, drawing the minimum wage of 3*s*. 4*d*. per annum, as compared with the fireman's 6*s*. 8*d*. and the carter's 20*s*. It is not clear what his functions were; possibly those of door-keeper.

establishments of all long-lived bodies. The visitation records, as well as the critics of the monks, show glimpses of houses dominated by one or more of the functionaries, or where the servants kept the monks in their place and took their ease in the monastic offices with all the assurance of householders. The evidence suggests, however, that the cause of any waste was not primarily luxury or display, but careless or slovenly administration, and while we may certainly think that economies could have been made, as always in large households when labour and service are plentiful and cheap, and though there may have been some justification in the current judgment that 'abbey lubbers' were the laziest of servants, there is no reason to suppose that a plethora of servants was a major cause of financial embarrassment, still less that the dissolution of the monasteries caused a crisis of unemployment and a race of sturdy beggars. When all those employed on the land, and all those re-employed by newly erected chapters, by ex-superiors and by the grantees of abbey lands, are deducted from the total, the remainder of men and women thrown out of employment cannot have exceeded if indeed it ever attained the numbers of the religious. We may say this, and yet be allowed to think that a monastic house may well set itself the ideal of dispensing with the ministrations of any paid servants.

The *Valor Ecclesiasticus* might also be expected to provide a clear answer on another matter that has long been controversial, namely, the extent of the charitable activities of the monks. Apologists in the past up to and including Dom Gasquet made much of these, principally as a means of showing what evils of pauperization followed in the wake of the Dissolution. More recently, it has been the fashion to minimize the charity of the religious almost to vanishing point. In the *Valor*, as has been said, expenses on charity which were in one way or another 'compulsory', as forming a condition of the reception of a gift or legacy, were, if duly certified by the commissioners, allowable as tax-free income. Savine, working his way through the figures in the *Valor*, was able to show that at two hundred monasteries, with an aggregate income amounting to more than half of the total monastic revenue, the average allowable expense on 'charity' was about 3 per cent of the income, while at more than a hundred other houses no alms at all free of the tenth were discoverable.[1] From these figures a number of scholars have argued that the total monastic expense on charity was considerably less than 3 per cent of the monastic income—a proportion which all would agree to be remarkably small, if not totally inadequate. Savine, indeed, loyally went on to point out that the commissioners, like other tax-collectors, were often both inconsistent and grasping; he added also that many bona fide eleemosynary expenses were technically inadmissible, while others would leave little or no trace in the accounts, but these reservations were not

1 Savine, 238–9.

always noticed by those who took all their facts at second hand.[1] It will therefore not be out of place to dwell for a moment on the point.

In the first place, Savine certainly did not overstate the inconsistencies and stringencies of the commissioners of the tenth. It may well be that the bona fide legal obligations of the monasteries were very considerably greater—perhaps as much as 50 per cent greater—than the allowances of the *Valor*. Next, there is good evidence, in addition to arguments of probability, to show that the sums spent on charity, even if not technically allowable, were considerably in excess of Savine's percentage. The commissioners of 1536 who dealt with the lesser houses recorded, for example, some ninety-seven children in their list of forty-seven houses of men with a population of three hundred religious. Some of these may have been in song schools, and therefore to a certain extent an asset to the house, but the monasteries concerned were small, and song schools were not common in small houses; most of these boys were probably maintained in small grammar schools founded either by the religious or one of their benefactors, and administered or at least patronized by the house. While the old myth of the Tudor monks as a great educational force has been rightly exploded, the real if unspectacular service of the monasteries in providing free education must not be forgotten. Similarly, hospitals and almshouses, for women as well as for men, were not unknown, as at Durham.[2]

Then, there were the daily day-to-day gifts and doles of broken meats, used clothing, and the like. It had always been a monastic tradition that food left from the monks' table should go to the poor.[3] In the days of strict observance and sparing administration, when each monk was given a fixed modest portion, this custom would not have implied waste and might even have encouraged self-denial; if a monk did not fully consume his ration of bread, he knew it would go to the poor. In later ages, with large households of guests and servants, there must have been much waste and pilfering of food, and very little thrift, but even so, considerable quantities of the basic foodstuffs must have filtered down to the poor of the neighbourhood, who would have fared no better without it, whatever we may think of indiscriminate relief.

Finally, there was the uncovenanted largesse of the abbot and major officials. The *Journal* of Prior More and some of the Durham accounts show that this was by no means negligible in quantity. Prior More, in the course of his priorate, not only bestowed moderate sums in private alms

1 *Ibid.* 240: 'It is impossible, from the *Valor Ecclesiasticus*, to judge of the voluntary charitable expenses of the monks...these may be very considerable and may equal or even exceed the alms free of tax.'

2 Thus, e.g., Durham was responsible for three hospitals, at Witton, St Mary Magdalen's, and one within the precinct. For the activities of a monastic almoner in the fifteenth century, *v.* the introduction by Professor C. N. L. Brooke to *The Book of William Morton*.

3 Cf. *Lanfranc's Monastic Constitutions*, 89. *V. ibid.* 131, for another practice that presumably continued to the Reformation, viz. the bestowal on the poor of a dead monk's full portion of food and drink for one month after his death.

to friars and to the victims of calamity,[1] but spent a much greater sum on gifts of plate and vestments to village churches. We can scarcely doubt that still more wealthy prelates, such as Islip or Bere, would have made similar and still more valuable gifts. Haphazard as many of these sources of charity may have been, and socially undesirable as they may seem to minds of our day, they must be allowed to swell the monks' account when percentages of income are being reckoned. Taken altogether they would certainly double and perhaps even treble the sums allowed by the commissioners, and thus would bring the total to something very near the tenth part traditionally apportioned to charity. But, indeed, much alike of the criticism and the defence of the religious in this matter is beside the real point. The true weakness of the Church in England in the later Middle Ages was not a failure to contribute a sufficiency of funds to poor relief, but a failure to provide scope, by means of organized bodies, to the kind of charitable service given in the modern world by so many of the teaching and nursing and missionary institutes of religious men and women of the type familiar in the Sisters of Charity, Little Sisters of the Poor, nuns of the Good Shepherd, Christian Brothers, and the like. Several such bodies appeared in Italy and South Germany in the fifteenth century, but neither their influence nor their example spread to England.

The monasteries have been accused of multiplying yet another class of parasites, the corrodians. A corrody was an allowance either of food and other necessaries, or of lodging, or of money, or a combination of several of these, granted or allowed to lay folk out of the monastic establishment for the closing years of their lives.[2] There were three principal classes of corrodians: first, an ex-superior of the house or (at a few of the larger houses) a distinguished ex-official; next, superannuated servants or dependants quartered or billeted on the monastery by those entitled to the privilege (e.g. the king, the founder, or the bishop of the diocese in the case of nuns); and thirdly, those granted a corrody by charter of the community. These last were of more than one kind: the religious might by this means make a small return to a benefactor who had given all his property to the house, or they might give security of livelihood to aged persons in return for a moderate cash payment. This last class was clearly of dubious religious significance. Towards the end of the medieval centuries, indeed, a corrody had become in effect a life annuity purchasable on terms which varied according to expectation of life or the need on the part of the monastery for ready cash. In the latter case, a corrody to an improvident superior might, like an entry fine, be a mortgage on the future which his successors would deplore. Corrodians figure largely

---

1 A year (1520) taken at random shows More as distributing about £1 on casual alms.
2 The *locus classicus* on corrodies is A. Hamilton Thompson, 'A Corrody from Leicester Abbey, A.D. 1393–4, with some notes on corrodies', in *Transactions of the Leicestershire Archaeological Society*, XIV. Savine, 240–5, has some pages on the subject.

in the visitation records of the fourteenth and early fifteenth centuries. 'Pensioners never die', and the burden that corrodians imposed no doubt often seemed heavier than it was in reality, though it is relatively easy to produce instances of a small house all but reduced to beggary by having to support a quondam and two or three corrodians. Nevertheless, the number of corrodians in existence just before the Dissolution was very small. In the forty-seven houses of men already mentioned, with a population of three hundred religious, only twenty-nine corrodians were noted, or less than one to every ten religious. A number such as this could never have been a major factor in the economy of the monasteries as a class, however hardly a small group of beneficiaries might have borne upon an individual monastery.

T

CHAPTER XXII

THE VISITATION OF 1535-6

I. THE VISITORS, THEIR AIMS AND PROCEDURE

The movement of events in these crucial years was so rapid and varied, and Cromwell, under the king, was putting into motion and steering so many projects at once, that it is difficult for the historian to keep them all separately before his mind, and it is often quite impossible for him to be certain why this one went forward swiftly, while another was delayed or abandoned. He is as one watching the passage of heavy traffic on a busy road half hidden by trees; now one vehicle is leading, now another, while a third has halted for some reason out of sight, or has turned down a side-road. As has been seen, all the machinery was ready to be set in motion for a visitation of the monasteries early in January 1535, but it was seven months before the brake was released. Though we are not explicitly given the reason for this delay, it would seem all but certain that the visitors were held back in order to give a clear road to the commissioners for the tenth. The two enquiries could not well have been conducted simultaneously, and of the two the financial survey clearly demanded priority. As we have noted,[1] it was concluded for all practical purposes in the early summer, but the late spring had been a peculiarly busy time for Cromwell, with the examinations and trials of the Carthusians, Fisher and More on his hands, and he delayed for some weeks before giving the signal for the visitation to begin.

Meanwhile, the enquiry issuing in the *Valor Ecclesiasticus*, coming as it did as a climax to many rumours of suppression and of new taxes, could hardly fail to cause the most lively feelings of uneasiness in the monasteries. Far-sighted superiors had read the signs of the times, and had acted accordingly; sheep and stock, the liquid capital that could be realized with the least difficulty, had begun to vanish from the downs and commons, and a process of leasing out lands on a heavy fine for a long term, and of selling or hiding plate and precious stones, had already set in. The exacting task which Cromwell had set himself, to 'remember all the jewels of all the monasteries in England',[2] would soon have a purely antiquarian interest. Speed was clearly essential. This was realized by the most energetic of his agents, Richard Layton, who repeatedly urged the minister to act. On 4 June he had forestalled possible rivals with a request for a commission for himself and Dr Legh to visit the northern parts.[3] Both of them, he

---

1 *V. supra*, p. 243.   2 *LP*, VIII, 475.

3 *Ibid.* 822 (= Wright, *SL*, lxxvi, wrongly assigned by editor to 1537), where Layton begins his letter: 'Whereas ye intende shortly to visite, and belyke shall have many sutters unto you for the same to be your commissares', etc.

says, 'have acquaintances within ten or twelve miles of every religious house in the North', and 'friends and kinsfolk' everywhere. He reminds Cromwell that he already has by him a set of articles of enquiry prepared by the writer many months previously. This letter was followed up by another proposing that Legh should deal with Lincolnshire and the diocese of Chester, while Layton went to York. 'If you defer the visitation', he warns Cromwell, 'till you have leisure, I am in great doubt when the day will come.' His compatriots need not expect favouritism. 'There can be no better way', he remarks, 'to beat the King's authority into the heads of the rude people of the North than to show them that the King intends reformation and correction of religion. They are more superstitious than virtuous, long accustomed to frantic fantasies and ceremonies, which they regard more than either God or their prince, right far alienate from true religion. The book of articles [i.e. the questionnaire for visitation] is clear written in the custody of Bartlett your clerk.' And he adds: 'You will never know what I can do till you try me.'[1] Matters in the North, indeed, had been somewhat complicated by the activities of Edward Lee, who since the last autumn had been making a visitation that was not only his primary, but the first to be made since the days of Bainbridge or before. This was finally superseded by the announcement that the visitor-general would be at York in mid-September.[2]

Silence then falls again on the records, to be broken only when the visitors are already at work. At the end of July the king was hunting on the borders of Gloucester and Hereford, and was at Winchcombe on the 24th of that month. A few days later Cromwell also was staying at Winchcombe, with which house he had an unspecified connection, while at Cirencester, not far away across the Cotswolds, Layton completed his visitation of the abbey at midnight on the 28th.[3] Thenceforward the visitors were on the road for exactly six months. Their activities fall naturally into two phases, divided by the progress of Layton and Legh across Trent at Christmastide. Before following them on their tour it will be well to enquire as to the aim of their inquest.

The older historians assumed that it was a bona fide attempt at reformation, and this view has not been without its exponents more recently. On the whole, however, what is almost a consensus of opinion has been reached on the view that partial suppression had already been decided upon, and that the visitors were expected to find abundant grounds for this. Yet even this may be to attribute to Cromwell and the king a strategic deliberation for which no evidence is forthcoming. In this matter, as on other occasions, Cromwell showed himself as the master-politician, who could seize the moment to make a decision of far-reaching consequence, and who based his actions on motives of expediency, not of

---

1 *Ibid.* 955. No date is given, but there is a reference to Lammas (1 August) as still some distance of time away.
2 *Ibid.* 965 (1 July).   3 *Ibid.* 1127.

principle or of statesmanship. There is no clear evidence that either minister or king had decided upon total or even partial suppression before the visitation began, whereas there is some slight indication that a drastic reform was intended. Very soon, however, the temper of the visitors and the reports of their findings led to a crystallization of policy. The primary aim now was to extract damaging confessions, to open the door of dispensation as wide as might be, and to interpret the injunctions literally so as to increase the feeling of dependence upon Cromwell. It was only after an interval that the alternative of surrender, rather than the acceptance of the injunctions in all their literal force, was used as an instrument of suppression. Thus from a tentative start the procedure gradually stiffened into a method well calculated to achieve the end that had at length come to be clearly envisaged; that Cromwell himself had desired it from the beginning is probable, but cannot be proved.

Cromwell's visitors, who received a handsome testimonial from Froude, have come in for a great many hard words from historians, antiquarians, and writers of romances of the last two generations.[1] It is, however, a mistake to regard them as a group of unusually odious and brutal persecutors and informers of the family of Titus Oates. The five or six agents most active in the business were all men of intelligence who made for themselves careers of some distinction and considerable profit quite apart from their connection with the monasteries. They were in fact, as a group, neither worse nor better than the agents of the government of every degree from the Chancellors Audley and Rich downwards: adulatory, pliant, time-serving, they were wholly materialistic in outlook, and ready to accuse or ruin any man, friend or foe, stranger or relative, in order to retain the favour of Henry or Cromwell, but they were often sagacious, moderate and good-natured in their personal dealings when neither career nor cash was at stake. All were either canonists, civilians or common lawyers, and were used, after the fashion of Henry's servants, for every kind of business, administrative, judicial and diplomatic. Among them, priests and laymen were in almost equal numbers.

Richard Layton,[2] the most energetic and resourceful of them all, was

1 Froude remarked of Legh and Layton (*History of England*, II, 438), 'that they were young impetuous men [Layton was about 38, Legh perhaps under 35], likely to execute their work thoroughly rather than delicately, but, to judge by the surviving evidence, they were as upright and plain-dealing as they were assuredly able and efficient'. Canon Dixon and Dom Gasquet led a reaction from this, and the subsequent abuse in the articles of local antiquaries often bordered on the hysterical. Catholic apologists, in their defence of the monks, seemed on occasion to forget, or to slur over, the priesthood of Layton and London and Bedyll. Baskerville, *EM*, 123 *seqq.*, while ostensibly deprecating rehabilitation ('a vast amount of abuse has been levelled at…his agents …a great deal of which is justified'), endeavours in fact to elude an adverse moral judgment by likening the visitors to types of men in the modern world unpopular by reason of their minor social defects. Thus Layton 'was a clergyman of that detestable type, the "man's man"' and Legh is pictured as 'a clever and conceited young don', thus disarming the censorious.

2 Summary biographies of Layton, Legh, London, Ap Rice, Tregonwell and Bedyll are in *DNB*; that of Ap Rice in particular requires correction.

a Cumberland man of good family, kinsman to Robert Aske and Cuthbert Tunstall. A D.C.L. of Cambridge, he had been a colleague of Cromwell in Wolsey's service and as early as 1522, when he was perhaps rising twenty-five, had a foot on the ladder of preferment; by 1534, besides a number of benefices and sinecures, he was a clerk in chancery and clerk to the privy council. He was used to bring Syon into compliance, and to interrogate Fisher and More. After his success as a visitor he was one of the commission to try the northern insurgents in 1536–7, and had previously taken part in the trial of Anne Boleyn. From 1537 he held the rich rectory of Harrow-on-the-Hill, from 1538 he was master in chancery and from 1539 dean of York. His last mission was as ambassador to Brussels in 1543, and he died there a year later, probably before attaining his fiftieth year.

Layton's lack of principle is shown with sufficient clarity by the haste with which he revised his sincere and favourable judgment on Abbot Whiting when Cromwell hinted at a *faux pas*,[1] as also by the language in which he invited the vicar-general to Harrow as a guest more welcome than ever Christ had been at Bethany.[2] His reckless and wholesale charges against monastic communities, together with his inquisitorial methods and salacious anecdotes, show well enough his own moral outlook. He was, however, active and enterprising, with a gift for swift action, as may be seen in his exploits with the poleaxe at Langdon and in the speed and obvious gusto with which he took charge when fire broke out at Canterbury. His letters, with their racy phrasing and unfailing verve, stand out from all others in the great collection of Cromwell's correspondence and can scarcely have failed to provide welcome relief in the midst of the minister's heavy and often distressingly arid mail; many of their phrases, indeed, almost all of them defamatory, linger obstinately in the memory and, like the sallies of Charles II or John Wilkes, do much to win for their author an indulgence which his character does little to deserve. His vignettes of the abbot's lodging at Langdon, 'evyn lyke a cony clapper fulle of startyng hoilles', where the only vocal response to his knocking was 'thabbottes litle doge that within his dore faste lokked beyede and barkede';[3] of his posse of 'iiij monks with bandoggs to kepe the Shryne' of St Thomas at Canterbury and other 'monks in everie qwarter of the Churche with candills';[4] of 'one Mr Grenefelde, a gentilman of Bukynghamshire', gathering up folios of the evicted Scotus in the windy 'quadrant court' of New College, Oxford, 'to make hym sewelles or blawnsherres [i.e. scaring-sheets] to kepe the dere within the woode, therby to have the better cry with his howndes';[5] of the abbot of Bisham,

1　Ellis, *OL*, III, 3, ccclii (16 September 1539); *v. infra*, p. 380.
2　*Ibid*. no. cclxxx: 'Simeon was never so glade to se Chryst his master, as I shalbe to se your Lordeshipe in this your owne house, and all that ever shalbe in hit for my lyffe.'
3　*LP*, IX, 668 (23 October); Wright, *SL*, xxxiii.　　4　*LP*, IX, 669.
5　*Ibid*. 350 (12 September); Wright, *SL*, xxx. Is Layton's 'quadrant court' the nearest a Cambridge man could get to 'quadrangle'?

çi-devant of Chertsey, selling his house's goods 'for white wyne, sugar, burage leves and seke [sack] wherof he sippes nyghtly in his chamber tyll mydnight';[1]—these, and many other passages, deserve on grounds of style a place in any selection of English letters.

When Layton dashed off his vivacious missives, he could not forseee that they were to be a principal document in the brief-case of prosecuting counsel at the trial of the monks in centuries to come, but in fact they have had an influence on the subconscious mind of historians greater, perhaps, than that of the *comperta*, and they have undoubtedly done much to corroborate the latter in many minds. We shall never know the precise proportions of fact and *ben trovato* in them; each reader must make the judgment for himself, remembering that they were written without a thought of their survival and that common experience belies any assumption that the most vivid version of an episode is also the most reliable. The present writer, after very prolonged reflection, bearing in mind Layton's evident impurity of mind and confessed desire to please, would hesitate to give full credence to any accusation of his, however plausible or amusing it might be.

Thomas Legh, his principal colleague, was a Cheshire man with connections in Cumberland, and probably a distant cousin of Rowland Lee, bishop of Coventry and Lichfield. If a probable identification is accepted,[2] he was an alumnus of the sister foundations of Eton and King's College, Cambridge, and 'of a very bulky and gross habit of body'. Though still comparatively young at the time of the visitations, he had proceeded D.C.L. in 1531, had been used as ambassador to Denmark in 1532, and had been employed in various ways at home and abroad where he would have heard at first hand of the results of the suppression of religious houses. A humourless, overbearing man, colder but more incisive of mind than Layton, conceited in behaviour and sharp to brutality in manner, he was an unsympathetic character, disliked by both Norfolk and Chapuys. Together with Layton, he became *bête noire* to the northern insurgents and was subsequently used in their trials; he emerged from the whole episode the better for the lands of Calder and Nostell. Like Layton, he helped to bring Anne Boleyn to the block and later shared in bringing Dr London to book for his share in the Prebendaries' plot. He was knighted in 1544, and died soon afterwards.

The two principal visitors that remain were more substantial men who brought their careers in the world to a more successful conclusion. John ap Rice or Price, scion of an ancient Welsh family, was reared at the Inns of Court and became a notary public. He was in Cromwell's service by 1532, when he searched Tunstall's house at Auckland; by 1534 he was registrar of Salisbury and took part in the examination of the Carthusians, Fisher and More. Besides his work in the visitation and suppression of monasteries he took an important part in drafting the statutes by which the

1 *LP*, XIII, i, 1239.
2 *The Cheshire Sheaf*, 3 ser.vol.iv p.13.

administration of Wales was assimilated to that of England; his activities for the government were requited by his acquisition of Carmarthen and Brecon priories. He was knighted in 1547 and in 1551 was on the Council of the Marches. Settling himself down in the monastic buildings at Brecon he founded a county family, collected an admirable library, and wrote a number of solid works on English and Welsh history, besides dedicating a book on coinage to Queen Mary. He has acquired a posthumous and spurious title to a niche in literary history as the reputed patron of Sir Hugh Evans, whom he (despite difficulties of date) was said to have drawn into Shakespeare's orbit.[1] His descendant, Colonel Price, was a royalist of note at a time when loyalty to the monarch entailed sacrifices as real as the advantages it had brought to his ancestor. Ap Rice was a shrewd, critical man, prejudiced against the religious, who appears to have carried through in East Anglia the programme outlined by Layton for the North.

John Tregonwell was perhaps the most notable figure among the visitors. He was by birth a Cornishman, and like Price he was a layman. After proceeding D.C.L. at Oxford in 1522 he became Principal of Vine Hall (Peckwater Inn). Sworn of the Council in 1532, he was king's proctor in the divorce suit and on diplomatic missions in the Netherlands and in Scotland. His talents, like those of Layton and Ap Rice, were used at the trials of the Carthusians, Fisher and More, and later at that of Anne Boleyn. In 1535 he was a principal judge in the court of admiralty. In the sequel, he filled many lucrative posts and secured a fair prize from the monastic spoils which he continued to hold as Member of Parliament under Queen Mary, who knighted him in 1553. Like Ap Rice, he founded a family on a monastic estate, and added a tomb to what is now one of the most exquisite monuments of the monastic past, where green lawns and ancient timber make more beautiful the church of Milton Abbas. Tregonwell, though acquisitive and in sympathy with the new world, was the most independent of the visitors, and did not hesitate to plead the cause of a house which in his eyes seemed deserving.[2]

In addition to these four principals, others were employed, such as John Vaughan and Ellis Price in Wales, of whom little trace remains in the Cromwell papers. In England the only other name to appear at all frequently is that of Thomas Bedyll, whom we have met earlier in these pages. Bedyll would seem to have stood a degree lower in the social scale than those previously mentioned. He was a New College man, and proceeded B.C.L. in 1508, rising no higher on the academic ladder. From 1520 to 1532 he was secretary to Archbishop Warham, but the archbishop, when testifying to his 'approved fidelity and virtue'[3] was either using a

---

1 The art. in *DNB* is ambiguous here and the date (1573) given for Ap Rice's death is probably too late.
2 There are some excellent pages on Tregonwell and his career in A. L. Rowse, *Tudor Cornwall*, 187–93.   3 *V.* art. in *DNB*.

set of conventional terms or had mistaken Bedyll's industry and submissive manner for something more admirable. Bedyll, indeed, though not actively malicious or brutal, is one of the least attractive of Cromwell's minions. He was counsel for the king in the divorce suit, and employed both in interrogating Fisher and More and in extracting the oath of Supremacy from the Charterhouse and Syon. A clerk to the Council in 1532, he turns up repeatedly in examinations and state trials and odd jobs of inspection, in all of which his coarse texture of mind and snuffling accents show to peculiar disadvantage against the foil of hard decisions and physical suffering accepted and endured by his victims; the most obsequious of men, he was quite untouched by finer issues.[1] Bedyll became a pluralist on a considerable scale, but his early death in 1537 prevented his attaining preferment higher than the archdeaconry of London.

Such were the varied careers of some of Cromwell's visitors; men distinguished in no way from a hundred others in the public life of the age; grasping, worldly and without a trace of spiritual feeling. They were to be, all unconsciously, principal agents in the most sudden and wholesale transformation that English social life has ever undergone between the Norman Conquest and our own day. As they rode over the rainswept English countryside in the late summer of 1535 the life of some eight hundred religious families, great and small, was continuing, at least in external show, to follow the rhythm that had endured for centuries and that had been familiar to Englishmen from the very dawn of national history. From the grey turrets and lichened gables, set among the red roofs of a town or framed by the ricks and elms of the open country, bells still rang to Mattins and Mass, and the habits, white or black, still crossed the great courtyard or passed down the village street. When, five years later, their work was done, nettles and the fire-weed were springing from the dust, and the ruins of Hailes and Roche and Jervaulx were already beginning to wear the mantle of silence that covers them to-day.

The visitors carried with them two documents, a list of 'instructions', which was in fact a long questionnaire to be administered to each of the religious, and a set of injunctions to be issued at the end of the visitation.[2] As these have been interpreted by historians in various senses, it may be well to examine them more closely.

The questionnaire differed little, if at all, from those which had been in use by ordinaries for centuries, save that it was, so to say, an 'omnibus' containing a section applicable to women only, and using in the case of men terms which could be applied as easily to regular canons as to monks. It covered the whole range of duties of the religious life, as well as containing a very full section dealing with the superior and his administra-

---

1 Bedyll's methods and sentiments at Charterhouse and Syon have been noted above, pp. 219, 232. His letters are almost universally repellent.
2 They are in Wilkins, *Concilia*, III, 786–91.

tion. There was no emphasis on sexual faults, and no trace of encouragement for the inquisitorial methods which were in fact employed. Reasonably administered, it could have proved as efficient an instrument as any
of its predecessors had been in the hands of a bishop.

The injunctions, on the other hand, had the familiar 'new look'.[1] They
began by reminding the abbot and community of the two oaths they had
recently taken in respect of the Acts of Succession and Supremacy, and
the first injunction laid down that 'the abbot...shall faithfully, truly and
heartily keep and observe, and cause, teach and procure to be kept' all the
laws and instructions relating to these two great issues, and that superiors
'shall observe and fulfil by all the means that they best may, the statutes
of the realm made or to be made for the suppression and taking away of
the usurped and pretended jurisdiction of the bishop of Rome within this
realm'. This let the religious know where they stood clearly enough, but
it was no more than the logical consequence of the oaths that they had
taken; they might dislike it or regret it, but they could not complain that
they had been taken unawares.

The injunctions dealing with the daily life of the house were on the
whole neither novel nor remarkably severe, and most of them were either
repetitions of traditional legislation or were at least similar to earlier
episcopal injunctions. As with all such reassertions of generally admitted
principles, everything would depend on the degree of urgency and rigidity
with which they were enforced. Two classes of injunction, however, call for
remark: those which, without being novel, were, or at least could be interpreted as being, severe, and those which in one way or another were new.

In the first class was a short article 'that no monk or brother of this
monastery by any means go forth of the precincts of the same'. This, as
a general law, has always been, as it still is, traditional in all monastic
orders. In itself, however, as here enunciated, it was ambiguous. Was it
a regulation binding all under all circumstances, or was it simply a general
principle admitting of exceptions sanctioned by necessity, custom and dispensation? Did the term monk include lawfully appointed obedientiaries,
with estates to manage? Did it even include the abbot himself, who had
always, from the very origins of monasticism, enjoyed a reasonable
freedom in this respect? Or did it merely assert a general principle for
'monks of the cloister' and others when not engaged in official work?
If the last, it was traditional; if the former, it would not only create an
administrative crisis, but would in effect deprive the house of autonomy.
A monastery in which an abbot could not give either his monks or himself
permission, under certain circumstances, to leave the precinct, would have
been in practice quite unworkable, unless a higher superior were to take

---

1 G. G. Coulton, at the end of two chapters (LVIII and LIX) in vol. IV of *Five Centuries of
Religion*, observes (p. 661): 'Thus, apart from the question of Royal supremacy, which was
a *chose jugée*, it is difficult to find anything in Cromwell's injunctions which St Louis might
not have decreed, and Innocent III approved.' *Judicet lector*.

the abbot's place in all respects as a giver of dispensations. No analogy can reasonably be drawn between a Tudor monastery, or even a medieval monastery of the strictest observance, and a fully enclosed house of women. It would therefore seem antecedently probable that the framer of this injunction had no intention of revolutionary innovation; had he so intended, he would have inserted 'abbot' or 'master' before the word 'monk'. Nevertheless, as we shall see, the issue was raised as a practical one almost immediately by the visitors.

This article was followed by one enacting 'that women...be utterly excluded', and it was doubtless intended that a similar prohibition should apply to men in nunneries. This again, though strong in emphasis, was no novelty and in itself most salutary, but again the phrasing was ambiguous. Did it bind *semper et ubique*, or were such traditional exceptions as distinguished ladies and near relations to be excluded from the abbot's board and the guests' dining-hall? Here again, a legal exegesis, with tradition behind it, would have favoured the broader interpretation.

In addition to these articles, which, though probably intended simply to reassert firmly what was already law, were in fact ambiguous and disquieting, there were four or five which were a direct consequence of the New Learning, and one which reflected clearly the new organization of the Church in England.

Of the former class the first was an injunction that every day, for the space of one hour, a lesson of Holy Scripture was to be read to the brethren. By this, doubtless, a commentary on the New Testament, of the type of Colet's on St Paul, was intended. So far as words went, this was little more than a development of the lecture on divinity, more than two centuries old, and we have seen how at Winchcombe Richard Kidderminster had given new life to a traditional practice. But the emphasis on the Scripture, as against divinity or the fathers, was a sign of the times; it was intended to encourage a new spiritual outlook, and could scarcely help but breed controversy as the world then was.

Still more novel was the next article, a long disquisition in the Erasmian manner on the unprofitable nature of ceremonies, that is, of the traditional monastic observances of offices, processions, fasts, penances, and the rest. The brethren were to be instructed that these of themselves were not pleasing to God, but merely remote preparations for the interior and spiritual service of Christ. The long article was phrased moderately, and would have been theologically unexceptionable if delivered in private, with due reservations, by a novice-master. Given, however, as a solemn injunction, it was clearly directed against what was assumed to be a common abuse and an undesirable frame of mind, and it could not but give to a master, and still more to a novice, addicted to the new learning, a platform from which to criticize and ridicule the traditional framework of monastic life, of the Rule itself, and of religious obedience. A further article was still more revolutionary. This was a command, again based on

Erasmian teaching, that no one under twenty-four years of age must be professed. This, in practice, was made retrospective by the visitors who held plenary powers under the vicar-general, and could therefore claim the right to dispense from monastic vows. There followed an article against superstition, another bogey of Erasmus. Relics were not to be exhibited for 'increase of lucre', and if visitors or pilgrims wished to make a donation at a shrine, the money was to go to the poor. A less important, but significant, command laid on priests the obligation each day of remembering Queen Anne in their Mass.

Finally, there was an article, entirely without precedent, that if the superior, or any subject of the house, should infringe any of the injunctions, any other member might denounce him at once to the king or his visitor-general or his deputy, and the abbot was to provide him with money and all facilities for his journey to headquarters.

The document ended with the statement that the visitors had power to add to these injunctions in accordance with their *comperta* and the needs of individual houses.

There has been in recent years some discussion as to the motive behind these regulations. As it would not be realistic to attribute to Cromwell an ardent pastoral concern for the spiritual welfare of the religious, our task is merely to decide whether the injunctions were intended as a sharp but practical disciplinary measure, or as a *reductio ad impossibile* for the monks: a demand for a severity of observance which would drive them either to a petition for release or to a disobedience which could be punished by suppression. It has indeed been argued that the injunctions were no more than reasonable deductions from the first principles of monasticism, and that the monks by their protests subscribed to all the charges of laxity that had been made against them.[1] Some of the injunctions, no doubt, were of this type, but to apply this line of thought to the regulation confining even superiors to unbroken residence within the gates is surely a serious failure of both practical and spiritual understanding. Such a regulation had never been the law or practice in the monastic or canonical order from the days of St Benedict to those of Cromwell, and, though unquestionably the abuse of freedom on the part of abbots and obedientiaries had been a principal cause of decline and scandal for centuries, the imposition of a rigid, universal prohibition would have rendered the administration of estates and courts an impossibility, and would have deprived the religious at a stroke of all opportunity for recreation which was probably desirable in itself and which in any case had a prescriptive claim of several centuries' validity throughout Europe. Even the Carthusians in country districts were allowed on occasion to walk outside their precinct. The long-needed reform on this point should have taken

---

1 Coulton, *op. cit.* 633, even puts the rhetorical question: 'Must we not recognize that his [i.e. Henry VIII's] initial move would have put him high among Popes, if not in the first place?' Baskerville, *EM*, 132–3, makes, by way of insinuation, a very similar suggestion.

the shape of a considerable, even of a severe, but not of a total restriction. Regulations imposed from without are only wise when they are reasonably practical, which this was not. A spiritual rebirth is not accomplished by a set of strict rules, nor by the agency of such men as Legh and Layton. In the event, the numerous petitions from abbots and priors, sometimes supported by the visitors themselves, seem to have been favourably received by Cromwell. He knew how to make the best of every situation, and the abbots had to pay for their freedom, but such dispensations would have been scarcely logical if the injunctions had been primarily intended as a return to primitive discipline.

On the other hand, the suggestion first made, or at least first firmly adopted, by Gasquet,[1] that the injunctions were from the beginning aimed solely at driving the monks to desperation and capitulation, would seem to be untenable. Layton, who was as deeply engaged as anyone in the preparations for the visitation, clearly knew nothing of such a policy, for during the first weeks of his visitatorial activity he urged restraint in applying the injunctions, and gave dispensations freely.[2] Moreover, the suggestion made by Ap Rice at Denney on 30 October, when the visitation was three months old, that a clearance could be effected without scandal by applying the injunctions literally, cannot be made to bear the weight of argument that Gasquet rests upon it when he suggests that the visitor was a confidential agent putting Cromwell's deepest designs into practice. The context makes it clear that the suggestion was thrown out as a post-script to a letter with the hope of hindering Legh's design of dispensing all who (as he alleged) wished to depart.[3] Doubtless the alternative of keeping the Rule to the letter or of departing was proposed to the friars in 1538, almost three years later, and achieved the result that was desired, but in these years of rapid change an argument reaching back three years is of little force. There is, in fact, no evidence whatever either that the injunctions emptied the monasteries in 1535 or that they were intended to do so. What little evidence there is goes to show that the severity of the injunctions was due to the king, who always took a strict view of other people's obligations, but who quickly lost interest in the matter and left it to Cromwell to apply the injunctions as he thought fit, partly to keep the abbots duly subservient and partly to secure the advantages of a lucrative dispensation.

Although what was accomplished by Cromwell's commissaries is always called a visitation, and although the facts and figures sent up to headquarters were styled *comperta* after the traditional fashion, the visitors were far from following the ponderous but essentially fair canonical procedure that had been in use for three centuries. According to this, after long preliminary formalities, religious and legal, the members of the community were examined singly, from the abbot downwards, on a long questionnaire. The *detecta* thus acquired were then controlled by a further

---

1 Gasquet, *Henry VIII*, 80–1.   2 *V. infra*, p. 281.
3 *V. infra*, p. 285. Ap Rice's postscript is in Ellis, *OL*, III, ccciv; cf. *LP*, IX, 708.

examination, often very lengthy and detailed, and the specific accusations were then sifted, and all accused of serious offences were given opportunity of canonical compurgation. Finally, often after an interval of weeks or months, injunctions were issued adapted to the situation as disclosed by the *comperta*, which was the name given to the final shape taken by the *detecta* after they had been controlled and analysed.[1]

Cromwell's visitors acted in a more summary fashion. They did indeed carry with them a long questionnaire, but there is no evidence that they employed it in all, or indeed, in any, cases, and the religious and canonical prologues were probably altogether neglected.[2] The liking displayed by Legh for a processional reception by the community, though an integral part of the episcopal visitation, was slightly ridiculous when the visitor was a young layman, and was in fact regarded as a foible even by his colleagues. As for the injunctions, these were not framed after the visitation to meet the individual case, but were carried round by the visitors, presumably on a printed broadsheet, and served on all the communities before the visitor left—only a few hours, it might be, after his arrival. So far as the *comperta* and the visitors' letters tell the story, it would seem that, after a few early experiments, the interrogatories were directed towards acquiring a summary statement of the financial and economic position of the house, and to eliciting from the individual religious, by means of relentless questioning of the kind which almost all the visitors concerned had been practising with state prisoners during the past year, statistics of sexual immorality and 'superstitious' practices in vogue at the house. The commissaries then dismissed, by authority of the king's vicar-general, all religious under a certain age, and, as the visitation proceeded, dispensed from their vows others who made petition for this. They then presented the superior and community with the injunctions, took their fee, and departed.

II. THE COURSE OF THE VISITATION

We can follow the visitors on their travels in so far as their letters to Cromwell, with accounts of their doings, permit. We may imagine them, if we will, riding under the louring skies and heavy foliage of an unusually wet summer.[3] Layton was at Evesham on 1 August, and thence passed to

---

1 For an account of the procedure, *v. RO*, 1, 81–3, and authorities there cited.

2 The reader may judge for himself the justice of Baskerville's statement (*EM*, 130, 132) that 'it cannot be said that [Layton and Legh] did not follow precedents, both generally and in detail, or that their methods differed much from those of former visitors, except that they were more thorough-going.... The royal visitors followed the precedents of episcopal visitors down to the last detail.'

3 Early in August Stephen Vaughan had remarked upon 'these great humidities' and shortly before 12 August old Edmund Brocke, of Crowle, going home in the rain from Worcester market, opined that 'it is long of the King that this weather is so troublous and unstable. There was never good wedringes since the King began this business'. He drew the conclusion that 'it maketh no matter if he [the king] were knocked or patted on the head'. Others noted that the bad weather began when the Carthusians were executed (4 May). Cf. *LP*, IX, ii, 47, 74.

Tewkesbury; a week later he was at Bath and Farley; thence he circled by way of Lacock, Witham and Bruton to Glastonbury and Bristol, where he arrived on 22 August.[1] After that, he is lost to sight for more than a fortnight, reappearing on 12 September at Oxford and Abingdon, whence he proceeded to join Cromwell at Winchester three days later. On 22 September he was at Southwark, and thence by a rapid stage to Durford near the Hampshire border of Sussex (24th). In the three following days he dealt with Waverley, Shulbrede and Essebourne; on 1 October he was at Boxgrove, and the next day at Lewes. He then swept round the south-eastern coast of Kent by way of Dover, Folkestone and Langdon, arriving at Christ Church, Canterbury, on 23 October. A week later he was at Rochester and Leeds, and about this time also at Bermondsey. Then he disappears again, perhaps engaged on other business, till he reappears on 12 December at Syon.

Meanwhile, Legh and Ap Rice had set out from near Worcester at the beginning of August, and Legh had dealt with the cathedral priory, Great Malvern and Winchcombe. Ap Rice does not appear at these houses, but within a few days they were working in double harness at Malmesbury, and thenceforward were together for more than a month. After visiting some houses in north Wiltshire they followed on the heels of Layton at Lacock (20 August) and Bruton (23–4); this overlapping, which caused some friction, was apparently a consequence of Layton's commission as a free-lance, whereas Legh had a list of specified houses to visit. From Bruton the pair travelled into central Wiltshire, where they dealt with some of the great nunneries, and thence to Hampshire and the Thames valley, with Reading (25 September), Chertsey and Merton. Legh was then commissioned to visit some London monasteries, and both he and Ap Rice can be traced at Westminster and Holywell (28 September), but if they completed the visitation of the metropolis, it was in a matter of a fortnight or less, for by 16 October they were at Warden in Huntingdonshire, having apparently put St Albans behind them on the way. After a short circle to Royston and Walden, the pair were at Cambridge for a week or so at the end of October, where they reformed the university with commendable despatch, finding time also to visit Denney and Swaffham and the bishopric of Ely. Thence on 4 November they departed to Bury St Edmunds and to a broad sweep in the coastal parts of Norfolk, which they had traversed by 20 November, leaving some three weeks for Suffolk, where Legh can be traced at Ipswich and St Osyth. They then parted, Ap Rice to other work and Legh to join Layton a few days before Christmas at Lichfield.

The fourth visitor, Tregonwell, had started work at Oxford with Layton on 12 September, Cromwell having in each case tactfully given a

---

1 The movements of the visitors can be followed in *LP*, ix, x; in addition to dated letters, indications are often given by references to future plans or past actions. *V.* also App. vi, *infra.*

member of the sister university a share in the congenial and remarkably simple task of academic reform. While at Oxford the two commissaries completed a joint visitation of Oseney, but then they separated. Tregonwell made a rapid circuit of minor houses in Buckinghamshire, south Northamptonshire, and Oxfordshire; he then disappears from sight, en route for Thame, and does not reappear for almost a month when, early in November (4th), he is at Athelney in Somerset, passing thence to Cleeve near Watchet, and then by way of Barnstaple to Bodmin and his native Cornwall, where he disappears from the monastic scene.

Simultaneously, but more slowly, two other commissioners, Adam Beconsaw and Dr J. Vaughan, were endeavouring to reform public morals, as well as the monasteries, in Wales. They can be seen on 22 August at Valle Crucis, on 14 October at Gresford, on 11 November at Llandaff, and four months later they are at Llandaff again, after dealing with Brecknock. Of this tour, however, very few details can be gleaned.[1]

The visitation did not pass without an occasional contretemps. As we have seen, Layton was first off the mark with a roving commission, whereas Legh and Ap Rice had their objectives fixed for them by Cromwell. Consequently, the abbot of Bruton who, after some initial unpleasantness, had succeeded in giving a fairly favourable impression to Layton, had a disagreeable shock a few days later when Legh arrived at the gate with a written commission. Some plain speaking followed, for the abbot, having already parted with a substantial fee and a venerable relic, in addition to hearing the comments of his canons on his régime, had no desire for a repetition of the experience within a fortnight. Nevertheless, he was only in part successful in avoiding it, for Legh, though refraining from a formal visitation, demanded to see Layton's *comperta* and proceeded to stiffen up his injunctions.[2]

These last, indeed, provided matter for friction on more than one occasion. As has been suggested, they were, if strictly interpreted, quite impracticable. Layton who, for all his railing and bawdy talk, could be reasonable on occasion, began by allowing heads of houses to sit lightly to them pending further instructions. Legh, on the other hand, who was by nature more rigid and self-important, enforced the rule of perpetual enclosure from the first, even for heads of houses, as also the exclusion of all laymen and women from the precinct, and as early as 20 August wrote to Cromwell urging uniformity of treatment.[3] Ap Rice, who was in some ways the most thoughtful of the visitors, wrote the same day in the opposite sense, setting out with fairness the reasonable case of the superior. Many of the houses, he said, 'stand by husbandry', and they must fall to decay if their heads are not allowed to go out. Even the Carthusians had been forced to give their priors and procurators this permission, and it was unavoidable that a Martha should be provided to care for her contemplative

1 Beconsaw and Vaughan can be seen in glimpses at work in *LP*.
2 *LP*, IX, 159.   3 *Ibid*. 138; Wright, *SL*, xxiii.

sisters; superiors could be chosen who had shown themselves worthy of trust in this regard.[1] Legh, however, reiterated his complaints, and by the time that Cromwell had replied to his first letter by giving him power to remit the injunction he had become obstinate on the point. The other monks would be jealous, he wrote; it would be a pity to grant dispensations only a few days after the injunctions had been served on them; let the monks wait a little, and they would be ready to pay more for it.[2] From what can be seen of subsequent events, this last argument appealed to Cromwell.

Another quarrel broke out on the question of dispensation and dismissal. The injunctions forbade any religious profession to be made by those under the age of twenty-four, and the visitors were from the start empowered to dispense those under age who might request it. Disagreement arose, however, as to whether those under the specified age should be compulsorily dismissed, or as Legh put it 'disvested', or should merely be given the choice of going. Layton at first did not force them out and Ap Rice allowed those over twenty-two to stay, thus falling foul of Legh, who was willing to let the monks stay, but not the nuns, despite Ap Rice's argument *a fortiori* that 'women come to maturity two years before men'. Legh also took it upon himself to grant dispensations to those of any age who might apply. Finally Cromwell decided after due reflection that none over the age of twenty was to be compelled to go.[3]

The differences of policy sprang from differences of personality. Relations between Legh and Ap Rice became less and less harmonious, and Legh expatiated to Cromwell on the Welshman's shortcomings. The vicar-general in return asked the latter for his views on his colleague, against whom complaints had been coming in, and Ap Rice, though 'not eloquent in accusation as some men be', succeeded in giving a very adequate impression of Legh's limitations. This drew some expressions of pained surprise from the aggrieved doctor. Complaints of 'my triumphant and sumptuous usage and gay apparel', he says, are misplaced. 'I used myself no otherwise than I did before, and wear no garments but such as I have worn in London these two years.' 'And as by your means I had of the king an old gown of velvet', he adds, 'what more reasonable than to wear it?' On the very day that Legh was penning this letter at Warden, his colleague was taking up his parable again. Legh, he wrote to Cromwell, is 'very insolent and pompatique', and of a 'satrapic countenance'. He has 'handled the fathers very roughly', with the result that he has spread 'more terror than ever Dr Alen did'. In addition, he goes about in a velvet gown with a dozen men in livery besides his brother, and takes a commission of £20 whenever he presides over an election, in addition to other

---

1 *LP*, ix, 139.

2 This dispute is hard to follow, and the abstracts in *LP* may sometimes have obscured the details. Cf. *LP*, ix, 167, 265, 423, 621, 622, 661; also Legh's query, *ibid.* 735 (November): 'What to be done for those who desire to be dismissed from religion?'.

3 *Ibid.* 423, 661.

less regular perquisites. His custom is to refuse the normal fee and depart in a huff, to be followed immediately by an emissary from the convent with an acceptable offer.[1]

Legh somehow got wind of his partner's activities and gave indications of 'ruffling', whereupon Ap Rice forwarded some second thoughts to Cromwell. Legh, he said, had for his acquaintances 'many rufflers and serving-men'; he was still young and 'by nature of a high courage', and if he were admonished might still turn out well.[2] A further admonition from Cromwell had in fact already reached Legh, who adopted a tone of injured innocence. 'As to my lordly countenance', he wrote, 'I have little cause so to look, for I have been sick since I left you and very ill at ease.'[3] Before this sad story could have reached headquarters a second candid note came down from Cromwell, and Legh wrote again at length in reply. He is willing to abandon the velvet gown, and only wears one of fur 'light and warm...that Richard's wife bought for me...fur and all, for £4'. As for the charge that he had a long train, he has only one old servant and his brother whom, since he had 'buried his wife of late and is not very expert in the world', he had 'willed to ride with [him] to see the countries and manners of men'.[4] Ap Rice, we may feel, was indeed justified in his apprehension that Legh, 'with bold excuse, in which he is very ready, should overcome me who have little audacity'. The quarrel blew over, but Legh was at pains to inform Cromwell of the gratifying reception which had been given to the Chancellor's injunctions to the University of Cambridge. 'They say', he writes, 'that nothing was ever better for the students, except three or four Pharisaical Pharisees', and three days later he repeats: 'they say you have done more for the advancement of learning than ever Chancellor did'.[5] In the intervals of reforming the university the two commissioners found time to deal with a few neighbouring nunneries, and Legh, still anxious to get on the right side of the vicar-general, forwarded a 'supposed' love-letter of the prioress of Sopham 'to make you laugh'.[6] Whatever complaints might have been made against Legh, Cromwell decided that he was an efficient agent.

The tiffs and bickerings of the visitors are of interest only as a testimony of their characters. Their letters are equally revealing of their authors' designs. Here Layton, sanguine and uninhibited, is seen most clearly. His primary aim from the start is to collect as quickly as possible serious matter for the *comperta*, and to keep Cromwell amused by scandal. His letters abound in opprobrious phrases. His description of the abbot of Battle is well known: 'the veriest hayne, beetle and buserde, and the arentest chorle that ever I see'.[7] On his return three years later he repeats

---

1 *Ibid.* 621, 622.   2 *Ibid.* 630.
3 *Ibid.* 640.   4 *Ibid.* 651; cf. Ellis, *OL*, III, ii, ccxlvii, etc.
5 *LP*, IX, 708; Ellis, *OL*, III, iii, ccciv.
6 *Ibid.*
7 *LP*, IX, 632. 'Hayne'=mean wretch. 'Beetle'=blockhead, numskull. 'Buserde'= stupid person (often with adjective 'blind'). So *OED*.

'so beggary a house I never see, nor so filthy stuff...the stuff is like the persons'.[1] It is only rarely that he is complimentary, as at Waverley, where the abbot is 'honest, but none of the children of Solomon', and even here he adds 'it will be expedient for you to tell the poor fool what he should do with his monks' who, it appears, had failed to make the royal visitor comfortable.[2] His comment on Durford, that it had 'better be called Dirtford', is typical.[3] Jocosely explicit when he scents evil, Layton has a ready explanation when all seems well, as at Glastonbury: the monks are too straitly kept to offend, 'but faine they wolde if they myght, as they confesse, and so the faute is not in them'.[4] Elsewhere he has another reason; there is a conspiracy of silence. Thus at Leicester 'the abbay is confederyde, we suppose, and nothyng will confesse', though they are 'the moste obstinate and factious chanons that ever I knowe'.[5]

His colleague, Ap Rice, who had shown himself discriminating in the west, where he had twice praised the large and aristocratic nunnery of Lacock,[6] has a similar story at Bury St Edmunds. 'I firmly believe and suppose that they had confedered and compacted before our comyng that they shulde disclose nothing.' Likewise at St Albans he 'found little, although there were much to be founde', and of East Anglia in general he notes: 'at the greatest houses they are so confederate by reason of their heads being mere Pharisees that we can get little or no compertes'.[7] Such conspiracy, if indeed it existed, argues a degree of self-control and loyalty in a large community such as is rarely found in those guilty of serious misconduct and the moral and psychological weaknesses which accompany it.

Of all the commissioners Tregonwell is perhaps the most reliable. He does not mince his words at Eynsham, whose latter end was like its middle age, 'a raw sort of religious persons, and all kinds of offences, *etiam crimen pessimum*', nor at Clattercote, where the house is 'old, foul and filthy', but he finds good to say of the nuns of Godstow and Catesby, and the canons of Ashby and other houses.[8] Even Bedyll, after a handsome compliment to Ramsey, adds piously, 'I pray God I may fynd other houses in no worse condition, and than I wolbe right glad that I tok this journey'.[9] A knowledge of Bedyll's character, however, and his repeated statement that the Ramsey monks are 'feythful obedienciaries' to the king as Supreme Head, make it conceivable that more material considerations had contributed to his satisfaction. Similarly Layton's resounding testimony to the respectability of Durham, though probably consistent with the facts, no doubt also bore relation to his kinship with Tunstall,

1 *LP*, XIII, i, 1085.   2 *Ibid.* IX, 452.   3 *Ibid.* 444.
4 *Ibid.* 168; Wright, *SL*, xxiv; Archbold, *SRH*, p. 39.
5 *LP*, IX, 1005; Wright, *SL*, xlii.   6 *LP*, IX, 139, 160.
7 Wright, *SL*, xxxviii; *LP*, IX, 772 (Bury); 661 (St Albans); 808 (general).
8 *LP*, IX, 457; Ellis, *OL*, III, iii, cclxvii.
9 Wright, *SL*, xlvi; *LP*, X, 90, 103.

who was his patron into the bargain.[1] Such testimonials did not receive a warm welcome from either Cromwell or the king, as Layton was to find in the case of Abbot Whiting. Legh did better with his story of 'half a dozen' nuns of Denney 'with tears in their eyes begging to be dismissed', to which the realist Ap Rice added in a postscript that 'they will all do this if they are compelled to observe these injunctions',[2] though in the event the nuns of Denney begged for, and obtained, exemption from suppression in 1536.

It is possible to see changes of procedure in the course of the visitation. Legh began as a pompous martinet, but seems to have been shaken by reproofs from Cromwell. Ap Rice, on the other hand, began sympathetically but coarsened after a time. As for Layton, who began in a spirit of coarse good-humour, a sense of power seems to have awakened in him the qualities of a bully. The episode at Lewes, recounted by himself, can scarcely have been unique. There, having been assured by the prior that he knew nothing of a risky sermon delivered by the subprior, he forced the latter to admit the former's complicity, and then went through a kind of parody of the rite of excommunication in the chapter-house:

I have declared the prior to be perjured [he writes to Cromwell], *per haec verba. Auctoritate Dei Patris Omnipotentis, et Regia Auctoritate, et auctoritate Magistri Thomae Cromwel, cujus officii in hac parte fungor, te priorem, &c., pronuncio perjurum.* That done, I laid unto him concealment of treason, called him heinous traitor in the worst names I could devise, he all the time kneeling and making intercession unto me not to utter to you the premises for his undoing.[3]

It is usually assumed, explicitly or tacitly, both by historians and (in consequence) by their readers, that the four visitors whose activities we have followed were the only commissioners at work, and that consequently the houses which they did not visit were left undisturbed. An exception, as we have seen, is clearly to be made for Wales, where Adam Beconsaw and John Vaughan were at work for six months or more, and there may have been other agents whose letters have not been preserved. The appearance of Bedyll in East Anglia, signalized by a couple of letters, shows that at least one other agent was busy. Bedyll toured the Fens and at Ramsey lighted upon a royal charter from Saxon times which suggested to him that the abbot and convent of the Confessor's day had accepted the royal supremacy,[4] while at Croyland he came upon 'a young fool... not past fifteen, who is every day new to the hearer'. He proposed, therefore, that since 'the king's fool is getting old', the brethren should be deprived of their enjoyment in the royal interest, adding that 'though I am

---

1 *LP*, X, 183 (to Cromwell): 'Your injunctions can have no effect in Durham Abbey in some things; for there was never yet woman in the abbey further than the church, nor they [i.e. the monks] never come within the town.'

2 *Ibid.* IX, 708.

3 *Ibid.* 632. Readers of R. H. Benson's novel, *The King's Achievement*, will remember the vivid scene at Lewes.

4 *Ibid.* X, 103. He adds: 'good notes might be gathered out of this'.

made of such heavy matter that I have small delectation in fools, he is one of the best I have heard'.[1]

Hitherto, throughout the autumn, the visitors had rambled in a somewhat aimless fashion about the country. A change came towards the end of December, when Cromwell decided to send Layton and Legh on the mission which the former had solicited some months earlier. They were therefore directed to make contact at Lichfield and to go together to the northern parts. The northern tour began about the turn of the year, and before the end of February, Legh and Layton, working sometimes apart but more often in double harness, had visited at least 121 religious houses and covered well over one thousand miles, and that in northern counties, over heather, stream and bog, in the short days and clinging mists of winter. During that time they had passed down Trentside, threaded Sherwood and its heaths, visited the houses that lay thick in the Vale of York, circled the East Riding and penetrated the Dales, reaching Bamburgh on the coast of Northumberland and Blanchland hidden in the moors where Northumberland and Durham meet. Returning south at least as far as Richmond, they then took the fork at Scotch Corner and made for Barnard Castle. Thence it is possible that one of them rode up Teesdale between the high fells and so down the Eden valley to Armathwaite and Lanercost, while the other passed into the Vale of Westmorland and so across to Shap. In any case, they were together at Carlisle, and thence passed along the coasts of Cumberland and Lancashire, with a detour to Whalley and Sawley, ending up in late February at Combermere and Chester.

So ended Cromwell's visitation of the monasteries. Events were already in train in London that would make it, within a matter of weeks, ancient history. We must, however, look at it a little more closely, for it is, in the last analysis, by the findings of these visitors that writers in the past have, with whatever reservations, judged the monks.

First, as regards its completeness, it may be remarked that several districts are without any record of visitation. Thus Lincolnshire, particularly rich in religious houses, was apparently not covered; many of the monasteries of Leicestershire, Warwickshire, north Worcestershire, Shropshire and Herefordshire seem to have escaped; and there are other isolated pockets of land which the visitors did not touch, unless we suppose others to have been at work who left even less trace in the records than Bedyll.

Secondly, there is the speed with which the visitation was accomplished. Endeavours have recently been made to show that the visitors were scarcely more expeditious than certain bishops and other prelates in the past,[2] but no one can read the letters of the Cromwellian visitors and

---

1 *LP*, x, 181.

2 In particular by Mr Warren Sandell, who composed the two appendices to vol. 4 of Coulton's *Five Centuries of Religion*. Even granted that the assumptions there made on somewhat slight evidence (e.g. for the separate itineraries of Layton and Legh) are valid, the conclusion, that the average daily mileage covered by the two visitors, viz. 17 miles,

follow their itinerary on the map without receiving an impression of haste, and the arguments against this impression are not convincing. Though bishops and their commissaries may have been speedy at times, no diocesan bishop ever covered in a single tour the distance travelled by Legh and Layton in the north, and the longer the distance, the greater the difficulty of maintaining the pace. As for the two Premonstratensian prelates, whose itineraries can more fairly be compared with the northern tour, they were following a familiar routine and a familiar itinerary, and were dealing with a single type of religious, those of their own order, while Redman, at least, knew intimately from long experience every house and almost every religious. Moreover, their responsibility was in a sense less, and their procedure different. On the one hand, bishops and their officials often accepted without question a unanimous *omnia bene*, whereas the Henrician visitors were searching for discreditable information by which the house might be ruined once and for all; moreover, both Redman and earlier bishops often adjourned their visitation, especially when the charges were serious, and reconsidered the whole affair at leisure. On any showing, a visitation which was to decide the fate of all the religious in the country should in justice have been conducted with unusual deliberation and care. Indeed, whether the ostensible purpose of the visitation, viz. serious reform, or its real purpose, the amassing of incriminating evidence, is considered, the speed achieved will seem to show a total lack of principle. The principal offenders were Layton and Legh, particularly in their tour of the north, but even as early as 26 September, Layton could write to Cromwell one Sunday from Waverley that on the following day he intended to go to Chichester, more than thirty miles distant over Hindhead, 'despatching by the way...a priory of nuns and canons close together',[1] and he fulfilled his intention. Shulbrede and Essebourne (at least five miles apart) were doubtless small houses, but on any showing this was quick work.

This despatch was in fact made possible only by a rigorous economy of words and a blunt directness in the interrogation of the inmates. Both the letters and the *comperta* of the visitors indicate that, after getting a general impression of the financial state of the house (for which, it may be, they could use the figures of the *Valor* as a control) and after making a shrewd and realist estimate of the superior's character, they restricted their enquiries to personal interrogatories of the monks on a few points (for they cannot have used the whole questionnaire) and a brief search for

is not notably more than the average of about 13 m.p.d. covered by five other earlier visitation rounds of comparable length, does not seem very strong. A daily addition of four miles for two months is considerable, and the Cromwellian visitors examined five or six times as many communities as the prelates with whom they are compared. Above all, there is the extremely serious (alleged) purpose of the visitation. If it was really the purpose of the visitors to bring about a thorough reform, why this haste? The waters of Shiloh run softly.

1 *LP*, IX, 444.

objects and practices that could be labelled as superstitious. Thus, on 7 August, Layton wrote from the cathedral priory of Bath:

We have visited Bath, and found the prior a very virtuous man, but his monks more corrupt than any others in vices with both sexes... the house well repaired but £400 in debt....I send you *vincula S. Petri*, which women put about them at the time of their delivery....I send you also a great comb called Mary Magdalen's comb, and St Dorothy's and St Margaret's combs. They cannot tell how they came by them....I send you a book of Our Lady's miracles, well able to match the Canterbury tales, which I found in the library.[1]

Three months later Ap Rice and Legh write from Bury St Edmunds:

As for thabbot, we found nothing suspect as touching his lyving, but it was detected that he laye moche forth in his granges, that he delited moche in playing at dice and cardes, and therin spent moche money....As touching the convent, we coulde geate little or no reportes amonge theym, although we did use moche diligence in the examination....And yet it was confessed and proved, that there was here suche frequence of women commyng and reassorting to this monastery as to no place more. Amongst the reliques we founde moche vanitee and super-stition, as the coles that St Laurence was toasted withall, the paring of St Edmundes naylles, St Thomas of Canterbury penneknyff and his bootes, and divers skulles [?skills, i.e. quasi-magical prayers] for the hedache, etc.[2]

The *comperta* give the same impression. Thus two or three items may be taken, almost at random:

Grace Dieu. Two nuns charged with incontinence. Superstition: they hold in reverence the girdle and part of the tunic of St Francis, which are supposed to help lying-in women. Founder, lord Ferys. Rents, 109 marks; debt, 20 lib.

Basedale. Joan Flecher peperit. Superstition: Virgin's milk. Founder, Sir Ralph Evers. Rents. 18 lib.

Bromholm. Will. Lakenham the prior and three others incontinent. A cross called the Holy Cross of Bromeholme. They say they have the girdle and milk of St Mary.[3]

From these documents, and indeed from every indication given in the course of the visitation, it is clear that the *comperta* were recorded and assembled not, as in canonical visitations, as a basis for remedial punish-ments and injunctions, but as information to be sent to Cromwell and used for any purpose he might think fit.

As regards the methods used by the commissaries, considerable informa-tion survives. Whereas in all the voluminous visitation documents of the past there is no instance or complaint of improper questioning or brow-beating, the records of the Cromwellian visitation provide examples of both, and imply very many more. Layton was probably the worst offender when it came to bullying the monks. The incident at Lewes, related with evident relish by himself, has already been mentioned. Of his inquisitorial methods we have good evidence in his notorious letter to Cromwell from Leicester: 'this mornyng I will objecte against divers of them bugrie and adulteries, *et sic specialiter discendere*,[1] wiche [*sc.*, the accusations] I have lernede of other, but not of them; what I shall fynde I cannot tell'.[2]

As for Legh, there is the testimony of Ap Rice which there is no reason to disbelieve:

> I was minded at divers times to mention certain abuses and excesses committed by him...at Bruton he behaved very insolently...at Bradstock and elsewhere he made no less ruffling with the heads than he did at Brueton...wherever he comes he handles the fathers very roughly.[3]

This harsh, bullying treatment was not only part of the visitors' policy of intimidation, but was extended to the examination of the individual religious. While it is fair to reject as baseless and biased gossip the later reports that the visitors assailed the virtue of some of the nuns, they certainly made a practice of obtaining from within and without the monastery what sinister reports they could concerning individuals, and proceeded to a brutal interrogation of those concerned with a view to obtaining admissions of guilt. It is clear from the *comperta* that the visitors demanded, at least of the male religious, an admission of secret sins, and while it is a mistake to suppose that this knowledge was obtained in sacramental confession, it must be emphasized that such interrogations were wholly uncanonical and, on elementary ethical principles, unlawful. Nor is it difficult to picture the condition into which such questioning would reduce a weak, neurotic or discontented man or boy.

Suppression had formed no part of the visitation as originally designed. Nevertheless, by the time that the act suppressing the lesser monasteries became law half a dozen houses had become casualties in the wake of the visitors. Four of these were in Kent, and Yorkshire and Essex contributed two others.

Langdon, a small Premonstratensian abbey near Dover, had been the scene of one of Layton's most exuberant exploits. It was clearly rotten to the core; according to the visitor the abbot was 'worse than all the rest, the drunkenest knave living', while 'his canons are as bad as he, without a spark of virtue'. There was probably exaggeration in this, for Layton was in a rollicking mood when he wrote to Cromwell from Canterbury, ending his account with more vivacity than grammar: 'send word whether I shall depose him and turn the priory into a parsonage with a vicar, and make the King patron, and give it to me for a parsonage'.[4] Cromwell adopted part of this programme, and Langdon surrendered on 12 November. The abbot, whom Layton had lodged in jail at Canterbury, acknowledged his guilt by throwing in his hand, thereby obtaining the

---

1 I.e. if he fails to establish the most heinous charges he will go down the scale (or species) to lesser ones, e.g. secret sins.

2 *LP*, IX, 1005.   3 *Ibid*. 622.

4 *Ibid*. 668–9 (23 October); Wright, *SL*, xxxiii.

relatively small pension of £7. The procedure adopted was similar to that of Wolsey's 'offices'. The canons confessed the house to be decayed and moribund, and therefore restored it to its patron and founder, the king. Folkestone, a minuscule priory, and Dover, a dependency of Canterbury, went the same way a few days later, though Bedyll, when winding up Dover, gave it a better testimonial than Layton's. In each case the religious were given the option of a transfer or a 'capacity'.[1] Three months later Layton took the surrender of the small Austin priory of Marton in Yorkshire and the Premonstratensian cell of Hornby in Lancashire, but the suppression of the latter was held up, and the canons remained till the mother-house of Croxton surrendered in 1538.[2] Finally, Bilsington, a small Kentish house of Austin canons and Tiltey, a decayed Cistercian abbey in Essex, collapsed independently at the end of February, only a few days before they became legally forfeit.[3] Insignificant in themselves, these sporadic instances of surrender, effectuated only a few weeks before the formal measure of wholesale confiscation was passed, are one more proof of the empirical, unpremeditated decisions that are characteristic of Cromwell in all his dealings with the monasteries.

1 The procedure is described by Bedyll and his colleagues; cf. *LP*, IX, 816, 829; Wright, *SL*, xl.

2 *LP*, XIV, i, 598.

3 The deeds of all these surrenders are in Rymer, *Foedera*, XIV, 555 *seqq.*, and *Deputy Keeper's Reports*, VIII (1847), Appendix II, 4–51.

CHAPTER XXIII

THE ACT OF SUPPRESSION AND THE
CASE FOR THE DEFENCE

Before the visitation was over, before any attempt could have been made to codify and weigh its findings, and while perhaps half of the monasteries of England still remained unvisited, Cromwell had decided how to act. He had recently considered an opinion of counsel that monasteries of the king's foundation that had failed in numbers or duty might be seized to the king's use, and had been informed that 'this good law duly put in execution would bring back to the Crown lands worth £40,000 a year'.[1] This opinion, which was an extension of the old feudal doctrine that land given for military service or sergeanty of any kind escheated when that service was not given through default either of will or of person, was not new, and had been put forward on behalf of lay owners of church property in the days of the Lollards and before.[2] Such a scheme, however, was not comprehensive enough, and Cromwell is found reminding himself of 'the abomination of religious houses throughout this realm and a reformation to be devised therein'.[3] Early in 1536, while his visitors were still at work, he had begun the final process and had drafted the bill, and on 3 March a friend could write to Lord Lisle that it was 'bruited that abbeys and priories under 300 marks by year, not having twelve in convent, shall down'.[4] The rumour was trustworthy, but the addition by another friend that the suppression was to be for the benefit of 'certain notable persons of learning and good qualities about his Highness' left room for a wide discretion on Henry's part and for pleasurable expectation among his familiars.[5] The bill would seem in the event to have come before the Commons on 11 March. In the debate that followed no doubt a lurid picture was presented by speakers for the government, and very probably selections from the *Comperta* were read out, though there is no good evidence that the Black Book of legend ever existed, or even that the outcry was as loud and unanimous as Latimer implied, though a fairly long extract from the *Comperta* would draw cries from any normal assembly prepared to believe in its authenticity. There is a possibility (it cannot be called a probability) that Henry left nothing to chance and himself intervened when the bill was about to be presented to the Commons, impressing upon a deputation that they must decide for themselves, and not let themselves be influenced by thoughts of what he might wish. Such an exhortation, followed up by an announcement that the King's Grace would come again to see what they had decided, was a familiar

---

1 *LP*, x, 242.   2 *RO*, II, 97–8 and notes.   3 *LP*, x, 254.
4 *Ibid.* 406.   5 *Ibid.* 445.

piece of technique with Henry, and may well have been employed here.[1]
There was a likelihood that some would 'grudge'; the friends as well as
the foes of the monks would see the wedge getting into the crack. As those
present were not slow to perceive, the first fire might take only the thorns
and brushwood, but the 'putrified old oaks', the 'great and solemn
abbeys', would fall all the more easily when there was a space clear about
them.[2] In the event, the bill passed;[3] that the king had actually to threaten
dire pains to those who might oppose it is a late tradition which may, or
may not, be authentic.[4]

As soon as the rumour of suppression had spread, and before the act
had passed, the air was thick with wings making for the carrion. The
methodical Tregonwell was one of the first off the mark with a petition
for one of a list of nunneries.[5] Lord Lisle at Calais did not lose a day after
hearing the news, but wrote by what must have been return of post to
Cromwell, 'beseeking you to help me to some old abbey in mine old days'.[6]
Soon the whole pack was in full cry: John Whalley wants Burnham or
Folkestone; the Earl of Essex would like Beeleigh; the Duke of Norfolk

1 A private letter (*LP*, x, 462; printed in full by Wright, *SL*, xiii) from a priest, Thomas
Dorset, to the mayor of Plymouth, relates how the king recently presented an unspecified
bill to the burgesses of parliament 'and bade theym loke upon it and waye it in conscience,
for he wold not, he saide, have theym passe on it nor on any other thyng because his grace
gevith in the bill, but they to see yf it be for a comyn wele to his subjectis'. It has been
supposed (as against Froude, who sees a reference to the Vagrants Act, which the letter goes
on to describe) that this was the bill suppressing the smaller religious houses. It may well
be so, but the evidence is too slender as it stands to take the weight of a firm assumption.
There is no certain instance of the king visiting the House of Commons, though occasionally
(as in 1532 on the Supplication of the Clergy) he summoned a deputation. The language is
certainly that commonly used by Henry (and many another autocrat) when he was deeply
concerned to have a measure passed. For the origin of the legend (if it be one) of the Black
Book, *v.* the Elizabethan narrative in Wright, *SL*, p. 114, and Coulton, *Five Centuries of
Religion*, IV, 680–1. Latimer's words (*Sermons*, ed. Parker Society, I, 123), 'When their
enormities were first read in the parliament house, they were so great and abominable that
there was nothing but "Down with them"', have often been quoted without reference to
their context. Latimer is speaking of the great abbots, since promoted to bishoprics and
other preferments; on any showing, therefore, his recollections are somewhat confused, as
the animus in parliament was directed against the smaller houses.

2 The phrase is Hall's (*Chronicle*, II, 167): 'But even at that time one said in the Parliament
House that these were as thorns, but the great abbots were putrified old oaks, and they must
needs follow.'

3 The act is in *Statutes of the Realm*, III, 733, 27 Hen. VIII, c. 28; it has often been printed,
most conveniently in J. R. Tanner, *Tudor Constitutional Documents*, 59–63. The operative
words are: 'Forasmuch as manifest sin, vicious, carnal, and abominable living is daily used
and committed among the little and small abbeys, priories...where the congregation of
such religious persons is under the number of twelve...the King's most Royal Majesty...
considering also that divers and great solemn monasteries...wherein, thanks be to God,
religion is right well kept and observed, be destitute of such full numbers of religious persons
as they ought and may keep...the Lords and Commons...most humbly desire the King's
Highness that he shall take into his possession all houses which have not...above the clear
yearly value of two hundred pounds.' A retrospective clause gave to the king all houses
that had surrendered during the past year.

4 Sir Henry Spelman, *History and fate of sacrilege* (ed. 1698, p. 183).

5 *LP*, x, 388. Hughes, *Reformation*, I, Appendix VI, prints a list of these petitions.

6 *Ibid.* 486 (16 March); the letters of his informants are dated from London, 3 and
9 March.

is unwilling to seem pushful but feels that 'where others speak I must speak too', and indents for Bungay and Woodbridge; Cranmer thinks that Shelford would suit his brother-in-law; Humphrey Stafford could manage with Fineshead for himself if his father could have Worspring; Lord de la Warr, writing from his 'powere howse' with apologies for troubling Cromwell 'for so powere a thinge', hopes that Boxgrove will be spared, where his ancestors lie entombed, and where he himself has 'made a powre chapell to be buryed in', but if not, may he have it?[1] Sir Simon Harcourt would prefer the family foundation of Ranton to continue, and would give the king and Cromwell £100 apiece for the licence; failing this, he indents for the place. Lady Elizabeth Ughtred, a sister of Jane Seymour, asks with less precision for 'one of those abbeys, if they go down'. Richard Zouche, Cromwell's 'howne pore servantt', dwells near a 'pore pryery, a fundacion of my nawynsetres', where the 'pore howseholde' is in a bad way; he therefore asks the minister to 'gett me the pore howse'. Sir Thomas Eliot, who confesses to more than his fair share of 'naturall shamefastness', hopes that his friendship with the late Sir Thomas More, which was in fact 'but *usque ad aras*', will not stand between him and a 'convenient porcion' of which he will give the 'first yeres fruites' to Cromwell.[2] The Lord Privy Seal, in fact, stood to gain either way: if the religious went, he took a commission (or more than one) for the first refusal of the lands; if they stayed, he had a gift for obtaining the licence; meanwhile he still had such windfalls as £100 (say £3000 or £4000 to-day) from a newly appointed abbot of Leicester.[3]

As it turned out, most of these diffident and penurious petitioners were doomed to disappointment, at least for a time. There was much administrative work to be done before the market could open, and Cromwell had no mind to prejudice his own or his master's free choice. Very few sites were granted before the summer, and more than one successful suitor in early days had his grant withdrawn when the house was after all given a further lease of life. But before the story is taken further, it may be well to consider briefly the charges on which the lesser houses were condemned.

The reliability of the evidence on which the lesser monasteries were condemned to suppression has been debated with some warmth during the past eighty years. If it is considered in its immediate historical con-

---

1 Lord de la Warr became the owner of Boxgrove, and his 'poor chapel' remains in all its splendour, but his body rests elsewhere, at Broadwater.

2 *LP*, x, 491, 531, 547, 551, 552, 557, 572, 607, 613, 643, 754; xii, i, 678. Zouche's letter is also in Archbold, *SRH*, 55; those of de la Warr, H. Stafford and Eliot are in Wright, *SL*, lii, liv, lxv; Eliot's phrase *usque ad aras* is clearly taken from an entry under *Amicitia* in Erasmus's *Adagia* (ed. 1643, p. 44). It apparently = 'short of perjury (or sacrilege)' and is a translation of a phrase in Plutarch's *Pericles*. It would seem to refer to More's refusal to follow the king's wishes; Eliot's words are a bitter commentary on More's estimate of human fidelity (e.g. in letter 206, ed. Rogers, p. 524). Lady Elizabeth's letter should probably have been calendared in March 1536.

3 *LP*, x, 690.

text, the question is superfluous. As has been seen, all available indications go to show that financial, and not spiritual or ethical, considerations were responsible for the move against the monasteries; the religious families who on universal testimony kept their rule to admiration were not saved by this fidelity, but were driven from the country or extirpated on entirely different grounds. Nevertheless, even if a desire for funds rather than reform was the prime motive of the suppression, it might still be argued that the measure could have succeeded only if the whole system had in fact been proved to be rotten; otherwise, it is said, public opinion, and the protests of the religious and their friends, would have been too much for the government. In any case, the evidence of the visitors was the principal instrument that secured the passing of the Act of Suppression, and the historian has a duty to examine its truth.

In one sense, the answer to this inquiry has already been given. Throughout this work, and particularly in a previous part of this volume, evidence has been provided in plenty of the state of observance and discipline in the various orders, as disclosed by disciplinary visitations, and materials for a general judgment have gradually accumulated. The reader who has had the patience to consider these chapters will have become in some measure immune to moral shock, while at the same time he may have learnt to balance against this disclosure of frailty the evidence of other and healthier activities. He will perhaps feel that he has a tolerably adequate picture of the state of early Tudor monasticism. Yet for all this, if he comes upon the *Compendium compertorum* and reads through its nauseating columns,[1] it will be strange if he does not feel something of the horror that struck chill into the heart of Lingard when he first read the Cottonian manuscript which contains a transcript of the original record,[2] and if he makes his way to the end he may well exclaim: 'If this be true, no wonder they were swept away'—

Ὣς ἀπόλοιτο καὶ ἄλλος ὅτις τοιαῦτά γε ῥέζοι.[3]

Strange as it may seem, the reliability of the visitors' account has hitherto never been discussed with a full consideration of the evidence. Gasquet, who was the first to treat it with any amplitude, made some telling points which have had a permanent effect upon opinion even though their originator's reputation has suffered an eclipse, but he was too clearly an advocate to satisfy later critics; moreover, he failed to play several of the excellent cards he held.[4] Coulton was as clearly biased in the opposite sense and, like Gasquet, was quite incapable of presenting a sober critical dialectic, but his reiteration of serious charges which could not be denied

---

1 *LP*, x, 364, pp. 137 *seqq.*
2 Cf. Lingard's letter to a friend printed by Coulton, *Five Centuries*, II, 458. Coulton, however, notes very truly that Lingard had not the means of criticizing the evidential value of the *Comperta*.
3 Homer, *Odyssey*, I, 47: 'So may everyone else perish who does such things!'
4 As, for example, in the matter of the Norfolk and southern reports; *v. infra*, p. 306.

ad great cumulative force.[1] Baskerville, professing to stand aloof from
l extremes, succeeded in imposing on the reading public what seemed
o be a cool and scholarly judgment, but his arguments, when closely
egarded, are seen to be themselves rhetorical; he often uses innuendo
ather than proof, and ignores numerous aspects of his subject.[2] The result
as in consequence been for writers to adopt a kind of mean between
asquet and Coulton, and to avoid precise statements. There is therefore
need for yet another assessment of the evidence. In what follows there
ill be no attempt to present anew the wider arguments drawn from the
haracter of the visitors or their method of procedure. We are here con-
erned simply with their statements.

   The defenders of the monks have used a number of indirect arguments
o invalidate the *Comperta*. It has been pointed out that nothing in them or
n the letters of the visitors or in other visitation records justifies the sharp
ivision made in the preamble of the Act of Suppression between greater
nd lesser houses. The reply may be made, however, that some of the worst
nd most unjustifiable cases of decadence had in the past been found among
he smaller houses, and that the letters, if not the *Comperta*, of Cromwell's
isitors bear witness to the continued existence of decaying priories, whereas
hey testify in one way or another to the respectability of a number of the
argest houses, such as Glastonbury and Durham. But in truth, this whole
ebate is unreal. The preamble of a Tudor statute cannot, for all the brave
vords of a great historian, be taken as unimpeachable evidence;[3] in the case
n point, Cromwell had strong practical reasons for wishing to ruin one
lass of monastery while sparing the other. The preamble to the Act of
uppression is propaganda. And in fact the words alleged do not assert
hat all the great and solemn abbeys are observant, but that divers of them
re, and that transferences are to be made to such among them as are so.[4]

   A second argument has been drawn from the action of the government
n giving pensions and even high ecclesiastical preferment to individuals
vho had been accused of grave moral offences by the visitors. The facts
re certain enough, and have their own significance, but of themselves they
lo no more than show that reasons of practical policy and not of spiritual
eform were uppermost in the minds of Cromwell and his associates.[5] If

---

1 Coulton's comments in chs. lxii and lxiii, and the two appendices to vol. IV of *Five
Centuries of Religion*, make it necessary to follow him into the dismal swamp of the *Comperta*.
2 Baskerville's *English Monks and the Suppression of the Monasteries* in fact contains
naccuracies as well as omissions and suggestions which falsify the picture. This needs to be
aid, because Baskerville was an academic historian, with a record of scholarly work behind
im, who wrote throughout as an enlightened critic surveying romantics and sentimentalists
de haut en bas.
3 J. A. Froude, *Short Studies on Great Subjects*, 1st ser., 425: 'After some experience [the
present writer] advises all persons who are anxious to understand the English Reformation
:o place implicit confidence in the Statute Book.'
4 Cf. 27 Hen. VIII, c. 28, §§ 1, 8; *Statutes of the Realm*, III, 575; Tanner, *Tudor Consti-
:utional Documents*, 59, 62.
5 Latimer, *First Sermon before Edward VI*, already notices both the inconsistency and its
:ause.

wholesale suppression was to be carried through expeditiously and un
obtrusively, the only way was to pension the religious *en bloc*. It woul
have been an impossible task for the hard-pressed Augmentations men
who had no visitatorial jurisdiction, to separate the sheep from the goat
on the strength of laconic *comperta* which had never been sifted for use in
a canonical process and which would certainly have been challenged, in
good or bad faith, by those concerned, above all by superiors.[1] What was
wanted was a speedy winding-up with the minimum of disturbance, and
the only practicable way of securing this was to treat the whole process
as a routine distribution of pensions. Similar practical considerations, when
it came to the surrender of the greater houses, prevailed in the treatment
of superiors. The most desirable head was one who would meet the
government half-way and would show himself pliant in surrender, and
one whose honesty or reputation had been blown upon would be more
likely to do what was wanted than a rigid or scrupulous man. He was
paid well for his complaisance, and when once he was drawing a large
pension it was all to the advantage of government that this should be
extinguished as soon as possible by the emoluments of another office.

A third argument has been drawn from the character and aims of Cromwell's visitors as seen in their actions and letters. This is undoubtedly a
powerful line of attack, though it may easily become a mere reflection of
a personal or prejudiced opinion, but it should be kept clear of an objective
examination of the evidence they provide. This should be directed to two
purposes: a criticism of the *Comperta* themselves, and a comparison between
them and other evidence. We shall first look at the *Comperta*; unpleasant
as the subject is, we cannot avoid it, as some apologists have done, by
mentioning no details or by rhetorical references to its unspeakable
depravity. We have ourselves in this country recently (1957) supped full
of matter of this kind, and whereas our Victorian forebears burked distasteful facts we are disposed to flaunt them; this may at least enable an
historian to attempt a factual review without seeming either to condone
evil or to brand as depravity what may be in part or wholly a psychological or a pathological phenomenon.

The *Comperta* achieve their effect by a pitiless enumeration of what
seems an unending list of sexual offences; with only an occasional reference to other charges, these fill the whole indictment against both the men
and women religious. These offences are distinguished by different terms
in the northern and in the East Anglian lists. In the northern district the
distinction is made between 'sodomy' and 'incontinence'; in the East
Anglian between solitary sin (*pollutio voluntaria*) and incontinence. Casual
readers of the *comperta* receive their principal shock, which cannot but
affect their attitude to all that comes after, from the very numerous entries
of sodomy in the northern houses, which come first in order. These

---

1 There is, in fact, no reason to think that any of the commissioners or Augmentations
men had ever seen the *Comperta*.

amount, for the north only, to the massive total of 181. Regarded with a little care, however, these entries become somewhat less overwhelming. In the first place, the East Anglian houses, where homosexual practices are explicitly distinguished from solitary vice, provide only four instances of the former offence. If we then return to the northern lists we note that on the very first occurrence of 'sodomy' it is explained as solitary sin, and it is so defined in eighty-four instances out of the total given above. Moreover, the occasions where it is so defined occur, with the exception of the first entry of all (i.e. Repton), in a steady run of houses in the middle of the list.[1] Finally, 'sodomy' is in a few instances, eight in all, with a further unspecified number at one house, explicitly defined as homosexuality. The inference seems therefore permissible that in many, perhaps even in all, of the cases where the word is left undefined it denotes solitary vice only. If so, this leaves us with a total of only twelve clear instances of homosexuality in the whole *Comperta*, four of them in East Anglia and eight in the North. This total is indeed so low as almost to be surprising, but since the East Anglian figure is a firm one, there would seem to be no *a priori* reason for distrusting the northern.

This leaves us with a very large total of those confessing (for there could be no question of accusation and evidence) solitary vice. This figure, it must be remembered, abstracting altogether from its accuracy, rests upon information to which neither the visitors nor any superior, still less any historian, had any right of access. At no visitation before or since has a visitor been canonically empowered to elicit it, and we have no standard of comparison in any age or profession by which to judge it. We need not indeed suppose that Layton or Legh obtained the information under the seal of confession.[2] A visitor is not a confessor and, in any case, Legh was not in priest's orders, while Layton has himself described his technique clearly enough.[3] No one, however, with any experience, either as a priest or as a medical man, will fail to be aware that a large proportion of any such total is made up of psychological or pathological cases who need the divine or the physician rather than the judge or the executioner. This is not to suggest that all, or even the majority, of the instances alleged are without any foundation. If we would be realistic, and if we have any knowledge of human nature, whether in the Tudor age or in the twentieth century, we should expect to find neurosis, psychosis, frailty and malice in varying proportions even amongst those vowed to the religious life, but we may at least feel some certainty that the number of grave faults was not as large as the totals in the *Comperta* would suggest. Moreover, we have no certainty whatever that the faults or habits were persistent or even that they were recent.

---

1 To be precise, from Newburgh (p. 139) to Martyn (p. 142).
2 Gairdner, *Lollardy and the Reformation in England*, II, 78, strangely enough thought this to be a necessary assumption, forgetting that Legh was not in Holy Orders.
3 *V. supra*, p. 289.

There remains the very large total of cases of incontinence: the breaking of the vow of chastity by fornication or adultery. Here once again we cannot take the figures precisely at their face value. Some of the cases are explicitly given as 'defamed' (that is, charged by report but not formally convicted), and we have no certainty that the faults alleged were recent; whatever else may be deducible from the speed of the visitors' movements, it may at least be thought that the full canonical trial of those accused was not in every—perhaps not in any—case observed. But when all reservations have been made, the long list of charges of incontinence still confronts the apologist of the monks.

When dealing with the nuns the royal visitors confined their investigations to public faults, and in particular to the loss of maiden honour. Here both the northern and the East Anglian records usually confine themselves to the statement that the accused had born a child (*peperit*). The number of individuals thus branded is thirty-eight. Here, granted that the visitors were moderately accurate and truthful, there can be no doubt as to the facts. There is, however, a probability, amounting in more than one case to a certainty, that a lapse from virtue in the past, however distant that past and however sincere the expiation, counted against the individual concerned.[1] In this, the visitors had some support in current sentiment.[2] Nevertheless, to add all ancient, recent and present delinquencies into a single consolidated total is to give a wholly misleading impression.

This long argument on a distasteful subject has not been conducted with a view to exonerating the religious. Sufficient evidence has indeed been provided in other chapters to show that the monasteries of England, taken as a whole, were far from fervent, and the experience of seventeen hundred years has shown clearly enough that where there is no fervour there can be no security. It seemed necessary, however, to come to close quarters with the *Comperta*, however inadequately, and to discover whether the impression of utter depravity was justified.

Besides criticism based upon the method of presentation of the data, the *Comperta* can be controlled, to some extent at least, by other documents and in particular by contemporary visitations and by the reports of the commissioners for the suppression. These last, though long recognized as existing, have never been methodically exploited. They lay unnoticed among the Augmentations documents until a bundle of them was examined almost simultaneously by James Gairdner and Dom Gasquet. The latter was the first historian to use them, which he did without great emphasis. Gairdner contented himself with remarking that 'the country gentlemen who sat on the commission somehow came to a very different conclusion from that of Drs Layton and Legh'.[3] Some years later, Gasquet turned

---

1 Mr G. W. O. Woodward has noted in his thesis (*v. infra*, p. 299 n. 2) that two Yorkshire nuns accused of becoming mothers were aged 70 and 49 and were declared as of good name and living by the Suppression Commissioners.

2 Thus, e.g. in the affair of the Wilton election of 1528, alleged misconduct in her youth was brought up against the elderly prioress.   3 *LP*, x, introd. p. xlvi.

up a further series of reports which he summarized in an article in 1894,[1] but as he made no attempt to display this new evidence in subsequent editions of his first book it made little impact. More recently, individual scholars have found and used other reports of the commissioners, especially for a group of Yorkshire houses,[2] and doubtless others await discovery. It may be well, therefore, to set out a general picture of all this evidence, but before doing so, a word of introduction may be allowed. Gairdner, as noted above, made a reference to the 'country gentlemen', and the phrase has been taken up by several subsequent writers, and in particular by Baskerville, with the implication that these reports were the work of local gentry with no official connections, who might therefore be supposed to be more tolerant, less inquisitorial and more open to the influence of personal relationships than Cromwell's visitors.[3] Actually, as Gasquet noted quite correctly, though without emphasis, the commission for each county was by the terms of its appointment to be composed of an auditor, a receiver, and a clerk of the register of the last visitation (i.e. that of the tenth commissioners of 1535), all of whom would have been Augmentations men or their friends, assisted by three other 'discreet persons'. From such lists of commissioners as are available, it does not seem clear that the former clerk of the register was always available, and sometimes more than three local gentlemen were appointed, but on the other hand the quorum of the commission (to judge from the terms of appointment in Yorkshire) consisted of the auditor, the receiver, and any third party, and in fact many of the visits were made by three commissioners only.[4] Moreover, if the names are examined, the commissions will be found to contain several gentlemen with very close relations with Cromwell or with the court, in whose interests, indeed, they were employed. There is no reason, therefore, to consider these commissioners as wholly regional or 'unofficial' in their sympathies. All that can be said is that their number, and the known standing of some at least among them, make it unlikely that they would as a body show the inquisitorial bias of Layton or Legh.

The force of their testimony is cumulative, and is derived from its ubiquity and unanimity. There are at present available full reports on some seventy religious houses, together with a few summary notes which cannot be used for statistical purposes. They cover large parts of York-

---

1 *DubR*, CXIV, 245–77. After discovering and printing this, Gasquet made no attempt to use the evidence in the many subsequent editions of *Henry VIII and the English Monasteries*, contenting himself with a casual allusion (without references) in a footnote.

2 *Miscellanea*, III, ed. J. S. Purvis (YARS, LXXX); *Yorkshire Monastic Suppression Papers*, ed. J. W. Clay (YARS, XLVIII); *The Benedictines and Cistercians in Yorkshire in the Sixteenth Century*, a doctoral thesis at Trinity College, Dublin, 1955, by G. W. O. Woodward. I am greatly indebted to Mr Woodward for allowing me to use this.

3 Baskerville, *EM*, 145: 'The leading spirits in [the commissions] were not lawyers but country gentlemen, with a wide and tolerant outlook on life, and an extensive knowledge of the internal affairs of the monastery...they gave as a rule a sort of general certificate of good character.'

4 Clay, *Yorkshire Suppression Papers*, 21–2 (= *LP*, X, 721 (5)). Lists of the commissioners, private and professional, will be found in Appendix VII, *infra*, pp. 478–9.

shire, Leicestershire, Warwickshire, Rutland, Norfolk, Sussex, Hampshire and Wiltshire, and a few houses in Huntingdonshire and Gloucestershire.[1] The commissioners were asked to report on the good fame of the house, to note the number who wished to remain in religion and to declare, besides the actual financial state of the house, the general state of its buildings. It may be said without hesitation that in all districts concerned the commissioners, both in their reports and their correspondence with Cromwell, are more favourable to the religious than were the royal visitors. Indeed, if one certain conclusion can be drawn from their words, it is that neither the regional gentry nor the immediate neighbours had any animus at all against the lesser houses. The commissioners do indeed give a bad character to certain houses and to a few individuals, and wherever this can be checked it is seen to be deserved, but the houses so stigmatized are very few indeed. Similarly, their total of those desiring release from their vows is far smaller than that of the visitors, and when it is checked against pension lists is seen to be the more reliable, though doubtless in some cases offenders and young religious had already been dismissed by the visitors. Elsewhere in this volume a list is given of some of the cases when visitors and commissioners disagree most sharply, but a few of the most noteworthy may be mentioned also here.[2] Thus at the Cistercian abbey of Garendon, Layton and Legh report five addicted to 'sodomy', one of them with ten boys, and note that three seek release from their vows. The commissioners state that all are 'of good conversation, and God's service well maintained; all desire to continue in their religion or be assigned to some other house'. In the event, Garendon was allowed to continue. At Gracedieu, a priory of Austin canonesses, the visitors charged two nuns with incontinence and of having borne children; the commissioners note that they are 'fifteen with the prioress, of good and virtuous conversation and living; all desire to continue their religon there and none to have capacities'. The convent was in fact reprieved.[3] At Pentney (Norfolk) Ap Rice found the prior guilty of sin with the prioress (?abbess) of Marham, basing the accusation on the lady's assertion; five other canons were guilty in one way or another. The commissioners found the priory 'of very honest name', while castigating Marham as 'of slanderous report'. Shortly after we find Cromwell writing to the prior of Pentney suggesting the possibility of a reprieve, at a price, and reprieved Pentney duly was.[4] Layton's ribald letter concerning the prior of Maiden Bradley has often been cited; it has not been noted that the commissioners found the canons 'of honest conversation; church and mansion in good reparacion, newly repayred and amendyd'.[5] At Handale and Yedingham

---

1 They are summarized in *LP*, x, 1191 (Leics, Warws, Hunts, Rutland and Lancs) and xi, App. 2 (Sussex).
2 References will be found in Appendix VIII, *infra*, pp. 480–2.
3 *LP*, xi, 385 (23) (8 August 1536).   4 *Ibid.* x, 563; xi, 518.
5 The prior in 26 Henry VIII (April 1534–5), Richard Jennings, became rector of Shipton Moyne (Glos), where he died in 1553 (*Monasticon*, vi, ii, 643; cf. *VCH, Wilts*, iii, 300–1).

(Yorks) the visitors noted that Alice Brampton and Agnes Butt had each given birth to a child. The commissioners reported all as 'of good living', and had occasion to note that the two ladies were aged respectively seventy and forty-nine.[1]

Occasionally, as in Yorkshire and Sussex, an almost contemporary visitation provides a check. Archbishop Edward Lee visited some of the houses in his diocese in the autumn of 1534, a little over a year before the royal visitors arrived. At St Mary's, York, he challenged the abbot with reports of compromising relations with a woman (which the abbot denied), but had no further grave charges to make.[2] Layton, saying nothing of the abbot, found seven monks guilty of 'sodomy', including one specific case of unnatural vice. At the nunneries of Nunappleton, Sinningthwaite and Nunburnholme the episcopal visitation found none but routine faults. Layton accused two at each house of bearing children. It is difficult to avoid supposing that at all these houses, as at Handale and Yedingham above, the fault, if fault there was, dated from the distant past, perhaps even from the secular career of the parties. At Boxgrove (Sussex) Layton remarked airily that the prior had only two mistresses and that his monks were of the same pattern. Visitations in 1524 and 1527 disclosed no grave irregularity and the commissioners in 1536 reported that none of the community was incontinent.[3] At Shulbrede (Sussex) Layton wrote that the prior had seven mistresses and his monks four or five each. The visitations in 1524 and 1527 reported that all was well, and the commissioners in 1536 noted no case of incontinence.[4] At Denney, in November 1535, Legh wrote that half a dozen of the nuns came to him with tears in their eyes begging to be dismissed. It may have been so, for Denney had a large community, but the abbey pleaded for, and obtained, a reprieve, and when it finally fell the abbess retired to her home at Coughton with two of her sisters and followed the religious horarium till her death.[5] Perhaps the strangest case of all is that of Chertsey. The abbey had been duly visited in 1501, when all was reported to be well, and in 1535 Gardiner of Winchester and Sir William Fitzwilliam, appointed royal visitors by one of the commissions that were soon superseded by the inner group of Cromwell's henchmen, gave a good report again, apparently in midsummer, 1535. Within a few weeks, however, Legh was there, and sent to Cromwell *comperta* charging seven with illicit relations with women and two (or possibly six) with unnatural vice. Yet in the following summer this remarkable community, due for suppression as a lesser house, was trans-

1 The commissioners in 1536 were required to give the ages of the nuns. For the details in text, *v.* Woodward, *op. cit.* 135, citing PRO, Suppression Papers, 5/2, fos. 1, 76.
2 For Lee's visitation, *v. supra* and an unsigned article with documents 'Archbishop Lee's Visitations, 1534–5', in *YAJ*, xvi.
3 *LP*, ix, (1535), 509: 'Prior habet tantum duas...ejus monachi omnes sunt eiusdem farinae.' Cf. *Register Shirborn*, ii (Ep. 1/1/4, 94 *b* and 98 *b*).
4 *LP*, ix (1535), 533 (*Reg. Shirborn*, ii, 92 *a*, 101 *a*).
5 *Ibid.* 708. Denney was granted letters patent 17 August 1536 (*LP*, xi, 385 (25)). For Elizabeth Throckmorton, *v. VCH, Cambs*, ii, 301–2, and *Warwicks*, iii, 78.

ferred to Bisham to man the king's new abbey, and the abbot was duly mitred by Henry himself.[1]

Besides giving a religious house favourable mention in their official returns, the commissioners frequently pause to allot praise of commendation, or to record that the religious have a good name for hospitality or charity. As we have already seen, in Yorkshire, Leicestershire and Warwickshire they occasionally put forward very strong recommendations for respiting a house. In the southern and eastern counties the commissioners do not go so far as this, but their commendation of a monastery can have no other motive than a desire to see it continue.

It is not easy to pronounce upon the relative reliability of these two copious and in many respects contradictory bodies of evidence. Certainly both should be examined with care by all who wish to come to a personal decision on the comparatively narrow issue as to whether the picture given to contemporaries by the royal visitors was in its main lines a fair and true one. If a personal opinion may be allowed, the present writer confesses that for many years he was persuaded that the reports of Layton and Legh were in substance justified, and that the decay which episcopal visitors had long been deploring and exposing had spread at last to almost every member of the monastic body. When, however, he came to consider the commissioners' reports in the mass, together with other contemporary evidence, he could not banish the impression that another picture was appearing, and one not wholly compatible with the first. This incompatibility cannot fully be resolved by distinguishing, with Baskerville, between the realist, efficient, worldly visitor and the tolerant, kindly country gentleman with his local associations. The opposition is rather between four or five visitors and numerous groups of commissioners. Perhaps the following conclusions emerge from the evidence.

First, it would seem clear that there was no animus against the religious on the part either of the local gentry or of the monks' neighbours. Their preference would probably have been for the continued existence of most of the monasteries and nunneries as useful and harmless elements of local activity. That many of the same men were ready, two or three years later, to apply for a grant of what was heretofore monastic property is no proof that they had hitherto been opposed to the monastic way of living or convinced of the corruption of its practitioners. Next, events seem to show that Cromwell's drive against the monasteries, though implemented with great efficiency in all its practical stages, was not integrated at every level into the official programme. Every indication, for example, goes to show that the Augmentations men of 1536 went about their enquiries without carrying with them—perhaps wholly ignorant of—the catalogue of vice compiled by the visitors. Thirdly, whatever may be the precise degree of truth in the statistics of the *Compendium Compertorum*, they cannot be accepted as reliable evidence of what at first they seem to assert, viz. the

1 For Chertsey, v. *LP*, XII (1537, ii), 220, 1311, no. 22.

universal depravity of more than half the religious houses. To an extent that cannot now be ascertained, but which is certainly significant and perhaps preponderant, the charges of sexual immorality are based on unproved charges and on a system of reckoning that makes no distinction between present and past culpability. Moreover, when Layton is concerned, the term 'sodomy' need mean no more than confession of solitary vice, which no visitor had a right to elicit or to publish. In brief, the conflict of evidence leaves us without a clear, simple and overwhelming proof of the general depravity of the monasteries, and we are left to make our final judgment after evidence of every kind has been reviewed and assessed. It may well be an adverse one, but we cannot in justice glance at the *comperta* and exclaim: 'What need have we of further evidence?'

CHAPTER XXIV

THE DISSOLUTION OF THE LESSER HOUSES

In the Act of Suppression as it was passed the preamble made mention of the corruption prevailing in communities less than a dozen strong, but the enacting clause adopted as a yardstick for good and evil the sum of £200 net income. The number twelve had been for centuries the traditional number of a perfect community, with the abbot as thirteenth; the Cistercians had given statutory force to it by making it the essential number for a new foundation, and the papal bull of 1528 to Wolsey had specified that the houses suppressed by him should contain less than twelve inmates.[1] The sum of £200 may have been the notional dower for a community of thirteen, but it was more probably taken as a convenient round figure which would include a large number of houses, and the number twelve does not appear in the body of the act. In 1536 the two criteria were far from coincident: thus of the thirty-five Yorkshire houses seventeen had less than twelve inmates, but twenty-four had less than £200 of income. It was further enacted that those religious who might elect to persevere in their vocation were to be allotted to such of the greater monasteries as were observant; the rest could be dismissed with a dispensation and a small gratuity.[2] The act reserved to the king the right of staying the suppression of any house he might choose to except from the list. Apologists of the monks have not failed to emphasize the futility of attempting to enclose spiritual worth within an income-bracket, and they have noted, truly enough, that the evidence of visitations, royal and episcopal, by no means bears out the suggestion that the larger monasteries were always, or even commonly, the more fervent. Yet such observations, true as they may be, do no more than corroborate what is already certain, that the preamble is mere propaganda, put together somewhat more carelessly than was Cromwell's wont. Any reformer would have begun by doing away with the houses that were only nominally conventual, but Cromwell needed above all some cash to show for everyone's pains, and the dividing line was fixed at £200 with this end in view. The figure of the income was to be the net figure of the *Valor ecclesiasticus*, and the aggregate value of all the houses in the 1535 list under the value of £200 amounted to about £19,000, or considerably less than a fifth of the whole.[3]

1 *V. supra*, p. 163.

2 The act has often been cited as asserting that the greater monasteries were as a class above reproach; in fact it does no more than authorize transference to 'divers great monasteries...wherein, thanks be to God, religion is right well kept and observed'.

3 Estimates differ widely, from the £32,000 of Stowe, adopted by Gasquet, Fisher and Constant, to the £18,000 of Hughes, *Reformation*, I, 322; the latter figure is apparently dependent upon the individual incomes as given in the (not absolutely comprehensive) list in Savine's appendix. The lower total is certainly nearer the mark, but in fact the aggregate

No time was lost in implementing the act. On 24 April instructions were issued under the king's hand to a commission in each county, bidding them repair to each house and there put superior and officials on oath to answer a questionnaire specifying the number of religious, their 'conversation' (that is, their moral repute) and the nature of their choice between going to another house of the order or 'taking capacities', that is, accepting dispensation from their vows of poverty and obedience. They were also to state the number of servants and dependants, the value of the lead and bells, the amount of valuables, stores and stock, and the debts owing by or to the religious. Further, they were to prepare a fresh assessment of the revenues, estimating the value of the demesne and woodlands. Having done this, they were to instruct the superior to conduct the routine administration of the property till he had heard the king's pleasure. They were then to send in their report to the Court of Augmentations.[1]

These instructions specified that the commissions were to be composed of an auditor, a receiver and a clerk of the registry of the last visitation (that is, of the commissioners of the tenth) together with three other discreet persons. These last, as the names show, were usually gentlemen of standing in the neighbourhood; the commission therefore consisted of an equal number of these latter and of 'Augmentations men'.[2] When a quorum was specified, the ratio was one of two 'professionals' to one 'amateur', and the detailed evidence available for Yorkshire shows that in that county, at least, the representatives of the government, several of whom had served previously as assistants to Legh and Layton as well as commissioners of the tenth, were the effective agents of this third enquiry, whatever the nominal position of the 'gentlemen' may have been.[3] We should, however, be on our guard against transferring classifications of to-day or yesterday to Tudor times. The majority of the 'Augmentations men' were in fact members of the class of local gentry who had found a career in the rapidly expanding bureaucracy of Wolsey and Cromwell. Only the lawyers, great and small, were in the modern sense of the word

income of the lesser houses has little significance, for many of them were reprieved, while those marked for destruction did not by any means all fall in 1536, and before the last of them went other plums were coming in by way of surrender and attainder. The significant figure is the yearly income of the Court of Augmentations.

1 *LP*, x (1536), 721. It is not clear why these commissioners were asked to report on the morals of the religious, as the houses were already forfeit and there was no question of pension. If it was intended to guarantee that only respectable persons obtained a capacity it must be said that the commissioners made no attempt to refuse applicants of evil repute. If the government wished for some confirmation of the reasons for suppression that had been given, the commissioners failed to provide it. It may be noted that G. Constant, *The Reformation in England*, I, 169 n. 143, confuses this commission with that of 1535 which established the *Valor Ecclesiasticus*.

2 For the names of the commissioners responsible for the reports, *v. infra*, Appendix VII, pp. 478–9.

3 Cf. Woodward, *The Benedictines and Cistercians in Yorkshire*, 238–9. Of the five 'gentlemen' commissioners for Yorkshire four had served on the commission of the tenth. Most of the suppression work was done by two Augmentations men and one (varying from place to place) gentleman.

'government servants'. While, therefore, it is well to avoid the mistake, originating with Gairdner and Gasquet, of opposing the 'country gentlemen' of 1536 to the 'government agents' of 1535, we should also bear in mind that many of the country gentlemen were also in government employment when we come to assess the value of their testimony.

The reports of several of these commissions survive, and most of them have been printed in greater or less detail.[1] They cover in all some eighty houses from eleven counties, ranging from Lancashire and Yorkshire to Hampshire and Sussex, and from Norfolk to Warwickshire and Gloucestershire, thus giving a fair cross-section of the country as a whole. They fall for our purpose into half a dozen groups, differing somewhat both in the form of their presentation and in the amount of information given. The fullest, as well as the longest, lists are those of the commissioners for the midland counties of Leicester, Rutland, Warwick and Huntingdon; those for Norfolk; and those for Hampshire, Wiltshire and Gloucestershire. All these give ample information in almost every case in answer to their headings of enquiry. For Sussex the answers are much more concise, and for the handful of Lancashire houses no personal details are included. For Yorkshire the information is full, but differs in the form of presentation and is only partially available in print.[2] The returns for the Midlands, Norfolk and Yorkshire and the western counties are particularly interesting, for they include a number of houses that figure in the letters and *comperta* of Legh, Layton and Ap Rice. Even in these formal documents the individuality of the commissioners appears. Thus the papers covering Warwickshire, Leicestershire and Rutland, for which the government agents George Gyfford and Robert Burgoyne were largely responsible, go into considerable detail over the buildings, besides going out of their way to praise certain communities and to give personal details about individual religious. The groups differ also in nomenclature and arrangement, particularly in the enumeration of servants and dependants. Though the existence of these lists has long been common knowledge, and though several of them have been worked over by research students, they have never been reviewed as a whole by historians of the Dissolution, and it will therefore not be out of place to consider them more closely. A be-

---

1 The reports of the commissioners, entitled 'Certyficate' or (as with Sussex) 'brief Certificat' or (in the case of the Lancashire abstract) 'the Breviate of the Breefe Certyffycate', are in the following documents: *Leicestershire, Rutland and Warwickshire*: PRO, E. 36/154/ 48–63; *Huntingdonshire*: BM, Cott. Cleo. E. IV, fos. 280–4ᵛ; *Norfolk*: PRO, S.C. 12/33/29; *Sussex*: PRO, S.P. 5/3/128; *Hampshire, Wiltshire and Gloucestershire*: PRO, S.C. 12/33/27; *Lancashire*: BM, Cott. Cleo. E. IV, 288. A summary is given of all save the Hants, Wilts, and Glos documents in *LP*, X, 1191 and XI, App. 2. The remainder, discovered by Gasquet, were printed by him, with a few omissions and errors, in an article with a somewhat misleading title, 'Overlooked testimonies to the character of the English monasteries on the eve of their suppression', in *DubR*, CXIV, 245–77.

2 For Yorkshire I have used J. W. Clay, *Yorkshire Monasteries Suppression Papers* (YARS, XLVIII), J. S. Purvis, 'A selection of monastic rentals and Dissolution papers' in *Miscellanea*, III (YARS, LXXX), and above all the thesis by Mr G. W. O. Woodward, *The Benedictines and Cistercians in Yorkshire in the Sixteenth Century* (1955).

ginning will be made with the personal and religious data of their evidence, after which some economic points may be considered.

The commissioners were asked, after having stated 'the clere yerly value of their laste valuacion [i.e. for the tenth in 1535] with the encrease new surveyed', to give 'the number of religious persones with their lyff & conversacon...& how many wyll have capacyties'.

As for numbers, out of the eighty houses only sixteen (equally distributed between men and women) held a community of twelve or more. No doubt by the spring of 1536 the religious population had reached its nadir, what with dismissals and defections, and it is interesting to note that a contemporary (perhaps a clerk in Cromwell's office) entered the difference in numbers at six Norfolk houses between 1535 and 1536, and that the total fall is from thirty-eight to seventeen.[1] At the houses not noted we may perhaps assume little or no change, but we should probably be justified in adding throughout one or two to every ten to arrive at what may be called the peace-time figure; even so barely a quarter of this numerous group of houses would have contained a community large enough to lead a dignified liturgical and domestic life.

As to the next part of the question, all the commissioners who answer it are in striking agreement. Without exception, and from whatever part of the country they hail, the commissioners give a far more pleasing impression of the life of these small monasteries than do the visitors of the previous autumn and winter. To four houses only do they give a downright bad name; all these are in Norfolk: Thetford is 'of slendre reporte', and indeed could scarcely have been otherwise, for five canons had decamped under a cloud and only one was left to ask for his capacity; of Wendling it is said 'ther name is not good'; Weybourne contained only '2 prysts of slaunderous name as yt ys sayde'; and Marham, a nunnery whence six had departed, is 'of slaunderous repute'.[2] Of all the rest the verdict 'all of good name' is repeated with verbal variations and inflexions of warmth save for Owston in Leicestershire, where 'relygion was not verry duely kepte for lake of nomber [six besides the abbot] & for because one of them is a verry aged man & a nother not havyng his wytt verry well but fantastycall & more than halffe ffrantyke'.[3] Often detailed commendation is added. Thus at Ulverscroft we hear that the prior 'is a wyse discrete man' and his canons 'good vertuous religious & of good qualities as writters ymbroderers & paynters & lyvyng & desireth the kynghis highnes to establysshe them ther yff it may stond with his graceyous pleasur'.[4] At the Benedictine house of Langley 'the prioress who is of

---

1 Gasquet, *art. cit.*, did not print these notes.
2 PRO, S.C. 12/33/29, M. 3, 4, 6, 7. It should be added that several of the Sussex priories were clearly in a bad way, but no verbal report on their character is given beyond the numbers of those alleged to be incontinent.   3 PRO, E. 36/154/49.
4 *Ibid.* 51 (cf. Wright, *SL*, lxii). Gairdner in printing this, reads 'lymnyng' for 'lyvyng', but the latter is the correct reading; 'as...paynters' is treated as a parenthesis. The canons of Ulverscroft clearly lived a full life, for a witness in a lawsuit some decades later remembered

great age and impotent, [is] of good & vertuous lyvyng & conversacon & so be her systers weroff one is sister to sir Richard Saccheuerell late decessed almost lxxx yeres, one other is in regarde a fole'.[1] At Polesworth the nuns '& one ancres of a very religious sorte and lyuyng bryng up uthers in vertue verie excellent, oon of theym beyng apon the poynt of a c yeres olde'.[2] Similarly, at St Mary's at Winchester, 'thole numbre in their ordre bene religious and in lyvynge vertuous'.[3] Sometimes the commissioners add a few words of special commendation. Thus the abbey of Netley 'beinge of large buyldinge scituate vopon the ryuage of the sees' is 'to the kings subgietts & straungiers trauelinge the same sees greate releef & comforte';[4] similarly Quarr, beside the waters of the Solent in the Isle of Wight, is 'by reaporte great refuge & comforte to all thinhabitants of the same yle and to estraungiers traueillinge the seid sees'.[5] Lacock, a 'large buyldinge sett in a towne', is 'to the same and all other adioynynge by common reaporte a greate releef',[6] as is also in similar phrase the Cistercian Stanley, while at the nunnery of St Mary's, Winchester, there is 'greate releef dayly ministred vnto the inhabitants of the seid citye'.[7] Ulverscroft 'standith in a wildernesse in the fforreste off Charnewood & refressith many pore people & waye faryng people'.[8]

Nor were the commissioners content with reporting only. On 12 May the Northamptonshire group wrote on behalf of Catesby nunnery, which they had 'founde in verry perfett order, the priores a sure, wyse, discrete and very religyous women, with ix nunnys ... as relygious and devote and with as good obedyencye as we have in tyme past seen or belyke shall see'; the nuns do much 'to the releff of the kynges people, and his graces pore subjectes their lykewyse mooche relewed'. A week later they write in similar strain of St James's abbey at Northampton, which they alleged with justice to have been undervalued by the earlier commissioners; the many poor of Northampton are greatly relieved by the canons, who have a good report through the whole town.[9] Ten days later the Yorkshire commissioners were writing of the Hull Charterhouse that the monks were 'well-favoured and commended by the honest men of Hull and others for their good living and great hospitality'.[10] This was not the kind of thing that the king's grace wanted, and when the letters from Northampton were shown him he took it amiss, saying that the writers had been bribed. Gyfford and his colleagues, however, not only stood their ground, but

them as great hunters; cf. Nicholls, *History of Leicestershire*, III, 1091. Baskerville's remark: 'They were not going to spend their time knitting when they could ride to hounds', is characteristically witty and misleading. He quotes Gyfford's letter (failing to note his report, which corroborates it) and omits to record that Ulverscroft was reprieved as a result of the commissioners' appeal (*EM*, 43–4).

1 PRO, E. 36/154/54.   2 *Ibid.* 56.   3 PRO, S.C. 12/33/27, M. 1.
4 *Ibid.*   5 *Ibid.*   6 *Ibid.* M. 2.
7 *Ibid.* M. 1.   8 PRO, E. 36/154/51.
9 *LP*, x, 858 (Catesby), 916–17 (Northampton). The reports of the commissioners for Northamptonshire seem to be missing.
10 *Ibid.* 980.

went on to a warm commendation of Ulverscroft, taking God to witness the truth of their words.[1] At the end of July the Warwickshire commissioners were pleading for Polesworth, begging Cromwell to speak to the king on behalf of the abbey, 'ffor, as we thinke, ye shall not speke in the preferment of a better nonnery nor of better women'.[2]

The commissioners, as already remarked, were instructed also to record the numbers of those who desired to abandon the religious state if or when their house should be suppressed. They do in fact give figures for all the houses for which the complete replies exist, and it might be supposed that this would give unimpeachable evidence as to the percentage of the religious in a fair-sized fraction of the monasteries who had preserved a sense of vocation or duty through all the many forebodings and alarums and defections of the past eighteen months. In fact, however, quite apart from the uncertainties of calculation and interpretation which beset all such attempts to elicit precise figures from casual records, there are a number of factors of uncertain value which render all conclusions to some degree perilous. In the first place, we have to remember that the religious had been harassed continually by government agents for more than a year, and that in the visitation of the autumn of 1535 most communities had lost a number of their members through dismissal or dispensation. How large a proportion this amounted to we have no accurate means of knowing; almost our only information is that given for eight Norfolk houses, where we are told that an aggregate of sixty-nine religious had decreased to thirty-two between 1535 and 1536.[3] It is not at all certain that at other houses a comparable decrease had taken place, but even if it had not, an overall loss of some 10 per cent would have been incurred by the lesser houses of the county, and it would be reasonable to suppose that a similar decrease had taken place elsewhere. Many, at least, of those who went were by definition the least settled and the least satisfactory members of the community, and we should therefore bear in mind that the commissioners of 1536 had to deal with houses which had already lost some of their weakest members. On the other hand we must remember that, since the act presupposed that suppression would take place, and as, according to the current convention, the superior (and he or she alone) was to be given a fixed pension, the possibility of the superior wishing to be transferred to another house was not allowed for, and thus it is only when the whole house petitioned for continuance that we can be sure of the disposition of the head. Doubtless in fact the great majority of priors and prioresses wished for a continuance of things as they were, and the figures that follow, in many (but not all) of which the superiors are omitted, should therefore show a slightly larger percentage of those who did not wish for a change of state.

1 *Ibid.* 1166. 2 *Ibid.* XI, 176.
3 The houses are Horsham, Buckenham, Thetford (monks), Pentney, Coxford, Thetford (nuns), Markham and Crabhouse.

One further general observation is perhaps permissible. Those who declared their desire to persevere in the religious life in 1536 must have felt a real sense of contentment with their vocation. They were the hard core of the community. Not only had they survived the difficulties of the recent past, but they had remained unshaken by the forebodings for the future that must have been rife. Beyond this, they were willing if necessary to leave their old homes to pursue their vocation elsewhere. A historian of the Dissolution has described their predicament vividly, if somewhat flippantly.[1] It was in all conscience a very real sacrifice, in those days of narrow local associations, for a monk who had lived all his life among his friends at a Leicestershire house, let us say, to go forth to a strange place in another county, where he might meet strange ways and sour glances.

According to the reports of the commissioners, including the papers available for Yorkshire, out of a total of 289 men and 265 women the numbers of those who desired 'capacities' or 'release', or what would now be called a dispensation from the vows of poverty and obedience (for the vow of chastity remained for the men in holy orders, and was soon to be reasserted by law in the case of the women) amounted to 117 and twenty-eight respectively, or about 40·5 and 10·5 per cent of the totals. Here, however, it is doubtful whether overall figures and percentages are of any great significance for the men, as there is a notable difference of proportion between the districts and between one religious order and another. Thus in the midland counties only twenty-seven men out of 124 (or about 21·8 per cent wished for capacities, whereas in Hants, Wilts and Gloucestershire the figures are twenty-eight out of eighty-six (32·6 per cent), in Norfolk thirty-one out of forty-three (72 per cent) and in Sussex no less than thirty-eight out of forty-one (93 per cent). This disparity can in part be easily accounted for. The Norfolk and Sussex houses were with few exceptions small houses of Austin canons. All indications go to show that East Anglia, Kent and Sussex were the least conservative and perhaps also the least devout regions of England, and it is certain that the small Austin houses were as a class the least observant of all the religious houses. In the Midlands and Wessex there was something of a better spirit in the monasteries; the figures also show the influence of several medium-sized Cistercian abbeys. Though the numbers of monks concerned is too small to allow any suggestion for a national average, the percentage (8·6 per cent) of the white monks who wished to leave is remarkably small[2] when compared with that of the Austin canons (48·5 per cent), while the Carthusians were unanimous for remaining. In the Sussex figures, the extremely low

---

1 Baskerville, *EM*, 149, suggests as a parallel the suppression of 'some of the smaller and more obscure colleges at Oxford and Cambridge' with the prospect for the Fellows of a choice between migration to a large and distinguished college and the abandonment of the academic profession. He thus, as so often, veils the personal dilemma and the spiritual issue in a sally and a laugh.

2 At Garendon, Stonely and Stanley the whole community opted for remaining; at Netley one, and at Quarr two wished to depart.

proportion of those electing to remain in the religious life rouses a suspicion that the local commissioners used a certain amount of persuasion to effect something like a clean sweep, but as their comments have not been preserved this must remain no more than a conjecture.

As for the nuns, the picture is notably different. Of the small total of thirty-five midland and south-country nuns who desired release from the religious life, no less than thirty-four came from eight small houses having a total population of forty-five; from the others, nine in number, with a population of 108, only one wished for release. From York-shire figures still more striking are available. Out of 108 nuns, all of them from small or very small houses, only one wished for a dispensation.[1] Thus the total figures from all the returns show only thirty-six out of 261, or about 14 per cent, desiring release, and this figure would be reduced almost to nil if the eight decayed and minuscule houses were left out of the reckoning. Evidence such as this would seem to be conclusive. Save for a relatively few small and unhappy families, the religious women of England desired to spend and end their lives in the monasteries where they had taken their vows. There is indeed nothing surprising in this; all spiritual motives apart, one would not expect a group of women, few of them young, to be anxious to break up their whole way of life and go forth into the unknown, to spend thirty years, perhaps, as begrudged pensioners with relatives. In the similar circumstances of the French Revolution, the women religious stood apart from the men in almost exactly the same way. Nevertheless, when we recall the readiness with which nunneries in many parts of central Europe had recently disbanded themselves, we may think it worth while to mark the contrast in England.

Thus of the lesser houses that were in the event suppressed, something in the neighbourhood of one-half of the religious went forth to become secular priests. This, it must be remembered, was the only alternative for those who had survived the purge of the royal visitors. They could not return to lay life, and the canon of West Dereham who, according to the royal visitor, 'wished with all his heart that all might be licensed...to resort to the remedy of marriage', and moreover expressed a hope 'that for this purpose his Royal Majesty had been divinely sent to earth', was doomed, at least for a time, to disappointment.[2]

In addition to the personal statistics they provide, the returns of 1536 yield a considerable amount of information regarding the economic condi-tion of the monasteries. The articles of instruction to the commissioners required them in the first place to state the net annual income of the house as estimated both by the commissioners for the tenth and by themselves. As has been noted when we were considering the figures of the *Valor*, it was expected by the government that the second valuation would show an increase in revenue over the first, if for no other reason than that the

---

1 The Yorkshire figures are from Woodward, 245–7.
2 *LP*, x, 1191; in full in Coulton, *Five Centuries of Religion*, IV, 697.

land held as demesne had in the previous survey been assessed at a conventional and conservative figure, whereas it was now to be assessed at its probable market value in a period of rising prices and rents. To mark this, the commissioners often note the new value of the demesne before indicating the result of other adjustments affecting the total, though unfortunately they do not in every case give a complete break-down of this new total. On the whole, and in every separate district, the new valuation of the income shows a marked increase over the old, but the differences between house and house, and district and district, are so great that the average obtained is purely statistical, showing a mean between extremes rather than a figure of common occurrence. The overall picture may be seen from the following table, where the first figure is that of the commissioners of the tenth, the second that of the suppression commissioners, and the third the increase expressed as a percentage:

	£	£	%
Leics and Rutland (eight houses)	729	811	11·2
Warwicks (ten houses)	857	1027	19·8
Hunts (three houses)	375	446	18·9
Hants (six houses)	637	795	24·8
Lancs (six houses)	480	657	36·8
Sussex (six houses)	603	619	2·7
Wilts and Glos (ten houses)	1003	1095	9·2
Staffs[1] (ten houses)	1055	1520	44·1
Norfolk (ten houses)	835	879	5·3
Total (sixty-nine houses)	6574	7849	19·4

Besides the revaluation of the demesne, there would seem to have been a fairly strict review of all sources of income, while in the case of the Cistercian abbeys the inclusion of additional granges and in that of Coventry realistic assessment of the urban site made considerable differences. It is not easy to explain the notably larger increases in Lancashire and Staffordshire, but as the latter seems to represent an overall stepping-up of estimates, it seems probable that the differences between the groups reflect different conceptions of their functions on the part of the commissioners.

Besides these statements of revenue, the commissioners were asked to assess the value, first, of the lead, bells, and other parts of the buildings that could be broken up before the sale of the 'mansion'; secondly, of all jewels, ornaments, moneys, stocks and stores; and thirdly, of the woods in the possession of the house. Lastly, they were asked for a list of all the debts owed by the house and of moneys claimed by it. The answers to all these questions differ so widely and irregularly from house to house that no useful conclusion can be drawn, save that the average saleable value of superfluous buildings, movables and stores taken together would seem to

1 The figures for Staffs are taken from F. A. Hibbert, *The Dissolution of the Monasteries*, 92–129.

have been something more than double and less than treble the annual estimated income, and that this average very nearly represented the actual state of affairs at numerous monasteries of very different aggregate wealth.

The valuations of the stock and stores are of considerable interest, and deserve further attention at the hands of an economic historian. On the whole it must be admitted that they do little to strengthen the evidence, drawn from contemporary expressions of opinion and from some precise records, that the religious had long been steadily realizing or consuming their perishable assets in view of an uncertain future. The value of the stock and stores held sometimes nearly equals or even considerably exceeds the annual revenue, and *a fortiori* exceeds the debts of the house. The Cistercians in particular still carried large reserves of stores and animals; the seven Cistercian abbeys for which we have information—Garendon, Stonely, Sawtre, Quarr, Netley, Stanley and Flaxley[1]—are all save the last (which had recently endured a disastrous fire) notably better found in stores, considered in relation to their income, than are the great majority of the other houses. The commissioners were chiefly at work in the late spring and early summer, before the crops of the year had been harvested, but they obtained estimates for the standing corn.[2] In general, as might be expected, the value of the stocks in Cistercian abbeys far exceeds the value of their lead and ornaments, while in the small Austin priories the latter are more valuable than the produce of agriculture.

Next, there is the woodland. This, more than any other asset, varies from house to house according to the natural resources of the locality. More than any other, also, it must have been assessed at a figure little more than notional. Variegated and ill-kept woodland is very difficult to estimate, and there was the additional problem of valuing forests, plantations, spinneys, copses and wildernesses in every stage of growth and showing every degree of care and neglect. The extremely high figures given for Ulverscroft (£745) and Garendon (£650) in Charnwood Forest must have been useful only in arriving at an estimate, for no owner would have been able or willing to realize, even over a period of ten or twenty years, such vast tracts of tangled woodland, much of which consisted of timber maturing in twenty or fifty years time; nor would a purchaser of forests at this price be readily forthcoming.[3]

---

1 In 'stokkes and stores' Quarr had £221, Netley £105 and Stanley £124. Garendon had £337 in goods, cattle and corn. The very detailed surveys of the three Hunts houses show that 'catell'='cattle' not 'chattels', as 'horses, mares, kyne, Bullocks and other Catell' are listed.

2 Often, as at Netley and Stanley, the commissioners make an estimate for 'corne not seuered'; occasionally, as at Stonely (Hunts), stores of grain are specifically mentioned; otherwise, no distinction is made.

3 E.g. Garendon (E. 36/154/52): '998 acres 3 roods whereof in spryngs & woods under 20 yers growe 10½ acres, in woods of 50 yers growe and upward 2 acres 1 rood, & in woods of 100 yeres growe and upward 3 acres growyng in the wast of the said mon. beyng withyn the fforrests of Chervey Wood 536 Acres.'

Lastly, there were the debts owed by and to the religious. Here again there is the widest degree of variation, due in this case more often to human vagaries than to the more impersonal forces of nature or economics. For the fifty-one houses for which figures are available the debts owing are £3025, as against those due of £640, being in the ratio of a little less than 5 : 1, and leaving a burden of debt of £2385 to set against an aggregate income of some £4200. Heavy as this is, it is not overwhelming, especially if we take into account the value of the liquid assets of stock and stores, as also the overlap of routine credit at any given moment. Moreover, the magnitude of the total is offset partly by the fact that a large proportion concerns a relatively few improvident houses,[1] and partly by the probability that even here (and still more with the efficiently run houses) much of the debt is either a reasonable one or a mere book-entry which might well have been written off. Thus, at Garendon, out of a debt of £142, no less than £100 represented a claim 'by the executors of one Thomas Stoks late of London by an obligacion under the covent seale dated Ao.xxv. Rs.H.Sexti' (i.e. 1447);[2] at Coventry £60 out of the £90 debt was owing to the king for first-fruits,[3] while at Lilleshall £9. 10s. out of £26 was a tailor's bill for the canons' habits.[4] Elsewhere, when details are available, any heavy debts are often in large individual sums to local gentry or clergy.[5] It is possible that many of them were loans which were 'serviced' by some agreed consideration such as a stewardship or tenancy, while some may very well have been practically bank-deposits or loans made without any expectation of immediate returns. One noteworthy fact may be mentioned. In several returns it is specified that there is no minted money among the assets, and records of the presence of cash are very few. It is true that we are concerned only with small houses, where some of the payments and wages may have been partly in kind, but it is difficult to believe that fair-sized houses were entirely without the small cash necessary for market purchases and for the innumerable 'rewards' expected by functionaries and familiars of every kind.[6]

The commissioners often give interesting details of the conditions of the buildings. Thus at Owston they note that 'the howse [is] a proper estatly and cleane howse well buylded & moch of yt new made with ffreston not fully fynneshed in good repayere & mete for a more company then there be'; at Ulverscroft 'the house [is] in good repayre & much of yt withyn this iij yeres newe sett upp & buylt'. At Garendon, on the

---

1 Eight houses, all relatively small, have a gross total debt of £1357, or more than half the grand total.
2 E. 36/154/52.   3 Ibid. 60.
4 M. E. Walcott in *Archaeologia*, XLIII, 203.
5 E.g. St Thomas, Stafford, in Walcott, *art. cit.*
6 St Mary of Winchester, almost alone of the houses in the reports, had £15. 13s. 'redy money'. Glastonbury in 1539 had £1100 according to a note by Cromwell in B.M. Titus, B. I, fo. 446, cited in *VCH, Somerset*, II, 96.

other hand, the house is 'greatt, olde and partly ruynous'.[1] At Gracedieu 'the Churche, the Quyer, the Cloysters be fayer & the rest of the house in very good repayer & well mayntayned and kept upp but of no stately buyldyng'. At Maxstoke the place is 'a very stately & goodly house in most parte buylded with hard stone and in good repaire'. At Stonely, however it is 'ruynous & in decaye'.[2] The other commissioners give similar details. At Buckenham (Norfolk) the house is 'newly built & in marvelous good reparacion';[3] at Ivychurch (Wilts) it is 'in very good state, with much new building of stone and brick'; at Flaxley (Glos) the church is 'brent & consumed with fire; the house in ruin & decay; the bells molten with fire & the metal sold for & towards the new building of the said church'.[4] Usually, but not universally, material 'ruine & decay' have their counterparts in spiritual tepidity or worse. Thus at Wendling (Norfolk) the house is 'in decay' and the canons 'not off good name'; at Marham the place is 'in sore decay', and the nuns are 'of slanderous report'; at Weybourne all is 'in decay' and the canons have a 'slanderous name'.[5] On the other hand, at both Easton (Wilts) and St Oswald (Glos) the church is in ruin while the canons are 'of honest conversation';[6] at Hinwood (Warwicks) the house is 'Ruynous & in much decaye', but although the nuns (one of them 'of thage iiij xiiii [= 94] yers & upwards') are 'of good conversacon & lyvyng' the community, with an income of £24, debts of £28, and movables valued only at £1 ('the price of iij litle manuelle bells'), was clearly on its last legs, and in fact it collapsed into the arms of the visitors, who 'theruppon tooke the same & discharged the Nones ymmediately'.[7] On the whole, however, the houses in fair fettle greatly outnumber those in decay. Out of fifty-three houses only thirteen are described in part or whole as 'ruinous' or 'in decay', and eight more as needing serious repair in particular places. The remaining thirty-two are noted as in 'competent', 'convenient', 'good' or 'very good' condition, while four or five excite the admiration of the commissioners. When it is recalled that all these were 'lesser' houses, and some of them having an economic life little above subsistence level, the significance of these statistics will be clear, especially when they are considered in close relation with the figures of debt. In brief, less than a third of the minor houses were in economic straits, and less than a third showed signs of grave neglect or mismanagement, and an examination of the individual cases shows, as might be expected, that as a general rule the two forms of distress were close companions.

The Act of Suppression had contained a clause reserving to the king freedom to permit any houses he might select to continue in being, and in the sequel some seventy or eighty, or nearly one-quarter of the total, did

---

1 E. 36/154/49, 51, 52.   2 *Ibid.* 53, 57, 61.   3 S.C. 12/33/29, m. 2.
4 S.C. 12/33/27, m. 2ᵛ. *Ibid.* m. 3.   5 *Ibid.* 29 m. 6, 4, 7.
6 *Ibid.* 27 m. 2, 3ᵛ.   7 E. 36/154/59.

in fact receive a respite.[1] This has been noted with some surprise by historians and various explanations have been given of this apparent infirmity of purpose in the king or his minister. The explanation that has found most favour, which Burnet, it would seem, was the first to put forward and which Gasquet adopted without reserve, was that Cromwell was willing to accept rich bribes. It is true that most, if not all, of the houses that survived paid heavily for the privilege, and it is true also that some heads of houses, both among those that survived and those that did not, wrote to Cromwell offering to pay handsomely for licence to continue.[2] Nevertheless, the number of survivors is too great to be the result solely of caprice or greed, and the explanation is probably in many cases more simple. The act guaranteed to all those who wished to continue in the religious life a transference elsewhere. In this it followed the model set by Wolsey's suppressions and indeed, with public opinion still uncertain, the bill might well have failed to pass without such a proviso. But in practice the placing of the religious who elected to persevere was soon found to present a graver problem than had been envisaged. It would have meant transferring a thousand or more, including whole communities with their superior, an eventuality not covered by the Act.[3] The pace of the whole proceeding was so swift, and Cromwell had so many pressing affairs claiming his attention (such as the trial of Queen Anne and her associates) that he was perhaps not able, and in any case did not take steps, to choose commissioners for every county who would cajole or bully the religious into taking their capacities. The only alternative, therefore, was to give a respite to houses in sufficient number to ease the problem of transference.

A rapid glance at the monasteries that survived seems to corroborate this view. To begin with, the Carthusians posed the problem in its most

1 Again, there has been disagreement as to the total, partly owing to the previous disagreement as to the total number of lesser houses, partly owing to the inclusion by some writers of Welsh houses, but chiefly owing to a failure to note the existence of the second of the two categories mentioned later, viz. those houses which received their seal back from the Court of Augmentations without any legal security of continued existence. Their number cannot be stated with absolute accuracy until all the Suppression Papers have been studied. Gairdner gives a list in the introduction to each relevant volume of *LP*, but there appear to be several omissions; for the various estimates, *v.* Constant, *The Reformation in England* (Eng. trans.), I, 168, notes 136–7. The figures vary between 52 and 123 (including nunneries); the total given by Hughes, *Reformation*, I, 295, viz. forty-seven, falls far below the mark, owing to the omission of the seventeen Gilbertine houses and some of those reprieved without letters patent.

2 *V.* list in PRO, E. 323/1, pt. 1, m. 2, quoted by Gasquet, *Henry VIII* (1 ed.), App. 1.

3 By the terms of the act the superior alone was given a pension, *ex regia caritate.* As the statute put it (27 Hen. VIII, c. 28, par. xiii, in *Statutes of the Realm*, III, 575): 'His Majesty is pleased and contented of his most excellent charity to provide to every chief head and governor...during their lives such yearly pension or benefices as for their degrees and qualities shall be reasonable and convenient.' For this there was no precedent in Wolsey's suppressions, which had (at least nominally) respected canon law, particularly when this told in favour of the spoiler. The pension to the prior is an instance of the Tudor lawyer's respect for proprietary rights of every kind.

acute form. Only three houses were liable to be suppressed—Hull, Beauvale and Coventry—and at these almost all wished to remain. A charterhouse was so constructed as to be unable to accommodate more than its quota and, as we have seen, Hull and Coventry, at least, were venerated by their neighbours. They were accordingly allowed to continue. Next, at least forty-three nunneries were allowed a respite.[1] This number, more than one-third of the total number of nunneries liable to suppression, was also a far greater quota than that of any order of men. As we have seen, practically all the nuns wished to persevere, and it was therefore necessary to spare enough houses to hold them. This, no doubt, was one of the reasons why the Master of Sempringham was able to secure continuance for his whole order. Of the rest, Cistercians and Premonstratensians had the greatest proportion of survivors, and here again there is evidence that whole communities had elected to persevere. Finally, the Court of Augmentations seems to have decided in several cases to let well alone, when a community was united in its desire to continue and was also well spoken of by the neighbours. It cannot be accidental that Ulverscroft, Garendon and St James, Northampton, survived, in spite of the king's irritation at the praise bestowed upon them.

Cromwell and the Court of Augmentations therefore made a virtue of necessity. The houses were respited and both the Crown and (in many cases) Cromwell himself received a handsome reward. The fee charged was in general in the neighbourhood of the annual value, but in some cases was much larger.[2] In all, more than forty houses received letters-patent of refoundation 'in perpetuity' by the king at different dates, but in addition to these an uncertain number, perhaps more than twenty excluding the Gilbertines, were exempted by word of mouth and did in fact continue in existence for two years and more. These 'unofficial' exemptions were particularly numerous among the nunneries of Yorkshire and were probably a direct consequence of the practical difficulty noted above. In addition, the seventeen Gilbertine houses received a block respite.[3] When no kind of exemption was granted the commissioners returned to dismiss the community, sell the cattle and movables, despatch the plate and jewels to London or to store, and dismantle the buildings or hand them over to the farmer or grantee.

If the year from August 1535 to August 1536 is considered in retrospect it provides what is perhaps the most striking example in the whole reign

---

1 Once more the totals vary, and that of Hughes, *loc. cit.*, viz. twenty-eight, again falls too low. There were at least the number stated in the text, including eleven Gilbertine nunneries.

2 It was usually a round sum in pounds or marks, e.g. £100 or £66. 13s. 4d. Thus in Staffs the following charges were levied on the revised incomes: Croxden, £100 on £157; Hulton, £66. 13s. 4d. on £67; Rocester, £100 on £129; St Thomas, Stafford, £133. 6s. 8d. on £141 (original assessment); cf. Hibbert, *Dissolution of the Monasteries*, 186.

3 Apparently no record of this reprieve exists, but the fact is certain, as we have the dates of the final suppression of the houses. Cf. R. Graham, *St Gilbert of Sempringham*, 174–6; *VCH, Lincs*, II, 186.

of an apparently haphazard, opportunist choice and employment of ways and means, which are nevertheless directed towards a single unchanging end, the realization of all possible sources of wealth for the Crown. The royal visitors had gone forth with their policy and procedure as yet not fully defined, uncertain whether they had come to mend or to end. As they went on their rounds the policy crystallized rapidly into an inquisition aimed at disclosing and presenting in vivid colours all the moral evils of the religious houses. Rapid as was their progress they had not completed their task before their newly won evidence was used to justify the Act of Suppression—but used arbitrarily, and against its own intrinsic force, to discredit only one section of the religious houses. These were condemned as a block, and many of them had actually been allotted to new proprietors when about one-fifth were drawn out of the fire and given a new lease of life, in some cases solemnly, in others more precariously. The whole process, in which a bout of inquisitorial violence was followed by treatment which, materially speaking, was in many ways equitable and even generous, was utterly devoid of any trace of religious or spiritual purpose; solemn obligations were dissolved and sacred places profaned by lay agents of the king, acting on the orders of his lay vice-gerent *in spiritualibus*. Critics have not failed to point out that among the surviving houses and their heads were several who had been selected for particularly unfavourable comment by the visitors a few months previously. A notable absurdity, which in retrospect has even a touch of burlesque, was the erection of an entirely new abbey by Henry, accommodated in the Augustinian house of Bisham, lately suppressed, and nominally endowed with the lands of Chertsey and half a dozen small priories to the value of £700. The community of abbot and fourteen monks was drawn from Chertsey which, if the royal visitor spoke the truth, was a peculiarly unsavoury establishment, and the abbot of that house was placed in charge of 'King Henry's new monastery of the Holy Trinity' and granted the use of the mitre; he and his sons were to pray for the good estate of the king and his late queen, Jane Seymour.[1] Henry, indeed, was also titular founder of another house at even less expense. This was Stixwold, whither Benedictine nuns were translated in 1536 from Stainfield after the first community had been disbanded; they in their turn were displaced to make room for a royal foundation of Premonstratensian canonesses in 1537. The newcomers were charged to pray for the good estate of the king and Queen Jane. The lack of all discrimination in the choice of these communities was matched only by the complete lack of interest on the part of the royal beneficiary when the prayers ceased in 1537 and 1539 respectively, but the mere existence of these two royal foundations would seem to prove conclusively that Henry, at least, had taken no final decision as yet concerning the fate of the larger and wealthier houses that still remained intact.

When the king or the Court of Augmentations had decided that a house

1 *LP*, XII, ii, 1311 (22).

was to fall the commissioners returned to perform the last rites. As they already had full information as to the economic and financial state of the place, and the wishes of its inmates, this function was often fairly brief. Thus the seven Yorkshire nunneries which had been allowed to continue without letters patent were all suppressed, in August 1539, at the rate of one a day. Doubtless, by that time the commissioners were masters of their technique, but even in 1536 the shears, abhorred or not, cut swiftly. Though the religious had for months been prepared for the thread to snap, some of them must long have remembered the day which began with the age-old routine of Lauds and Prime and Mass, and closed as they passed through the well-known gateway, leaving for ever the home where they had thought to abide in life and in death.

CHAPTER XXV

THE NORTHERN RISING

Had no new factor supervened, it is possible that Cromwell would have spent some years in realizing the profits from the smaller monasteries. The suppression of these houses had, however, been in train for less than six months when, with a sudden and ubiquitous upheaval that had almost the character of a seasonal change of nature, the whole of the north of England rose in revolt. This insurrection, so swift alike in its outbreak and in its complete collapse, has only in recent decades attracted the notice it deserves from historians, and even now, as happens with all unsuccessful reactionary causes, its significance has not been wholly laid bare. Unlike any other revolt in the Tudor period, its spearhead was directed by men of high principles and intelligence, entirely without personal ambition and unwilling to use violence save as a last resort, and who were capable of giving a reasoned explanation of their actions. In the words and manifestoes of the leaders of the Pilgrimage of Grace we hear, for the only time in the reign of Henry VIII, the free expression of opinion of a large body of men unmixed with any element of official propaganda and unaffected by considerations of a purely personal or sordid kind. The present pages are not directly concerned with the course of the revolt or its more general aims, but as the suppression of the lesser monasteries was in large part its occasion, and the dissolution of many of the larger ones its immediate consequence, something must be said of the fortunes of the religious during the troubles, and of the hopes that inspired the leaders of the discontented.[1]

Although the outbreak was so sudden as to take the government almost entirely by surprise, the fact that only a few days separated the outbreaks in regions more than a hundred miles apart, and that a few clear demands were universally made by the various leaders, shows both that it was a popular movement, and that men must have been long brooding upon,

1 For the northern rising in all its phases reference may be made to the work of M. H. and R. Dodds, *The Pilgrimage of Grace, 1536–37, and the Exeter conspiracy, 1538*. This lengthy and detailed survey, which gives what is almost a day-to-day narrative of the various outbreaks, is a work of accurate and well-informed scholarship that retains its value after more than forty years. It will not need to be replaced within the foreseeable future, and nothing less will be sufficient for a reader who wishes to see the pattern with its main lines. Though the authors did not bring forward any material that was previously unknown, and did not pretend to make any novel conclusions, their work, with its patient unravelling of a tangled skein, with its abundant and accurate references, and with the sanity and humanity of its judgments, was a notable achievement. It does not, however, make easy reading, and this, together with its length, may account for the fact that several writers who have used and praised the book nevertheless tacitly ignore some of its most valid judgments. In recent years (1952) it has inspired a moving historical novel, Miss H. F. M. Prescott's *The Man on a Donkey*. This chapter was already in print when Professor A. G. Dickens's *Lollards and Protestants in the Diocese of York* appeared (1959).

and discussing, what they felt to be their grievances. In its greatest extent, the rising in the autumn of 1536 covered almost the whole of the northern ecclesiastical province, that is to say, the counties of York, Durham, Northumberland, Westmorland and Cumberland, with the northern part of Lancashire—Nottinghamshire alone being unaffected—together with the adjacent regions of south Lancashire, Cheshire and Lincolnshire, but the last-named county, which was in fact the first to rise, was speedily reduced to order, and in consequence the movement there, though characteristic in more than one respect, forms a chapter apart from the rest.

The rising, as is almost invariably the case with a widespread and popular civil commotion, was the outcome of a mingling of numerous causes and motives, some of them religious, others purely social or economic. As almost always happens, the party with the highest and least material motives was often tempted or forced to constrain the hesitant and to ally itself with, and in part support, the cause of those whose aims were less pure and less disinterested, and although the various outbreaks were almost simultaneous, the difference both in character and aim was often great between the various regions at first, though very swiftly the control was taken by those who had the clearest and least sordid programme. In Lincolnshire the outbreak was primarily in the townships, or at least among the common people centring upon a town; the gentry in most cases either disappeared from view or joined the rising with patent uneasiness, and the whole movement collapsed before it was possible to achieve any further organization or alignment of front. In the wide Vale of York and the prosperous East Riding, on the other hand, which embraced by far the most populous and civilized area north of Trent, the movement, though quite spontaneous, was from the start supported and directed by the gentry, men of substance and education. This fact, added to the economic and strategic importance of central Yorkshire, gave to this element a decisive place in the movement, and the high character and ability of the Yorkshire leaders and those who joined them gave a colour and a significance to the whole rising which it might otherwise have lacked.

Although social and economic grievances were present over the whole area and preponderant in parts of it—the subsidies in Lincolnshire and Yorkshire, the exactions of landlords and enclosures in the north and north-west, the statute of uses among the gentry universally—it is equally certain that a motive present and expressed everywhere, and one which alone was powerful enough to unite and to inspire the various groups, was a conservative desire to abolish the recent changes and innovations in religion. In Lincolnshire this took the principal form of resistance to the spoliation of churches and the molestation of the clergy which was feared to be imminent; in Yorkshire and parts of Westmorland and Lancashire there was an instinctive reaction against the Act of Suppression and its consequences; among the more intelligent insurgents everywhere, there was a disapproval of the royal divorce, of the recent appointment of a group of bishops known to be heterodox, of the royal supremacy, and of the aims and methods of Cromwell and his associates. One general conclusion would seem certain: that everywhere the religious motive was present, though often only in solution, that in the part of Yorkshire that gave life to the whole movement the religious motive was paramount if not exclusive of all else, and that the event that focused the indignation of the adherents of the old faith was the visitation of the monasteries, followed by the Act of Suppression. This was the one constant in all the discussions and petitions: the dissolved monasteries were to be restored and the two obnoxious visitors were to be punished.[1]

We are not here concerned with the events and phases of the revolt, but it is necessary to note the part taken in it by the religious and the justification by the leaders of their petition on behalf of the monasteries.

The self-contained Lincolnshire rising may be considered first; it lasted for less than three weeks, from the first of October to the eighteenth of the month. In contrast to the Yorkshire rising—the Pilgrimage of Grace proper—the actions of the Lincolnshire men had throughout a riotous, violent character almost entirely absent from the other theatres of disturbance. There, alone, was bloodshed and mob murder—on a small scale, indeed, but still a noteworthy blot on a movement that was throughout the most orderly and bloodless revolt that England has ever seen.[2] The king's well-known characterization of the district as 'one of the most brute and beastly of the whole realm',[3] and the remark of Cromwell's servant Williams, that he had never seen 'such a sight of asses'[4] as the gentlemen of those parts, were perhaps unduly harsh, but not altogether without excuse. Lincolnshire had, however, suffered more than most counties during 1536 from the activities of royal commissions, one suppressing the monasteries, another collecting the subsidy, and a third about

---

1 One of the Lincolnshire articles of 8 October demanded 'that no more abbeys should be suppressed', another that the king 'should...give up...Legh and Layton to the vengeance of the commons, or else banish them' (Dodds, *op. cit.* I, 114). Aske's first article at York, 15 October, ran: 'By the suppression of so many religious houses the service of God is not well performed' (*ibid.* 177). Finally, the council at Pontefract, 2–4 December, had as its fourth article: 'The suppressed abbeys to be restored to their houses, lands and goods', and as the eleventh: 'that Drs Legh and Layton have condign punishment' (*ibid.* 348, 354). Of the first article at York the Misses Dodds say with truth (*ibid.* 177): 'The first article was really the root of the whole matter; Aske invariably declared that the religious troubles alone would have caused the insurrection.'

2 The murdered men were Lord Brough's servant Nicholas at Caistor Hill (Dodds, I, 98); the bishop of Lincoln's chancellor, Dr Rayne, at Horncastle (*ibid.* 101), and Thomas Wolsey, an ex-servant and probably a relation of the cardinal (*ibid.* 102). The story of Christopher Askew, presented also in garbled form by Chapuys's nephew, of the murder of Dr Legh's cook, and the baiting to death of one of Cromwell's servants (*LP*, XI, 576, 714, 567) finds no corroboration in any of the examinations or trials, where it is not even mentioned (Dodds, I, 133), though it is repeated by Baskerville, *EM*, 159. In the Pilgrimage of Grace itself, only one life was lost, a pilgrim killed by mistake by his friends (Dodds, *op. cit.* I, 155–6, citing Aske's declaration in *EHR*, v, 571–2).

3 *LP*, XI, 780 (2); *State Papers*, I, ii, 463.

4 *LP*, XI, 888.

to enquire into the sufficiency of the parish clergy. The region was rich in monastic houses and nunneries; it was the home of the Gilbertine order, which in fact had escaped the consequences of the Act *en bloc*; and a number of the discharged religious were at large, either on their way to other houses or seeking 'capacities' for themselves and others, or simply waiting for employment of some kind; it was therefore a potential centre of disorder.[1]

The Lincolnshire insurgents, on each of the three occasions when their grievances were formulated,[2] demanded either that the suppressed houses should be restored, or that no more should be suppressed, though they did not give their reasons or enlarge any further on the point. Yet though the commons were fighting the battle of the religious, it is a notable feature of the risings here and elsewhere that the religious themselves took little share in the activities and counsels of the insurgents, and constantly showed themselves unwilling to be drawn into the fray. Examples may be seen during the progress of the 'host' of Horncastle down the valley of the Witham to Lincoln, where several abbeys lay on or near their road. The first was the Cistercian abbey of Kirkstead, before which the insurgents arrived and threatened to burn it to the ground, monks and all, unless the community joined them. The brethren capitulated, and on the following day all save the abbot, who was able to plead sickness, went out; the cellarer and bursar horsed, with battleaxes, the rest on foot. They took with them victuals and twenty shillings from the abbot. After five days unadventurous campaigning they returned home, much to the relief of their spiritual father, who 'thanked God there was no business'.[3] The host next gave trouble at Barlings, a house of Premonstratensian canons a few miles east of Lincoln. Here the abbot was a more distinguished man, Matthew Mackerell, bishop of Chalcedon *in partibus* and suffragan of Lincoln. The insurgents met him and demanded provisions; he gave them bread and beef and the meat off the spit that was roasting for the canons' supper. Some of the troops broke into the abbey and slept in the offices and on the hay in the barns. The next day their leader insisted that the community should accompany them and rejected the abbot's suggested compromise of a party to sing the Litany for them; when he urged that it was contrary to their vow to wear harness he was received with oaths which caused him to tremble 'so that he could unnethe [scarcely] say his service'. Ultimately, when threatened, like Kirkstead, with fire and rapine, he gave way and came forth, as he related in biblical phrase, 'to meet the host at Langwase Lane End with his brethren and harness and victuals', which last included beer, bread and cheese and six bullocks. When these had been presented he begged leave to retire with his canons, but the

1 An example of the wandering monk is William Morland, late of Louth Park, whose long deposition (*LP*, XII (i), 380 *seqq.*) is a principal source for all narratives of the Lincolnshire rising. He was subsequently executed.
2 Cf. Dodds, *op. cit.* I, 102, Horncastle, 4 October; I, 111, Ancaster, 8 October; I, 114, Lincoln, 8 October.   3 *LP*, XI, 828 (viii).

leader, 'seeing they were tall men' refused, insisting that six at least should join the host, which they did.[1] The evidence regarding Kirkstead and Barlings was, it must be remembered, given by accused men long after the rising had collapsed; they may well have exaggerated their unwillingness to join the insurgents, or at least omitted any words uttered or enthusiasm shown in the contrary sense, but the impression given, and borne out by other incidents in the rising, is that the religious were apathetic to the point of opposition. They were, it must be remembered, peculiarly vulnerable: if the rising failed they could neither escape nor hide their assets, and recent experience had shown only too clearly that the government would respect neither their property nor their persons. Moreover, there was little in the words or methods of the host from Horncastle to stimulate any kind of rational enthusiasm. They were to find, however, that reluctance to join the insurgents was not imputed to them for justice.

Something of the same unwillingness was shown by the northern religious in the first weeks of the rising, but here their behaviour varied with the varying circumstances. At the northern and southern extremities of the disturbed territory serious resistance was offered to the commissioners for suppression, who did not arrive till late September. At Hexham priory, a disorderly house in a wild district, there had been considerable uncertainty for some months. Hexham, originally a proprietary church of the archbishop of York, was still the centre of an enclave or peculiar of the archbishop in the diocese of Durham, and the house still looked to York for governance. Earlier in the year Archbishop Lee had petitioned for the continuance of the priory on utilitarian grounds, and it seems that this was granted and then either revoked or forgotten. The prior then went up to interview Cromwell and had no success, but before he could return the commissioners for suppression had approached Hexham, only to find that the subprior had laid in a supply of weapons and had closed the gates. When the commissioners drew near for a parley the prior of the dependent cell of Ovingham, a warlike spirit, 'appeared in harness on the leads' and asserted that there were twenty brethren in the house who would all die rather than surrender; he also produced a document from the king allowing the house to continue. By way of further demonstration the entire community paraded two deep on the Green accompanied by sixty armed men.[2] This show of resistance was successful for the moment, and the general insurrection which supervened within a few days gave Hexham some months of grace. Away in the south near the Mersey, at the Augustinian abbey of Norton, a conservative abbot had been expelled and the house disbanded, but when the commissioners were about to leave with the movables and treasure the late abbot returned with a band of several hundred natives, forced the commissioners to

1 *LP*, XI, 805, 828 (v).
2 *Ibid.* 689 (Archbishop Lee to Henry VIII), 504. Cf. also J. Raine, *Memorials of Hexham Priory*, preface.

barricade themselves in a tower, and took possession of the abbey, where his troops proceeded to encamp, lighting numerous camp-fires in and about the house, and roasting an ox. This picturesque barbecue was interrupted in the small hours of the morning by the sheriff, the energetic Sir Piers Dutton, who arrived with a posse of his 'lovers and tenants'. Most of the abbot's party escaped in the darkness by way of 'pools and Waters', but the abbot himself and a few companions were arrested and lodged in Chester Castle. Their subsequent fate is uncertain.[1]

Emeutes such as these were, however, exceptional and due to peculiar local circumstances. In the districts directly affected by the northern rising the religious took up every attitude from opposition to active or passive support. In the North Riding, where the insurgents were the commons and the aims largely social, directed against the landlords including the religious, the attitude of the monks was similar to that adopted in Lincolnshire. Thus when a body of the commons approached Jervaulx abbey demanding that the abbot and his monks should join them, the abbot straightway 'conveyed himself by a back door to Witton Fell', where he 'tarried in a great crag' for four days, returning only at night. The commons meanwhile endeavoured to bring about a new election, with threats of burning the house down. This brought the abbot home, and he and two monks were forced to go campaigning for a few days. Once again it must be remembered that this account of events was given at an examination in the Tower six months later, and the abbot doubtless exaggerated his reluctance to join the march, but other evidence shows him using words of hesitation.[2]

Even in the Vale of York and the East Riding, where the religious motive was uppermost and the leadership most enlightened, the religious hung back. It is true that at York itself, on Aske's entry into the city on 16 October, a proclamation was made, chiefly owing to pressure from the commons, that the religious were everywhere to return to their convents.[3] Some especially, the smaller houses in or near the city, did so with alacrity, escorted by the pilgrims,[4] but the often-quoted statement that however late the hour they sang mattins that same night was in fact made some months later by an exuberant pilgrim in East Anglia.[5] Certainly, the important houses again stood aloof, under the impression that they had everything to lose and nothing to gain. Sir Thomas Percy, who did things in style, sent George Lumley, Lord Lumley's heir, on a tour of the monasteries to ask for contributions and 'to have the abbots and priors and two monks of every of those houses to come forward with the best

1 *LP*, xi, 681; Dodds, *op. cit.* i, 214; Baskerville, *EM*, 180; Gasquet, *Henry VIII and the English Monasteries*, 221–3.   2 *LP*, xii (i), 1035.
3 *Ibid.* 6. A striking example of Aske's remarkable moderation.
4 The only authority for this is the sub-contemporary poet Wilfred Home, *The Fall and Evil Success of Rebellion* (1572), quoted Dodds, *op. cit.* i, 179.
5 *LP*, xi, 1319. This is a most untrustworthy source. How many religious houses were there in or near York, already suppressed, that had such liturgical enthusiasm?

cross in their best array'. Bridlington, Newburgh and Whitby sent a small subscription and the abbot of Rievaulx and the prior of Guisborough offered to come in person, but Aske, with his usual sense of moderation and decorum, sent command that the religious should be left at home.[1] How far those who showed themselves so backward in moral and material encouragement played faithfully the part that belonged to them by wrestling in prayer for their champions, who shall say? At York, at least, Sir Thomas Percy had his way. When he rode 'gorgeously through the King's highness' city in complete harness with feathers trimmed as well as he might deck himself at that time', he and Sir Oswald Wolsthrope made the abbot of St Mary's, much against his will, walk at the head of the procession carrying the abbey's best cross, but when they reached the town's end the abbot excused himself and levanted, leaving his cross behind.[2]

On the other hand, the Cistercian monks in Cumberland and Lancashire gave warmer support. The abbot of Holm Cultram realized that if the rising failed the monks would go, and acted as envoy at Carlisle for the commons;[3] the abbot and monks of Furness were even more outspoken against the royal supremacy.[4] At Sawley, recently dissolved, the monks were restored by the insurgents and immediately became a centre of resistance and propaganda; the well-known marching-song of the pilgrims derives from a Sawley paper and may conceivably have been composed by a monk of the house. The king took the behaviour of Sawley very ill, and instructed the Earl of Derby 'without further delay', to 'cause the said Abbot and certain of the chief of the monks to be hanged upon long pieces of timber, or otherwise, out of the steeple'.[5] By contrast the neighbouring Whalley, which had not been suppressed, when summoned to open its gates to the force which Nicholas Tempest was leading against the Earl of Derby, behaved in exactly the same way as Kirkstead and Jervaulx; they refused until threatened with fire.[6]

If, then, a fairly wide view is taken a clear pattern is seen to emerge. The religious of the North, whether taken as a body or as individuals, had no share in inspiring, organizing, leading or counselling the rising. Apart from one or two pieces of violence, as at Hexham and Norton, that were in no sense typical, they remained inert. The large unsuppressed houses stood aloof, fearing for their future; the dispossessed religious, also, for the most part hung back, though in a few places, such as Sawley, they returned readily as a community. Only in the immediate vicinity of York was the general restoration, ordered by Aske, effected with alacrity and general consent.

This lack of generosity and enthusiasm stands in remarkable contrast to the consistent policy and many declarations of the leaders of the rising.

1 *LP*, XII (i), 369.   2 *Ibid.* 393.
3 *Ibid.* 1259.   4 *Ibid.* 652, 841.
5 *Ibid.* XI, 786; XII (i), 1034. Henry's letter is in Byrne, *Letters of King Henry VIII*, 144.
6 *YAJ*, XI, 253.

Whenever any kind of manifesto or petition was issued, the staying of the suppression and the restoration of the dispossessed religious, including even the long-vanished Observants,[1] was in the forefront of the programme. This demand was entirely sincere, and it was free from any sordid motive. No material reward would accrue to the champions of the monks, and the men of status among them were renouncing all prospect of enrichment in future confiscations. It is therefore lamentable that the religious for their part showed so little generosity of spirit, for their inertia was due, not to any high conception of their vocation as dedicated to silence and solitude, but to purely material and personal considerations of supposed security. Even in this they were deceived, for they were in the near future to be driven from their homes by forced surrender or by the more violent attainder.

If it be asked what motives lay behind the widespread desire to preserve the religious houses, a partial answer is no doubt to be found in the conservative outlook of the northern people. The monasteries and nunneries had for centuries been far-seen landmarks, focal points in the social life of the district, and their disappearance was felt to leave a void in the familiar scheme of things in some such way as would the obliteration of all old parish churches at the present day. Few of the northern monasteries were felt to be a restrictive force, an economic incubus, as were some of the urban monasteries of southern England. Moreover, contemporaries, at least in the North, were convinced that monasteries gave considerable help to the poor and needy.[2] On a deeper level, also, there was a feeling that the religious, however undistinguished their individual lives might be, were nevertheless representatives of a class that Christian tradition had for ages regarded as necessary to the proper expansion of holiness; they were those who stood for an ideal which all admitted but few accepted for themselves, and the people of the North, though not untouched by Lollards and reformers, had not yet come to regard this ideal as false or undesirable.

These considerations, and others more detailed and subtle, were set out in unforgettable phrases by Robert Aske at his examination six months later. When he wrote, Aske was a prisoner with no hope of life. He had nothing to gain and it may have seemed to him that he had much to lose from a frank exposition of his feelings in the previous autumn. Since then

---

1 Article 6 at Pontefract demanded, 'to have the Friars Observants restored to their houses'.
2 Not only Aske (cf. his answer), but the writer and singers of the Pilgrims' Song (in *EHR*, v, 561–2; cf. Dodds, I, 350 and *EHR*, v (April 1890), 345) and the anonymous author of the petition in *LP*, xi, 1182, held this view, and though they lacked the advantage of knowing the statistics compiled from the *Valor* by Savine and others, their opinion deserves notice. The ballad (stanzas x–xii) runs: (x) 'Alacke Alacke / For the church sake / Pore comons wake / And no marvell. / For clere it is / The decay of this / How the pore shall mys / No tong can tell. (xi) For ther they hade / Boith ale and breyde / At tyme of nede / And succer grete / In alle distresse / And hevynes / And wel intrete. (xii) In troubil and care / Where that we were / In maner all bere / Of our substance / We founde good bate / At churche men gate / Withoute checkmate / Or varyaunce.'

his world had crumbled about him, and a man of less integrity and generosity might well have been soured by his failure and might have remembered only the faults of those who had been no staunch allies. Instead, he set out in simple words what seemed to him the truth of the cause for which he was to die, without a thought that they would be read by any eyes save those of Cromwell and his servants. Aske was a chivalrous man; too simple and too trustful it may be in all his loyalties, but we may well suppose that such a one would be the better for what he saw in the Yorkshire abbeys, while a Layton, no less surely, would find only what he went to find. In any case, it would be hard if the monks lost the benefit of the words written by one who gave his life to vouch for their truth.

As to the statute of suppression [he wrote], he did grudge against the same and so did all the whole country, because the abbeys in the north parts gave great alms to poor men and laudably served God; in which parts of late days they had but small comfort by ghostly teaching. And by occasion of the said suppression the divine service of almighty God is much minished, great number of masses unsaid, and the blessed consecration of the sacrament now not used and showed in those places, to the distress of the faith and spiritual comfort to man's soul; the temple of God russed [ruined] and pulled down, the ornaments and relics of the church of God unreverent used, the towns [tombs] and sepulchres of honourable and noble men pulled down and sold, none hospitality now in those places kept.... Also divers and many of the said abbeys were in the mountains and desert places, where the people be rude of conditions and not well taught the law of God, and when the said abbeys stood, the said people had not only wordly refreshing in their bodies but also spiritual refuge both by ghostly living of them and also by spiritual information and preaching....for none was in these parts denied, neither horsemeat nor mansmeat, so that the people were greatly refreshed by the said abbeys, where they now have no such succour....Also the abbeys were one of the beauties of this realm to all men and strangers passing through the same; also all gentlemen were much succoured in their needs with money; their young sons there succoured, and in nunneries their daughters brought up in virtue; and also their evidences and money left to the uses of infants in abbeys' hands, always sure there; and such abbeys as were near the danger of sea banks were great maintainers of sea walls and dykes, maintainers and builders of bridges and highways, and other such things for the commonwealth.[1]

Eloquent and sincere as this tribute is, it is, apart from the purely material benefits mentioned in it, no more discerning than would be expected from a devout layman of any age. There are many religious houses of mediocre life in the modern world to which a well-disposed lay visitor would pay a similar tribute of praise. Aske's attitude certainly shows that the people of the North and their spokesman, an exceptionally

---

1 *LP*, XII, i, 901 (2); 'Aske's examination' in *EHR*, v, 561–2; Aske's main contention is corroborated by the Duke of Norfolk, writing to the king on 10 May 1537, of 'the howses greatlie beloued with the people'. *V. Yorkshire Monasteries, Suppression Papers*, ed. J. W. Clay, YASRS, XLVIII, 43.

intelligent lawyer, did not regard the monasteries of the North as scandalous abodes of vice, but we should not be warranted in taking his words as a testimonial to a high level of spiritual excellence. It was the glory and the tragedy of the Pilgrimage and of its Captain to fight for a spirituality that was too weak to fight for itself. 'What God abandoned, they defended', and their defence was vain.

Henry's brutal answer to the Lincolnshire petition may be set against Aske's challenge.

And where ye allege, that the service of God is much thereby diminished, the truth thereof is contrary; for there be none houses suppressed, where God was well served, but where most vice, mischief and abomination of living was used: and that doth well appear by their own confession, subscribed with their own hands, in the time of our visitations....And as for their hospitality, for the relief of poor people, we wonder ye be not ashamed to affirm that they have been a great relief to our people, when a great many, or the most part, hath not past four or five religious persons in them, and divers but one, which spent the substance of the goods of their house in nourishing of vice and abominable living. Now, what unkindness and unnaturality may we impute to you, that had lever [=rather] such an unthrifty sort of vicious persons should enjoy such possessions...to the maintenance of their unthrifty life, than we, your natural prince, sovereign lord and king, which doth and hath spent more in your defence, of his own, than six times they be worth.[1]

It would not be difficult to traverse more than one statement in this passage which, like all the king's utterances, is that of a man who can see no excellence save in himself. It is more to the purpose to note these two expositions of the issue by the leaders of the opposing causes, remembering that Aske wrote, knowing well what the king had said, yet throwing his words back on him in a last confession of faith.

Besides demanding the restitution of the religious, the insurgents both in Lincolnshire and in the North in general demanded the condign punishment of Doctors Layton and Legh 'for their extortions from religious houses and other abominable acts'.[2] This is a remarkable tribute to the impression which these two worthies had made upon one-third of England in the space of a few weeks.[3] But while it should certainly increase a reluctance to believe or to approve of any of their actions and statements, it would seem that the northern resentment was not precisely on account of the inquisitorial methods and reckless calumnies of the visitors, but rather because of the exactions and bribes which had marked their progress, and above all because of the spoliation of ornaments, images and relics.[4]

---

1 State Papers, I, ii, 463; LP, XI, 780 (2); Dodds, I, 136–8.   2 Dodds, I, 354.
3 They are also mentioned, along with Cromwell, Cranmer, Rich and Longland (or Edward Lee), in the pilgrims' ballad as offenders who never would be missed.
4 Aske, in his examination (EHR, v, 335), when Legh was present, alluded to 'the violating of the relekes by the suppressors, with the unreverent demener of the dewers therof, with almesse [? money spent on entertaining them] and their imposicions takin extra ordinary, and other ther necligensses in not dewing their dewtie'.

This would strike home to the people far more than the charges against individual religious and the injurious treatment suffered, most of which would scarcely be matter for publication. In all the voluminous collection of papers connected with the northern rising, there is no mention of any specific charges having been made against the religious.

At the second appointment at Doncaster on 6 December the formal petitions of the Pilgrims were presented to Norfolk, who gave the leaders to understand that the king would give gracious consideration to them. More specifically, he assured them that Henry would visit the North and that the parliament for which they asked would shortly be held, in which order would be taken to meet the principal demands, such as the modification of the royal supremacy[1] and constitutional reforms. It seems clear that at this conference, from which the Pilgrims returned with nothing in the way of document or pledge, but with undiminished hopes, Norfolk threw the greatest possible burden upon the parliament that was assumed to be forthcoming, thereby avoiding any immediate decision or concession on the particular points at issue; he had no powers to make such concessions, and he knew that Henry would not give way.

On one point, however, the Pilgrims refused to be put off. Whereas other matters might be left pending till the parliament, they insisted that the religious who had been restored to the suppressed monasteries should remain in possession till the Act of Suppression had been repealed.[2] In default of precise evidence as to what passed at Doncaster it is difficult to be certain; the Pilgrims were firm, but Norfolk was equally unwilling to commit himself. It would seem most probable that a compromise was effected; the religious who had been restored by the insurgents were to make a formal exit, but were then to be immediately restored by the grantee or 'farmer', who was to control the revenues, but to make an allowance to the religious until such time as parliament made a final decision. This was certainly what happened in many cases.[3] But while this compromise was being implemented in the North, the king, a few days before news of the Doncaster meeting reached him, expressed himself in no uncertain terms to Norfolk on the subject. He marvelled, he said, that Norfolk could write in such desperate sort as though it were not possible to appease the commons unless the king consented to the standing of the abbeys in those parts which were to be suppressed by Act of Parliament. 'To tell you our mind plainly as to the abbeys [he continued], we shall never consent to their desires therein, but adhere to our right, to

---

1 On this Aske remarked (*EHR*, v, 559, 565) that 'as touching the suprematie they [all the gentlemen and commons] wolde have anulled the whole statute, as he thinks, but that he hymself putt in "touching curam animarum", which shulde belonge to the busshop of Rome', and that 'all men much murmored at the same [*sc.* the statute of Supremacy] and said it could not stand with Goddes law . . . that neuer king of Ingland, sith the fayth comyn within the said realme, clamyd any such auctorite'.

2 Dodds, II, 14–16.

3 *Ibid.* 18–22. For the restoration of the Observants at Newcastle, *v. LP*, XI, 1372.

which we are as justly entitled as to the Crown, and while we enjoy the one, we will not suffer the other to be infringed.' And the king added sententiously, unconscious of the irony of his words: 'A patient cannot be cured who will not trust his physician.'[1]

As is well known, the simple trustfulness of the pilgrims, the king's skilful tactic of delay, and the 'unofficial' risings, such as that of Hallam and Bigod, to which this delay gave cause, completed the ruin of the Pilgrimage of Grace. In these sporadic risings several religious houses were involved, more by accident than by design. Thus Watton, a large Gilbertine house not far from York, which had for some time been suffering from domestic discord, was patronized by Sir Francis Bigod, who endeavoured to settle its affairs, and was visited there by Hallam; it was a house known for its conservative views on royal supremacy.[2] Similarly the abbot and monks of Jervaulx, who had been discommoded by the commons in the first rising, were now swept into the fringe of a minor commotion which the ex-abbot of Fountains, a lodger in the house, may have endeavoured to exploit in his own interest. It was in consequence of such implications that when the Duke of Norfolk was clearing up the débris of the conspiracy in Yorkshire he executed without further ado, as caught in the act, the subprior of Watton and two canons of Warter whose previous history is unknown.[3]

From York Norfolk proceeded to the north-western extremity of the county, with the king's banner displayed (thus indicating a state of war in which the usual processes of the law were suspended), to deal with Sawley and other suppressed houses where violence of some sort or another was alleged to have occurred during the restoration of the religious. He was sped on his course by a well-known missive from the king, in which Henry, after telling him that he 'must cause dreadful execution upon a good number of the inhabitants, hanging them on trees, quartering them, and setting their heads and quarters in every town', added a particular directive for the religious, whom he affected to regard as ringleaders:

Finally, forasmuch as all these troubles have ensued by the solicitation and traitorous conspiracy of the monks and canons of these parts; we desire and pray you, at your repair to Sawley, Hexham, Newminster, Lanercost, Saint Agatha, and all such other places as have made any manner of resistance, or in any way conspired, or kept their houses with any force, sithens the appointment of Doncaster, you shall, without pity or circumstance... cause all the monks and canons, that be in any wise faulty, to be tied up, without further delay or ceremony, to the terrible example of others.[4]

1 *LP*, XI, 1271. This is a good example of Henry's imperturbable assurance. The 'right' to the monasteries was less than a year old, and had been obtained entirely by his own violent initiative, without which parliament would never have taken cognizance of the matter.

2 *Ibid.* XII (i), 201.   3 *Ibid.* 1023, 1035.

4 *Ibid.* 479, and *State Papers*, I, ii, 539. Cf. the later letter referring to the monks of Sawley, *supra*, p. 326.

It is unfortunately impossible, owing to the dearth of records, to say what was the direct result of this command at the places mentioned.[1] The Sawley monks had been ejected by the farmer, Sir Arthur Darcy, and the abbot, Thomas Bolton, was subsequently attainted of treason and executed some time before 10 March 1537,[2] the date of the execution at Lancaster of Abbot John Paslew of Whalley. The latter abbot was indicted on a number of counts, including his association with the earlier rising, a crime which he might have covered by suing the king's pardon, and for more recently harbouring a monk of Sawley, Richard Estgate, brother of one of his own monks who was also indicted on the same day. Paslew was an old and tired man, and for some reason he pleaded guilty to all the charges, though it is possible that he might have given serious trouble to the prosecution by a resolute defence. With him suffered the fugitive Estgate and a monk of Whalley, William Haydocke. John Estgate of Whalley pleaded not guilty to the charges against him, and had the rare fortune of acquittal.[3] Along with them nine canons of Cartmel were tried (three of them *in absentia*) and four were condemned and executed.[4] As for the abbey of Whalley which, unlike Sawley, ranked as one of the greater abbeys, the king 'thought that as the house had been so corrupt it were better taken into the king's hand, the king being, by the attainder of the late abbot, entitled to it'. This was perhaps the first appearance of the convenient but novel plea which made use of the legal fiction, whereby the abbot was regarded as the *persona* of his church and community, to treat the whole house and its rights as part of his personal property, which escheated to the Crown like any other fief or possession.[5]

The earl of Sussex then turned to the great abbey of Furness, which he hoped to ruin as easily. At first, however, he met with difficulty, for only two out of the large community could be charged on any colourable pretext of treason since the pardon of 1536. His efforts to implicate the abbot likewise failed at first, but this functionary, who four months earlier had taken refuge with the earl of Derby when the commons approached his abbey, and had congratulated himself on being safe whatever happened, was even more accommodating. Sussex, almost at a venture, suggested that he might feel disposed to make a free surrender of his house.[6] He responded with alacrity, and straightway signed a document in which he

1 But cf. *LP*, xii, i, 416 (2).

2 *Ibid*. 1034. There has been much confusion as to the name and fate of the last abbot of Sawley, and a 'ghost' abbot, William Trafford, has for two centuries found a place in the *fasti* of the abbey, probably owing to a mistake of the antiquary J. Stevens, who for some reason inserted the name of the renegade prior of the London Charterhouse.

3 Here again there has been much confusion, which was finally resolved by the discovery of the kalendar of indictments at Lancaster by Canon Wallis, and the researches of Canon Wallis, 'The Narrative of the Indictment of the Traitors of Whalley and Cartmel', 10–11, and of W. S. Weeks in 'Abbot Paslew and the Pilgrimage of Grace'—an article which makes severe demands upon the reader's powers of concentration. Cf. also J. McNulty, *Sallay Cartulary*, ii, 196–7; *LP*, xii, i, 630; and Stow, *Chronicle, s.a.* 1537.

4 Cf. *LP*, xii, i, 632.   5 *Ibid*. 668; *State Papers*, i, ii, 540.

6 *LP*, xii, i, 840.

declared that 'knowing the misorder and evil life both unto God and our prince, of the brethren of the said monastery', he gave freely, 'in discharge of [his] conscience' to the king and his heirs and assigns, 'all such interest and title as I have had, have, or may have', in the abbey.[1] This simple proceeding, by which an abbot, entirely without the knowledge of his community, could dispose for ever of his monks, his abbey and all its possessions, was a distinct advance even upon the doctrine of escheat. Sussex was no lawyer, and might think it would do, but it so happened that Sir Anthony Fitzherbert, a very distinguished man of the law, arrived a few hours later. He entered into the plan, but saw at once that the deed must be signed by the monks also, and so it was done.[2] Sussex had thus shown once and for all how to deal with the greater abbeys. As for Hexham, it remained unsuppressed till the end of February in 1537 when it fell quietly, but apparently without bloodshed, into the hands of Norfolk.[3]

Meanwhile, with the North at last reduced to inaction, the king's agents were able to proceed to 'justify' their prisoners. The first to go were the men of the original Lincolnshire rising, who had never been explicitly covered by the pardon nominally given to the Pilgrims. Among those tried and condemned on 6 March at Lincoln were four canons of Barlings, six monks of Bardney, and the abbot and three monks of Kirkstead.[4] The abbot of Barlings and Dan William Morland, monk of Louth Park, were in the Tower; against them the Lincoln jury found a true bill for treason. The others were executed at Lincoln, Horncastle and Louth. As has been seen their only crime was that they had lacked will or courage to resist being pressed into following the commons for a day or two. By the procedure that had now become automatic Kirkstead and Barlings escheated to the king. The abbot of Barlings, Matthew Mackerell, bishop of Chalcedon, was tried with others at Guildhall and executed at Tyburn on 29 March. He was accused, and admitted the charge, of having counselled the monks to hide and sell the plate and ornaments of the house. It was suggested that this showed him to have had foreknowledge of the rising, and therefore to be guilty of misprision of treason, if not of treason itself. Mackerell replied that he had advised the liquidation of the abbey's assets because he anticipated that the larger houses would soon go the way of the smaller ones. He was probably speaking the truth, but to anticipate the king's unexpressed designs and endeavour to forestall them was as reprehensible as rising against him; in any case the abbot's action was both canonically and morally questionable. Still, it was not treason. The assistance he had given to the insurgents, on the other hand, might fairly be construed as such. An equitable court would no doubt have admitted

---

1 *Ibid.* 832.
2 *Ibid.* 840, 880, 903. For Fitzherbert, *v. DNB*. To Maitland (*Historical Essays*, 140) he appeared as the only great English lawyer of the reign, apart from More.
3 *LP*, xii, i, 546.   4 *Ibid.* 581.

the abbot's plausible excuse that he had acted under moral duress, and had given no help beyond victuals, but such a plea was unacceptable at a Tudor treason trial, and the bishop of Chalcedon who, with his canons, had strained more than one point to secure tranquillity, paid the same penalty as a martyr or a rebel.[1]

Five weeks after the trials at Lincoln the selected leaders of the Pilgrimage were condemned. When the juries at York found a true bill against the ringleaders, Norfolk made use of the court to despatch two monks of the London Charterhouse, John Rochester and James Walworth, who, though they had steadfastly opposed the royal supremacy, had for some reason escaped the fate of their brethren, and had been sent to the Charterhouse at Hull. Dan John Rochester, indeed, begged Norfolk to introduce him to the king, that he might face to face argue with him the evil of the royal supremacy, but the Duke contented himself with forwarding the letter to Cromwell and executing the writer and his companion, with the remark: 'two more wilful religious men in manner unlearned I think never suffered'.[2] These two victims at Hull completed the tale of witnesses to the Catholic faith from the House of the Salutation.

Meanwhile, the principal group of prisoners came up for trial in London on 17 May, including some of the religious who had been implicated either in the Pilgrimage or in the Hallam-Bigod conspiracy. They were James Cockerell, quondam prior of Guisborough, William Wood, prior of Bridlington, Friar John Pickering of Bridlington, a Dominican, Adam Sedbergh, abbot of Jervaulx, and William Thirsk, quondam abbot of Fountains. Of these, Cockerell had certainly been technically guilty of misprision of treason at the time of Bigod's revolt, but no more. The prior of Bridlington, who had as certainly aided the Pilgrims, was probably innocent of any offence subsequent to the pardon. Friar John Pickering had been a resolute and prominent member of the Pilgrimage, and has the distinction of being the only friar to give all his energies to the cause. He was foolish enough to give support to Bigod's revolt also, and he paid the legal penalty. Abbot Sedbergh, though a very unheroic figure, was probably, as he maintained, completely innocent of treason. His guest, the quondam of Fountains, equally mediocre in personality, was also probably innocent of anything that could be called treason.[3]

Although Robert Aske was not connected either professionally or personally with any religious house, he showed himself the most loyal and able contemporary champion and apologist of the Tudor religious, and his death cannot be allowed to pass without a memorial of words. He is indeed one of the few men of his age whom we recognize at once to have been utterly frank and single-minded. Although he appears on the stage of history for only six months of his thirty-six years of life, it is clear that

---

1 For Mackerell's trial, *v.* Dodds, II, 154–7.   2 *LP*, XII, i, 777–8; 1172.
3 For these trials, *v.* Dodds, II, 214 *seqq.* For the quondam of Fountains, *v.* article by G. R. Elton in *JEH*, VII.

he had an intelligence, a capacity for leadership, and a sense of justice and generosity quite out of the common. In religious as in political and legal matters he seized with precision the points that were vital, and it was his influence more than anything else that raised the Pilgrimage, alike on the spiritual and on the intellectual plane, to its unique position in Tudor history. While he directed it, and so far as his influence extended, it was the worthy expression of the devotion of a simple and intelligent people to their ancestral faith and to the free institutions which Englishmen before that time and since have valued more than life itself. Robert Aske, not Henry, was the true representative of all that was most characteristic and most sincere in England. He failed, in the eyes of men, because he was by temperament and desire one who lived by reasonable, fair and kindly dealing, and who trusted in the power of right reason. But over and above this, he failed because, when the call to build his tower had come suddenly upon him, he had not fully reckoned the cost. He had known that he was putting his career and his life to the throw, and was willing to take the hazard, but he had not reckoned with the call to abandon his trust in his king and to defy all human authority and law when they ran counter to the law of God. It is certain that nothing but force could have changed the direction of policy in England in 1536; it is probable, if not certain, that Henry's mind and character were then so fixed that nothing—not even force—would bend them. The leader of a rising should have been prepared, if need arose, to put his cause before his king; else were it better to have remained silent and hidden. Posterity passes harsh judgment on unsuccessful rebels, however good their cause. They fail both to reach the spiritual standard of a martyr, and to satisfy the worldly demand of success. At another and a more august tribunal, where sycophants and timeservers have no say, they may expect a fairer trial. Of all leaders of revolts that have failed, Robert Aske is one of the noblest. He was deceived and killed by the king whom he would gladly have served and whom he loved and trusted 'not wisely but too well'.

CHAPTER XXVI

THE LAST PHASE

I. SOME WORCESTERSHIRE PRELATES

With the departure of the visitors in the autumn and winter of 1535–6 there began, for such of the monasteries as were not liable to suppression under the Act of 1536, a short period of three to four years that may truly be called the last phase of their existence. Though their ultimate fate was still uncertain, they could have had few illusions as to the change in their condition. Any hopes that the inmates may have cherished of permanent survival became more and more forlorn with every new political event; domestic authority was impaired; sincere and sensitive spirits must have been assailed by every kind of doubt and despondency, while the discontented, the selfish, the neurotic and the malicious had every opportunity for restlessness and for intrigue. The visitation, coming as the climax of a series of harassing demands, had shown conclusively, even brutally, that the royal supremacy was not a matter of words alone. Their independence, their freedom of manœuvre, was gone for ever. They could not take any serious decision or make any notable change in their arrangements without coming into immediate contact with a master who, besides being powerful and efficient, was also entirely wanting in any appreciation of religious or spiritual values. His visitors had dismissed a whole section of the community, and thrown the machinery of recruitment out of gear; they had imposed a number of restraints which, if observed literally, would have brought the economic and social life of the monastery to a standstill, if not to an explosion; they had made it possible for any discontented subject to delate his superior's words or acts to Cromwell, or to obtain complete or partial dispensation from his monastic obligations. This rough usage would probably have slowly paralysed and starved the monasteries out of existence, as a somewhat similar treatment gradually extinguished monastic life in Scandinavia. In the few years that remained to them of life, however, the age-old momentum of their petrified fabric carried them along, as a storm-beaten vessel drifts before the wind till it founders at last.

The immediate problem for all superiors in the latter months of 1535 was how best to escape the injunction imposing complete and universal enclosure. Cromwell was assailed at once by numerous versions of the same tale of woe. One of the first to relieve her feelings was the abbess of Wilton who wrote, only forty-eight hours after Legh had promulgated his decrees, to ask for leave to go round her estates.[1] Ten days later the abbot of Oseney followed. His plea was more personal; Oseney stands very low, 'encompassed with waters', whereas he was brought up in the

[1] *LP*, IX, 280.

rarefied air of St Frideswide's and fears 'it will abbreviate his life' if he is confined to his island.[1] Then came a flood of letters from Bath, Abingdon, Christ Church Canterbury, Cleeve, Bury St Edmunds, Boxgrove, Hyde, St Swithuns Winchester, Whitby and Forde.[2] Well might Cromwell add to his 'remembrances' the note: 'Of the visitation, and how it grieveth the heads to be kept within their monasteries.'[3] Some of the sufferers made use of advocates: thus the abbot of Glastonbury enlisted the services of Sir John Fitzjames of Redlynch,[4] the steward of the abbey, while Cranmer himself pleaded the cause of the prior of his cathedral.[5] For the prior of Leeds in Kent his brother, Sir Anthony St Leger, appealed with disarming candour on the score of his having 'hitherto always been used to take recreation with his hounds for a certain infirmity with which he is troubled'.[6] Others, with the abbot of St Augustine's, Canterbury, were content to seek refuge beneath Cromwell's protecting wings.[7] Many of these requests were accompanied by gifts, and the vicar-general had no scruple in asking for what he wanted; though his alleged requests for money, accompanied by a blank form of receipt and a statement of minimum requirements are forgeries.[8] By reason of this, the injunctions have sometimes been seen as a purely financial measure, but it seems clear that this particular injunction was either due to an unrealistic effort at reform or to mis-interpretation by the visitors of a traditional prohibition; Cromwell soon realized that the decree of rigid enclosure as applied by the visitors was unworkable, and the *status quo* was gradually restored; the occasion was not missed of making a stiff charge, but this was not the primary object of the manœuvre.

Still more galling to abbots, though less immediate and universal in its incidence, was the injunction that established a system of delation:

If either the master [so ran the words] or any brother of this house do infringe any of the said injunctions, any of them shall denounce the same or procure to be denounced as soon as may be, to the king's majesty, or to his visitor-general, or his deputy; and the abbot or master shall minister spending money and other necessaries for the way to him that shall so denounce.[9]

This was to prove a godsend to factious and restless cloisterers; as Fitzjames wrote at once on behalf of Abbot Whiting:

Peradventure there be sume of his brodirs would be gladde to be abrode and to make untrew surmyse, so the abbot may paye for ther costes.... Wherfore, it may please you...to make it if the complaynannt prove his complaynt to be trow, than to have his costes, or elles not.[10]

1 *Ibid.* 375.   2 *Ibid.* 426, 455, 784, 790, 530, 724, 1039; X, i, 239.   3 *LP*, IX, 498.
4 *Ibid.* 253; Wright, *SL*, xxvii.   5 *LP*, IX, 686.   6 *Ibid.* 713 (31 October).
7 *Ibid.* 744; as he puts it, *sub umbra alarum vestrarum*, an allusion to the versicle and response at Compline.
8 Merriman, *Life and Letters of Thomas Cromwell*, II, 49 (letter 180 to prior of Coxford: cf. letter 161 to prior of St Faith's, and *LP*, XI, 484–5).
9 The injunctions are in Wilkins, *Concilia*, III, 786–91.
10 *LP*, IX, 253; Wright, *SL*, xxvii.

Here, however, the abbots had to do with an essential part of Cromwell's technique, and met with no satisfaction. Taking no interest whatsoever in the spiritual well-being of the monasteries, he wished his grip to
be felt throughout the community and, as we shall see, consistently used
unsatisfactory or disgruntled subjects both as informers and as agitators,
to bring about the downfall of an abbot or the surrender of a house.
A number of letters of complaint from such men survive, particularly from
the months immediately following the visitation. They come from all over
England, but they have been preserved in particular abundance in connection with a group of houses in the region between the Cotswolds and
the Malvern hills. The monasteries concerned are Winchcombe, Evesham,
Pershore and Worcester; three of the four were seen as homes of spiritual
energy in the late Old English monastic world;[1] we can see them again in
a different light before they pass finally out of existence.

Winchcombe had lost only three years previously the most distinguished
abbot of its history, but there is no evidence that Richard Kidderminster
had set any stamp upon the community; he had resigned in his old age,
and his successor, Abbot Munslow, was a moderate conservative who
ended his days as a prebendary of the new cathedral of Gloucester.
Cromwell, it would seem, had some personal connection with Winchcombe, for he is found staying there in the first days of August when the
king lay nearby in Gloucestershire and he was on the point of launching
the great visitation of the monasteries.[2] Three weeks later one of the
monks, John Placid, writes to him for counsel. He is troubled, he says,
about certain ceremonies which exalt the bishop of Rome, and wishes for
powers to confiscate books dealing with the pope, St Patrick's purgatory,
and miracles.[3] A fortnight later he returns to the charge and begs
Cromwell, 'for the love you have for the increase of faith and the destruction of papistical creatures', to 'set forth the Word. This truth', he continues, 'is not proclaimed so fully as it ought to be'. He himself has made
a little treatise against the usurped power of the bishop of Rome. In the
second letter we have some personal details. 'Whereas it pleased you, considering my infirmity, to excuse my rising at midnight', the abbot had
represented to him that this had caused grumbling in the community,
though 'he [the abbot] knows that I cannot endure the straitness of the
religion, the customary abstinence, the frayter, and other observances.
I have [he adds] the cure under him of a little village of forty souls. Such
a thing were most quiet for me, which I may serve and keep my bed and
board, and go to my book in the monastery'.[4] He therefore asks for a
capacity. He asks also that 'my brother Overbury be commanded to
preach the Supremacy every Sunday, and have his chamber, books and
fire'. Despite the phrase used of him, Overbury would seem not to have
been a monk, for he is soon found addressing Cromwell on his own

1 *MO*, 159–67.   2 *LP*, VIII, 1111; IX, 4.
3 *Ibid.* IX, 134 (20 August).   4 *Ibid.* 321 (9 September).

account in the best evangelical style. 'Faithful, trusty and dearly beloved minister unto the high power of Almighty God [he begins], of the which you have ministration under our sovereign lord the King, here in earth the only high and supreme head of this his Church of England, grace, peace and mercy be evermore with you: laud and thanks be to God the Father Almighty for the true and unfeigned faith that you have in our sweet Saviour Jesu.'[1] At about the same time Cromwell was hearing from another Winchcombe gospeller, one Anthony Saunders, whom he had appointed 'pastor' in the little town to 'set forth the King's title and pluck down that great whore of Rome'. 'I have small favour and assistance amongst the pharisaical papists', writes Saunders. He is preaching justification by faith alone, and in consequence the neighbouring abbot of Hailes has set up to preach against him 'a greate Golyas, a sotle Dunys man'. Nor do the monks appreciate his efforts; they come late to his sermons because 'they set so much by their Popish services'.[2] With such an entourage the abbot was sure to be in trouble whether he enforced or relaxed discipline. Early in September 1535, Dan Peter was delating him for entertaining the prior and the precentor at his table, and for failing to give a daily conference on the Rule,[3] while a few weeks later he writes to Cromwell that Dan Walter Aldhelm and Dan Hugh Egwin are eating flesh in Advent and when publicly reprimanded refuse to obey and declare their readiness to eat meat on the next Friday if they can get it.[4] After this, silence falls on these warring factions, but here, at least, the abbot, whom Cromwell must have known well personally, kept his seat to the end and retired on a good pension.

Ten miles to the north of Winchcombe the elderly abbot of Evesham, Clement Lichfield, was having a more trying passage.[5] Evesham, whether by good fortune or good management, ended its days in a glow of prosperity, and we have already seen that it was not without young men of ability and letters. The abbot, who had been elected as long ago as 1514, stood in the tradition of the successful abbots of the past. He sat in the House of Lords, served on the commission of the peace at Worcester, and took part in local business of all kinds. He had also set up memorials of his rule in the fan-vaulted chapels in the churches of All Saints and St Laurence, and above all in the richly panelled bell tower which, with its pinnacles and vanes, is still the town's landmark and most precious ornament. He seems, however, to have been feared rather than loved by his subjects, and this may partly account for the success of the intrigue that brought him down.[6] This was the work of the cellarer, Philip Hawford,

1 *Ibid.* 1134. 2 *LP*, VIII, 171; IX, 747.
3 *Ibid.* IX, 314 (9 September). These were infractions of the visitors' statutes.
4 *Ibid.* 934 (7 December).
5 Some interesting facts about Lichfield are collected by E. A. B. Barnard in *Clement Lichfield, Last Abbot of Evesham*, but there are several inaccuracies and omissions. For Robert Joseph's feelings, *v. supra*, p. 104.
6 *LP*, X, 930 (20 March 1536).

who in May 1536 had already been sounding Cromwell. 'I am advertised', he writes somewhat cryptically to the minister, 'by Mr Wells, of your furtherance of my suit and will gladly accomplish the promises made by my friends, which shall always be ready when you call me to preferment.'[1] The matter for some reason hung fire for more than a year, till in October 1537 we find a kinsman of the cellarer asking Wriothesley to remind Cromwell of his intentions. There was a motive for speedy action. The abbey's day of audit and receipt was approaching, and the cellarer feared that if nothing were done till the abbot had realized the year's yield, his successor would be hard put to it to find the first-fruits for the king. As the letter to Wriothesley is among Cromwell's papers, the reminder doubtless got home, but nothing was done immediately, and it was not till mid-March 1538 that the call came, when Dr William Petre arrived at Evesham with a letter from Cromwell suggesting that he would be obliged if Lichfield would withdraw. A sight of the envelope was sufficient; in the words of the Worcestershire antiquary the abbot 'struck sail to avoid shipwreck'[2] and resigned on the spot, desiring Petre 'very instantly that he wolde nott open the [letter] during the tyme of his being here, because (as he sayd) it would bee notyd thatt he was compelled to resign for fear of deprivation'.[3] He had previously bargained with Petre, and received a pension and his manor of Offenham, where, twenty-four years previously, he had been blessed as abbot. Thence in 1546 his body was carried to be buried at the entrance of the chapel he had built in All Saints church, where a brass commemorated him as the builder of 'the new tower'.[4] He probably knew well enough who had played him false; as for the cellarer, elected abbot forthwith, he paid what he had promised on the nail. 'Touching Mr Cromwell's matter,' wrote Petre, 'the abbot says it shall be paid to-morrow morning.'[5]

Six miles down the Avon from Evesham lay Pershore abbey where, in the latter years of Lichfield's rule, John Stonywell, bishop of Pulati *in partibus*, was in charge. Stonywell's career is typical of the age.[6] He was

1 *LP*, XII (ii), 902 (13 October 1536).
2 Habington, *Survey of Worcestershire*, cited by Barnard, *op. cit.* 47.
3 *LP*, XIII (i), 531 (17 March 1538) = Wright, *SL*, lxxxix.
4 Barnard, *art. cit.*, describes the chapel and grave.
5 *LP*, XIII (i), 974. This letter is misplaced by the editor of *LP*; it should follow close upon no. 531 (*v. supra*, n. 3). For Hawford, *v.* also 'Philip Hawford, Pseudo-Abbot of Evesham', by E. A. B. Barnard.
6 The career of Stony- or Stanywell has not hitherto been fully elucidated. There is much information in E. A. B. Barnard's 'John Stonywell', but the article contains numerous errors, and there are mistakes in the references under *Tynemouth* in the *History of Northumberland* and in the article 'William Hogeson Episcopus Dariensis', by A. Hamilton Thompson, in *YAJ. LP*, IV, ii, 2537, seems to be the source of the attribution to him of Polizzi in Sicily as his titular see; this mistake is repeated by Barnard and others. Eubel, *Hierarchia catholica*, III, 294, gives the place correctly as Pulati in Epirus, in the ecclesiastical province of Antivari. Even after the identification of the prior of Tynemouth with the abbot of Pershore had been made there was further confusion; thus Baskerville, *EM*, 67 and 73 n., makes him a protégé of Lady Mary Carey who in reality befriended his successor, with whom Baskerville confuses Stanywell. His whole story can be extracted from *LP*, I, 3497 (p. 435); III, i, 510; IV, ii, 2537, 3227, 4708; XII, i, 822.

a Staffordshire man who became a monk at St Albans,[1] whence he was
sent to Gloucester College, becoming in due course *prior studentium*.[2] In
1512 he was appointed prior to Tynemouth in Northumberland, a cell of
St Albans, where twelve years later he became suffragan to act for the
absentee cardinal in the city of York, with the title *in commendam* of
Poletensis.[3] In 1527 Tynemouth was needed as a home for a protégé of
Lady Mary Carey, sister of Anne Boleyn and the king's whilom mistress,[4]
and it was arranged, no doubt by Wolsey, that Stonywell should fill a
vacancy that had occurred at Pershore.[5] There are indications that he was
a harsh and grasping man, and he had trouble with his community more
than once.[6] After the visitation of 1535 they demanded a higher rate of
stipend than they had hitherto enjoyed, and the abbot sought a ruling
from Cromwell.[7] Almost at the same moment that troublesome customer,
Richard Beerly or Beely, addressed to Cromwell as 'second person yn
this rem of Englond, ynduyd with all grace and goodness', his 'lowly
and myck [meek] scrybullyng', in which he betrays both a 'gruggyng yn
my conchons that the relygyon wyche we do obser and keype ys no rull
of sentt Benett, nor yt [yet] no commandyment of God' and a sense of his
own moral frailty which led him to feel that he would be 'bettur owt than
yn'. He further offered to 'ynstrux your grace sumwatt of relygyus men,
and how the kynges grace commandyment ys keyp yn puttyng forth of
boches [?maintaining] the beyschatt of Roms userpt power. Monkes [he
adds] drynk an bowll after collacyon tell ten or xii of the clock, and cum
to mattens as dronck as myss [mice], and sume at cardes, sum at dyyss and
at tabulles, sume cum to mattens begenynge at the mydes, and sume when
yt ys allmost done.'[8] This curious farrago need not be taken too seriously;
as Beely does not appear on the pension list, he presumably secured his
release from the vicar-general; he would not have been missed. The bishop
of Pulati had to weather another squall in April 1538, when William

---

1 This seems clear from *LP*, III, i, 510 (14 November 1519), where Wolsey exempts
John Stonywell, S.T.P., for life from the jurisdiction of St Albans, while allowing him to
retain his right of voting, seat in choir, place in chapter, right of residence in the abbey, etc.
It is confirmed by an entry in a Pardon Roll of (?)1509–10 (*LP*, ed. Brodie, I, i, 438 (4),
p. 256), where he is referred to as 'late sexton of St Albans abbey and archdeacon of
St Albans'.

2 *LP*, ed. Brodie, I, i, *loc. cit.*: 'nuper prior de Studens in Oxynford...doctor de
Cathedra in Oxon.'

3 He was appointed 24 April 1524, 'in civitate Eboracensi propter latam diocesim', and
his revenue was to come from Tynemouth (Eubel, *loc. cit.*). In 1513 he was sheriff of
Newcastle (*LP*, ed. Brodie, I, ii, 2222 (p. 997)).

4 *LP*, XII, i, 822.

5 *Ibid.* IV, 2537 (30 September 1526) royal assent to election: 1562 (16 October) restitution of temporalities.

6 Barnard, 'John Stonywell', 33–8, cites various complaints and suits in which he was
implicated.

7 *LP*, XI, 1145 (23 November 1536).

8 *Ibid.* 1449 (= Wright, *SL*, lx), and *Monasticon*, II, 412. Barnard, *art. cit.* 33, states that
the name is Beely [= Beoley, Worcs] not Beerley [= Bearly, Warwicks]. Beely would have
been surprised and flattered to think that three centuries later he would be cited in the
OED, *s.v.* 'mouse', and appear in stained glass in his old abbey church.

Harrison, groom of the king's privy chamber, delated him for treasonous conversation in the presence of his old adversary Richard Sheldon.[1] Comment had been made on the executions after the northern rising, and Stonywell had relieved his feelings by remarking: 'I trust and I pray God that I may dye one of the chynderne of Rome.' For one who had on more than one occasion solemnly subscribed to a repudiation of papal authority it was perhaps an optimistic as well as a dangerous expression, but nothing came of it. Later in the year Cromwell suggested resignation, and apparently reminded the bishop that he owed his post to the writer. Stonywell took the point, though not without a reference to the position he had vacated,[2] but Cromwell did not press him. A year later the matter was still under discussion, and in the end Pershore was one of the last abbeys to surrender on 21 January 1540. The abbot secured a large pension and part of the monastic buildings,[3] but he retired to Longdon in Staffordshire, where he added a chapel to the parish church and in due course bequeathed his vestments and *pontificalia* to a clerical friend.

We may complete this tale of the houses in the Severn basin by a glance at Worcester, where we can follow from Cromwell's correspondence and other sources the fortunes of Prior More in the last uneasy months of his rule.

Explosive material had long been lying about in the priory of St Mary, but fifty years before it would probably never have been touched off. As so often happened, the train was fired by the royal visitation of 1535. This took place, as has been seen, on 1 August, and was conducted by Dr Legh and Ap Rice, for both of whom it was a new experience. Before them the various parties aired their grievances freely, above all Musard and Fordham, who besides their personal wrongs took the opportunity of denouncing one of their brethren, Dan Richard Clyve, for criticizing the statute of appeals, railing against the king and Queen Anne, alluding to the king as a weathercock and upholding Queen Katharine and the authority of the pope.[4] The visitors in their inexperience took a very reasonable view of all this, and agreed with the prior's poor opinion of Musard; he found himself in prison once more and his attempts to write to Cromwell were successfully frustrated for a time. Finally, he succeeded in getting letters off to both the king and Cromwell, denouncing his confrère, Dan Richard, and his prior. 'As a religious man', he remarked, 'I felt bound to send the words of treason and the cloaking of them by my master', and he swept up a long list of charges against More, 'my unkind master', including one of unlawfully deposing Fordham and Neckham 'for standing unto the right of the house'.[5] Fordham for his part joined in the denunciation and offered Cromwell one hundred marks if he might

---

1 *LP*, XIII, i, 822 (1538).

2 *Ibid.* ii, 1259: 'No doubt this benefice has been sweet to me, as your Lordship says, but remember what I left when I came to this.'

3 *LP*, XIV, i, 349.   4 *Ibid.* VIII, 51-2   5 *Ibid.* 6.

be restored to office.[1] A charge of treason against a superior was always acceptable to the government, as it simplified negotiations for surrender, and Cromwell lost no time in submitting the alleged treasonable words to Audley in London. The chancellor, however, gave a lawyer's cautious reply: the reference made by Clyve to the weathercock could hardly bear an interpretation of treason; misprision of treason was the most that could be hoped for. As for the criticism of the king and Queen Anne at Christmas time, the words had unfortunately been spoken a month too soon, as the date fixed for the operation of the penalties under the Treasons Act had been 1 February. The best course would be to have an indictment made out and then to take evidence and wait.[2] Audley followed this up by sending the necessary instrument down to Worcester.

The case was duly heard by Rowland Lee and the dossier sent up to London. Prior More meanwhile was sent to Gloucester abbey under house arrest, but Lee wrote to Cromwell that caution was needed in going to extremes with such a well-known figure in county society as the prior of Worcester; he was 'a great possessioner, and at assizes the gentry of the county had been familiarly entertained by him'. Meanwhile, wires were being pulled in every direction. The community of Worcester were in no mind to have Fordham back again as cellarer and sent a round robin with twenty-eight signatures to Cromwell telling him so.[3] On the other hand, Cranmer down at Canterbury only a fortnight after the visitation had got wind of what had happened. He understands, so he writes to Cromwell, that the priory of Worcester is shortly to be void; if so, he hopes the vicar-general will be good to Dr Holbeach, a monk of Croyland and prior of the student monks at Cambridge, where the archbishop had known him.[4] As for More, he found a good friend in his guest of other years, Lady Margery Sandys, whom we have seen in the past taking a glass of wine with the prior and sending him a valuable rosary. She wrote to Cromwell warmly on his behalf, demanding that the matter should be looked into at once, and judiciously adding to her forthright advocacy the assurance that the prior, 'a true monk to God and his King', would doubtless 'be glad to give you in ready money as much as any other man will give'.[5] She could speak with the greater boldness, for less than a week before writing she had acted as hostess to the king and Queen Anne at the Vyne.[6] She had probably brought More's name up during the royal visit, for the king was disposed, we hear, 'through pity' to restore More to office; before doing so, he told Cromwell to find out the views of the

1 *Ibid.* 90 (14 August), 165.   2 *Ibid.* 510.   3 *Ibid.* 653.

4 *Ibid.* 97. In a letter of John Gostwyk to Cromwell, 26 August 1535, Richard Gresham, the Lord Mayor, is said to desire Cromwell's favour for John Fulwell, monk of Westminster, to be prior of Worcester (*Ibid.* IX, 184); if he is appointed, Cromwell shall have £100 and Gostwyk £20.

5 *Ibid.* IX, 656. Lady Sandys (*née* Margery Bray) came of a family with Worcestershire associations; her uncle, Sir Reginald Bray the statesman (*v. DNB*), was a benefactor to Great Malvern.

6 *Ibid.* 619, 639. For Lord Sandys, *v. DNB.*

new bishop of Worcester, Hugh Latimer. Latimer for some reason was not More's friend, and with rather less than his traditional bluntness of speech he let it be understood that he did not want the old prior back.[1] More did in fact return early in 1536, but he seems to have shown some resentment towards those of his brethren who had caused all the trouble. In any case, Musard was active once again with a sheet of charges which readers of the prior's Journal will recognize as resting on a basis of fact, even if they are extremely stale and essentially unfair. The prior, Musard tells Cromwell, maintains his relatives and retinue of twenty-four attendants in comfort while the monks want. 'I wish you knew', he adds feelingly, 'of the poor service the convent has on fish days.' The prior takes land from his tenants to enlarge his parks, and wastes money on hospitality and litigation in London while 'your cloister' crumbles. Above all, he has bought quite unnecessarily a precious mitre and staff, and Musard who, as we have seen, took an interest in plate, adds that More had been forced to sell some to pay off the debt.[2]

The documents do not tell us what happened next. It may be that Cromwell felt that More, though clearly innocent of crime, had too many enemies and rivals for a quiet life. Possibly the prior himself realized that now or never was the time for a deal. He did in fact resign within a few weeks on favourable terms and, at the end of March 1536, Dr Holbeach succeeded him as Cranmer had wished.[3] Nevertheless, something had biased Cromwell in More's favour; it may be that Lady Margery remained in the background at the king's ear; certainly the word went round influential circles that More's debts would be paid, and the ex-prior himself is found laying down very precisely to Cromwell what he wants: the mansion at Grimley with a suitable amount of land; a pension to be paid quarterly, and all his gear and plate and chapel stuff to go with him.[4] An agreement was duly drawn up and signed by More, the convent and the representative of the king which embodied all these requests save one: Crowle, not Grimley, was allotted as his dower.[5]

There behind his moat, among the nymphs and shepherds of Crowle, 'between the vale of Evesham and the woodland, deepe in the one, and warme by the other',[6] the old man passed what years remained to him in that pleasant land of orchards, in his half-timbered manor house with its chapel and glass and its comfortable rooms, with the magnificent profile

---

1 *LP*, x, 56. Latimer refers to More as 'that simple man'. His basic objection was probably the prior's religious conservatism.

2 *Ibid.* 216. If Musard found it necessary to bring up a purchase stale now by fourteen years and by no means exceptional in itself (for similar purchases by Abbots Whethamstede and Wallingford of St Albans forty years earlier, *v. Reg. Whethamstede*, I, 423–33, 455–9), we may perhaps assume that no more serious charge would have seemed plausible.

3 *LP*, ix, 597 (8). The *congé d'élire* was given on 7 March; the election possibly took place *c.* 25 March; cf. Miss Fegan's note in *Journal*, 426.

4 *LP*, x, i, 1272.

5 Printed by Noake without reference *op. cit.* 203–4.

6 W. Habington, *Survey of Worcestershire*, I, 532.

of the Malvern Hills framing his horizon when he looked towards his old home at Worcester. Many years before he had ordered his tomb before the altar of the Jesus chapel in the cathedral of St Mary, but when his hour came it was at Alveston, a Worcester manor near Stratford-on-Avon, that he found a humbler grave.[1]

II. THE LAST VISITATIONS

When the backwash of the visitation had subsided, and the Act of Suppression of 1536 had removed for the larger houses the prospect of immediate extinction, the monasteries seem to have resumed their old disciplinary rhythm. Episcopal visitations were revived, and it is from these that much of our knowledge of the daily life at this time derives. They fall roughly into two classes: visitations of the conservative type, and those by the supporters of the new way of thinking whom Cromwell was now appointing to bishoprics. Of the first class the only extant example is Bishop Edward Foxe's paper of injunctions to the very unsatisfactory abbot and community of Wigmore. These, delivered in London in March 1537, rounded off the visitation by the bishop's vicar-general in the previous September, and had a long story behind them. Here we need only note that both in form and matter they might have been written a century or two earlier, and that there is nothing in them to suggest that Wigmore might not look forward to another two centuries of disorderly existence, instead of the bare twenty months that were to pass before its extinction. The visitation was the bishop's primary, and his commissary, Hugh Corwen, was in the somewhat unusual position of having been recently ordained by the prelate he was visiting and that, too, in his own abbatial church, for the abbot, John Smart, bishop of Panada *in partibus*, who had been appointed to office by Wolsey almost twenty years before, had for some time been acting as suffragan to the bishops of Hereford and Worcester. He had no good reputation, and the injunctions,[2] issued by Foxe after an interval of more than six months, imply that he had been guilty of incontinence and dilapidation, had been overbearing in his conduct towards his canons, and had pawned the abbey's jewels. Grave

1 Mr C. J. Hughes has kindly informed me that in the Alveston Parish Register of 1552, now in the Coventry Diocesan Registry Office at Warwick, the entry occurs: 'Willa More was sometyme Prior of Worcester was buried the xvith of September'. This disposes of the surmises of Noake and Canon J. M. Wilson as to More's place of burial, noted in the first (1959) edition of this book. In 1552 More would have been 81 or 82. As for Fordham, he fled to Scotland and joined the community of Dunfermline. See *Register of the Privy Seal of Scotland* (H.M.S.O.), vol. III, no. 1599 (23 March 1545/6). I owe this reference to Dr G. Donaldson of Edinburgh University.

2 The injunctions from the brief Register of Edward Foxe are in CYS, LXVIII, 372–4. The affair has had a controversial notoriety ever since J. A. Froude 'fished it up', to use his own phrase, as 'a choice specimen' of normal conditions in the monasteries at that time. Gasquet took up the challenge in *Henry VIII* and Coulton subsequently joined in the fray. The whole sordid skein at Wigmore is a tangle of private failings and intrigues; for a fuller account, *v.* article by the present writer, 'The Last Abbot of Wigmore', in *Medieval Studies presented to Rose Graham*, 138–45.

suspicion covered some of the canons also, and Richard Cubley, the abbot's chaplain, besides hunting and hawking, was a habitual brawler. Wigmore, in fact, in the last months of its existence, was, as it had been for a great part of the last two centuries, a thoroughly unsatisfactory house.

At an unspecified date subsequent to this visitation one of the canons of Wigmore, John Lee, drew up a long list of twenty-nine charges against the abbot for Cromwell's information. The indictment included simony, rape, manifold concubinage, the promiscuous ordination of a thousand priests, poisoning and the abetting of murder.[1] The motive of the accusation is obscure; many intrigues were afoot in the last years of monastic life, and it is probable that we have here a move in one of them of which the issue is not known. The more sensational features in Lee's indictment are undoubtedly fiction or gossip, but the bishop of Panada was in every way unworthy.[2] Nevertheless, he remained in office, performing all subsequent ordinations for Foxe, and made a successful bargain with Cromwell in the end.

In the same year that Foxe issued injunctions for Wigmore, Latimer visited his cathedral monastery at Worcester.[3] Unlike Cranmer, he appears as a frank innovator, and his act of visitation is characteristic of the bishop in its outspoken expression of opinion. Departing from common form, and opening with a preamble in the vernacular, Latimer, after a formal salutation, makes no attempt to mince matters:

> Forasmuch [he observes] as in this my Visitation I evidently perceive the ignorance and negligence of divers religious persons in this monastery to be intolerable and not to be suffered; for that thereby doth reign idolatry and many kinds of superstitions and other enormities: and considering withal that our sovereign lord the King, for some remedy of the same, hath granted by his most gracious licence, that the scripture of God may be read in English of all his obedient subjects,

the bishop duly proceeds to implement the royal wishes with a string of injunctions. Thus, a Bible in English is to be laid chained in church and cloister; every religious is to possess a copy of the New Testament at least; chant and extra offices are to be shortened whenever a sermon is toward; an English lecture on the Scriptures is to be given daily, attended by the whole community; the prior is to have a chapter of the Scripture in English read daily at his table at both meals, while the convent while eating are to listen to Scripture and its exposition. To these commands are added others of more general scope; the priory is to have a lay steward for all external business; there is to be a schoolmaster; and no one is to

---

[1] The list, in several recensions, is in *LP*, XII, i, 742. Froude's discussion of it is in *Short Studies*, 8th ed. I, 418–24.

[2] Gasquet's attempted rehabilitation of Bishop Smart cannot be accepted; *v.* Knowles, *art. cit.* 142 n. 2.

[3] Latimer's injunctions for Worcester Cathedral Priory are printed by W. H. Frere in Alcuin Club Collections, xv, *Visitation articles and injunctions of the period of the Reformation*, II, 12–14.

discourage any lay man or woman from reading any good book, whether in Latin or English. The first of these latter three injunctions appears as a general precept, and may have been a governmental order intended to make strict enclosure a practicable measure; the third, which cannot have had much relevance either in the priory or among the prior's gentlemen at Crowle or Grimley, may have been part of a private campaign on the part of the bishop.

Latimer's injunctions show us a reformer at grips with stolid conservatism; Clerk's *detecta* at Glastonbury a year later (15 July 1538) give us the other side of the picture, and show the kind of trouble that progressive spirits were giving to their superiors. This, the last glimpse of community life at that great and wealthy abbey, shows us a family that was no longer happy or united.[1] Out of a community of thirty-two some dozen, principally of the younger monks, were anxious to exploit the difficulties of their elders. Thus several complain that various royal injunctions are not kept, and that the grammar master (appointed, so it is alleged, just before a visitation and promptly removed afterwards) is underpaid, and his fee taken off the allowances made to the younger monks. Others are still more topical: two assert that the community has neither library nor books to read; no less than nine complain that the services in choir are 'soo tedius' that they have no time to study Scripture; three deplore the lack of books of Scripture 'and tyme to stodye the same', while others regret that the convent should be so 'much greved with mony processions and other seremonies'. Still others draw attention to the lack of lectures, as a result of which the brethren 'doth diverse tymes play at dice and cards'. There was also a remarkable consensus of opinion that brother Neot, our friend of the Evesham letters, had been at Oxford too long with no apparent result, though there is the widest disagreement as to the number of years he has kept in the university.[2] This agitation against him was apparently due to some of the younger monks who wanted his place, but there was clearly something of a division between the young and the old at Glastonbury; and the prior, a conservative, as well as the abbot, came in for criticism from the juniors. There is also the perennial criticism of the convent's ale, but the only serious charge is one of unnatural vice against one of the brethren who was himself one of the few examinates to aver that all was well.

At Athelney, a decayed house which we know from other sources to have been in financial difficulties, there was no public reading at meals and

---

1 This has been printed by Dom Aelred Watkin from the Proceedings of the Consistory Court in Wells Cathedral Act Book for the SRS, LVI, *Dean Cosyn and Wells Cathedral Miscellanea*, 159–65. Dom Aelred has kindly provided me with his transcript of the manuscript of the visitation.

2 For Neot, *v. supra*, p. 105, where he appears as a practitioner of *dolce far niente* at Oxford; the Evesham letters help to explain the indignation (or envy) of his brethren. Nevertheless, John Neot was one of those who petitioned Queen Mary for the refoundation of Glastonbury and he previously renewed his vows at Westminster (*infra*, pp. 426, 438).

the brethren ate in their private rooms. A grammar master was lacking, and no lectures on Scripture were given. Clerk made an injunction that the choir service was to be shortened so that the monks might have two hours every weekday for study and lectures.[1] And thus, in the last full year of monastic life in England, the long story of episcopal visitation in the monasteries, which had extended over more than three centuries, comes to an end. We may take leave of the visitation records with a recognition of the value of their evidence, but reminding ourselves once again that they were not composed for the use of historians or for the eye of posterity, and that their purpose was to correct and not to praise. If, over three centuries, their effect for good seems less than the contemporaries of St Bernard or of Gerald of Wales had hoped, the reason lies partly in the spiritual fact that no true reform can be imposed from without, but must always be the response from within to a vision of truth, justice and love, but partly also in the historical circumstance that these three centuries saw a progressive loosening of all disciplinary bonds within the Church.

The notes of this visitation, however, are not the last evidence we have of Tudor Glastonbury. Two other glimpses are given us of the abbot and the officials of the abbey continuing the routine acts of administration that had been repeated with little essential variation for almost six hundred years. An ex-monk, once the abbot's chaplain, deposed in a lawsuit some years later that a debtor, John Lyte, had paid £10 of a debt of £40 'to the said abbot in the little parlour upon the right hand within the great hall, the Friday after New Year's day before the said abbot was attainted [i.e. January 1539]... when the abbot's gentlemen and other servants were in the hall at dinner'. The balance was paid only a few months before the end of all things 'on St Peter's day being a Sunday [29 June] in the garden of the said abbot at Glastonbury, while high mass was singing... and... the abbot got him into an arbour of bay in the said garden [which rendered him invisible to Lord Stourton, who had been present but probably did not wish to be brought into the affair] and there received his money'. Abbot Whiting, it is added, 'asked the said master Lyte whether he would set up the said abbot's arms on his new buildings that he had made', and was given 'eight angels nobles' in consideration thereof.[2]

The second glimpse from the same year comes from the obedientiary rolls of 1538–9 which were checked after the dissolution by a royal clerk, Richard Amyce, and taken up to London to find a long home in the Record Office.[3] In them we can see the machinery of the abbey moving slowly onwards like the hands of a great clock. The enormous quantities of foodstuffs come in; the ditches and watercourses are cleansed of weeds

1　In *Dean Cosyn and Wells Cathedral*, ed. Watkin, 164–5.
2　Gasquet, *Henry VIII*, 369–70. Was Lyte a forebear of the distinguished archivist and antiquary, Sir H. C. Maxwell Lyte?
3　Dom A. Watkin, 'Glastonbury, 1538–9', 443–9.

and slime, the nettles round the chapel of St Michael on the Tor are scythed down, the abbey church is stripped of ivy, the candelabra are cleaned up, the girls' gild at St John's church receives a midsummer gift of beer; the plumber and porter between them, at considerable expense, veil the great rood in Lent. Who could know that it was for the last time? That what they and their forebears had done for centuries was never to be done again, that before the summer's foliage had withered the heart's beat of that vast body was to cease, that the weeds and nettles and ivy were to resume their kingdom, and that a silence was to fall?

CHAPTER XXVII

THE ATTACK ON THE GREATER HOUSES

The precise moment and occasion of the decision to have done with all the remaining monasteries, great and small, are almost as difficult to discover as are those marking the opening of the first attack. As late as July 1537, the king was elaborately re-founding Chertsey at Bisham[1] and the nunnery of Stixwold[2] in Lincolnshire, in order that they might offer their prayers for himself and his queen, and a whole batch of monasteries was being given formal exemption from the Act of Suppression. Indeed, the arrangements for Bisham were not completed and registered till 18 December,[3] and the trickle of lesser houses officially refounded 'in perpetuity' did not dry up till May 1538, when the nunnery of Kirklees received a patent to this effect.[4]

Long before this, however, a new policy was developing. On 11 November 1537, the wealthy priory of Lewes was surrendered to the king.[5] There was a long history behind this, and the prior was in a very vulnerable position, so that pressure could easily be brought to bear on him. Lewes took with it Castleacre, which duly conformed to the surrender on 22 November.[6] A few days later the Premonstratensian abbey of Titchfield in Hampshire followed suit, at the end of a long intrigue. The house was surrendered by its commendatory abbot, a Benedictine monk named John Salisbury, originally of Bury St Edmunds, who had taken up with the new ways when a student at Gloucester College, and had been made prior of St Faith's, Horsham, by Cromwell, and later, suffragan bishop of Thetford and commendatory abbot of Titchfield; he was later to become first dean of Norwich and absentee bishop of Man.[7] Clearly the surrender was the end of negotiations of which no trace has survived. Titchfield went to Wriothesley, who transmogrified it rapidly. Almost immediately there followed the surrender of Warden, an abbey long rent by domestic intrigue, probably fostered by Cromwell, which centred upon competition for the office of abbot.[8]

There was, during this phase of surrenders, some hesitation as to the legal procedure to be followed. Two years earlier, when Cromwell was in optimistic mood, and had taken counsel of 'some way to be devised, betwixt this and next session, by which young men should be restrained

---

1 Chertsey surrendered on 6 July 1537, 'on consideration of refoundation' (*LP*, xii, ii, 220, 411 (27)).

2 *LP*, xii, ii, 1311 (22).

3 Bisham was actually refounded on 12 December (*ibid.* 1228, 1311 (22)).

4 The Kirklees patent is dated 13 May (*ibid.* xiii, i, 1115 (19); in full in *YAJ*, xvi, 329).

5 *LP*, xii, ii, 1101 (16 November).   6 *Ibid.* 1119.

7 *Ibid.* 1153, 1274. For Salisbury, *v. DNB*.   8 *Ibid.* 1171.

from marriage... and tall and puissant persons stayed from marriage of old widows', he had had hopes of an even greater achievement, with 'some good way to be devised for the restraint and utter extinction of the abuses of lawyers'.[1] These, however, survived every revolution, social, religious and administrative, and as throughout the reign of Henry VIII the forms of legality were honoured however justice might fare, it was necessary to find a way that might put the minds of the lawyers easy. They distrusted the simplest and most expeditious formula, the deed of gift, presumably on the grounds that a community or a corporation could not legally give all its property away. They therefore preferred the more lengthy and dis-ingenuous, but nevertheless more familiar, method of fine and recovery.[2] This was a legal fiction long made use of in order to transfer entailed land or land held by a person (e.g. a woman) incapable under certain circum-stances of making a deed of gift. By this process a collusive suit was brought against the possessor, who acknowledged his want of title to the property and made a fine, which enabled the plaintiff to obtain recovery by judgment of court. Audley, on the whole, favoured the simpler method, but the more cumbrous one was employed on several occasions for greater security, and finally the act of 1539 gave retrospective validity to all surrenders.

Meanwhile, the pears were falling off the wall one by one. Voluntary surrender, however, was still largely confined to communities who sought a refuge in disgrace or distress, or were simply dropping early off the course. Towards the end of 1537 the next move was organized and a more active policy was adopted by the government. It was in three parts: a fresh visitation of the greater houses in order to induce surrender; a systematic pillage of the richer shrines; and a suppression out of hand of the friars. The remarkably well-informed steward of Lord Lisle, John Husee, writing to his master on 11 December, gives as a piece of news that 'the abbey of Warden is suppressed, and others are named to go down, as Peterborough, Ramsey, Sawtrey and St Albans. It is thought most will go down by consent of their abbots and priors; so I trust something will fall to your lordship.[3] Writing on the same day to Lady Lisle, Husee adds, after some more important information about ladies' dresses: 'no news but that divers abbeys are to be suppressed, and it is thought the most part will after'.[4] On 3 January he writes again: 'I pray Jesu send you shortly an abbey, with many good new years.'[5]

Husee's surmises were correct. No direct information as to the origin of the new policy is forthcoming, but it was certainly of Cromwell's planning, and Layton, when executing it, refers to 'your command to me in your gallery'.[6] Early in the New Year of 1538 Legh is found on circuit

1 *LP*, IX, 725 (ii).
2 Cf. Audley's letter to Cromwell apropos of Tichfield: *ibid.* XII, ii, 1153.
3 *Ibid.* 1209.   4 *Ibid.* 1210.
5 *Ibid.* XIII, i, 24.   6 *Ibid.* 102.

as a visitor in Somerset, and Layton in Norfolk, and their task is to bully or cajole superiors into surrender, those in the worst posture for defence being approached first. Legh received the surrender of the tottering Muchelney on 7 January,[1] and a week later Layton and two other commissioners took that of Westacre in Norfolk.[2] Here one Charles Wingfield, pretending royal authority, had anticipated the opening of the market by purchasing some of the property himself, but his claims were overridden. Others, nevertheless, might imitate him more successfully, for Layton wrote from Westacre that rumours were abroad everywhere that all monasteries would be suppressed, and in consequence the communities were preparing to lease or sell whatever they could. To counter this he spent some time calling together the communities on his road and assuring them that their fears were groundless. Meanwhile the surrenders continued. George Rolle, another of Lisle's agents, wrote on 8 February that 'the abbeys go down as fast as they may', and he adds loyally, 'I pray God send you one among them to your part'.[3]

Concurrently with the resumed visitations, groups of Cromwell's underlings were sent on tour to rifle some of the wealthiest shrines. This move was not started by any fresh act of parliament or royal proclamation; the last public act of hostility towards pilgrimages and offerings to the saints had been the Ten Articles of 1536,[4] but since then the influence of the radical bishops had been growing, while the needs of the government for money had been sharpened by the expenses incurred in putting down the northern risings. No doubt Cromwell had long contemplated his lists of the monastic treasures of the country, and considered that the time was now ripe for liquidation.

A beginning was made at Bury St Edmunds early in 1538, when the shrine of St Edmund, re-established by abbot Samson after the great fire described by Jocelin of Brakelond, was found 'very cumbrous to deface', but successfully relieved of 5000 marks' worth of gold and silver, besides many precious stones.[5] A little later in the year 'the bluddy abbott' (the phrase is Latimer's) of Hailes was trying to save his house by jettisoning its 'fayned relycke' of the Precious Blood.[6] After thanking God 'that he lived in this time of light and knowledge of His true honour, which he has come to through reading the Scripture in English', he denied that the relic had been tampered with within living memory, and asked for a commission to examine it. Meanwhile he returned 'immortale thancks for [Cromwell's] inestymable goodness', and packed the relic out of sight in

---

1 *LP*, XIII, i, 27.   2 *Ibid.* 101.   3 *Ibid.* 235.

4 Cf. also Cromwell's draft of an Act against pilgrimages and superstitious worship (*ibid.* X, 246 (16)).

5 *Ibid.* XIII, i, 192. For a list of the sums obtained from all these shrines, *v.* the accounts of the king's jeweller, Sir John Williams, printed for the Abbotsford Club by W. B. Turnbull, 1886.

6 *Ibid.* 347. As Gairdner notes (p. 74), the adjective has reference to the 'Blood of Hailes'.

a chest. According to Latimer, he also sold a number of the jewels.[1] The climax came in September, when the 'disgarnishing' of St Thomas's shrine supplied the king with several waggon-loads of precious metals and jewels; Cromwell's trusty agent Pollard was absorbed for days in his devotions at the blissful martyr's tomb.[2] From Canterbury Pollard, joined by Wriothesley and Williams, went on to Winchester where, after dismantling the shrine of St Swithun at 'three o'clock this Saturday morning' in order to discourage spectators, they proposed to 'sweep away al the rotten bones' as well, lest it should be thought 'we came more for the treasure than for avoiding of the abomination of idolatry'.[3]

With such spoliations in train and the crash of falling masonry echoing in the land, it is not surprising that the remaining monasteries took alarm and made friends on a lavish scale with what mammon of iniquity they still possessed. Their well-wishers urged the monks 'that better hit shulde be for them to make ther hands betyme then to late' by alienating property, granting long leases, and felling timber.[4] Cromwell found it necessary to reinforce his own exhortations with letters in the king's name to all heads of houses.[5] They must not listen to idle rumours of a general suppression. Nothing could be further from the truth. 'He [The king] does not intend in any way to trouble you or devyse for the suppression of any religious house that standeth.' Let them husband their resources carefully and delate to Cromwell any who spread such wild tales.

Nevertheless, surrenders continued thick and fast. The visitors were still uncertain of the legality of their acts, and endeavoured to confirm them by means of 'voluntary' confessions. Thus the brethren of St Andrew's, Northampton, expressed 'contrition for the enormities of their past living',[6] while the Cistercian monks of Bittlesden were willing to put their names to an unctuous recantation of popery, and discovered that they did 'profoundly consider that the manner and trade of living which we and others of our pretensed religion have practised and used many days, doth most principally consist in dumb ceremonies and in certain constitutions of Roman and other forinsical potentates'.[7] Failing this, the commissioners tackled the abbot alone, either with letters from Cromwell plainly demanding the surrender, as at Combermere, Faversham and Bisham,[8]

1 *Ibid.* XIII, ii, 186, 409.
2 The witticism is John Husee's; he repeats it more than once in his letters to Lord Lisle, e.g. *LP*, XIII, ii, 303 (8 September): 'Mr Pollard has been so busy night and day in prayer with offering unto St Thomas's shrine and hearse...that he could have no idle wordly time' for other business; *ibid.* 317 (10 September): Mr Pollard 'cannot yet intend to follow any idle causes'. For the twenty-six waggon-loads, *v. ibid.* 133 (a document of doubtful authenticity). The king and Cromwell were fellow-pilgrims of Pollard at Canterbury (*ibid.* 303, 317).   3 *Ibid.* 401–2; Wright, *SL*, cvi.
4 *LP*, XIII, i, 401; Ellis, *OL*, III, iii, cccxvii.
5 Some months previously he had reminded himself (*LP*, XII, ii, 1151) 'to send out my letters to all monasteries for their stay'. His (?draft of a) circular to abbots is in *LP*, XIII, i, 573. The acknowledgement of a letter of this kind by the abbot of Hartland is *ibid.* 893.
6 *Ibid.* 396.   7 *Ibid.* ii, 421 (Bittlesden).
8 *Ibid.* i, 1390 (Faversham), 969 (Combermere), 1208 (Bisham).

or with promises of office or a pension or both in case of compliance, and threats of deprivation and poverty in case of refusal. Occasionally, a surrender would seem even to have been staged behind the abbot's back.[1] Very few communities were proof against such attacks, though some, such as Shaftesbury and Cerne, tried once more to secure survival at a price.[2]

This final phase of the liquidation of the monasteries introduces us to the legendary figure of Dr John London.[3] He has often been treated by historians as a colleague from the beginning of Layton, Legh and Ap Rice, and the misapprehension has been perpetuated by Baskerville.[4] In fact, he was not employed till 1538 and played no part at all in the campaign of inquisition and calumny in 1535–6. Yet for all this, he has come to bear, somewhat undeservedly, the most unsavoury name of them all. He has had the misfortune to incur odium with every party; to the Catholics his activity in suppression, to the extreme Protestants his persecution of heretics, and to moderate Anglicans his insidious attack on Cranmer have rendered him detestable, and historians have often made the mistake of accepting as proved the sum total of all the accusations made by the various interested parties. He was older than the other visitors, a man of fifty or so, and it is not very clear how he came to find himself their shipmate, since neither before nor after was he employed as a government agent. A native of Buckinghamshire, and a Wykehamist of both foundations, he was Fellow (1505–18) and ultimately Warden of New College, Oxford, proceeded D.C.L. in 1519, held several benefices, and was treasurer of Lincoln cathedral. At New College he quarrelled with his Society and showed his conservatism both by his zeal against the Lutherans and by his refusal to manumit bondsmen on the estates of his college. He became canon of Windsor in 1540, and continued his severity against Lutherans, besides taking an active part in the plot of the prebendaries against Cranmer. For his share in this he was condemned for perjury, but a verdict of this kind against anyone on the losing side at this time should not be taken at its full face value. We need not, however, regard this combative man as a type of injured innocence. Dr London is not a prepossessing figure, and he seems to have made few friends. He died in the Fleet prison in 1543, and both Lutheran and Catholic apologists have taken care to point the moral. The charge of gross personal unchastity may well be sheer calumny.[5]

1 As at Vale Royal (*LP*, XIII, ii, 314), though the abbot there seems to have been a slippery customer (*ibid.* 315).

2 Ellis, *OL*, III, cccxliv; *LP*, XIII, ii, 1092.   3 The outline of his career is in *DNB*.

4 Baskerville, *EM*, 127: 'The third visitor of note [*sc.* after Legh and Layton] was . . . Dr John London.' The judgment of Mgr Hughes: 'one of the vilest men of all this vile time' (*Reformation*, I, 235), may serve as an example of the harsh judgments on London.

5 The chief source of the imputations against London's moral character is the biased and irresponsible Protestant of the next generation, John Louthe, cited in Nichols, *Narratives of the Reformation* (CS, 77, p. 35). His testimony is of the same worth as Layton's *obiter scripta* in his letters to Cromwell.

The bad name borne by the Warden of New College among the advocates of the monks rests partly upon his admitted energy in material destruction and partly on the interpretation of a single episode in his career as visitor. He certainly swept relics out of churches as ruthlessly as could be desired, among them, so he alleged, 'two heddes of seynt Ursula' from one district and 'a chowbone [jawbone] of saynt Ethelmold', but he does not seem to have attacked the fabric itself.[1] At Caversham he destroyed the pilgrimage shrine of Our Lady, sending up the image 'platyd over with sylver' in a nailed box 'by the next bardge that comythe from Reding to London'. This done, he 'also pullyd down the place she stode in, with all other ceremonyes, as lightes, schrowdes, crowchys [i.e. jewels] and images of wax, hangyng abowt the chapell, and defacyd the same thorowly in exchuyng [i.e. eschewing, preventing] of any farther resort thedyr'.[2] At Reading he 'rydde' the church of the grey friars of 'parcleses [=parcloses, screens], ymages and awlters', and recommended it for use as a town hall instead of the existing one, which was situated so near the common washing place that on 'cession dayes' there was 'such betyng with batildores' that juries could not hear the charge given them.[3]

The incident which has helped to earn his ill fame was his encounter with Abbess Bulkeley of Godstow, and it rests chiefly upon a misinterpretation of a phrase in her first letter to Cromwell, clearly written when she was in a highly excited frame of mind.

Doctor London [she writes], whiche, as your lordeship dothe well knowe, was ageynste my promotyon, and hathe ever sence borne me greate malys and grudge, like my mortall enmye, is sodenlie cummyd unto me with a greate rowte withe him, and here dothe threten me and my susters, sayeng that he hathe the kynges commyssyon to suppres the house spyte of my tethe. And when I ... shewyd him playne that I wolde never surrender to his hande, beyng my awncyent enemye, now he begynes to intreate me and to inveigle my susters one by one otherwise than ever I harde tell that any of the kynges subjectes hathe bene handelyd ... and will not taike my answere that I will not surrender till I have the kynges gratious commaundment or your good lardeshipes.[4]

This letter, taken out of its context, was construed by Sanders, and later by Gasquet, as a charge of solicitation against London. It is clearly nothing of the sort, but merely another instance of the pressure brought on communities to extract a surrender. The abbess did not know that on the very next day the object of her wrath was himself writing to Cromwell:

I am now at Godstow ... wher I perceyve my ladye to tak my commynge som thinge penciflye ... if the kinges grace pleasure be ... to tak the house by surrendre, than I besek your lordeschipp to admytt me an humble sutar for my

---

1 The two interesting exhibits in the text are from London's list of the Reading relics in Wright, *SL*, cx (*LP*, xiii, ii, 377 (ii)). It has not been possible to check Wright's reading of the text, but he is usually fairly accurate; 'chowbone' clearly=jawbone.
2 Wright, *SL*, cviii, cix, cx; *LP*, xiii, ii, 367, 368, 377.
3 Wright, *SL*, cviii; *LP*, xiii, ii, 367.
4 *LP*, xiii, ii, 758; Wright, *SL*, cxii. The letter of the abbess bears date 5 November.

lady and herre sisters and the late abbasse...specially my lady, whiche lately payd herre fyrst fruytes, and wass indaungeryd therfor unto herre fryndes. Many of the mynchys [=nuns, cf. Minchin Buckland] be also agyd...wherfor I besek your lordeschipp to be gudd lord unto them.[1]

Katharine Bulkeley, indeed, was far from being a confessor of the old faith. Three weeks later she begged Cromwell to

be well assuered that ther is nother Pope nor Purgatorie, Image nor Pilgrimage, ne prayinge to dede Saintes, usid or regarded amongeste hus; but all supersticious ceremonies set aparte, the verie honor of God and the trewithe of his holie wordes...is mooste tenderlie folowid and regarded withe hus.[2]

In the sequel, when Godstow passed quietly away twelve months later, Abbess Bulkeley retired on the munificent pension of £50. Her prioress received only £4 and the nuns £3 or less.

This was not the only occasion on which Dr London showed himself considerate and good-natured in his recommendations. A month after his visit to Godstow, and during the Christmas season, he presented the abbess of Delapré to Cromwell as 'a good aged woman' and, on 2 February 1539, he writes that the abbess of Polesworth 'with her virtuous reputation and great age...rather deserves more than less' than her pension, and the nuns also deserve consideration as 'aged, impotent and friendless'.[3] Finally, it should be added that Dr London nowhere makes a sweeping or ill-natured charge against the moral character of the religious.

As there was now no question of transference, the suppression commissioners who allotted the pensions had a sharp weapon to hand for those who boggled. The abbess of Amesbury, when first approached, had replied with spirit that if the king commanded her to leave the house she would gladly go, though she begged her bread; she cared for no pension, and prayed them to trouble her no further. In the event she resigned, and asked for due provision to be made for her—and failed of her request.[4] Similarly the abbot of St Albans, who in December 1538, had stated that he would 'rather choyse to begge his bredde alle the dayes of his lif than consent to any surrender',[5] did in fact accept some kind of pension when

1 Wright, *SL*, cxi (6 November); *LP*, xiii, ii, 767. It is not clear why Wright printed the letters in this order.

2 Ellis, *OL*, iii, iii, cccxlv; *LP*, xiii, ii, 911. Written on 26 November, this letter thanks Cromwell for intervening to stay London's hand. The abbess assures the vicar-general of a 'poor mayden is prayer duringe my life' and appoints an understeward at Cromwell's request. Eight months later she offered him the 'lyttle office of the Stewardship of this Monasterie', with the assurance that 'if it were a M. tymes better you should have it with all my harte and prayers'. On another occasion 'a couple of Banbury cheeses' went to Cromwell (*LP*, xiii, i, 441, 492, 1262).

3 For Delapré, *v.* Wright, *SL*, cxiv; *LP*, xiii, ii, 1153. For Polesworth, *LP*, xiv, i, 207.

4 *LP*, xiv, i, 629; ii, 27.

5 *Monasticon*, ii, 249; Wright, *SL*, cxxiv. This letter is not calendared under its date (10 December 1538) in *LP*, where there is some confusion of the last abbots of St Albans (cf. *LP*, xiii, ii, 385).

he was deposed. In many cases, indeed, the religious felt a relief when the final break-up came. At Beauvale Dr London 'founde the prior of the Charterhouse in hys shortt gowen and velvytt cappe, redy befor our commyng', and he noted that at all houses 'as well of men as of wemen, they be in maner all gon that night I have taken ther surendre and streightway in new apparell'.[1] From Bisham Layton gave a vivid account of the last hours of the 'king's new monastery', now less than two years old. The aspect of the fields awoke his enthusiasm: 'whete of the gronde, barly, with all kynds of grayne, the fayrest that ever I see. . . the godelieste demaynes that I have sene', but the abbot was 'a very simple man; the monks of smale lerning and muche lesse discretion'. The place was in utter poverty, and the monks anxious to be off, so that 'whan we were makyng salle of the olde vestments within the chapitre house, they [*sc.* the monks] cryede a newe marte in the cloister; every man bringing his cowle caste upon his nec to be solde, and solde them in dede'.[2]

Thus by persuasion, manipulation and the hard logic of the changing times the great monasteries were brought to surrender one by one throughout 1538 and 1539, and were accompanied by many of the lesser ones that had purchased a respite two years earlier. Hitherto the proposals originally used to justify suppression, that the revenues and buildings might be transferred to educational or other ecclesiastical uses, had been allowed by Cromwell to remain in oblivion. The method of voluntary surrender made all apologetics superfluous and was itself the most profitable that could be devised. Towards the end of 1538, however, when the great landslide was beginning and it was clearly a case of now or never, bishops and others began to appeal for certain houses, that they might remain in another guise. Thus the abbot and community of Evesham petitioned for continuance as one of the royal educational establishments they had heard of; inns at Evesham were few and bad; the place was on the main road to Wales and there was plenty of scope for hospitality and charity; it was an exempt monastery, and the only one left in the district, the very place for a college.[3] Were Dr Feckenham and his correspondents behind this move? Whatever its origin, it was pigeon-holed by Cromwell and Evesham fell. Then Latimer is found petitioning Cromwell, 'tamquam non tibi natus soli, sed multorum commodo', that the priory of Great Malvern may continue, 'natt in monkrye, God forbyd', but for learning, preaching and hospitality, and to this end the present prior would put up 'ccccc markes to the kynges hynesse, with cc markes to your selffe for your good wyll'.[4] A few weeks later Dr London noted that Rowland Lee of Lichfield and others wished that Coventry might be a college of learned men for preaching. To commend the project he added that 'the King might cause

1 *LP*, xiv, i, 1321; Wright, *SL*, ciii.
2 *LP*, xiii, i, 1239; Ellis, *OL*, iii, iii, ccclviii. This description may be taken as a *locus classicus*.
3 *LP*, xiii, ii, 866.   4 *Ibid.* 1036.

abbots thereabouts, as Kilingworthe [=Kenilworth], that be pensionate, to spend their pensions there and not lie lurking in corners.'[1] Nothing, however, was done to establish a communal centre for quondams or a college for preachers, and in the spring of 1539 (13–23 May) Parliament passed an act vesting in the Crown all monastic possessions surrendered or henceforth to be surrendered subsequent to the Act of 1536. This was an application on the grand scale of the procedure recommended by Audley in 1532 for St Aldate's. Some twenty of the great abbots were present in the Lords' house, some of them with proxies, but they raised no protest. The bill went through its stages in the customary leisurely way, but on the day of its final passage a brief bill was introduced by Cromwell and rushed through all its stages between the two Houses in a single day.[2] Herein, after a preamble written by Henry himself, which alluded to 'the slothful and ungodly life which hath been used among all those sort which have borne the name of religious', and which outlined a long and comprehensive list of good causes and social services towards which the revenues of the monasteries might be devoted, the enacting clause gave the king power to erect as many bishoprics as he might think fit.[3] There is no record that the abbots present did anything to hinder its passing; it would indeed have been the height of temerity in them to do so; but it was the last occasion that they were ever to have of exercising their powers of voting in parliament.

Various schemes were considered during the summer, several of them very ambitious, and there is some evidence that the group of conservative 'Henrician' bishops, which included Gardiner, Tunstall and Sampson of Chichester, were particularly interested.[4] Cromwell was naturally anxious to keep the cost of these new establishments as low as possible, and a note of his survives as a memorandum 'to dymyshe [*sic*] sum of the busshop-ricks'.[5] In October he gave his views on the subject to the king,[6] and finally six large abbeys were erected into bishoprics: Westminster, Bristol, Gloucester, Oxford, Peterborough and Chester, while Thornton and Burton became colleges. Precedents already existed for the necessary

1 *LP*, XIV, i, 183,

2 *Journals of the House of Lords*, I, 110. Sixteen abbots were present.

3 This preamble has often been printed, e.g. by Wright, *SL*, pp. 262–3 (in part), and by H. Cole, *King Henry the Eighth's Scheme of Bishopricks* with facsimiles of the king's writing. Both these state that it is in the king's hand.

4 Cole prints two such lists, one in the king's own hand. In this almost every county that is not already allotted a bishopric has one allotted to it, and very careful calculations are made for the various new establishments, with provision for chapters, clerk, choirs, hospitality, education, pensioners (veterans and servants), and the expenses are balanced against the income of one or more suppressed house or houses amalgamated for the purpose. Some interesting experiments were to be made, e.g. Fountains was to be made the seat of a new bishopric, and Bodmin, Launceston and St German's priories were to be thrown together to provide for a Cornish see. For other lists, *v.* also *LP*, XIV, ii, 428–30. One is in the hand of Sampson of Chichester (a conservative) with a note 'the book of the erections of all the new houses as they came from the Bishop of Winchester (Gardiner)', and there are indications that Tunstall of Durham had a hand in the matter.

5 *LP*, XIV, ii, 424. 6 *Ibid.* 427.

changes, since from the spring of 1538 onwards the cathedral priories which surrendered had been transformed into secular chapters wherein were retained the more serviceable of the old personnel. In the new creations the arrangements were as a rule still more conservative: an abbot became bishop, a prior dean, and many of the monks canons and prebendaries. Sometimes, as at Gloucester, there was a short intermediate stage of collegiate existence, and there and elsewhere an endeavour was made to give an educational colour to the new foundation, together with a connection with the universities. Many of the currents of feeling at work are evident in the case of Canterbury, where the conservative prior Goldwell had fallen foul of Cranmer, who considered that 'no one has hindered the word of God so much as he, or maintained superstition more'.[1] Goldwell, therefore, anxious to be first dean, wrote to Cromwell: 'I have been Prior of the seid churche above xxii years, wherfore it shuld be moche displeasure to me in my age to be putt from that my levyng or from my chamber and lodgying which I have hadd by all the seid xxii yers'.[2] Cranmer, however, was obdurate, and the septuagenarian Goldwell had to leave. The archbishop also criticized Cromwell's scheme for the establishment of twelve prebendaries and preachers with good stipends. It was his experience, he said, speaking with a prophetic distrust of the class, that prebendaries were as a rule neither learners nor teachers, but good vianders; he therefore suggested twenty divines and forty students in tongues and sciences and French with smaller stipends.[3] In the event, all the new sees and converted priories, with the exception of the short-lived Westminster, quickly conformed to the normal type of cathedral establishment.

---

1 *LP*, xiii, ii, 97 (15 August 1538). A letter from the prior to Cromwell (*ibid.* 139) helps to explain Cranmer's dislike.
2 *Ibid.* 676; Ellis, *OL*, iii, ccclxiii.   3 *LP*, xiv, ii, 601.

CHAPTER XXVIII

THE SUPPRESSION OF THE FRIARS

The third part of the campaign of 1538 was directed against the friars. These, it will be remembered, had been the first to be taken in hand and sworn in to support the new regime in 1534; they had lost their independence as separate orders and had been placed under two nominees of Cromwell. They had, however, not fallen under the jurisdiction of the visitors of 1535 and had not figured in the Act of Suppression of 1536. They had little property and no treasure, and their dissolution, which brought very little revenue to the Court of Augmentations, was part of the process, begun already by Cromwell and urged on by the supporters of the new religion, of 'cleaning up' after the severance from Rome. Unlike the monks, the friars were, however loosely, centralized upon the papacy; they had now no *point d'appui* and could only be a nuisance. Accordingly, from February 1538, onwards, they were dealt with by Richard Ingworth, sometime prior provincial of the Dominicans and now suffragan bishop of Dover, who received his commission as visitor of the four orders of friars on 6 February.[1] When he first appears on his rounds in Cromwell's correspondence, it is already 23 May 1538 and he is at Gloucester, having passed from Northampton by way of Coventry into the Severn basin. 'In every place is poverty', he writes, and the friars are using every shift to raise money by selling jewels and leases.[2] It is interesting to note that even at this late stage the visitor's approach was tentative, and a rhythm similar to that of the visitation of 1535–6 is perceptible, though there is some evidence that now, at least, the initial hesitation was due to the ambiguity of Cromwell's instructions rather than to the uncertainty of his plans. In any case, Ingworth writes from Gloucester that he is for the present leaving the friars in existence, after sequestrating the convent seal, in the expectation that they will thus be starved into surrender before the year is out. He notes that at Droitwich the community consisted of the prior alone; during the past year he had felled and sold 'vii score good elmys' in addition to realizing a gilt chalice, a censer, 'ij gret brasse pottys eche abull to sethe an holl oxe as men sey', together with spits, pans and all the household gear, 'so that in the howse

---

1 *LP*, XIII, i, 225. The narrative that follows is largely the result of piecing together the letters of Ingworth and London which are printed in full by Ellis and Wright in exactly equal proportions. This division and still more the erroneous arrangement and chronology of the two editors, have caused infinite trouble and confusion in the narratives of subsequent writers. The correct order of the letters, together with notices of others omitted by Ellis and Wright, will appear in the sequel. A minor additional confusion has been caused by Ellis misreading *Ric. Dovorensis* for *Richard Devereux* and printing the letters under the latter name.

2 *LP*, XIII, i, 1052; Wright, *SL*, xcviii.

ys not left on bede, on schete, on plater or dische'. Despite this clearance three gentlemen are 'labouring' to get a grant of the site from the king.[1]

Ingworth's comparatively gentle treatment of his erstwhile brethren drew a rebuke from Cromwell. He had, the vicar-general told him, changed his habit, but not his friar's heart; he was writing kindly about the friars and allowing them to continue. The bishop of Dover was hurt at the imputation. 'Good my lorde', he wrote, 'juge me not so, for God shall be my juge, my fryers hart was gone ij yeres befor my habet.' His cautious approach had been due rather to an inability to ascertain Cromwell's wishes; now that these are clear, he 'koulde by juste and fayer menys, and do no wronge, dyspache a gret parte off the fryers in Ynglonde or my yere off vysytacyon was endeyd', if only he might be given powers of dispensation and some guarantee of employment for the friars, 'for off trewthe ther harttes be clere from the relygyon the more parte, so they myght change ther cotes'; and he adds a few scandalous details to prove his lack of prejudice. He has now despatched the Bristol Carmelites and the three houses at Gloucester.[2]

Ingworth had indeed now perfected his technique, which is succinctly described in a memorandum written on 28 July by the mayor of Gloucester and three of his aldermen. The bishop of Dover, they write,

befor the meyar and aldermen in the howseys of freeres ther at ij tymeys in ij days putt the seyd freers att ther lybertys, whether they wold contynew in ther howseys and kepe ther relygyon and injuxcyons accordeyng to the same, or ellys gyff ther howseys into the kynges handdes. The injuxcyons he ther declareyd among them, the whyche war thowthe by the seyd meyar and aldermen to be good and resonabyll, and also the seyd freeres seyd that they war accordeyng to ther rewlys, yet as the warlde ys nowe they war nott abull to kepe them and leffe in ther howseys, wherfore voluntaryly they gaffe ther howseys into the vesytores handes to the kynges use. The vesytor seyd to them: 'thynke not, nor hereafter reportt nott, that ye be suppresseyd, for I have noo suche auctoryte to suppresse yow, but only to reforme yow, wherfor yf ye woll be reformeyd accordeyng to good order, ye may contynew for all me'. They seyd they war nott abull to contynew. Wherfor the vesytor toke ther howseys, and charytabully delyvered them, and gaff them letteres to vesyte ther fryndes, and so to goo to oder howseys, with the whyche they war wery well contentt, and soo departeyd.[3]

This formula usually worked well enough, though even Ingworth noted that 'many be lothe to departe, and specyally off the graye Fryeres; they be so close eche to other that no man can cum within them to know ther hartts. I have more besynes with them then with all the Fryers besyde.'[4] He had trouble, however, at Shrewsbury with his own brethren, the black friars. It was a house of some size and good observance, against

1 Ibid.   2 Ibid. 1484; Wright, SL, xcviii.
3 LP, xiii, i, 1484 (3); Wright, SL, xcix.
4 LP, xiii, ii, 49; Ellis, OL, iii, iii, cccxxviii.

which he could find no charge, and when he made the usual offer they called his bluff. The bishop of Dover was in a quandary, and wrote to Cromwell more than once for advice;[1] we do not hear of the immediate result, but the final sentence could not be long delayed; it was with the friars of Shrewsbury as with the ancress in the churchyard of the black friars at Worcester, of whom he wrote that he 'had not a lytyll besynes to have her grauntt to cum owte, but owte sche ys'.[2]

Ingworth passed from Worcester to Bridgnorth, where he found the grey friars 'the porest Howse that I have seyn'. Thence, he circled through Staffordshire, shutting down a number of friaries. At almost all there is the same story of poverty: the Austin friars at Stafford have 'a pore howse with small implements'; the black friars at Newcastle-under-Lyme are 'all in ruyne, and a pore howse'; the Austins at Shrewsbury in 'a howse all in ruyne, and the more parte falleynge downe; no thynge in that howse ...no chaleys to sey masse...no fryeres ther but the prior', and he a lunatic, assisted by 'ij Erysche men'.[3] From Shrewsbury he went by way of North Wales to Brecknock, Carmarthen and Haverford, whence he took ship to Mount's Bay to deal with Cornwall and Devon.[4]

Meanwhile, Dr London came into action in the Midlands. He is first heard of at Oxford on 8 July, surveying the friars' houses in the city. The Carmelites had been insuring themselves against a rainy day by selling an annuity of £4 for the reasonable sum of £40 to the abbot of Eynsham, by letting out their grounds and by selling their elms and their jewels; the fabric of the friary was 'notably ruynose'. The same words are used of the buildings of the Austins, where the late prior, George Browne, now archbishop of Dublin, had felled the best timber and departed with the jewels and plate. The grey friars, with 'praty Ilonds behund the Howse well woddyde...oon fayr orcherd, and sondry praty gardens', have also been selling out, and have even dug up and melted down the lead pipes of their conduit. They have 'a great hoge [=huge] Howse conteyning moche ruynose bylding'. Finally the black friars, also possessed of well wooded islands, are in better fettle, with a newly built church and a 'prety store of plate and juellys'. There was also an 'Anker' there, 'a well disposyd man', who had 'byldyd his Howse owt of the grounde' and begged to be allowed to stay there for the rest of his life. The Warden of New College then went on to suggest, with a generous appreciation of the need for industrializing Oxford, where there 'ys no great thorowfare', that it would be a 'blessyd acte' on the part of Cromwell if the four friaries were given to 'thys poor towne' to be turned into fulling mills; a still further advantage would be the consequent saving to the king of the hundred marks *per annum* which were now paid in alms to the grey and black friars.[5]

1 *LP*, XIII, ii, 92; Wright, *SL*, c.   2 *LP*, XIII, ii, 49; Ellis, *OL*, III, iii, cccxxviii.
3 *LP*, XIII, ii, 92; Wright, *SL*, c.
4 *LP*, XIII, ii, 200; Wright, *SL*, cii. 'and so over to Sent Mykelles Mownte, and so brynge all Cornwall and Denschyar with me.'
5 *LP*, XIII, i, 1342; Ellis, *OL*, III, iii, cccxxxvii.

Something has already been said of London's activities at Reading.[1] He reappears again at Northampton on 29 October, having been on circuit in the Midlands, and is still feeling the effects of a letter from Cromwell. Stories have reached the king of his works of destruction, and he hastens to defend himself. He has, he says, done no more than take down and realize for the king what the neighbours would else have helped themselves to in 'som very beggarly Howses'. He gives some details: at Reading he 'dydd oonly deface the Church; all the windows being full of Fryers'; the same was true of Aylesbury, another poor house; he had 'pulled down no Howse throwly at noon of the Fryers, but so defacyd them as they shuld nott lyghtly be made Fryerys agen'. And he adds: 'amongs many blessed reformations don by the King's Grace, I suppose thys be nott the lest, utterly to suppresse theis Fryars'.[2] London, who presumably had the same commission as Ingworth, and was ostensibly a reformer, not a suppressor, saved appearances by persuading the brethren to endorse a sanctimonious manifesto; thus the minors at Aylesbury 'did profoundly consider that the perfection of a Christian living doth not consist in dumb ceremonies, wearing of a grey coat, disguising ourselves after strange fashions, ducking, and becking, in girding ourselves with a girdle full of knots [i.e. the three knots of the Franciscan girdle, symbolical of the three vows of poverty, chastity and obedience] and other like papistical ceremonies, wherein we have been most principally practised [i.e. deceived] and misled in the past'.[3] Occasionally the friars took action even before the visitor arrived, as the warden of Greyfriars, London, writing to Cromwell asking that he and his brethren might be dispensed 'of their papistycall slanderous apparell'.[4]

A week after London's letter from Northampton he was back in Oxford, having dealt with Warwick on the way. There he found it difficult to protect the property for the king, for 'the power people...in every place be so greedy upon these Howsys...that by night and daye, nott oonly of the townys, butt also of the contrye, they do contynually resortt as long as any dore, wyndow, yren or glasse or lowse [=loose] ledde remaynythe in any of them'.[5]

This ended London's share in suppressing the friars; henceforth his activities were concerned with the possessioners. While Ingworth, however, was working up from the west, some of the friars were trying to settle their future for themselves. Layton, who was spending the last weeks in September in his rectory at Harrow, birding over the fields and relishing the pears grafted by his distinguished predecessor and kinsman, got wind of a scheme on foot among the small community of Trinitarian friars at

1 *V. supra*, p. 355.   2 *LP*, XIII, ii, 719; Ellis, *OL*, III, iii, cccvii.
3 *LP*, XIII, ii, 501; Rymer, *Foedera*, XIV, 611.
4 *LP*, XIII, ii, 808; Rymer, XIV, 609.
5 *LP*, XIII, ii, 757; Ellis, *OL*, III, iii, cccx.

Hounslow who, he told Cromwell, 'as the commyne reporte is, drinke wichely [=weekly] all the toune dry' and are led home nightly 'by the inhabitaunce'. They would be, he adds, 'not a lytle myssyde of the ale typelers'.[1] They had bargained with a Mr Cheeseman to lease their house to him for ninety-nine years in return for a pension of £10 for the minister and £5 apiece for the brethren. Unfortunately for them, the resourceful Layton soon had the affair under control.

Meanwhile, Ingworth had appeared again at King's Langley, his old headquarters. He has been closing down the friaries of East Anglia and corroborates London: 'the substans before my cuming was conweid and gone; sum sollde, sum stollen, and sum plegeid'. He has now ejected his late brethren from Langley, and makes a doleful plea to Cromwell that he may have the place himself. He has lost money in the business of visiting and will have no home or income. 'My good Lorde, for Goddes sake, have pitey on your true and feithfull seruante.'[2] A fortnight later he was at Canterbury where he had an unusual experience. One of the brethren at the Austin friars 'very rudely and trayterusly useyd hym be for all the cumpany...and at all tymes he styll hylde and styll woll to dey for yt, that the Kynge may not be hede of the Chyrche of Ynglonde, but yt must be a spyrytuall father adpoynted by God.' Ingworth sent him straight up to Cromwell and he was duly sent down again to Canterbury for execution; his name was John Stone.[3] We are not told how (if at all) he had avoided taking the various oaths admitting the royal supremacy, nor do we know by what interior debates and combats he made himself ready for his stand. We know only that this confrère of Luther and Barnes came forward at the very end of the day as a steadfast witness to the faith that had been handed down to him.

When Christmas was past, the bishop of Dover moved north from London at the end of February; his goal was Boston, but on his way thither he 'found' a house of Austin friars at Huntingdon, 'very pore', which he 'received'. At Boston he confiscated the four friars' houses; they were 'very pore howseys and pore persons...with pore implementes'. The properties were delivered to 'master Taverner and master Johnys, servanttes to the kynges grace'.[4] Ingworth would no doubt have been surprised had he been told that he had encountered one whose pleasant voices would outlive so many specious creations of the age and entrance a very different world. So perhaps would their composer, for he had recently been converted from polyphony to good works, and was one of Cromwell's lesser agents for the work of suppression in Lincolnshire; a letter from

1 *LP*, xiii, ii, 481; Ellis, *OL*, iii, iii, cccxl–cccxli. Layton sends Cromwell 'perisse [=pears] of Harowe graffede by my Lorde of Duresme [Tunstall was rector 1511–22] his owne hand, and suche parterige as my hawke kylle'.

2 *LP*, xiii, ii, 1021; Ellis, *ibid*. cccxvi.

3 *LP*, xiii, ii, 1058; Ellis, *ibid*. cccxxv. A. G. Little in *VCH, Kent*, ii, 201, cites the civic accounts with details of expenses for the execution.

4 *LP*, xiv, i, 348; Wright, *SL*, xcvi.

him is extant which corroborates Ingworth's account of the general poverty of the friars.[1]

From Boston the visitor attained Lincoln, where he received another 'iiij powre howseys, non thyng lefte but stonys and pore glasse'. He proposed to proceed into the northern parts and act with a despatch that would 'leve but fewe in Ynglond before Ester'. From Lincoln he went to Grimsby, where he found 'all in pouertye and lytell lefte';[2] a fortnight later he was at Scarborough, having dealt with Hull and Beverley; there he 'receyved iij pore Howses...so pore that they have solde the stall and partclossys in the Churche'. He is bound now for Carlisle and Lancaster and any other friaries 'that I can here off', recommending to Cromwell that George Lawson should be commissioned to deal with Berwick and other houses in the far north. In this, his last extant letter of this tour, Ingworth repeats once more, and with urgency, his plea that 'all curats myght have warnynge to suffer soche pore men that have gyff upe ther Houses, to synge [i.e. say Mass and officiate] in ther Churches'.[3] Within a few weeks of this letter the English province of the four orders of friars had ceased to exist.

Thus, without noise or outcry, almost without a whimper, a familiar class of men disappeared from English life. Three hundred years ago they had come, the brethren of Agnellus of Pisa, of Jordan of Saxony, of Haymo of Faversham and of Simon Stock, the vanguard of a great movement that had covered the land with its fame. From the English friaries had issued forth a wave of learning that had captured the universities and given a decisive and permanent wrench not only to the teaching of the schools but to the whole course of European thought. They had seemed to their adversaries, little more than a century before their end, as numerous and as ubiquitous as flies in summer or as motes in the sunbeam. And now they vanished overnight, like flowers of a day.

Ingworth and London, indeed, had to do with little more than a rump. In the previous twenty years the friars had lost almost all their notable men at the extremes of the right wing or of the left. Many of their most active minds had followed the call of Germany to new things, with Bale and Barnes and Coverdale, whether the way led to the stake or to a mitre. At the other pole the staunchest had been swept away to death or exile with the Observants. Of those who remained, some of the ablest had left friar's habit and friar's heart to take office under Henry and Cromwell. It was left to the remnant to suffer the bitter experience of being turned out of their houses by their own renegade superiors, a Hilsey or an Ingworth. From all the accounts that the visitors give, those remaining in the friaries were the proletariat of their class, without enterprise or

1 *LP*, xiv, i, 348; Wright, *SL*, xcvi. Taverner's letter (*LP*, xiv, i, 101; cf. xiii, ii, 328) is printed in full by E. H. Fellowes, *Tudor Church Music*, i, lv.
2 *LP*, xiv, i, 413; Ellis, *OL*, iii, iii, cccxxiv.
3 *LP*, xiv, i, 494; Ellis, *ibid.* cccxxvii.

zeal or parts. They were, of all the religious, least able to stand against the final assault, for they had no centre and no fulcrum save Cromwell, no superior save his agents, and no hope of material existence for the future.

Historians have rightly noted their extreme poverty. Whatever charge might be made against them, it could not be that of indulgence in wealth and luxury. But the positive indigence and squalor of 1538 was abnormal. It was not due to the lack of a fixed income, for this they had never had, but to the failure of their world to support them any longer and the failure on their part to hold or recapture the favour of their world. The pages of their earliest chronicler, Thomas of Eccleston, are full of the names of townspeople and civic authorities who had given the friars their first plots of land and small tenements, and he records the protest of their zealous provincial William of Nottingham, against their too elaborate cloisters and churches. Now, when they had left, their houses and halls often passed back into the possession of the municipality and townspeople; their churches and cloisters almost invariably perished altogether.[1]

1 For excellent accounts of the remains of Dominican and Franciscan friaries, v. A. Hinnebusch, *The Early English Friars Preachers*, and A. R. Martin *Franciscan Architecture in England*.

CHAPTER XXIX

THE CANKERED HEARTS[1]

The great enterprise of the suppression of the monasteries, which intimately affected the lives of thousands of the educated men and women of the land, which transferred a large fraction of the wealth of the country from the possession of religious corporations to that of the king, which brought about the rifling and demolition of so many churches, and which eliminated from England a traditional way of Christian life, went forward during four years with a minimum of personal violence. Few revolutions of comparable importance, whether in the sixteenth or in later centuries, have been accomplished with so little bloodshed or judicial barbarity. Indeed, throughout the process little or no animus was displayed against the religious as such. It was their wealth that Henry and Cromwell wanted, not primarily or professedly the extinction of their order, though this was soon seen to be an inevitable consequence. The apologists of the monks, therefore, who have written of the reign of terror, or of the cruel tyranny of Cromwell, have misread the situation, or transferred to the sixteenth century in England the mentality of reformers and revolutionaries of other lands and times. It would be almost permissible to say that the king and his minister had no more ill-will towards the monks than the gay highwayman of legend had towards his victims.

Yet it is equally unhistorical to treat the Dissolution as no more than the first scheme of nationalization in English history. Beneath the harmless façade of legalism, pensions and bargaining for terms there lay, only half hidden, the mailed fist of the minister who was prepared to strike down without shrift or mercy any who hindered the smooth working of his design. The religious had, perhaps without fully knowing it, renounced all right of appeal to pope or bishop or principle of justice by the oaths they had taken to the king and his claims; if they showed any signs of a change of mind or heart they were liable to the barbarous penalty of treason; if they refused for too long to bow to the inevitable trend of policy they were liable to be suddenly removed out of the way on any pretext that might serve the purpose of the all-powerful vicar-general. In the first stages of the religious revolution, as we have seen, a few determined and clear-sighted groups of men resisted, and were promptly removed from the stage. They were in the truest sense martyrs to the beliefs they had absorbed in their early lives. In the course of the Sup-

1 This was a trade term in Cromwell's circle for anyone hostile to the regime; cf. the letter of Layton and others to Cromwell in *LP*, xiv, ii, 272 (=Wright, *SL*, cxxvi): 'whereof shall appear his [*sc.* Abbot Whiting's] cankered and traitorous heart'; also 'inwardly cankered' (also of Whiting) in *LP*, xiv, ii, 185; and Sir John Seyncler of Abbot Marshall: 'I like not the man. I fear he hath a cankered heart' (*LP*, xiii, ii, 887).

pression a few others, perhaps no more than a dozen or fifteen all told (if we leave aside those who had been associated with the northern risings) were done to death on one pretext or another but in fact because they had opposed or hindered or at least questioned the power of the king and the justice of the Dissolution. One or two of these were true martyrs to their inmost convictions, others had schemed or repined ineffectually, while a third group, neither fully heroic nor merely factious, had been caught in the toils and died, half unwillingly, for what they had felt rather than for what they had proclaimed. All these evoke feelings of sympathy, and even of admiration. In any case, no account of the Suppression would be complete without a brief account of the acts of violence that accompanied it. If they are rare enough to prove the absence of any policy of terror or of religious or 'ideological' persecution, they are numerous enough to show that no considerations of humanity or personal worth or even of the insignificance of an exceptional and uninfluential dissenter had any weight to shield the offender from the pitiless exaction of the extreme penalty. In the pages that follow the story shall be told of George Lazenby, of Friar Forrest, of Anthony Browne, of the sufferers at Lenton, of the abbot of Woburn and of the three abbots of Glastonbury, Reading and Colchester.[1]

I. GEORGE LAZENBY

It has often been noted that the religious of Yorkshire showed little resistance to the king's designs. Neither before nor during the Pilgrimage of Grace did they take a leading part in the counsels of the defenders of the old faith. There is, however, one exception to this indifference, though he has hitherto received little notice or sympathy from historians.

The story of Dan George Lazenby's last days begins with a letter to Cromwell dated 12 July 1535, from that unstable young man, Sir Francis Bigod.[2] He wrote from Jervaulx Abbey, whither he had accompanied Master Thomas Garrard, one of the preachers sent by government to diffuse the doctrine of the royal headship of the Church. Garrard in the course of his sermon had declared 'that every prieste, by the worde of God, had as myche authoritie to remitte syn as had the bishop of Rome', when he was interrupted by one of the monks. After the sermon Bigod examined Dan George Lazenby before the abbot and certain gentlemen; the examinate declared the pope to be the head of the militant Church and 'thanked God who gave hym spirite and audacitie so to say'. He went on to state that he neither could nor would 'take the Kynge's highnesse for to be the only and supreme heade of the cherche of Englond', and straightway subscribed his name to a duly attested account of the

---

1 The case of Nicholas Mileham, subprior and treasurer of Walsingham, need not detain us. He was embroiled in a conspiracy, brewed early in 1537 by a knot of malcontents and inspired by the northern rising. The motive was resentment at the religious changes and spoliations, regarded principally as creating a danger of unemployment. Cf. *VCH, Norfolk*, II, 256–8, with references to *LP*; and J. C. Dickinson, *Walsingham Priory*.   2 *LP*, VIII, 1025 (i), 1033.

proceedings.[1] Bigod took the monk with him to Middleham Castle where he examined him again and found him ready to defend 'yonder same idol and blood sucker of Rome so loudly and stiffly as I never in all my days saw the like'. In the course of the examination it appeared that he had had close relations in the past with the Carthusians of Mount Grace and claimed to have seen an apparition of Our Lady in the pilgrimage Chapel there.[2] On 6 August he was tried at the York assizes by Sir John Spelman and Christopher Jenney, and the latter wrote that his execution would speedily follow. 'He is', added Jenney, 'a wilful fool of little learning.'[3] There is no record of his death, but on 6 October Dr Ortiz wrote from Rome to the emperor that a letter from the ambassador in England (Chapuys) of 25 August had informed him that a friar had been martyred in the archbishopric of York in the same manner and for the same reason as the Carthusians.[4] There are several other confused references to Lazenby; one especially, in which an old monk of Jervaulx, Thomas Madde, who lived till 1579, is recorded as saying that he 'did take away and hide the head of one of his brethren of the same house, who had suffered death for that he would not yield to the Royal Supremacy'.[5]

Dan George has received little attention from the martyrologists, and the historians of the Pilgrimage of Grace, usually so sympathetic to the defenders of the traditional faith, appear to have been scandalized either by the alleged visions or by the forthrightness of speech of the monk. His visions we cannot judge; we can only record that he confessed his faith even to the shedding of his blood. There seems to be no reason why he should not take his place in the scanty band of martyrs to the Catholic cause.

II. FRIAR FOREST AND FRIAR BROWNE

John Forest[6] was born c. 1470 and entered the Franciscan convent at Greenwich at the age of twenty;[7] in due course he studied at Oxford. There seems to be no record of his degree, but he is consistently alluded

1 *Ibid.* 1025 (ii); printed in full in Walbran, *Memorials of Fountains*, I, 269 n.
2 *LP*, VIII, 1069.   3 *Ibid.* IX, 37.
4 *Ibid.* 557. For Lazenby, see also L. E. Whatmore, 'George Lazenby, monk of Jervaulx: a forgotten martyr?', in *DR*, 184 (October 1942), 325–8.
5 Cited by Foley, *Records of the English Province of the Society of Jesus*, III, 239 (noted by Whatmore, *art. cit.* 328).
6 There are abundant references to Forest in the contemporary documents among Cromwell's papers, and in the letters of Cranmer and Latimer. There are also sketches of his life and last days by Thomas Bourchier, a Marian Franciscan, and by the Spaniards Garzias and Fra Marcos. For these, *v. infra*, 371 n. 3. In his Life Bourchier printed six letters to and from Forest and Queen Katharine, one of her ladies and Thomas Abell. These he gives in Latin, and they may have been touched up a little, but they can be taken as in the main authentic, and give a vivid glimpse of the friar. The queen refers to Forest as of 'noble and ancient family', and it has been suggested that he may have been of French extraction. There is a good and critical account of him by Fr John Morris, S.J., and Fr J. H. Pollen, S.J., in *Lives of the English Martyrs*, ed. Dom B. Camm, 1904 (cited hereafter as *Morris*).
7 It is commonly stated (e.g. *Morris*, 275, and *DNB*) that Forest became a friar when seventeen. In his letter to Queen Katharine, however, in *Morris*, 286, he says that he is in his sixty-fourth year (in 1534) and has been in the Order for forty-four years.

to as Doctor both by the chronicler Wriothesley and by Bishop Latimer,[1] who also considered him one of the most learned men of the realm. He was confessor to Queen Katharine and became warden of the Greenwich house, where he took a leading part in the early opposition to the divorce. He was in consequence removed from office by Cromwell in 1533 after repeated denunciations of his activity on the part of the discontented friars Laurence and Lyst, and sent to a northern convent, perhaps Newark or Newcastle.[2] Early in 1534 he was in prison,[3] possibly under a charge of having given support to Elizabeth Barton, along with his confrères Rich and Risby, though his name is not mentioned in any of the printed documents of the case. He was still in durance at the end of the year,[4] and at one moment was expecting to be put to death within three days.[5] This we know from a letter he wrote to Queen Katharine from prison, replying to one from the queen; there were also exchanges between Forest and Elizabeth Hammon, one of the queen's attendants, and Thomas Abell, a chaplain and confessor of the queen, then in the Tower for opposition to the divorce. Forest, however, did not die, and is next found, more than two years later, at liberty in the convent of the grey friars at London. It seems probable, though not certain, that he had made some sort of acknowledgement of the royal supremacy and the validity of the Boleyn marriage, unwillingly indeed, but still sufficiently, so far as words went.[6] Early in 1538, however, he was again in trouble. He had been sought after, so it would seem, as confessor by those of a conservative temper, and there were suspicions in official circles that he was advising his penitents to resist the title of Supreme Head of the Church. After an unsuccessful attempt to get evidence out of a *bona fide* penitent, Lord Mordaunt, an agent of Cromwell succeeded in obtaining dangerous pronouncements about the pope, and Forest was arrested and examined.[7] As a result he seems to have made statements which gave a handle for a charge of heresy, and this was arranged by Cranmer early in April.[8] On 8 May Forest was condemned, principally, it would seem, for his support of papal claims to supremacy. As before, when the crucial moment came, he seems to have yielded for the moment and abjured his 'errors',[9] but

---

1 So *Morris*, 317, citing Garzias, *A Chronicle of King Henry VIII*, ed. M. A. S. Hume.
2 *LP*, VI, 334, 512.
3 Thomas Abell, writing in the Tower to his fellow-prisoner Forest, says that he has been thirty-seven days in ward. He was committed, according to an official list, on 24 February 1534 (*LP*, VIII, 1001), but Chapuys, writing on 27 December 1533, says that he was already there (*ibid.* VI, 1571). If the list is to be followed, Abell's letter would have been written on 31 March 1534.
4 Cf. the list of Observants in prison in *LP*, VII, 1607.
5 He asserts this in his letter to the queen (*Morris*, 287).
6 *LP*, XIII, i, 1043: 'excerpte out of the confessions of Friar Forest...that he told one Waffener in confession "that he had denied the bishop of Rome by an oath given by his outward man, but not in th'inward man"'.
7 *Ibid.*
8 Cf. letter to Cromwell from Cranmer in *Remains*, I, 239–40 (*LP*, XIII, i, 687).
9 Wriothesley, *Chronicle*, 79.

while still in prison he came into contact with Friar Laurence Cooke, of the Carmelite house at Doncaster, and William Horne, the last survivor in prison of the London Carthusians. They confirmed him in the faith, and he refused to abjure publicly at the gathering that had been arranged for the purpose. He was therefore sentenced to death by burning as a relapsed heretic, and a wooden image from Llandarvel, a noted object of pilgrimage and 'superstition', was used to make the fire.[1] On 22 May, in the presence of a great crowd and after a long sermon and an exchange of arguments between Latimer and Forest, the friar was burnt in circumstances of unusual barbarity.[2] Immediately before his death he had made a bold declaration of his faith:

> That if an angell should come downe from heaven, and show him any other thing than he had beleeved all his liffe tyme past he would not beleeve him, and that if his bodie shold be cutt joynt after joynt or membre after membre, brennt, hanged, or what paine soever might be donne to his bodie, he would neaver turne from his old sect of [=former adherence to] this bishopp of Rome.[3]

Friar Cooke, referred to above, is sometimes listed as a martyr. He was certainly in the Tower for three months in 1538,[4] and in 1540 was attainted for adherence to Aske and exempted from a general pardon.[5] Marillac and Sanders chronicle his execution, though with inconsistent details, and reckon him a martyr,[6] but there is no clear evidence that he died on a purely religious issue. Moreover, a pardon for him exists, dated 2 October 1540, just two months after the date of his alleged execution.[7]

The case of Friar Anthony Browne follows naturally after that of Friar Forest. The story begins and ends abruptly with a long letter of the Duke of Norfolk and Sir Roger Townshend to Cromwell, written at Framlingham and completed at 11 p.m. on 4 August 1538.[8] Friar Browne in happier days had been a member of the Greenwich community of Observants, and nothing is known of his fortunes in the years following the suppression of his Order until he appears in Norfolk's letter as one 'late takyng upon hym as an hermyte', who had on an unspecified occasion declared his opposition to the royal supremacy and put his name to the charge as true. For this he was indicted, cast, and judged accordingly, but execution was stayed for ten days in order that the occasion might be improved by a sermon by the bishop of Norwich 'as was by the bishop of Worcester at the execucyon of Forrest'. The duke had doubted whether

---

1 *Ibid.* 78, 79; Hall, *Chronicle,* 280–2.
2 *Remains of Latimer,* 391; Ellis, *OL,* III, iii, cccxxxi; *LP,* XIII, i, 1024.
3 Wriothesley, *Chronicle,* 80. For a discussion of Bourchier, Garzias and Fra Marcos, *v.* Morris, 322–6.
4 *LP,* XII (ii), 181.   5 *LP,* XV, 498, pp. 215, 217.
6 *Ibid.* 953, and Sanders, *Anglican Schism,* trans. Lewis, 877.
7 *LP,* XVI, 220. For other details, *v.* relevant vols. of *LP* index; Ellis, *OL,* III, ii, 202; and Gasquet, *Henry VIII* (ed. 1893), II, 366.
8 Ellis, *OL,* I, ii, cxxxi, pp. 86–9; *LP,* XIII, ii, 34.

the veteran Nykke, known to have conservative leanings, would perform to satisfaction and had therefore catechized beforehand both prisoner and bishop. According to his own account, he and Townshend had succeeded in shaking the friar's insistence on papal claims, but had failed utterly to get him to admit the supremacy of the king, for he insisted on 'sayng that no temporall Prynce was *capax* of that name and auctorite'. Dr Call, a grey friar brought in by the Duke, was equally unsuccessful, whereupon the bishop, who had arrived, was sent into the lists. Nevertheless, though Nykke on two separate occasions so handled the matter 'that it was sufficient to have torned th'oppinion of any man that was not yevyn to wilfulnes as this fole is', Friar Browne stood firm and was sent back to die, unless Cromwell should wish him to be 'more streyghtlye examyned and to be put to torture' in the Tower. There the story ends, but there is no reason to suppose that the friar failed to stand fast to his confession to the end. If so, and if evidence of his execution is ever forthcoming, he would seem to be in like case with Friar Lawrence Stone of Canterbury, a martyr, and a steadfast one, to the fundamental belief of Christians that Christ gave the supreme guidance of his Church to no temporal authority.

III. LENTON AND WOBURN

The fate of the prior and at least one of the monks of Lenton in Notting-hamshire cannot fully be explained in default of clear evidence.[1] The origin of the trouble is probably to be found in conversations such as that reported to Cromwell as having taken place in December 1536. On that occasion Dan Ralph Swenson, sitting on a form by the fire in the misericord along-side of Dan Hamlet Pentrick, an unsatisfactory character who had thrice abandoned the monastic life, observed: 'I hear say that the King has taken peace with the commonty till after Christmas, but if they have done so it is alms to hang them up, for they may well know that he that will keep no promise with God Himself, but pulls down His churches, he will not keep promise with them; but if they had gone forth onward up and stricken off his head, then had they done well, for I warrant them if he can overcome them he will do so by them.' 'Peace,' said the nervous subprior, 'you rail you wot not whereof.' 'Nay', replied the prescient Dan Ralph, 'I say as it will be.'[2] A second conversation in the misericord is repeated from Easter week, when Dan John Houghton and Dan Ralph Swenson were sitting at the board's end, and the former remarked: 'It is a marvellous world, for the King will hang a man for a word speaking now a days.' 'Yea', replied Dan Ralph, 'but the King of heaven will not do so, and He is King of all kings; but he that hangs a man in this world

---

1 The story is told by Gasquet, *Henry VIII*, 282–3, and J. C. Cox, *VCH, Notts*, LI, 99–100; both use original documents which are still in part unpublished.

2 *LP*, XII, i, 892. The arrangement and dating of the documents of this case in *LP* are unusually arbitrary and inaccurate.

for a word speaking, he shall be hanged in another world his self.'[1] This was duly carried up to headquarters by the subprior, who added that many of the monks had spoken ill of the king and queen and of the Lord Privy Seal 'whom they love worst of any man in the world'. This was not forgotten, but more than a year passed before action was taken; then, in February 1538, Prior Heath was seized and imprisoned. He does not figure in any of the extant accusations, though the precise date of the alleged treason is given, being 29 June 1536. Gasquet suggested, with some documentary support, that he had sold some of the monastic plate; Baskerville, that he had fallen foul of 'certain men of Nottingham' who figure in the records.[2] The date of the offence, the feast day of St Peter in Rome and the patronal feast of Cluny perhaps suggests verbal treason in a sermon. In any case, Cromwell had decided that he was to die,[3] and in March 1538 he was indicted for treason, along with eight of his monks. In the event only he, and one or perhaps two others, were executed at Nottingham.[4] The priory was then dissolved by attainder.

The fate of the abbot of Woburn, Robert Hobbes, is of greater significance. His story was first made familiar in the sympathetic and moving pages of one of Froude's *Short Studies*,[5] whence it passed, with some changes and elaboration, to Dixon and Gasquet.[6] Froude was misled by Stow[7] and Speed, followed by Burnet, into thinking that the ultimate cause of the abbot's condemnation was his complicity in the northern rising; this led him to assume the existing depositions to have been taken in 1536 despite clear evidence of dating to the contrary.

Woburn Abbey, as we see the glimpses of its daily life in the depositions of its monks, was a respectable house of fair observance.[8] The abbot, Robert Hobbes, was a man of some learning and knowledge of theology, with a clear mind and a kindly, reasonable disposition. He was on friendly terms with Lord Grey of Wilton and his wife, as well as with his own high steward, the gifted, susceptible, dissolute, 'eternally young' court poet

---

1 *Ibid.*

2 Gasquet, *Henry VIII*, 283; Baskerville, *EM*, 178.

3 *LP*, XIII, i, 877. Among Cromwell's 'remembrances' is 'The suppression of Lenton and the execution of the prior'.

4 Gasquet cites the indictment of the prior and eight monks (including Swenson, but not Gylham); he also cites the record of the conviction of the prior and Dan William Gylham from the relevant Controlment Roll. Cox refers to *LP*, XIII, i, 786, of 11 April (actually 787 of 16 April), for a letter of the commissioners from Lenton to Cromwell announcing the execution of the prior and Dan Ralph Swenson. He also gives details from the municipal records which imply that the execution took place at Nottingham.

5 Ed. 1878, I, 430–41.   6 *Henry VIII*, 283–90.

7 Stow, *Annales* (ed. 1615), 573.

8 The story of Abbot Hobbes was first narrated clearly and with chronological exactness by a writer (Sister Elspeth) in *VCH, Beds*, I, 367–70; the place of trial and a summary of the indictment were supplied by Miss Gladys Scott Thomson, 'Woburn Abbey and the Dissolution of the Monasteries', in *TRHS*, 4 ser. XVI (1933), 129–60. The bulk of the depositions are in *LP*, XIII, i, 981, but the confession of the subprior, which was in fact slightly later in date than most, is misplaced in *LP*, X, 1239.

and intimate friend of Henry VIII, Sir Francis Bryan.[1] He had a conservative, wholly Catholic outlook and saw, with both clarity and sorrow,
the disappearance of the religious life and of the old orthodoxy. He had
taken the oath to accept the king as Supreme Head in 1534, but it had been
against his conscience and, unlike others, he had never thereafter enjoyed
complete peace of mind.[2] Before giving up his papal bulls he had caused
copies to be taken, and when commanded to erase the pope's name from
service books he had preferred to strike it out, believing that sooner or
later the tide would turn; he read and passed on to his friends a tract
De potestate Petri composed by a priest in the neighbourhood. When the
Carthusians were executed he had pronounced solemnly to his monks in
chapter: 'Brethren this is a perilous time; such a scourge was never heard
since Christ's passion', and he had ordered them to recite the psalm *Deus
venerunt gentes* prostrate daily before the high altar. A year later, when the
lesser houses were suppressed, he had enjoined the singing of the anthem
Salvator mundi salva nos, with special prayers at Mass. When preaching
he stated that the pope's jurisdiction had been abrogated 'by common
consent of the realm', but never alleged Scripture to prove the king's title
or the justice of the act that had taken away the power of the bishop of
Rome. At Passiontide, 1538, he was seriously ill and in great pain with
strangury, and when he heard that hard things were being said against
those who still held for the pope he exhorted the monks round his bed to
keep charity, quoting a passage from St Bernard's letter to Eugenius III:
'Other churches have each their own shepherd; thou art shepherd of the
shepherds themselves', and he exhorted them never to surrender their
monastery or change their religious habit. When in great physical pain
from his illness, he was heard to reproach himself for failing to die with
the good men who had died for holding with the pope, and he repeated
that his conscience grudged him daily for his failure; whereupon one of
his monks rejoined (or said that he had rejoined): 'If he be disposed to
die for that matter, he may die as soon as he will.'

It is indeed clear that Abbot Hobbes was consistently opposed to all
religious innovation, and that he had criticized the Boleyn marriage, the
suppression of the lesser monasteries, and the tacit encouragement of
heretical books. His community was divided. Some were favourable to
the New Learning, and successfully objected to any public manifestation
of sympathy with the cause of the Carthusians. Others had been equally,
though more intemperately, outspoken in their criticism of the government; among these the subprior and Dan Lawrence Blunham were notable,
and the latter had paraded his achievement in evading the formal act of
swearing to the king as Supreme Head; there had been a press of monks

---

[1] For Bryan, *v. DNB*. His friend Roger Ascham is witness to his eternal youth and to
his personal charm.

[2] All the details that follow are taken from the abbot's depositions and those of his monks
and chaplain in *LP*, xiii, i, 981.

touching the book of the gospels and he had not put out his hand.[1] Altogether, six monks besides the abbot were noted as 'papists'.

With a community thus divided against itself the chances were great that sooner or later the recalcitrants would be delated to Cromwell. The fateful step was in fact taken by an ex-friar,[2] William Sherburne, who for almost a year had been curate of the parish chapel[3] at Woburn. He was, like so many of his brethren, of the New Learning, and had had several brushes with the abbot, who took him to task for his violent language:

Sir William, I heard say ye be a great railer. I marvel that ye rail so. I pray you teach my cure the scripture of God, and that may be to their edification. I pray you leave such railing. Ye call the Pope a bere and a bawson.[4] Either he is a good man or an ill. *Domino suo stat aut cadit.*[5] The office of a bishop is honourable. What edifying is this to rail? Let him alone.[6]

The chaplain bore malice, and discovered some papal bulls in his chapel that had not been surrendered. With them, and a letter setting forth the abbot's pro-papal utterances, contributed by the discontented Dan Robert Salford, he went up to London to call upon the Lord Privy Seal. On his return, he informed the abbot of his errand, and was forthwith dismissed from his cure. It was too late. Cromwell sent down Dr Petre and John Williams to take depositions and the abbot and two monks, the subprior and Dan Lawrence, were duly tried at Abbot's Woburn a month later (14 June). There was no difficulty in securing a conviction; the legal case was clear. The two monks retracted all they had said, pleaded a change of heart and asked for mercy, all to no purpose. It has been alleged that Abbot Hobbes likewise gave way. He was certainly an ailing, broken man, and it is extremely difficult to extract a precise meaning from the long and sometimes rambling depositions, or to separate what he was alleged to have said or done from what he actually admitted, and to distinguish between retractations on matters of principle and apologies for bluntness of speech and misunderstandings. He certainly retracted an opinion he had expressed as to the 'unlawfulness' of Cranmer's acts of jurisdiction. On the other hand, he committed himself, apparently without recantation, to some very strong statements about the suppression of monasteries, the distribution by Cromwell of heretical books, and the royal divorce. His indictment at least is clear. He had stated, as recently as the previous 10 January, that 'The Bysshop of Rome's Auctorite is good and lawful

---

1 The subprior (*LP*, x, 1239) had 'heard Dan Laurence, the sexton, say that when he was first sworn, for the multitude of swearers he could not lay his hand on the book, and so thought himself free, though he had signed the "carte of profession"'.

2 This detail is supplied by the subprior *loc. cit.*

3 This was presumably the *capella ad portas*, the layfolks' chapel.

4 Bere=bear; bawson=badger. The two words are found in conjunction in another example in *OED, s.v.* bauson.

5 'To his own master he standeth or falleth.' Cf. Rom. xiv. 4.

6 *LP*, xiii, i, 981, p. 357.

within this Realme accordyng to the old trade, and that is the true waye. And the contrary of the kynges parte but usurpacion disceyved by flattery and adulacion.'[1] He had likewise on the same occasion said: 'Yt is a mervelous thyng that the Kynges grace could not be contented with that noble quene his very true and undowted wyffe quene Kateryn.'[2] At his trial he attempted no defence and admitted his technical guilt on both counts. No appeal for mercy or recantation of his has been preserved, nor is there record of his asking pardon for these specific statements. In the past he had certainly failed to hold to his convictions; he may have failed again, but there is no proof that he did so. Writers in the past, unaware of the precise terms of his indictment, have dwelt, perhaps unduly, on his weakness of character. They have failed to do justice to a certain elevation of mind, and absence of levity, that distinguishes him from most of the gossips and grumblers of the cloister. More than this cannot be said. *Domino suo stat aut cadit.* He was duly executed, and his abbey confiscated by attainder. The architects and landscape gardeners in their work on and about the majestic ducal mansion that perpetuated the name of Woburn Abbey were successful in obliterating every trace of the medieval past, but the oak from which the last abbot, according to a venerable tradition, was hanged continued until the early decades of the nineteenth century to stand within a stone's throw of the house.

IV. THE THREE BENEDICTINE ABBOTS

A peculiar interest, not devoid of controversy, attaches to the fate of the three abbots of Colchester, Reading and Glastonbury.[3] Though often linked together by historians from Hall downwards, as they are also in their modern liturgical commemoration, the circumstances of their condemnations are quite dissimilar and the first, at least, had no personal tie of cause or friendship with either of the other two.

The case of Thomas Beche or Marshall, abbot of Colchester since 1533, is a clear one, as most of the essential documents survive.[4] Little is known of his early career, save that he had studied at Gloucester College, where he proceeded B.D. in 1509 and D.D. in 1515;[5] several references to his theological expertise occur in the depositions against him. On his election in 1533 he found it advisable to forward to Cromwell a bond for £200 to the king's use in order to secure the swift restoration of his temporalities.[6] A year later, in April 1534, one of his monks delated his subprior to

1 This brought him in danger of the Act of Supremacy and the Treasons Act of 1534 (26 Hen. VIII, c. 1 and c. 13).

2 By this he was in danger of the Succession Act of 1536 (28 Hen. VIII, c. 7).

3 For a discussion of some further points, and for passages from the documents, *v. infra*, Appendix IX.

4 *LP*, XIII, ii, 887; *ibid.* XIV, ii, 438, 439, 454, 458, 459, and Appendix 45 : these are printed in full in the excellent account by R. C. Fowler in *VCH, Essex*, II, 97–100.

5 C. W. Boase, *Register of the University of Oxford*, 63.

6 *LP*, VI, 621. He had previously been abbot of St Werburg's, Chester.

Cromwell as having declared the king and his council to be heretics on account of the recent book of articles,[1] but the charge was not followed up, and the subprior joined his abbot and the rest of the community in subscribing to the royal supremacy on 7 July of that year.[2] In spite of this external submission, however, the abbot continued to express his views on current events in a way that showed him to be a conservative in every way. He spoke with reverence of Fisher and More; he sympathized with the northern insurgents; and he deplored the suppression of the religious houses.

In the summer of 1538 Audley is found petitioning Cromwell for the preservation of the abbey as a college,[3] but the house had been marked down for suppression in the autumn of that year, when Legh and Cavendish were commissioned to repair to Colchester for that purpose,[4] but apparently they were called off for the time being, possibly on account of information received by Cromwell that the abbot would stick at surrendering. Abbot Marshall, indeed, showed no sign of budging, and either because of this or for some other reason which is not mentioned, investigations were set on foot which issued in the abbot's lodgment in the Tower at some date before 20 November 1539.[5]

The charges against him were varied. A servant had deposed to having received valuables and money from him to hide, and to his having expressed a wish in 1536 that the northern insurgents might lay their hands on Cranmer, Audley and Cromwell.[6] Thomas Nuthake, a mercer and physician of Colchester, had heard him declare in 1534 that the bishop of Rome was Supreme Head of the Church, and Robert Rouse, another mercer of the town, agreed in having heard the abbot deny the royal supremacy and declare that the avarice of the king was such that if the Thames were flowing gold and silver it would not suffice to slake his thirst for money.[7] Finally, Sir John Seyncler or St Clere, who had collected this evidence, had himself quoted the abbot as saying that the king could never take his house by right and law and should never have it but against his will.[8]

No doubt this testimony was substantially true, but Abbot Marshall, more clearly than Abbot Hobbes, lacked the courage of his convictions. He denied that he had spoken against the royal supremacy or criticized the king's avarice; in his opinion, he said, the supremacy of the bishop of Rome was established merely *jure humano* in the early Church and subsequent papal usurpations had justified the king in making his claim to supremacy. He would certainly have given up his house if commanded, but had delayed in hopes of increasing his pension.[9] Such a defence,

1 *LP*, vii, 140, 454.
2 *Deputy Keeper's Reports*, vii, 287; *LP*, vii, 769.
3 *LP*, xiii, ii, 306. 4 *Ibid.* 764.
5 His name is on the list of prisoners on that date in *LP*, xiv, ii, 554.
6 *Ibid.* 438–9. 7 *Ibid.* 454, 458.
8 *Ibid.* xiii, ii, 887. 9 *Ibid.* xiv, 459.

whether or not it represented his genuine frame of mind, was useless in face of the evidence against him; he was tried at Colchester and executed on 1 December. Sir Christopher Jenney wrote to Cromwell that before his execution the abbot asked for forgiveness of the king, of Audley and of Cromwell, and 'knowledged himself, in substance, to be guilty', though he 'stood somewhat in his own conceit that the suppression of abbeys should not stand with the law of God'.[1] Too much must not be made of such a report, but from other evidence it seems clear that the abbot of Colchester clung in his heart to the orthodox faith in which he had been reared, but repeatedly lacked the inner strength and clarity of vision to hold to his profession at the crucial moments of trial.

Hugh Cook, abbot of Reading since 1520, was a more distinguished figure. He had been in favour with the king, who used him on official and ceremonial occasions,[2] and whatever may be thought of the testimony to his conservative orthodoxy borne by an anonymous pamphleteer,[3] he had received to the habit at Reading John Holyman, a fellow of New College, Oxford, and an opponent of Lutheranism,[4] and Cromwell's letters show him successfully vindicating his control of the doctrine to be preached to his monks against a married priest of the New Learning supported by Shaxton of Salisbury.[5] At a crucial moment in April 1533, he was one of the sixteen theologians who had the courage to stand to the opinion that marriage with a dead brother's widow was permissible, since the impediment of affinity could be removed by papal dispensation.[6] On the other hand, he had unquestionably sworn to accept the royal supremacy both in 1534 and at the visitation in 1535,[7] and even if the pamphleteer's charge is true, that Abbot Cook declared that his heart had never consented to his oath, this is no proof that he ever publicly recanted. The same writer's assertion, that he offered Mass weekly for the pope, if true, shows where the abbot's hopes lay, but does not imply any overt action. More significant, perhaps, was his friendship with the Marquis of Exeter and Lord Montague, and the presence at Reading of Prebendary Rugg of Chichester, another familiar of the Poles.

What happened at Reading in the early autumn of 1539 is not clear.

1 *LP*, xiv, Appendix 45.
2 E.g. at the obsequies of Queen Jane Seymour, when he sang Mass on the fourth day, the most honorable office. Cf. *LP*, xii, ii, 1060.
3 For this, *v.* Appendix ix, *infra.* Gasquet (*Last Abbot of Glastonbury, passim*) and J. C. Cox, *VCH, Berks*, ii, art. 'Reading Abbey', use this document freely and uncritically.
4 That Holyman was received to the habit at Reading *c.* 1530, and that he was a conservative in belief is certain, but the assertion that his motive was a desire for solitude and austerity, and that he rapidly acquired a monastic reputation corresponding to his name, seems to rest on the unsupported word of Anthony Wood, writing more than a century later.
5 *LP*, xiii, i, 147, 264, 571.
6 Pocock, *Records of the Reformation*, ii, 457. He carried his three proxies with him. At the second vote, however, on the fact of consummation, he was absent.
7 The list of those at Reading who accepted the royal supremacy is not extant, but there can be no reasonable doubt that the oath was administered there, both in 1534 and at the visitation of 1535.

In the previous summer Dr London, engrossed in suppressing the friars of the town, remarked that the abbot had said some time since that he would surrender if the king commanded him,[1] but neither then nor subsequently had Abbot Cook shown any signs of making the first move. As late as 15 August 1539, he was still in possession, and said to be selling off sheep, grain and timber,[2] but on 8 September Moyle was there drawing up an inventory for Cromwell[3] and on the 12th Sir William Penizon had received possession of the abbey and its demesne 'as the late abbot left them'.[4] On 17 September Layton was there with the others, and by the 19th the abbey was recognized as formally suppressed and the abbot as deprived of office.[5] No formal surrender is extant, but as the abbot was already under arrest his condemnation may already have been taken for granted and the house considered as forfeited by attainder. The community received pensions.[6]

The precise charge against Abbot Cook cannot be discovered. Marillac, the French ambassador, writing at the end of November, could only suggest that it was part of the process of cleaning up after the Exeter conspiracy.[7] It may well have been so; the abbot was a friend of some of the principal victims, and those rounded up with him were a Reading group who may be supposed to have had some connection with the Poles. The anonymous pamphleteer clearly has in mind a charge of active conspiracy in sympathy with Cardinal Pole rather than an individual stand against the royal supremacy.[8] Whatever the precise charge, the abbot was condemned by a commission appointed on 27 October.[9] No trustworthy details of his trial and execution are preserved; it may reasonably be supposed that his condemnation was unjust by any normal standard of justice but there is nothing to show that he died precisely as a witness to the Catholic faith.

The third black monk to suffer at this time was the aged Richard Whiting, appointed abbot of Glastonbury by Wolsey in 1525. The date of his birth is uncertain, and the opinion that he graduated at Cambridge in 1483 is untenable.[10] Until the day of trouble, all who mention Whiting do so with respect, though there is nothing to suggest that he was distinguished by any unusual force or integrity of character or holiness of

1 *LP*, XIII, ii, 346.   2 *Ibid.* XIV, ii, 49; Wright, *SL*, cxxvii.
3 *LP*, XIV, ii, 136.   4 *Ibid.* 202.
5 J. C. Cox in *VCH*, Berks, II, 71. On 19 September the burgesses of Reading elected a mayor; hitherto they had presented three names to the abbot.
6 Cf. Moyle's letter of 8 September (*LP*, XIV, ii, 136); '230l. will serve for the pensions', and Baskerville, *EM*, 179 n.
7 *LP*, XIV, ii, 607; *Correspondance politique de MM. Castillion et Marillac*, ed. J. Kaulek, 144.
8 *LP*, XIV, ii, 613. 'Weeneth the abbot of Reading...with...pestilent and cankered counsel to overthrow a prince most puissant, etc....Could not our English abbots be contented with English forked caps, but must look after Romish cardinal hats also? Could they not be contented with the plain fashion of England, but must counterfeit the crafty cardinality of Raynold Poole?'   9 *Ibid.* 435 (45).
10 Venn, *Alumni Cantabrigienses*, I, iv, 395, refers to Cooper, I, 71, but notes that 'the D.D. of 1505 was John' and not Richard. Mr A. B. Emden agrees with text above.

life. His abbey was in some ways the most renowned, as it was still for all practical purposes the most wealthy, in England; it had recently been rendered even more beautiful and illustrious by Abbot Bere, and under Whiting the discipline had been such as to escape criticism from the visitors of 1535, though the records of a subsequent visitation show traces of discord and failing. Leland, the antiquary, who had been hospitably entertained by Whiting, wrote of his host with a warmth which he later found it expedient to regret.[1] Even Layton was betrayed into a similar enthusiasm; though his original letter has perished, his recantation survives in that great collection in which the thoughts of so many hearts are revealed, and, like all similar palinodes, it is fatal to the reputation of the writer, while it does nothing to sully Whiting's name.[2] Though unsympathetic to the royal divorce, he did not in fact make a stand, either in parliament or in his abbey, against the revolutionary legislation and the oaths framed in its support. He had signed the petition to the pope against the Aragon marriage and subscribed to the oath accepting the royal supremacy. He had, moreover, done his best to keep the royal favour for his house by a number of gifts and offers to Henry and Cromwell. In this he acted like all his fellow-abbots, but it is a little surprising to find him asking the Lord Privy Seal to act as his procurator in the spring session of parliament in 1539, from which he asked leave of absence owing to a physical infirmity which made travel of any kind a suffering.[3]

The end of his abbey is, like that of Reading, covered by a certain obscurity. Cromwell must long have been desirous of grasping such a prize and his agents become almost lyrical in tone when they first rest their eyes on its delights.[4] Trouble was certainly brewing in the middle of September when Layton was asked angrily by Cromwell what he had meant by praising the abbot of Glastonbury so unconscionably to the king. His abject recantation was found satisfactory and a week later he was in Somerset with Pollard and Moyle badgering the abbot, 'being but a very weak man and sickly', with admonitions 'to call to mind what he had forgotten and tell the truth'. As Whiting's answers showed 'his cankered and traiterous heart'—the phrase used in government circles for any kind of independence of speech—he was sent up to the Tower 'with as fair words' as the commissioners could bring themselves to use.[5] It is clear

---

1 Leland, *Collectanea*, VI, 70: 'Homo sane candidissimus et amicus meus singularis.' Leland later cancelled these words.

2 *LP*, XIV, ii, 185 (16 September 1539); Ellis, *OL*, III, iii, ccclii.

3 The letters are in *LP*. Some are printed also in Ellis, *OL*, III, iii, cclviii, cccxlix, and Archbold, *SRH*, 37, 40, 49, 67, 90, 92–3.

4 E.g. Wright, *SL*, cxxvi–cxxvii: 'We assure your lordship that it is the goodliest house of that sort that ever we have seen...a house mete for the kinges majesty and for no man else: which is to our great comfort.... The house is greate, goodly and so pryncely as we have not seen the lyke; with 4 parkes adjoynynge...a great mere...well replenished with greate pykis, breme, perche and roche; 4 fair manour placis belonginge to the late abbott, the furthest but 3 myles distante, beyng goodly mansions', etc. (=*LP*, XIV, ii, 232).

5 *LP*, XIV, ii, 206, 232; Wright, *SL*, cxxvi–cxxvii.

from other expressions in this letter that proof of treasonable correspondence, perhaps with the abbot of Reading and the Exeter group, was
being sought; it was not forthcoming, but a book was found written
against the divorce, as also a number of precious objects which the abbot
had secreted from the spoilers. Glastonbury, the trio added, 'is the
goodliest house of the sort we ever saw...meet for the King and no man
else; and we trust there shall never come any double hood within it again'.
Within a few days of this letter the abbot was out and the abbey was in
the king's hands, and the energetic treasure-seekers had made a rich haul
from 'walls, vaults and other secret places' where they found as much
precious stuff 'as would have sufficed for a new abbey', and had imprisoned
two of the monks responsible. Four days later they had secured depositions alleging treasonable conduct on Whiting's part.[1]

The sequel cannot be known with any certainty; we hear of examinations in the Tower before Cromwell, but on 25 October Marillac had
heard of nothing save the book against the divorce.[2] Then followed the
familiar 'remembrance' of the Lord Privy Seal: 'The abbot of Glaston
to be sent down to be tried and executed at Glaston.' Pollard and Moyle
were to give evidence and Cromwell reminds himself 'to see that the
evidence be well sorted and the indictments well drawn'.[3] None of this
dossier has survived, but the names of the witnesses suggest that the charge
of conspiracy had been abandoned in favour of the simpler one of
'robbery'. In any case, a letter of Russell, who had charge of the subsequent trial and execution, makes it clear that the capital charge on which
the verdict was found by the uncommonly 'worsshipfull' jury, who displayed unprecedented willingness 'to serve the kyng', was that of 'robbing
Glastonbury church'—a charge of which the ironical overtones seem to
have escaped Russell's perception.[4] Marillac's suggestion that the accusation was one of complicity in the Exeter conspiracy, as also Hall's state-

1 *LP*, xiv, ii, 272; Wright, *SL*, cxxviii.   2 *LP*, xiv, ii, 389; Kaulek, 138.
3 *LP*, xiv, ii, 399; Gasquet, *Last Abbot of Glastonbury*, 99, with facsimile. Gasquet,
following Froude, *History of England*, iii, 436, saw here a palmary instance of flagrant
injustice: Cromwell 'acting as prosecutor, judge and jury' decides before the trial that the
prisoner is to be executed. Baskerville, *EM*, 177, following K. Pickthorn, *Henry VIII*,
374 n. 1, deprecates this interpretation placed upon a private memorandum, and sees in it
a piece of shorthand, viz., 'when he is condemned (as I know he will be)'. Who, in fact,
ever doubted the issue when, e.g., Sir Roger Casement or William Joyce was captured by
British hands? It is in fact anachronistic to apply the standards of modern criminal justice
to a Tudor political trial. Cromwell had discovered, or extracted, what he and his expert
advisers knew to be cast-iron evidence for a jury of the day; the consequences would follow
automatically when the machinery was set in motion; and Cromwell's realist mind appreciated this. The injustice does not lie primarily in the absence of procedural forms, or in
the exercise of a supposed ruthless tyranny, but in the basic evil of the legislation on the
issues of religion and treason, and in Cromwell's ruthless exploitation of the letter of the
law for political and financial purposes.
4 *LP*, xiv, ii, 530; Ellis, *OL*, i, ii, 98; Wright, *SL*, cxxix. A few days before the monks
expiated their 'robbery', Cromwell noted (*LP*, xiv, ii, 427): 'The plate from Glastonbury,
11,000 oz. and odd, besides gold. The furniture of the house of Glastonbury. In ready money
from Glastonbury, £1,100 and odd. The rich copes from Glastonbury. The whole year's
revenue of Glastonbury.'

ment that Abbot Whiting died for denying the royal supremacy, can scarcely, therefore, be accepted as literally true. Had convincing evidence been available on either of these charges, it would have been used; had the indictment been based on it Russell would have said so.

The trial had taken place at Wells; on the following day, 15 November, Whiting was taken across the moor to Glastonbury and dragged on a hurdle from his abbey's gate through the town and up the Tor Hill, which is for many to-day his far-seen memorial. At the last moment Pollard did his best to obtain evidence for future use against others, and information as to more hidden treasure, but the abbot would incriminate nobody and would make no further admission. 'He took his death patiently, asking pardon of God and the King for his offences', and asking Pollard and Russell 'to mediate with the King for his forgiveness'.[1]

Mentem mortalia tangunt. The statesmen and public servants of the early Tudors had little sense of the tears of things, or of the rich historic past preserved in the book they were closing for ever. They would have marvelled that the imagination of later generations could have found cause to linger over the memory of that autumn gathering on Tor Hill. When Whiting rode up to London his orchards had been red with fruit; now, the last splendours had been swept even from the sheltered woods of Dinder, and the trees near the abbey were bare. The old man's eyes, as he stood beneath the gallows, would have travelled for the last time along the slopes of the clouded hills to Brent Knoll and Steep Holm; over the grey expanse of mere to the sharp outline of the Quantocks and the darker Poldens; over the distant ridges to the south where the Glastonbury manors near Domerham had been white with sheep, and over those to the north once hallowed, so the story ran, by the footstep of the 'beauteous Lamb of God'. No other landscape in all England carried so great a weight of legend. To the island valley at his feet the dying Arthur had been ferried. Through the sedges from the Parrett had come Joseph of Arimathea bearing the Grail. On the pleasant pastures of Mendip had shone the countenance of the Child Jesus. Below him lay now the majestic pile of his abbey, desolate, solitary, and about to crumble into ruins. Did he, the last of a long line, think, as we do, of the seed planted at Glastonbury by the first of his predecessors, Dunstan 'the resolute', and of the narrow cloister that was to be the nursing-mother of bishops and abbots, so many and so great? Such a question finds no place in Pollard's interrogatory. We know only that the abbot and his companions took their deaths very patiently, and that Abbot Whiting's head was set up over the gateway of the abbey which he had robbed, not before hands other than his had stolen thence the life of the building.

1 *LP*, xiv, ii, 531; Wright, *SL*, cxxx; Ellis, 1, ii, cxxxvi. It may perhaps be noted that while many of the good men unjustly executed by Henry, such as Aske, begged his forgiveness, those who died for and on behalf of their religious faith did not do so. More, Fisher, Reynolds, the Carthusians and Forest might pray for Henry, but they had no reason to ask his pardon.

CHAPTER XXX

THE TRANSFORMATION OF THE BUILDINGS

At all the monasteries, great and small, save for the few that were converted into cathedrals or colleges, the business of turning the buildings
and their contents into cash was begun as soon as the suppression of a
lesser house had been finally ratified, or when a greater house had signed
the deed of surrender. When an abbey fell by attainder, or through the
disgrace and anticipated condemnation of its abbot, the process often
began before the monks were out.

First, all the plate and jewels that had survived the two preliminary
combings were sent up either to the royal treasury[1] or temporarily to the
local receiver's strong-room, together with a few of the books that might
be of value for the royal library. These last were not necessarily those
that were richest in illumination, for these were often service books which
were now otiose, if not positively distasteful in many quarters.

Next, all the church furniture and domestic stuff was sold by auction
on the spot, often in the cloister or chapterhouse.[2] Everything that could
be priced was put up for sale: paving-stones, glass, alabaster retables,
sets of vestments, missals, candlesticks, censers, cupboards, pans, ladders,
organs, pulpits, bricks and tiles. No object was inappropriate, no offer
too small. Thus at the Austin friars of Stafford a Mr Stamford picked up
an alabaster retable, a door, and the high altar for seven shillings the lot,
while Margaret Whytfyld secured a table from the brewhouse at the
bargain price of twopence.[3] Meanwhile, the surveyors had decided what
parts of the monastery were to be left as a nucleus for the establishment
of the new owner or farmer of the property. Such parts as had been
condemned as 'superfluous' were then stripped of everything saleable

---

1 For the jewels, *v.* John Williams, *Account of the Monastic Treasures.* For a short
summary of the fate of such books as survived, *v.* N. Ker's preface to *Medieval Libraries of
Great Britain*, xi–xv, and C. E. Wright, 'The dispersal of the monastic libraries and the
beginnings of Anglo-Saxon studies'. The selection for the royal library, made under the
direction of John Leland and now for the most part in the Royal Collection in the British
Museum, consisted largely of books by English authors and biblical, legal and theological
commentaries. A request from Leland may have lain behind Cromwell's application to the
prior of Christ Church for Bede's *Ecclesiastical History* and William of Malmesbury's
De Gestis Anglorum (*sic*; *LP*, IX, ii, 529). Other survivals were partly the result of salvage
by individual religious as, e.g., that of the proir of Lantony. The fate of such books as did
not survive is vividly described by Bale in a passage often quoted (e.g. in *Archaeologia*,
XLIII, 203) and in the account of the destruction of Roche abbey by the old Yorkshireman
(Ellis, *OL*, III, iii, 33). A fuller study by Dr Wright, 'The Dispersal of the Libraries in
the Sixteenth Century', has now (1958) appeared.
2 The *locus classicus* of this procedure, as portrayed by Layton in his letter from Bisham,
has already been quoted (*supra*, p. 357). The accounts of many such sales remain, e.g. the
auctions at Bordesley, etc. (*LP*, XIV, ii, 236; Wright, *SL*, cxxxii), and the sales at Stafford,
Dieulacres, etc., in Hibbert, *Dissolution of the monasteries*, App. IV–XI.
3 Wright, *SL*, 272.

such as lead, woodwork, benches, grates, locks and the rest, and this also was sold on the spot or packed for transport to London. The leaden roofs of the great churches, halls and barns were particularly valuable, as were also the bells. Whenever possible furnaces were set up alongside, and the metal melted into pigs. Where livestock remained on the demesne or on the sheep and stock farms they also might be sold, though they often formed part of the purchase price to the grantee. The general outlook of the commissioners is well seen in the letter written by Sir A. Darcy to Cromwell on the amenities of Jervaulx, 'oon off the fayrest chyrches that I have seen; ffayr medooze, and the ryver running by ytt, and a grete demayne', in fact, the ideal spot for the royal stud of mares, 'ffor ssurly the breed off Gervayes ffor horses was the tryed breed in the northe... ffor ther is large and hye groundes ffor the ssomer, and in wynter wooddes and low ground to serve them'.[1] Similarly the Duke of Norfolk was in admiration of the priory at Bridlington, 'it has a barn all covered with lead, the largest, widest and deepest roofes that I ever saw', not to speak of the shrine of St John, from which 'if I durst be a thief I would have stolen [three wrought retables] to have sent them to the Queen's Grace'.[2]

The official instructions were that the commissioners should 'pull down to the ground all the walls of the churches, stepulls, cloysters, fraterys, dorters, chapter howsys' and the rest.[3] Occasionally this was done to perfection, as at Lewes, where the demolitions of Giovanni Portinari and his gang of Italian technicians from London were as expeditious and complete as could be desired. It was imperative to have the place ship-shape as soon as possible, for Gregory Cromwell and his wife were going into residence and wished to make a good impression upon the county. Portinari, with twenty-five men, every one of whom 'attendith to hys own office' went at it with a will, and 'x of them hewed the walles abowte ... thother brake and cutte the waules'. Lesser masonry and columns they could undercut, shoring up with timber as they went, till all was ready to set light to the wood and bring everything down, but some of the piers needed gunpowder to shift them. Portinari hoped that Cromwell would 'be moch satisfied with that we do', and the great church of St Pancras, with its high steeple and its vault ninety-three feet over the high altar was soon 'pulled down to the ground', where the foundations remained till they were found to be in the way of the London, Brighton and South Coast Railway three hundred years later.[4] Similar activities took place

---

1 *LP*, XII, ii, 59; Wright, *SL*, lxxvii.   2 *LP*, XII, i, 1172; ii, 34.

3 So Cromwell's agent John Freeman in Ellis, *OL*, III, iii, ccclix; *LP*, XI, 242. In *LP* this letter is calendared under 1536, but the year is clearly 1539.

4 The priory of Lewes was granted to Cromwell *père* on 16 February 1538, and was given by him as a residence to his son Gregory. Portinari, an Italian gangmaster, began work shortly before 20 March (Wright, *SL*, xci; *LP*, XIII, i, 554, 590) and on 11 April Gregory wrote to his father that Mrs Cromwell found the place 'so commodious that she thinketh herself to be here right well settylled'. Lord and Lady Dacre, Sir John Gage and his lady, with others, had already called (*LP*, XIII, i, 734). Baskerville (*EM*, 124, 277), who refers to 'the Rev.

elsewhere, as at Chertsey[1] and at Stanley in Wiltshire; the stone of the latter church was needed by Sir Edward Baynton, the grantee, to build his house at Bromham, and one of the working-party lost his life under a premature fall of stone.[2] More often, however, the commissioners found that the work of destruction would not pay its way. Though it is easier to destroy a church than to build it, demolition, then as now, cost money, and John Freman, faced with the task of 'plokyng down' all the monastic churches of Lincolnshire, estimated that it would cost at least £1000. He proposed therefore to content himself with 'defacing' the church and making the buildings uninhabitable by removing roofs and stairs. The ruins could then be leased as a quarry for all and sundry.[3] It is perhaps a tribute to the success of Freman's policy that few districts in England have scantier monastic remains than the county which contained, for its area, more houses than any other in England. At Sempringham the work was done so well that the very site of the church, with its great tower, its shrine of St Gilbert, and the adjoining complex of two large cloisters, was forgotten till yesterday, though it stood in a flat, open and solitary countryside.[4]

When the state of defacement had been reached the neighbours descended on the site to pick up any unconsidered trifles that might remain. 'As soon as I hadde taken the Fryers surrendre', wrote London from Reading, 'the multitude of the poverty of the tone resortyd thedyr, and all things that might be hadde they stole away, insomyche that they hadde convayd [stolen] the very clapers of the bellys'.[5] As one of the beneficiaries of the suppression at Hailes remarked, it was 'there now catch that may catch'.[6] A conservative of another generation, who had the story from his uncle, has left a vivid and oft-quoted description of the process of destruction at Roche Abbey, with the monks seeking to raise cash on the contents of their cells, and the natives filching missals to patch the covers of their waggons, and pulling iron hooks out of the walls. One of those favourable to the old religion and a friend of the monks, who had bought much of the timber of the church, when asked long after how he could bring himself to do it, expressed the view of his contemporaries when he replied: 'I did see all would away; and therefore I did as others did.'[7]

When the commissioners themselves did not destroy the church and main conventual buildings, one of the conditions of the lease or sale was that they should be destroyed by the new owner or occupier within a fixed

Mr Portinari', confuses the contractor with his namesake who held the living of Algarkirk, Lincs. Giovanni Portinari appears regularly in Cromwell's wages bill; it may be noted that he writes to Cromwell in Italian.

1 *LP*, XIII, i, 1238.
2 There is an account by H. Brakspear in *Archaeologia*, LX (1907), 493–516.
3 *LP*, XI, 242; Ellis, *OL*, III, iii, ccclix.
4 For Sempringham, *v.* R. Graham in *Journal of the British Archaeological Association*, 3 ser., V, and plates in *Monastic Sites from the air*, 243–4.
5 *LP*, XIII, ii, 367; Wright, *SL*, cviii.
6 *LP*, XVII, 8.   7 Ellis, *OL*, III, iii, pp. 33–5.

space of time. The reason for this is clear. In the religious climate of the times Cromwell, like others, could not be sure of the changes of weather, and he did his best to ensure that there should be no return for the monks. As a new owner put it after he had pulled down the church, the nest had been destroyed lest the birds should build there again.[1] It was left to the individual to choose his own method. Some frankly recoiled before the expense or the danger, and the dismantled church survived in large part till the weather and the ivy had bitten into the masonry and caused an avalanche; in some cases, as at Fountains, the church and tower remain to-day a roofless skeleton. Of the canons' churches, a number were parochial in whole or part, and thus remain standing, as at Lanercost and Brinkburn. A few were bought by the parish or township and used as a parish church, after the monastic portion had been shorn off, as at Bolton, Pershore and Malmesbury. At Tewkesbury the whole fabric thus escaped destruction when this seemed imminent.[2] More rarely still, the whole or part, contrary to instructions, was turned into a private chapel, as by Tregonwell at Milton Abbas.[3] In most cases, however, even stranger transformations took place. At the Cistercian Buckland, Sir Richard Grenville, some decades after the Dissolution, found a use for the dismantled church by converting it, tower and all, into a dwelling house; the grantee at Denney, Cambridgeshire, made an equally ingenious use of the nave and transepts of the nuns' church.[4] Wriothesley, to whom the Premonstratensian abbey of Titchfield was allotted, went rapidly to work upon an imaginative large-scale transformation. Leland, passing that way a few years later, could remark that 'Mr Wriothesley hath buildid a right stately house embatelid, and having a goodely gate and a conducte castelid in the middle of the court of it'.[5] The court was the cloister garth, but Leland does not tell us that Wriothesley's great gate, which still stands a roofless shell, was sited exactly in the middle of the nave of the church, with lodges occupying the bays to east and west. The choir and presbytery, where for three centuries the round of liturgical worship had been performed, were pulled down as superfluous, and the central tower, which had been allowed to stand for a short time at the south end of the west wing of the mansion, had ultimately to be brought down to enable Wriothesley's chimneys to draw.[6] Elsewhere in towns, the offices were

---

1 Fuller, *Church History*, VI, 558; *VCH, Derby*, II, 62.
2 At Tewkesbury both the church and library were originally 'deemed to be superfluous' (*Monasticon*, II, 57–8). Such buildings were indeed worse than superfluous to the grantee, as their maintenance would have been a heavy standing charge on his income.
3 *Monastic Sites from the air*, 34–5.
4 *Ibid.* 146–7, 266–7, descriptions and plates of Buckland and Denney.
5 J. Leland, *Itinerary*, ed. L. Toulmin Smith, I, 281.
6 Cf. W. H. St J. Hope, 'The Making of Place House at Titchfield'. The reconstruction was accomplished very speedily and was almost complete by midsummer, 1538. John Crayford, who seems to have been clerk of the works, wrote on 12 April: 'Every man wold have the steple downe as a thing in the mydest of your forefront Defacing tholl [the whole] & of no profeit nor pleasure.'

used as warehouses or tenements. Henry himself used the chapel of the London Charterhouse as a store for his tents and garden gear, and at Malmesbury, when Leland was there a few years after the monks had left,

the hole logginges of thabbay be now longging to one Stumpe, an exceding riche clothier that boute them of the king....At this present tyme every corner of the vaste houses of office that belongid to thabbay be fulle of lumbes to weve clooth yn, and this Stumpe entendith to make a stret or 2 for clothiers in the back vacant ground of the abbay.[1]

Such adaptations were, however, the exception. In the main, and especially in the numberless small houses in field, forest and dale, the work of destruction was swift, and the church and cloister of yesterday were left a stripped and gutted ruin. This process of destruction was not devised for the first time by Cromwell; at the earlier suppressions of Wolsey something of the kind had taken place, not without the protests of those who were shocked at the spectacle of the desecration of buildings solemnly dedicated to God by previous generations. The scale of these later proceedings, however, was beyond measure more vast, and the majesty of the churches destroyed incomparably greater; this could not but alter the whole character of the act, and men might well wonder if any reverence towards the things of God remained in those who ordered this pillage, and if any human faith could be looked for in those who desecrated great abbeys dedicated to the divine service, and trafficked in their treasures. It was the swift, callous irreverence of the Augmentations men, at work on the relatively few small houses of Yorkshire and Lincolnshire, and the not unnatural fear that everything venerable and sacred might soon likewise be snatched away, that precipitated the explosion of wrath in the northern risings.

Nor were there lacking, even in that age, those who deplored, on the merely human level, the destruction of things fair and precious. Aske, writing in the Tower when all the greater abbeys still stood, could speak of the few that had gone as 'one of the beauties of this realm',[2] and Leland, who was no conservative in religion, more than once paused in his journeys to observe, as at Plympton, that 'the glory of this towne stoode by the priorie of Blake Chanons'.[3] Visible beauty of form and line and hue is as nothing in comparison with the eternal beauty of things unseen, but those who wantonly destroy the one will not readily be supposed to value the other. The country and its Church were deprived in the space of two or three years of a multitude of monuments of architectural beauty, and of innumerable masterpieces of every smaller art and craft. The loss to what may be called the aesthetic capital of the land was very great; certainly it

1 Leland, *Itinerary*, 1, 132.
2 *LP*, XII, i, 901(23); *EHR*, v, 561–2; Dodds, *Pilgrimage of Grace*, 1, 348–9.
3 Leland, *Itinerary*, 1, 215; cf. of St Germans, Cornwall: 'the glory of it stoode by the priory' (*ibid.* 210).

was the greatest single blow of the kind that England, secure till yesterday from hostile shocks, has ever sustained. History, which tells of the slow rise of civilized peoples, and of many fortunate epochs in which things of beauty were created in profusion, has also many a melancholy record of the wholesale destruction of the beautiful works of man, all too rare in any age. In the long list of those who have thus destroyed things fair and lovely—a list that has seen a lamentable increase in length even while these volumes have been in the writing—Henry VIII and Thomas Cromwell, who rid themselves also of many just men, must find a place of note.

CHAPTER XXXI

THE NEW CATHEDRALS AND COLLEGES

A small group of the monasteries, some sixteen in all, stood in a class by themselves by reason of their continued or revived existence in a different shape. They were not destroyed but (to use the official term) 'changed'. They were of three types: first the cathedral churches, eight in number, served by monks or canons, viz. Canterbury, Rochester, Winchester, Ely, Norwich, Worcester, Durham and Carlisle;[1] next the abbeys, six in number, which became, with or without a period of collegiate existence, cathedrals of newly founded sees, viz. Westminster, Gloucester, Peterborough, Chester, Oxford and Bristol; thirdly, the two abbeys turned into colleges, Burton and Thornton. Though few in numbers this group contained some of the wealthiest houses of all, such as Westminster and Canterbury, and the aggregate net income amounted to no less than £19,283, or almost 15 per cent of the total income of all houses. Considered as a group, therefore, they represent the sum total of the material benefit accruing to the official Church from the great monastic confiscation or, to put the matter in other and more realistic words, the sum total of the salvage effected from the great wreck. Even so, the total amount relinquished by the king and Cromwell did not add up, when all the permutations were over, to a quarter of the sum just mentioned. Existing cathedrals, including the metropolitan church and such venerable fanes as Durham and Winchester, could not be left without any establishment merely because they had been staffed by monks. The cost of the new chapters and their dependants had therefore to be met out of the existing monastic revenues, and though this was considerably more modest than the cost of running the cathedral priory, it was nevertheless a substantial item to be lost to Augmentations. In the event, however, Henry recouped himself in large part by the sacrifices in lands and income that he exacted from the bishops concerned. Next, the foundations enumerated above were not all permanent. Westminster lasted only ten years as a bishopric, and the college which replaced the chapter was a more modest establishment. The two colleges of Burton and Thornton endured only for five and seven years respectively; they were soon found to be 'superfluous', as were also the scholars at the universities originally attached to Canterbury and Winchester cathedrals. Burton and Thornton thus came duly to Augmentations. In short, the only permanent piece of genuine salvage was the group of five new bishoprics, Gloucester, Chester, Peterborough, Bristol and Oseney (later Oxford), of which the first three inherited the

1 The two monastic churches that shared rights with secular chapters, viz. Bath (with Wells) and Coventry (with Lichfield), were treated as autonomous communities and dissolved on surrender.

buildings of a black monk abbey, and the last two those of an abbey of Austin canons. The total net income of the five houses concerned was £5236, and even on this considerable savings on behalf of the Crown were effected by severe economies in the scale of the new cathedral establishment, which in every case was considerably more modest than that of even the smallest and poorest of the old secular cathedrals.

The conversion of the cathedral monasteries into secular chapters took place in a haphazard manner, with intermediate stages or eclipses, over three years. The first conversion was that of Norwich, a see to which the abbot of St Benet's, Holme, had recently (1536) been appointed, retaining his abbey *in commendam* until the community ceased to exist in 1539, when the revenues were annexed to the bishopric. The cathedral priory had been an unhappy house for many years, and in 1538 the community surrendered, coming into being again on 2 May as part of a secular establishment; the prior became dean, five of the monks prebendaries, and sixteen others petty canons.[1] Early in 1540 the priories of Canterbury, Worcester and Durham surrendered, and a new establishment was created of a dean with eleven prebendaries (canons), petty canons, a gospeller (deacon) and epistoler (subdeacon). At Durham there was also an arch-deacon, and the minor canons were replaced by twelve students in divinity, who did not long remain. Rochester, always a satellite of Canterbury, received a similar constitution a few days after its mother-church.[2]

At Winchester and Ely a somewhat different process took place. Immediately upon surrender the house was 'altered' into a 'new college', which at Winchester consisted of a guardian, twelve seniors, twelve commoners and four priests. After little more than a year, however, both these colleges were converted into a cathedral establishment of the usual pattern, save that at Winchester the original scheme allowed, besides prebendaries and minor canons, twelve students divided equally between Oxford and Cambridge. These last were soon found to be a burden and were discarded.[3]

As for the new cathedrals, they also were established in a haphazard way after the fall of Cromwell. All the abbeys concerned had appeared on the various draft lists circulated by the king and others in the past few years.[4] At Westminster the change took place soon after the surrender, and an establishment on the scale of Durham and Winchester was created.[5] The other churches had to wait for a time. At Gloucester on the surrender (5 January 1540) a college was formed with a guardian, a sub-warden, three assistants, a reader in divinity, eight seniors, ten resident commoners, and four students at Oxford, but this lasted less than two years, and on

---

1 *VCH, Norfolk*, II, 258; *LP*, XIII, i, 867; ii, 1115 (4).

2 For Canterbury, *v. LP*, xv, 452, and Woodruff and Danks, *Memorials of Canterbury Cathedral*, 288 n. For Rochester, *LP*, xv, 474; Worcester, *ibid.* 81; Durham, *VCH, Durham*, II, 101, and D. Hay, 'The dissolution of the monasteries in the diocese of Durham'.

3 For Winchester, *v. LP*, xvi, 678, no. 53, p. 719; 878, no. 1.

4 For these, *v. supra*, 358–9   5 H. F. Westlake, *Westminster Abbey*, 208–9.

3 and 4 September 1541, a cathedral establishment was created with a dean, archdeacon, six prebendaries, and eight petty canons.[1] Peterborough and Chester, on the other hand, were left after surrender in a state of suspended animation, with the late abbots administering the property and some, at least, of the former community still in residence. They were re-established about the same time as Gloucester (3 September and 4 August respectively) with a similar set-up of dignitaries and officials, minus the students.[2] At Bristol and Oseney the break was more complete, and over two years elapsed before the cathedral came into being, with considerably less continuity in personnel.[3] At Carlisle, the interval was of sixteen months and the new establishment a very modest one of four prebendaries and eight minor canons, all of them old inhabitants.[4]

Finally, of all the colleges proposed in one or other of the schemes in circulation or suggested by individuals, only two came into existence. Both were in churches which had been selected for bishoprics, though both were awkwardly placed for that purpose, Burton being a fairly near neighbour of both Lichfield and Coventry, and Thornton lying near the Humber, the natural limit of any diocese, and at no great distance from Lincoln. Both were established as colleges with four prebendaries, perhaps originally as an interim measure; Burton had six minor canons, and Thornton had also a reader in divinity. Burton enjoyed four, and Thornton seven years of life; this was long enough to show them 'superfluous', whether as colleges or prospective cathedral churches, and they were suppressed.

The houses that were transformed into cathedral chapters or colleges stood in a class apart from the other religious houses as regards the provision made for their inmates. Where the change was immediate, as at Canterbury, Rochester, Durham and Worcester, a division was made between those to be retained on the new foundation, and those who had become 'superfluous persons late religious'. The latter were pensioned and 'despatched', the former lived on at their old home, though in new quarters around the precinct. Generally speaking, the new establishment was half the size of the old, and appointment to the prebends was divided more or less equally between the king and the bishop; among the latter's nominees were a number of the ex-religious, while others found posts as minor canons, or as deacon and subdeacon. Thus at Norwich, as we have seen, more than twenty monks remained; at Canterbury, despite Cranmer's dislike of monasticism, six of the twelve original prebendaries were monks; at Winchester all the monks save four remained in the 'altered' interim establishment, and at Durham twenty-six out of fifty-four.

1 For Gloucester, *v. LP*, xv, 24, and G. Baskerville in *TBGAS*, xlix (1927), 81–4.
2 For Peterborough, *v. LP*, xv, p. 549, and xvi, 1226 (8), p. 573; also Northants Record Society, vol. 13. For Chester, R. V. H. Burne, 'The Dissolution of St Werburgh's Abbey' and 'The Founding of Chester Cathedral'; also *LP*, xvi, 1135 (4).
3 For Bristol, *v. LP*, xvii, 443 (9); for Oxford, *ibid.* 881 (3).
4 For Carlisle, *v. ibid.*, xvi, 878 (15).

At Gloucester the resident community was halved exactly: fourteen were 'despatched' and fourteen remained, with four others maintained as students at Oxford; in the final cathedral establishment the dean was not a monk, but the late prior of St Oswald's, an Austin canon, and only seven monks were retained, though among the remaining prebends one went to ex-abbot Munslow of Winchcombe, and one to an ex-monk of Ramsey, while an ex-Franciscan became archdeacon. At Peterborough the monks had a larger share. All the six prebends and seven out of the eight petty canonries went to members of the old community, and the bishop (late abbot), dean (late prior) and gospeller were likewise ex-monks. At Ely also a dozen or so remained in the 'New College', and of these ten or eleven were appointed a year later to the cathedral establishment. At Chester the first dean was the late prior, Thomas Clarke, but he died within a month of his appointment and his successor was the late prior of Sheen Charterhouse, Dr Henry Man. Man's compliance had been useful, and he had a large pension, which the government were glad to extinguish. The subdean was not a monk, but the young ex-warden of the grey friars in the city,[1] and the ex-prior of St Werburgh's had to be content with the post of senior prebendary and treasurer. Three of the four remaining prebendaries were ex-monks, and five out of the six minor canons, while yet another monk became gospeller in 1542. As at least two other ex-monks of St Werburgh's held livings or curacies and several had been aged in 1540 the brethren had not done badly for themselves in a material way out of the Dissolution. At Bristol, on the other hand, where the community had all been pensioned off two years earlier, only one ex-canon secured a prebend; the bishopric went to the late master of the Bonhommes of Edington, and the deanery to the ex-prior of the Austin canons of Bradenstoke. At Carlisle, which had surrendered on 9 January 1540, to be refounded on 2 April 1541, the dean, four prebendaries and eight petty canons were members of the old community.

In this way the change-over at the cathedrals, old and new, was effected with a minimum of dislocation. The monks who remained, the most intelligent and generally useful members of the old community, found themselves living a life that differed little from that in the monastery, save that they gradually came to dwell in separate lodgings carved out of the old buildings. It was not for a generation or so that wives and families began to appear in the precinct. When that happened, the wheel had come full circle. Almost six centuries earlier the zealous monastic reformers had ejected the married clerks from the cathedral of Winchester. Now, it was the monks' turn to go or, if they stayed, to be merged in their middle age in the ranks of the new clergy and live to see, as at Durham, a Dean's wife going about her lawful occasions in what had been the great court of the priory.

1 Burne, 'The Founding of Chester Cathedral', 40, notes that he did not die till 1574.

CHAPTER XXXII

THE DISPOSAL OF THE LANDS

The Act of March 1536, which provided for the suppression of the lesser monasteries, was accompanied by another, which erected a 'courte of Thaugmentacions of the Revenues of the Kinges Crowne' to conduct the business of suppression and to administer the former monastic property.[1] The responsibilities of the new court were greatly increased by the operation of the attainders and surrenders from 1537 onwards, which were confirmed by the Act of May 1539,[2] and they received still further additions in 1540 and 1545, when the lands of the Knights of St John and of the non-academic colleges were confiscated.[3]

The new court, the equivalent of a new 'ministry' in a modern scheme of government, was an extension of the administrative revolution which Cromwell had initiated, and was framed after the pattern of the existing court of the Duchy of Lancaster.[4] It was controlled in London by a chancellor, Sir Richard Rich, the solicitor-general, and by a treasurer, Sir Thomas Pope, who was later to found Trinity College, Oxford; they were assisted by an attorney and a solicitor, and the work in the country was carried out by seventeen particular receivers, each allotted to a specified region, and ten auditors, each associated with one or more of the receivers. The salaries of all were to be on a generous scale,[5] and the opportunities for advancing private fortunes were obviously promising. The 'Augmentations men' were in great part those who had taken part in previous surveys of monastic property, first for Wolsey and then for Cromwell, and many of them went on to still higher positions in the government machine and became the founders of county families or noble houses. The court was responsible for taking the surrenders, whether nominally free or secured by statute or attainder,[6] for realizing or protecting the liquid assets, and for administering the estate until it was farmed out or granted away.

1 27 Hen. VIII, cc. 27, 28; *Statutes of the Realm*, III, 569–78.
2 28 Hen. VIII, c. 13; *Statutes*, III, 733–9.
3 32 Hen. VIII, c. 24 and 37 Henry VIII, c. 3; *Statutes*, III, 778–81, 988–93.
4 The history of the Court of Augmentations has yet to be written. Meanwhile, the reader may consult G. R. Elton, *The Tudor Revolution in Government*, 203–19; J. Conway Davies, *Records of the Court of Augmentations relating to Wales and Monmouthshire*, introd.; and, for the relationship of the Court of Augmentations to that of the Duchy of Lancaster, R. Somerville, *History of the Duchy of Lancaster*, vol. I, chs. v and vi. Miss Joyce Youings has provided excellent studies of the working of the court in a regional context in her article, 'The Terms of the Disposal of the Devon Monastic Lands', in *EHR*, LXIX, and in *Devon Monastic Lands: Calendar of Particulars of Grants, 1536–1558*, introd. Cf. also Tanner, *Tudor Constitutional Documents*, 336–9.
5 The annual expense on salaries, according to a document cited by Fuller, *Church History*, III, 465, was £7250.
6 Some of the estates of attainted superiors were administered by the General Surveyors, who in consequence were responsible for the pensions.

Originally, when policy was still fluid and the intake of property was relatively small, the intention of Cromwell was undoubtedly to retain the lands for the Crown and to merge the income with current revenue, but when the stream had swollen into a great river, and the personal and political interests of the king had cut across the minister's planning, grants were made on long lease or by sales which in effect gave freehold limited only by the retention of knight service in chief and a small reserved rent. From the beginning, permission to alienate often followed a large grant, and very soon the residue of the property began to come on to the open market.

To deal with the business created by this new situation a series of commissions were set up, empowered to sell Crown lands, whether monastic in origin or not, to a specified annual value, usually £10,000.[1] The Chancellor of the Augmentations was always one of these commissioners, and the first appointment in September 1539 consisted of Rich and Cromwell only. After Cromwell's disgrace Rich was alone in charge till 1543, when he was joined by a group of government agents who were for the most part past or present Augmentations men. By its original constitution the court could grant leases for life or for a term of years under its own seal, whereas alienations always required letters patent under the Great Seal of England. In early years there was a good deal of haphazard granting, either to convenient or persistent local buyers or as rewards or retainers of servants and supporters of the Crown, but as the situation stabilized itself a fixed and lengthy procedure became the norm. The request of the would-be purchaser, if accepted, was followed by a valuation of the property, the assignment of a price,[2] the drafting of warrants, and the final sueing out of letters patent from Chancery, all of which cost money.

In the business of administration, as indeed throughout the whole process of suppression, the general policy was conservative and tolerant of vested interests. The existing agreements between monks and tenants were generally honoured, often even when, as with leases of less than a year's standing, the agreements were statutorily voidable, and the new leases and sales were usually at first calculated on the valuations of the Suppression Commissioners or even of the *Valor*. The fact that so much of the land was already leased and rented, often to the prospective buyer of the manor or demesne, helped to steady the whole transaction with respect to both parties, and to keep the new rents in step with the old. Though the climate of constant and universal inflation gradually drove up rents and prices, there seems to have been little attempt on the part of the

1 There were no less than twenty of these commissions between 1539 and 1558. In 1547 the Court of Augmentations and the Court of the General Surveyors were merged, after a formal suppression of both and the constitution of a new body.

2 The request of the petitioner for a grant, the auditor's certificate of value, and the terms proposed by the commissioners together made up the bundles known as 'Particulars for Grants'.

commissioners to rig the market or to sell the lands by auction, nor was the market notably worsened by the amount of land which was potentially for sale.

As is clear from the flood of requests, there was in general no lack of demand for the lands. The casual reader of history has in the past often received the impression that the stampede of 1536 reflected in Cromwell's correspondence was largely that of courtiers who could receive, or at least hope to receive, estates for the asking. This was not so: most of the early applicants were in fact disappointed or at least kept waiting till the process of dissolution was complete; in a few cases, indeed, farmers who had obtained a lease saw it cancelled as a result of a successful bid for a respite on the part of the inmates. Moreover, very few received grants on terms that were notably easy. Rather, the eagerness was that of a wealthy and land-hungry class, who had hitherto been able to buy only occasionally and locally, and who now saw an avalanche of desirable properties about to descend into the lap of the fortunate, and could only hope that by approaching Henry or Cromwell with all speed they might be among those in the running for a bid.

Three classes, not wholly exclusive each of the other, were the principal beneficiaries of the earliest transactions: the local landowners, often patrons or titular founders or stewards of a particular house, and therefore in a position to know exactly what they wanted and to ask for it first; individual courtiers in high favour or government agents whose support was needed, such as Charles Brandon, Thomas Howard, Edward Seymour, William Wriothesley and John Russell; and officials of the Court of Augmentations, who knew the good points of a particular property and were in an advantageous position when it came to pressing their claim.[1] Though in very early days a few of these, and some others who had not applied, obtained the land as a gift or on advantageous terms, it has been calculated that of the monastic property disposed of, only some 2½ per cent was given away. Indeed, no grant was an absolutely free gift.[2] An annual rent of one-tenth of the income was reserved to the Crown on all property over the value of one hundred marks freely granted before 1543. The Crown also retained the right to knight-service *in capite*, with the accompanying feudal incidents and wardships on all property of £2 or more annual value.[3] In addition, many of the grants for which no cash payments were demanded were in fact heavily burdened in one or more ways. Some were conditional upon an exchange of estates with the Crown

1 For an analysis of the classes of buyers, *v.* Savine's table in Fisher, *Political History of England*, v, 499–501. This, however, is vitiated by a failure to allow for (*a*) speedy resales, (*b*) escheats to, or resumption by, the Crown, and (*c*) the probability that the 'land-jobbers' were in fact agents buying for principals.

2 So J. Kennedy in his unpublished thesis, 'The Dissolution of the Monasteries in Hampshire and the Isle of Wight', 171.

3 For knight-service, *v.* J. Hursfield, 'The Greenwich Tenures of the reign of Edward VI', in *Law Quarterly Review*, 65.

amounting to a quarter or more of the total value, others were burdened with the pensions of the ex-superior and religious, others again with the outstanding debts and corrodies of the house. Nevertheless, a favoured few, such as Russell in Devon and Wriothesley in Hampshire, acquired without trouble or great outlay of capital a large block of estates which they certainly could not have afforded to buy in a single batch on the open market, and which gave them at once a predominant influence in the district. These formed, however, a small group, if a powerful one; the great majority of the applicants paid, if they were purchasers, at the ruling rate appointed by the commissioners, which was, from 1539 onwards for the next twenty years, the rating, long conventional in the land market, of twenty years' purchase for landed estate and ten or twelve years' for urban property.[1] Those who became farmers of demesne by lease, or who leased parcels of land or urban property, paid rent at the old annual rate with a fine which in most cases was less than the annual rent. Recent research would seem to have established that these ratings were economically justifiable, at least in 1540, and were based on a fairly realistic survey of the lands. It must be remembered that the purchase, even if it included the whole of a monastic estate, gave 'vacant possession' only of the buildings and such demesne as had been in hand at the time of suppression. Over the rest of the land various forms of leases, tenancies, and rents were running, and the rates even of rack-rents and tenancies at will were in practice fairly tightly bound by convention or by economic sympathy with the pattern of similar holdings in neighbouring non-monastic estates. Consequently, if on the one hand no clear evidence exists to show that the release of so much land upon the market resulted in a lowering of price, there is on the other hand equally scanty evidence that the new owners were able, or attempted, to step up rents and fines as soon as they took possession.[2] It was, however, an age of creeping inflation, in which any calculations of the value of real property from estimates or surveys ten or twenty years old were sure to be unrealistic; to that extent the market in land at the disposal of the Crown favoured the early grantees and farmers, even if rack-rents and leasehold rates on the whole lagged behind prices in the general rise.

This fact did not escape the commissioners, and early in the 1550's the rate for property was raised to twenty-four years' purchase, which became thirty in the early 1560's and higher still before the end of the century. Similarly the entry fines were increased to three or more times the annual value of the land. On the whole, then, it may be said that the lands, apart from the original freshet of gifts and occasional subsequent largesses,

---

1 Kennedy, *op. cit.* 162, and H. J. Habakkuk, 'The Market for Monastic Property', 364 *seqq.*

2 H. P. R. Finberg, *Tavistock Abbey*, 271, notes successful attempts of Lord Russell's agents to make new leases on favourable terms.

were sold at a constant fixed rate which was that normal on the land market of the day, while the grantees made no spectacular profits out of increases of rent. The market was preserved from sagging partly by the constant pressure of a force of purchasers with capital to invest, partly by the force of convention, and partly by the lack of any organized system of information throughout the country as to the fluctuation of prices and rents. That the buyers continued to come forward shows that capital was plentiful, even if we allow for a certain amount of borrowing. In the early years much of this may have come from reserves of cash accumulated by landowners and farmers in the days when sales were scarce; in the 1540's the vast sums spent by the government in the war with Scotland and France must have given many of the king's subjects new capital to invest.

In the first year or two of the sales most of the land went to courtiers, government agents and existing landowners, and fifty years ago it was a commonplace to attribute the rise of a new nobility to the partition of the spoil from the monasteries; more recently still, the same cause has been invoked to account for the rise of a much larger class of gentry within the following eighty years.[1] That a considerable number of men connected with the court and government now for the first time joined the ranks of the landed proprietors and remained for centuries among the most powerful of the aristocratic families need not be denied. Besides the court favourites, whose possessions were rarely permanent, the great houses of Bedford, Hertford and Salisbury rose into the first rank on a basis of land originally monastic, and others, such as Wriothesley, Audley, Rich and Cromwell himself came in for very large shares. Nevertheless, much of the monastic land went to men who already held considerable estates (as indeed did some of those just mentioned), while not a few of those so enriched were found later among those families who were most zealous for the old religion, such as the Howards and the Arundells. Many of those who have been taken at one time or another as typical new men grown rich on the spoil of the Church had this reputation either because they set up what was ever after to be the family seat on the site of a religious house, perhaps their sole modest purchase, or because they bought heavily of monastic land at its second or third appearance in the market. In short, three considerations at least must modify the opinion commonly held that the bulk of the monastic land went cheap and remained with a few courtiers and politicians. First, as has been seen, the number of estates freely or cheaply bestowed was small. Next, many, perhaps most, of the grantees at court either sold part of their land almost at once to pay for the expenses

---

1 For early discussions of the gifts and sales, *v.* Savine, *The English Monasteries,* 258 *seqq.*; H. L. Fisher, using Savine's tables, *Political History of England,* 500 *seqq.*; S. B. Liljegren, *The Fall of the Monasteries and the Social Changes of England,* especially 109 *seqq.*; and for particular regions, the monographs and theses referred to on pp. 306, 406. For recent conclusions, *v.* the work of Habakkuk, Hodgett, Kerridge and Youings (in Bibliography).

of their careers, or fell into disgrace in one of the conspiracies or turns of fortune in the middle decades of the century, thus causing their lands to escheat in part or in whole to the Crown. Thirdly, the Crown for long reserved radical ownership of more than half the estates concerned, which the grantees held on leases of varying length; in early grants the lease was usually for a period of twenty-one years. Had this policy been pursued firmly and constantly from the start, the later Tudors and early Stuarts would have been possessed of large tracts of country throughout England, and the controversies which found a neuralgic focus in the attempts of the Crown to pay for government out of taxation might have taken a different course. In fact, however, Henry VIII led the way in turning his capital assets into cash, and throughout the century his successors continued from time to time to follow his example, so that at the death of Elizabeth I, little more than sixty years after the Dissolution, only a small part of the lands once monastic remained the property of the Crown.[1]

As for the land granted and sold, it too was speedily parcelled or reassembled. Very many of the earliest grants were accompanied by permission to alienate, and the courtiers in particular were quick to take advantage of this. Finally, from c. 1542 onwards, there appeared, singly or in pairs and groups, a new class of buyers who bought up large estates and scattered properties all over England, and sold them almost at once in bulk or in parcels. When this type of sale was first noticed by those investigating the records of the Court of Augmentations it was assumed that they were land-jobbers exploiting a buyers' market with a view to re-sale at a profit.[2] They were not a homogeneous group for among them were found members of the nobility and officials of the Court of Augmentations, but the most constant and conspicuous were private men of commerce such as Richard Andrews and Leonard Chamberlain of Woodstock, William Romsden, Nicholas Temple and others. Closer investigation has shown that the re-sale often followed so closely upon the grant, even before the price had been paid or the final documents drawn up, that the price paid by the ultimate owner was little if any more than that received by Augmentations, and that this owner was often one who had himself applied previously for grants in person. For all these reasons it would appear that the transaction was one between agent and principal rather than one between speculator and customer. There remain, however, at least some cases where a group of small men, usually Londoners, are seen to buy a bunch of insignificant properties all over England and Wales, with no evidence of re-sale, and it is natural to see them as a syndicate

---

1 K. Pickthorn, *Henry VIII*, 382–6. Careful allowance must, however, be made for the property that reverted to the Crown by escheat, etc.

2 Liljegren, *op. cit.* 118–24, was the first to consider these transactions in detail. G. J. Hodgett, 'The Dissolution of the Religious Houses of Lincolnshire and the Changing Structure of Society', continued the examination. For the view given in the text, *v.* H. J. Habakkuk, 'The Market for Monastic Property', 378–80.

investing in real property as a source of private income.[1] As a result of all these transactions, the monastic lands were soon split up among a very numerous class of owners and lessees,[2] and the final result of the division was perhaps rather to increase the holding of land of every existing class of landed proprietor than to favour the growth of a few great families or to plant a generation of new men or London merchants on the land. Much further research is necessary before the final detailed picture appears, but it is already clear that over the whole of England and Wales a primary result of the transfer of land was the betterment of the well-to-do yeoman and of the younger sons of country gentlemen.

Much has been written of the wastage that occurred in the course of realizing the gigantic haul. It was indeed very great, as is almost always the case when a wholesale confiscation takes place. The Court of Augmentations had been established in 1536 in order to isolate and control the litigation and administration connected with the property newly fallen into the king's hands; neither the Exchequer nor the ordinary courts were to have anything to do with it. The task from the beginning was difficult. To the inevitable problems of action and policy caused by so much property of various kinds coming upon the market, or at least being *en disponibilité*, within a very brief space of time, the court was hampered by gifts or deals made outside its doors by the king or Cromwell, and by the natural anxiety of its members and their friends to make the most of a golden opportunity and to get in on the ground floor. Furthermore, its efficiency was notably impaired by what may be called the original sin of Tudor administration, which no genius in planning or firmness in action could wholly exorcize: the atmosphere of bribery, flattery, pillage and avarice which the new master and his personnel had inherited from the days of the cardinal. It is true, and should be duly recorded, that the dealings of the commissioners and Augmentations men are remarkably free from the acts of brutality, heartlessness and violence towards individuals that have distinguished almost all processes of revolutionary confiscation. With few exceptions, so far as the records show, they behaved as one group of Englishmen dealing with another. Yet at the same time the investigator does not have to go far in the records and accounts to see frequent instances of waste and appropriation of funds.[3] With all its efficiency in coercion and espionage the governmental machinery lacked the clean bite given by the training and traditions of the bureaucracies controlled by a Colbert or a von Roon; just as the social and police regulations of the early Tudor Council tended to break down at the circumference when

1 In particular, the instance given by Hodgett, *art. cit.* 91.

2 This seems true of many regions, but any generalization is dangerous in the present fragmentary state of our knowledge. Kennedy, in his study of Hampshire, notes (p. 203) that *c.* 1559, 'three-quarters of the former monastic manors were in the hands of the original grantees'.

3 Examples of petty extravagances and more important irregularities are chronicled in Gasquet and Hibbert, both advocates of the monks.

applied by the decentralized local justices, so the economy and strict accountability which Cromwell desired could not be realized with a staff venal and acquisitive from head to heel. Nor was the master himself primarily a great finance minister or a far-sighted statesman of genius. He worked in a materialistic world to satisfy an insatiable and capricious master. If need was, he burnt the candle at both ends; when it went out he might, as he well knew, be where he would no longer benefit by its light.

Into the books of the Court of Augmentations flowed enormous sums.[1] It has been calculated that the total yearly net income of the monasteries in 1535 was in the neighbourhood of £136,000 to £140,000, and this is undoubtedly a conservative estimate.[2] The average net receipt of the Court of Augmentations for the decade 1536–47 was in the neighbourhood of £140,000 per annum. As the normal recurring revenue of the Crown in c. 1535 was £100,000 it will be seen that Cromwell had indeed secured for Henry a very considerable additional income. Had this new accession been pure revenue, that is, mere income from capital, the king would have had every reason to be satisfied. In fact, however, an annual average of £82,300 of the sum of £140,000 represented the alienation of capital by sales of land, materials and precious objects, or by non-recurring fines for long leases; only about £61,300 was normal recurring revenue.[3] Nor was this all. As gifts and sales began at once there was, after the great tidal wave of suppressions, a steady ebb of resources. The sale of monastic goods and movables reached its peak (£13,787) in 1541–3, and thereafter rapidly decreased to vanishing point. The sales of lands were at their maximum in 1544 and 1545, with totals of £164,495 and £165,459, and thereafter declined sharply to £66,186 in 1546–7. Most significant of all, rents reached their peak at once in 1542, with £177,806, and thereafter fell at first gradually and then sharply for the next half-century.[4] In other words, motives of every kind existed from the beginning which inspired a constant gradual alienation of capital, with the inevitable shrinkage of revenue. While Cromwell was in charge this was controlled, so far as administration could control the king, but afterwards especially from 1542 onwards, less prudent counsels prevailed. Yet when all due reservations have been made, the sums accruing to the Crown were very large, and so far justified the Dissolution as a short-term financial expedient; regarded,

1 For the receipts of the Court of Augmentations, *v.* F. C. Dietz, *English Government Finance*, appendix, tables iii and iv, pp. 217–19.

2 For the significance of 'net' in this connection, *v. supra*, p. 242. All calculations are uncertain, as a few houses are missing from the *Valor*, and the gross income is often wanting; historians in the past have varied greatly in their estimates. That in the text is from Savine, *op. cit.* 98–100; it includes nunneries but not friaries and agrees roughly with the £135,000 of Dietz, 137 (with a reference to B.M. Cott. Cleo. E. iv, 446–56).

3 Dietz, 139, 140; Pickthorn, 372. The common length of a lease was twenty-one years, but when funds were needed in later years the period was extended to sixty, eighty-one or ninety-one years.

4 Dietz, *loc. cit.*

however, as a piece of long-term planning, intended to nationalize super-fluous wealth in the interests of government and social service, it cannot be regarded as financially successful. Even before the end of the reign, the recurring regular revenue from the spoils was less than half the original monastic income, and the capital of land and precious objects had been repeatedly raided for needs that were purely passing, without being used at all to endow the Crown with a permanent revenue, or the country with religious, educational or social assets.

CHAPTER XXXIII

THE TREATMENT OF THE DISPOSSESSED

In addition to the liquidation of the estate and the destruction of the monastic building, the commissioners had also to deal with the inhabitants of the monastery and their dependants. The fate of the dispossessed religious has often in the past provided a topic for inaccurate general statements. Historians and antiquaries of a romantic or conservative temper, attributing to Tudor England the sentiments and modes of action common in other countries and ages where the suppression of a monastery has been an incident in the bitter conflict of creeds and ideologies, have assumed that to the religious as a class dissolution meant the violent wrench from a life given to God in seclusion, and the ejection into a hostile world with only a meagre and irregular pittance.[1] This view, it must be acknowledged, receives some support from isolated contemporary witnesses who, through prejudice or insufficient information, may have exaggerated the misfortunes of the monks and nuns;[2] it cannot, however, be maintained in its original simplicity in face of all the evidence now available. That the lot of some of the religious was hard, and undeservedly hard, need not be questioned. At some houses, at least, there must have been individuals with a vocation and an aptitude for an observant religious life who had, knowingly and willingly, set aside other hopes when first devoting their lives to God and who had a right, therefore, on every score to live those lives out in congenial surroundings. The number of such

1 The oft-quoted account of the old Yorkshireman (Ellis, *OL*, III, iii, 33-5), 'for it would have made a heart of flint to have melted and wept to have seen the breaking up of the House [Roche] and their sorrowful departure', is clearly an example of the 'sob-stuff' castigated by Baskerville, though the date of writing (1591) does not of itself wholly invalidate the testimony, for the writer goes on to say (p. 34) that he himself saw the bells hanging in the belfry a year or so after the suppression. No conservative or romantic antiquary, however, has ever outbidden the poet Wordsworth, with his picture (*Ecclesiastical Sonnets*, II, xxii) of the exiled nun

'unveiling timidly a cheek
Suffused with blushes of celestial hue.'

2 The statement of Chapuys to Anthoine Perrenot on 8 July 1536 seems at first sight trustworthy: 'It is a lamentable thing to see a legion of monks and nuns, who have been chased from their monasteries, wandering miserably hither and thither, seeking means to live' (*LP*, XI, 42), but his next words, 'and several honest men have told me that what with monks, nuns, and persons dependent on the monasteries suppressed, there were over 20,000 who knew not how to live', make one pause. Fuller, a century later, was somewhat more restrained: 'Ten thousand persons were by this dissolution sent to seek their fortunes in the wide world' (*Church History*, III, 374). Sober historians who have cited these passages seem to have forgotten that all those who were at a loose end in 1536, save for a few young people under twenty, had chosen freedom rather than transference, and we have seen that the number of nuns actually leaving the cloister at this time was minimal. Nor could the number of displaced dependents of the lesser monasteries have been large. In such a society as that of early Tudor England even small displacements could start rumours, and exiles with a grievance would naturally pass on exaggerated stories.

men and women must have been considerably greater than the number of those who bore external witness to their fervour and constancy by exile or by joining one of the houses refounded by Queen Mary. While it is right to remember that all of the religious had, in greater or less degree, knowingly departed from what they had been brought up to believe in the matter of papal authority, some of them, at least, might have made the plea that they knew not what they did, and when they accepted the royal supremacy they had certainly no thought that their new Supreme Head would so soon put an end to their way of life. It would be reasonable to suppose (and the evidence bears this out) that this type of mind would be most common in the stricter orders of men and among the women religious; of these two classes the former had been greatly reduced by active persecution, while the latter do indeed give most evidence of the real hardship of their later life outside the cloister. What proportion of the remainder, that is, the great bulk of the religious, had what in modern phrase would be called a real or fervent vocation, must remain a matter of uncertainty, and only those who have pondered the visitation records of the past century, together with all the documents of the Suppression, will be in a position to hazard an opinion. The present writer, after thirty years in which he has from time to time reflected on the evidence, can only say that he believes the number of those who were, in the traditional ascetical phrase, 'seriously striving after perfection', to have been relatively, if not even absolutely, small.

Between the two extremes of fervour and unworthiness there was undoubtedly a large body of respectable men and women who were contented and useful members of the society to which they belonged. To these dissolution meant at least an unpleasant and unforeseen break in their life's even tenor. Such people were unfortunate to the extent that any members of a corporation or profession are unfortunate if their personal career is interrupted by political or social reform or revolution. The contention of some apologists of the past, that the purely physical amenities of a great abbey, such as majestic buildings, rich liturgy, comfortable living, opportunities for study, the interests of administration, and so forth, are in any sense a part of the bargain in a truly spiritual religious profession, can scarcely be seriously maintained.

When reviewing the resettlement of the ex-religious three moments in the process of secularization must be distinguished, and four classes among the religious. The three moments are: first, the suppression of the lesser houses by the Act of 1536; secondly, the 'voluntary' surrenders made between 1536 and 1540; and thirdly, the small group of houses that fell by the attainder or disgrace of their heads during these years. The four classes are: first, the communities that were transformed into cathedrals or colleges; secondly, the rank and file of the other houses suppressed; thirdly, the orders of friars; and fourthly, the abbots and priors of autonomous houses.

By the Act of 1536 statutory provision was made, as we have seen, for the inmates of the doomed houses. Allowing for the possibility that those under the age of twenty at least had been dismissed, and that dispensations had been obtained by the visitors for the rare individuals who had petitioned for release, the remainder might elect either to apply for transference to one of the greater houses or, if they were in holy orders, they might receive a small bonus *ex caritate* and apply for 'capacities' or dispensations from their religious vows (save that of chastity) in order to apply for or to accept an ecclesiastical benefice or chaplaincy. Statistics of the choice made at this moment are not available for the whole of England, and have been analysed only in a very partial way. They would not, it must be remembered, be identical with those compiled from the replies of the commissioners of 1536 which we have already considered, for in these latter the choice of the inmates was hypothetical, and in several instances the houses concerned were in fact reprieved. Whatever the numbers concerned, they were certainly not very large, and as they were the first religious to appear in the market in search of employment they were probably absorbed without great difficulty. Moreover, they had made their choice freely, even though the alternative may not have been very alluring. At the same time, many of them were in the nature of the case dissatisfied persons without a permanent source of income, and they undoubtedly spread abroad a sense of grievance.

When a house, great or small, had surrendered with the consent, expressed or at least implied, of all its members, and often with an expression, however artificial, of regret for past faults or delusions, no question of perseverance could arise. The religious were assigned a pension, together with a small *ex gratia* 'reward', which was often the equivalent of some months' unpaid 'wages', and a capacity which was now issued gratis to all in orders on application.

In the cases of attainder for treason, which occurred principally as a sequel of the northern risings, there was no question of a pension. Such of the community as survived after suspects had been arrested and malcontents had fled were transferred willy-nilly to other houses. Some years later, however, a different treatment was accorded to the three black monk abbeys of Glastonbury, Reading and Colchester. By this time transference to another house would have been wellnigh impossible and in any case futile. The monks were therefore pensioned off by the commissioners as an administrative act. This procedure was abnormal and possibly technically illegal, as the houses concerned were dissolved without formal instruments of surrender and before the trial of their respective abbots. The houses were rich and speed was essential; no general disaffection existed among the monks, who had no desire to find themselves at the bar with their abbots, and Cromwell probably felt that criticism would best be silenced and a liquidation of the assets cheaply ensured by securing a body of contented pensioners; *ex hypothesi* no allotment would be needed for the head of the house.[1]

As for the four classes mentioned above, that of the cathedrals and colleges has been considered separately, and we may proceed at once to the largest class of all, that of the inmates of the houses that surrendered between 1536 and 1540. Here the ruling principle was that all professed religious were regarded purely as members of a society possessed of real estate; there was no question of forfeiture owing to past or recent misconduct, and newcomers transferred from smaller houses received an equal portion with members of the community they had joined.

There has in recent years been considerable difference of opinion as to the fate of the rank and file of the religious and as to the degree of sympathy to which they are entitled.[2] Two aspects of the matter must be distinguished; first, the adequacy and reliability of the scheme of pensions; and secondly, the success of the religious in finding for themselves alternative or supplementary sources of income. Considerable research has been undertaken on both these topics during the past thirty years, but the mass of documents to be sifted and the wide gaps in the information that they present have not yet made it possible to reach a final and agreed conclusion. Gasquet, who was the first to penetrate beyond the literary evidence to the pension lists, painted what all now agree to have been a picture in which the distress of the pensioners was exaggerated. Coulton and Baskerville reacted against this, and the latter in particular, in the course of much valuable work among the Augmentation papers, bishops' registers, and parochial registers, came to the conclusion that the pensions were on the whole adequate, and sometimes generous, and that a large number, perhaps the great majority, of the young and middle-aged religious found within a few years congenial and lucrative employment as chantry priests (before 1546), chaplains, curates, prebendaries and incumbents of parochial livings.[3] More recently,

---

1 Gasquet maintained to the end that the monks of these three houses received no pensions, and Archbold was inclined to agree with him for Glastonbury (*SRH*, 101), even though he himself printed (p. 117) the letter in which Pollard and his colleagues state that they have 'assigned the pentyons', as also (pp. 161–2) the Glastonbury contingent from Pole's pension list. Baskerville noted ('The Married Clergy and Pensioned Religious in the Norwich Diocese, 1555', p. 204) the occurrence of pensioned members of the Colchester and Reading communities; *v. supra*, p. 379.

2 Between the extremes of Gasquet, who suggests that widespread hardship and poverty afflicted the monks after the Dissolution, and Baskerville who, after remarking that the fate of the religious is rarely discussed 'except in vague terms of ululation' (*EM*, 246), asserts roundly (256) that 'a detailed investigation of any surrender list will show that all but the very old pensioners were soon beneficed', there is room for a more careful statement.

3 Some of Gasquet's most valuable work at the PRO was done among the pensions documents, and his pages in *Henry VIII* on the subject still deserve attention, though caution is needed in adopting his conclusions and general observations. The whole matter was taken up with greater attention to method and superior critical acumen by G. Baskerville, who after many years of work presented some of his findings in 'The Dispossessed Religious after the Suppression of the Monasteries', in *Essays in History presented to R. L. Poole* (1927), and in 'The Dispossessed Religious of Gloucestershire', in *TBGAS*, vol. 49. A summary of these papers, with new matter, was provided by the same writer in *EM*. Baskerville

Professor A. G. Dickens, while accepting Baskerville's detailed evidence, has questioned the validity of the general conclusions based upon it.[1] Finally, much useful information has been drawn by research students from the records of four or five separate regions of England.[2] These last, when their findings are compared and consolidated, give perhaps the clearest indications hitherto available of the answers that will finally be forthcoming.

The amount to be allotted to the pensioners was not fixed either by statute or by any ruling of the Court of Augmentations, but was left to the discretion of the commissioners appointed for the various suppressions. In spite, however, of this absence of precise directions, there was a very fair measure of agreement in practice all over England; this no doubt reflects the consensus of opinion among the Augmentations men. In allotting the pension some regard was generally had to the wealth of the house, especially in the case of the superior and senior officials.[3] For the private religious the award, in any case modest, could differ only by the matter of a pound or two between one house and another, though it must be remembered that in such small sums the addition of even £1 per annum might well make the difference between penury and a modest subsistence. Some regard was paid to age: at the one end two or three of the oldest received £2 more than the others, while the juniors, including some as yet not in priest's orders, would receive £1 or £2 less than the average. Sometimes, also, especially in the case of the nuns, an infirm and aged individual was treated with studied consideration. The average annual pension for the houses of men was somewhere in the region of £5. 10s., though this precise figure is rarely found, since the pensions were generally calculated in marks and half-marks even when expressed in pounds and shillings. In Lincolnshire, out of the sixty-two religious men noted in a county report of 1554, thirty-five had pensions between £5 and £6. 13s. 4d.[4] For Somerset seventy pensioners out of ninety-six fall within

undoubtedly reacts too strongly against what he calls 'the tear-stained pages' of Gasquet, and his picture of comfortable annuitants makes little or no allowance for the hard cases, conscientious objectors and official jobbery that must have existed; moreover, even he covers a very small section of the total religious population of England. Nevertheless, his findings, to which may be added Professor D. Hay's account of the monks of County Durham and Prebendary Clerk-Maxwell's notes on the monks of Wenlock (*infra*, p. 410), certainly tell very strongly against Gasquet's view.

1 'The Edwardian Arrears in Augmentations Payments', in *EHR*, LV.
2 Especially A. J. Hodgett, 'Dissolution of the monasteries of Lincolnshire' (London, M.A. Thesis, 1947); J. Kennedy, 'The Dissolution of the Monasteries in Hampshire and the Isle of Wight' (London, M.A. Thesis, 1953); and G. W. O. Woodward, 'The Benedictines and Cistercians in Yorkshire in the Sixteenth Century' (Trinity College, Dublin, Ph.D. Thesis, 1955). To these may be added the older regional studies of Archbold (Somerset), Hibbert (Staffs) and Hay (Durham).
3 This may be clearly seen by comparing the pensions from the wealthy house of Gloucester (average £8 to £10) with those of the poorer house of Kingswood (average £4) in Baskerville's 'Dispossessed Religious of Gloucestershire'.
4 These figures are calculated from Hodgett's thesis, appendix V, compiled from a list in PRO Exch. 101, 76/26. Five had pensions above the limit, and ex-superiors are not reckoned in. It may be added that fourteen of the ninety-six enjoyed a chantry pension as well (Hodgett, 111).

the same limits.[1] The average figure given by Baskerville, and accepted by Dickens, is therefore probably a shade too low. For chantry priests a few years later the award oscillated between £4 and £5.[2] For women the average was £3.

Opinions as to the adequacy of £5 as an annual income have differed. To Baskerville it is 'really quite adequate on which to live', and he cites a document showing it to be 'apparently the scale of payment for serving a cure'.[3] Professor Dickens, who looked up Baskerville's reference, found that in fact £5 was there regarded as 'a beggarly income for a curate'; he noted with justice that the value of money was falling owing both to inflation and to a debasement of the coinage, and that in the decade 1541–51 £5 'scarcely equalled the income of an unskilled labourer'.[4] For the moment, however, subsequent inflation need not be taken into consideration; the commissioners of 1539, like their descendants in the Inland Revenue in 1939, could only reckon with the current value of the money of the day. They must, one would think, have had the subsistence level in their minds, and the constantly recurring figure of £4 for the chantry priests suggests that this was bedrock, and that £5 for a single man was a low, but not an unreasonably low, subsistence wage. It is perhaps worth noting that the pensions allotted to the monks of the rich abbey of Glastonbury, where legal claims to the pension had been technically forfeited, was likewise £4.[5]

The pensioner, however, did not touch the whole of his sum. Besides the statutory fee of 4d. per £1, payable to the Court or to the commissioners on the receipt of each instalment, there were repeated levies of the ecclesiastical tenth, occurring in all years save ten between 1540 and 1600. This was regularly assessed upon these pensions even when stipends of £5 or less were exempted.[6] Moreover, this tax was 'deducted at source'. In the case of the larger pensions to superiors and others this taxation, though vexatious, would not seem to modern eyes to imply a greater hardship than modern pensioners have suffered at the hands of the Exchequer, but an annual loss of eleven shillings on an income of £5 was an appreciable diminution.

The pensions, so it seems, were paid with fair regularity by successive governments, whatever their shade of religious belief. It is one of the

---

1 Calculated from the pension lists printed by Archbold.
2 Calculated from the lists in Archbold.
3 *EM*, 256 n. 1. Baskerville's example (in *LP*, XIII, i, 94) does not convince, as it is there noted that £5 was a pension that did not attract curates.
4 Dickens, *art. cit.* 415–16.   5 Archbold, *op. cit.*
6 Woodward, *op. cit.* 412 n. 2. Mr Woodward's subsequent assertion, for which he gives the authority of 37 Hen. VIII, c. 24, that the pensioners benefited by the exemption mentioned in the text, contradicts what seems to have been established by Professor Dickens, *art. cit.* 417. In any case Baskerville's remark (*EM*, 257), that the pensions 'were liable to income tax...just as all sources of income were', is scarcely justified. Very few sources of income were thus subjected to heavy direct taxation, least of all incomes of such small annual value.

minor paradoxes of the times that different parts of the Elizabethan financial machine were receiving fines from Catholic recusants and paying life-pensions to ex-Carthusians. There were, of course, irregularities and arrears and cases of illegal exaction on the part of the pay-office. In 1549 these were made the subject of a statute imposing heavy penalties for extortion,[1] and in 1552–3 a fact-finding committee was set up to investigate complaints both of illegal delays on the part of officials and landowners and of sharp practice on the part of beneficiaries.[2] The investigation was conducted in each county, and in several there were neither arrears nor frauds. In others, especially where pensioners were numerous, arrears were frequent, if not normal, and affected at least one-third of the recipients, but they very rarely extended for more than a year; this, however, would have caused serious hardship to one who had no other source of livelihood. When property carrying pension-charges was sold, the liability passed to the purchaser, and it would seem that private owners tended even more frequently than Augmentations to make the pensioner wait.[3] Fraud was rare, but cases occurred of pensions having been obtained by relatives of deceased pensioners or of those who had gone abroad into exile. On the other hand, sales of interest in pensions, though not common, were accepted as legal. The terms varied greatly, for the short-term risk was all on the side of the purchaser who had, in addition, to furnish some sort of certificate of existence in respect of the original grantee before each payment. Despite the risk, there were instances of a speculator (sometimes the owner of the estate) buying up three or four pensions. The list of pensioners was checked at intervals, the last recorded commission sitting for the purpose in 1575, thirty-five years after the original assignments, and recipients who happened also to be clergymen holding benefices can be traced still later; a few of the beneficiaries survived into the seventeenth century.[4] According to Fuller, the last pensioner died in the reign of James I in 1607–8, two years after the Gunpowder Plot. He, at least, had had good value out of Augmentations.[5]

Whatever may be thought of the normal pension as a livelihood, it was always possible for an ex-religious to augment it, and it was a reasonable supposition of the government that he would do so. There was no 'means test' and a pension was only extinguished if the government or private person responsible for payment of the pension appointed the individual

---

1 For this, v. Dickens, art. cit. 385.　　　2 Ibid.

3 It should in fairness be added that the Crown took over responsibility for the pensions paid by private grantees of monastic property when the latter were condemned by attainder (as, for example, Cromwell and Sir Thomas Seymour); v. Baskerville, 'The Dispossessed Religious', in Essays presented to R. L. Poole, 444 n. 2.

4 E.g. the Dominican Thomas Mekus who lived till 1598 (Baskerville, EM, 245) as parson of Ashleworth, and the Cistercian monk of Bittlesden who died rector of Dauntsey in 1601. Cf. also the aged monk of Evesham, William Lyttleton, who lived on until 1603, v. infra, 417 n. 1.

5 According to Fuller, Church History (ed. 1845), III, 462, the last surviving pensioner died in 5 Jac. 1 (1607–8).

concerned to an office of equal or superior value. There is no possibility of discovering how many of the religious took to secular employment either at once or later, but an occasional case turning up in a lawsuit or elsewhere shows this not to have been unknown. Those of the younger monks who were not in major orders may well have put themselves immediately on the market, for their pension would certainly not keep them in perpetuity, nor can one conceive the normal young man as being satisfied with an unearned pittance. Of the priests, also, a certain number disappeared into secular life. The great majority, however, would be led by motives of every kind to seek clerical employment, and there has been much discussion as to the proportion of those who succeeded in obtaining it and thereby supplementing their assignment.

Great as was the number of ex-religious to be absorbed, there can be no doubt whatever that the religious changes of Cromwell's decade of power, with its spoliations and rumours of more to come, had led to an almost complete drying-up of the stream of ordinands, just as it led to a complete standstill in the building of churches. Practical reasons, also, were added to prudential in the minds of aspirants to the priesthood. For centuries a large proportion of those to be ordained had obtained their title from a monastery, which presumably made thereby a loose undertaking to find some kind of a billet for its protégés. This avenue to ordination had now disappeared, and bishops were no doubt showing themselves less ready to find a title for mere 'mass-priests'. In any case, it is certain that for fifteen or twenty years after 1535 many of the diocesan bishops held next to no ordinations. The way, therefore, lay open to the ex-religious, who were in other respects also at an advantage. Almost every house had the patronage of a number of rectories and vicarages, and there is plenty of evidence that shortly before the Dissolution the religious had parted with advowsons to influential friends on the understanding that if need arose the benefices should be bestowed on members of the house. The canons had also the initial advantage of having themselves owned or served churches. Thus a small number of black canons, and a larger number of Premonstratensians, could continue in their own right as incumbents of the churches they had been serving on behalf of their communities. Similarly, the cathedral chapters of ex-religious had considerable patronage in their gift, and made use of it to provide a home for former colleagues who had not been carried over into the new foundation. Finally, it was to the advantage of the Crown, or the private owner with the responsibility of disbursing the pension, to extinguish it by presenting the pensioner to a living of equal or greater value.

It is impossible to say what percentage of the pensioned religious, other than the class of ex-superiors, secured livings, curacies or other ecclesiastical offices and employments. A benefice, though it was doubtless the haven desired by all, was not the only door that might open to an unmarried priest seeking a passable means of livelihood. The clerical proletariat had always been more numerous than the beneficed clergy, and many of the ex-monks entered its ranks. There were, in the first place, the chantries, which outlived the monasteries by half a dozen years, and the office of chantry priest, which would more than double his pension, would not be uncongenial to a monk of the cloister without ambition or expensive tastes. It is possible that as many as one in a dozen found a temporary resting-place of this kind and thus, by adding one pittance to another, were in tolerably good case. Even when the chantries went the way of the abbeys in 1546, and those concerned were once more 'on the dole', they could now enjoy a second pension of £4 or £5.

From the nature of the case, any investigation into the fate of a community is subject to the law of diminishing returns. It is easy to find at once half a dozen monks of a large house settled in neighbouring churches, and a little research will probably reveal another six. After that the task becomes less rewarding, and there is no firm basis on which to establish a statistical average. Accidents of migration or patronage might give a monk a billet in London, or in a county half-way across England from his monastery, and only lucky chance could reveal this to one conducting research on a regional basis. If we were to judge by some of the comparatively few cases hitherto examined in detail, we should suppose that within a few years of the surrender almost all the able-bodied priests of a house had found some sort of perch for themselves.[1] Thus out of the fourteen private religious of Much Wenlock no fewer than twelve can be traced as sooner or later occupying some clerical post or other, and of the two remaining one was reputed a centenarian in 1540 and the other was still a poor scholar at Oxford when the Dissolution occurred.[2] At Dunstable, out of the twelve canons besides the prior, ten can be identified as incumbents in 1556; at Winchcombe thirteen out of sixteen, at Hailes sixteen out of twenty, and at St Augustine's, Bristol, seven out of ten can be found in lucrative employment of one kind or another within a decade or so of the Suppression.[3] These should perhaps not be reckoned as average figures; all the houses concerned had enjoyed patronage and good connections, and lay in districts thickly set with churches. For the religious of the smaller and less wealthy upland houses there were fewer sources of benevolent patronage, and even of the ex-religious just enumerated many had spent several years in the wilderness before attaining to security. If all the religious had been equally well provided for it would be necessary to suppose that two-thirds or more of the parishes of the country were harbouring them either as rectors, vicars or curates when the chantries and hospitals had gone. There are indications that in the North, where the proportion of religious houses to the number of churches and

1 Baskerville gives many examples, e.g. in *Essays presented to R. L. Poole*, 449, and *EM*, 199, 294.
2 Cf. Prebendary Clerk-Maxwell, 'The Monks of Much Wenlock after the Suppression', in *Trans. Shropshire Archaeol. Nat. Hist. Soc.* 4th ser. IX.
3 Cf. G. Baskerville, 'The Dispossessed Religious of Gloucestershire', 86–90.

general wealth was greater than in the southern parts of England, the ex-monks were less successful in finding employment. Thus one scholar, who has examined the black and white monk houses in Yorkshire, containing altogether 292 religious, has been able to identify with absolute certainty only seventeen in clerical posts after the Suppression, with seven others highly probable and an indefinite, but by no means vast, number of further possibilities.[1] This is probably a minimum result in a very difficult field, but another skilful worker has only succeeded in finding six certain and three probable holders of posts among the twenty-eight ex-monks of the great abbey of Rievaulx, and only two certainties and seven possibilities from the twenty-odd inhabitants of Byland.[2] We may contrast these findings with those of Lincolnshire, a county unusually rich both in small religious houses and in parishes, where some fifty-three religious out of a total of ninety-six examined have been identified as incumbents or curates in 1554.[3] When allowance is made for future identifications and for the migration of individuals to other regions this would represent the very high proportion of two in every three. Such a state of things, though surprising at first sight, is not absolutely inconceivable.

Within the economically fortunate class of beneficed priests a fair-sized minority were pluralists. Thus of the ten canons of Dunstable already mentioned four held two livings concurrently before their death,[4] but Dunstable was a prosperous house for its size and the prior was a member of a family that had lands and patronage. Out of the fifty-three Lincolnshire incumbents noted above only two held three livings, though two more were pluralists.[5] It is among the ranks of ex-superiors that the most impressive instances of prosperous pluralism are to be found, but a few of those who had never risen to the headship of a house succeeded in making themselves extremely comfortable in a financial way. Thus Canon Roger Dallson of Thornton Abbey, who had been appointed Professor of Theology in the college which replaced the abbey for a few years, received a pension of £50 on its suppression, and ultimately succeeded in augmenting this with the rectory of Lanceby (£13. 6s. 8d.) and the vicarages of Hoxing (£13. 6s. 8d.) and Stonden (£2).[6]

Compared with the possessioner religious, the lot of the friars was materially hard. They had neither real property nor treasure of any significance, and many of the friaries were poor to destitution. It was no part of Cromwell's policy to promote social security at the expense of government funds; the friars were therefore cast on the world with nothing but their capacities and such small gratuities as the commissioners could afford. We have seen that Dr London and Bishop Ingworth felt their

---

1 Woodward, *op. cit.* 433.
2 H. Aveling, 'The Monks of Byland', and 'The Rievaulx Community'.
3 These are Mr Hodgett's figures, *op. cit.* 108–11.
4 Baskerville, *EM*, 293–6.   5 So Hodgett, *op. cit.* 111.
6 Hodgett gives this case on pp. 111–12. Such an income would have a purchasing power of at least £2500 net to-day (1958).

responsibility, and did what they could to give practical help. In a sense the friars, who were in the ordinary course shifted about by their superiors from house to house, and whose professional success depended largely on their own wits and social tact, may have felt the parting with regular life less keenly than the monks, and were better fitted to fend for themselves than those who had spent twenty or thirty years in the security of a single family. In the event, they showed themselves fairly successful in the competition for livings, though the friaries had no benefices in their gift into which the brethren might step with little difficulty. Here, as with the others, there is a great difference between the great men and the proletariat, but whereas with the monks and canons it was those already in high place who received the richest plums, with the friars it was those of the highest intellectual gifts or with the greatest talent for self-advancement who became bishops and deans.

With the exception of an unknown number of the Observants and other friars, particularly Dominicans, in the early days of trouble, and of the Carthusians and Bridgettine nuns after the Dissolution, there is little or no evidence that the ex-religious in any number sought to follow their vocation in exile. For the monks and canons of autonomous houses indeed there was no obvious procedure for accomplishing this. Neither the authorities in Rome nor religious opinion in France or Spain was awake to the real trend of English affairs, and individual exiles would have had to fare far to find a warm welcome. Even the centralized orders such as the white monks and canons had long ago ceased to be in any practical sense international, and in all orders the individual house with its inmates had sunk so deep into the earth of its neighbourhood that the passage of an individual or even of a group to a foreign land would have been all but unthinkable.

There are a few known instances of small groups of religious hanging together, usually with the ex-superior as its nucleus and material support. Thus three or four of the community of Monk Bretton (by no means a fervent house) lived with the prior in the neighbourhood, having with them some of the library and muniments of their old home, and several instances have been noted of a single companion living with his ex-superior.[1] The practice, as might be expected, was commoner among the nuns, and has been revealed chiefly by the evidence of wills. A well-known instance of a conscious endeavour to pursue the religious vocation is that of the small group of nuns who followed their abbess, Elizabeth Throckmorton, from their Cambridgeshire cloister to her family home at Coughton in Warwickshire.[2] The group of five from Kirklees in Yorkshire, who lived with their prioress at Mirfield for many years on a consolidated income of £20, is less familiar.[3] Such groups, however, were

---

1 Woodward, op. cit. 419–21; cf. YARS, LXVI, Chartulary of Monkbretton, 5–9.
2 VCH, Cambs, II, 302; Warwicks, III, 78, 85.
3 Woodward, op. cit. 422–3.

exceptional and almost all the ex-religious lived their own lives after they had left their houses, though not a few remembered their brethren or sisters in their wills, or even bequeathed a vestment or a chalice to their old home, should it ever come again to life.[1]

Thus, what with those who held clerical preferment, those who had from the beginning adopted secular employment, those who had died within the first few years and, finally, the faithful few who had gone into exile, at least two-thirds of the pension-worthy religious can be accounted for at least in broad categories. There remain the rest, perhaps 1500 or less in number. They would inevitably include a large proportion of the ex-religious who were least fitted by physical, moral and mental disabilities to cope with the world's shocks. It was in this group, silent and unseen, that the social hardships of the Dissolution were most keenly felt.

The monks and nuns of the dissolved houses, though secularized as regards their obligations of obedience and poverty, were still legally bound by their vow of chastity, which had been given a new lease of life by the Act of Six Articles; priests, moreover, whether in religious vows or not, were still bound by the law of canonical celibacy. Early in the reign of Edward VI the Act of Six Articles was repealed, and a few years later clerical marriage was legalized.[2] Although it is quite impossible to hazard a guess as to the number of ex-religious who took advantage of their legal liberty, it was certainly very considerable. Nicholas Harpsfield, the Catholic apologist, makes a distinction between the men and the women; marriages among the former were many, among the latter, few. This is what might be expected both from the deeper sense of vocation shown by the nuns, and from any reasonable consideration of the age to which many of the religious women would have attained within ten years of the Dissolution. Nevertheless, Lincolnshire statistics show at least eighteen out of sixty-one nuns as married ($=29 \cdot 5$ per cent), compared with twenty-eight out of 108 religious and chantry priests ($=25 \cdot 9$ per cent).[3] In the diocese of Norwich alone (which comprised the counties of Norfolk and Suffolk) almost one hundred ex-religious appear on a list of clergy deposed for marriage by Mary's government, and to these must be added an unknown percentage of those holding no ecclesiastical office.[4] These figures, partial and local as they are, do no more than show that the marriage of ex-religious was common, and cases occur in which the marriage was between an ex-monk or canon and an ex-nun; they would thus be able to set up house on a double pension.

In general, familiarity with the sources confirms the first impression that the dissolution of the monasteries was accomplished with com-

1 For examples, v. Gasquet, *Henry VIII*, 454, and Baskerville, *EM*, 253–4. Similarly, Henry Man, the last prior of Sheen, left his books to that house 'if it should be re-edified'; Edmund Hord, last prior of Hinton, did likewise.
2 2 and 3 Edw. VI, c. 21; *Statutes of the Realm*, IV, 67.   3 Hodgett, *op. cit.* 114.
4 G. Baskerville, 'Married Clergy and Pensioned Religious in the Norwich Diocese, 1555'.

paratively little personal hardship. It would not be easy to point to any revolution of the sixteenth century, or indeed to any comparable secularization of modern times, in which compensation on such a scale and with such security was offered.[1] It is indeed one more indication that in the eyes of the government the whole affair was one of finance, in which the rights at common law were to be respected as far as seemed reasonably possible. Suppression for Cromwell was neither a measure of reform nor a move in religious warfare; it was a matter of revenue, the suppression of wealthy corporations. It was as if in the modern world the colleges of Oxford and Cambridge were to be liquidated by confiscation, with pensions or college livings to the existing Head and Fellows, and the tenure of one of the college estates secured to the former for life. The government did indeed make use for purposes of propaganda of what hostility to the monastic life existed among those of the New Learning, and Layton cannot have been consistently mistaken over so long a space of time as regards Cromwell's private bias when he pitched his stories and comments in a particular key, but the violence and injustice that entered into the process of suppression were not due primarily to religious prejudice, but to the ruthless methods of securing acquiescence employed by Cromwell and the king, which were applied indiscriminately to every part of their policy.

Perhaps the most surprising feature of the Dissolution, to those familiar only with Catholic or Protestant apologetics and polemics of past centuries, is the ease with which the ex-superiors and the more able among the religious adapted themselves to the new conditions of their changing world. The abbots and priors of autonomous houses could expect to receive a pension ten or twenty times as great as that of their subjects, together, in many cases, with a house and land and stock. Primarily, as has been noted elsewhere, this reflected the attitude of the later medieval sentiment towards the master or mistress of a house, who was regarded as being in a very real sense the governor and proprietor. Nevertheless, it had a practical aspect at the moment of dissolution, since it stood as a golden prize before the eyes of an abbot faced with a demand for surrender. Though preferential treatment for superiors was taken for granted by all, the relief of the commissioners at meeting with a ready compliance from an abbot is often reflected in the lavish grant they made, and there is evidence that abbots occasionally obtained a higher price by finesse, though clearly the utmost care was needed not to cross the line beyond which promises and gratuities would be replaced by charges of treason.

If he could manage to keep his head and his counsel, an able superior of an important house was in a very strong position for bargaining. Owing to the peculiar mixture of rascality and legalism with which the suppression

---

[1] E.g. in France at the Revolution (where the course of events has so many striking points of similarity) pensions were indeed offered to those who wished for release from their vows, but they were cancelled a year or two later.

was conducted he had several good cards in his hand: his bargaining power before surrender; his experience and reputation as an administrator; and the anxiety of the government to extinguish a large pension. As a result of this combination of motives numerous heads of houses were transferred at once into bishoprics or deaneries. The new cathedrals, with scarcely an exception, had an ex-religious as bishop and dean, and between twenty and thirty other abbots or priors became bishops within a few years of the Dissolution. Others were appointed by the government or by relatives to one or more posts, such as the mastership of a college or hospital or a rich living, which carried a salary equal to or greater than their pension. At the very worst a superior could get a pension and a house, and the pensions ranged from the £330 of the abbot of Bury St Edmunds, through the £160 of Abbot Stonywell of Pershore and the £133 of the abbess of Shaftesbury to the £30 of a small house of canons and the £10 of a decaying nunnery. We have seen how Prior More of Worcester, though in comparative disgrace, secured a favourite house and his books and chattels, and the abbot of St Augustine's a pleasant home not far from Canterbury. Though such grants were usually made for a single life, a good farmer or business man could usually manage to buy in the land he lived on or another estate; sometimes, also, he had managed to make friends of the mammon of iniquity while there was yet time and had prepared a refuge for himself against a rainy day. The last abbot of Basingwerk in Flintshire and the last abbot of Alnwick in Northumberland were surely not the only ones to found county families, nor was Abbess Temmes of Lacock the only one to do her family proud with the abbey lands just before the final surrender.[1]

Thus the abbots and priors found themselves established in comfort, if not in affluence, for the rest of their days, with a position among the smaller country landowners with whom they had consorted on equal terms in the past. The more conservative among them, and those who appreciated leisure and independence, lived on in some state in their quiet manor houses. Not a few even among those whose monastic life had been pure married and left their sons among the middling gentry. There was, however, no need for an active abbot to feel that his working days were over. The government was always concerned to extinguish these large pensions; Henry and his advisers among the bishops were conservative in their theological opinions, and the established order had nothing to fear from men who had surrendered their principles and their trust already. In consequence, many of the abbots and priors became bishops both of the old and of the new sees, or deans of the newly erected cathedral chapters. Altogether, as has been said, some twenty monks and canons became bishops within ten years of the Dissolution, and there were further pro-

---

1 For ex-religious as bishops, *v.* Appendix x *infra*. For the last abbot of Basingwerk, *v.* A. Jones, 'Basingwerk Abbey'; for Alnwick, *v.* Baskerville, *EM*, 253; for Abbess Temmes, *ibid.* 196–7. Cf. also A. L. Rowse, *Tudor Cornwall*, for similar cases.

motions both of conservatives in Mary's reign and of conformists in Elizabeth's. Of the eight cathedrals with chapters of monks or canons seven received as dean the late prior; the single exception was Canterbury, where Dr Nicholas Wotton was appointed. Similarly, all the six new cathedrals had ex-superiors for their deans, though some of these were drafted in from outside; thus the prior of St Andrew's, Northampton, became dean of Peterborough, since the last abbot had become bishop, and at Bristol the prior of Bradenstoke was given the post. The black monks were not the only recipients of official patronage. Cistercians, Austin canons, Gilbertines and even Carthusians had their representatives among the higher clergy, and the friars, especially the Dominicans, held an even greater proportion of English sees, though of the friar-bishops a greater number had thrown in their lot with the new way of thinking. Nothing, perhaps, is more disconcerting to those who would wish to see a clear-cut religious division of the modern type in Tudor England than this passage into the higher clergy of the Anglican Church of so many notable ex-religious, some of them with reputations a little the worse for wear, who, by a paradox not without parallel in religious history, usually retained conservative opinions in matters of theology and church government even though they had abandoned all the more spiritual ideals of their calling. *Plus ça change, plus c'est la même chose.* There was in fact little interior change between the rich, easy-going abbot and the ageing, comfortable dean; he had been the victim neither of reform nor of persecution. In the country parsonages and deaneries and masters' lodgings in the early decades of Elizabeth's reign there must still have been a number of such survivors from the *ancien régime*. We think of Talleyrand in his last phase, conservative and respectable, attending Sunday Mass at Valençay with his niece beside him, and at the last carefully presenting his consecrated hands, palms downward, for the sacramental anointing. Nothing, perhaps, in the whole business of the Dissolution is more revealing and more sordid than the unanimity with which the abbots and priors, abbesses and prioresses, of hundreds of houses, great and small, accepted rich prizes for the abandonment alike of the service of God which they had vowed and of the flock for whom they stood responsible at the last account to the great Shepherd of souls.[1]

We should indeed be unwise to picture to ourselves the seven or eight thousand dispossessed religious living as did so many of the religious and priests in revolutionary France after the secularization and the Civil Constitution of the Clergy, when for those who refused to conform there remained only a tenuous existence and a dependence on charity either as *ci-devants* or as *émigrés*. The reality was less distressing in a social, if not in a religious, reckoning. The vast majority of the monks had accepted the accomplished fact and had fended for themselves as best they could.

---

1 *Regula S. Benedicti*, c. 2: 'Agnoscat [abbas] pro certo quia in die iudicii ipsarum omnium animarum est redditurus Domino rationem.'

Perhaps one of these old men, a relic of the ruined choir of Hailes or Merevale, may have caught the curious eye of the young Shakespeare, whose aunt had been a nun; perhaps another lived still longer, to see the gay Campion riding past, with his *Exercises* and his *Agnus Deis*, and to resent the newcomer with his strange wares. A few at least, although they had lived on into a brave new world, never wholly lost their monk's heart when their monk's coat went, and were gathered home by a seminary priest or even, when the day was nigh spent, by an English monk of the new generation, whose lot had fallen along lines so different from theirs.[1]

1 E.g. the aged monk of Evesham, William Lyttleton, who lived on at Hindlip in Worcestershire until 1603, when he was reconciled to his Church and his profession by Dom Augustine Bradshaw (Oxford Bodleian Wood MS. 8. 6. f.16).

Part Four

REACTION AND SURVIVAL

CHAPTER XXXIV

THE MARIAN RESTORATION

Queen Mary entered upon her reign with one overmastering determination and desire, to restore in England the Catholic religion in full communion with and obedience to the pope, and to undo all the measures taken by her father to subjugate or to despoil the Church. She was, perhaps, in a simpler position in this matter than any of her subjects in public life, for not only had she never deviated, save once in a moment of agony and desperation,[1] from the beliefs which she had absorbed with her mother's milk, but also her fundamental belief throughout her happy girlhood and sour adolescence had been deepened and hardened by the teaching and companionship of the one person in England who had remained motionless among all the tempests and earthquakes of the time, with all the single-minded purpose of a daughter of the Spanish monarchs. Whatever Mary might have been had her lot fallen in more pleasant places, her own sufferings and the sorrows and exhortations of the only being to whom she could turn for love and counsel had made her more than half a Spaniard in outlook, and from both father and mother she had inherited a strength of will that bordered on obstinacy if not on folly. It was her fate to encounter as her coadjutor and father in God in the business of religious restoration, the only notable Englishman who had, by his own resolute action at a moment of crisis, escaped from the clutches of a king whose policy he deplored, and who had thrown in his lot both with the papacy and with the party of extreme conservative reform.[2]

In the forefront of the problems confronting the queen, and indeed overshadowing all others in the eyes of the landed classes in England, was that of the confiscated monastic property, whether made up of the recently suppressed chantries and colleges or of the first great spoliations now fifteen or twenty years old. To Mary, all this transference of wealth was robbery and sacrilege, and her anguish was all the keener since by a cruel irony she, as inheritress of the Crown of England, was now the chief beneficiary of what she regarded as her father's sin. We of to-day, even if we condemn the motives and methods of the spoliation and deplore the removal of so much good timber along with the rotten wood, have

---

1 Mary took the Oath of Succession and signed a renunciation of papal obedience in 1535 under extreme pressure from her father and Cromwell. She applied for absolution to the pope almost at once. Cf. *LP*, x, 1137, 1186, 1203 and *Cal. St. Pap. Spanish*, 1536–8, 270–2.

2 Miss H. F. M. Prescott, in her careful and sensitive analysis of the queen's character in *Mary Tudor* (2nd ed. 1952), suggests with considerable plausibility that Mary, deeply wounded by her lapse, which she attributed to the fallacious motives of policy or human respect, tended in later life to follow her religious intuitions (or scruples) almost blindly, distrusting all reasoning from expediency. Miss Prescott, however, is perhaps too well disposed to Pole, who cannot escape all responsibility for some of the calamitous decisions of the reign.

witnessed or read of so many similar revolutions, and have become so inoculated with the ideas of socialism and nationalism, and are so sharply aware of economic forces, that we are able to regard the confiscation of the monastic wealth with equanimity as an adjustment which was, in part at least, inevitable, but neither Catholics nor Protestants of the mid-sixteenth century were capable of such a dispassionate approach.

Mary's difficulty was increased by the impossibility of half measures and by her own deep, if unwilling, participation in the canonical guilt. There would have been general agreement, then as now, that while many of the monasteries had forfeited all moral right to their wealth, others, either by blameless life or by good husbandry, had continued to deserve their income. All, however, had been lost, all had become with equally good legal title the property of the Crown, and parts of almost every estate had, by a rapid process of fragmentation, devolved by equally strong title into the hands of innumerable lay owners, great and small. Even if the queen could have afforded, as she would certainly have desired, to abandon all claim to the monastic lands, the portion still under Crown control would have formed a most unsatisfactory cross-section to hand back to the religious, while to 'unscramble' (in the current modern term) the results of twenty years of private ownership and repeated sales to private individuals was clearly out of the question.

There was, therefore, no half-way house between a complete and complicated expropriation 'in reverse' and a complete condonation; and indeed, if *per impossibile* a return of property had been contemplated, where were the monks and canons, and what were now their rights, apostates as they technically were, if a restoration were to be made? The queen, therefore, was in a genuine dilemma of conscience; to insist on a restoration would have been both practically impossible and politically disastrous, while to recognize the *fait accompli* would be to give implicit approval to a great wrong done, not to man, but to God.

There was only one way out which could satisfy all demands, at least in the external forum. Since the original owners, with whatever excuse, had in fact defaulted, the immediate as well as the ultimate right of decision lay, from the canonical point of view, with the pope, who could declare or disclaim his intentions of resuming the Church's rights. In modern times it has often happened that the papacy has shown itself far less intransigent in matters of property than have those on the spot who have fought for the *status quo ante*, and so it was now. In his first decisions, when the news came of a Catholic sovereign's accession in England, Julius III had shown a grasp of at least some of the realities of the situation. He had decided to accept the *fait accompli* in England, and to include in the powers of his legate that of expressly condoning the possession of lands once belonging to the Church, and of absolving the owners, along with all other Englishmen, from the censures and penalties of sacrilege and heresy. The letters of the pope to Pole, the earliest of which date from only a month after the death of Edward VI, as well as the ample faculties subsequently given, make this quite clear. With the pope, at least, there was no question of hesitation or bargaining.[1]

Nothing, however, could be done in England in the matter before the arrival of the legate, Cardinal Pole, and this was delayed for over a year, principally by reason of the hindrances caused by the emperor, Charles V, to whom Pole, as an opponent of the projected Spanish marriage, was not *persona grata*, but also in the later months precisely on account of the abbey lands, regarding which Pole, with the characteristic mixture of scruple and unpracticality which more than once marred his fortunes and achievement, felt more strongly than the pope, dreading lest the concession should seem to be a bargain, and hoping to leave in any accommodation a sting to trouble the consciences of the landowners. When he arrived at last in London on 24 November 1554, parliament lost no time in presenting to the sovereigns a petition that the legate might grant to all those concerned untroubled possession of property, sometime belonging to the Church but now by Acts of Parliament and decisions of the common law conveyed to individuals. Pole replied on Christmas Eve granting the request, save for movable goods, such as plate, ornaments and vestments belonging to churches, which were to be restored, and saving also the duty of the new owners to make some provision for the support of the clergy, which had been the purpose of the original benefactions. Parliament then passed an act legalizing the legate's dispensations and recording the legal rights of the present owners of property anciently ecclesiastical.[2] The legate then applied to Rome for confirmation of what he had done, and this was granted by Julius III in the Bull *Praeclara* of 20 June 1555. By these two instruments of legate and pope the religious houses of old became canonically extinct. There is no suggestion that any monk or canon existed to claim any rights. Pole, however, stuck obstinately to his original principles and three years later, in a public sermon on the anniversary of the great reconciliation, reminded his hearers that they held the lands on sufferance only, and provided they showed worthy fruit of penance.

The prayers and hopes of the legate met with scant response, save in the heart of the queen. Mary had determined from the first to make what satisfaction she could for her father's sacrilege, and now that the realm was officially reconciled she could begin to act. Towards the middle of March 1555 an incident is recorded which must have been inspired, if not actually directed, by Mary or Pole or both together. This was the appearance at Court of sixteen Benedictine monks clad in the habit of their

---

1 The letters are cited with references by Philip Hughes, *The Reformation in England*, II, 222–4.

2 Cf. Mary's Second Statute of Repeal, i.e. 1 and 2 Phil. & Mary, c. 8 (J. R. Tanner, *Tudor Constitutional Documents*, 125–9); Pole's Dispensation of 24 December 1554 in *Documenta ad Legationem Cardinalis Poli spectantia*, 31–4; *Statutes of the Realm*, IV, i, 246. Cf. also *CalSPV*, 1555–6, no. 14.

order; they were led by Dr Feckenham, Dean of St Paul's and confessor
to the queen, and all of them, though actually holding preferments of
greater or less value, declared that they had decided to renounce them in
order to re-enter the monastic life.[1] The queen, we are told, could not
restrain her tears at the sight of the group (did she remember the spring
days at Worcester long ago?) and immediately appointed a strong committee of the Council including the Chancellor (Stephen Gardiner), the
Treasurer (William Paulet, Marquis of Winchester), the Comptroller
(Sir Robert Rochester)[2] and the Secretary (Sir William Petre) who,
together with the legate, might decide what best to do for these monks
and for the other projects of restoration, and in general how to deal with
all the church property now vested in the Crown. The queen herself
desired that all such property should be restored in its entirety to the
original owners, should any of them appear as a body to claim their part;
her ministers, and her husband, with their eyes on the governmental
revenues, were less enthusiastic.

Apart from lands directly held by the Crown, and in the case of almost
all the greater abbeys of the past, the processes of sale, destruction and
conversion had gone so far that the initiative of restoration had been taken,
not only out of the hands of the queen, but out of the realm of practical
politics, for not a single one of the new owners of such lands made so
much as a gesture of restoration. There was, however, one monastery
where a resumption of the regular life would be both practicable and
eminently desirable. This was Westminster Abbey, the royal *eigenkirche*
of the sainted Confessor, which ever since its enrichment by him had
been the traditional scene of royal coronations and obsequies, and indeed
of all public displays of royal devotion. Even here the process of erosion
and destruction had begun. The abbot's house and the adjacent walk of
the cloister had been let to Sir Edward North, the kitchen and infirmary
had been destroyed, and the remaining monastic buildings had been carved
into houses for the dean and prebendaries. But the clergy still had control
of the great church and some of the living quarters, as well as of a tolerable
endowment, and they were in no position to resist pressure from the
Crown. That Westminster had been selected for restoration by the
beginning of 1556 is clear from a letter of Pole to the President of the
Congregation of Monte Cassino, of which Pole was cardinal protector.[3]
This congregation sprang from a movement instituted more than a century
before (1409) through the agency of the monk, Ludovico Barbo, in the
abbey of Santa Giustina at Padua. His reform was a thoroughgoing
attempt to break with the abuses endemic in late medieval monasticism,
and in particular with the system of commendatory abbots, and of superiors

---

1 An account of the incident occurs in a letter of the Venetian ambassador to the Doge of
19 March (*CalSPV*, *ibid*. no. 32).
2 Rochester had a brother among the martyred Carthusians, and was a generous
benefactor of the Marian Sheen and Syon.
3 *CalSPV*, *ibid*. no. 334.

living apart from the community in apartments of their own. It also had more constructive and genial aims, such as the fostering of private prayer, silence and study that should be of use to the Church in the new age dawning in Italy. Pole was an ardent reformer, and he intended that Westminster should be a fresh growth with a life based on these principles. To ensure a good beginning he hoped to divert to England two leading officials of the Cassinese congregation who were engaged on a visitation in Spain, John Baptist Folengo of Mantua and Eutychius of St Angelo from Placentia.[1] His efforts, for some reason, were fruitless, and in the end he had to arrange matters himself, but it was probably the expectation of help from these monks that delayed matters at Westminster. By the end of September all seemed ready and the formal re-entry was considered imminent;[2] the secular chapter was dissolved on the 27th of that month;[3] but again there was a hitch, and it was not till the end of November that all was ready. Then, on Friday, 20 November, the monks took possession, some sixteen in number, clad in their habits, and on the following day, the Presentation of Our Lady, a group of postulants was 'shorne in', and on the Sunday solemn procession was made from cloister to choir for even-song, the monks walking 'after the old fassyon in ther monkes wede, in collys [cowls] of blake say'.[4] Pole had insisted that the election should be after the Cassinese model, free, and without royal nomination or congé d'élire, and for three years only.[5] Feckenham had not relished the last proviso, but had accepted it, though, unlike the Cassinese priors, he was solemnly consecrated by Bonner on Saturday, the 29th, and on Sunday, 6 December, visitors could see the procession of abbot, monks and 'sanctuary men', all in their traditional garb.[6]

1 Ibid. no. 403 (February 1556): Pole to the President of the Congregation of Monte Cassino, hopes the visitors will render good service in the restoration of the monastery [Westminster] which is about to be effected.

2 Ibid. no. 634 (28 September, same to same): 'the monks of St Benedict...in God's name, will make their entry [sc. into the Abbey] to-morrow'.

3 Pole's legatine act of Restoration (25 September) is in his register (Douai, Bibliothèque Municipale), tome 6, fo. 110. Bonner's consent was given the same day, it is in his Register, ccccvii (W. H. Frere, The Marian Reaction, 250), and Westminster Abbey Muniments, 12792. The chapter demised on 27 September (cf. H. F. Westlake, Westminster Abbey, I, 222), but the royal letters patent rehearsing and confirming all this were not issued till 10 November (CPR, 3 and 4, Phil. & Mary, pt. 5, p. 348).

4 There is some confusion as to the precise day, possibly because the physical and ceremonial entries were separated. Thus the Venetian ambassador writes, 23 November (CalSPV, 1556–7, no. 723): 'On Friday last, the 20 inst., and not until then, the Black Monks of St Benedict were put in possession of the Abbey of Westminster.' Henry Machyn (Diary, ed. J. G. Nichols, 118–19), notes on 21 November: 'Moo [more] monks shorne in', and gives details of the Sunday procession. Wriothesley (Chronicle, II, 136) gives 21 November as the date.

5 Cf. letter of Aloysius Prioli to Ludovico Boccatelli, archbishop of Ragusa, in Epistolarum Reginaldi Poli...Pars V, Appendix, p. 346: 'Quello che contra sua voglia è stato Abbate triennale al modo d'Italia, e non perpetuo, come si soleva far qui, era Decano, etc.' Pole, it will be remembered, had long ago favoured this arrangement (v. supra, p. 155).

6 Machyn (Diary, 119–20) records the blessing on 29 November, after which the new abbot, true to himself, preached the sermon, and the subsequent procession.

It is usually assumed without question by historians that the Marian Westminster was the medieval abbey aroused from a state of suspended animation. This would seem far from certain. The original community, who had in 1534 fallen into schism, if not heresy, by their repudiation of the pope and their acceptance of the royal supremacy, had subsequently surrendered their abbey and all their rights to the king, had ceased to cohere as a body or to have any expectation or desire of revival, and had accepted both pensions and various preferments. Canonically speaking, therefore, Westminster was almost certainly 'extinct'. If any title to existence remained, it was extinguished by the legate's Dispensation and the confirmatory Bull *Praeclara*, which confirmed the grantees in their tenure of the property and the existing dean and college in their status and rights. Of the original Westminster community only two returned in the early days of the new venture, and it is never suggested that they claimed or were recognized as able to transmit any rights. The restoration therefore was an act of ecclesiastical authority equivalent to a new foundation. To take an analogy, it was the creation of a new peerage with an old title, not the calling of a dormant peerage out of abeyance. As to the further question, whether a single newly founded abbey could be said canonically to be *ipso facto* the nucleus of a re-established Congregation, that is a matter to which neither Pole nor anyone else gave any attention at the time, though later, as we shall see, it was to become of some significance.

The nucleus of the community would seem to have been provided by the sixteen who had approached the queen in the previous March, and they were joined either on 20 November or within a few days by ten or a dozen more.[1] During the short life of the abbey some fifty monks were or became members of the community, and several died in the habit. The names of some forty are known (and it so happens that the community was forty strong in 1559) and an early list preserves the names of some twenty-five professed monks of 1556–7.[2] We cannot be certain of all the original sixteen, but it is probable that among them were four monks of Glastonbury, three of Evesham, two from Westminster, St Albans and Ramsey, and one or two from Sherborne and Christ Church, Canterbury. Among the first recruits were monks of St Swithun's, Winchester, and perhaps Bury, and a little later came ex-members of Croyland and other houses. It is interesting to note the presence not only of two or three Cistercians but also of at least two Austin canons. One of the white monks, John Redbourne, was probably the last abbot of Dore, a com-

---

1 Here again, there is a slight confusion. The Venetian ambassador (*CalSPV*, 743) records abbot and twenty-six monks on 30 November, and twenty-eight all told on 20 December (*ibid.* 771). Prioli (*loc. cit.*) gives twenty-eight.

2 The list provided by E. H. Pearce, *The Monks of Westminster Abbey*, Appendix, 214–17, has been enlarged and elucidated by Dom Hugh Aveling, of Ampleforth Abbey, both in *Ampleforth and its Origins* (London, 1952), Appendix A, 271–9, and more fully in notes generously supplied to the present writer in 1956. A contemporary list (?beginning of 1557; certainly before the autumn of that year) is in Westminster Abbey Muniments, 9327.

munity that had continued some at least of its religious observance after the Dissolution. He must have been an old man in 1556 and in the event he died soon.[1] It is possible to see the background and relationships of most of the monks. Thus the abbot and four or five others were among the group of young Oxford monks with whom Robert Joseph of Evesham had corresponded a quarter of a century previously,[2] and the two canons seem to have come in through connections with Winchester cathedral priory and other black monk houses. The most influential bond appears to have been the academical one. At least fourteen of the first twenty or so, including two of the Cistercians, are known to have been at Oxford, many of them in the last decade of the existence of Gloucester College. They provide interesting evidence that the academic life in the early years of religious change, at least at Oxford, was not subversive either of traditional beliefs or of a monastic vocation. Besides knowing the ultimate provenance, we also have information as to the recent careers of the band. Thus William East, the first prior, had been in early life a monk and monastic archdeacon of St Albans, had subsequently become rector of St Albans and later royal chaplain and canon of St George's, Windsor. The Cistercian, Richard Edy, had been vicar-choral at Wells, rector of North Petherton, and canon of Salisbury. Stephen Baily, another monk of St Albans, had acquired three livings; the two Canterbury monks had been on the new foundation of the cathedral and others had held preferment of one sort or another. Thus, though there were no names (apart from the abbot) of any great distinction, the monks of Westminster were on the whole a very well-educated community and, what is more, had for the most part abandoned secure, comfortable and respectable positions in order to re-enter religion.[3]

The new abbot stands apart from and above the rest, both in distinction of mind and in varied achievement, as also in the abundant documentation with which his career can be illustrated. We have met him as a young monk at Oxford, but this would seem a fitting place to review the earlier part of his life.[4]

1 For him, v. Aveling, Ampleforth, 273. He was blessed as abbot in 1529 (Hereford Reg. C. Bothe, CYS, 208). For Dore, v. D. and A. Mathew, 'The Survival of the Dissolved Monasteries in Wales', 70–81.

2 E.g. John Neot, John Fagan, Thomas Athelstan (Glastonbury), Thomas Coventry (Evesham), Thomas Lovewell (Westminster).

3 For their careers, v. Aveling, Ampleforth, 271–9, and later notes. Prioli (loc. cit. 345) notes them to have been: 'tutte persone benissimo qualificate di dottrina, e di gran pietà, della quale hanno dato testimonio con muoversi volontariamente a lasciar gradi onorevoli ed entrate comode, etc.'

4 No complete study or biography of Feckenham exists, save for the good but outdated article in DNB, but references to him and details of his activities are remarkably frequent in the documents and narratives of the time. His controversial skill attracted the notice of both Catholic and Protestant writers, and his works have been catalogued by antiquaries and bibliographers such as Anthony Wood, Fuller and Pits, while his monastic career attracted the attention of the early scholars of the revived English Congregation such as Baker and Maihew. In recent times modern Benedictines and others, such as Gasquet and

John Homan, or as he was known from his noviciate onwards, John Feckenham, was a native of the small village of that name on the eastern border of Worcestershire in the heart of the Midlands. From the Ridgeway, a mile or so distant, which marks the western limit of Warwickshire, the eye can travel over the forest of Arden eastwards to the uplands of Northamptonshire and Oxfordshire, and westwards across the wooded Severn valley to Brown Clee in Shropshire and the Malverns throwing their shadow over Herefordshire. Though he left his home in boyhood, and knew many vicissitudes of fortune, this man of Worcestershire was to return to Feckenham in manhood and to remember it in the last days of his extreme old age.

John Homan was born *c.* 1512–15 and came of well-to-do yeoman stock.[1] His father and uncle, both with large families, died possessed of considerable property scattered about the district and often held in partnership; they were clearly the second or third generation of a peasant ancestor who had bettered himself. The boy John, possibly patronized by the Throckmortons of Coughton, four miles away in the Arrow valley, entered Evesham Abbey and proceeded as a young monk to Gloucester College.[2] There we have made his acquaintance in the years between 1533 and 1538, when he was already the admired leader of a group of monks, slightly younger than himself, from several houses. He proceeded B.D. in 1539, having, as has been pointed out, passed through most of his theological course immediately after Cromwell's commissioners had purged Oxford of Duns and his likes. Feckenham, on the fringe of Erasmian humanism but never one for the New Learning of Germany, had accepted the royal supremacy with the rest and had presumably acquiesced in the surrender of Evesham. He had indeed shown himself a child of this world wise in his generation, for on the very day of the surrender of the abbey a proxy was being admitted on his behalf to the vicarage of Feckenham.[3] He held the benefice for at least fourteen years, though the evidence for his residence in the village is scanty and indirect.[4] He certainly employed a curate, and for a number of years after *c.* 1545 this post was held by two ex-monks in succession, the one of Evesham, the other a Cistercian from nearby Bordesley; there were two chantries in the church, and here again

Ethelred Taunton, have done good work; the latter in particular devoted to him a chapter of his work, *The English Black Monks of St Benedict*, which is perhaps the best in an uneven book. Finally and principally, in the last ten years Dom Hugh Aveling has examined anew every phase of Feckenham's career and has amassed materials for a full-length study. The pages that follow owe much to Dom Hugh, and I wish to acknowledge both his generosity and the great pains to which he has put himself in response to enquiries.

1 His father, uncles, brothers and sisters can be traced in Worcester wills in the Birmingham Probate Registry.

2 Wood, *Athenae Oxonienses*, ed. 1813, vol. 1, col. 507, gives various hearsay pieces of information.

3 Worcester Diocesan Archives, *Regist. Bell*, fo. 5ᵛ (27 January 1540). The presentation was made by two private persons; the church had been impropriated by the Charterhouse of Sheen.

4 E.g. in court rolls and wills.

two ex-monks of Evesham were beneficiaries. That the parish of Fecken-ham, a large hamlet rather than a village, could support three priests and an absentee vicar, all of them at one time ex-monks, is a notable, though no doubt a common, phenomenon. As for John Feckenham, he made good use of his time to become chaplain, first to John Bell, bishop of Worcester, of whose cathedral Philip Hawford, last abbot of Evesham, was dean, and then, by 1547 at latest, to Edmund Bonner, another Worcester-shire man, bishop of London. In 1544 he was presented by Sir George Throckmorton of Coughton to the north Warwickshire vicarage of Solihull, which he retained in plurality with Feckenham till 1553/4. Here again there is no direct evidence that he ever served the cure in person. He did, however, take a practical interest in his parishioners, for at both places he instituted a charity fund for advancing loans to poor people, heading the list of donors in each case with a gift of £10. The deeds of erection survive, and at Solihull there is an interesting list of subscribers over a series of years, including Feckenham's parents, a group of Throck-mortons and other county families, and a number of ex-monks and ex-servants of Evesham.[1] Meanwhile, the vicar of Solihull, Bonner's chaplain, was entering the lists of controversy in the capital. On 16 January 1547, a few days before the death of Henry VIII, he preached an anti-Protestant sermon at Paul's Cross deploring heresy and German novelties.[2] For this, and also probably for refusing to accept the new doctrine of justification and the abolition of fasting in Lent, as well as by reason of his close con-nection with Bonner, he was sent to the Tower. There he remained till he was 'borrowed' to take part in a series of disputations in London and Worcester on the conservative side.[3] His final release took place very early in Mary's reign, for he preached at Paul's Cross at the coronation on 23 September 1553.[4] His fame and reputation for orthodoxy must have grown during his imprisonment, for from the very beginning of Mary's reign he was the official preacher in London, and on 6 October he was one of those chosen by Convocation to defend the doctrine of the Real Presence and Transubstantiation, and for the next six years sermon followed sermon at close intervals. Early in 1554 he visited the imprisoned

---

1 The book of the Solihull charity is printed by Pemberton, *Solihull and its Church*, 61 seqq. The Feckenham Charity Book, couched in almost identical terms, is in the Worcs. Record Office. There is also an original letter there (Worcs. Rec. Off. MS. B. 116/18, 1, 2).

2 *LP*, xxi, ii, 710; PRO/SP, 1, vol. 228, no. 55: 'Item he openly enveyed agaynst the Germaynes notyng them to be seditious heretykes and of iijc [three hundred] sectes and above...also fynding him greaved in summe part of the statute of fyrst fruttes, etc.'

3 The word 'borrowed' (*mutuatus*), which has amused historians from Fuller downwards, seems to originate in T. Stapleton's *Counterblast against M. Horne's vayne blast* (ed. Louvain, 1567, 36ᵛ). Feckenham's activities in Mary's reign can be followed in ambassadorial despatches, Machyn, Wriothesley, Foxe and Strype.

4 Dom Hugh Aveling states that there is no document extant regularizing Feckenham as an ex-monk in 1553, though there are numerous deeds of the kind in Pole's register (*v. Archaeologia*, viii, 51 seqq.). These require the religious to wear his habit under the dress of a secular priest. No doubt Bonner had faculties to grant such absolutions.

Princess Elizabeth and advocated clemency to the queen,[1] and a little later was sent to exercise his gifts of persuasion upon Lady Jane Grey. The prisoner acknowledged his eloquence but remained unmoved, and the two parted with mutual assurances that they would never meet beyond the grave, but it is pleasant to hear that when on the day of execution Feckenham attended her on the scaffold, the seventeen-year-old victim of the ambitions and follies of her elders took his hand and thanked him: 'God will requite you, good sir, for your humanity to me, though it gave me more uneasiness than all the terrors of my approaching death', and that she turned to him to ask whether she might say the *Miserere* before she died.[2]

Thenceforward for the rest of the reign he was constantly in demand for sermons and disputations, and as a member of royal commissions, and he took a share, as the friend of the two founders, Sir Thomas White and Sir Thomas Pope, in the establishment of St John's and Trinity Colleges at Oxford, receiving the D.D. from the university in 1556 as a token of gratitude. In other quarters, too, his services received rapid recognition. The queen made him Dean of St Paul's in March 1554,[3] and he received a bunch of benefices—a prebend at Kentish Town, a canonry at Canterbury, and the livings of Finchley and Greenford. With these in hand he resigned Feckenham and Solihull.

We have no means of knowing whether Feckenham's decision to return to the monastic life was wholly spontaneous or whether it was inspired by a suggestion from Pole or the queen. With his position and reputation, he would inevitably be the leader of any group he joined, and it would seem probable that the first suggestion came from without. The decision was a momentous one for him, for it meant renouncing a lucrative and influential post. Wise after the event, we may think that he gave a hostage to fortune, and lost the stake, but in fact he had already mortgaged the future by his active and resolute defence of Catholic orthodoxy and by his share in the trials of leading heretics. The advent of Elizabeth would have been as disastrous for the dean of St Paul's as it was for the abbot of Westminster. Nevertheless, the sincerity of Feckenham need not be questioned. Though little external change of life was demanded of him as abbot, he accepted all the responsibilities and radical obligations of a monk, and he was aware of the legate's intention that the revived Westminster should provide a life more regular and austere than that of Evesham thirty years before.

The restored community of Westminster was in many ways an unusual one. All the 'founding members' were over forty years of age, and though there was a steady flow of recruits these also were for the most part

---

[1] Strype, *Memorials*, III, i, 129; Stapleton, *Counterblast*, 27–27ᵛ.

[2] Foxe, *Acts and Monuments* (ed. 1877), VI, 415–17, 424; H. F. Westlake, *Westminster Abbey*, I, 226. Jane, at the end of their interview, remarked to Feckenham: 'He [God] hath given you his great gift of utterance, and if it please him also to open the eyes of your heart.'

[3] Elected 10 March (W. Dugdale, St Paul's, 227); perhaps rather 12 March (Frere, *Marian Reaction*, 249); installed 18 March (Wriothesley's *Chronicle*, II, 114).

ex-religious of equal maturity. A majority of them had lived for the greater part of their previous monastic life in one or other of the Oxford monastic colleges, and had subsequently passed many years as secular clergymen. Nor was Westminster an ideal home for a monastic reform. It lay at the heart of the political and social life of the nation, and the abbey church was the theatre of recurrent royal ceremonials and displays. If Pole had hopes of inaugurating a monastic revival in which silent prayer and diligent study were to have a place of privilege, Westminster was scarcely the house in which it might expand.

In the event, the monastic life of the restored abbey seems to have been sober and dignified rather than austere, looking backward rather than forward in its aims. It was compared by a very well-informed monk fifty years later, who had himself lived at Santa Giustina, to the life of a college or an inn of court, to which was added the routine of a group of cathedral clergy.[1] This monk, Father Augustine Baker, did his best to elicit from the last survivor of the abbey, Fr Sigebert Buckley, what was the polity and what the daily way of life of Marian Westminster. He was disappointed in both respects, and was often heard to 'complain, that the old man was through age much decayed in all respects, and especially in his memory'. He judged also 'that he had never bin curious in searching or observing the monastick politie or manner of government of his own days, and much less of more ancient times'. Nor was Fr Buckley very helpful on details of daily life; all that he could tell were insignificant scraps 'not worthy the recounting'. Only one such happened to stick in Fr Baker's memory. 'I yet remember', he wrote many years later, 'that he told me, that they rose at midnight, that they did eate flesh, that at refection in the refectory they satt face to face on both sides the table beinge fowre to every messe as they do in the innes of court; that at supper they had so in common betweene every fowre, first a dish of cold sliced powdred beefe, and next after a sholder of mutton rosted. I do not remember what postpast they had, but it is likely thay had cheese and perhaps allso an apple or two, or peare. I do not remember', he adds, 'what thay had at dinner, but remembered what they had at supper, because it seemed a fare somewhat heavy for digestion to them that rise at midnight to me, who had lately before only experienced the monastick fare of Italy.'[2] The abbot was always busy preaching and organizing, and was not either by character or experience the kind of man to lead or to direct a secluded community in the ways of the spirit, nor were his monks, all men of formed minds and

---

1 Fr Leander Prichard, early in the seventeenth century, had heard Fr Baker opine that 'Dr Fecknam had not insisted much upon monastick regularities, at what time he was restored to the Abby of Westminster, but contented himself to have sett up there a disciplin much like to that which he saw observed in cathedral churches, as for the Divine Office; and for other things, he brought them to the laws and customs of colledges and inns of court'. *V.* Life of Father Baker in *Memorials of Father Augustine Baker* (Catholic Record Society, 33 (1933), ed. J. McCann and R. H. Connolly), 95–6.

2 *Ibid.* 95 and 181 (the latter passage is from Fr Baker's history of the English Mission).

habits, and of most diverse provenance, likely to have the enthusiasm and the elasticity needed for an enterprise of spiritual daring. Pole supplied a few ordinances and the community made some steps towards a greater austerity of life, but the venture had too short an existence to develop a spirit of its own.[1] Very little is known of the activities of the monks. Recruits came, and besides the novices there were postulants at the gate, students preparing for the secular priesthood, the boys of the school, choristers and singing men about the place. We are told that the monks visited the prisons, especially to treat with heretics,[2] and no doubt they preached and disputed in less distinguished circles than those in which the abbot moved. Some of the old obediences were revived, but the collection of revenue and management of property was in the hands of a layman, John Moulton, as general receiver and auditor. The income available was paid by him to the cellarer, who himself disposed of most of the funds, passing on relatively small amounts to a few obedientiaries.[3] The abbey had inherited the revenues of the college, and these had been augmented by the queen; in 1557 the receiver handed over £1258, and in the following year £1655, but in the latter year the gross income was assessed for the clerical tenth at £2064, the difference between the greater and lesser figures being largely accounted for by legal expenses and fees to the exalted lay officials.[4] It will thus be seen that Westminster under Mary enjoyed less than half its net pre-Dissolution income of £3470, and from the reduced sum the cellarer had to pay pensions to the late dean and prebendaries, and to support a school of forty boys, with master and usher as well as twelve choristers and twelve almsmen. The community, as the account of 1558 shows, now numbered forty, excluding any postulants who might be in commons with them. Ordination lists of these years show also that the abbey, as of yore, allowed numerous clerics to be ordained to its title, and the names of some of these, and of some of the servants, show that the abbot did not forget either his family or his neighbours at Evesham and Feckenham.[5]

Abbot Feckenham continued to be one of the prominent figures of the reign, speaking in parliament and Convocation, preaching at Paul's Cross and in the Abbey at the opening of parliament, disputing with heretics, assisting at the refoundation of other communities, serving on royal

1 Prioli, in the letter cited above (p. 425 n. 5) of 15 December 1556, records (p. 347) that the Cassinese visitors are shortly to arrive 'per comunicare a questi buoni Monaci tutti i buoni instituti della loro Congregazione d'Italia, i quali essi si mostrano pronti a voler imitare, benchè sappiano che sieno molto più stretti che non erano i loro qui, i quali però da se hanno cominciato già in parte a ristringere'. Cf. Pole's letter to the President of the Cassinese Congregation in February 1556 (*CalSPV*, 1555–6, 403).

2 Prioli, *ibid.* 346: 'Gli altri suoi Monaci averanno cura di visitare, e consolare li prigionieri, ed in particolare quelli che sono incarcerati per conto d'eresie.'

3 Pearce, *The Monks of Westminster Abbey*; Westlake, *Westminster Abbey*, and above all notes supplied by Dom Hugh Aveling.

4 From transcripts by Dom Aveling.

5 E.g. Thomas Studley (from a village four miles from Feckenham) appears as a curate of St Margaret's, and William Feckenham as a monk of Westminster.

commissions of sewers and of exports and imports. In 1557 he secured the release of the old abbot's house by Lord Wentworth, and although he does not seem to have had any property allotted solely to his support, as in olden days, he kept considerable state with a chaplain and fifteen gentlemen and servants. His principal and lasting service to the Abbey was the rebuilding in simple style of the damaged shrine of the Confessor, and the solemn translation thither of the body of the saint from the place of security in which it had been hidden when the rich shrine was plundered.[1] He received a few jewels from the queen but he was not granted time in which to see to its ornamentation. For this reason, and perhaps also because it was the tomb of a king as well as of a saint, the shrine was left unmolested in the next reign and still remains a place of pilgrimage in October.

We know nothing of the forebodings of the abbot and his monks when it became clear that the days of Mary and Pole were numbered. The queen was duly buried at Westminster, and the abbot preached from a text which may have borne heavy undertones for the preacher: 'Wherefore I praised the dead which are already dead more than the living which are yet alive. Yea, better is he than both which hath not yet been.'[2] A month later Elizabeth was crowned in the Abbey, and Feckenham and his monks must have been there, though their ceremonious movements were not, as the sequel showed, appreciated. It may have been on the occasion of the visit which by old custom the abbot of Westminster paid to the sovereign in connection with the coronation service that Elizabeth expressed her gratitude to Feckenham and made him the offer of the primatial see.[3] Shortly after the coronation the queen came to the Abbey for the opening of parliament, and the Mantuan ambassador relates the sequel. 'On arriving at Westminster Abbey the Abbot, robed pontifically, with all his monks in procession, each of them having a lighted torch in his hand, received her as usual, giving her first of all incense and holy water; and when her Majesty saw the monks who accompanied her with torches, she said: "Away with those torches, for we see very well".... Thereupon Dr Cox, a married priest...preached the sermon in which, after saying many things freely against the monks, he proved by his arguments that they ought to be persecuted and punished by her Majesty, as they were impious for having caused the burning of so many poor

1 Machyn records the event on 20 March 1557 (*Diary*, 130): 'Was taken up at Westmyster agayn with a hondered lyghtes kyng Edward the confessor in the sam plasse wher ys shrine was, and ytt shalle be sett up agayne as fast as my lord abbott can have ytt don, for yt was a godly shyte to have seen yt, how reverently he was cared from the plasse that he was taken up when he was led when that the abbay was spowlyd and robyd.'

2 Eccles. iv. 2, 3.

3 Stapleton, *Counterblast*, 27–27ᵛ, records the visit: 'But this I certaynle knowe, that he hath reported...that her hyghnesse had [his kindness towards her] in remembraunce at the firste and laste talke that ever he had with her, in her palace at Westmyster not longe before her highnes Coronation.' The story of the offer of Canterbury rests on the authority of Sanders (J. Stevens, *Monasticon*, I, 289) and may be true. Elizabeth adopted a similar tactic with Campion.

innocents under pretext of heresy, on which he expatiated greatly.'[1] Feckenham must have seen well enough the way the wind was blowing, even apart from these inauspicious incidents, but he did not allow his forebodings to influence his actions. For almost three months he was in his place in the House of Lords, using his talents in defence of his beliefs. He voted against the Act of Supremacy and the First Fruits Bill and took part on the Catholic side in the Westminster Conferences at the end of March. He spoke against the Act of Uniformity and the bill dissolving the refounded monasteries.[2] This was clearly the end, and by the last week in May it was reported that most of the monks had doffed their habits. Early in June Feckenham received an offer from the queen that if he would take the Oath of Supremacy and promise to conform in the Abbey to the new order of services he and his monks might stay. He had no hesitation in refusing, and when 29 June, the last day for taking the oath, had passed he prepared, in the words of a contemporary, 'to go about his business'.[3] The abbey as a legal entity ceased to exist on 10 July; the late abbot remained in or about the place for almost a year, arranging the transference of property; at last on 22 May 1560, Feckenham was taken to the Tower 'at about viii o'clock of the evening'.[4]

On that evening began what may be called the fourth act of his adult life.[5] During the twenty-four years that remained to him he was in prison or under house arrest save for a few relatively brief intervals. The government, had it so wished, could in due course have driven him into a position where he must either have recanted or died, but for some reason this extreme step was never taken. It was not on the whole the policy to go to extremes with those who had been priests or monks before the troubles began, and Feckenham, like other çi-devant Catholics, had little direct communication with the seminary priests or the Jesuits. He spent several years in the Tower, along with some of the Marian prelates who had refused to conform, and with his customary amiability helped the new

1 *CalSPV*, 1558–80, 15.

2 Cf. Strype, *Annals*, I, App. 24, no. ix (Dodd-Tierney, II, App. 38); letter from Jewell to Zürich in *Zürich Letters*, I, 20; J. E. Neale, 'The Elizabethan Acts of Supremacy and Uniformity', in *EHR*, LXV, 331, and C. J. Davis, 'Journal of the House of Lords for April and May, 1559', *ibid.* XXVIII, 538. Feckenham spoke against the Act of Uniformity at the second reading, but was apparently absent from the third.

3 Il Schifanoya wrote to the Castellan of Mantua on 6 June (*CalSPV*, 1558–80, 78: 'The Abbey cannot last long, as the Abbot made a similar reply [to that of Bonner] when it was offered to him to remain securely in his Abbey with his habit, and the monks to live together as they have done till now, provided that he would celebrate in his church the divine offices and the mass, administering the sacraments in the same manner as in the other churches of London: and that he would take the oath. To these things the Abbot would by no means consent.'   4 Machyn, *Diary*, 235.

5 Oddly enough, this is also the phase that is best documented. Dom Hugh Aveling, supplementing Gillow, *DNB* and Taunton, has assembled a long list of movements and activities. A specimen of Feckenham's prose and short bibliography are in A. C. Southern, *Elizabethan Recusant Prose, 1559–82*, 169–70, 405–7, 526–33. His debating manner may be sampled in an article by Dom R. Webster, '"Conference" at Wisbech' (1580), in *DR*, xxxv. Dom Aveling has prepared a full bibliography, at present in typescript (1957).

dean, Gabriel Goodman, to straighten out the accounts at Westminster and get a grasp of the administration. He took part again in the sharp and useless controversies that were such a feature of the intellectual life of the times; he was quartered on Anglican bishops at Waltham Abbey and Ely and tired them both out with his wealth of argument. Andrew Perne, the well-known Cambridge weathercock, later Master of Peterhouse, also took a hand at disputing with him. For a time he was allowed to live on parole in Holborn, and later, when his health gave serious trouble, he was even allowed to spend some time at Bath, taking the waters.[1] Finally he was sent to Wisbech Castle, where a kind of concentration camp of priests was about to be established, and where, after his death, the bitter controversy broke out that was to have such tragic consequences for the Catholic cause in England. In consequence, Feckenham spent the last years of his long life at the margin of the tides where in his day fenland and salt-marsh met, in the bishop's castle lapped by water and mists in winter, searched by the east winds in spring, and touched with colour by dandelion and snapdragon in the summer.[2] He was never idle, and when not engaged in controversy wrote tracts and commentaries on Scripture, or put together for the use of those too poor to pay an apothecary the book of remedies that he had picked up during his life.[3] He resisted all attempts to force or trap him into accepting the Elizabethan religious demands and to the last answered his opponents good-temperedly but without withdrawing from what he had learned in his youth to be the faith of the Church. He was never wholly at a loss for funds. Either by saving or investing surplus moneys in the days of preferment, or by salving something from Westminster, or from family legacies, he was comfortably off, and his estate, while he was in prison, was administered by a friend or a relative. He was even able, at every period of his life, to spend money on the poor. It may be that he felt it a duty as a monk to give away all his superfluity in this way. We have seen what he did at Feckenham and Solihull. At Westminster he set up a distribution of alms that lasted long after his day. When at Holborn he gave the milk of twelve cows to the sick and poor and constructed an aqueduct for the people, besides providing prizes for the athletes of the locality. When at Bath he built a hospice for the poor, and even at Wisbech he gave money for a causeway and a market cross.[4] Curious as they are, these benefactions seem to be for the most part authentic, and Fuller, sixty years later, had still heard the tradition, 'so that flies flock not thicker about spilt honey than the beggars constantly

1 *V.* E. Bishop, 'In Laudem Joannis Feckenham, O.S.B.', in *DR*, I, and F. A. Gasquet, 'Abbot Feckenham and Bath', *ibid.* xxv.

2 For the 'flower in the crannied wall' at Wisbech, *v.* E. Taunton, *The English Black Monks of St Benedict*, I, 218–19. E. Bishop helped Taunton in this chapter.

3 *The Book of sovereign remedies...collected of Mr Doctor Fecknam late Abbot of Westminster*, exists in B.M. Sloane MS. 167 (the earlier and better form), and in Cambrai Municipal Library, 910 (later, augmented version compiled for the English Dames there). Feckenham gives his sources, e.g. 'my cosen Hatly', 'my Aunt Lytton', etc.

4 J. Stevens, *Monasticon*, 289, is the authority for this.

crowded round him'.[1] He was able to keep two relatives at the university and to leave substantial legacies to those who had been good to him. He died at last, probably towards the end of 1584, and tradition relates that he was enabled to receive Viaticum devoutly shortly before his death. The last abbot of Westminster lies somewhere in Wisbech churchyard.

As will have been seen, we have a very considerable knowledge of the background and external events of Feckenham's life; it is evident that from his early days at Oxford till the end of his life he was one with whom contemporaries had to reckon, and to whom they deferred in the daily affairs of life. He rose naturally, despite mischances, to a position of eminence and authority which he did not abuse, and had his life been passed in an epoch when a man's career could go smoothly forward, there can be little doubt that he would have reached a commanding position in the Church. In the qualities looked for in an archbishop or a secretary of state in times of peace he would have been surpassed by only a few of those who did in fact reach eminence between 1540 and 1580. At the same time he remains, as do so many of his fellows, something of a dim figure. We have samples of his sermons and works of controversy, but no intimate letters or autobiographical details, and no indications whatever of his emotions, his apprehensions or his personal religion. His long adult life covers almost exactly the generation of ceaseless controversy, when Englishmen were engaged in bitter theological strife of a kind unfamiliar to the modern world and conducted with improvised weapons in an ill-lit and ever-changing scene. The generation before Feckenham, that of Fisher, Erasmus and More, had grown to maturity in a relatively settled world, and met the religious storm with the outlook of the traditional theologian or the tolerant humanist. The generation after him, that of Campion and Whitgift and Hooker, knew that the religious divisions were permanent and used new weapons and a new technique. To Feckenham and his contemporaries the issues were still confused, the result was still unsettled and the theological positions not yet sharply and irrevocably defined; the disputants, in England at least, are neither integral Tridentines nor fully Protestant or Calvinist; they are indeed not wholly clear in their own minds where they stand, or whither the world is moving; it is only as time goes on that they harden, and even then they have the illusion that intellectual conviction can be reached by debate.

Feckenham, whose formative years at Oxford had been spent in the twilight of scholastic theology and Erasmian piety, had followed the world in the matters of the royal supremacy and the dissolution of the monasteries and had, without apparent repugnance, taken up with a normal clerical career. There was in him, however, not a vestige of continental Protestantism, and even while Henry was still alive he was deploring the advances of heresy. His imprisonment and the acrid theological and liturgical disputes of the time seem to have convinced him, as they con-

[1] T. Fuller, *Church History*, v, 97.

vinced Gardiner and many other 'Henricians', that a Church tied to the monarch and severed from Rome could not long escape chaos and error. From 1553 onwards Feckenham was consistent in all his actions, maintaining and defending what he considered to be Catholic truth. He was, however, a controversialist rather than a theologian, but of an accommodating temper rare in that age. His mind moved in terms of practical concessions and adjustments; he had neither Pole's forward-looking zeal for reform nor the unworldly, single-minded devotion of a Campion; he appears sometimes to continue an argument or to suspend decision when a Jesuit or a seminarian would have broken sharply off. Seen in the whole picture of his life, however, and as a man of his generation, he appears an admirable and sympathetic figure, if not wholly a heroic one. As a young man he and his friends had felt no call to follow More and the Carthusians; twenty-five years later the choice was clear, but even now Feckenham had no thought of exile; he remained to endure a long and wearing period of imprisonment, never a martyr, but certainly a confessor for the faith.

There is more than one personal description of him. A tradition records that 'he was of mean Stature, somewhat fat, round fac'd, beautiful, and of a pleasant aspect, affable and lovely in Conversation'.[1] A well informed contemporary saw in him a 'man of an extremely kindly nature, sanguine temperament and thoughtful cast of mind',[2] and we may picture him, in the portrait of which Father Baker had heard, 'with a cornered cappe on his head, and some furre appearinge at the end of his cassock sleeve at his wrist'.[3] His good temper in controversy, his merciful demeanour in his days of power, his generosity to the poor and his long durance for conscience sake have won the praises of bibliographers, antiquaries and the historians of the recusants. Camden and Pits set the tone which all their successors have adopted. There is no reason to believe that he would ever have made a great reformer or a deeply spiritual father of his monks, but he is at least a worthy and dignified figure to end the long line of medieval abbots. An eighteenth-century antiquary, repeating an older tradition, records the familiar anecdote, that when Queen Elizabeth wished to speak with him, 'the first Messenger sent to him found him planting Elms, which are still growing in the Garden at Westminster Abbey; nor would he go with the Messenger till he had finish'd the Work he was about'.[4] Whatever the truth of the story, it is fitting that the last old English abbot, the man of Worcestershire, should be associated in the Abbey precinct two centuries later with the tree that in its gracious and majestic dignity veils and beautifies so many midland villages and lanes.

1 This is from J. Stevens, *loc. cit.*
2 Prioli's letter (*supra*, p. 425 n. 5) of 15 December 1556, 346: 'Uomo d'una natura benignissima, e complessione sanguigna, e mente malincolica, dotto assai in Teologia, ed ottimo Predicatore.' There is a remarkable concurrence of testimony from all sources and at all times to Feckenham's courtesy and humanity.
3 *Memorials of Father Augustine Baker*, 182.
4 So Fuller, *Church History*, v, 97, deriving from Reyner, *Apostolatus*, 234–5.

Westminster Abbey was the only house of the black monks to achieve restoration under Queen Mary. Other schemes had been on foot, but material difficulties stood in their way and the space of time granted was too short. Along with Westminster, if not above it, two other abbeys had always disputed the primacy of honour among the Benedictines: Glastonbury and St Albans, both of venerable antiquity and great wealth. As has been seen, a knot of Glastonbury monks were among the earliest members of the revived Westminster, and at a subsequent date, probably in 1557, four of them, John Fagan, John Neot, William Adelwold and William Kenwyne, petitioned the queen to refound their old home. 'Already', they say, 'our friendes there hath buylded and bestowed moche upon reparation', and they stress the unwillingness of their departure in 1539 from the abbey which they had never surrendered.[1] Hopes of a restoration seem to have been in the air, for wills both at Westminster and in Somerset contain bequests to Glastonbury, should it be restored.[2] The project, though it must needs have been costly, was not wholly impracticable; though the destruction had been great, the conventual buildings and their environs had not been devoted to secular uses. Nothing, however, was done before Mary's death. The scheme at St Albans made even less headway.[3] Two of the Westminster monks (one being the first prior, sometime archdeacon of St Albans) came from the house, and the ex-abbot Richard Boreman, assisted by the queen, had bought in the abbey church. Nothing further, however, is known to have happened. Most probably, it was the monks themselves that failed. Every indication goes to show that the refoundation of Westminster depended upon the assembling of volunteers from every quarter possible; other foundations could only have been made when the Abbey had a superfluity of men.

Westminster has been given pride of place on account of its celebrity. It was not in fact the first religious house to be re-established. When the Venetian ambassador wrote of the imminent refoundation of the Abbey at the end of September 1556, he noted that this would be the third monastery of strict observance to be established, and that a fourth, of Carthusians, was pending.[4] Two months later (15 December), Prioli reported that four besides Westminster were in being: of Franciscans, Dominicans, Bridgettines and Carthusians, and that a fifth, of regular canons, was imminent.[5] Five months later still (13 May 1557), the late Venetian ambassador noted that when he left England seven houses were in being, viz. the five just mentioned, together with King's Langley and Dartford.[6]

---

1 *Monasticon*, I, 9. 2 *VCH, Somerset*, II, 96.
3 *VCH, Herts*, IV, 413. 4 *CalSPV*, 1555–6, no. 634.
5 *Epistolarum Reginaldi Poli...*, pars v, App. 347. Prioli remarks: 'E presto se ne resti-tuirà uno [monastero] de Canonici Regolari.' It is not clear what this proposal was, but it had no issue.
6 *CalSPV*, 1556–7, no. 884, p. 1074. The number of seven can only be reached by counting Langley and Dartford separately, though in fact they existed in succession.

The first to come were the two mendicant houses in the capital. The friars were clearly a simpler proposition than the monks. In the first place, now, as ever, they needed but modest buildings and small revenues. Next, some at least of both Dominicans and Franciscan Observants had escaped twenty years before and settled in convents of the Low Countries, where they had been joined by a few English recruits. Finally, an international order could make arrangements for a foundation and afforce the native nucleus with foreign friars. The first to return were the Observants.[1] Towards them the queen's feelings must have been particularly warm. She had been christened in their church, and they had always been among her mother's advisers and staunchest champions; their sufferings had indeed begun in her cause. The Greenwich house, Crown property, was revived on 7 April 1555, and among those in residence was the aged Friar Peto, nominally bishop of Salisbury by papal appointment and soon to be cardinal; likewise Friar Elstow, another stalwart of olden days, and Thomas Bourchier, later to become martyrologist. Here in their church Pole was consecrated bishop on 23 March 1556, two days after the burning of his predecessor. At about the same time the Dominicans were established in St Bartholomew's, Smithfield. The Carthusians of London,[2] like the friars, had active representatives; in 1546–7 several had escaped to Bruges, where one of them, Maurice Chauncy, had composed his early versions of the martyrdom of his old companions. Chauncy, Foxe and a converse, Hugh Taylor, returned to England on 29 June 1555. They had a friend at court in the person of the Comptroller, Sir Robert Rochester, a brother of Dan John Rochester, one of their martyrs. He and Pole presented the monks to the queen, and they were temporarily housed in the hospital of the Savoy. As the House of the Salutation had been in part destroyed and in part converted into a mansion, return thither was impracticable. The queen therefore looked to Sheen, still Crown property, where the sitting tenant, the Duchess of Somerset, was difficult about moving. Meanwhile Chauncy's hopes had been dashed by the death first of Foxe and then of Dan Richard Crofts, sent over to take his place. He persevered, nevertheless, and gradually a group was formed of ex-monks who took possession of Sheen on St Hugh's day (17 November), 1555, and made their solemn entry on 25 November. Rochester, Sir Richard Southwell and others gave help, and the place regained much of its monastic plan. The community, like that of Westminster, was an elderly one, fifteen in all and of varied provenance. From Witham came the ex-prior and two others, from Mount Grace the ex-prior, Dan John Wilson, who had capitulated to Archbishop Lee, together with two monks and two converses. From Hinton came two, from Sheen three, and one each from Beauvale and Coventry, while Chauncy himself, their prior, represented

---

1 A. G. Little in *VCH, Kent*, II, 198.
2 There is a full and documented account of the refoundation of Sheen by E. M. Thompson in *The English Carthusians*, 500–9.

London. They quickly re-established the full Carthusian way of life and pressed on with the rebuilding.

Meanwhile, the Bridgettines[1] had returned to Syon, another Crown estate. They, as will be remembered, had never formally surrendered their house, and when, by a legal quibble, it fell under a praemunire in 1539, several of the nuns crossed the Channel and were received at Termonde, having taken with them their convent seal and some of the most precious of their relics, vestments, muniments and books. The returning exiles were joined by some of their sisters who had remained in England, and they made up a community of seventeen under Abbess Catherine Palmer, with three priest-brothers. They were enclosed on 1 August 1557, by Bishop Bonner and Abbot Feckenham, assisted by brothers of the order with habits 'of shepe coler as the shepe bereth', and charged 'never to goo forth as long as they do lyffe'.[2]

Finally, there were the Dominicanesses, late of Dartford.[3] They also had hung together, though not in formal religious life, and in 1557 they were housed at King's Langley to the number of eight, including their prioress, Elizabeth Cressener. Dartford, though belonging to the Crown, had been settled upon Anne of Cleves, and entry could not be obtained till that lady ended her placid life in 1557, when the nuns went back to their old home on 8 September, to enjoy little more than a year of conventual life.

There were thus by 1557 four houses of men and two of women in being, with a total population of a little above one hundred religious, of whom possibly a dozen friars were aliens. This, it may be thought, was not a great number out of the fifteen hundred or so ex-religious who must still have been living up and down the country, and it is noteworthy that three great religious bodies—the Cistercians, the Premonstratensians, and the Austin Canons—showed no sign of revival. No doubt we should remember that the monasteries and friaries had been alienated or destroyed, and that both spiritual and economic motives had driven most of the male religious to find occupation in clerical posts, withdrawal from which would have needed a very lively sense of vocation. Doubtless, also, ten or twenty years of quiet under a Catholic sovereign would have seen an increase in the number of houses and an intake of young recruits. Nevertheless, a general conclusion seems to impose itself; while twenty years of religious turmoil and secularization had not extinguished the sense of vocation in a few individuals, the conception of the religious life as an occupation for a young man in the neighbourhood of a monastery had gone for ever, and the appearance of anything like a widespread desire for the monastic life as a vocation would never be seen in England until a fresh epoch of fervour had dawned. When this occurred, under the

---

1 Pending the appearance of the relevant volume of *VCH*, *Middlesex*, the best account is still in Aungier, *Syon Monastery*, 97–8.

2 Machyn, *Diary*, 145.   3 A. G. Little in *VCH*, *Kent*, II, 188–9.

impulse of the Counter-Reformation thirty years later, there was indeed a notable flowering of English religious life, but it took place beyond the Channel and was maintained by those who had left forever their country and the home of their father's house.[1]

After Mary's death it soon became clear how the world was going, but it was more than six months before the end came. Then, with the Acts of Uniformity and Supremacy passed, together with that dissolving the religious houses, there was clearly no future for the life in England. This time the inmates knew where they stood, and few took the oath. The last day for swearing was 29 June, and before that the majority had taken themselves off. The Spanish ambassador, the Count de Feria, obtained permission for the friars and nuns to leave the country, but there was some doubt if this applied to all, or only to those who had been religious under Henry VIII.[2] Pensions were granted only to those who remained and conformed to the new religious settlement. The Carthusians of Sheen and the Bridgettines of Syon waited till the officers came to undertake the suppression, and then departed on, or shortly after, 1 July, as did also the convent of Dominicanesses. The friars of Greenwich followed on the 12th, and the Dominicans of Smithfield on the 14th.[3] The Carthusians went to Val de Grace at Bruges, where they remained as a distinct community till they ultimately settled at Nieuport.[4] The Dominicans were for the most part either Spanish or Dutch; the four English friars remained and submitted; the only English black friars to be true to their vocation were the three priests from Dartford, one of whom, Richard Hargrave, who had been elected prior of Smithfield shortly before Mary's death, and asked for as vicar-general of the Order in England by Pole, escorted the nuns in their flight. These last, to the number of ten with prioress, four nuns, four sisters and a postulant, settled at Seland near Antwerp in a state of penury. All save the postulant were survivors of the Henrician community; in 1559 three were octogenarians, and the youngest was over fifty; among them was a sister of the martyred John Fisher, of like spirit to her brother. The duchess of Parma and English friends helped them, but they could not hope to survive as a community.[5] The nuns of Syon, leaving their sister, Clementia Tresham, to die at her family home in Northamptonshire, crossed the Channel with the Dominicanesses, and at first returned to Termonde, where they had found

---

1 This 'second spring' deserves to find an historian worthy of the theme. The English Benedictine Congregation alone numbered some 120 monks by 1630.

2 *CalSPVen*, 1558-80, no. 81 (Tiepolo to the Doge).

3 Machyn, *Diary*, 204, records these departures, but there is some confusion in the dating in the printed text.

4 This phase can be followed in Thompson, *The English Carthusians*, 510-15.

5 There is an interesting account of this in a letter from Hargrave to the Dominican master-general, quoted in Pio, *Delle Vite degli Huomini di San Dominico*, 377-80. His description of St John Fisher's sister is as follows: 'Tra loro v'è la sorella del Vescovo Roffense martire, di non mena constanza, se si potesse provare, di quello che già fosse il suo fratello.'

refuge previously, but soon began their odyssey of wandering which led them to a stay of almost two centuries in Lisbon and more than one approach to extinction, till at last they returned to England, where they still remain.[1]

As for the community of Westminster, they made no attempt at corporate flight. As black monks they had no 'order' to care for them, and they would have found neither funds nor function abroad. The break-up was leisurely;[2] Feckenham, with his characteristic moderation and good temper, remained to assist in the transfer, and obtained for his brethren the contents of their cells and a small dividend from the sale of the goods of the house when debts had been paid. For a few months the late abbot seems to have been treated as if he were still the administrator of the property, and large sums were paid over to him by the receiver. Feckenham for his part made no difficulty when vestments and furnishings passed into the keeping of Dean Gabriel Goodman, the president of the new chapter. In the end, however, he departed without a pension, as did his monks. The latter, so far as can be discovered, stood firm. There is no record of a Westminster monk of this vintage conforming or holding a benefice in the established Church, and for this very reason the brethren are difficult to trace.[3] Dan Richard Eden the cellarer, once a Cistercian of Hailes, returned to his old Oxford college, now transformed into St John's, where he became a fellow. His name last appears as senior fellow in 1565–6, and it is interesting to note that one of his colleagues in that year was the young Edmund Campion. Two, at least, tried to flee abroad and were hindered: of these one, Hugh Philips, once a monk of Ramsey, was in 1576 indicted for saying Mass in London; the other, John Langdon, was similarly indicted in Essex in 1561, but this time made good his escape to Flanders. Henry Style, a young monk who had come from Trinity College, Cambridge, returned to Caius College, a nest of papists, whence, after some years, he escaped to Douai. Thomas Figge, a Winchester monk in origin, escaped to France. Thomas Cooke, once an Austin canon of Christchurch, was in the Marshalsea in 1570 and died in prison two years later. William Feckenham, another young monk, possibly a relative of the abbot, was in Newgate in 1586. The others, perhaps, lived on in the capital or in the country, ministering to those who, even if sometimes outwardly conforming, held privately to the old ways. Since more than half the community of Westminster had taken their vows before c. 1535, few can still have been active in 1580.

Thus the Westminster community and their abbot lingered on, dwindling slowly to extinction, but not with dishonour, in the middle decades of the Elizabethan age. One monk, however, survived the queen and lived to become, by reason of his status rather than of his personality,

---

1 Aungier, *Syon Monastery*, 100 *seqq.*; *Archaeologia*, XVII, 326.
2 Here once more the generosity of Dom Hugh Aveling's help must be recorded.
3 H. Aveling in *Ampleforth and its origins*, 74–8 and Appendix A, 271–9.

a figure of history. Dan Robert Sigebert Buckley, or Bulkeley,[1] was in his eighty-sixth year on the day when Queen Elizabeth was alive and dead. Clearly defined, almost visible, as Fr Buckley is in the Baker narratives, his early years are hidden in the dark backward of time. If he was born in 1517–18 he might conceivably have taken monastic vows before the Dissolution, but a phrase of Fr Baker's seems to rule this out.[2] He received minor orders at Westminster on 17 December 1557, and was priested on 4 June 1558;[3] it is therefore very probable that he was one of those 'shorne in' on 21 November 1556. Apart from the ordination lists, where he figures as Robert Seberte, nothing is known of him unless he is the unidentified 'Selbie' of the earliest Westminster list, and Fr Baker certainly felt that he had never been a man of parts. Dull or not, he remained staunchly loyal after the Suppression, and was in prison for twenty years, perhaps for more; he was in the Marshalsea (1582–6), Wisbech (1588–99) and Framlingham (1599–1603). Firm in faith, he remained also firm in hope, and prayed for the restoration of the monastic life in England.

1 His name appears in more than one form and 'Bulkeley' has given rise to the conjecture that he was of the well-known Anglesey family of that name. There seems no doubt that Buckley is the correct form. Cf. Baker, *Treatise of the English Mission*, in CRS, XXXIII, 177, where he speaks of the Cassinese monks as having 'buckled [i.e. made contact] with fa. Buckley'.

2 *Ibid.* 181, where he writes: 'I...might have understood of him...what was the monastick discipline in Westminster after the foresaid restoration...for of elder times he of his own experience could have said nothing.'

3 The dates are from the Liber Ordinationum (23 June 1550 to 23 March 1577, in London Diocesan Records, Library of St Paul's Cathedral, fo. 161 b). I owe this reference to Dom Hugh Aveling, who has also kindly supplied a reference in the Simancas archives, stado leg. 583, to two Westminster monks, Figg and Langham, 'propter fidem in Belgia exulantes', 8 February 1570.

CHAPTER XXXV

THE OLD AND THE NEW

With the suppression of Marian Westminster monastic life came to an end, for the time being, not only in England but among Englishmen. For more than thirty years scarcely any English Catholics left their fatherland to become monks abroad, and if a rare individual did so, he was absorbed as an adopted son into a family of blood alien to his own. Those who, either in England or in exile, felt drawn to the priesthood or to the religious life, normally found a haven either in one of the English seminaries abroad or in the houses of the Society of Jesus. In the last decade of the sixteenth century, however, a number of Englishmen and Welshmen were taking the Benedictine habit either in the Cassinese Congregation of Italy or in the Valladolid Congregation of Spain. The motive that actuated these men, who were almost without exception either priests or students preparing for the priesthood, was not solely, perhaps not even principally, a resolve to have done once and for all with secular life and persecution by retiring abroad into the regular life of an observant and 'contemplative' monastery, but a desire to work in England for the conversion of their countrymen. To understand their motives and aims it is necessary to look for a moment at the circumstances of the English Catholics at the time.

When it had become clear that the reaction of the queen and the official classes away from the Marian revival and from what may be called integral Catholicism was permanent, and that unless action were taken from without those still affected to the old faith and to the papal obedience would either conform outwardly to the establishment or gradually dwindle to extinction, a twofold attack was directed against this danger by the forces of the fervent religious counter-Reformation. On the one hand William (later Cardinal) Allen founded a seminary college at Douai in 1568 (moved to Reims in 1578 and back to Douai in 1593) which soon began to send into England a stream of missionary priests pledged to the reconversion of their country, and on the other the young and dynamic Society of Jesus directed to this land small groups of its subjects who were of English birth, beginning with the celebrated mission of Campion and Persons in 1582.

At first missionary priests and Jesuits worked together in amity and with abundant fruit. Then, through a series of deplorable mistakes and mischances, divisions began to appear that ultimately caused great and permanent harm to the cause for which each party was working and suffering. As it had been with the Cistercians and mendicant friars at their first appearance centuries earlier, so now the Jesuits acted as a strong polarizing force, attracting desirable recruits from all sides not only by their novel efficiency of government, their great success, their unquestionable fervour, and their appeal to the spirit of the times, but also by penetrating, directly or indirectly, into religious institutes of all kinds. In particular, the fathers of the Society had come, by the end of the century, to have the direction, actual or virtual, not only of the English College at Douai, but also of those at Rome, at Valladolid and at Seville. Gradually, therefore, the division among the English clergy ceased to be one between the Jesuits and the secular clergy and became more complex. The Jesuits and their secular supporters both in the colleges and on the English mission were joined together in opposition to a party made up of the older secular mission priests, on the one hand, and of an anti-Jesuit minority of the professors and students of the colleges on the other. The latter party were inevitably at a great disadvantage; they were not only without centre, organization and cohesion, but also without any influential superior or representative, and their position was rendered still weaker by their failure, in the so-called Archpriest controversy, to obtain from Rome a bishop or vicar-apostolic for England, and by the subsequent lamentable division of opinion on the lawfulness of the new oath of allegiance in the early years of James I.

It was in these circumstances that a number of able and zealous young priests and students in the various English colleges looked towards the monastic life as a solution, partly moved by a desire for a spiritual formation and a way of life other than that of the Society, and partly hoping that as members of a reformed and influential branch of the ancient monastic order they might return to England with a status and independence that might free them from the allegiances and the quarrels which existed there.[1] They began, therefore, quite independently, to seek admis-

---

1 The best contemporary account of the genesis and early days of the revived English Benedictine Congregation is Fr Augustine Baker's 'Treatise of the English Benedictine Mission', printed and annotated in *Memorials of Father Baker*, ed. J. McCann and H. Connolly. Fr Baker's sketch has, however, as all such things must have, an individual and personal 'slant'; moreover, he does not attempt to give an account of the interminable negotiations and the various false starts which preceded the arrangement of 1619. There is a good short sketch by Abbot McCann in *Ampleforth and its Origins* (London, 1952), 81–106. Dom Justin (later Abbot) McCann has for thirty years and more edited and studied the writings and biographical material of Fr Baker and has in recent years devoted his attention to the early history of the Congregation in general. Dom R. H. Connolly of Downside (d. 1948) gave much time and pains in the last two decades of his life to congregational history, to the study of which he brought the fine critical powers and sober judgment that distinguished his patristic work. Finally, Dom Stephen Marron of Douai (d. 1954) was at the same time engaged on the same material. The three original houses of the Congregation were thus represented, and the results of the labours of these three scholars will be found principally in the three periodicals of their respective abbeys, viz. *The Downside Review*, *The Ampleforth Journal*, and *The Douai Magazine*. In addition, Dom Connolly provided a firm foundation for future students with *Some Dates and Documents for the Early History of our House* (i.e. St Gregory's, now Downside Abbey), privately printed in 1930, and he and Abbot McCann collaborated in a valuable *Report* on 'The Abbots of the ancient monasteries and the Cathedral Priors', printed privately in 1942, and travelling over a far wider field than its title would suggest. [Abbot McCann died early in 1959, when this note was already in print.]

sion into the monasteries of Italy and Spain, which had the greatest repute in the Europe of the day. The monastic authorities of those two countries, sympathetic to the militant flood of the counter-Reformation, which was now at full tide, gave ready support to their projects. It was, however, necessary to obtain direct papal approval and permission for the missionary project. Whatever may have happened in the far-off days of the evangelization of Europe, missionary work by monks, not only 'in the world', but under the extraordinary circumstances of active persecution, had been unheard of for centuries. The request, made by the agents of both the Cassinese and Valladolid Congregations acting independently, was warmly supported by high Roman ecclesiastics, by students of the English College at Rome,[1] and by exiled English laymen, animated both by a love of the traditional monachism and by the desire of opening a door to a body that was not the Society of Jesus. It was at this point that Fr Sigebert Buckley, in his prison at Wisbech, had, all unknowing, an effect on the movement of affairs at Rome.

Somehow, most probably by means of Dr Christopher Bagshawe, a secular priest imprisoned in Wisbech Castle from 1593 onwards, the Italian monks had heard of the old man's existence. Bagshawe, an alumnus of the English College and a correspondent from prison with some of its members, took Buckley to be 'the last survivor of those monks who once lived in Catholic England',[2] and spoke with him as to the prospect of a Catholic and monastic revival 'a thing which he earnestly prayed for with many sighs, as I myself know'.[3] These words occur in a letter to the Spanish Benedictine abbot-general, in which he urged him to continue sending monks to England, and were probably written shortly before the death of Queen Elizabeth, but it is at least very probable that he had, on a previous occasion, passed the news about Buckley on to those at Rome whom he knew to be devising the return of the monks to the English mission. However the information may have come, it was used in the Curia as an argument on behalf of the English Cassinese. The pope was told that there still existed in England a representative of the ancient monastic order to whose sons, sent by St Gregory the Great, that country owed its first faith: the order, therefore, whose very existence was a living testimony to the continuity of that faith and to the antiquity of the Roman

---

1 In particular by Fr Edward Maihew who, when about to go on the English mission as a secular priest, addressed an appeal to the Cassinese abbots printed in *Memorials*, 185–9.

2 Fr Buckley may well have been the last surviving monk of Westminster in 1603, but there was in that year at least one survivor of the Henrician monasteries, the old monk of Evesham named Lyttleton, who was reconciled to the Church by Fr Augustine Bradshaw (*v. supra*, p. 417). What, we may wonder, was his canonical position *vis-à-vis* Fr Buckley when he had been duly absolved from all censures?

3 'Id quod multis cum suspiriis expetiisse eum scio.' The letter from Bagshawe to the General of the Spanish Benedictines was registered for some reason in the acts of the general chapter of 1633 of the English Congregation; so Marron, 'Dom Sigebert Buckley and his Brethren', in *Douai Magazine*, VII, 3 (1933). For Bagshawe, *v.* Gillow, *Dictionary of the English Catholics*.

obedience. It was even said that the advocates used a more personal argument with Clement VIII, who was known to be devoted to the interests of his nephews, the Aldobrandini. If he allowed the ancient family of monks to die out, it was suggested, his own family would also disappear.[1]

Whatever the reasons alleged, the pope gave the required permission, first by word of mouth (1601) and later by formal grant (5 December 1602). Almost immediately afterwards, probably some months or weeks before the death of the queen (24 March), the first monks entered England from Spain; a little later, perhaps in the summer or autumn, those from Italy arrived. These latter made landfall at Yarmouth; shortly before, Fr Buckley had been released by order of the new king from the neighbouring Framlingham Castle, and the new and the old order met at the house of a Norfolk recusant. There, according to Fr Thomas Preston, one of the two, Fr Buckley renewed his monastic vows,[2] and thenceforward the two Cassinese monks provided for the old man's sustenance in the seven years of his long life that remained.[3]

The first stage of the project had now been achieved. The English monks of Italy and Spain were back in England. The second stage still remained to be completed. How were they to achieve a status as a group and to show themselves as the undoubted heirs and successors of the monks of medieval England? These objects, which at first had been regarded in the light of sentiment and prestige in the mission field, seem by this time to have assumed a practical, almost a material importance. When the long reign of Elizabeth I was drawing towards its inevitable close, there came within the purview of the exiles and the schemers, if not of the practical politicians, the vision of an England once more officially restored to the obedience of Rome. Illusory and baneful as the dream may appear to modern eyes, wise after the event and able to survey the whole English scene from the point of vantage of the historian, it was certainly cherished by many of the English exiles and of the English Jesuits, and even found favour in the Roman Curia, and the interested parties began to make arrangements for dividing the lion's skin. Among the possibilities that occurred to all were the restitution of at least some of the monastic property and the problem of the capitular rights of the cathedrals that had once been abbeys or cathedral priories. The Jesuit Persons was strongly of the opinion that the new world would best be served by new methods, and that the Society of Jesus should have a large share in any distribution of property that might take place.[4] It seems clear that by 1603, at least,

1 So Fr Baker, *Treatise*, 170.   2 For this, *v. infra*, p. 450.
3 Letter of Fr Anselm Beech, quoted from B. Weldon, *Collections*, I, 34–5, by Connolly in 'The Buckley Affair', in *DR*, XLIX, 61. Weldon probably had it from the chapter acts of 1633, where the letter is copied.
4 Cf. his *Memorial for the Reformation of England*. This was written in 1596, and a contemporary copy is in the archiepiscopal archives at Westminster; it was printed in London in 1690. Granted that property was likely to be available on a large scale, there was much to be said for Persons's contention, but coming from such a source at such a time it was bound to be controversial.

the question was mooted among the English monks, and it was realized that they would stand in a far stronger position for future bargaining if they could in some way establish a juridical succession between themselves and the English monks of pre-Reformation days.[1] It is possible that various expedients were suggested, and even in time executed. One such may have been the transference of Fr Buckley to the Cassinese allegiance; another, the continuation of Westminster by means of professions made to the old monk in person. At this crisis, the monks from Italy were fortunate in having at their disposal the learning and services of Augustine Baker, a professed monk, not yet a priest, of their congregation, who was at that time living in England for reasons of health. Baker was a lawyer of experience and distinction, and he immediately caught hold of the legal principle that the last survivor of a college or corporation enjoys all the rights and privileges of that body, and can therefore transmit them to others. *Ex hypothesi*, Fr Buckley was the last surviving monk of the old dispensation; he could therefore transmit any rights he might possess to his brethren from Italy. As many of the rights which were then being canvassed belonged to houses other than Westminster, it was clear that Buckley needed to be regarded, not only as a monk of Westminster, but as the last representative of the old English Benedictine body.[2] Fr Baker, for his part, was probably influenced by the conditions of his own day in Italy and Spain and elsewhere. In these countries, recently reformed groups of monasteries existed; these, in order to safeguard their way of life and to prevent the return of old abuses, had delegated to a central governing body many of the rights and powers previously retained by the abbot and community of each house; with them, the Congregation was quite clearly a legal entity, with a life and officers of its own, which could be considered apart from the individual monasteries and as being, in a sense, superior to any one of them. In pre-Reformation England, there had been no organization of this elaborate rigidity. The English monasteries, as we have seen, did indeed apply to themselves the legislation of the Fourth Lateran Council more closely than did those of many other provinces of the Church, and the amalgamation of the two provincial chapters in the fourteenth century had given the meeting a national character, but the conception of a Congregation as a legal entity in its own right was foreign to the thoughts of the monks of the day in England; the organ of union was the chapter, and the abbots-president who executed its decisions and who had certain powers in the intervals between chapters were presidents precisely of the chapter, not of a Congregation; indeed, the latter word was not in use in its technical sense. The visitors, likewise, were appointed by the chapter, not by the presidents, who did not themselves exercise visitatorial powers unless directly authorized. The only institution that did not exist *sui juris* but in common was the house of

1 So Fr Baker, *Treatise*, 171.
2 *Ibid.* 177–9, 180–1; Prichard, *Life of Fr Baker*, 95–6.

studies at Oxford, Gloucester College, and even this was for some time under the aegis of a neighbouring abbey and was in fact a congeries of separately owned lodgings, over which the presidents had only a general right of supervision. No papal bulls or privileges had ever been directed to the chapter as such; it had no titles or privileges in its gift, and such very real privileges as existed for some of the houses, e.g. exemption and immunity, were never regarded as anything but grants to individual monasteries. The medieval Congregation, in short, stood to the post-Reformation Congregation in much the same relationship as the whole Benedictine body of to-day stands to a fully articulated and centralized religious order—as the representative, that is, of an earlier stage in the evolution of a species.

Augustine Baker, at this period of his life, knew nothing of this, and could not have been expected to know it, and he himself tells us that his attempts to elicit information of this kind from Fr Buckley were not successful.[1] It so chanced, however, that just about this time he discovered, written in a copy of Turrecremata which he had bought secondhand, the decrees of the Benedictine general chapter of 1444.[2] Very naturally, and in a sense rightly, he took this as a proof that the monks of England had been organized in a Congregation. Possessed of these ideas and these data, he proceeded to arrange a ceremony to suit the case. Two English priests on the mission, Fr Robert Sadler and Fr Edward Maihew, who had decided to become monks of the Cassinese Congregation and had duly passed through their year of noviciate, were introduced into the presence of Fr Buckley, probably at his lodgings in Clerkenwell, on 21 November 1607.[3]

Despite a mass of evidence and two formal instruments purporting to be issued by Fr Buckley himself, one of which has notarial attestation, it is not at all clear what precisely took place.[4] If we take the solemn declaration, running in the name of Fr Buckley but clearly drawn up for him by a notary, we learn that the two priests, Sadler and Maihew, already professed members of the Cassinese Congregation, were 'received and admitted as brethren and monks of Westminster and of the Congregation of England...[and were granted] all rights, privileges, ranks, honours, liberties and graces which in times past the monks professed and dwelling in the said monastery did enjoy'.[5] A legal document is not an historical

---

1 Prichard, *Life of Fr Baker*, 95–6: 'He therefore undertook the business to git out of the old man all knowledg of the rights, manners, customs and whole state of the Benedictine monachism in England, under Queen Mary, and other knowledges also of elder times.... But indeed I have heard him complain, that the old man was through age much decayed in all respects, and especially in his memory.'

2 Baker, *Treatise*, 180.

3 *Ibid.* 181, where Fr Baker, writing of this period, speaks of visiting Fr Buckley at 'his lodgings at St Johns his', i.e. St Johns, Clerkenwell.

4 For a discussion, careful but involved, *v.* Connolly, 'The Buckley Affair'.

5 Connolly, *art. cit.* 51–2, from C. Reyner, *Apostolatus Benedictinorum in Anglia*, Script. 1.

narrative. Of its very nature it retails an event or series of events with the intention of establishing a particular right or claim. It is, so to say, the film that is shown to the public; it is a photographic record of actions that took place, but many other actions may have taken place which it does not record. So it is with what has been called 'the Buckley affair'. There is more than one indication, if the parallel already used may be extended, that 'shots' were made which were afterwards discarded or suppressed. In the first place, Fr Maihew has two stories to tell. In a semi-official account written some years later he repeats almost exactly the declaration of Buckley.[1] Elsewhere, however, he tells us that Fr Buckley received the profession of one monk for his own abbey of Westminster, and it seems certain by a process of exclusion and inference that this was none other than Fr Maihew himself.[2] On the other hand, it was later alleged, on the authority of Fr Thomas Preston, the acting superior of the Cassinese monks in England, that Buckley, at his first meeting in Norfolk with Fr Preston and Fr Beech, renewed his monastic profession to them with the purpose of joining the Cassinese Congregation himself.[3] No historian has hitherto succeeded in resolving these apparent contradictions satisfactorily, and it may be noted that a well-informed contemporary writer hints that mistakes were made; probably here lies the key of the matter.[4] In corroboration of Fr Maihew's second version of the story, it should perhaps be emphasized that the *corpora vilia*, so to say, of the day at Clerkenwell were two men who had not yet made their monastic profession. It seems a legitimate inference that they had been chosen in order that they might take their vows for Westminster and so form a nucleus of the reborn English Congregation, even if in the event they made their profession for the Cassinese Congregation and were only subsequently aggregated to Westminster.

For in fact two objects were being pursued: the perpetuation of the English Congregation, now represented only by Fr Buckley, and the

1 Connolly, *art. cit.* 56, from E. Maihew, *Trophaea*, tom. II, p. 387.
2 Connolly, *art. cit.* 54, from *Trophaea*, I, 141–4.
3 The statement occurs in a rare controversial book, *Strena Catholica, seu explicatio . . . novi Fidelitatis Juramenti. Ab E. I. Sacrae Theologiae studioso composita. Apud B. Fabum. Augustae 1620.* The imprint is almost certainly a fabrication. Dom Thomas Preston, the author (1563–1640), wrote also under his alias of Roger Widdrington. He was a self-opinionated and quarrelsome person, who developed a strong bias against the revived English Congregation, and his book on the Oath was ultimately placed on the Index. This story of Buckley was used by John Barnes in his *Examen Trophaeorum* (1622) and is also found in an unpublished *narratio* delivered to the Nuncio Cardinal di Spada c. 1625–6 (Vatican archives, Francia, 412) which contains also comments by Dom John Barnes and answers by Dom Clement Reyner. The truth of the story remains a little doubtful; it seems probable that Buckley made some sort of profession to Preston, and probable also that this was not taken at the time to be a transfer of rights, though whether canonically it was so is another matter. It is difficult to understand the powers given to the Cassinese monks by Fr Buckley in 1607 save on the assumption that they were already in some way his confrères.
4 Prichard, *Life of Fr Baker*, 96: 'And as for those things, that seemed to have been done by them [*sc.* the English Cassinese monks] unskilfully or less legally . . . I dare say they were done without, or against, his counsell.'

continuance of its supposed rights, of which he was the sole depository. The rights, whether personal or corporate, could presumably have been transferred by him to another Congregation, such as the Cassinese, but if the English Congregation itself were to be perpetuated it was necessary to have a body of monks, if not an actually existing monastic family, to form the nucleus. In the present case, therefore, a group of men was needed to perpetuate both Westminster Abbey and the English Congregation; this might conceivably be effected either by the aggregation to Westminster of those professed already for other houses, or by fresh professions for Westminster itself, and there seems to be evidence that what actually took place was either a mixture or the sum of both methods.

The original intention may well have been for the two priests, Maihew and Sadler, to make their profession to Fr Buckley in order to secure, so to say, the 'apostolic succession' from the English monks by receiving the habit from him. Then Augustine Baker may have doubted either the validity or the wisdom of this course. In any case, it was in the end decided to stand upon the platform of aggregation, and steps were taken to facilitate a speedy multiplication of monks within the revived Westminster. Fr Buckley therefore appointed four Cassinese monks as his delegates to receive any whom they might choose. This is another strange feature of the business, for none of these delegates became a member of the English Congregation, and none in fact exercised his right of aggregation, which expired with the death of Buckley two years later. [1] Subsequent aggregations were made by the three new Westminster monks, the third being Augustine Baker himself whom Fr Buckley received after the original two.

Though accomplished with such care, recorded with such solemnity and subsequently ratified (though with all due caution) by Rome,[2] the Buckley affair in fact bristles with problems, both of fact and law. First of all, it is doubtful whether the medieval 'Congregation' had any rights, etc., as distinct from the rights of the individual houses, just as at the present day it would be hard to say what rights the Benedictine 'order' possesses as distinct from the houses and Congregations of which it is composed. In particular, the right which the revived Congregation came most eagerly to maintain, the right, that is, of supplying monastic chapters to so many

1 The four delegates were Frs Thomas Preston, Augustine Smith, Anselm Beech and Maurus Taylor. According to the *Apostolatus*, Script. v, there were only three professed monks of the English Congregation on 14 December 1609. No aggregations had therefore been made.

2 The brief *Cum sicut accepimus* of Paul V, after stating that Fr Buckley had imparted to Frs Sadler and Maihew '*as far as he could*, the rights, privileges, dignities, etc., of Westminster and of the Benedictine Order in England', goes on to decree that 'the aforesaid Congregation of England and its rights, privileges, dignities, etc., do truly and really subsist in the aforesaid English monks thus aggregated, *according as they subsisted in the said Congregation of England* at the time of such admission and concession and not otherwise'. (Translation by Connolly; I have added the italics.) Were the Roman canonists thinking of the Bull *Praeclara*, or of the questionable existence of the ancient Congregation?

cathedrals, was never in pre-Reformation days regarded as having anything to do with the chapter and the presidents: in fact, the cathedral priory of Canterbury steadfastly and successfully refused to belong to the chapter precisely because of its superior position as chapter to the primate. Next, it would seem certain that the old English 'Congregation' came to an end before the refoundation of Westminster. If it had not become extinct by the implied consent of all its component members to the abolition of the monastic life in England, it is hard to see how it could have survived Pole's legatine Dispensation, confirmed by the bull *Praeclara*, which effectively decreed the non-existence of all the religious houses of England. Thirdly, it is not at all clear that an English Congregation, old or new, came into being with the refoundation of Westminster. Both the pre-Reformation 'Congregation' and the recent Congregations were by definition and decree a gathering of many together, and it is hard to see how a single house, which was itself a fresh start, could have this collective or representative character. Moreover, Pole's intention, known to all at the time, was probably some sort of alliance with, or imitation of, the Cassinese Congregation. Finally, even if there had been continuity from 1540 to 1603 over the gulf of the Reformation and counter-Reformation, what were the rights and privileges to be transmitted? It is difficult to see that Fr Buckley could transmit anything save the basic canonical rights of a single house—Westminster—together with the real but barren right to be a member of any English Congregation that might come into being. In the event, no attempt was made to assert even such a fundamental right as that of Westminster monks to a house possessing the abbatial status.

As things turned out, and for all practical and canonical purposes, the end which Fr Baker and his associates hoped to attain by means of Fr Buckley was secured beyond question by the papal brief *Ex incumbenti* of Paul V (23 August 1619).[1] In this the pope united the restored English Benedictine Congregation and the larger body of English monks of the

---

[1] The brief *Ex incumbenti* of 23 August 1619 has been called by Dom Connolly 'the foundation-charter of the present English Benedictine Congregation'. The new Congregation, it is there stated, is a coalition between the monks aggregated to the English Congregation by Fr Buckley and the English monks of the Spanish Congregation who elect to join with them: 'monachi Anglici... Congregationis Hispanicae et Anglicanae coalescerent ita ut per hanc coalitionem et corpus sic unitum continuaretur, et restauraretur, ac si opus esset de novo erigeretur, antiqua Congregatio Anglicana Ordinis S. Benedicti'. The brief is here confirming, in identical terms, what was asked for by the Paris Definitory of the English monks in 1617, and Fr Leander (Jones) of St Martin, the principal framer of their request, explains in his *Apostolatus* (Tract III, pp. 180–1) the meaning of the Latin passage cited above. Three alternatives were expressed: (a) if the old English Congregation has been in fact preserved, without interruption, in the person of Fr Buckley, it shall be *continued*; (b) if it has suffered interruption through the schism it shall be *restored*; (c) if there had never been an English Congregation, now, at least, *it shall be erected*. Further on, the brief refers to 'the ancient English Congregation of the same Order, *or the same Order in England*' (italics mine), thus once more safeguarding the rights granted, if indeed there never had been an ancient Congregation. The same *caveat* is repeated in the Bull *Plantata* of 1633. In other words, the first fathers were not prepared to stake all their hopes upon Fr Baker's reading of history and the Buckley succession.

Spanish Congregation into a single body which he declared to be 'a continuation and restoration and (if necessary) a re-erection of the English Benedictine Congregation', and he conceded to this body the enjoyment of all 'privileges, graces, indults, faculties', etc., which the English Congregation, or the Benedictine Order in England, had been granted in the past; if need be, they were now granted anew.

As for the Westminster succession, this had been allowed to fall into the background and disappear when four autonomous priories of English monks came into being, viz. St Gregory's at Douai (1606), St Laurence's at Dieulouard (1608), St Benedict's at St Malo (1611) and St Edmund's in Paris (1615), of which the third disappeared, while the first, second and fourth are now represented by the abbeys of Downside, Ampleforth and Douai (Woolhampton). At the union of 1617 that marked the permanent union, after several failures, of all those desiring independence from continental Congregations, it was expressly enjoined that the merger between the 'English Congregation' [i.e. the aggregated 'Westminster monks'] and the English members of the Spanish Congregation should be complete, and in fact the 'Westminster' monks never subsequently formed a house by themselves or considered themselves as standing apart from the rest.[1] When once the four houses had been established, all professions were made in the normal Benedictine way, and the monk became a member of the existing monastery in which he took his vows. Dieulouard, indeed, after 1612–13 came to count as its sons most, if not all, of the thirty-odd monks who were accounted members of the 'English Congregation' (i.e. who had been aggregated to Westminster) at the time of the union of 1617, and in the general chapter of 1621, in which the four monasteries were 'appropriated' to four celebrated medieval abbeys, Dieulouard was naturally allotted to Westminster. This, however, was properly speaking a lien on the future, not on the past; it had no practical or legal effect, nor did St Laurence's claim to preserve anything of the spirit or customs of Fr Buckley's old home. Dieulouard, canonically speaking, was not Westminster *redivivus*, nor a filiation of Westminster; the direct link was personal to the group that had been 'aggregated', and when the last of these, Fr Richard Huddleston, died in 1655[2] the link that remained was precious indeed, but one of sentiment only.

The 'Buckley affair', which in its historical setting is so difficult to analyse, became almost immediately something of a myth, attracting to itself picturesque addition. One detail, indeed, is not mythical. The

1 Had the first project been carried through to its logical issue, viz. that of simply perpetuating the line of the old monasticism through Fr Buckley, the result would have been purely and simply a revived Westminster. As it was, the desire to perpetuate the *congregation* with all its supposed rights, and the necessity of a coalition with members of duly founded houses in those houses, led to the submergence of the Westminster identity and individuality, if indeed it had ever been conceived as existing apart, so to say, from its congregational quality. Any attempt to describe this complicated phase of monastic history must take account of the contemporary 'climate' and prepossessions.

2 *Memorials of Fr Baker*, 238.

aggregation had taken place on the feast of the Presentation of the Blessed Virgin, 21 November, which, as has been noted in its place, was the accepted date of the refoundation of Westminster in 1556. This passed unnoticed at the time, but Fr Maihew subsequently made much of it,[1] and the day has since been celebrated by the Congregation as its *dies memorabilis*. But if the date is historical, the location of the act within the Gatehouse prison, current in many modern accounts, is almost certainly mythical. There is no evidence, and little likelihood, that Fr Buckley was again in prison after his release in 1603,[2] and none of the eyewitnesses of the ceremony remarks either on his captivity, or the name of his prison. While it is conceivable that the parties repaired of set purpose to the precinct of the Abbey, it would be surprising that none of them should note the circumstance if it had been a deliberate move. Finally, the worthy but unromantic figure of Fr Buckley himself has received poetic treatment. Dr Bagshawe may have had grounds for seeing him ready to meet death 'with Holy Simeon's joy because he has seen his Order reviving once again'; Fr Maihew, who had an eye for the dramatic, took the matter further by remarking that the sight of the old man, which had long been failing, was extinguished forever immediately after he had seen his sons before him.[3] Fr Buckley was certainly blind two years later,[4] and there is nothing to suggest that he was already sightless in early November 1607, so that we may perhaps accept Fr Maihew's statement if we remove from it the hint of a marvel. It was left for an orator of yesterday to picture the old man as seeing with the inward eye the line of his progeny, like Banquo's issue, stretching to the crack of doom:

> He saw: but blasted with excess of light,
> Closed his eyes in endless night.[5]

Seen more soberly in the contemporary Jacobean daylight, the meeting of late November appears as a moment laden with little of either romantic or spiritual significance. Neither Maihew nor Baker had illusions as to the shortcomings of the old English monks[6] or the limitations of

1 Maihew, *Trophaea*, II, 377, cited by Connolly in 'The Buckley Affair', 57.
2 Fr Anselm Beech, in a letter cited by Connolly, *art. cit.* 61, from Weldon, *Collections*, I, 34–5, writes: 'From that time [i.e. 1603] Dom Thomas Preston and I took care of the old man till his happy death, which took place on the 22 February in the year 1610.' This rather loose statement—for Fr Beech was out of England for a considerable part of the time —would certainly seem to exclude the possibility of a term of imprisonment.
3 *Trophaea*, II, 377, cited as above (n. 1): 'When this work was completed, immediately he became blind.' Fr Maihew goes on to testify that Fr Buckley could see on 21 November 1607, but he does not state precisely how soon afterwards he lost his sight.
4 He signs the declaration of 15 December 1609, as a blind man: 'Nomen meum subscribo, quantum ab homine caeco fieri potest' (Reyner, *Apostolatus*, Script. IV Appendicis, prima pars, p. 4).
5 Gray's allusion to Milton was applied to Buckley in 1914 by the then Bishop of Clifton, George Ambrose Burton, when preaching at Downside on the occasion of the centenary of St Gregory's settlement on that site.
6 Maihew's opinion is in the epistle dedicatory of the *Trophaea* (I, vii–xv). Fr Baker's is in several passages of his *Treatise*, e.g. 181–2.

THE OLD AND THE NEW

Fr Buckley himself; they were indeed concerned not so much with a spiritual heritage and a solemn covenant as with the transmission of valuable and tangible privileges and rights. Yet even so it was a memorable day in the age which to us is Shakespeare's. Six days after that meeting in Clerkenwell a scribe was to enter the first performance of *King Lear* in the Stationers' Register, and the dramatist had within a few weeks or months passed *Antony and Cleopatra* to the players. Augustine Baker, who himself had been a playgoer fifteen years earlier, may have known something of this, but he had other thoughts now—'for every man hath business and desire'—and he, like Hamlet, had turned to prayer. Fr Buckley, half blind and a little dazed in his wits, was yet a 'venerable peice of antiquity'.[1] Though he had been a monk of Westminster for so short a space he had never denied his vows or his priesthood. For more than forty years, in prisons often, in cold and in weariness, he had kept the faith. Nor were his visitors ordinary men. Fr Maihew, to whose energy and determination the success of the appeal to Rome and the entry of the monks upon the mission was largely due, was a notable scholar who left a worthy monument in his *Trophaea*, and a monument of another and a more durable kind in the tradition of bracing austerity and firm discipline that he transmitted to his monastery of Dieulouard. Even more remarkable was the master of ceremonies. Lawyer, scholar and monk, though not yet priest, Augustine Baker had not at this time fully realized what was to be his vocation. Only a little above thirty years old, with his trim beard and doublet and hose, he had not yet become that intense and solitary counsellor who could send to the cloister the brother and sisters of Falkland, and Hugh Cressy himself; who could guide Dame Gertrude More so firmly and so wisely; who could give comfort to so many, and yet meet with such opposition and enmity among those of his own household. He was not yet 'that mysterious man'

> Whose secret life and published Writings prove,
> To pray is not to talke, or thinke, but love.[2]

He was to become one of the greatest masters of the life of the spirit of a great age, and to transmit all that was best in the teaching of medieval England to his countrymen in the seventeenth century and to the modern world. It was fitting that he should have been one of the three to receive the succession of Westminster from the old monk, and thus to be one of the founders of the English Congregation, for he had a true understanding of the nature and demands of the life that Abbot Isaac and John Cassian and St Benedict himself had led, and his words will ever remain to challenge and to stir, to repel or to attract, his readers; words of eternal life, that the thoughts of many hearts may be revealed.

1 The phrase and spelling are Fr Prichard's in his *Life of Father Baker*, 95.
2 From the verses by Fr Leander Norminton on the page following the title-page of *Sancta Sophia* (2nd ed.).

CHAPTER XXXVI

EPILOGUE

At the conclusion of a work that has presented the history of the monastic order and of the religious orders in England from the revival of the tenth century to the dissolution of the monasteries almost exactly six centuries later, it is natural to look back upon the path that has been traversed, as climbers might look back upon the silhouette of an *arête*.

Before doing so, we should do well to remind ourselves that the monastic way of life, to which all the medieval religious orders were assimilated in greater or less degree, had been in existence for more than six centuries before the age of Dunstan, and continued to flourish in Catholic countries during and after the age of the Reformation. Indeed, in the previous chapter we have seen how the last spark of the old fire remained in this country to be merged in the new flame. The monasticism of the counter-Reformation had in its turn an eclipse in the age of enlightenment and revolution; it witnessed a third spring in the nineteenth century and still flourishes; indeed, it has expanded yearly even while these volumes have been in the writing.

Yet for all this, the assumption of English antiquarians and historians in the past, that monasticism was something medieval, and had passed 'like the baseless fabric of a vision' with the medieval world, had in it a part, at least, of the truth. Monasticism as an integral part of society, and as an economic and cultural factor of the first importance, was a specific element in the medieval world between the decline of the Roman empire and the Reformation: as such it passed wherever and whenever the medieval framework disappeared, and it is hard to see how it could ever again come to take such a place in society, save perhaps in a comparable state of utter disruption and depopulation following upon the collapse of a world civilization of which Christianity was the only surviving element. Much of what has been written in the past of medieval monasticism has indeed been vitiated by a failure to realize that it had within it elements that were temporary together with those that were permanent, and while Catholic and romantic writers have confused social, cultural or institutional features of medieval monasticism with the religious life in itself, Protestant and secularist historians have often treated the permanent, essential elements as if they were as perishable as the medieval garments in which they were clothed. Only if this distinction is borne in mind can it be seen how the purely religious and spiritual institute, such as was conceived by a Cassian, a Benedict, a Columba, or a Bede, was caught up into the very fabric of a continental society, of which it became and remained for many centuries a wealthy, powerful and even a dominant part.

When Dunstan and his companions initiated a great revival in England, society throughout western Europe was in need of, and docile to, spiritual and intellectual leadership. Monks, and monks principally and often monks alone, were the repositories of religious doctrine and educational opportunities; in consequence, they multiplied exceedingly, and rapidly attained an economic as well as a religious and cultural supremacy, and it was natural and inevitable that society outside the walls of a monastery should look to it for its spiritual leaders and receive from them an imprint of their own qualities. During the eleventh and the greater part of the twelfth centuries monasticism reached its peak of influence and dynamic force at Cluny and Cîteaux, and its light was focused upon Christendom by a Lanfranc and a Bernard, by a Gregory VII and a Eugenius III. If it was something of a rhetorical exaggeration to say, as contemporaries said, that the world had become one great Cîteaux, it was but the bare truth to say that the whole Western Church had received such an infusion of the monastic spirit as to colour its whole spiritual and devotional life.

The material result of this was seen in the numberless religious foundations, in the vast and ever-increasing army of monks and *conversi*, in the great buildings that began to dominate the landscape and the rich estates controlled by the monks. From being in the early eleventh century primarily a religious and an educational force, they became towards its end, both by force of numbers, by virtue of their appeal to all classes, and by sheer economic weight as landlords (and somewhat later as producers) an immense social power. It should perhaps be added, that the character and outlook of the older monastic and canonical orders deprived their power of any political force, even within the sphere of ecclesiastical policy. The medieval monks never became, as did the Byzantine monks on occasion, and religious orders in later times, a 'pressure group' or a party within the Church.

The 'Benedictine centuries' are generally thought to have ended with the death of St Bernard in 1153. Thenceforward, while on the one hand the monarchies of France and England were consolidating their power and developing their judicial and financial control of their people, while the Church, centred upon the papacy, was perfecting a legal and financial system, and an extensive bureaucracy of its own, the intellectual life of Europe was shifting from the monasteries to the cathedral schools and the young universities. Concurrently, the growth of population, the increase of trade, and the expansion of all forms of agrarian exploitation were lessening the relative importance of the monasteries in almost every region. For a time, indeed, the tendencies of the age were masked by the emergence and wide diffusion of the friars, who seemed to contemporaries (what indeed they set out in part to be) the ultimate issue of the monastic spirit, the communication of the religious life to the last groups hitherto untouched by it, the urban populations and the poor throughout the land. In fact, however, the friars dealt a heavy blow to monastic prestige, at first by outbidding the monks in fervour, then by draining many of the reservoirs of talent and virtue that would otherwise have served the older orders, next by giving an entirely new challenge to the monks by their intellectual celebrity, and finally by attracting so many recruits, good, bad and indifferent that the edge of their ideal was blunted, and in course of time, both by their direct opposition to the monks and by the criticisms which they themselves incurred, they became the weakest and most vulnerable corps in the army of the religious. All orders, in fact, had in the days of expansion gone beyond the frontiers that could be permanently held. Already in the late thirteenth century the numbers of monks and canons were slowly diminishing; those of the friars reached their peak about 1300, when both the number of religious establishments in the country and the population within them touched a high-water mark which was never again to be attained or even approached.

Indeed, from about the middle of the thirteenth century the old orders of monks and canons were losing their commanding position in medieval society. They had ceased for some time both to be a dynamic, formative element, and to be regarded as the upholders of Christendom by their prayers and penances; they had hardened into what was merely a constituent part of the national life, half religious, half economic, alongside of the landowners, great and small, and the growing craft and commercial interests of the towns. In a society still conventionally, and in part actually, dominated by religious modes of thought they were regarded as an essential part of the body politic, just as the friars were still indispensable in the schools and pulpits, and if their social function of intercession was no longer reckoned important, individuals still hoped to benefit by their prayers and Masses, nor were they as yet (1350) seriously regarded as unprofitable proprietors of desirable lands. Towards the end of the fourteenth century, in fact, they attained within their walls an architectural and material splendour greater than ever before, and in the artificial society and new-won wealth of the decades of war with France and domestic intrigues among the great families they, or at least the greater ones among them, were a kind of extension of the contemporary world of chivalry.

Thereafter, when that world faded and was succeeded by a world in which money and property meant everything, and in which deep intellectual or spiritual interests were wanting, a world which was shortly to be shaken by the impact of new doctrines and new ideals, the monasteries and religious orders in general receded more and more from the forefront of society. Though those who uttered their criticisms of the monks were perhaps neither many nor influential, there was a new feeling of resentment abroad. The monks were accused of sloth, and of being the drones of the community; those who leased or managed their lands were land-hungry, and the slow but significant growth of population and mercantile wealth put a new pressure upon the land market. Though there was little increase in the aggregate wealth of the religious and little change in the use they made of it or in their own habit of life, a feeling was abroad that great revenues were being used selfishly or aimlessly. Few of those who felt thus had any programme for a better distribution or use of wealth, and in the event the transference of property at the Dissolution did not to any significant extent benefit other religious, educational or charitable institutes, or assist impoverished classes; no social injustice was in fact remedied or any national end served. Nevertheless, in the last decades before the end the new generation of gentry and government servants lacked altogether the conservative reverence towards the Church that had prevailed a century earlier. As for the friars, though they held no property of any value and were probably living on a bare subsistence income from charity past and present, they also were accused of draining the country's wealth.

While the social and economic position of the religious was thus changing and ultimately deteriorating, the energy and spirit within the Orders were following something of the same curve. In the two centuries that followed the revival under Dunstan the monks had an ideal and a message which both they and those around them could see and appreciate. The monastic and the canonical life was a clearly defined, severely disciplined one of prayer and work, sufficiently austere to inspire respect in those outside and to produce the fruits of the gospel promises in those who followed it with perseverance. The careful reader of the *Regularis Concordia*, of Lanfranc's monastic constitutions and of the early Cistercian constitutions cannot fail to perceive that these documents were composed to be followed, and that a life based upon them would have been not unworthy of the ideals of the gospel; it would have been a life only comprehensible or defensible on the supposition of the truth of the Christian revelation, a life in which natural human satisfactions, interests and activities were abandoned by those who believed that they had here no lasting city, but sought one to come. This high endeavour was reiterated and emphasized by the manifestos of the new Orders of the twelfth century, and again by the early friars of the thirteenth, and despite the failures, the scandals, and the criticisms of the age it is probable that even as late as the middle of the thirteenth century the religious life in all its forms was normally maintained in its essentials at most of the larger conventual houses. In the fourteenth century, however, changes were made in the tenor and structure of the life which materially affected its character. The frequentation of the universities, the increased part taken by a greater number of officials in administering the estates and funds, the mitigation of the Rule in the matter of meat-eating, the introduction of periods of relaxation and excursion, of holidays and of pocket-money, seriously altered the rhythm of life for the majority of the adult community. Further changes, unauthorized by any legislation, but arising when the bonds of discipline were loosed by the Great Schism, gave numerous individuals exceptions and privileges of all kinds which lowered still further what may be called the normal spiritual temperature of the house. While it was no doubt still possible for an individual to live a strict and holy life, he could only do so by refusing in practice to take advantage of relaxations or to solicit any favours. Whereas the monk in private place of the early twelfth century would have needed to take deliberate action to escape the full regular life, the monk of the late fourteenth century would have needed equal determination to remain within its ambit. Finally, in the last fifty years before the end, though no further official mitigations of observance took place, an indefinable spiritual rusticity took hold of a majority of the houses; recruits expected and even demanded the normal amenities of the day—the wage-system, official privilege, regular times of holiday, and the rest. With the exception of the Carthusians, the Bridgettines and the Observant Franciscans, the religious life in England was humanly speaking easier and less spiritually stimulating in 1530 than it had been a century earlier.

What, we may ask, were the causes of this, and at what point in the long story did the religious orders miss their way, or at least begin to stray down the primrose path whence a return to the ascent of the mountain was hard if not impossible? A general answer, and one true within very wide limits, would be that the religious throughout these centuries did but follow the general rhythm of Christendom. Not only upon the monks, but upon the higher and lower clergy and perhaps even upon the layfolk religious convention made less austere demands in 1530 than it had done in 1100. The penal and penitential discipline, the precepts of fasting, the strictness of overhead control, the levels of comfort and wealth had all moved in the direction of mitigation, and there had been no compensatory developments of sacramental devotion, preaching, social works of charity or private methods of prayer such as become so common among all classes and all confessions in the latter part of the sixteenth century. When all allowances and reservations have been made, we must still say that the Church throughout Europe was at a lower level of discipline and observance, and exhibited more symptoms of mental and moral sickness than at any time since the Gregorian reform. Though England on the whole showed less alarming signs of decline than most of the continental countries it is certain that here, too, the faith and charity of many were cold and that, if a phrase used on an earlier page may be repeated, the Catholic religion was being reduced to its lowest terms. If this was true of the whole body ecclesiastic, it could not but be so with the religious orders, which were now nothing if not racy of the soil.

If, however, we insist on asking what were the contributory factors to this decline within the Orders themselves, and what their responsibility, the following considerations may be proposed.

There was, first, the great wealth of the religious and (what is another aspect of the same circumstance) the vast number of their houses. The wealth, indeed, they shared with all other ecclesiastical institutions, with bishoprics, benefices, chapters and the Curia itself. It had come to them in the first place unasked, and it had grown to vast dimensions partly by natural increase and economic development, and partly by prudent administration, but in the long run it had been a prime cause of spiritual weakness to the monasteries as to all the ministers and organs of the Church, great and small. It was not necessary for the proper functioning of the monastic life, and it was the parent of luxury, of strife and of worldliness. Yet it clung like pitch, if only because no individual or group of individuals could in fact do anything to rid themselves of it. Nothing but a completely fresh start, or a social revolution, could have changed things. The numbers also had come unasked, and every age has taught anew the lesson which no institution has been willing to learn, that in the long run quality fluctuates in inverse relation to quantity. Even the wisest of saints have been unable to decide when the duty of preserving a precious heritage takes precedence over the duty of offering a spiritual treasure freely to all. In fact, saturation point had been reached in England even in the century of greatest fervour; there were not enough true vocations to go round; and the religious life became gradually and insensibly an occupation, an apprenticeship to a craft, rather than a 'conversion' or a dedication to the service of God and the imitation of Christ.

In addition to these general sources of weakness, there were others that affected the black monks most, and others through sympathy or imitation. There was, first of all, what may be called the original sin of English black monk polity after the Conquest: the feudal ties of the heads of houses, of which a sequel, if not a result, was the immersion of the abbots in affairs external to their abbey, together with their gradual separation, physical, financial and psychological, from their monks, and their consequent inability to stand to their sons in the only true relationship, that of spiritual fatherhood and mutual love. Like the theological condition from which the metaphor has been taken, this situation was no fault of the individual, and it could be overcome to a greater or less degree, but never fully. The medieval abbot could not be among his monks as one that served. This defect passed also by kinship or inheritance to the other orders, such as the Cistercians, who were founded in free alms. There too, though less markedly, the abbot acquired a state apart from his monks, and it was the status of the black monk abbots which gave rise to the convenient legal fiction that the abbot was the proprietor of his abbey: a concept that weighed heavily in favour of a sitting abbot when deposition was mooted, that ensured for a quondam an establishment of his own, that in the final cataclysm gave a superior a pension often larger than that of all his subjects put together, and that allowed the legal chicanery by which the abbey of a treasonable superior was held to escheat to the Crown.

Of quite another kind was a weakness that was a misfortune rather than a fault. Throughout the Benedictine centuries the basic employment of the monks of the cloister had been the making and decorating of books. Once granted that agricultural and craft work was not for priests, this was an ideal employment. It was necessary for the continuance of the daily life, liturgical, spiritual, intellectual and administrative; it was in itself often either mentally or devotionally satisfying; by including all the processes of book manufacture and ornament it made use of various talents; it could be taken up and laid down again and again without hurt or loss; it furnished a literature for the whole of the educated class and in its finest forms it gave full scope for artistic talent of the very highest order. Moreover, it was an easy transition from the copying of literary masterpieces and biographies to pass to the imitation of their style and to original composition. But from the middle of the thirteenth century its unique position was assailed. Writing of all kinds was now a common attainment and a lucrative employment outside the monastery, and in the more settled and complex conditions of life scribes and artists, clerical and even secular, began to compete with and even to supplant the claustral writer and illuminator. Writing in the monastery became more utilitarian and for domestic ends, till in the late fifteenth century it was a fossilized and artificial occupation from which the sense of urgency and of achievement had disappeared. No substitute occurred to take its place; indeed, no perfect substitute has been found to this day. In the monasteries of the counter-Reformation teaching and works of theology and scholarship were pursued as the normal monastic employment, but nothing has been found to fit all types of ability, while these and all alternatives imply sooner or later frequent physical absence from the cloister and considerable distraction of life which tells against monastic recollection and solitude. One of the troubles in monasteries in the late fifteenth century was undoubtedly the absence of satisfactory and satisfying occupation.

Another disability came from the lack of a spiritual doctrine, an *ascèse* to fit the changing world. In the simpler and more silent world of the Benedictine centuries a meditative reading of the Scriptures and the Fathers, and the liturgical prayer in choir were able almost alone to mould the character and spirit and lead it to recollection and prayer. The rise of the schools and the training in law and dialectic gradually increased all mental activity while at the same time life in the monastery itself became less remote and more distracted. A new spiritual approach was needed to supplement the training given by exercises in deportment, by the customs of the house, by Victorine doctrine, and by the memorizing of the psalter, but it was not forthcoming. The monks made little use either .of the scholastic analysis of the acquired and infused virtues or of the later and fuller teaching of the mystics of Germany and Flanders or of the still later *devotio moderna* of the Brethren of the Common Life. To the end they seem to have preserved a ghost of the method, or lack of method, of a simpler age, and in practice this implied the lack of any personal training or direction in the ascetic and spiritual life for the individual during the later Middle Ages. Not until the days of the great Spaniards, Franciscans, Carmelites and Jesuits, was the monastic world recalled to the cultivation by the individual of the life of prayer, and given the instruction fitted to a generation familiar with the printed book and the formal method.

Yet if some of the ills of the religious were due to misfortune, they cannot escape all responsibility for others. Of these three perhaps were primary causes of the decline in fervour: the escape from the common life made easy and normal by the proliferation of the obedientiary system, by which the single procurator of the Rule was replaced by numerous officials and sub-officials charged with the administration of estates and funds; the gradual relaxation of the prescriptions of the Rule in the matter of fasting and abstinence, a relaxation not in itself directly evil but indicative of a weakness of faith and spiritual purpose; and, most corrosive of all, the introduction of private ownership and privilege and exemption in numberless occasions of daily life. Small and apparently trivial as all these mitigations may have seemed when regarded individually, and negligible as may have been their effect on this or that fervent individual, they nevertheless despiritualized the whole life of the house, divorced common practice from the precepts of the Rule, and reduced the monk's life from that of a school of the service of God to that of a tolerably easy-going collegiate body. Though an earnest individual under such circumstances might lead an edifying existence, the life as such was no longer of itself a means of sanctification, a way of perfection, a following of Christ.

The friars must be considered apart from the possessioners in any estimate, for their problems were not the same and they present peculiar difficulties to the historian. As they were liable to frequent transference from house to house, we cannot regard any friary as having a moral or spiritual character of its own; moreover, we know next to nothing of any community at any time save for the friaries of Oxford, Cambridge, London and perhaps Canterbury. Certainly what little we know suggests that the friars were intellectually more restless and susceptible of external influence than the monks, and that the rank and file up and down the country had a narrower background and were of simpler, perhaps of coarser, fibre. There is no clear evidence that the four orders differed greatly among themselves in discipline or characteristics, though there are suggestions that the Dominicans were mentally the most alert. As we have seen, the Roman committee of reform was for extinguishing altogether the conventual or unreformed branches of the Orders, particularly the Franciscan, which was very numerous in Italy. Clearly the friars of all the orders were too numerous in England for good governance, but there is no clear evidence that a large majority were undisciplined beyond all hope. The real difficulty would have been to find for them a focus and agency of reform.

With all these weaknesses and handicaps the English monks and friars had the hard fate of remaining untouched by any reforming hand, any breath of the creative Spirit. From the mid-thirteenth century onwards there was a dearth of founders and saints in England. No new orders like the Servites, no new branch like the Minims or the Carmelite nuns, no reform like that of the Celestines or the Olivetans appeared; no saint arose such as the Catherines of Siena and Genoa, no mystics like Suso and Ruysbroeck, no preachers like Bernardine, Antoninus or John Capistran. The religious of England, separated from the rest of Europe by the sea, by the Hundred Years War, and by nationalist sentiment, produced no champion of their own to renew their youth. The later monastic reforms, several of which, instinct with new life, antedated the Reformation by many years, such as those of S. Giustina di Padova, Bursfelde and Hirschau, and the reforms of the canons and friars, such as Windesheim and the reformed Carmel of Rubeo, together with the Minims and Colettines of France, did not penetrate to this country. Here the old machinery still ran on, though the rhythm was gradually slackening.

The foregoing pages may seem to some readers to be nothing but

> a melancholy tale of things
> Done long ago, and ill done.

They may feel that the splendours of the dawn and noonday have done no more than serve as an introduction to the description of a falling day and lengthening shades. No historian would claim that his picture can adequately reflect the myriad colours of the past, and he may easily falsify its light or its gloom, but it is only right to remember that in the three hundred years before the Reformation the fortunes of monasticism followed those of the whole Western Church. The writer of to-day, aware as he is of the catastrophes and revolutions of the sixteenth century, is justified in seeking to trace in its main lines the gradual deterioration of quality in the institutions and methods and practices of external church life, and in pointing to the abuses of the Curia, to the luxury and venality of Avignon, to the rivalries and jealousies of the Schism, and to the worldliness and ambitions of the popes of the Renaissance, as symptoms and causes of the sickness that attacked head and members. In so doing he does not forget or deny the existence of upright and saintly men and women at Avignon and Rome, and the blameless and devout lives of thousands upon thousands of the faithful, still less the slow but marvellous awakening by which the papacy and the Church in general rose from its long illness with a new vigour. So with the monastic and religious orders there were at all times men and women, both among the superiors and the private religious, of goodwill and spiritual achievement. We may not be able to disguise the general trend of the period with which we have had to deal, but we may remember the words of St Gregory the Great, echoed by St Thomas More, that there is little credit for living well in good company, but praise indeed for those who are worthy when all around is ill.

The writer of these pages has often been asked, and has often asked himself, whether the monks of the Tudor Age deserved the hard fate that overtook them. He has tried to answer by presenting the reader of the

earlier chapters in this volume with evidence on which to base his judgment. It may well be that important pieces have been overlooked, but
these chapters contain what seemed, after thirty years of reflection, to be
a representative assemblage. The reader has indeed had before him records
of visitations that do little credit to the religious, and has heard the criticisms of contemporaries, including such eminent judges as Erasmus and
More, but on the other hand he has entered the cloister of the Charterhouse
with Maurice Chauncy, he has seen something of the achievement of
Marmaduke Huby and Richard Kidderminster, he has watched Prior
More summering and wintering at Worcester and Grimley, and Robert
Joseph and his friends discovering Plautus and Virgil. He has seen something of the dignified and richly apparelled liturgy and chant at Durham
and Waltham, and has noted the new and beautiful buildings rising at
St Osyth, at Forde and at Westminster, and the words of praise given by
their neighbours to many a house great and small.

If the question is still urged, the opinion (it can be no more) of the
present writer, if he were to set himself as one surveying the English scene
in 1530, would be as follows. In the first place, there were a number of
houses—the Charterhouses, Syon, the Observant friaries, many of the
larger nunneries, one or two of the cathedral priories, and several other
abbeys of the black and white monks—which no temporal or ecclesiastical
sovereign would have dreamt of destroying unless he was prepared to
deny the right of existence to any monastic house, and to consider solely
the cash value of a church and its treasures. Secondly, there was a larger
number of houses (though with a smaller aggregate population) whose
continued existence served no good purpose whatever. In this category
would be found all priories and cells of monks and nuns with less than ten
or a dozen inmates, and, in addition, almost all the houses of Augustinian
canons. Within no foreseeable future and by no practicable scheme of
reform could they have been rehabilitated spiritually. Between these two
fairly large groups about which there could have been little serious
difference of opinion among men of average insight and probity, there
was still a large *bloc* of medium-sized and large houses upon which it would
have been difficult to pass judgment. None of them was fervent, but many
were harmless and, at least to a good-natured observer from outside,
respectable enough to pass muster. The nature of the judgment passed on
them would have depended upon the condition of the judge: a tolerant
man of the world would have allowed them to continue, a severe spiritual
reformer would have found them wanting.

It is not an historian's task to predict the issue of a course of action that
never took place, under conditions which were never realized, but if we
are allowed, with a momentary flight of fancy, to suppose that in early
Tudor England a breach with the papacy and an invasion of Reformed
principles and theology were not of themselves inevitable, and that the
existence of a strong, prudent and orthodox monarch may be allowed as

a hypothesis, it is conceivable that a minister with the powers of Wolsey and the character of a Cisneros or a Pole might, by a judicious combination of suppression and disciplinary reform, have provided the monastic world in England with a purge and a tonic that would have prepared the survivors for the reception of the Tridentine regulations and the constitutions of the contemporary reformed orders of Italy and Spain.

In several chapters of this book the immediate personal and material consequences of the Dissolution have been set out in some detail. It is natural to suppose that the long-term consequences, religious and social, of such a wholesale extinction of a way of life, and such a vast transference of property must have been great indeed. Yet after a century's debate historians are by no means agreed as to the nature or extent of these results. Three hundred years ago the sober and intelligent historian, Thomas Fuller, tabled a series of consequences based not so much on historical evidence as on his own opinion of the needs and sorrows of his country, and historians almost down to our own day have, whether consciously or not, done little more than echo or embroider his words. There was a time when apologists of the Middle Ages attributed to the Dissolution almost every ill which they deplored in the sixteenth and later centuries: the secular and servile state, the upstart nobility, the parliamentarian gentry, the later oligarchy, pauperism, capitalism, avarice and atheism. More recently still, there has been a tendency to minimize the extent of the revolution. It has been said that the religious were so earthbound that their disappearance left no spiritual void, while at the same time the existing landowners had already such a footing within the monastic estates either as leaseholders or administrators that the Dissolution had little social or economic effect. It would indeed seem true that it is very difficult to distinguish any save the most superficial results in these spheres from those of other disturbing influences of the time, religious, social and economic, but a summary review may not be out of place.

On the spiritual level, the dissolution of the monasteries was not of itself a great catastrophe. By and large the whole body ecclesiastic was lukewarm, and the monasteries had little warmth to spare for others. Nevertheless, their disappearance had considerable consequences. The suppression of the Carthusians, the Bridgettines and the best of the nunneries removed from the national purview an ideal and a practice of life that had always attracted a spiritual *élite* and, in things of the spirit, as in works of art, the best has a value and a price which no quantity, however great, of the mediocre can supply. Next, the witness of Aske and of others shows, what we might expect, that even a tolerably observant religious house could have had an encouraging influence upon good men of the neighbourhood, to say nothing of its real practical use as a school, an almshouse, a bank, or an inn. Thirdly, when the monasteries had been followed to destruction by the colleges, there disappeared from the country almost every home of that rich liturgical life of chant and ceremony of which we have seen glimpses on earlier pages. There remained only the parish church and the minished cathedral; there was no cushion to take the impact of reforming, iconoclastic zeal when it came. Finally, and most important of all, there was the negative result. Good or bad, the monasteries were an important and integral part of the traditional church life of the Middle Ages. Had they stood, the tide of Protestantism in this country would have been, if not halted, at least checked and divided. Their disappearance, especially when their lands and wealth were held by a great number of all the higher classes, rendered any complete revival of the old ways extremely difficult. Without the support and example of the revitalized religious orders on a fairly large scale, Mary, had she lived to be eighty, would have had a hard task to reestablish Catholicism, and any large-scale restitution would have been met with sullen hostility and fear on the part of the landowners of the country. Probably neither Henry VIII nor Cromwell fully realized in this respect what they were doing. They thought of the religious orders primarily as a source of wealth, and only very occasionally as a potential enemy of change. But the monasteries, with all their weaknesses, were more than landowners. They were not indeed, as has sometimes been repeated, fortresses of the papacy, but their existence in a healthy condition was necessary, if not for the *esse*, then at least for the *bene esse*, of a church that was to be part of Catholic Europe, and when they went, something had gone that might have been good or bad, but would never have been Protestant.

On the social and economic level the results are not so clear. There was the great but imponderable loss in things of beauty devoted, or at least erected, to the glory of God. How great the loss was we can but guess from what remains still in partial use or utterly ruined. Those to whom the great churches and cathedrals stand apart from all other buildings in their power to move and to inspire will never say that enough has been spared. On the purely professional level of architect and craftsman the Dissolution meant the end of an art-form. Gothic art, not yet as strained and flamboyant in England as it was abroad, came to an end as it were overnight, if only because churches were not built any longer. It survived for a generation or two in craft traditions, and then became a curiosity or a survival. Social changes remain hard to assess. A few great families of *nouveaux riches* emerged, and remained for the next half-century near the controls of government, but the new rich were not always new men; for the most part their rise was of a modest landowner to the rank of a magnate, and they were far less numerous than was asserted in the past. They were not precisely a new class or a new way of thought breaking into a charmed circle. The real beneficiaries of the change, once the dust of the suppression had settled, were innumerable men of small or moderate fortunes, who bought themselves a small estate or augmented an existing one. It was this multiplication of country landowners that had its effect in time. The map of England was no longer, like those of Catholic France and Germany, marked by numerous islands, the privileged lands great and small of religious corporations. Everywhere laymen were in possession, potential cultured gentlemen of the latter decades of Elizabeth's reign or parliamentarians of a later period. Some of them might well be Catholics, and zealous ones, like the Arundells or the Paulets, but all were, economically speaking, supporters of the 'new deal'; all would have been equally apprehensive of a return of the monks. Here, as often in this matter, the analogy with revolutionary France is close. There also the beneficiaries of the change remained sullen opponents of the old régime, and it needed a papal act of power, which seemed to many as a betrayal of friends, to break the solidarity of the old form of things with the old faith. In England, as we have seen, the pope pronounced early, but, in the shifting policies of the years that followed, the renunciation of claims was allowed to fall into oblivion, and for almost three centuries the rights of the dispossessed remained as a spectre that defied exorcism. In a still more powerful way the ghost of medieval monasticism remained and remains to haunt this island. The grey walls and broken cloisters, the

> bare ruin'd choirs, where late the sweet birds sang,

speak more eloquently for the past than any historian would dare, and pose for every beholder questions that words cannot answer.

At the end of this long review of monastic history, with its splendours and its miseries, and with its rhythm of recurring rise and fall, a monk cannot but ask what message for himself and for his brethren the long story may carry. It is the old and simple one; only in fidelity to the Rule can a monk or a monastery find security. A Rule, given by a founder with an acknowledged fullness of spiritual wisdom, approved by the Church and tested by the experience of saints, is a safe path, and it is for the religious the only safe path. It comes to him not as a rigid, mechanical code of works, but as a sure guide to one who seeks God, and who seeks that he may indeed find. If he truly seeks and truly loves, the way will not be hard, but if he would love and find the unseen God he must pass beyond things seen and walk in faith and hope, leaving all human ways and means and trusting the Father to whom all things are possible. When once a religious house or a religious order ceases to direct its sons to the abandonment of all that is not God, and ceases to show them the rigours of the narrow way that leads to the imitation of Christ in His Love, it sinks to the level of a purely human institution, and whatever its works may be, they are the works of time and not of eternity. The true monk, in whatever century he is found, looks not to the changing ways around him or to his own mean condition, but to the unchanging everlasting God, and his trust is in the everlasting arms that hold him. Christ's words are true: He who doth not renounce all that he possesseth cannot be my disciple. His promise also is true: He that followeth me walketh not in darkness, but shall have the light of life.

APPENDIX I

SIR THOMAS MORE'S LETTER 'TO A MONK'

More's letter 'to a monk' was published in *Epistolae aliquot eruditorum* (1520), and thence by Miss E. F. Rogers, *Correspondence of Sir Thomas More*, no. 83, pp. 165–206. More does not name his correspondent, nor is there any direct clue to his identity in the letter itself. Strangely enough, neither the latest editor nor, so far as I am aware, any previous writer, has made any attempt at identification. All that the letter tells us is that More had known his correspondent 'in the world'; that he was an autodidact; that he was a monk of a 'contemplative' Order and a priest; and that he was still young (cf. Rogers, pp. 167, 190, 193: 'Tu juvenis αὐτοδίδακτος'). We know from other sources of one and only one English monk who attacked Erasmus's New Testament, the Carthusian John Batmanson of London, who died in office as prior in 1531. This Batmanson has been identified, tentatively in *DNB* and with more assurance by later writers, with John Batmanson, D.C.L., who appears in the records of the time as a figure of some importance in public life, from which he disappears c. 1516. That Erasmus should have referred to his opponent slightingly as a young man has been taken by P. S. Allen[1] and others as an instance of the humanist's wilful discourtesy towards his critics. To the present writer it had long seemed that Batmanson must be More's correspondent, but the identification of the prior with the aged lawyer appeared to be an insuperable difficulty. Recently, however, Dom Andrew Gray, of St Hugh's Charterhouse, Parkminster, has acquainted me with the following facts in the possession of his community: (*a*) a brass, once in the (vanished) church of Itchen Stoke, Hants, and now in the modern building, commemorates Joan Batmanson (*ob.* 1518), widow of John Batmanson, Doctor of Laws of Seville; (*b*) in Joan's will, preserved at Winchester, she refers to her late husband and leaves instructions for her burial in the London Charterhouse; (*c*) in 1511 John Batmanson and his wife *Margaret* received letters of confraternity at Durham; (*d*) John Batmanson the Carthusian was ordained deacon by Bishop Fitzjames on 31 March 1510 (Reg. Fitzjames in the Library of St Paul's); he would then have been rising twenty; he was prior of Hinton 1523–9 and of London 1529–31. This clearly eliminates the identification of the old lawyer with the Carthusian, but makes it probable that the younger John Batmanson was a son of the elder by his first wife, Margaret. It may be added that no John Batmanson appears in the degree lists of Oxford and Cambridge in the early sixteenth century; thus the youth and the self-educated state of More's correspondent would tally with what we know of John Batmanson junior.

1 *Erasmi Opus Epistolaram*, IV, 259.

APPENDIX II

RELIGIOUS HOUSES SUPPRESSED BY CARDINAL WOLSEY

Name	Order	Income (net) £	Numbers	Papal bull	Royal writ	Execution
		(1) 1524–5				
Bayham	Pre.	125	?10	—	8. ii. 26	1525
Blackmore	Aug.	85	4	—	1. xii. 25	1525
Blithbury	Ben. nuns	?	?	14. v. 28	—	1525–8
Bradwell	Ben.	47	3–4	—	—	1524–5
Canwell	Ben.	25	1	—	8. ii. 26	1525
Daventry	Ben.	236	?10	—	8. ii. 26	1525
Dodnash	Aug.	44	?4	—	1. xii. 25	1525
Horksley	Ben. (Cl.)	27	2	—	—	1524–5
Lesnes	Aug.	189	6 or ?11	—	8. ii. 26	1525
Littlemore	Ben. nuns	33	?5	—	8. ii. 26	1525
Oxford St Frideswide's	Aug.	220	?15	3. iv. 24	10. v. 24	1524
Poughley	Aug.	71	4	—	8. ii. 26	1525
Pynham	Aug.	43	1	—	8. ii. 26	1525
Ravenstone	Aug.	66	?2 or 5	—	8. ii. 26	1525
Thoby	Aug.	75	3	—	1. xii. 25	1525
Tickford	Ben.	57	6	—	8. ii. 26	1524
Tiptree	Aug.	22	2	—	1. xii. 25	1525
Tonbridge	Aug.	169	8	—	8. ii. 26	1525
Sandwell	Ben.	38	?1–2	—	8. ii. 26	1525
Snape	Ben.	99	?	—	1. xii. 25	1527–8
Stansgate	Ben.	43	3	—	1. xii. 25	1525
Wix	Ben. nuns	92	4	—	1. xii. 25	1525
		(2) 1527–8				
Bromehill	Aug.	25	5	14. v. 28	—	1528
Farewell	Ben. nuns	33	?	13. iv. 28	—	1527
Felixstowe	Ben.	?40	3	14. v. 28	—	1528
Ipswich, St Peter	Aug.	(c. 80)	7	14. v. 28	—	1527
Mountjoy[1]	Aug.	?	2	14. v. 28	—	1529–30
Romburgh	Ben.	30	?3	14. v. 28	—	1528
St Mary de Pré	Ben. nuns	65	3	15. v. 28	—	1528
Wallingford	Ben.	134	c. 5	31. v. 28	—	1528

1 The suppression of Mountjoy, though authorized in 1528, did not take place while Wolsey was in power.

APPENDIX III

THE WITNESS OF THE CARTHUSIANS

J. A. Froude, in a justly celebrated passage of his *History* (II, 350), compares the Carthusians preparing for death to Leonidas and his followers combing their golden hair on the morning of their heroic defence of Thermopylae. The analogy, which Froude proceeds to draw, between those fighting for the political freedom of Hellas and those who died for the freedom of conscience, has appealed to many historians. Whatever may be true of other victims of religious persecution in the sixteenth century, however, it is unhistorical to regard the Carthusians as dying for freedom of belief. They died because they refused to abandon what they were convinced was the secular traditional teaching of the Church, based on the words of Christ. The sources are unanimous on the point.

THE THREE PRIORS

Chauncy, *Historia martyrum*, 100. When asked by the Council to take the oath of supremacy, they replied: 'Ecclesiam Catholicam aliter semper tenuisse ac docuisse.'

Ibid. 103. Houghton speaking at Tyburn proclaimed that he died because he refused to obey the king 'eo quod sancta mater Ecclesia aliter decrevit et statuit quam ipse Rex vester cum suo Parlamento'.

LP, VIII, 565 (20 April 1535). Robert Laurence and Augustine Webster are asked by Cromwell 'whether they...would be content to obey the king as supreme head in earth under Christ of the Church of England? To which both answered they could not consent nor believe that he is so.'

Ibid. 566. John Houghton says he cannot take the king to be supreme head of the Church of England. Ric. (*sic*) Lawrence says there is one Catholic Church, of which the bishop of Rome is the head. Augustine Webster also denies the supremacy.

Ibid. 661 (from Vatican archives; *v. supra*, p. 231 n. 1). Houghton asks Cromwell: 'Seeing that our Lord gave power to men upon earth by the words Et tibi dabo claves Regni Caelorum, which no doctor understood to be addressed to any other than St Peter alone, then to the Apostles, and consequently to the Pope and bishops, how could the king, a layman, be Head of the Church of England?' The Secretary replied, 'You would make the king a priest, then?' and commanded him to speak no further.

Ibid. 666 (5 May, Chapuys to Charles V). 'Three Carthusians and a Bridgettine monk were executed yesterday, only for having maintained that the Pope was the true Head of the universal Church, and that the king had no right in reason or conscience to usurp the sovereign authority over the clergy of this realm.'

Ibid. 856 (11 June, articles of examination concerning Fisher). George, Fisher's servant, deposed to his master having made him cut some leaves out of one of the monks' books (almost certainly these were Houghton's notes, *v. supra*, p. 231). 'In one was written "pasce oves meas, etc.", and I am sure that these words Christ spake himself, and dare take that quarrel to my death.' In another place he read: 'My Lord [this was either North or Audley; both were of the Court (cf. *LP*, IX, 666)] ye should not judge me to death this day, for, if ye should, ye should first condemn yourself and all your predecessors, which were no simple sheep in this flock, but great bellwethers. And, my Lord, if ye would, in detestation of this opinion, dig up the bones of all our predecessors and burn them, yet should not that turn me from this Faith.'

MIDDLEMORE, EXMEW AND NEWDIGATE

Hist. mart. 108: 'Hi tres...audacter allegantes de Scripturis Sanctis ante tribunal juris divini [?esse] illam supremitatem et primatum Ecclesiae quam Papae et sacerdotibus tribuit Jesus Christus Dominus noster.'

LP, VIII, 886 (17 June 1535). The indictment at the trial ran that the three monks 'did say "I cannot nor will consent to be obedient to the king's highness as a true, lawful and obedient subject, to take and repute him to be Supreme Head in earth of the Church of England under Christ"'.

THE REST

Hist. mart. 110: 'Terminos quos posuerunt Patres nostri noluerunt transgredi, sed ut sancta Mater Ecclesia eos docuit, hac firmiter se tenere semper decreverunt et ore confessi sunt.'

APPENDIX IV

HOUSES WITH INCOMES EXCEEDING £1000 IN THE 'VALOR ECCLESIASTICUS'

House	Order	Gross income £	Net income £
Westminster	Ben. (abbey)	3912	2409
Glastonbury	Ben. (abbey)	3642	3311
Canterbury, Chr. Ch.	Ben. (cathedral pr.)	2909	2423
St Albans	Ben. (abbey)	—*	2102
Reading	Ben. (abbey)	—*	1938
Abingdon	Ben. (abbey)	—*	1876
Bury St Edmunds	Ben. (abbey)	2336	1659
York, St Mary's	Ben. (abbey)	2091	1650
Peterborough	Ben. (abbey)	1979	1721
Syon	Bridgett. nuns	1943	1735
Ramsey	Ben. (abbey)	1849	1643
Winchester, St Swithun's	Ben. (cathedral priory)	1762	1507
Gloucester	Ben. (abbey)	1744	1419
Canterbury, St Augustine's	Ben. (abbey)	1733	1431
Durham	Ben. (cathedral priory)	1572	1328
Tewkesbury	Ben. (abbey)	1478	1319
Worcester	Ben. (cathedral priory)	1444	1296
Cirencester	Aug. can. (abbey)	1325	1045
Shaftesbury	Ben. nuns (abbey)	1324	1149
Evesham	Ben. (abbey)	1313	1138
Ely	Ben. (cathedral priory)	—*	1084
Fountains	Cist. (abbey)	1178	1004
Chester	Ben. (abbey)	1104	1030
Lewes	Clun. (priory)	1091	921
Leicester	Aug. can. (abbey)	1056	946
Norwich	Ben. (cathedral priory)	1061	871
Croyland	Ben. (abbey)	1050	947
Merton	Aug. can. (priory)	1036	957

It is interesting to note the relative wealth of abbeys at the Dissolution and at the date (c. 1085) of *Domesday*. If Reading, Syon, Durham and York (which do not figure in *Domesday*) are omitted from the above list, and Ely (which lost a large portion of its wealth when the bishopric was founded) is ignored in that of *Domesday*, it will be seen that ten names are common to the two lists among the eleven richest houses in each. The single absentee from the later list is Winchester, New Minster (later Hyde Abbey), always an unfortunate house, which was transferred, burnt out, and sacked in the twelfth century. The new house to improve its position is Gloucester Abbey. (See next page.)

* The *Valor* does not provide gross figures for these houses; their position in the above list is therefore only approximate.

House	Position and income 1535 £		Position and income 1085 £	
Westminster	(1)	3912	(6)	583
Glastonbury	(2)	3642	(1)	827
Canterbury, Christ Church	(3)	2909	(2)	768
St Albans	(4)	—	(11)	269
Abingdon	(5)	—	(7)	462
Bury St Edmunds	(6)	2336	(3)	639
Peterborough	(7)	1979	(10)	323
Ramsey	(8)	1844	(9)	358*
Winchester, St Swithun's	(9)	1762	(5)	600
Gloucester	(10)	1744		—
Canterbury, St Augustine's	(11)	1733	(4)	635

* In the complete list of *Domesday* values on pp. 702–3 of *MO* (1940) the figure for Ramsey was given by mistake as £658, thus giving the house a place too high in the list. This was corrected in the 1949 reprint.

APPENDIX V

THE SACRIST OF BEAUVALE

It is difficult to believe that the monk of Beauvale escaped in this way if the oath was tendered to his community as it was to other houses, for in such cases the monks were not asked their views, but told to take the oath. It may be, however, that after their experience at London, the government decided not to force the Carthusians up to the brink, but to get some sort of acknowledgment out of them. In fact, no Carthusian house, other than London under Prior Trafford, appears in the lists of those who took the oath printed in the Deputy Keeper's Report VII. Beauvale duly appears as surrendering in Report VIII, but the sacrist's name (Dugmer) is not among the signatories. He rejoined the order at Sheen and died twenty years later in exile in the odour of sanctity. One of his confrères related the following incident of his early life (Hendriks, *The London Charterhouse*, 304):

Our good Father Dugmer told me that when he was young and Sacrist, and one day had washed the Church Corporals, and had laid them in the garden upon the lavender borders to dry, in the midst of his dinner he went into his garden to see the cloths, and he saw our Blessed Lady sitting beside the Corporals tending them, and our Blessed Lord in the likeness of a little child, pulling the lavendar knops and, as little children will do, casting them upon the Corporals. 'Then', thought the good Sacrist, 'I may well go to my dinner again, for the cloths are well kept.' The tears poured forth of his eyes as the good Father told me this.

APPENDIX VI

ITINERARY OF THE VISITORS, 1535–6

[Places in italics were inspected by more than one visitor.]

1535 LAYTON	LEGH	AP RICE	TREGONWELL
JULY			
28 Cirencester			
	29–31 Worcester		
	31 Great Malvern		
AUGUST	*Malmesbury*	*Malmesbury*	
1 Evesham			
Tewkesbury	Bradstock	3 Edington	
7 Bath			
Farley			
Keynsham			
Maiden Bradley			
Witham			
20 Bruton	20 *Lacock*	20 *Lacock*	
23–4 Glastonbury	23–4 Bruton		
25 Bristol			
SEPTEMBER			
	3 *Wilton*	3 *Wilton*	
	11 *Wherwell*	11 *Wherwell*	
12 *Oxford*			12 *Oxford*
Oseney			*Oseney*
13 Abingdon	? Waltham		
15 Winchester *with*			
Cromwell			
22 Southwark			Circuit of Oxf. and Bucks
24 Durford	24 *Wintney*	24 *Wintney*	
25 Waverley	25 Reading		
	Chertsey		27 Studley (Oxon)
28 Shulbrede			
Essebourne	*Haliwell*	28 *Haliwell*	
29	29		
	Merton		
	Westminster	*Westminster*	
OCTOBER			
1 Boxgrove			
2 Lewes			
Battle			
16 Leiston	16 *Warden*	16 *Warden*	
Dover			
	17 *Royston*	17 *Royston*	
Folkestone			
	19 Saffron Walden		
	21–30 *Cambridge*	21 *Cambridge*	

1535	LAYTON	LEGH	AP RICE	TREGONWELL
OCTOBER				
23	Canterbury, Ch. Ch. and St Aug.'s	22 Denney		
	Bermondsey			
	St Mary Overy			
	Maidstone			
	Faversham			
27	Rochester	27 Swaffham		
		30 Denney		
31	Leeds			
NOVEMBER				
1		Ely	Ely	
4		*Bury*	*Bury*	Athelney
		Dereham	*Dereham*	
		St Faith's	*St Faith's*	
		Crabhouse	*Crabhouse*	
8				before 8 Cleeve
9				9 Barlinch
11		*Westacre*	*Westacre*	
				Barnstaple
				Bodmin
19		Norwich		
27		Ipswich		
		St Osyth		
DECEMBER				
12	Syon			
	Chicksand			
	Harrold			
	St Andrew's, Northampton			
22	Leicester	22 Sawtre		
23		Hinchinbrook		
	Lichfield			
	Trentside			
36				
JANUARY				
13	*York*	*York*		
	Fountains			
20	*Richmond*	*Richmond*		
	Durham	*Durham*		
26	*Newcastle*	*Newcastle*		
FEBRUARY				
2–3	*Whitby*	*Whitby*		
	Guisborough			
		Hull		
7	York			
	together on 8 Feb.			
	Marton	Mount Grace		
9–10	Fountains			
10	*Richmond*	*Richmond*		
	Carlisle	*Carlisle*		
28	*Ludlow*	*Ludlow*		

APPENDIX VII

THE COMMISSIONERS FOR THE SURVEY OF THE LESSER HOUSES IN 1536

The instructions specified that the commissioners for each county or district were to be six in number: the auditor, receiver and clerk of the registry reappointed from the commission for the tenth of the previous year, and three gentlemen of the locality. A quorum, where specified, was to consist of two 'professionals' and one 'gentleman'. In fact, the professional element was rarely the same as in 1535, and often only one or two gentlemen attended. In the lists that follow, the professionals, now mostly 'Augmentations men', are italicized when identifiable; an asterisk denotes those who are known to have served as commissioners for the tenth. In view of the favourable reports made by these commissions, it is worth noting that almost all the names appear sooner or later as grantees of monastic lands.

BRISTOL (S.C. 12/33/27, m. 3ʳ)

Thomas White, ?the T. W. (1492–67) of *DNB*
Nicholas Thorne, ?son of Robert Thorne, *ob.* 1527 of *DNB*
Richard Paulet
William Berners

GLOUCESTERSHIRE (ibid.)

John Walshe
Edmund Thame (merchant family from Fairford)
Richard Paulet
William Berners

HUNTINGDONSHIRE (B.M. Cott. Cleo. E. IV, fo. 336)

John Goodryk*
William Legh
Thomas Combes

HAMPSHIRE (S.C. 12/33/27, m. 1)

Sir James Worseley*
John Paulet*
George Paulet*
Richard Paulet
William Berners

LEICESTERSHIRE (E. 36/154/48, m. 1)

Sir John Nevell*, ? later third Baron Latimer, 1490–1543, *DNB*
Roger Ratclyff*
William Asheby
John Beaumont*, fl. 1550, ?master of rolls, *DNB*
George Gyfford
Robert Burgoyn

NORFOLK (S.C. 12/33/29, m. 1)

Sir John Towneshend*, ?s. of Sir R. T. judge, *ob.* 1493; f. of Sir R. T. 1543–90: both *DNB*
Sir William Paston* 1479?–1554, lawyer and courtier, *DNB*
Richard Southwell* (auditor of tenth; *Valor*, iii, 489), 1504–64, *DNB*
Thomas Myldemaye, f. of Sir Walter M., 1520–89, chancellor of exch., *DNB*

RUTLAND (E. 36/154/64)

Thomas Brudenell* ?s. of judge Rob. B., *DNB* (auditor of tenth *Val.* iv, 279)
David Cecill
John Harrington, ?*DNB*, m. the enigmatic Etheldreda, d. of Henry VIII
George Gyfford
Robert Burgoyn

WARWICKSHIRE (E. 36/154/56)

John Grevyll
Roger Wygston
Symon Mountford
Thomas Holte, ?gf. of Sir T. H. 1571–1654, *DNB*
George Gyfford
Robert Burgoyn

WILTSHIRE (S.C. 12/33/27, m. 2)

Sir Henry Long*
Richard Paulet
John Pye
William Berners

NORTHAMPTONSHIRE (S.P. 1/104, fo. 33 *a*)

Edmund Knyghtley, *ob.* 1542, sergeant-at-law, *DNB*
John Lane* (auditor of tenth), ?gf. of Sir Rich. L., lord keeper, *DNB*
George Gyfford
Robert Burgoyn

YORKSHIRE (B.M. Harl. 364, 60, 21)

Sir Ralph Ellerker*, jun. For Sir R. E. sen., *v. DNB* (*ob.* 1542)
Sir Marmaduke Constable, *DNB* (*ob.* 1545)
Sir Roger Cholmley, judge; *ob.* 1565, *DNB*
William Babthorpe
Robert Chaloner*
Leonard Beckworth, later Knight and Sheriff of Yorks
*Hugh Fuller** (on tenth commission in Herts), auditor of Augmentations

ARCHDEACONRY OF RICHMOND (S.C. 6 Hen. VIII, 7467, m. 7)

Sir William Mallory
Sir George Lawson
Robert Bowes
*William Blitheman**
*James Rokeby**

APPENDIX VIII

THE CONFLICT OF EVIDENCE ON THE MONASTERIES

The following are the most striking examples of the differing estimates of various houses supplied by Layton and Legh on the one hand, and other sources of evidence on the other. No attempt is made to reconcile the conflicting verdicts, but it must be remembered that in any age the judgments on a community made by a hostile critic and a benevolent outsider will differ widely.

BOXGROVE, SUSSEX (black monks)

28 July 1524:

Visited by Mag. J. Worthall for Robert Shirborn, bishop of Chichester; details from Register Shirborn II = Ep. 1/1/4 in County Record Office, Chichester.
Ten present; several say *omnia bene*; a few make small complaints, none of them with any moral bearing. Two injunctions meet these. (Ep. 1/1/4, fo. 94*b*.)

19 June 1527:

Twelve present. House 'in mediocri statu' and greatly in debt. Monks obedient 'et religiose vivunt' (Prior's declaration). One other repeats first clause; subprior testifies to Prior's good conversation. All others say *omnia bene*. No injunctions. (Ep. 1/1/4, fo. 98*b*.)

1 Oct. 1535:

Layton to Cromwell (*LP*, IX, ii, 509): 'the prior of Boxgrove habet tantum duas... ejus monachi omnes sunt ejusdem farinae [= of the same brand]'.

Spring 1536:

Commissioners for suppression in Sussex (P.R.O. S.P. 5/3/128) remark: 'religious persones ix...incontinent none'.

CHERTSEY, SURREY (black monks)

29 Sept. 1535:

Legh to Cromwell (*LP*, IX, ii, 472): 'Whereas of late the King sent my lord of Winchester [Stephen Gardiner] and Mr Treasurer [Sir William Fitzwilliam] to see the order of Chertsey abbey, and they reported all was well, you will see somewhat more by the compertes I send...incontinentes 7, incontinentes et sodomitae 4, patientes sodomiticum 2.'

6 July 1537:

Surrender of Chertsey on understanding that abbey will be refounded by the king at Bisham. (*LP*, XII, ii, 220.)

18 Dec. 1537:

Refoundation at Bisham, with community from Chertsey; abbot given privilege of wearing mitre. (*Ibid.* 1228 and 1311 (22).)

DENNEY, CAMBS (Franciscan nuns)

30 Oct. 1535:

Legh to Cromwell (*LP*, IX, ii, 708): 'At Denney we found half-a-dozen who, with tears in their eyes, begged to be dismissed.... They will not need to be put forth, but will make instance to be delivered. They at Denney say that they live against their conscience.'

17 Aug. 1536:

Petition of Denney to continue granted. (*LP*, XI, 385 (35).)

FARLEY, WILTS (Cluniac monks)

7 Aug. 1535:

Layton to Cromwell (*LP*, IX, ii, 42): 'At Farley cell to Lewes the prior has only 8 whores, the rest of the monks fewer.'

1 July 1536:

Certificate of Suppression Commissioners (PRO, S.C. 12/33/27, m. 2): 'vi monks all beinge preests of honest conuersacon holley desyrynge contynuance in religion'.

GARENDON, LEICS (Cistercians)

Feb. 1536:

Comperta in *LP*, X, i, 364. Five names noted as sodomites, one with ten boys.

June 1536:

Commissioners' report (PRO, E. 36/154/52): '...of good conuersacon and gods seruyce well maynteyned and desyre all to contynewe ther in ther religion...& other wise to be assigned ouer to other howses of the same religion'.

GRACEDIEU, LEICS (Austin canonesses)

Feb. 1536:

Comperta in *LP*, X, i, 364. Two nuns charged with incontinence (*pepererunt*).

June 1536:

Commissioners' report (PRO, E. 36/154/53): 'of good and vertuous conuersacon & lyuing as apperyth by examynacon and by report of the Countreye desiering all to contynewe in ther relygyon ther'.

MAIDEN BRADLEY, WILTS (Austin canons)

24 Aug. 1535:

Layton to Cromwell (*LP*, IX, ii, 168): 'Maiden Bradley, where is a holy father prior, with but six children...his sons be tall men waiting on him...the Pope gave him licence *sub plumbo* to keep a whore.'

1 July 1536:

Commissioners report (PRO, S.C. 12/33/27, m. 2): 'Preests vi and nouesses ij by reporte of honest conuersacon. Whereof desyringe contynuaunce in religion v and to haue capacites iij.' The prior obtained a benefice as noted in text, p. 300 n. 5.

PENTNEY, NORFOLK (Austin canons)

Nov. 1535:

Visitors report prior incontinent, as appears from the confession of the abbess of Marham, and five others with women (*LP*, X, i, 143).

27 March 1536:

Richard Southwell and Robert Hogen to Cromwell (*LP*, x, 563): 'We beseech your favour for the prior of Pentneye, assuring you that he relieves those quarters wondrously where he dwells, and it would be a pity not to spare a house that feeds so many indigent poor, which is in a good state, maintains good service, and does so many charitable deeds.'

Spring 1536:

Commissioners report (PRO, S.C. 12/33/29, m. 4): 'Religious persones in the said howsse ix all prysts of very honest name & goode religious persones who done desire the kyngs highnes to contynue & remayne in religion.'
Pentney was respited till 1537.

SHULBREDE, SUSSEX (Austin canons)
6 July 1524:

Visitation by J. Worthall (Register Shirborn, II, Ep. 1/1/4, fo. 92a). Five present; two absent, one in apostasy. Four depose *omnia bene*. Injunction to prior to show accounts.

3 July 1527:

Visitation (Reg. Shirborn, II, Ep. 1/1/4, fo. 101a). Six present. All say *omnia bene* but three complain that prior is sparing with food and one adds he is remiss with stipend. Injunctions to correct above failings.

4 Oct. 1535:

Layton to Cromwell (*LP*, IX, ii, 533): 'The prior of Shulbrede...has seven [women] and his monks four or five each.'

Spring 1536:

Commissioners for Sussex report (PRO, SP 5/3/128): 'Religious parsones v all preests, incontinent none.'

STANLEY, WILTS (Cistercians)
20 Aug. 1535:

Ap Rice to Cromwell (*LP*, IX, ii, 139): 'At Stanley the abbot confessed incontinence before he was abbot, and six or seven of the convent here confessed the same.'

1 July 1536:

Commissioners report (PRO, S.C. 12/33/37, m. 2): 'Preests ix and nouesse j by reaporte of honest conuersacon all desyringe contynuaunce in religion...by reaporte to all the cuntrye a greate releef.'

APPENDIX IX

THE LAST ABBOTS OF COLCHESTER, READING AND GLASTONBURY

The fate of these three abbots, without parallel among the black monks of the dissolved houses, and the paucity of our information as to their last days, give a peculiar interest to their case. What follows is an attempt to set out in reasonable fullness all the evidence that is available to historians in the matter. It will be convenient to divide it into two categories, which may be labelled roughly as 'literary' and 'record' evidence. It is worth noting that the first class alone was available until the middle of the nineteenth century, and that therefore Catholic apologists and historians based all their accounts upon it.

Charles Wriothesley, 1508?–1562. *Chronicle*, ed. W. D. Hamilton, p. 109.

In this moneth [November 1539] the Abbottes of Glastonburie, Reding and Colchester were arraigned in the Counter, and after drawen, hanged and quartered for treason.

Wriothesley was a contemporary with a house in the City; the single detail he supplies is therefore probably correct, though he implies that the whole process of trial and execution took place in London. There were at least three Counters or Compters in the City; this is probably that containing the prison and the court of the Sheriff.

Edward Hall, ?–1547. *Chronicle*, ed. C. Whibley, II, 294.

The xiiii day of November Hugh Feringdon Abbot of Redyng and two Priestes, the one called Rug and the other named Onyon, were attainted of high treason, for denying the king to be supreme head of the churche, and was drawen, hanged and quartered at Redyng. This Abbot was a stubborne Monke and utterly without learning. The same day was Richard Whityng Abbot of Glascenbury likewise attainted and hanged on Tower hyll beside his monastery for the said case and other great treasons, which was also quartered; and the first day of December was Jhon Beche Abbot of Colchester put to execucion for the same confederacy and treason.

Hall, though a contemporary and a valuable source, has an anti-Catholic bias and is often demonstrably inaccurate. He is remarkably vague as to the charges against Whiting and Beche. Moreover (*a*) he wrongly describes Faringdon as ignorant; (*b*) he equates the charges against the three abbots—as we shall see, wrongly; and (*c*) he attributes a wrong Christian name to Abbot Beche *alias* Marshall.

Nicholas Harpsfield, 1519?–1575. The *Pretended Divorce*, ed. Pocock, 300–1.

Such as would voluntarily give over were rewarded with large annual pensions and other pleasures. Against some other there were found quarrels as against Hugh Faringdon, abbot of Reading, which was there hanged, drawn and quartered. Against Richard Whiting, abbot of Glastonbury, that was hanged on the Torr hill, beside his monastery. Against John Beche, abbot of Colchester, put also to death, which dreadful sight and hearing made other some so sore afraid that they soon entreated to yield over all to the king's hands, and some thought they escaped fair when they escaped with their lives. So that after a few years there needed no Parliament at all for the great abbeys—they came in otherwise so thick and so roundly—but only to confirm such as had been already relinquished and yielded up to the king.

Harpsfield, a judicious writer, seems not to have heard of the charge of conspiracy, nor does he claim the abbots as martyrs. He also has the name John. He wrongly supposes that their harsh end was intended *pour encourager les autres*, whereas by November 1539, very few houses remained to surrender, and in three months (not a few years) all had gone.

Nicholas Sanders, 1530?–1581. *De Schismatis Anglicani Origine ac Progressu Liber*, ed. 1585, 91–91ᵛ.

Octauo idus Iulias Vicarius rector paroeciae Vandsuorti & presbyter qui eum iuuabat & famulus qui ministrabat, itemque monachus quidam cognomento Mayrus, & ad decimum octauum calendas Decembris eodem anno, Hugo Feringdonus Redingensis, Ricardus Vitingus Glasconiensis, & ip/sis calendis Ioannes Becus Colcestrensis, omnes ordinis S. Benedicti Abbates, itemque duo presbyteri Ruggus & Onio, ob negatam Henrici pontificiam potestatem, martyrii coronam adepti sunt.

Sanders was a controversialist, writing forty years after the event in Rome with no access to English records. He appears to consider the two sets of executions as in some way connected. In subsequent editions the clause *ob negatam...potestatem* disappears and in its stead there is a long and apocryphal account of Whiting's last days. This was rightly rejected by Gasquet, and responsibility for it has been very plausibly attributed to Robert Persons, a Somerset man by birth, who may be repeating the myth current in Whiting's own county. Sanders may have been following Hall, but it is not impossible that he was summarizing the very account that was later substituted for his.

To these witnesses may be added that of Father William Goode, 1527–86, who was a native of Glastonbury, where as a boy he served Mass in the abbey; he became a priest and was a canon at Wells under Mary; passing into exile, he joined the Society of Jesus and at Rome *c.* 1580 supervised the painting of the fresco, commissioned by George Gilbert, representing the English martyrs, among whom the three abbots appear. How far he wished, or was competent, to vouch for Abbot Whiting as a martyr, as distinct from a victim of tyranny or a supporter of the conservative cause, is not at all clear; he certainly had no personal knowledge of the fate of the other two abbots.[1]

Taken together, this succession of witnesses has considerable apparent force, and it is easy to understand that to Catholic historians of the past the case seemed proven. The record evidence, however, has another story to tell. Before dealing with each abbot in turn, three early letters, which mention all three abbots, may be quoted:

Zürich Letters. I, cxlviii, pp. 316–17. Bartholomew Traheron to Henry Bullinger; London, 20 February 1539/40.

...three of the most wealthy abbots were led to execution a little before Christmas, for having joined in a conspiracy to restore the pope.

Ibid. II, cclxxxi, p. 614. Nicolas Partridge to Bullinger. Dover, 26 February 1539/40.

Punishment has lately been inflicted upon three principal abbots who had secreted property and had conspired in different ways for the restoration of popery.

Ibid. II, cclxxxviii, p. 627. John Butler to Bullinger. Basle, 24 February 1539/40.

... ...the two abbots [*sc.* of Glastonbury and Reading] have been condemned for treason.

I. Thomas Marshall, alias Beche, abbot of Colchester

His name appears among those petitioning the pope to decide the king's suit in favour of nullity (*v.* list in Herbert, *Henry VIII*, p. 306) and he duly took the oath accepting the royal supremacy (*LP*, VII, 1024, 7 July 1534; *Deputy Keeper's Reports*, VIII, App. 2, 279).

---

1 For Goode (who is said to have influenced Robert Persons to join the Society of Jesus), *v.* Gillow, *Dictionary of the English Catholics*; F. A. Gasquet, 'A Glimpse at Glastonbury before its destruction', in *DR*, XVI, and R. H. Connolly, 'Fr Maihew and Glastonbury', *ibid.* L.

6 Nov. 1538:

Legh and Cavendish commissioned to dissolve and pension monks of Colchester (*LP*, xiii, ii, 764). This was not executed.

1 Nov. 1539:

Sir John St Clere and others write to Cromwell that a servant of the abbot, Edmund Troman, has inculpated the abbot (*LP*, xiv, ii, 438. = SP 1/154, fo. 100*a*).

1 Nov. 1539:

The examination of Edmund Troman (same reff.). He admits to having received some precious objects and £40 in cash twelve months since, and a 'trussyng cofer' eight or nine days since. He did not know the destination of these valuables. The deposition of the same (*LP*, xiv, ii, 439, SP, 1/154, fo. 103*b*). '. . .he hathe herd the said abbot [of] Colchester [d]ivers tymys withyn on yere next afore thys examynacion takyn [say that the] Kynges grace could not at ony tyme lafully [*sic*] nor by ony lawe subpresse ony howse of [reli]gion that were above the yearly value of thre hundred markes, saying also that he shuld never surrender upp hys howse and landes to the Kynges handes saying then also that he had as leave dye as to forsake his levyng, saying also that hyt koud not stond with hys consyens to forsake hys howse'. Had also heard the abbot say: 'I whuld to god that every abbot were of my mynd [fo. 104*a*] concernyng the subpression and surrenderyng of ther howses.' Asked whether he had ever heard the abbot speak against the Royal Supremacy, answered 'that he never herd the said abbot saie ony thyng ayenst the Kynges grace theryn'; moreover, he had never heard him say 'that the bysshop of Roame whas ymmedyat successor unto seint peter. . .[?unto who]m cryst gave the full Actorytie'. Had heard the abbot say 'withyn thys halff yere at Colchester this wordes folowyng. Well, god wyll take vengeance at lengythe for the puttyng dowan of the howses of Religion saying then also that god whas lykyn unto the bocher whoys properte ys to suffer his Catell to be ffatt afore that he wyll kyll them'. [fo. 105*b*] Asked whether he had heard the abbot say that two or three of the king's council had brought his grace to such a covetous mind that if all the water in Thames did flow silver and gold it would not suffice to quench his grace's thirst, he answered that 'he hathe herd. . .abbot saie the same wordes or suche moche lyke in effect'. Asked whether he had heard the abbot say that he thought the Bishop of Rochester, Thomas More and the monks of the Charter-house died holy martyrs answered that he had heard the abbot at the time of their death say 'that they dyed lyke good men and that hyt whas pety of ther dethes for they [fo. 106*a*] were great lerned men and wyse men and more he never herd hym saie therof. . .'. Asked whether he had heard the abbot say anything about the Northern Rising, answered that the abbot had said 'that the same northeryn men were goad men mokyll in the mothe great cracars and nothyng worthe in ther deades and more he dyd not here therof'. Asked if he had heard the abbot say 'I whuld to cryst that the rebelles in the northe contrye had the bysshop of Canterbury, the Lord Chanceler and the lord privy-ceyall amongst them and then I trust we shuld have a mery world ayen. Wherunto this examynat sayth yn hys conciens that he hath herd the said abbot sae the same divr (?). . .at Colchester at the tyme of the said Insurreccyon and more he rememberyth not.'

3 Nov. 1539 (*LP*, xiv, ii, 454):

Thomas Nuthake, mercer and physician of Colchester, examined, said he had heard the abbot say that the cause why the king forsook the bishop of Rome was that he might be divorced '. . .and that the bishop of Rome is the only supreme head of the Church by the laws of God. . .'. At the time the supremacy was treated in Parliament, he said he could prove that the bishop of Rome was supreme head of the Church, and that those who made the king so were heretics. The abbot also said, 'Alas, what wretched tyrants and bloodsuckers be these that have put to death and murdered these blessed clerks and best learned men that were in this realm. They died martyrs and saints, in my conscience, for holding with our holy Father, the Pope, for the right of all Holy Church'. He also said that those who held with the new acts against the bishop of Rome were accursed; with much more to the same effect.

4 Nov. 1539:

Robert Rouse, mercer, of Colchester, examined, said he left the abbot's company because he reasoned against the king's supremacy and the Acts of Parliament for extinguishing the authority of the Bishop of Rome...and that the King and his Council were driven into such inordinate covetousness that if all the water in Thames were flowing gold and silver, it were not able to slake their covetousness...that he would to God the northern lads had them [sc. Cranmer, Audley and Cromwell] for they were three arch-heretics (ibid. 458).

20 Nov. 1539:

The abbot's name is on a list of prisoners in the Tower (ibid. 554).

No date:

The abbot's answers. LP, xiv, ii 459 = SP 1/154, fo. 128a. No heading.

(Questions):

What he hathe spokne at any tyme concernyng y⁰ kinges supremicie.
and concernyng y⁰ byshyp of Romes usurped autorytie.
Item that all y⁰ water in Temes wolde not sleke y⁰ kinges covitousnesse.
yᵗ god wold take vengeance for suppressing of houses of religion.
what he hath spokne tochyng Sir Thomas Mores deth and byshop of Roff [i.e. Roffensis, John Fisher] and y⁰ monkes of Syon (sic) with other.
what he hathe spokne of y⁰ Northern men in y⁰ tyme of y⁰ commocion.

(Answers—in the abbot's hand throughout):

As concernyng the first and 2 interrogatories. for as moch as I have reade in episte of Saint Jeromi wer he sayth that all byschoppes have lyke autoritie but ob scismatis remedium in thos parties elegerunt Episcopum Romanum in summum. By the which sayying I take and understand the byschoppe of Rome hadde his suppremecye jure humano. And afterward usurpid moch more autorytie then ever was gyve to hym by any law, wherfor now I affirme that our most godly prince [fo. 128b] electith by the fre consent of all his hoole Reawme hath good autoryte to be and is suppreme head of the same. And this I have sayd as I am well rememberyd.

As concernyng the 3 interrogatory I never sayd nor thought that yff all the water un the Temaes was gold it wold nott qwench or sleke the conveytysse mynd of the kyng or his consell nor any sentence lyke the same. I have sayde that the nature of coveytise is lyke to the dropsy it is insaciable and never content but I never referith the same saying to the kynges grace nor yet to his most honorable consell.

As concernyng the 4 interrogatory in suppressyng Relygious hooses I have sayd (as I Remember) and yff it be the wyll of god so to be it is well doon. yff nat god woll ponyssh at lengyth and as towchyng my oon hoose (I take god my jugge) yff the kynges visitours hedd cum to suppresse the same I wold have gyve it uppe rather then to have the kynges displeasyr but I thowght sumwhat to stond in it for that I wold my pensyon schold be the more.

As concernyng the 5 interrogatory I have sayd that the bisshoppe of Rochester and Sir T. More were grett lernyd men and with the grace of god they myght have contricion for their...(illegible) goodness. And as concernyng the 6 interrogatory I have sayd the northernmen woll spek moch with ther tong but with the grace of god they shalbe venqwysshith as the cornysshtmen were or else it welbe wrong (?) with us for whe shalbe spoylid in our howses. And heare is all that I have sayd (as I remember). Most mekely besechyng the kynges most gracius magiste and his most honorable consell to be good to me for the love of god.

Per me Thomam Beche alias marciall.

No date (?1 Dec. 1539). Sir Christopher Jenney to Cromwell (*LP*, xiv, ii, app. 45 = SP1/156, fo. 183*a*):

Sir Christopher Jenney, one of those in charge of the trial (cf. commission of oyer and terminer in *LP*, xiv, ii, 435 (46)) writes to Cromwell that

the prisoner after his Judgement axed the kynges highnes your Lordshippe and my Lord Chauncelor forgiveness and knowelegid hym self in Substaunce to be giltie Accordynge to theffecte of thendictment and shewyd hymself to be very penytent savynge he stoode sumwhat in his own conceyte that the subpression of Abbeys shuld not stonde with the lawes of god And therby and by other circumstaunces I thought hym an evill man in myn own concyens and opynyon *yf ther had apperyd noo more but his own confession.* (words in italics interlineated).

By the last words Jenney wishes to say that judging merely by the abbot's answers, given above, and his last words, and abstracting from other evidence given at the trial, he would have considered him guilty.

II. Hugh Cook alias Faringdon, abbot of Reading

His name likewise appears on the list of petitioners for the decree of nullity (*V. supra*, p. 175).

14 Sept. 1538 Dr London to Cromwell:

My Lord here doubteth my being here [*sc.* at Reading, where he was suppressing the friars] very sore, yet I have not seen him since I came...the last time I was here he said, as they all do, he was at the King's command, but loth they be to come to any free surrender (*LP*, xiii, ii, 346).

15 Aug. 1539 Sir William Penizon to Cromwell:

Has moved Cromwell, not long agone, of the dissolution of Reading Abbey; the abbot, preparing for the same, sells sheep, corn, woods etc., to the disadvantage of the king, and partly also of the farmer (*LP*, xiv, ii, 49).

6 Sept. 1539 onwards:

Layton, Moyle and Pollard are at Reading, taking inventories.

19 Sept.:

Entry in town minute book, *à propos* of the newly elected mayor, who was by custom presented to the abbot. It is noted that the abbey is suppressed and the abbot deprived (*VCH, Berks*, ii, 71).

21 Sept. Sir William Penizon writes to Cromwell:

On 12 Sept. I received possession, from Mr Pollard and the other commissioners, of the abbey of Reading and the demesnes as the late abbot left them (*LP*, xiv, ii, 202).

No date, but before 27 Oct. Cf. *LP*, xiv, ii, 435 (45). Cromwell's remembrance:

For the indictment against the abbot of and other (*sic*), a commission of *oyer and terminer* into Berkshire for his indictment and trial....The abbot Redyng to be sent down to be tried and executed at Redyng with his complices...counsellors to give evidence against the abbot of Redyng, Mr Hynde [sergeant-at-Law and the king's attorney], John Baker...To see that the evidence be well sorted and the indictments well drawn (*LP*, xiv, ii, 399, 424, 427).

27 Oct. Commission for Berks as above.

30 Nov.:

Marillac writes to Francis I that two abbots have been lately executed for high treason ...he could learn no particulars of what they were charged with, except that it was 'les reliques' of the late lord marquis [*sc.* of Exeter] (*LP*, xiv, ii, 607, and Kaulek, 144).

III. RICHARD WHITING, abbot of Glastonbury
16 Sept. 1539:

R. Layton, from Reading, recants to Cromwell his former praise of Whiting,

whiche now apperithe nether then, nor now, to have knowyne God, nether his Prynce, nother anny parte of a good Christin man his religion...I am a man, and may err, and cannot be sure of my judgementt to knowe the inwarde thoughte of a monke, beinge fayre in wordly and outward apparaunce, and inwardly cankerede as now by your discrete inquisition apperithe...from henesforthe I shalbe more circumspecte...this shalbe an experience for euer in suche behalfe (*LP*, xiv, ii, 185).

22 Sept. 1539:

Pollard, Moyle and Layton write to Cromwell that they came to Glastonbury on Friday last (19th) and examined the abbot at Sharpham on certain articles.

As his answer was not to our purpose, advised him to call to mind what he had forgotten and tell the truth. Visited the abbey, searched his study and found a book against the King's divorce...and divers pardons, copies of bulls, and the counterfeit life of Thomas Bequet in print; but could not find any letter that was material. Examined him again on articles received from Cromwell. His answers which we send, will show his cankered and traitorous heart. And so, with as fair words as we could, we have conveyed him from hence unto the Tower, being but a very weak man and sickly. Will now proceed to discharge his servants and the monks...have found a gold chalice and other articles which the abbot hid from previous commissioners, and as yet he knows not we have found it (*LP*, xiv, ii, 206; Wright, *SL*, cxxvi).

28 Sept:

The same to Cromwell that they have discovered money and plate hid in walls, vaults, and other secret places...have committed to jail, for arrant robbery, the two treasurers, monks, with two clerks of the vestry, laymen. The abbot and monks had embezzled and stolen as much plate and ornaments as would have sufficed for a new abbey (*LP*, xiv, ii, 232; Wright, *SL*, cxxvii).

30 Sept:

Pollard writes to Richard Cromwell that the monastery of Glastonbury is now in the king's hands (*LP*, xiv, ii, 290).

2 Oct. The three commissioners as above to Cromwell:

Since writing last, have come to the knowledge of treasons committed by the abbot of Glaston, Enclose a book thereof, with the accusers' names, 'whych we thyngke to be verye haut and ranke treasons' (*ibid.* 272; Wright, *SL*, cxxviii).

25 Oct. Marillac to Montmorency:

It will be seen...what will be done with the abbot of Glastonbury, who had recently been put in the Tower because they found a written book of the arguments in behalf of Queen Katherine (*LP*, xiv, ii, 389: Kaulek, 138).
[*Note.* It is not clear which book Marillac knows of, or whether he is confusing the two; it seems probable that he refers to the book of the letter of 22 Sept.]

No date. Cromwell's remembrance (earlier than 27 Oct.):

Certain persons to be sent to the Tower for the further examination of the abbot of Glastonbury...the abbot of Glaston to be sent down to be tried and executed at Glaston...Counsellors to give evidence, Richard Pollard, Lewis Forstew [Fortescue], Thomas Moyle. To see that the evidence be well sorted and the indictments well drawn (*LP*, xiv, ii, 399).

16 Nov. John, Lord Russell to Cromwell:

On thursdaye [an error for Friday] the xiiii daye of this present moneth, the Abbott of Glastonburye was arrayned, and the next daye putt to executyon, wyth ii other of his monkes, for the robbyng of Glastonburye churche, on the torre hull next unto the towne of Glaston. ...And here I do sende your lordeshipp enclosed the names of thenquest that passed on Whytyng, the seid abbott; whiche I ensure you my lorde is as worsshipfull a jurye as was charged here thies many yeres (*ibid.* 530; Ellis, *OL*, I, ii, 98; Wright, *SM*, cxxix; Archbold, *SRH*, 120–1).

16 Nov. Pollard to Cromwell:

The same xv daye the late Abbott of Glastonberye went from Wellys to Glastonberye and there was drawyn thorowe the towne upon a hurdyll to the hyll callyd the Torre wheare he was put to execucon. Att whych tyme he askyd god mercye and the kyng for hys great offensys towardes hys hyghenes, And also desyred my servauntes beyng there present... that they wold be meane to my lord presydent and to me thatt we shold desyre the kynges hyghenes of hys mercyfull goodnes and in the waye of charytye to forgyve hym his great offensys by hym commytted and done ageyneste hys grace, and thereapon toke hys deathe very pacyently...and lykewyse the other ii monkys desyred lyke forgyvenes, and toke there deathe verye pacyently, whose sowllys God pardon...afore hys execucon [the abbot] was examyned apon dyuers artycles and interrigatoryes to hym mynystered by me but he cowld accuse no man but hymselfe of any offense ageynst the kynges hyghnes, nor he wold confesse no more goold nor sylver nor any other thyng more than he dyd afore youre lordshyp in the Towre (*LP*, xiv, ii, 531, Wright, *SM*, cxxx; Archbold, 118).

30 Nov. Marillac to Francis I:

Two abbots have been lately executed for high treason...could learn no particulars of what they were charged with, except that it was 'les reliques' of the late lord marquis (*LP*, xiv, ii, 607; Kaulek, 144).

A few general remarks may be made in conclusion:

1. Historically speaking, the record evidence, i.e. the contemporary depositions and official letters, which are strictly contemporary and are themselves part of the web of history, must be given priority of importance wherever it is peremptory. The chroniclers are only good evidence in so far as they agree with, or eke out, the records.

2. It may be accepted as certain that the case made out against the abbot of Colchester has no intrinsic connection with the cases against the other two. The only link is extrinsic, viz. all three died about the same time and in consequence of a move on the part of government to bring about the surrender of the great houses still standing. Although the four chroniclers and the anonymous pamphleteer (for whom *v. infra*) join the three abbots together, there is not a single mention of the other two in the dossier of Abbot Marshall, and the charges against him are purely personal. It is conceivable that Cromwell hoped at first to include all three in a charge of conspiracy, and that this was the charge proffered against them when first arraigned at the Counter. If so, the programme was changed for some reason, and two at least of the abbots were prosecuted on a purely individual charge.

3. Abbot Marshall was certainly a conservative in all his opinions; he was originally, and perhaps remained always at heart, a supporter of the traditional Catholic beliefs. It would appear, however, that he was indiscreet and unrestrained in his talk. Under stress of danger in the Tower he withdrew his previous expressions, and declared his willingness to surrender, but it was too late to save his life. He had said quite enough to ensure his conviction, and it was his conviction, and not his conversion, that was desired. It is always possible that, like Cranmer, he repented of his weakness and confessed his faith before death, but his character as seen in the depositions, and the letter of Jenney to Cromwell, make this a very unlikely supposition. On every public occasion he had accepted the royal supremacy, and we have no evidence, public or private, that he openly revoked his assent.

4. There is no need to question the general statement of the anonymous writer, which is corroborated by other indications, that the abbot of Reading was at heart a supporter of the traditional faith, even though he had sworn more than once to implement the

royal supremacy and had even given his countenance in parliament to the long series of antipapal measures. It would also appear certain that he was connected in friendship and sympathy with several of those implicated in the so-called Exeter conspiracy, and it is possible that he had expressed hopes for the success of Cardinal Pole's missions against Henry. All sources agree in attributing to him 'complices' outside his monastic family, and this places him apart from his two fellow-abbots and suggests that the charge against him was not purely personal. In default of any reliable information as to the charges made against him and his replies we can be certain of nothing save the fact of his execution, unless we are prepared to rely upon the anonymous pamphleteer. That he died on account of his eleventh-hour denial of the royal supremacy cannot, in default of evidence, be disproved; but it certainly cannot be proved.

5. The case of the abbot of Glastonbury is clearer, though in some respects more complicated. His alleged correspondence with the abbot of Reading does not depend wholly upon the anonymous pamphleteer, but receives some support both from Cromwell's rebuke to Layton (cf. *LP*, xiv, ii, 185) which clearly argued 'treason' in Whiting before any of the discoveries at Glastonbury, and from the juxtaposition of the names of the two abbots in several of the 'remembrances' of the minister. It would seem that the original intention was to involve Whiting in the alleged treason of the Reading group; that Layton hoped to reinforce this by his discovery of a book against the divorce (the retention of which was at least misprision of treason); but that these lines of prosecution were abandoned in favour of the simple and irrefutable charge of robbery. In one sense, therefore, the execution of Whiting, though the most brutal, was the least unjust of the three, for he had condoned (if indeed he had not commanded) an act which was inconsistent with his continued professions of submission to the king, and which he knew to be technically liable to a capital charge. In view of the letters of Russell and Pollard there can be no reasonable doubt that Whiting at Wells was charged with and convicted of robbery and nothing more; it is difficult to understand how Gasquet (*The Last Abbot*, 112) could persuade himself 'that there was no trial of the abbot...at Wells', and could write that 'of any verdict or of any condemnation of the abbot and of his two monks nothing is said by Russell and Pollard'.

6. A word must be said about the anonymous pamphleteer or preacher (*LP*, xiv, ii, 613) from whom most of the details of Abbot Cook's life and trial have been drawn since the document came to light some sixty years ago. Gasquet (*op. cit.*) and J. C. Cox (*VCH, Berks*, ii) proceeded on the twofold assumption (*a*) that as a contemporary he knew the facts and presented at least some of them, and (*b*) that as he was a 'hostile witness' to the abbots full belief might be given to such of his assertions as in his view tell against the abbots, e.g. that the abbot of Reading celebrated Mass weekly for the pope. But in fact such assumptions rest on a misapprehension of the nature of such documents. Sermons and pamphlets of this kind were part of the life of the day, and were suppressed, tolerated or inspired by the government as policy might dictate. They are utterly unreliable, and their authors are often so ill-informed and so careless of the truth that it is impossible to be certain of any statement they may make. A reader may feel fairly sure that this or that statement 'rings true', but this is merely his guess and of no more historical value than another's. In this case, the anonymous writer seems to have some personal knowledge of Abbot Cook's behaviour, and to assume some sort of association among the various Reading clerics and between this group and the abbot of Glastonbury in a kind of plot in support of Pole's activities, but even this cannot be proved, and the only safe course is to disregard the writer altogether. It should be noted that he always refers to the 'prior' of Colchester and to 'John' Whiting.

7. Finally, in all these and similar events of the time it must be borne in mind:

(*a*) that the monks (and *a fortiori* the abbots and the parliamentary abbots) had over and over again accepted the royal supremacy with all its implications, and had assented to the most violent anti-papal declarations and actions. Unwillingness to surrender, therefore, and alienation or concealment of treasure, however understandable, was certainly *in foro externo* indefensible, while on the other hand it cannot of itself be construed as an assertion of Catholic doctrine; and

(*b*) that whereas in the latter part of Elizabeth's reign the Oath of Supremacy was a permanent test which could be applied immediately and repeatedly, and which when taken often carried a pardon with it, in Henry's reign oaths were imposed on certain occasions only and were not thenceforward used as tests. Those who subsequently acted and spoke against the Boleyn marriage or the royal supremacy were liable to conviction thenceforward for that word or action as for any other criminal act; recantation was not demanded and could not serve as a defence.

To sum up a long and perhaps tedious argument. The three abbots were almost certainly singled out for attack because they showed no signs of readiness to surrender. The abbot of Colchester was accused of treasonable words, among which was a denial of the royal supremacy; had he stood by his utterances he would have died primarily for his faith. In fact, in the latest extant document he retracted and begged for mercy, thereby making it at least probable that his earlier words were not inspired by deep religious conviction. The abbot of Reading, along with others, was accused, justly or unjustly, of some sort of conspiracy. Despite his previous actions and words, he may now have spoken against the royal supremacy and died for his words, but there is no reliable evidence for this. The abbot of Glastonbury was attacked on more than one count, but was apparently not very vulnerable until the 'embezzlement' of treasure came to light. This was a straightforward criminal offence, and he was executed for it. That the three abbots, and especially the abbot of Glastonbury, were the victims of unscrupulous, brutal and (on any true assessment) unjust treatment seems certain, but the historical evidence available does not suffice to prove that they died, like Sir Thomas More, 'in and for the Catholic faith'. The abbot of Colchester denied papal supremacy; the abbot of Glastonbury was executed on quite a different charge; the abbot of Reading may have stood up for the papal claims at his trial, but this cannot be regarded as historically proven.

POSTSCRIPT (18 July 1959)

When the printing of this book had already begun, I learnt that Dr J. E. Paul, in the course of his research at the Public Record Office, had recently had the good fortune, denied to all his predecessors in the field, to discover the indictments of the abbots of Colchester and Reading, together with some further details of the trial of the latter. Dr Paul hopes to publish his findings in the near future, and meanwhile he has given me permission to call attention to his discoveries, in order to warn my readers that this new evidence has come to light. As regards the abbot of Colchester, the newly discovered indictment does not appear to affect in any essential way [the judgment expressed in Appendix IX, but the evidence now available concerning Abbot Cook of Reading would seem to show conclusively that he died because he had not only expressed, but also firmly maintained, a clear assertion of the papal supremacy, and that conspiracy formed no part of the charge against him and his two associates.

Dr Paul's paper has now [1960] appeared as 'The last abbots of Reading and Colchester', in *Bulletin of the Institute of Historical Research*, XXXIII, no. 87 (May, 1960), 115–19.

APPENDIX X

REGULARS AS BISHOPS

The following lists continue those in previous volumes (*MO*, Appendix XII, pp. 709–10; *RO*, I, Appendix II, pp. 321–2; *RO*, II, Appendix III, pp. 369–75). The average of the previous century is maintained to the end; thus in 1500 and 1525 there were three regular bishops in English and Welsh sees. For the Irish bishops I am once more indebted to Professor Aubrey Gwynn, S.J. An attempt has been made to list the ex-religious who became bishops, whether as Henrician conservatives, Edwardian Protestants, Marian Catholics or Elizabethan Anglicans. Those who owed their appointment to Mary are italicized.

I. 1485–1533

(a) ENGLAND

BLACK MONKS

[Thomas Milling]	abb. Westminster	HEREFORD	1474–1492
[Richard Bell]	pr. Durham	CARLISLE	1478–1495
William Senhouse	m. Durham; abb. York	CARLISLE	1495–1502 [tr. Durham]
"	"	DURHAM (fr. Carlisle)	1502–1505

AUSTIN CANONS

Henry Dean	pr. Llanthony	SALISBURY (fr. Bangor)	1500–1501 [tr. Canterbury]
"	"	CANTERBURY (fr. Salisbury)	1501–1503
John Penny	abb. Leicester	CARLISLE (fr. Bangor)	1508–1520

PREMONSTRATENSIANS

Richard Redman	abb. Shap	EXETER (fr. St Asaph)	1495–1501 [tr. Ely]
"	"	ELY	1501–1505

FRIARS PREACHERS

John Howden		SODOR AND MAN	1523–1538

(b) WALES

AUSTIN CANONS

Henry Dean	pr. Llanthony	BANGOR	1494–1500 [tr. Salisbury]
John Penny	abb. Leicester	BANGOR	1505–1508 [tr. Carlisle]

PREMONSTRATENSIANS

[Richard Redman]   abb. Shap   Sᴛ Asᴀᴘʜ   1471–1496 [tr. Exeter]

FRIARS PREACHERS

George de Athequa   Lʟᴀɴᴅᴀꜰꜰ   1517–1537

FRIARS MINOR

Richard Edenham   Bᴀɴɢᴏʀ   1465–1494
Henry Standish   Sᴛ Asᴀᴘꜰ   1518–1535

(c) IRELAND

1. *Resident bishops*

FRIARS PREACHERS

John Payne   Mᴇᴀᴛʜ   1483–1507

FRIARS MINOR

Philip Pinson   Tᴜᴀᴍ   1503

CARMELITES

John Bale   Ossᴏʀʏ   1553

2. *Non-resident bishops English suffragans*

BLACK MONKS

Florence Woolley   m. Abingdon   Cʟᴏɢʜᴇʀ   1475–1500   Norw.
Robert Blyth   abb. Thorney   Dᴏᴡɴ ᴀɴᴅ Cᴏɴɴᴏʀ   1520–1541   Eli.

PREMONSTRATENSIANS

John Maxey   abb. Welbeck   Eʟᴘʜɪɴ   1525–1536

AUSTIN CANONS

Thomas Ford   Aᴄʜᴏɴʀʏ   1492–1504   Lich. Linc.
Richard Wilson   pr. Drax   Mᴇᴀᴛʜ   1523–1529   Ebor.

FRIARS MINOR

[James Wall]   Kɪʟᴅᴀʀᴇ   1475–1494   Lond.

AUSTIN FRIARS

[William Egremond] (uncertain order)   Dʀᴏᴍᴏʀᴇ   1463–1501   Ebor.

John Bell   Mᴀʏᴏ   1493–1541   Lond. Sar. Ex. Lich. Cant. Bathon.

(d) SUFFRAGAN BISHOPS IN PARTIBUS
BLACK MONKS

	Provenance	Title	Diocese served	Appointed or consecrated
Thomas Chard	pr. Montacute	Selymbria	Exon. Bathon.	1508
Thomas Wele		Panada	Lond. Lich.	1484
John Brainsford	m. Bury		Linc.	1517
William Sutton	pr. Avecote	Panada	Lich.	1524
John Stonywell	pr. Tynemouth	Pulati	Ebor.	1524

AUSTIN CANONS

Andrew Whitney	pr. St Bart's, Gloc.,	Chrysopolis	Wig. Wint. Glos. Her.	1525
Thomas Carr	pr. Brinkburn	'Carenen.'	Dur.	1504
Thomas Wells	pr. Bicknacre	Sidon	Cant. Lond.	1505
William Grant	—	Panada	El.	1515
Thomas Hallam, al. Swillington	—	Philadelphia	Linc.	1532
Thomas Vivian	pr. Bodmin	Megara	Exon.	1517
William Gilbert	abb. Bruton	'Majoren'.	Wint.	1519
Thomas Chetham	pr. Leeds	Sidon	Cant. Lond.	1526
Thomas Bale	can. St Mary without Bishopsgate	Lydda	Lond.	1521
John Smart	abb. Wigmore	Panada	Wig. Her.	1526

CISTERCIANS

Augustine Church	abb. Thame	Lydda	Exon. Sar. Linc.	1488
Robert King	abb. Thame	Rheon	Linc.	1527

PREMONSTRATENSIANS

Richard Burgh	abb. Shap	'Syrenen.'	Carl.	1519
Matthew Mackerell	abb. Barlings	Chalcedon	Ebor.	1524
Christopher Lord	abb. Newhouse	Sidon	Cant.	1533

FRIARS PREACHERS

Richard Wycherley	pr. K. Langley	Olenus	Her. Wig.	1480
William Hogeson	—	Dara	Wint. Ebor.	1520
William How	—	Avara	Cant. Cicest.	1520

FRIARS MINOR

?Francis Sexello	—	Castoria	Bathon.	1507
Thomas Wolf	—	Lacedemon	Bathon.	1510
William Duffield	—	Ascalon	St As. Ebor	1531

BONHOMMES

	Provenance	Title	Diocese served	Appointed or consecrated
John Pinnock	pr. Edington	Syene	Sar. Her.	?1518

O.S.J. JERUS

Thomas Cornish	—	'Tinen.'	Bathon. Ex.	1480
?William Bachelor	—	'Carvagha- zonen.'	Chich.	1515

II. EX-RELIGIOUS BISHOPS, 1533 ONWARDS

BLACK MONKS

John Capon or Salcot	m. Colchester; abb. St Benet's, Holme; abb. Hyde	BANGOR	1534–1539
—	—	SALISBURY	1539–1557
William Repps	m. Norwich; abb. St Benet's of Holme	NORWICH	1536–1549
Robert Warton or Parfew	pr. Wenlock; abb. Bermondsey	ST ASAPH	1536–1554
—	—	HEREFORD	1554–1557
Thomas Sparke or Durk	m. Durham; pr. Holy Isle	BERWICK	1536–1572
John Salisbury	pr. Horsham St Faith	THETFORD	1536–1570
—	—	SODOR AND MAN	1570–1573
William More	abb. Walden	COLCHESTER	1536–1541
John Bird	abb. Hyde	PENRITH	1537–1539
—	—	BANGOR	1539–1541
John Bradley	abb. Milton	SHAFTESBURY	1539–
John Chambers	abb. Peterborough	PETERBOROUGH	1541–1556
John Wakeman	abb. Tewkesbury	GLOUCESTER	1541–1549
Henry Holbeach	pr. Worcester	ROCHESTER	1544–1547
—	—	LINCOLN	1547–1551
Richard Thornden	m. Ch. Ch. Canterbury	DOVER	1545–1557
Anthony Kitchin	m. Westminster; abb. Eynsham	LLANDAFF	1545–1566
John Holyman	m. Reading	BRISTOL	1554–1558

CISTERCIANS

Thomas Morley	abb. Stanley	MARLBOROUGH	1537–
Lewis Thomas	abb. Kymmer	SHREWSBURY	1537–1561
Robert King	abb. Thame	OSENEY	1542–1545
—	—	OXFORD	1545–1557
John Hooper	—	GLOUCESTER	1551–1554
—	—	WORCESTER	1552–1554

CARTHUSIANS

Henry Man	pr. Sheen	SODOR AND MAN	1546–1556

AUSTIN CANONS

William Barlow	pr. Bisham	ST ASAPH	1535–1536
—	—	ST DAVID'S	1536–1548
—	—	BATH AND WELLS	1548–1553
—	—	CHICHESTER	1559–1568
Thomas Manning	pr. Butley	IPSWICH	1536–
Robert Sylvester *or* Pursglove	pr. Guisborough	HULL	1538–1579
Robert Ferrar	—	ST DAVID'S	1548–1554
Edmund Freke	can. Waltham	ROCHESTER	1572–1575
—	—	NORWICH	1575–1584
—	—	WORCESTER	1584–1591

FRIARS PREACHERS

John Hilsey	pr. provincial	ROCHESTER	1535–1539
Richard Ingworth	—	DOVER	1537–1545
John Hodgkin	—	BEDFORD	1537–1560
John Scory	—	ROCHESTER	1551–1552
—	—	CHICHESTER	1552–1553
—	—	HEREFORD	1559–1585
John Hopton	pr. Oxford	NORWICH	1554–1558
Maurice Griffin	—	ROCHESTER	1554–1558

FRIARS MINOR

Gilbert Berkeley	—	BATH AND WELLS	1560–1581

CARMELITES

John Bird	pr. provincial	BANGOR	1539–1541
—	—	CHESTER	1541–1554

AUSTIN FRIARS

George Browne	—	DUBLIN	1535–1554
Miles Coverdale	—	EXETER	1551–1553

GILBERTINES

Robert Holgate	master of Sempringham	LLANDAFF	1537–1545
—	—	YORK	1545–1554

BONHOMMES

Paul Bush	pr. Edington	BRISTOL	1542–1554
William Downham	can. Ashridge	CHESTER	1561–1577

BIBLIOGRAPHY

The lists which follow are in no sense a complete bibliography of the subject. They are intended to include all, and only, those manuscripts, books, articles and theses that have been used or quoted in the text or notes of this book. The omission of any work, therefore, does not necessarily imply that it has not been consulted, or that it is of slight value, but simply that it has not been used by the writer in this particular connexion.

An asterisk (*) denotes that the book referred to is in another section of the bibliography.

I. CONTEMPORARY SOURCES

(a) MANUSCRIPTS

Aberystwyth
National Library of Wales.
Peniarth MS., 119, fos. 604–735. Evesham letters.

Chichester
County Record Office.
Register Shirborn I = Ep. 1/1/5. (Visitations of 1521.)
Register Shirborn II = Ep. 1/1/4. (Visitations of 1524, 1527.)

Dijon
Archives de la Côte d'Or.
Fonds de Cîteaux, 11 H. 19. Transcripts from Cîteaux MSS. Correspondence between England and Cîteaux.

London
British Museum.
Cott. Cleop. E IV 280–284ᵛ (old pagination); 336–340ᵛ (new). (Commissioners' certificates, Hunts; 288 (old); 343 (new). Commissioners' certificates, Lancs.)
Guildhall Library.
MS. 1231. (Chauncy's 1546 account.)
Public Record Office. Commissioners' certificates, 1536.
E. 36/154/48 (Leicestershire, Rutland, Warwickshire).
S.C. 12/33/29 (Norfolk).
S.P. 5/3/128 (Sussex).
S.C. 12/33/27 (Hampshire, Wiltshire, Gloucestershire).
Evidence against Abbots.
S.P. 1/154, FF. 100a–128a. (Evidence against Abbot Hugh Cook of Reading.)
S.P. 1/155, fo. 55 d seqq. (Anonymous invective against the same.)
S.P. 1/156, fo. 183a. (Letter of Jenney to Cromwell.)

Oxford
Bodleian Library.
MS. Twyne xxiv. (Writings of Richard Kidderminster.)

KRO III

(b) Printed Works

Amundesham, Annales Joannis de, ed. H. T. Riley (*MSAC*, v, i–ii).

Anglo-Premonstratensia, Collectanea, ed. F. A. Gasquet (CS, 3 ser., VI, X, XII, 1904, 1906).

Baker, Memorials of Father Augustine, ed. J. McCann and R. H. Connolly (Catholic Record Society, XXXIII, 1933).

Bale, J., *Index Britanniae Scriptorum*, ed. R. L. Poole and M. Bateson (Oxford, 1902).

Benedicti, S., Regula Monasteriorum, ed. C. Butler (2 ed. Freiburg-i-B., 1927).

Bourchier, T., *Historia Ecclesiastica de Martyrio Fratrum* (Paris, 1582).

[*Bristol*], *Two Compotus Rolls of St Augustine's Abbey*, ed. G. Beachcroft and A. Sabin (Bristol Record Society, IX, 1938).

Burchardi, J., Rerum urbanicarum commentarii, ed. L. Thouasne (Paris, 1883).

Bury, Memorials of the Abbey of St Edmund at, ed. T. Arnold (RS, 96, 3 vols. 1890–6).

Butleigh Priory, Suffolk, 1510–1535, The Register or Chronicle of, ed. A. G. Dickens (Winchester, 1951).

Calendar of Letters and Papers, Foreign and Domestic, of the reign of Henry VIII, ed. J. S. Brewer, J. Gairdner and R. H. Brodie (RP, London, 1862–1932).

Calendar of Patent Rolls (RP, London, 1903–   ).

Calendar of State Papers, Spanish (RP, London, 1862–   ).

Calendar of State Papers, Venetian (RP, London, 1864–98).

Canterbury College, v.s. *Pantin.

Cantuarienses, Literae, ed. J. B. Sheppard (RS, 85, 3 vols. 1887–9).

de Castillon et de Marillac, Correspondance politique de MM., ed. J. Kaulek (Paris, 1885).

Chapters of the Augustinian Canons, ed. H. E. Salter (OHS, LXXIV, 1920; and CYS, LXX, 1921–2).

Chapters of the Black Monks, ed. W. A. Pantin (CS, 3 ser., XLV, XLVIII, LIV, 1931–7).

Chauncy, M., *Historia aliquot martyrum*, ed. V. M. Doreau (Montreuil-sur-Mer, 1888).

—— Texts and portions of, ed. F. Van Ortroy in *AB*, VI, 36–51; XIV, 268–83; XXII, 54–75.

—— *The Passion and Martyrdom of the Holy English Carthusian Fathers* (CHS, 1935).

Chichester Visitations, *v.* list of original sources (MSS.).

Christ Church Letters, ed. J. B. Sheppard (CS, n.s., XIX, 1877).

Cisterciensis Ordinis Statuta, v.s. Statuta.

Clifford, H., *Life of Jane Dormer, Duchess of Feria*, ed. J. Stevenson (London, 1887).

Cranmer, T., *Works*, ed. J. E. Cox (2 vols., Parker Society, 1844–6).

Deputy Keeper's Reports, VII (1846). Acknowledgments of Royal Supremacy, App. 2, pp. 279–307.

—— VIII (1847). Deeds of Surrender, App. 2, pp. 1–51.

Documenta ad Legationem Cardinalis Poli spectantia, ed. E. Moyes, F. A. Gasquet and D. Fleming (Rome, 1896).

Dugdale, W., *v.s. Monasticon.*

Dunelmensis scriptores tres, Historiae, ed. J. Raine (SS, IX, 1839).

Durham, Accounts of the Bursar of the Monastery of, ed. J. Raine (SS, XVIII, 1844).

—— *Extracts from the Account Rolls of the Abbey of*, ed. J. T. Fowler (SS, XCIC, C, CIII, 1898, 1900).

—— *Household Book = Accounts*, etc., above.

—— *Rites of*, ed. (1) J. Raine (SS, XV, 1842); (2) J. T. Fowler (SS, CVII, 1903).

Edward the Confessor, Lives of, ed. H. R. Luard (RS, 3, 1858).

Ellis, H., *Original Letters* (three series, 11 vols.; London, 1824–46).

Erasmi, Desiderii, Roterodami, *Colloquia* (Cambridge, 1685). *Enchiridion* (Cambridge, 1686).

—— *Opera* (Basel, 1540).

—— *Opus Epistolarum*, ed. P. S. and H. M. Allen (12 vols., Oxford, 1906–58).

Evesham, Chronicon Monasterii de, ed. W. D. Macray (RS, 29, 1863).

Fish, Simon, *A supplicacyon for the beggars*, ed. J. M. Cowper (EETS, extra s., XIII, 1871).

Fountains, Memorials of St Mary's Abbey of, ed. J. Walbran (SS, XLII, 1863).

Fox, Edward, Bishop of Hereford, *v.s. Registrum*.

Gardiner, Stephen, *The Letters of*, ed. J. A. Muller (Cambridge, 1933).

Grey Friars Chronicle, ed. R. Howlett, in *Monumenta Franciscana* (RS, 4, 1882).

Hall, E., *Chronicle*, ed. C. Whibley (2 vols., London, 1904).

Harpsfield, N., *A treatise on the pretended divorce*, etc., ed. N. Pocock (CS, 2 ser., XVI, 1878).

Henry VIII, The letters of, ed. M. St C. Byrne (London, 1936).

Hexham Priory, Memorials of, ed. J. Raine (SS, XLIV, XLVI, 1864–5).

John of the Cross, St, *Works*, ed. and trans. E. A. Peers (3 vols., 1 ed., London, 1933–4).

Journals of the House of Lords (RP, London, 1846–).

Lanfranc's Monastic Constitutions, ed. M. D. Knowles (Edinburgh, 1951).

Leland, J., *Commentarii de Scriptoribus Britannicis* (Oxford, 1707).

—— *Itinerary*, ed. L. Toulmin Smith (5 vols., London, 1906–8).

—— *de rebus britannicis collectanea*, ed. T. Hearne (6 vols., Oxford, 1715).

Letters and Papers of Henry VIII, v.s. Calendar.

Letters and Papers illustrative of the reigns of Richard III and Henry VII, ed. J. Gairdner (RS, 2 vols., 1861–3).

Luther, M., *Werke* (Weimar, 1883–).

Machyn, The Diary of Henry, ed. J. G. Nichols (CS, XLII, 1848).

Maihew, E., *Congregationis Anglicanae Ordinis Sanctissimi Patriarchae Benedicti Trophaea* (4 vols., Rheims, 1619–24). For an account of this, *v. DR*, L (1932), 108 *seqq.*

Martiloge in Englysshe, The, ed. F. Procter and E. S. Dewick (HBS, 3, 1893).

Melsa, Chronicon Monasterii de, ed. E. A. Bond (RS, 43, 3 vols., 1866–8).

Monasterii S. Albani Chronica, ed. H. T. Riley (RS, 28, 12 vols., 1863–76).

Monasticon Anglicanum, ed. W. Dugdale (re-ed. J. Caley, H. Ellis and B. Bandinel; 6 vols. in 8, London, 1817–30).

Monasticon Anglicanum, ed. J. Stevens (2 vols., London, 1718).

Monkbretton, Chartulary of, ed. J. W. Walker (YARS, LXVI, 1924).

More, Journal of Prior William, ed. E. S. Fegan (WHS, 1914).

More, the Correspondence of Sir Thomas, ed. E. F. Rogers (Princeton, 1947).

More, The Life and Death of Sir Thomas, by N. Harpsfield, ed. E. Hitchcock and R. W. Chambers (EETS, o.s., 186, 1932).

More, *v.s.* *Voght, de*.

Morison, R., *Apomaxis Calumniarum* (London, 1527).

Musica Britannica, X, *v.s.* *Harrison, F. Ll*.

Original Letters, v.s. Zürich letters.

Peterborough Monastery, The Last Days of, ed. W. T. Mellows (Northants Record Society, 12, 1947).

Plumpton Correspondence, The, ed. T. Stapleton (CS, 4, 1839).

Pole, R., *Apologia ad Carolum Quintum*, in *Epistolae*, pars I, pp. 66–171.

—— *Epistolae*, ed. A. M. Quirini (5 vols., Brescia, 1744–57).

—— *Pro ecclesiasticae unitatis defensione* (Rome, 1536).

—— Register, *v. Archaeologia*, VIII, 51.

also *v.s. Documenta*.

Prichard, L., *Life of Father Baker, v.s. Baker, Memorials of*.

Reformation, Narratives of the days of the, ed. J. G. Nichols (CS, 77, 1869).

Registrum Caroli Bothe Ep. Herefordensis, ed. A. T. Bannister (CYS, 1921).

Registrum Eduardi Fox Ep. Herefordensis, ed. A. T. Bannister (CYS, 1921).

Reyner, C., *Apostolatus Benedictinorum in Anglia* (Douai, 1626).

Rymer, T., *Foedera*, etc. (London, 20 vols., 1704–35; re-ed. 7 vols. (RP), 1816–69).

St Augustine's, Canterbury, Chronicle of a Monk of, in *Reformation, Narratives of, supra.*
Sallay in Craven, The Chartulary of the Cistercian Abbey of St Mary of, vol. II, ed. J. McNulty (YARS, XC, 1934).
Sanders, N., *De schismatis Anglicani Origine et Progressu Liber* (Cologne, 1585).
Spanish State Papers, v.s. Calendar.
Stapleton, T., *A counterblast to M. Hornes vayne blaste against J. Fekenham* (Louvain, 1567).
Starkey, T., *A Dialogue between Reginald Pole and Thomas Lupset,* ed. K. M. Burton (London, 1948).
State Papers during the reign of Henry VIII (RP, 11 vols., 1830–52).
Statuta Capitulorum Generalium Ordinis Cisterciensis, ed. J. M. Canivez (8 vols., Louvain, 1933–41).
Statutes of the Realm (RP, 11 vols., 1810–28).
Stone, *Chronicle of John,* ed. W. G. Searle (Cambridge Antiquarian Society Publications, XXXIV, 1902).
Stonor Letters and Papers, ed. C. L. Kingsford (CS, 3 ser., 29, 30, 34; 1919, 1924).
Stow, J., *Annals of England* (London, ed. 1615).
[Twyne] *Joannis Twini Bolingdunensis Angli, de rebus Albionicis, Britannicis atque Anglicis libri duo* (published 1590, London).
Valor Ecclesiasticus, ed. J. Caley and J. Hunter (RP, 6 vols., 1810–34).
Venetian State Papers, v.s. Calendar.
Vergil, Polydore, *Anglica Historia,* ed. D. Hay (CS, 3 s., LXXIV, 1950).
Visitations of the diocese of Lincoln, 1517–31, ed. A. H. Thompson (Lincoln Record Society Publications, 33, 35, 37, 1940–7).
Visitations of the Diocese of Norwich, 1492–1532, ed. A. Jessopp (CS, n.s., 43, 1888).
Visitation Articles and Injunctions of the Period of the Reformation, ed. W. H. Frere (Alcuin Club Collections, XIV, 1910).
'Visitations, 1534–5, Archbishop Lee's', an unsigned article in *YAJ,* XVI (1902), 424–58.
Wells Cathedral, Dean Cosyn and, Miscellanea, ed. A. Watkin (SRS, LVI, 1941).
Whethamstede, Registrum J., ed. H. T. Riley = *MSAC,* VI, i (RS, 28).
Wilkins, D., *Concilia Magnae Britanniae et Hiberniae* (4 vols., London, 1737).
Williams, J., *Account of the monastic treasures confiscated at the dissolution of the various houses in England,* ed. W. B. Turnbull (Abbotsford Club, 1836).
Winchelcumba, Landbok de, ed. D. Royce (London, 1892).
Worcester, 1531–2, Accounts of the Priory of, ed. J. M. Wilson (WHS, 1907).
Worcester, The Almoner's Roll of the Priory of, ed. J. H. Bloom (WHS, 1911).
Wright, T., *Three chapters of Letters relating to the suppression of monasteries* (CS, 26, 1843).
Wriothesley, C., *A chronicle of England,* ed. W. D. Hamilton (2 vols., CS, n.s., 11, 1875–7).
Zürich Letters, The, Original Letters relative to the English Reformation, 1531–1558, ed. H Robinson (2 vols., Parker Society, 1842–5).

II. MODERN WORKS

(a) PRINTED WORKS

Archbold, W. J., *The Somerset Religious Houses* (Cambridge, 1892).
Aungier, G. J., *History and Antiquities of Syon Monastery* (London, 1840).
Aveling, H., 'The Monks of Byland Abbey after the Dissolution', in *Ampleforth Journal,* vol. 60, pt. i (Feb. 1955).
—— 'The Rievaulx Community after the Dissolution', *ibid.* vol. 57, pt. ii (June, 1952).
—— H., *v.s.* *Evesham Letters.
Aveling, H., and McCann, J., *Ampleforth and its origins* (London, 1952).

Barnard, E. A. B., 'Clement Lichfield, last Abbot of Evesham', in *Transactions of the Worcs. Archaeological Society*, 1927–8; repr. Worcester, 1929.
—— 'John Stonywell', *ibid.* 1937; reprinted 1938.
—— 'Philip Hawford, Pseudo-Abbot of Evesham', *ibid.* 1927–8; reprinted 1929.
Baskerville, G., 'The Dispossessed Religious after the Suppression of the Monasteries', in *Essays in History presented to R. L. Poole* (Oxford, 1937).
—— 'The Dispossessed Religious of Gloucestershire', in *TBGAS* XLIX (1927), 63–122.
—— *English Monks and the Suppression of the Monasteries* (London, 1937).
—— 'The Married Clergy and Pensioned Religious in the Norwich Diocese, 1555', in *EHR*, XLVIII (1933), 43–64, 199–228.
Bataillon, M., *Erasme et Espagne* (Paris, 1937).
Bateson, M., 'Archbishop Warham's Visitation of Monasteries, 1511', in *EHR*, VI (1891), 18–35.
—— *Catalogue of the Library of Syon Monastery, Isleworth* (Cambridge, 1898).
—— 'The Pilgrimage of Grace and Aske's examination', in *EHR*, V (1890), 330–45, 550–73.
—— *v.s.* *Bale.
Bennett, H. S., *English Books and Readers, 1475 to 1557* (Cambridge, 1952).
Bishop, E., 'In Laudem Joannis Feckenham, O.S.B.', in *DR*, I (1882), 430–2.
Britton, J., *The History and Antiquities of Bath Abbey Church* (London, 1825).
Brooke, C. N. L., Introduction to *The Book of William Morton* (Northants Record Society, XVI, 1954).
Burne, R. V. H., 'The Dissolution of St Werburgh's Abbey', in *Journal of the Cheshire Archaeological Society*, XXXVII, pt. i (1948).
—— 'The Founding of Chester Cathedral', *ibid.*
Butterworth, C., *The English Primers, 1529–45* (University of Pennsylvania Press, 1953).
Camm, B., with J. Morris and J. H. Pollen, *Lives of the English Martyrs* (2 vols., London, 1904–5).
Caroë, W. D., 'The later history of the priory and the gatehouse [at Butleigh]', in *AJ*, XC, 229–81.
Chambers, E. K., *The Medieval Stage* (2 vols., Oxford, 1903).
Chambers, R. W., *Thomas More* (London, 1935); also *v.s.* *More, Sir Thomas.
Chauncy, H., *The Historical Antiquities of Hertfordshire* (London, 1700).
Cheney, A. D., 'The Holy Maid of Kent', in *TRHS*, n.s., XVIII (1904), 107–39.
Clay, J. W., *Yorkshire Monasteries Suppression Papers* (YARS, XLVIII, 1912).
Clerk-Maxwell, W. G., 'The Monks of Wenlock after the Suppression', in *Transactions of the Shropshire Archaeological Society*, 4 ser., IX (1923), 169–75.
Cole, H., *King Henry the Eighth's Scheme of Bishopricks* (London, 1838).
Collier, J., *An Ecclesiastical history of Great Britain*, ed. T. Lathbury (9 vols., London, 1852).
Colvin, H. M., *The White Canons in England* (Oxford, 1951).
—— 'The *Registrum Premonstratense*: a lost MS. recovered', in *JEH*, VIII, i, 96–7.
Connolly, R. H., 'The Buckley Affair', in *DR*, XLIX (1931), 49–74.
—— 'Fr Maihew and Glastonbury', in *DR*, L (1932), 502–4.
—— 'A rare Benedictine book: Father Maihew's *Trophaea*', *DR*, L, 108–25.
—— *Some dates and documents for the early history of our House* [St Gregory's, Downside] (privately printed, 1930).
—— with J. McCann, *The Abbots of the Ancient Monasteries and Cathedral Priories* (privately printed 1942).
—— *v.s.* *Baker, Memorials.
Constant, G., *La Réforme en Angleterre* (Paris, 1930; Engl. trans. London, 1934).
Coulton, G. G., *Five Centuries of Religion*, vol. IV (Cambridge, 1950).
—— *Ten Medieval Studies* (3 ed., London, 1930).
Creighton, C., *A History of epidemics in Britain* (2 vols., Cambridge, 1891).

Davies, J. Conway, *Records of the Court of Augmentations in Wales and Monmouthshire* (University of Wales, Cardiff, 1954).

Davis, E. Jeffries, 'The Beginning of the Dissolution: Christchurch, Aldgate, 1532', in *TRHS*, 4 ser., VIII (1925), 127–50.

—— 'The Journal of the House of Lords for April and May, 1559', in *EHR*, XXVIII, (1913), 349–61.

Dickens, A. G., 'The Edwardian Arrears in Augmentations Payments', in *EHR*, LV (1940), 384–418.

—— *v.s.* *Butleigh.

Dickins, B., 'Premonstratensian Itineraries from a Titchfield Abbey MS. at Welbeck', in *Proceedings of the Leeds Philosophical Society*, IV, vi, 349–71.

Dickinson, J. C., 'Early Suppressions of English Houses of Austin Canons', in *Medieval Studies presented to Rose Graham* (Oxford, 1950), 54–77.

—— *Walsingham Priory* (Cambridge, 1956).

Dictionary of Music and Musicians (G. Grove), ed. H. C. Colles (London, 1927–8).

Dictionnaire de théologie catholique (ed. A. Vacant *et al.*, Paris, 1915–50).

Dodd, G. and Tierney, M. A. [= Dodd-Tierney], *The Church history of England* (5 vols., London, 1829–43).

Dodds, M. H. and R., *The Pilgrimage of Grace, 1536–7, and the Exeter Conspiracy, 1538* (2 vols., Cambridge, 1915).

Douie, D. L., *The Nature and Effects of the Heresy of the Fraticelli* (Manchester, 1932).

Duff, E. G., *English Provincial Printers to 1557* (Cambridge, 1912).

—— *Fifteenth Century English Books* (Bibliographical Society: illustrated monographs, XVIII, Oxford, 1917).

Dugdale, W., *Saint Paul's* (London, 1818).

—— *v.s.* *Monasticon.

Dunkley, E. H., *The Reformation in Denmark* (London, 1948).

Durrant, C. S., *A Link between the Flemish Mystics and the English Martyrs* (London, 1925).

Elton, G. R., *The Tudor Revolution in Government* (Cambridge, 1953).

——, The Quondam of Rievaulx', in *JEH*, VII, i (1956), 45–60.

Eubel, C., *Hierarchia catholica medii aevi* (Münster, 1898–1901).

Fellowes, E. H. and Buck, P. C., *Tudor Church Music* (10 vols., London, 1923–30).

Finberg, H. P. R., *Tavistock Abbey* (Cambridge, 1951).

Fisher, H. A. L., *The History of England from the accession of Henry VII to the death of Henry VIII* (London, 1906).

Foley, H., *Records of the English Province of the Society of Jesus* (7 vols., London, 1877–84).

Foxe, J., *Actes of the Martyrs* = Acts and Monuments (London, ed. 1576).

Frere, W. H. *The Marian reaction* (CHS, XVIII, 1896).

—— *v.s.* *Visitations.

Froude, J. A., *History of England* (4 ed., 12 vols., London, 1862–70).

—— *Short Studies on Great Subjects* (8 ed., London, 1890).

Fuller, T., *Church History of Britain*, ed. J. S. Brewer (6 vols., Oxford, 1845).

Gairdner, J., *The English Church in the sixteenth century* (London, 1902).

—— *Lollardy and the Reformation in England* (4 vols., London, 1908–13).

—— *v.s.* *Letters and Papers.

Gasquet, F. A., 'Abbot Feckenham and Bath', in *DR*, XXV (1906), 242–60.

—— *Abbot Wallingford* (London, 1912).

—— *Eve of the Reformation, The* (ed. 1919, London).

—— *Glastonbury, The Last Abbot of* (London, 1895).

—— 'A Glimpse at Glastonbury before its destruction', in *DR*, XVI (1897), 57–60.

—— *Henry VIII and the English Monasteries* (London, ed. 1906).

—— 'Overlooked testimonies to the character of the English monasteries on the eve of their suppression', in *DubR*, CXIV (April, 1894), 245–77.

Gasquet, F. A., *v.s.* *Anglo-Premonstratensia, Collectanea.*

Gautier, P., 'De l'état des monastères cisterciens anglais à la fin du xve siècle', in *Mélanges d'histoire offertes à Charles Bémont* (Paris, 1913).

Gillow, J., *A...bibliographical dictionary of the English Catholics* (5 vols., London, 1885–1903).

Godwin, F., *De presulibus Angliae*, ed. G. Richardson (Cambridge, 1743).

Graham, R., *English Ecclesiastical Studies* (London, 1929).

—— 'The English Province of the Order of Cluny in the Fifteenth Century', in *TRHS*, 4 ser., VII (1924), 98–130; reprinted *EES*.

—— 'Excavations on the Site of Sempringham Priory', in *Journal of the British Archaeological Association*, 3 ser., V (1940), 73–101.

—— 'Roland Gosenell, Prior of Wenlock, 1521–6', in *Transactions of the Shropshire Archaeological Society*, XLII (1923), 151–68; reprinted *EES*.

—— *St Gilbert of Sempringham* (London, 1903).

Green, V. H. H., *Bishop Reginald Pecock* (Cambridge, 1945).

Habakkuk, H. J., 'The market for monastic property', in *EcHR*, 2 ser., XI, 362–80.

Habington, T., *A survey of Worcestershire* (WHS, 2 vols., 1895–6).

Hamilton, A., *The Angel of Syon* (Edinburgh, 1905).

Harris, J. W. *John Bale, a study in the minor literature of the Reformation.* (University of Illinois Studies in Language and Literature, 25, Urbana, 1949).

Harrison, F. Ll., 'The Eton Choirbook', in *Annales Musicologiques*, I (1953).

—— *Musica Britannica*, X: 'The Eton Choir Book' (London, 1956).

Hay, D., 'The Dissolution of the Monasteries in the Diocese of Durham', in *Archaelogia Aeliana*, 4 ser., XV (1938), 69–114.

—— *v.s.* *Vergil, Polydore.*

Heales, A., *The Records of Merton Priory* (London, 1898).

Hendriks, L., *The London Charterhouse* (London, 1889).

Herbert of Cherbury, Lord E., *The life and raigne of king Henry the Eighth* (London, 1649).

Hibbert, F. A., *The Dissolution of the Monasteries* [of Staffordshire] (London, 1910).

Historical Monuments, Royal Commission on, vols. cited by counties.

Hodgett, G. J., 'The Dissolution of the Religious Houses in Lincolnshire and the Changing Structure of Society', in *Lincs. Architectural and Archaeological Soc. Reports and Papers*, 4 ser., pt. i (1951), 83–99.

Hoffmann, J. G. H., *La Réforme en Suède.*

Holmquist, H. F., *Die schwedische Reformation* (Leipzig, 1925).

Hope, W. H. St John, 'Fountains Abbey', in *YAJ*, XV (1900), 269–402.

—— 'The Obituary Roll of John Islip, Abbot of Westminster 1500–32, with Notes on other English Obituary Rolls', in *Vetusta Monumenta*, VII, pt. iv (Society of Antiquaries, London, 1906).

—— 'The Making of Place House at Titchfield', in *AJ*, LXIII (1906), 231–43.

Hughes, P., *The Reformation in England*, I (London, 1950).

Hurstfield, J., 'The Greenwich Tenures of the reign of Edward VI', in *Law Quarterly Review*, 65 (1949), 72–81.

Imbart de la Tour, *Les Origines de la Réforme*, I (Paris, 1905).

Jacob, E. F., *Essays in the Conciliar Epoch* (Manchester, 1943).

Jarrett, B., *The English Dominicans* (London, 1921).

Jedin, H., *The Council of Trent*, I (Engl. trans. E. Graf, Edinburgh, 1957).

Jenkins, C., 'Cardinal Morton's Register', in *Tudor Studies presented to A. F. Pollard* (London, 1924).

Ker, N. R., *The Medieval Libraries of Great Britain* (Royal Historical Society, 1941).

Kerridge, E., 'The Movement of Rent, 1540–1640', in *EcHR*, 2 ser., VI (1953).

Kidd, B. J., *Documents of the Continental Reformation* (Oxford, 1911).

King, Archdale A., *Liturgies of the Religious Orders* (London, 1955).

Knowles, M. D., 'The case of St Albans in 1490', in *JEH*, III, ii, 144–58.

Knowles, M. D., 'The last abbot of Wigmore', in *Medieval Studies presented to Rose Graham* (Oxford, 1950), 138–45.
—— *The Monastic Order in England* (Cambridge, 1940).
—— *The Religious Orders in England*, vols. I, II (Cambridge, 1948, 1955).
—— '"The Matter of Wilton" in 1528', in *Bulletin of the Institute of Historical Research*, XXXI, 83 (1958), 92–6.
Knowles, M. D. and Grimes, W. F., *Charterhouse* (London, 1954).
Knowles, M. D. and Hadcock, R. N., *Medieval Religious Houses* (London, 1954).
Knowles, M. D. and St Joseph, J. K., *Monastic Sites from the Air* (Cambridge, 1952).
Latimer, H., *Works* [=*Remains*], ed. G. E. Corrie (Parker Society, 1844–5).
Liljegren, S. B., *The Fall of the Monasteries and the Social Changes in England* (Lunds Universitets Arsskrift, N.F. Adv. i, Bd. 19, Nr. 10, 1924).
Lindley, E. S., 'Kingswood Abbey, its Lands and Mills', in *TBGAS*, LXIII, 115–41; LXIV, 36–59.
Little, A. G., 'The Introduction of the Observant Friars into England', (1) in *PBA*, x (1923), 455–71; (2) *ibid.* XXVII (1941), 157–66.
—— *The Grey Friars in Oxford* (OHS, XX, 1892).
McCann, P. J. (editor), *Ampleforth and its Origins* (London, 1952).
—— *v.s.* *Baker, *Memorials*, and Connolly, *The Abbots*, etc.
McCusker, H., *John Bale, dramatist and antiquary* (Bryn Mawr, 1942).
MacKinnon, J., *Luther and the Reformation* (4 vols., London, 1929).
Maitland, F. W., *Historical Essays*, ed. H. M. Cam (Cambridge, 1957).
Marron, S., 'Dom Sigebert Buckley and his Brethren', in *Douai Magazine*, VII, 3 (1933), 130–8.
—— various short articles in *Douai Magazine*, 1922–33.
Mathew, D. and G., *The Reformation and the contemplative life* (London, 1934).
—— 'The Survival of the Dissolved Monasteries in Wales', in *DubR*, January 1929, 70–81.
Maxwell-Lyte, H. C., 'Visitations of Religious Houses and Hospitals, 1526', in SRS, *Collectanea* I, vol. XXXIX (1929), 207–25.
Merriman, R. B., *The Life and Letters of Thomas Cromwell* (2 vols., Oxford, 1902).
Moorman, J. R. H., *The Grey Friars in Cambridge* (Cambridge, 1952).
Moreau, E. de, in *Histoire de l'Eglise* (Fliche et Martin) XVI (Paris, 1950).
Myres, J. N. L., 'Butley Priory', in *AJ*, XC (1933), 177–228.
—— 'Butley Priory', in *Oxford Essays in Medieval History presented to H. E. Salter* (Oxford, 1934), 140–206.
Neale, J. E., 'The Elizabethan Acts of Supremacy and Uniformity', in *EHR*, LXV (1950), 304–32.
Noake, J., *The Monastery and Cathedral of Worcester* (London, 1866).
Northumberland, A History of (Newcastle, 1893–   ).
Nugent, E. M., *The thought and culture of the English Renaissance* (Cambridge, 1956), 304–32.
Ogle, A., *The Tragedy of the Lollard Tower* (Oxford, 1949).
Oxford Companion to Music, ed. P. Scholes (Oxford, 9 ed. 1955).
Oxford, Register of the University of, ed. C. W. Boase and A. Clark (OHS, I, IX, XI, XII, XIV, 1884–9).
Pantin, W. A., 'Abbot Kidderminster and Monastic Studies', in *DR*, XLVII (1929), 198–211.
—— *Canterbury College* (OHS, n.s., 6–8, 1947–50).
—— 'English Monastic Letter-Books', in *Historical Essays in honour of James Tait* (Manchester, 1933).
—— Also *v.s.* *Chapters of the Black Monks.
Peacock, E., 'Injunctions of John Langland,' in *Archaeologia*, XLVII (1875), 49–64.
Pearce, E. H., *The Monks of Westminster* (Cambridge, 1916).

Pemberton, R., *Solihull and its Church* (Exeter, 1905).
Perry, G. G., 'Episcopal visitations of the Augustinian Canons of Leicester and Dorchester', in *EHR*, IV (1889), 304–13.
—— 'The Visitation of the Monastery of Thame, 1526', in *EHR*, III (1888), 704–22.
Pickthorn, K., *Early Tudor Government*: vol. 2, *Henry VIII* (Cambridge, 1934).
Piò, G. M., *Delle Vite de gli Huomini illustri di San Domenico* (parte prima: Bologna, 1607).
Pocock, N., *Records of the Reformation* (2 vols., Oxford, 1870).
Pole, Cardinal, *v.s.* *Documenta* and *Pole, R.
Pollard, A. F., *Henry VIII* (London, ed. 1913).
—— *Wolsey* (London, 1929).
Pollard, A. W., *A Short-title Catalogue of books printed in England...1475–1640* (Bibliographical Society: London, 1926).
Prescott, H. F. M., *Mary Tudor* (London, 2 ed. 1952).
Purvis, J. S., 'Notes from the Diocesan Register at York', in *YAJ*, XXXV (1943), 393–403.
—— 'A selection of monastic rentals and Dissolution papers', in *Miscellanea*, III; YARS, LXXX (1931).
Renaudet, A., *Etudes Érasmiennes (1521–29)* (Paris, 1939).
Robinson, J. A., *The Abbot's House at Westminster* (Cambridge, 1911).
—— 'The Benedictine Abbey of Westminster', in *CQR*, LXIV, 58–80.
—— *Two Glastonbury Legends* (Cambridge, 1926).
Rowse, A. L., *Tudor Cornwall* (London, 1941).
Rupp, E. G., *Studies in the making of the English Reformation* (Cambridge, 1947).
Sabin, A., 'Compotus Rolls of St Augustine's Abbey, Bristol', in *TBGAS*, LXIII, 191–207.
Savine, A., *The English Monasteries on the eve of the Dissolution* (Oxford Studies in social and legal history, ed. P. Vinogradoff, I, 1909).
Schirmer, W. F., *Der Englische Frühumanismus* (Leipzig, 1931).
Scholes, P., *v.s.* *Oxford*.
Seebohm, F., *The Oxford Reformers* (Oxford, 1887).
Simpson, J. B., 'Coal-mining by the monks', in *Transactions of the Institute of Mining Engineers*, 39 (1910), 573–98.
Skeat, T. C., 'Letters from the Reign of Henry VIII', in *British Museum Quarterly*, XXI, i (March 1957).
Smith, R. A. L., *Canterbury Cathedral Priory* (Cambridge, 1943).
Sole, S. H., *The Jesus Psalter* (London, 1888).
Somerville, R., *History of the Duchy of Lancaster*, I (London, 1953).
Southern, A. C., *Elizabethan Recusant Prose, 1559–82* (Cambridge, 1950).
Stanley, A. P., *Memorials of Westminster Abbey* (London, 5 ed. 1882).
Strype, J., 'Ecclesiastical Memorials', in *Works* (Oxford, 1820–40).
—— *Annals of the Reformation* (4 vols., Oxford, 1820–40).
Syon Abbey, *v.s.* Aungier, Bateson, *Martiloge*.
Sweet, A. H., 'John de Feckenham and the Marian Reaction' (n.d., reprinted from *Persecution and Liberty*).
Tanner, J. R., *Tudor Constitutional Documents* (Cambridge, 1922).
Taunton, E., *The English Black Monks of St Benedict* (2 vols., London, 1897).
Teresa (of Avila), St, *Works*, and trans. ed. E. A. Peers (3 vols., London, 1946).
Thérèse (of Lisieux), St, *Histoire d'une Ame* (Lisieux, 1925).
Thompson, A. H., 'A Corrody from Leicester Abbey, A.D. 1393–4, with some notes on corrodies', in *Transactions of the Leicestershire Archaeological Society*, XIV (1926), 114–34.
—— 'William Hogeson Episcopus Dariensis', in *YAJ*, XXIV, 236–57.
Thompson, A. H., *v.s.* *Visitations*.
Thompson, E. M., *The Carthusian Order in England* (London, 1930).

Thompson, E. M., *A History of the Somerset Carthusians* (London, 1895).
Tour, Imbart de la, *Origines de la Réforme* (Paris 1905–9).
Venn, J. and J. A., *Alumni Cantabrigienses*, Part I (4 vols., Cambridge, 1922–7).
Victoria History of the Counties of England (London and Oxford, 1900–   ), cited by county and volume.
Voght, H. de, *Acta Thomae Mori* (Louvain, 1947).
Walcott, M. E. C., 'Inventories and Valuations of religious houses', in *Archaeologia*, XLIII (1871), 201–49.
Wallis, J. E. W., 'The Narrative of the Indictment of the Traitors of Whalley, 1536–7', in Chetham Society, XC, *Miscellanies* V (1931).
Watkin, A., 'Glastonbury, 1538–9, as shown by its Account Rolls', in *DR*, LXVII (1949), 437–50.
—— *v.s.* *Wells.*
Webster, R., '"Conference" at Wisbech (1580)', in *DR*, XXXI (1935), 323–45.
Weeks, W. S., 'Abbot Paslew and the Pilgrimage of Grace', in *Transactions of the Lancashire and Cheshire Antiquarian Societies*, XLVII (1930–1), 199–223.
Weiss, R., *Humanism in England during the Fifteenth Century* (Oxford, 1941).
—— 'Humanism in Oxford', in *The Times Literary Supplement*, 9 Jan. 1937.
Weldon, B., *Chronological Notes on the English Congregation of the Order of St Benedict* (London, 1881).
Westlake, H. F., *History of Westminster Abbey* (2 vols., London, 1923).
Wharton, H., *Anglia Sacra* (2 parts, London, 1691).
Whatmore, L. E., 'George Lazenby, monk of Jervaulx: a forgotten martyr?', in *DR*, LXI (1942), 325–8.
—— 'The Sermon against the Holy Maid of Kent and her Adherents', in *EHR*, LVIII (1943), 463–75.
White, H. C., *The Tudor Books of Private Devotion* (University of Wisconsin, 1951).
Widmore, R., *History of Westminster Abbey* (London, 1751).
Wilson, J. M., 'The Visitations and Injunctions of Cardinal Wolsey and Archbishop Cranmer', in *Associated Architectural and Archaeological Reports*, XXXVI (2), 1922.
—— and Ede, W. Moore, *Worcester Cathedral: its Monuments and their Stories* (Worcester, 1925).
—— *v.s.* *Worcester.*
Wood, A. à, *Athenae Oxonienses* (ed. P. Bliss, 6 vols., Oxford, 1813–20).
—— *Historia et Antiquitates Universitatis Oxoniensis* (ed. J. Gutch; Oxford, 1674).
Woodruff, C. E., and Danks, W., *Memorials of Canterbury Cathedral* (London, 1912).
Wordsworth, J., *The National Church of Sweden* (London, 1911).
Wright, C. E., 'The dispersal of the monastic libraries and the beginnings of Anglo-Saxon studies', in *Transactions of the Cambridge Bibliographical Society*, III (1951), 208–37.
—— 'The Dispersal of the Libraries in the Sixteenth Century', in *The English Library before 1700* (London, 1958).
Youings, J., *Devon Monastic Lands: Calendar of Particulars of Grants, 1536–55* (Devon and Cornwall Record Society, n.s. I, 1955).
—— 'The Terms of the Disposal of the Devon Monastic Lands', in *EHR*, LXIX (1954), 18–38.
Zimmermann, B., *Monumenta Historica Carmelitana*, I (Lérins, 1907).

(b) UNPUBLISHED THESES AND DISSERTATIONS

Hodgett, G. J. The Dissolution of the monasteries of Lincolnshire (M.A. London, 1947).
Kennedy, J., The Dissolution of the Monasteries in Hampshire and the Isle of Wight (M.A. London, 1953).
Woodward, G. W. O., The Benedictines and Cistercians in Yorkshire in the Sixteenth Century (Ph.D. Trinity College, Dublin, 1955).

INDEX

The following abbreviations are used: A=Augustinian; abb.=abbey, abbot, abbess; archb.=archbishop; b.=bishop; B.=Benedictine; c.= canon; Carm.=Carmelite; Carth.=Carthusian; cath.=cathedral; Cist.= Cistercian; Cl.=Cluniac; Gilb.=Gilbertine; m.=monk; n.=nun; O.=Order; Obs.=Observant; OFM=Franciscan; OP=Dominican; OSA=Augustinian (Austin); Pr.=Premonstratensian; pr.=priory, prior, prioress; prov.=provincial.

Bury St Edmunds, B. abb., 101, 129, 280, 284, 288, 337, 350, 352
building at, 21, 352
last abbot of, 415
monks in Westminster revival, 426
Butley, A. pr., 127–9
organs at, 20, 128
servants at, 260
Butts, Sir William, M.D., 219
Byland, Cist. abb., 411
servants at, 260

Calder, C. abb., 272
Call, William, OFM, prov., 59
Calwich, A. pr., 200 n.
Cambridge
Buckingham College, 96 n., 98, 343
Christ's College, 213, 225, 226
Corpus Christi College, 214
Jesus College, 57, 157
King's College, 16, 163, 272; chapel, 21
Pembroke College, 213
Queens' College, 152, 213
St John's College, 213
St Radegund's, B. n. pr., 14, 157
White Horse Tavern, 55, 57
Cambridge University
Lutheran influence at, 55
reform of, 280, 283
Campeggio, Cardinal, 159, 164, 199, 200, 215 n.
Campion, Edmund, S.J., 417, 433 n., 436, 442, 444
Campsey, A. n. pr., 75 n.
Canterbury
Austin friars, 60
Christ Church, B. cath. pr., 87–90, 191, 251, 280, 337, 416; buildings, 22, 87–90; library, 90; monks in revived Westminster, 426; numbers at, 80; secular chapter at, 391; shrine of St Thomas at, 249, 271, 353
Monks, see Bocking, Dering
Observant friars, 13
Priors, see Chillenden, Goldstone I and II
St Augustine's, B. abb., 20, 95, 191, 251, 337, 415
monk, see Dygon
St Gregory's, A. pr., prior of, 176
St Sepulchre's, B. n., 183; prioress of, 187, 191
'capacities', number of canons and monks desiring, 310
number of nuns desiring, 311
when issued, 404
Capistran, St John, OFM, Obs., 11–12
Capon, John (alias Salcot), abb. Hyde later b., 187 n., 188 n., 189 and n.

Cardiff, B. pr., 13
Cardmaker, John, OFM, 59
Carey, Lady Mary, 340 n., 341
Carlisle, A. cath. pr., conversion to secular cathedral, 391, 392
Carmelite friars, the, and music, 20
Carthusian order, the
and enclosure, 227
and music, 20
perseverance in 1536, 310, 316–17
Cartmel, A. pr., 332
cash in hand, monastic, 246, 254–5, 314 n., 381 n.
Cassino, Congregation of Monte, OSB, 424–5, 431, 444, 446, 449–51
officials of, 425, 432
Castleacre, Cl. pr., 350
Catesby, Cist. n., 284, 308
cathedral priories, conversion into bishoprics, 359, 389–92
claims of religious in after times, 447 and n., 451–2
Catton, Robert, abb. St Albans, 26
Caversham, A. cell, 355
Cerne, B. abb., 354
Chacombe, Aug. pr., 70
Chalcondylas, Demetrius, 88, 89
chantry priests, ex-religious as, 405, 407, 410
chapter, monastic general, 10
Chapuys, Eustace, imperial ambassador, 184 n., 187 and n., 188, 201, 202, 207 n., 210, 272, 369, 370 n., 402 n., 471
Chard, Thomas, O. Cist., abb. Forde
as builder, 24, 37
as commissary, 37
charity, monastic expense on, 264–6
Charnock, Richard, OSA, pr. St Mary's College, Oxford, 152 and n.
Chartreuse, Grande, prior of (Dom John Gaillard), 234
Chauncy, Maurice, O. Carth., 222 n., 223, 226, 227, 228, 231 n., 232–3 nn., 235, 237, 240, 439
his Historia Martyrum, 222 n.
Chertsey, B. abb., 97, 280, 301, 318, 350, 385, 480
abbot of, 272
visitation at, 301, 480
Chester, B. abb., 23, 376 n.
bishopric in, proposed, 358
conversion to secular chapter, 391, 392
Chillenden, Thomas, pr. Chr. Ch. Canterbury, 22
choirmaster, the
at colleges, 16
at monasteries, 17–18
church ales and bonfires, 116

Sweden, suppression of monasteries in, 167–9
Switzerland, suppression of religious houses in, 170
syndicates as buyers of monastic estates, 398–9
Syon, Bridgettine abb., 212–22, 227 and n., 230
  and the Carthusians, 234, 235, 237
  music at, 20
  refounded under Mary, 440, 441–2
  wanderings of, 442

Talbot, C. H., 28 n.
Talley, Pr. abb., 41
Tallis, Thomas, musician, 18–21
Tattershall College, 20
Taverner, John, musician, 18, 20, 364
Tavistock, B. abb., 101, 249
  monk, see Richard
  printing at, 25–6
Teresa of Avila, St, 185 and n., 186 and n.
Tewkesbury, B. abb., 175 n., 280, 386
Thame, Cist. abb., visitation at, 70–2
Thetford, A. pr., 307
Thompson, A. Hamilton, 63 n., 340 n.
Thorney, B. abb., abbot of, 175 n.
Thornton, Aug. abb., 411
  college in, 358, 389, 391, 411
  visitation at, 68
Throckmorton, family of, 124, 428
  Elizabeth, 301 and n., 412
  Sir George, 206 n., 215, 429
Tiltey, Cist. abb., 290
Titchfield, Pr. abb., 40 n., 42, 51, 350
  buildings, 386
Tonbridge, A. pr., 162
Torre, Pr. abb., 40, 41 n., 45 n., 48 n., 51 n.
  buildings at, 51
Towne, John, OSA, 60 and n.
Tracy, Sir William, 100 n., 101
Trafford, William, O. Carth., 238, 332 n., 475
Traheron, Bartholomew, OFM, later dean Chichester, 59, 484
Treasons, Act of (1534), 180, 190 n., 230
Tregonwell, John (later Sir), D.C.L., 202, 292, 386
  career, 273
  methods as visitor, 284
  tour as visitor, 280–1
Tudor, Mary, Queen of France and Duchess of Suffolk, 128, 129
Tunstall, Cuthbert, b. Durham, 55, 57, 153, 233, 239, 271, 272, 284, 358 and n., 364 n.
Tupholme, Pr. abb., 45 n., 49 and n.
Twyne, John, 95
Twyning, Thomas, OSB, abb. Winch-combe, 91

Tynbygh, or Tenbi, William, O. Carth., pr. London Charterhouse, 223–4, 228, 235
Tyndale, William, 59
Tynemouth, B. pr., 250 n., 340 n., 341

Ulverscroft, Aug. pr., 307, 308, 309, 313, 314, 317
  buildings, 24
university, monks and canons at, 50, 65, 73, 101–7, 123
  see also Cambridge, Oxford

Vale Royal, Cist. abb., 354 n.
  abbot as commissary, 30
Valladolid, Congregation of, OSB (Spanish Congregation), 444, 446, 452–3
Valle Crucis, Cist. abb., 281
Valor ecclesiasticus, the, 241–54, 394
  accuracy of, 244–5
  analysis by Savine, 246–7
Västerås, recess of, 169
Vaughan
  John, 281, 285
  Stephen, 273, 279 n.
vestments and church furnishings, 112, 121–2, 132–6
Visitations
  Austin canons, 66–8, 74–5
  Austin friars, 60–1
  Benedictine, 64–6, 73–4, 77–80, 81, 84–5, 125–6, 347
  Cistercian, 33–4, 70–2
  Cluniac, 82–3, 160
  of Cromwell (1535–6), 268–90; its speed, 286–7
  diocesan, Bath and Wells, 80, 83–4, 347–8; Norwich, 73–5; Lincoln, 62–72; Worcester, 346–7; York, 85–6, 301
  friars, 77–8
  metropolitan, 80–1, 85–6
  Premonstratensian, 40–51
visitors of 1535–6, 270–4
  articles of, 202 n.
  itinerary, 476–7 (Appendix VI)
Vitrier, Jean, OFM, 150–1
Vyntoner, John, A. c., abb. St Osyth, as builder, 23

'wages' of monks, 80, 83 n., 122 n., 123 n., 404
Walden, B. abb., 280
Wallingford, William, OSB, abb. of St Albans, 8–9, 77–9
  his buildings, 23
Walsingham, A. pr., 152, 368 n.
  prior of, 176
  shrine of Our Lady, 249
  visitation at, 74–5